IMPLACABLE FOES

WALDO HEINRICHS
AND MARC GALLICCHIO

IMPLACABLE FOES

War in the Pacific, 1944–1945

OXFORD
UNIVERSITY PRESS

OXFORD
UNIVERSITY PRESS

Oxford University Press is a department of the University of Oxford.
It furthers the University's objective of excellence in research, scholarship,
and education by publishing worldwide. Oxford is a registered trade mark of
Oxford University Press in the UK and certain other countries.

Published in the United States of America by Oxford University Press
198 Madison Avenue, New York, NY 10016, United States of America.

Library of Congress Cataloging-in-Publication Data

Names: Heinrichs, Waldo H., author. | Gallicchio, Marc S., 1954– author.
Title: Implacable foes : war in the Pacific, 1944–1945 / Waldo Heinrichs and
Marc Gallicchio.
Other titles: War in the Pacific, 1944–1945
Description: New York : Oxford University Press, [2017] |
Includes bibliographical references and index.
Identifiers: LCCN 2016040696 | ISBN 9780190616755
Subjects: LCSH: World War, 1939–1945—Campaigns-Pacific Area. |
World War, 1939–1945—Naval operations, American.
Classification: LCC D767 .H43 2017 | DDC 940.54/26-dc23
LC record available at https://lccn.loc.gov/2016040696

1 3 5 7 9 8 6 4 2

Printed by Edwards Brothers Malloy, United States of America

I am deeply grateful to my wife for help in making this book. Thereby I give my part in its dedication to Dr. Audrey S. Heinrichs, for testing and encouraging me in my writing and for many years maintaining an open path for it.

—*Waldo Heinrichs*

CONTENTS

MAPS

ACKNOWLEDGMENTS

As I was preparing *Threshold of War: Franklin D. Roosevelt and American Entry into World War II*, I was struck by the limitations that imposed themselves on FDR's delicate policies leading up to Pearl Harbor. He battled mightily for every inch of wiggle room, to keep his options open. Yet his opportunities diminished as he was repeatedly forced by circumstances to make high-risk decisions that he could back with only limited resources. He was constrained to make up his mind about such matters as aid to Great Britain (and after June 1941 the USSR), how much of an "incident" to stage with a German submarine, and his placement of U.S. warships.

Some scholars have pointed fingers at his supposed vacillations and lack of clear purpose. To claim those faults concerning FDR, however, neglects the context and environment in which he operated. Worse, it ignores the degree to which he remained consistent and with clear purpose. It is as if the critics posited a smooth war machine in which all the parts were fully operational and equal to the need—if only the president could keep from vacillating. Now, in bookend fashion, we come to the end of the war (from February 1944 on). Crucial, high-risk decisions have to be made once again. Policy-makers are up against a real wall of limitations, one that becomes painfully clear as the war splashes on.

I thank those who helped us make the book, at the archives, libraries, and our home. At Carlisle, where I needed much help, I want especially to thank Micheal Knapp, Isabel Manske, Tom Buffenbarger, David Keough, Dr. Richard Sommers, Shaun Kirkpatrick, and Youngae Raymond. My thanks also goes to Ed Drea for reading some of my chapters, suggesting additions, and encouraging me to go on. When it came to finishing the book, my wife Audrey, joined with an expert friend, Marion Canning, to read the text for clarity, grammar, and spelling errors. Many, many thanks. Much thanks to Barbara Blank for helping me learn how to draw maps. Finally I want to thank our sons: Dr. Timothy Heinrichs, our historian, for assisting me at Carlisle, Pennsylvania, and advising and correcting the text, and Rick Heinrichs, production designer of many fine movies, who has given us artistic treatment to maps for the book. I am delighted in having such a fine historian as Marc Gallicchio for my coauthor. Thank you, Marc.

This book's existence has depended on grants from the Earhart Foundation for travel to the necessary archives and libraries from Norfolk, Virginia, to Independence, Missouri, and longer stays in Washington, D.C., and Carlisle Barracks, Pennsylvania.

Waldo Heinrichs
South Hadley, Massachusetts
August 23, 2015

I begin by thanking my long-time mentor and friend Waldo Heinrichs for inviting me to work with him on this book and help bring it to completion. The entire experience has been intellectually stimulating, professionally rewarding, and, speaking for myself, immensely enjoyable.

I am especially grateful to Villanova University for generously supporting my research and writing with a sabbatical and with faculty development and research grants. I also benefited greatly from the support provided by the Department of History's Albert Lepage Research Fund. A travel grant from the Harry S. Truman Library proved especially helpful as I was getting started on this project. I also wish to thank the Earhart Foundation for providing me with a grant that allowed me to take time from teaching responsibilities to write.

I am indebted to numerous friends and colleagues who patiently, or so it seemed to me, listened to me discuss this book. Space does not permit a full accounting, but I wish to make a special point of thanking Professor Yujin Yaguchi for kindly giving me the opportunity to present some of the research done for this book to a seminar at the University of Tokyo and Professors

David Schmitz and Mark Stoler for helping me obtain funding for this project. Professor Thomas Zeiler of the University of Colorado read the initial proposal and generously provided helpful advice all along the way.

Both authors wish to thank our editor, Timothy Bent, for the extraordinary time and effort he put into improving the manuscript, and his assistant, Alyssa O'Connell, for guiding us through the editorial process. We also wish to thank George Chakvetadze for designing many of the maps, Martha Ramsey for her excellent copyediting, and Gwen Colvin, senior production editor at Oxford University Press, for making sure that everything came together in the right place and on time.

Marc Gallicchio
Havertown, Pennsylvania

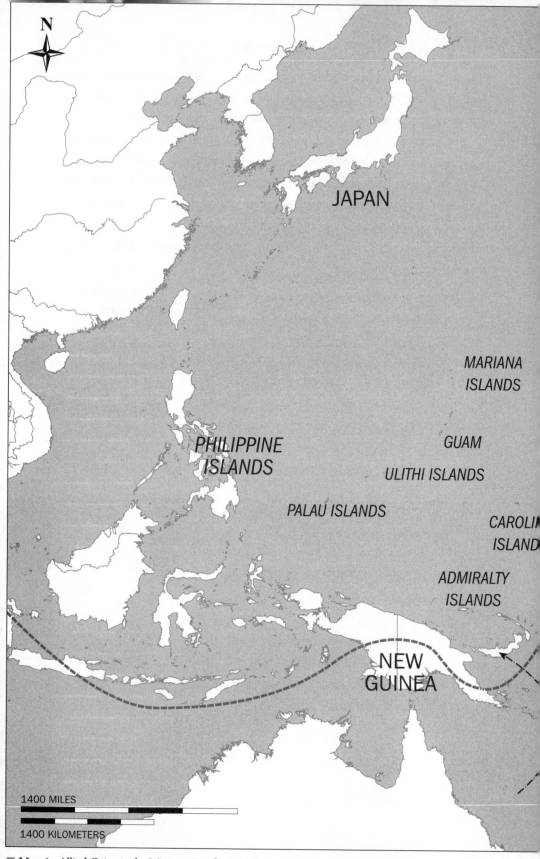

N

MARIANA
ISLANDS

JAPAN

GUAM

ULITHI ISLANDS

PHILIPPINE
ISLANDS

PALAU ISLANDS

CAROLI
ISLAND

ADMIRALTY
ISLANDS

NEW
GUINEA

1400 MILES

1400 KILOMETERS

■ **Map 1** Allied Gains in the Western Pacific, March 1944. Drawn by George Chakvetadze.

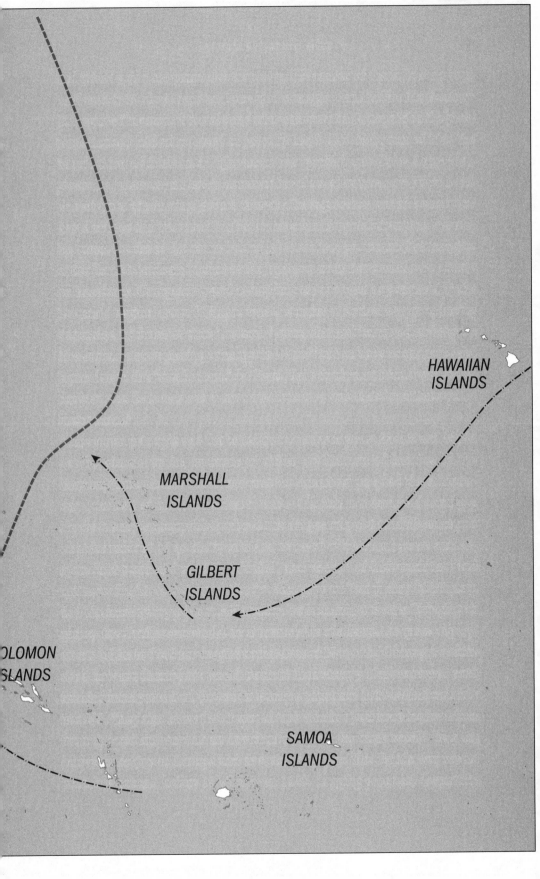

IMPLACABLE FOES

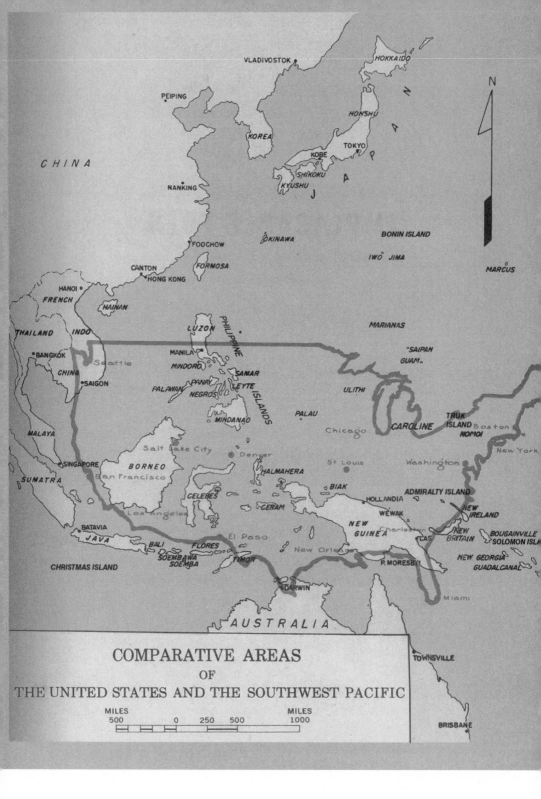

COMPARATIVE AREAS
OF
THE UNITED STATES AND THE SOUTHWEST PACIFIC

MILES
500

0   250   500

MILES
1000

Introduction

The Reckoning

"The capitulation of Hirohito saved our necks," recalled Colonel S. L. Weld, a staff officer in Army Ground Forces, referring to the Japanese emperor's decision on August 14, 1945, to surrender to the United States. "With things being as they were, it would have been absolutely impossible for us to have sent well-trained teams to the Pacific for participation in the scheduled invasion of Japan."[1] How had it come to this? What had happened to make the American victory—seemingly assured after the Battle of Midway in 1942—reliant on two atomic bombs and the belated intervention of the emperor—just half a year after the defeat of Germany?

■ **Map 2** Comparative Areas of the United States and Southwest Pacific. From Office of the Chief Engineer, General Headquarters, Army Forces Pacific, *Engineers of the Southwest Pacific, 1941–1945*, vol. 1, *Engineers in Theater Operations*. Reports of Operations, United States Army Forces in the Far East, Southwest Pacific Area, Army Forces, Pacific, Historical Reports (Washington, DC: U.S. Government Printing Office, 1947).

To answer these questions, we need to understand the constraints on American war-making in the Pacific in the last year of the conflict. First and foremost among these was the American people's unwillingness to endure the sacrifices required to wage war over such vast distances against such a determined enemy. Second, the war effort was hampered by interservice rivalries and congressional challenges to authority over manpower and procurement policies. To operate within these constraints, American strategy placed a premium on rapid advance and a rising tempo of military operations against the enemy, ending in invasion of Japan's home islands. But this strategy harbored serious contradictions, contradictions that would have to be reconciled on the eve of the final campaigns.

By August 1945, American troops scheduled for the invasion of Japan had been through a grueling island campaign. Fresh replacements were yet to arrive. After the surrender of Germany, the Army had begun a massive redeployment of GIs from Europe to the Pacific, but these men would not be available until the second stage of the invasion, the assault on the Tokyo area set for March 1946. In the meantime, the Army had also initiated the discharge of two million GIs who had fought in Europe and the Pacific. This partial troop demobilization worked at cross-purposes with the simultaneous redeployment of GIs from Europe—one suggesting the war's end and the other its continuance—and stimulated growing criticism at home. In the midst of this transition to a one-front war, the Army began to encounter stiff opposition over its continued demands on the national economy and its refusal to countenance changes in its policies governing the discharge of GIs. Months before the first invasion was to take place—in November 1945—the commitment of the American Joint Chiefs of Staff (JCS) to bringing overwhelming force to bear against Japan was straining American logistical resources, testing the limits of military resourcefulness, and raising concerns across the political spectrum of impending economic disaster.

This book will weave together analysis of grand strategy with ground-level narrative, depicting the brutal and often terrifying experience of combat in the Pacific from the perspective of American soldiers, sailors, and Marines. It will highlight the interaction between operations, logistics, and strategy, always keeping in mind that a speedy completion of the war was the driving imperative for American commanders.

In 1943, as soon as it was possible to look ahead toward victory and persistently thereafter, General George C. Marshall, Army chief of staff, warned that there were limits to public support for the war, in the amount of sacrifice exacted and the length of time required. In the summer of 1943, Marshall cautioned a conference of the nation's governors, "We are just getting started. The great battles lie ahead. We have yet to be proven in the agony of enduring heavy casualties, as well as the reverses which are inevitable in war."[2] President Franklin D. Roosevelt also doubted Americans' understanding of what was ahead and worried about the public's mood, which oscillated between overconfidence and despair. The policy of unconditional surrender, announced in January 1943, provided a concrete objective, one that was easily comprehended and emotionally satisfying. From a military standpoint, however, it would require an American invasion of the Japanese homeland. Marshall fastened on the goal of invasion because, despite its many risks and overwhelming challenges, it offered a quicker path to victory than did a strategy of blockade and bombardment. Waging a protracted war meant risking the loss of public support, which in turn would encourage a negotiated and incomplete peace.

The narrative begins with the quickening pace of operations in the Pacific in early 1944 and the development of the campaigns that would bring American forces to the doorstep of the Japanese homeland. The whole effort was one of establishing a functioning fighting system, of taking hold of all the complex and intricate war components and moving from the South Pacific to the shores of Japan. It was all put together and transformed again and again in the crucible of battle. By 1944, the tide of the war in the Pacific had definitively turned. The American fleet, the Marine Corps, and some Army infantry, as well as Australian and New Zealand forces, had stopped the Japanese advance in the Southwest Pacific. The oceanic supply line to the American West Coast was protected, while U.S. war capacity was providing enough arms, ammunition ships, landing craft, planes, food, and manpower to press back against Japanese forces. Under the command of General Douglas MacArthur, supreme commander of the SWPA, American troops, with air and naval assistance, hopped from island to island, captured the thousand-mile northern face of New Guinea, defended it against Japanese attempts to recapture it, and landed troops in the Philippines. American submarines devastated Japanese shipping in the South China Sea. The Pacific Fleet rapidly gained new carriers, battleships, cruisers, and destroyers, all under the command of Admiral Chester Nimitz, who shifted north toward capture of the Mariana Islands—Guam, Saipan, and Tinian—in the mid-Pacific, finally making possible long-range air attacks on Japan itself.

MacArthur turned the other way, toward the middle and southern Philippine Islands and the East Indies, though Marshall refused him permission on the latter. The sparring between Marshall and MacArthur over other items on MacArthur's ambitious wish list plays an important part in the story. MacArthur's persistent demands for prioritizing the liberation of the Philippines limited the possibility of more daring movements closer to Japan and meant that in some ways the quality of U.S. strategy could never rise above his level.

Then there was the war itself. The war in every theater was hell; but war in the Pacific was its own special kind of hell. Weather could vex operations in North Africa, Italy, and northwestern Europe, especially during the hard winter of 1944–1945, and GIs in those areas fell prey to disease and endured privation at the end of long supply lines. But those conditions were intermittent and could be relieved by rehabilitation of existing infrastructure: roads, sanitation systems, and rail lines. In contrast, the climate in the Pacific was a steady source of hardship and danger. The GIs in the Pacific suffered from a panoply of insect and waterborne diseases that resulted in the highest non-combat-related casualty rates in the war. A GI guide to New Guinea warned soldiers that "the country itself will fight you with all its forces.... You must be forever on your guard against this silent enemy, your environment. It is relentless."[3] Supplying America's advancing forces posed its own set of challenges. First and foremost was distance. The vast expanses of the Pacific mocked American efforts to bring the war to a speedy conclusion. A round trip voyage from San Francisco to Manila took three times as long as a circuit from the East Coast to France. When the

Allies launched the invasion of Normandy, they had the advantage of gathering their forces in England, an industrially advanced nation, roughly fifty miles across the channel from their destination. Luzon, from which American forces would stage in preparation for the invasion of Japan, was approximately 1,400 miles from Kyushu, the southernmost of Japan's main islands. War in the Pacific was a war of bases, air and naval, but the Americans had to build them as they advanced, bringing with them the necessary construction materials, equipment, and manpower as they moved forward. In the Pacific, once the Allies moved beyond Hawaii and Australia, there were no modern ports capable of handling the large quantities of men and matériels needed to sustain an advancing army. Often, supplies had to be shuttled in from ships anchored off the coast of an island and then hauled across the beaches on tracked vehicles. Scarcity of shipping and shortages of trained construction and engineer battalions hampered movement and became increasingly serious as American forces closed in on Japan in the final year of the war.

Americans being shipped out to the Pacific could be at sea for weeks before they reached their ultimate destination. Once there, they confronted a grimly determined enemy intent on making them pay dearly for every inch of territory yielded to the invaders. Japanese military doctrine emphasized spiritual zeal as a counter to American matériel superiority. Tactically, the Japanese stressed night fighting, infiltration, and skilled use of terrain for last-ditch defenses in which the only outcomes could be victory or death. Surrender was unthinkable. In Tunisia, when the Afrika Corps surrendered in 1943, the British captured more than 120,000 German soldiers, including a colonel general and his staff, twelve generals in all. The Allied liberation of France in the summer of 1944 netted another 200,000 Germans. As the war progressed, the Allies captured so many German officers that the British set up a special residence for them in the English countryside. During the final weeks of the war in Europe, more than 1,500,000 Germans surrendered to the Western Allies. In contrast, no organized unit of the Japanese Imperial Army surrendered during the entire Pacific war until they were ordered to do so by the emperor, after Japan had formally agreed to capitulate. This was a record unprecedented in the annals of modern warfare.[4] Japanese officers chose death over surrender, ending their lives by suicide or by leading desperate banzai charges against the Americans. Japanese soldiers fought with the same fierce fatalism demonstrated by their officers. Toward the end of the war, Japanese soldiers surrendered individually or in small groups, but most continued to fight on well past the point when the outcome of the battle was decided. This meant that American soldiers and Marines had to flush the remaining Japanese from fortified positions in caves or ravines or track them through the jungles and forbidding mountains of the Philippines. The dangers encountered in such "mopping up" exercises contributed greatly to a sense among GIs who risked their lives sealing caves or destroying bypassed strongpoints that they were engaged in a war of annihilation against an enemy resigned to his own death and determined to fight on for the sole purpose of killing as many Americans as possible.

In Europe, the power of the enemy incrementally declined as the battle moved in on Germany. In the Pacific, as one advanced from island to island to the home islands, the task grew more formidable. By the spring of 1945, as noted, the liberation of the Philippines and the battles for Iwo Jima and Okinawa had taken their toll on American combat personnel. The tropical conditions as much as the enemy had weakened the infantry. The Twenty-Fourth Division on the Philippine island of Leyte, for example, had endured continuous drenching rain. Mud and water-filled foxholes soaked the skin of one's feet, which shriveled and tore when shoes came off. The fighting was sometimes hand to hand. If a soldier fell ill he could only be taken to the hospital when his temperature reached 103. Often, food did not reach troops in the field until dropped by airplanes. The longer the infantry fought, the greater the number of cases of combat fatigue.

This account of the last year of the war in the Pacific will pay close attention to both physical and strategic restraints on American conduct of the war. Among the latter perhaps the most important were the demands of the Europe First strategy, the policy outlined at the outset of the war effort to allocate the most American resources to the fight against Nazi Germany. Once the focus of effort shifted to the Pacific the United States still had to contend with an enemy whose main land forces had yet to be engaged.

Looming over all was the realization shared by the military leaders in both nations that the greatest obstacle to an American victory would be the willingness of U.S. citizens and their representatives to support the extraordinary measures needed to subdue Japan. These concerns about the home front drove the Army's decision to implement partial demobilization following V-E Day (Victory in Europe Day). The program, announced in 1944, was devised with substantial input from GIs and reflected their belief that the rate of discharge should be based on a combination of factors, including an individual's length of service, exposure to combat, military valor, and family obligations. Apart from disregarding the overall readiness of the units from which individuals were discharged, the policy, with its announcement of a critical score required for discharge, served as an incentive in the wrong direction, toward home, for the GIs already in the Pacific and the three million soldiers and airmen in Europe scheduled for redeployment against Japan.

Germany's surrender in May 1945 created widespread expectations on the home front that there would be a lifting of wartime rationing and a loosening of economic regulation. But the Army's Pacific strategy permitted little letup. And although the war entered a seemingly uneventful interlude following the costly victory on Okinawa, the public remained fearful that even bloodier campaigns lay ahead. All the while, Radio Tokyo cooed that a softening of the policy of unconditional surrender might bring Japan's warlords to the table.

And then, in the summer of 1945 came the reckoning, causing American strategy to be thrown into turmoil. Delay or even cancelation of the scheduled invasions seemed possible, opening the way at the eleventh hour for the embrace of alternative strategies and diminished war aims. The use of the atomic bomb in August cut short a growing debate over the war's purpose, producing swift decision where none had seemed likely and obscuring the extent to which American strategy had been unhinged by Japanese resistance and the fissuring of unity at home.

Gaining Momentum

The Pacific Theater of World War II is roughly divisible into two parts: a defensive phase in 1941–1943 and an assault phase in 1944–1945. The first was one of limited resources and constant peril, of seeking to halt the Japanese advances after Pearl Harbor; protect Hawaii, Australia and the supply routes between them; preempt further advance; and stabilize the military imbalance by limited attacks and counter-pressure along the perimeter of the front. Characteristic of this early phase were prolonged, debilitating jungle campaigns and costly naval battles (Papua and the Solomons) fought by inexperienced, ill-trained troops, with inadequate supplies and transport, spotty naval and air support, and thin margins of victory (Midway and Guadalcanal). American forces advanced, but at a painfully slow pace. The dominant concerns were holding on, building up, adapting to climate and terrain, and learning from experience.

In February 1944 the balance shifted as American forces moved into unceasing offensive action on a front stretching across the Southwest and Central Pacific. Symbolic of this shift was a tiny invasion that took place February 29, 1944, on the eastern shore of Los Negros Island, which lay cheek by jowl with the Manus Islands in what was known as the Admiralty

Group, an archipelago of eighteen islands located 200 miles north of New Guinea and 723 miles southwest of the principal Japanese naval base at Truk Island, a seemingly impregnable atoll with a reef encircling islands. Coming ashore that morning from destroyers and transports were 1,000 American soldiers of the Fifth Cavalry (Robert E. Lee's regiment), First Cavalry Division. In the afternoon, General MacArthur himself came ashore to inspect the perimeter defense the troops were digging against an anticipated Japanese counterattack and left, confident his reconnaissance-in-force would hold until reinforcements arrived.[1] It did hold, against repeated and heavy attacks that night, and the remaining squadron and regiments of the First Cavalry arrived from New Guinea in time. The division cleared the island and moved over to Manus, where heavy fighting continued throughout March 1944. The campaign cost 326 Americans killed and 1,189 wounded. Most of the 4,000 Japanese defenders were killed. The prizes were airfields and one of the finest harbors in the Pacific. Los Negros thrusts northwestward, with a peninsula and trailing islands parallel to Manus, forming Seeadler Harbor, a deep anchorage some twenty miles broad and five miles wide.

This swift lunge into the Admiralties represented a radical departure from the tempo and manner of MacArthur's operations thus far. Advances to the northern coast of New Guinea and westward along that coast during 1942 and 1943 had been measured and cautious, constrained by meager resources and Japanese air and naval power on the flank. Plans now called for full-dress invasion of the Admiralties on April 1. An advance on a much larger scale had occurred earlier, in the first week of February, when Central Pacific forces under Admiral Chester W. Nimitz struck into the Marshall Islands. Rather than follow standard procedure, securing the nearer islands first, Nimitz decided to bypass them and seize Kwajalein atoll at the center. Having accomplished that expertly and quickly, Nimitz moved on immediately with fresh reserves to take Eniwetok on the northwestern fringe of the Marshalls, which was secured by February 23. In three weeks, the Pacific Fleet had leaped ahead a thousand miles; they now were a thousand miles from Saipan in the Mariana Islands, and 700 miles east of Truk. They had moved from the fringes of the great Pacific basin to within reconnaissance distance of its strategic center. How does one explain this shift from an essentially defensive role in the Pacific to a fast-paced, aggressive posture?

The immediate cause was the advent of the fast carrier forces of the Pacific Fleet. With most of its aircraft carriers lost, one by one, in the desperate defensive battles of 1942, the Navy was scraping by with only the *Saratoga* and *Enterprise,* one of which was often under repair. That began to change in May 1943 with the arrival at Pearl Harbor of the battle-ready *Essex,* the first completed in its class of thirteen attack carriers ordered in 1940 after the fall of France. In the following months came sister ships: the new *Yorktown,* the new *Lexington, Bunker Hill, Intrepid,* and more on the way. Joining the fleet as well was a new class of light carriers, built on cruiser hulls, featuring one-third the tonnage of the *Essex* and one-thrid the planes but just as fast. They served to supplement any attack and provide defense for their formations. Furthermore, eight battleships, completed after 1940, had joined the Pacific Fleet, including the 45,000-ton *Iowa* and *New Jersey,* as well as many cruisers and destroyers.[2]

As the carrier element of the fleet swelled, naval aviators pressed their case that the aircraft carrier be accepted as the centerpiece of the fleet. Promotions and key assignments increasingly went to attack-minded air officers. Slipping the leash of Pearl Harbor, the fleet moved forward, with its supply and repair ships establishing an anchorage and base at Majuro atoll, the first acquisition in the Marshalls. Strikes by larger and larger carrier task forces on Marcus, Baker, Tarawa, Wake, Rabaul, and the Gilbert Islands permitted experimentation with tactical formations and strike doctrine.[3] In the latter months of 1943 emerged Task Force 58, the striking arm of the Pacific Fleet. Commanded by Rear Admiral Marc A. Mitscher, one of the attack-minded naval officers, it consisted of six heavy and six light carriers formed into four multicarrier task groups, each with accompanying battleships, cruisers, and destroyers. After supporting the initial landings in the Marshalls, Mitscher headed west for Truk with three of his task groups. Truk's lagoon was so vast that gunfire outside the reef could not reach the anchorage inside.[4] In addition to being the principal base of the Japanese Combined Fleet, Truk had been a critical staging point for Japanese air reinforcements moving to the South Pacific.

The new carrier task forces gave the Navy a striking power that made the once formidable defenses on Truk vulnerable to attack. By mid-February 1944 most of the Japanese fleet had left, fearing such an attack. Waves of American fighters, bombers, and torpedo planes, in 1,250 combat sorties, destroyed 250 Japanese planes and about 200,000 tons of Japanese shipping and inflicted extensive damage on the base, airfields, and supplies. Truk was neutralized. Mitscher then swung northwest for raids in the Marianas that destroyed another 168 planes and 45,000 tons of shipping. As a result, Japanese garrisons on New Guinea were starved for reinforcements and supplies, and the Marianas were laid open to invasion. These Truk-Marianas raids dramatically transformed naval air warfare.[5] It was apparent to American commanders from Pearl Harbor to Brisbane that Japan's weakness along its defensive periphery begged for a faster, bolder tempo of advance. Because of the Truk attacks, the threat against MacArthur's flank had been substantially reduced. MacArthur responded by discarding plans for his own attack and immediately ordering reconnaissance in force into the Admiralties.

The new fleet vividly illustrated the capacity of the American war economy as it reached full throttle in the latter part of 1943. Between 1942 and 1945, it produced over six times the warship tonnage built for the Japanese navy. In 1943 alone, the U.S. Maritime Commission delivered over eighteen million tons of merchant shipping (Liberty and Victory types, mass-produced and assembled in sections, as well as standard cargo ships and tankers). Gross national product increased by half. Production was based on a firm bed of national support for the war, although debate over allocation of resources was incessant, with labor and management bitterly contesting work rules and wages. Nevertheless, however much Americans differed on domestic issues involving the war, they agreed on its necessity and generally understood that they were participating in a common effort to achieve victory. Conflict was abated with the dictum "Let's get on with the war."

National unity goes a long way in explaining the success of the American war effort, together with a rich endowment of natural resources, agricultural and mineral, and the nation's immunity from attack. So do "the strengths of the American industrial tradition," pointed out by Richard Overy; "the widespread experience of mass production, the great depth of technical and organizational skill, the willingness to 'think big,' the ethos of hustling competition."[6] Although all-out mobilization did not begin until early 1941, the country's major shipyards in the Delaware and Chesapeake bays, New York, and Boston were already fully engaged; eight battleships and five aircraft carriers were on the way by the time Pearl Harbor was attacked on December 7. A year and a half earlier, on May 16, 1940, Roosevelt had called for a production capacity of at least 50,000 airplanes a year, then an unimaginable goal. Again and again he challenged the economy by raising his expectations, creating in the public and bureaucratic mindset an image of industrial potential consonant with the nation's capacity.

Achievement of that capacity depended on establishing systems for allocating available raw materials and plant space among the competing programs and on juggling the needs of the military services, wartime allies, and the civilian sector. Only after months of trial and error—and bitter bureaucratic contention—did the War Production Board, the entity created in 1942 to oversee the war effort, bring the American economy up to speed. Governing the Board and the production process was a combination of military procurement officers and industrial executives on loan. By late 1942, the government had effectively imposed a whole new war economy on top of the existing civilian economy, first squeezing the latter, especially in consumer durables, and then putting it on hold, turning the increase in gross national product over to the military.[7]

Behind the rise in American war production was a 25 percent increase in the productivity of American labor from 1940 to 1944, twice the rise of German labor productivity and five times that of Japan. Since the U.S. government contracted primarily with corporations that had experience in large-scale manufacturing and standardization of product, over half of the contracts between 1940 and 1944 were placed among merely thirty-three corporations out of the nation's approximately 175,000 industrial concerns. These corporations were of course among the nation's largest, hence worker productivity benefited from application of efficiency techniques on the assembly line. The assembly process in the Ford Motor Company's Willow Run bomber plant in Michigan, for example, stretched through a building nearly one mile long and emitted, at peak performance, a B-24 bomber every sixty-three minutes.[8] In the Kaiser shipyards at Richmond on San Francisco Bay, one assembly process served six building ways, with parts moving from railway cars, fabrication and assembly buildings, and storage toward the rising hulls on the ways, then lifted aboard by cranes. Efficiency improved with standardized design (the Liberty and Victory ships), substitution of welding for riveting, subassembly outside the yard of components, such as portions of the deck house and forepeak-prow, and disassembling the labor process into simplified and repetitive tasks so that inexperienced workers could be quickly trained. In March 1942 the average building time for a Liberty ship from keel-laying to delivery was 207 days; by June 1942 it was 118 days. For the Kaiser Richmond yard, it was 69 days.[9]

By the third quarter of 1943—July to September—the American war economy shifted from a steady, steep climb in production to a plateau of full production. The war economy conceived in 1941—to incredulity—had substantially been realized. The armies, fleets, and air forces and the huge supply and transportation equipment that supported them were already overseas or lining up in depots, rail yards, and staging areas ready for shipment. Pacific commanders constantly complained about the predominant strategic role assigned to the European Theater, which entitled it to top priority in acquisition of troops and matériel, leaving the Pacific shorthanded and undersupplied. And indeed in the last year of the war, the requirements of the European Theater overshadowed those of the Pacific. Nevertheless, in the early months of the war the JCS shipped troops almost exclusively to the Pacific, to garrison the lifeline to Australia. Beginning in late 1942 it had assigned or approved increasingly expansive campaigns in the Solomons, New Guinea, and the Central Pacific for which it supplied troops in large numbers.

The Pacific Theater benefited from uncertainty about European strategy. Soon after Pearl Harbor, Winston Churchill and Roosevelt met and agreed that Germany presented the greatest threat and had to be defeated by invasion of northwest Europe. However, two years passed before the Cairo-Tehran conferences in late 1943, at which they set a date—May 1944—and named a commander, General Dwight D. Eisenhower. Holding that offensive action in the Pacific was slightly less important than across the English Channel, and far more valuable than gambits beyond Italy into the eastern Mediterranean, such as the British were urging. The JCS nonetheless kept up a steady westward flow of divisions, containing anywhere from 10,000 to 15,000 men each, well into 1944.[10] However, once Eisenhower was fully in charge, accumulating forces for the invasion of France, Washington brought Pacific reinforcement to a halt and directed deployment toward Europe. After D-Day, plans for Pacific reinforcement revived but expired with the German counteroffensive in the Ardennes in December 1944. Two divisions staging for the Pacific were redirected to Europe. After July 1944, no additional division embarked on the Pacific for the rest of the war.

By that point, however, the Pacific commands had gathered in a substantial portion of the United States Army while they could. Nine divisions were stationed in the Pacific at the end of 1942: four in the Central Pacific (including Hawaii); three in the South Pacific; and two in the Southwest Pacific. By the end of 1943 there were thirteen divisions. By the end of 1944 there were twenty-one, not including six Marine divisions and Australian and New Zealand forces. In fact not until October 1943 were there more divisions in the European Theater than in the Pacific. Furthermore, at the end of 1943 there were 8,807 Army and Navy aircraft deployed against Germany and 7,857 against Japan. Still, the disparity was apparent. Ultimately, Eisenhower commanded sixty-three American divisions; the Pacific peaked at twenty-seven.[11] These numbers don't tell the whole story, however. Critical to the equation between theaters was the United States Navy, entirely concentrated against Japan except for antisubmarine warfare in the Atlantic and limited bombardment and amphibious lift responsibilities in the Normandy and Mediterranean invasions. The Pacific Fleet essentially got what it needed in ships and supplies, as did the Marine divisions. Despite the priority of Europe, the Pacific collected enough forces for powerful, accelerated advances in 1944.

Reorganizing the forces they had gave the Pacific commands even more offensive punch. The progressive weakening and isolation of Japanese forces on the periphery brought about by rising American sea and airpower provided sufficient safety along the line of communications to Australia to release troops from garrison duty for further training and action. The Pacific lacked a large landmass, such as England provided for the European Theater, where troops could be concentrated in preparation for an offensive. The Pacific troops' bases would always be scattered, and there would always be oceanic voyages between preparation and assault. Nevertheless, the center of gravity of American divisions in the Pacific shifted at least 2,000 miles westward in the period 1942–1944. Thus the Americal Division, a name derived from shortening "American troops in New Caledonia"—an island lying between Australia and New Zealand—was formed from separate garrison regiments in May 1942, after the Battle of Coral Sea, which, though a narrow victory, relieved fears of Japanese invasion. The Americal followed the First Marine Division into the Battle of Guadalcanal in October 1942, while the Forty-Third Division arrived to take its place on New Caledonia. Similarly, the Twenty-Fourth and Twenty-Fifth Divisions, the Hawaiian garrison, moved to the South and Southwest Pacific, making way for divisions stopping in Hawaii for jungle warfare and amphibious training (and quieting local residents' fears of being left unprotected). Later, following a more systematized model designed to save shipping, the Sixth Division took over the transports, bringing the Thirty-Eighth Division into Hawaii along with its own equipment already aboard and in place for the Thirty-Eighth. In this way incoming divisions met training and garrison needs while steadily shunting westward toward battle in a sort of caterpillar movement of concentration and then extension.[12]

The apportionment of military resources for the Pacific was a matter of grand strategy agreed on at the highest levels of government. The JCS would provide what they could; the theater's commanders might ask for more but had to settle for what they got. The Joint Chiefs were also the ultimate arbiters of what strategy to follow in using these resources to defeat Japan. However, on questions of theater strategy the Pacific commanders had more say, and the Joint Chiefs adopted a supervisory role. This meant that strategy was subject to bone-deep bureaucratic conflict and the indeterminate debate between the Army and Navy, in the Pacific as well as in Washington.

Nobody was more fully engaged in playing a mediating role than Army chief of staff George Marshall, the most influential and respected military leader in Washington.[13] Marshall was born in 1880 at Uniontown in rural southwestern Pennsylvania. Young George learned less from school than from reading at home, especially being read to by his father, who, he said, read aloud "very well, and liked to do it." In retirement he remembered that the books he most admired were William H. Prescott's *The Conquest of Mexico*, the James Fenimore Cooper frontier stories, the G. A. Henty books for boys, such as *With Clive in India,* and especially *The Young Carthaginian* (Hannibal). Arthur Conan Doyle's *The Refugees,* was a "thrilling" tale of French Huguenots fleeing the Indians in the Canadian wilderness. (He found much later, to his delight, that Queen Elizabeth II shared his enthusiasm for Conan Doyle's *Sir Nigel.*) Tales of daring and conquest in faraway places inspired by Victorian imperialism not only raised thoughts of a military career but also widened his horizons.[14]

History abounded in the glades and hills east of Uniontown, where the Marshalls, father and son, hunted and fished. His father showed him the outline of the trench at Fort Necessity, where George Washington surrendered to the French in 1754, and, Marshall reminisced: "the first shot was fired . . . which was literally heard round the world in those days—upset the thrones of Europe and pretty much changed the face of political Europe." Settlers heading west to the Ohio River in Conestoga wagons passed through Uniontown. "So there was a great deal of history, and very, very important history . . . written in that vicinity," he recalled, "and there was this great life of the nation which flowed through the National Pike and stopped overnight at the inn, just two blocks beyond the house that I lived in as a boy."[15] Quite naturally young Marshall saw himself in the stream of American history.

For many, the military profession had a narrowing effect on the mind, with its settled theory, bureaucracy, and imperatives of command. Not so Marshall. He had a powerful and perpetually inquisitive mind and an awareness beyond the garrison, of things in time, changing and unchanging. His soldierly skills operated within this worldly context. He graduated from Virginia Military Institute in 1901 and entered the Army the following year. His first posting was to the Philippines, both in Manila and the island of Mindoro, just south of Luzon. During a second tour there in 1913–1916, he acquired a set of combat reports on the Philippine Insurrection, studied them carefully, and visited the principal battle sites. He also participated in maneuvers on Luzon and survived a typhoon at sea on a small interisland ship. He was by no means unschooled on the Philippines. In World War I, he earned a reputation for his brilliant staff work at the division, corps, and army levels and at General John J. Pershing's headquarters, particularly his planning for the Meuse-Argonne offensive, the largest of the American engagements. Preparation required withdrawing 220,000 Allied troops from the front while sending in 600,000 Americans, over three rail lines and three roads, at night.

In the interwar period Marshall served in China with the American contingent of the international garrison at Tianjin. He widened his experience during tours of duty training National Guard troops in Illinois and running Civilian Conservation Corps camps for unemployed youth in Oregon. On September 1, 1939, President Roosevelt, in a critical step toward his revamping the nation's military leadership, appointed Marshall chief of staff of the Army.

The shock of Pearl Harbor and the daunting challenge of a two-front war against Germany and Japan demanded, and at the same time facilitated, a fundamental reorganization of the Army high command. Within eight weeks Marshall and his senior staff devised a radically different "command post" that proved effective and remained in place until the end of the war.

The existing structure consisted of a host of War Department staffs and agencies, all of them reporting independently and directly to the chief of staff, and many of them having little direct relevance to what Marshall took as his central responsibility—the direction of American military operations in a global war. The solution involved a devolution of responsibility that meant establishing three new semiautonomous commands whose functions were more prescribed, self-administration was more practical, and practices were more standard. The first of these three commands was the Army Air Forces (AAF), an entity that already enjoyed relative autonomy. The second was the Army Service Forces: the principal procurement agency of the military that managed the housing, feeding, medical care, transport, and other needs of troops as well as the operation of various independent agencies.[16]

The responsibility for training Army troops lay with the third of these commands, Army Ground Forces Command. Into 1944, the procurement and training of infantry to fill the ranks of the nine rifle battalions in a division proved disappointing.[17] To avoid stationary warfare, the planners of the World War II infantry division had dropped the number of regiments in a division from four, as there had been in World War I, to three, with the idea of producing a more mobile force, advancing alongside armor and airpower. Besides their own weapons, the 6,000 or so infantry in a division of over 14,000 would carry and use parts of heavy and light machine guns and their ammunition; mortar base plates, tubes, and shells; and grenades, shoulder-fired rocket launchers, and flamethrowers. They learned weapons skills, bayonet attack and defense, squad and platoon tactics, and camouflage. They carried heavy packs, stood night watches, and made long marches. They needed good vision, dependable memory, aptitude, and, for leadership, initiative and judgment. Infantry had powerful support, especially from the artillery, but they were the ones who physically engaged the enemy; they were the teeth of the division. Ground Forces wanted its men intelligent, strong, and, for endurance, young. Draftees did not rush to enlist; given that it did the dirty work, the infantry was not popular. Preferable were the Navy, the Marines (for the bold), the Air Cadets, the Officer Training Schools, the Army Specialized Training Program, and the Service Forces. Others stayed home, exempted from national service by family farm work. In the physical and mental classifications, the Army Infantry Replacement Training Centers found their trainees somewhat below Army averages.

As mobilization of the Army progressed, the outlook for infantry, if anything, darkened. The Air Force, undergoing a huge buildup and needing recruits with the intelligence to develop technical skills, insisted that 75 percent of those sent to the Air Force have induction scores in the top brackets of the Army General Classification Test. This drained much of the pool that Army Ground Forces looked to for troop leadership. When

Congress lowered the draft age from twenty to eighteen in late 1942, Ground Forces was particularly hopeful of gaining new infantry recruits. The infantry indeed got a share of them, but not without burden. To the Army they were young men full of vigor and stamina; to their families and Congress they were still boys. The Army thought they should go overseas when training was complete, like the rest. The War Department, however, with Congress in mind, kept shifting restraints that usually kept the "boy" out of battle at least until the age of nineteen.[18] As the war went on, draft calls were yielding fewer recruits, and these were physically inferior. Furthermore, the Army had grown to 8,000,000, past an authorized strength of 7,700,000, so infantry replacements would mostly have to come from within the Army.

In late 1943 and 1944 the bulk of the Army moved overseas, establishing and extending battlefronts into western Europe and the western Pacific, and in that migration the role of the infantry within divisions and as replacements became critical. Before the Ardennes breakout, in December 1944, the battles in Italy, the Normandy hedgerows, and especially along the German border in October and November 1944 all made it evident that the Army had failed to anticipate the strain of combat, especially for infantry.[19]

For the preparation and direction of the Army's combat operations, Marshall established the Operations Division of the General Staff (OPD), building on the existing War Plans Division, which had been created in 1921. Established in March 1942, beginning with over 100 officers, mostly field grade with a sprinkling of generals and reporting directly to Marshall and his deputy, the OPD took up quarters in the Pentagon, which had just been constructed. The OPD dealt in specifics. Its central purpose was to design military operations that reflected both the realities facing the president and relations with allies and the Army's and Navy's strategic premises. Its job was also to estimate, gather, and dispatch the necessary resources, balancing the need against operations elsewhere; to determine timing and objective; and to supervise the action and assist in the outcome. The OPD combined the flexibility and versatility of a field command with the resources of a supreme headquarters. It both maintained its own classified records and managed the War Department's worldwide communications net. Composing the OPD were the planning section (Strategy and Policy); the Theater Section, with experts in the circumstances and needs of each war theater; the Troop Control section, for arranging deployments; and the Logistics Section, for estimating and providing the necessary supplies for an operation. The OPD also manned the committees of the Joint Chiefs and Combined Chiefs of Staff. It absorbed much of the personnel and functions of three of the traditional staff sections collateral to it: G1 (Personnel), G3 (Operations and Training), and G4 (Logistics). Only G2, on which the OPD remained dependent for intelligence, operated independently. Working on common projects created, if not collegiality, at least a lessening of formalities that had existed before the creation of the OPD: fewer written concurrences, for example, and quicker access to the chief of staff and his deputy.

The shapers of strategy for an army in global conflict were bound to encounter political issues and had to deal with them. American military leadership and their planners internalized Carl von Clausewitz's famous dictum that war is an instrument of policy and they recognized the need for politico-military coordination and political input on strategy and operations.[20] Marshall was highly sensitive to the boundary between civilian and military authority and often testified before committees of Congress on issues in which the boundary was blurred, such as Selective Service, manpower, war production, and budgets. It was in the nature of his job to take into account the political aims and constraints imposed by the president and Congress and if necessary to defend the critical programs of the Army in that context. The same was true of deliberations, mostly with the Navy and in the JCS and its committees as well as the British-American Combined Chiefs of Staff, created just after Pearl Harbor, and especially of the intensely political environment of the meetings, held every few months in Washington and abroad, at which Roosevelt and his staff met with Churchill and others.

In mid-1943, as the tide turned against the Japanese, American military planners, particularly Marshall, began to give greater focus to how best to defeat Japan. Settling in the minds of the Joint Chiefs was a set of informal and interdependent principles that, over the course of the following year, hardened into convictions and powered strategic planning for the Pacific.[21] To begin with, unconditional surrender was essential, a condition the president himself had announced in January 1943. His definition of it as the "elimination of German and Japanese war power" suited the Army well, given the Japanese military's domination of its government.[22] To end the war without eliminating Japan's capacity for aggression would be an utter waste of lives and treasure. To effect such a fundamental change in mentality, given the do-or-die resistance of Japanese troops, meant that invasion of the home islands and defeat of the Japanese army there would very likely be necessary. Conquering and occupying enemy territory, especially the industrial region around Tokyo, was the most effective way of inducing surrender. At the same time, the term "unconditional" sounded sufficiently dire and all-encompassing to reflect the American public's hostility toward Japan due to the "sneak attack" on Pearl Harbor. Unconditional surrender, the planners believed, was a concrete objective, one that Americans could understand.[23]

A second principle was the belief that popular support for the war would not be without limits, in terms of either the amount of sacrifice or the length of time. Roosevelt worried that the American people did not understand the level of sacrifice needed to defeat the Axis in a worldwide struggle. He frequently spoke publicly about the danger of public indifference and what he referred to as the "peaks and valleys" of overconfidence and despair. In the summer of 1943, Marshall also warned of false optimism and the need for "stoic determination."[24] Secretary of War Henry L. Stimson and Undersecretary Robert P. Patterson both shared this view. Bringing an end to the Pacific war would be a formidable challenge. As mass deployments began in 1943 for the great offensives of 1944, the JCS began to consider how much longer it would be until final victory. If all went well with the Normandy invasion, the war in Europe might end in 1944 and certainly in 1945. They also knew that it would take another year to redeploy forces from Europe and mount an invasion of Japan. So there would be a lag between victory in Europe and invasion of Japan. The Pacific war would probably not end before 1946 or even 1947. Lagging progress, despiriting

casualties, and unfulfilled objectives would dissolve national unity and produce pressure for a compromise peace, one that would leave Japan essentially unchanged. In the estimation of JCS leaders a five-year war would be
problematic, a six-year war—one that went into 1947—unacceptable.[25]

A third principle among Marshall and the JCS planners followed from
these first two. To achieve unconditional surrender while maintaining public
support, speed was going to be essential. Marshall felt that the United States
could not afford to spend lives and time on preliminary or secondary operations that did not lead in a measurable way toward the goal of invading
Japan; one needed a yardstick that provided what he termed "incremental
dividends," insular milestones on the road to Tokyo, to keep the American
public engaged.[26] Marshall therefore opposed projects promoted by allies
for the Mediterranean and Southeast Asia that in his mind would fritter
away resources from the overriding objective of defeating Germany and
then Japan.[27] British arguments for the postponement of the invasion of
France drew from Marshall the counterargument that American resources
reserved for that event would not be otherwise available because of the
need in the Pacific for maintaining unrelenting pressure on the Japanese.[28]

These three interrelated principles—unconditional surrender, awareness of American public opinion, and the need for unrelenting pressure on
Japan—formed a strategic paradigm for the War Department, underlying
specific campaign planning. Thus intensifying operations against Japan
would shorten the war, maintain public support, and preempt completion
of Japanese defenses, thereby reducing casualties. Increasingly in 1944, military strategy followed a tight schedule. The approach to Japan, victory in
Europe, redeployment from Europe, and invasion of Japan had to occur
within a time frame tolerable to the American public.[29]

The Navy had a different planning perspective, which, when it conflicted
with the Army's, had to be mediated through the JCS. The Navy's view was
more limited and traditional and was formulated after Japan had initiated
the war and seized the Philippines. At the heart of naval strategy was the
destruction of the Japanese fleet. The American fleet, once concentrated
and supplied, would strike for the western Pacific, capturing bases in the
Japanese mandates along the way and drawing the Japanese into a decisive

main fleet engagement. This concept guided the Marshalls and Marianas campaigns of 1943–1944, the main fleet being the new, fast carrier-battleship forces of the Pacific Fleet. After it had met and defeated the Japanese navy in the decisive fleet action, the Navy, controlling the Pacific, would encircle and besiege Japan from nearby island bases, thereby forcing surrender. The Navy recognized that the length of such a siege would be indeterminate and an invasion of the home islands might be necessary, but once the troops were landed, that would be an Army show. What to the Army would be the climax of the war would be to the Navy an anticlimax—a mere mopping-up operation. Nor did the Navy dwell on public opinion as a limiting factor. Their planners were engaged in a more technical and esoteric profession, less concerned with the American public than the Army, with its National Guard training responsibilities and public works projects.

However, the Navy was in no way laggard about demanding that pressure on the enemy be unrelenting, and pressing hardest was the commander-in-chief of the United States Fleet and chief of naval operations, Admiral Ernest Joseph King. Roosevelt chose King to command the Atlantic Squadron (soon to become a fleet) in 1940 because he considered him just the man to shake the Navy out of its peacetime psychology.[30] King, born in Lorain, Ohio, of Scots parents, was a dour and driving commander, harboring "a storm within him"—as a *Time* piece described him—and merciless toward sloth and incompetence.[31] He quickly and skillfully brought the fleet to war readiness and convoy duty on the Atlantic, gaining the unswerving support of the president, who placed him in charge of a Navy stunned by Pearl Harbor. King was probably the most versatile and knowledgeable commander-in-chief Roosevelt could have chosen, with experience as an engineering officer, destroyer division commander, and assistant chief of staff to the commander of the Atlantic Fleet in World War I. In the interwar period, after duty in submarines, King attended the Naval War College, earned his wings as a naval aviator, and served as captain of the carrier *Lexington*, chief of the Bureau of Aeronautics, and commander of the Aircraft Battle Force.[32]

King was also a brilliant strategist and aggressive proponent of the Navy's path to victory in the Pacific. In the early months of 1942, when the Japanese advance southward seemed unstoppable, he pressed not just for defense of the line of communications to Australia but beyond that for a preemptive move into the Solomon Islands. In the ensuing naval battles around Guadalcanal that proved so costly to both sides, he insisted on reinforcement, wagering precious aircraft carriers, one after another, and finally battleships, until the Japanese withdrew and their overall retreat began. King was quite different from Marshall. King's world was bounded by war at sea; he had no interest in civilians and felt little respect for them. If he believed that speed was essential in moving in on Japan, it was not to appease the American public but to prevent Japan from consolidating its defenses and to establish the Navy as a dynamic and critical player in the war.

Like Marshall, King reorganized his seat of command to suit his needs but less broadly and substantively, and mainly to enhance his personal authority and discretion. He consolidated his personal authority by assuming the positions of both commander-in-chief of the fleet and chief of naval operations. In this fashion he exercised more explicit command authority over fleet operations in the Pacific than Marshall held over theater commands of the Army, though, of course, both were bound by the decisions of the JCS. He kept close watch over the Pacific Fleet, meeting its commander, Admiral Chester W. Nimitz, on a bimonthly basis in San Francisco. Unlike Marshall, King did not create the equivalent of an OPD. His control mechanism was more spare and personal, depending heavily on key staff officers, such as Vice Admiral Frederick C. Horne for logistics and Rear Admiral Charles M. Cooke for planning. Otherwise he rotated officers out to the fleet and back to his staff.[33] Nor did King integrate and leash the technical and supply bureaus of the Navy, as Marshall had done by establishing the Army Service Forces. The Navy Department remained essentially a "hyphenated and atomistic structure,"[34] requiring extensive coordination and stopgap solutions.

By the end of 1943, as we've shown, the American leadership had decided to raise the tempo of war in the Pacific even as it gathered divisions for the invasion of Europe. Existing forces in the Pacific, joined by the new carrier fleet, were to draw out the Japanese fleet and sink it. Assault forces—air, land, and sea—were to move the Pacific "front" from the equatorial region to within bombardment and invasion range of Japan itself, there to be joined by air and land forces redeployed from Europe after the defeat of Germany. If Japan still refused unconditional surrender, invasion would be necessary. King, however, remained confident that a siege would bring Japan to its knees and viewed invasion as a remote possibility.[35] However much the Army and Navy might disagree over the necessity of invasion, King, Marshall, and the JCS were in total agreement on the need for developing momentum—unstoppable momentum—toward Japan itself.

On March 12, 1944, two weeks after Nimitz's seizure of Kwajalein in the Marshall Islands and MacArthur's advance into the Admiralties, the JCS sent the two Pacific area commanders a directive, setting forth their next stage of advance. The Pacific Fleet would occupy the southern Marianas (Saipan, Tinian, and Guam) on June 15, three months hence. It would then advance southwestward through the Carolines and by September 15 seize the Palau Islands, only 600 miles from Mindanao, the large island in the southern Philippines, there to establish air and sea bases for further advance.[36] Meanwhile, on April 22 MacArthur's Southwest Pacific forces were to occupy the Japanese post of Hollandia, located some 500 miles westward along the northern coast of New Guinea and within heavy-bomber range of the Palaus. By November 15, these forces, supported by the Pacific Fleet, would occupy Mindanao. Bypassed and isolated would be several Japanese garrisons along the intervening coast as well as Japanese bases in the Carolines, particularly Truk. Kavieng on New Ireland and Rabaul on New Britain would be neutralized rather than invaded. Thus the two Pacific forces of Nimitz and MacArthur would run westward, roughly parallel to each other, to Mindanao, with the fast carriers first supporting one and then the other. American forces who had spent two years fighting in eastern New Guinea and the Solomons were now to leap some 2,000 miles in nine months.

The March 12 directive did not mention—and did not need to—one major objective of the assault on the Marianas: the expectation of a major fleet engagement with the Japanese navy. The Saipan/Tinian/Guam cluster lay at the center of the western Pacific, at the midpoint of a gigantic insular crescent barring the way to Asia, stretching southward from the home islands of Japan and through the Ryukyu chain, Formosa, the Philippines, the Moluccas, and New Guinea. Aside from vessels in home ports, the Japanese fleet had largely retired from the Pacific, abandoning Truk for Singapore and Tawi Tawi, a Philippine island close to the Navy's oil supply in Borneo and to passages eastward through the sheltering island chain into the broad Pacific. It was unlikely that Japan could ignore the challenge presented by an attack on the Marianas, which American planners saw as a choke point in the air reinforcement "pipeline" running south from Japan and which, as the March 12 directive specified, would provide the Americans with "sea and air bases for operations against the Japanese homeland."[37] Victory in a main fleet engagement, something the Pacific Fleet was confident it could achieve, would extend sea control to the expanse of ocean lying between the Philippines and the Marianas, known as the Philippine Sea, and perhaps much more.

The final objective of the 1944 Pacific advance, as set forth by the March 12 directive, was to gain a foothold in the area of Luzon—Formosa—China. Naval leadership did not deny that an invasion of Japan might ultimately be necessary but believed that encirclement, blockade, and bombardment would bring Japan to submission at far less cost. The Navy's view in early 1944 was that encirclement should begin with Formosa, cutting off Japan from its troops and resources in southern China and Southeast Asia like a cork put into the neck of a bottle. Then, through nearby ports on the China mainland, the United States would supply the Chinese with arms for attacking strategic Japanese territories to the north—Shantung, Korea, and Manchuria—thus, in the words of Admiral "Savvy" Cooke, "utilizing their manpower as the ultimate land force in defeating Japan on the continent of Asia."[38] This was scarcely a formula for speedy surrender.

The issue in debate among commanders and planners in Washington was whether to go the Navy way—directly to Formosa—or, as MacArthur insisted, to go by way of the Philippines. The inclusion of Mindanao was a handicap to the Formosa project: American forces would be far to the south in that attack, subject to prolonged air attack from Luzon when they moved north.[39] On the other hand, inclusion of Mindanao returned MacArthur to the Philippines and kept him in the strategic picture. Furthermore, the directive allowed that while Formosa was scheduled to be taken by February 15, 1945, "should such operations prove necessary prior to the move on Formosa," occupation of Luzon would occur on February 15 with no further date assigned to Formosa. The purpose of the directive was to keep open both the Army's and the Navy's strategic objectives. The JCS wanted large-scale and swift action on immediate objectives in the Pacific. Its concentration of power and depth of thrust promised to change radically the configuration of the war in the Pacific. The competitive nature of the twin drives provided an incentive for speed, and its open-endedness allowed for the seizing of opportunities provided by a changing battlefield.

The Pacific war of World War II was a war for airfields.[40] Army and Navy air forces were essential to offensive operations and followed the same procedures, whether over land or water. Navy pilots would attack Japanese airfields until enemy forces were isolated, neutralized, and bereft of capacity to interfere with American operations. These would be bypassed or assaulted, depending on circumstances. Seizure was followed by airfield repair or construction. The fleet train would follow and build bases. Planes would move forward to these new bases and set out on missions, extending the reach of American power several hundred miles farther, and the process would repeat itself. The same process occurred with Army pilots over the enormous jungle-covered island of New Guinea. Army planes would beat down Japanese defenses. Assault troops would arrive and carve a chunk out of the vast wilderness to make room for an airfield, depots, and a defensive perimeter. An American "island" would emerge from the jungle, and the process would continue, with planes hopping from island to island over jungle or ocean. It was not frontal and territorial but point-to-point and web-like, yet creating an expanding zone of control.

Both strategies required substantial reorganization and concentration of Pacific troop strength. With the completion of the Solomons campaign in February 1943, the South Pacific area command was superfluous. The JCS eliminated it and divvied up its resources between the Southwest Pacific and Central Pacific commands: the Army divisions, Thirteenth Air Force, and smaller vessels went to MacArthur, and the Marine divisions, Navy and Marine air units, and larger warships to Nimitz. To Nimitz also went Admiral William F. Halsey as a fleet commander and, from the Aleutians, now a backwater, the Seventh Infantry Division.

Hence by 1943 the Pacific operations were being run by McArthur and Nimitz. Nimitz's headquarters overlooked Pearl Harbor, which seemed to one onlooker to be "almost paved with steel" by the ships of the "big blue fleet," until it left for the Marshalls campaign in early January 1944.[41] Even after they had left, Hawaii teemed with soldiers and sailors and repair, supply, and command facilities, not to mention airfields, hospitals, and training bases. Nimitz had administrative responsibilities for all Navy and Army personnel in the Pacific except for the Southwest Pacific, where MacArthur reigned supreme. Nimitz had been chosen to command the Pacific Fleet by the president and Secretary Frank Knox ten days after the attack on Pearl Harbor. Nimitz's first job was to restore confidence in a demoralized fleet, and he had the personality and skills to do so. Possessed of "a sunny disposition and an unruffled demeanor," he relaxed with classical music, regular exercise, swimming, walking, and target practice with a pistol. Samuel Eliot Morison describes him as "the most accessible, considerate and beloved of fleet commanders," calm, confident, and courteous, prompt and firm in decisions, and having an "almost impeccable judgment of men."[42] Born in Fredericksburg in the hill country of west Texas (near Lyndon B. Johnson's birthplace) Nimitz had graduated from the Naval Academy in 1905. He had served in submarines, cruisers, battleships, and, most recently, as chief of the Bureau of Navigation, in effect head of personnel in the Navy.

As a fleet and theater commander, Nimitz had been given seventy million square miles of ocean to rule or conquer and by 1945 a force growing finally to 1,500 ships with which to do it.[43] Threading his way through the precarious decision-making of the period from Pearl Harbor through Guadalcanal, 1941 until February 1943, he had managed the vast enlargement and reconstitution of his fleet and then launched it into unceasing offensive campaigning. This he did under the scrutiny of his most exacting and demanding superior, Admiral King, on one side and a suspicious and contentious rival on the other, General MacArthur.

Nimitz's principal weapon was the fast carrier force of eighty-eight warships, including battleships, cruisers, and destroyers, described by Morison as it sortied from Majuro atoll on June 6, 1944, and headed west to initiate the Marianas campaign: "In a setting of sparkling blue water, the long reef stretching out of sight [the ships] form a column that steams proudly through the pass at 15 knots. With much making and executing of long hoists of brightly colored flags, they deploy into a circular cruising formation."[44] A formidable weapon, it still had limitations. Naval air strategists believed carriers needed plenty of sea room so that they could appear out of nowhere to strike the enemy, as the Japanese fleet did at Pearl Harbor, and then disappear. Carriers were vulnerable to land-based air attack and should not be tethered to a particular military operation or trapped in narrow passages among islands, such as the Philippines. Furthermore, ships, crews, pilots, and planes experiencing prolonged combat conditions required frequent harboring for resupply and repair, beyond what could be transferred at sea.

A no less formidable weapon was the amphibious assault force, whose composition engaged most of the fleet.[45] The number of divisions assigned to an invasion generally increased as the fleet moved closer to Japan: from one division at Tarawa in November 1943 to several in the Marshalls in January 1944, five in the Marianas in June 1944 and seven at Okinawa in April 1945. Usually the ground force included both Marine and Army divisions, and before Okinawa the overall ground command was Marine. All divisions took special, indispensable amphibious training either in southern California or Hawaii, and all rehearsed forthcoming landings. The amphibious assault was a minutely scripted drama of multiple and sequential firepower used in the seizure of a beachhead. The preparatory phase began with several days of attacks by fast carrier forces: raids on the airfields, then bombing of invasion defenses, then bombardment by the new battleships with their 16-inch guns. The day before and the early morning of the day of landings drew a full-throated roar from older pre–Pearl Harbor battleships as well as cruisers, destroyers, and planes from escort carriers. The assault troops came ashore in waves of landing craft, strictly monitored by control boats on the flanks. The first waves had sailed partway by transports and then by landing ship tanks (LSTs), 300-foot vessels with bow ramps, in which were stowed amphibious tractors (amphtracs). At the invasion site, with the troops aboard, these clattered down the ramp to line up before crossing the reef encircling the island. Behind them came troop transports with their own landing craft hoisted aboard. These were lowered and filled with troops, who climbed over the sides of the transports and down cargo nets as they rose and fell on the waves. The landing craft then circled, formed waves, and moved after the amphtracs toward the beach, passing bombardment ships, including the cruisers and destroyers lined up outside the reef and the gunboats farther in. The schematics were meticulous, the reality always different.

A third weapon was the submarine, a service slow to hit its stride but devastatingly effective in the last half of the war. Many of the obstacles during the first half were to be expected: too few submarines, a shortage of torpedoes, the huge distances from bases to Japanese shipping routes, the extensive training required for specialists. What was perhaps most surprising was the widespread malfunction of torpedoes, made worse by the Navy Bureau of Ordnance's failure to take charge of the problem and fix it, illustrative of the autonomy of bureaus in the Navy Department. Finally, after interventions by both Nimitz and King, testing showed that the guidance and exploder systems were defective. Remedies weren't found until the end of September 1943, halfway through the war, after which they proved effective.[46] Next to torpedo failure and perhaps affected by it was a conservative mindset among submarine commanders. In World War I, the United States stood against unrestricted submarine warfare and in the interwar period did not anticipate waging war against enemy commerce. Instead the submarine was tied to the main fleet and used for scouting and attacking enemy warships. With the advent of underwater sound tracking (sonar) and airplane surveillance, the submarine seemed much more vulnerable. Naval strategy held that it must not be sighted on the surface and should fire by sonar from depths below periscope level. Such advice encouraged a defensive mindset and meager results. In 1942, 30 percent of submarine commanders were relieved for "unfitness or lack of results" and replaced by younger, more aggressive officers.[47]

A huge boon to the U.S. submarine program was the breaking of the Japanese convoy code, as it opened the way to concerted operations against the enemy merchant marine. As American power in the Pacific expanded westward, submarine tenders moved with it to refuel and rearm the boats (submarines are categorized as boats, not ships) at Pearl Harbor, Fremantle—located near Perth on the west coast of Australia—and Brisbane on Australia's east coast. Those stationed at Pearl Harbor (around 100 in total) headed for Japanese waters, the East China Sea, and Formosa; those at Fremantle to the South China Sea and minor seas in between; and those at Brisbane to the Solomons, New Guinea, and the Philippines, together forty more submarines. They were at sea for periods of between fifty and fifty-five days, on station roughly half of those days. Those from Australia ran supplies and liaison personnel to Filipino guerrilla forces and returned with refugees; from time to time others scouted Japanese fleet movements.[48]

By late 1943 the submarine campaign was better coordinated. The fleet was forming small packs sent in rotating assignments on a checkerboard of patrol zones in the China Seas. By then the submarines posed a major threat to the resource supply of Japan. They were maneuverable, long ranged, and silent when submerged, boasting sturdy hulls, reliable armament and engines, excellent air and surface search radars, and, with air conditioning, minimal crew discomfort. The Japanese navy, short of escort vessels, had no adequate defense.[49] The rate at which submarines sank Japanese merchant vessels rose steadily in 1942 and 1943 and then sharply after the torpedo problems were fixed: 180 were sunk in 1942, 296 in 1943, and over 600 in 1944. In the last months of the war the fast carrier forces and aerial mining increased sinkings substantially. Altogether, American forces sank 2,117 Japanese merchant ships in the war, with submarines responsible for about 55 percent of the total.[50] Japan's prewar merchant fleet of six million tons, swelled by wartime construction and seizures, was reduced to less than two million tons. The submarines also sank 201 warships, including eight aircraft carriers. By 1945 Japan had lost most of its ships and the oil they carried and 40 percent of its resource imports; its five main Pacific ports were handling one-eighth of their 1942 traffic.[51] The American submarine campaign was a decisive factor in the destruction of Japan's ability to make war, but it proved costly. Out of a total of 288 boats, between forty-one and forty-four were lost to enemy action. Loss of a boat to any cause meant loss of the crew, and nearly a quarter of the submarine crews failed to return, the highest loss for any branch of the service.[52]

Sustaining the momentum of all Central Pacific offensive operations was the huge and versatile fleet Service Force developed and managed during the entirety of the war by Vice Admiral William L. Calhoun. Since standard pre–Pearl Harbor strategy called for sending the fleet across the Pacific for a decisive battle with the Japanese fleet, the Navy had already invested in a fleet train—repair, provision, and ammunition ships, destroyer and submarine tenders, oilers—and had learned the technique of fueling at sea. That was only the beginning.[53] The fleet moved forward by stages: while Calhoun's service squadrons distributed matériel and provisions for the current operation, he and Nimitz's logistic staff were already ordering the ships and cargoes for the next one. The pace quickened by early 1944, leaving shortening intervals between operations. The number of troops and ships employed in operations grew as American forces moved closer to Japan. As casualties grew, more hospital ships were needed, with landing craft being outfitted to evacuate the wounded. Then each operation took the fleet farther away, at a cost in fuel, food, and time. The base needed a huge stock of spare parts to fix machinery worn down by prolonged cruising and combat, as well as skilled personnel to adjust and repair gun sights, radar, coding machines, and other complex instruments. Furthermore, secure harbors with room to spread out ashore were few and far between on the Pacific; atolls offered shelter from the sea but only strings of encircling land.[54]

In order to keep ships in action and avoid time-wasting voyages to Pearl Harbor or the West Coast, Calhoun needed to move the components of a harbor and base to an island or atoll as close as possible to the fleet's operation area and stock it with as many remedies and replacements as practicable. Supply service had to send the right mix of ships and platforms to make a particular harbor and base: craft for surveying, net tending, and minesweeping; sectional docks; lighters; scows; concrete barges towed across several thousand miles of ocean at four knots to serve as barracks and stores purveying 5,000 of the most wanted items. The Navy operated a retail distributing system not unlike that of Sears Roebuck.[55] In addition to all the other equipment were cranes, sectional and floating dry docks (including one for a battleship), and repair ships that would either fix battle and storm damage or patch it so the ship could return to the West Coast. The floating base sheltered ammunition ships, provision ships, some with food refrigeration, water distilling ships, a fleet post office, and a movie exchange.[56] These were the sorts of fittings used for Majuro, Kwajalein, and Eniwetok in early 1944.

To keep ships at sea, fleet supply took the moveable base idea one step further. Fuel arriving at the forward base in commercial tankers directly from Aruba and Curacao filled fleet oilers there, which then sailed to meet combatant ships in the vicinity of operations to refuel them, often simultaneously and on both sides of the oiler. In July 1944 tankers moved almost 4.5 million barrels of fuel oil and 8 million gallons of aviation gas to the fleet's forward bases. In 1945, the fleet service squadron expanded the at-sea transfer system by adding ammunition, fresh and frozen provisions, general store items, and disposable aircraft fuel tanks. Small escort carriers joined in the process with replacement airplanes, catapulted and flown to the fast carriers.[57] The fast carrier, amphibious assault, and submarine forces of the Pacific Fleet, propelled by the fleet's service squadrons, constituted offensive power of the most innovative and devastating kind.

Nimitz had the advantage over MacArthur of being closer to and current with Washington through his regular visits with Admiral King and headquarters at Pearl Harbor and Guam. He had a talented planner in Rear Admiral Forrest Sherman and an excellent joint staff of Army and Navy officers. His subordinates were not generally like the "quiet warrior," Admiral Raymond A. Spruance, Fifth Fleet commander. There were Admiral "Bull" Halsey and Vice Admiral Richmond Kelly "Terrible" Turner, and Marine Lieutenant General H. M. "Howling Mad" Smith as subordinates, none of them shy in voicing their opinions. Neither was Vice Admiral John H. Towers, fleet air commander and later Nimitz's deputy, the brilliant, aggressive father of naval aviation, who more than any other individual established the primacy of the fast carrier forces in the Pacific Fleet.[58] The aviators had largely gained the key commands in the fast carrier forces, but Nimitz was a gradualist about change and liked to maintain a balanced persuasion around him. Thus "battleship admirals" like Spruance, who were coming, however grudgingly, to accept the carrier as the dominant element of the fleet still retained some of the conservative, prewar attitude toward its use. The airmen, not denying static and defensive uses, regarded the essential value of the fast carrier forces as its striking power and its character as essentially independent, aggressive, and strategic and regarded its defining function as attack on the enemy fleet and airpower. The nonairmen held a broader conception that included defensive roles and close support, with guns and planes, of amphibious assaults.

A further element of stress in the Nimitz command was the employment of Army alongside Marine troops. He required more troops than the four (rising to six) Marine divisions and was getting them: the number of Army divisions in his command was rising to six as well. Army combat methods differed from those of the Marines, and the Army's slow advances in the Makin and Kwajalein landings raised questions about leadership and training.

Overall, however, one word describes the United States Pacific Fleet of mid-1944: predictability. It had overcome distance by learning how to move its assorted elements together so that they were in the right strengths at the right places and times. The question was whether it could sustain that capability in rising magnitudes (its cargo loadings in 1944 went up 62 percent)[59] and as combat spread, accelerated, and intensified. A second question was whether it could sustain it not only in competition but in cooperation with General MacArthur's forces moving alongside. Could it adapt to rapid changes that would occur under a JCS Pacific strategy that was opportunistic and bound to create uncertainty? MacArthur's headquarters lay 3,500 miles away from Nimitz's headquarters at Pearl Harbor, and Brisbane was like the last apartment at the far, far end of a long corridor. His SWPA command extended across New Guinea and the Bismarcks, westward through the Netherlands East Indies as far as Sumatra, and northward through the South China Sea and the Philippines. This was where most of the fighting occurred and in difficult terrain. Stretching the distance from Boston to Minneapolis, New Guinea had both jungle-clad mountains rising above 10,000 feet and skimpy beaches that were home to razor-sharp kunai grass, unmapped swamps, and uncharted reefs.

MacArthur's command had nothing like the fast carrier, amphibious, or service forces that powered the Pacific Fleet. He started with two Australian divisions and two ill-trained, poorly equipped American divisions, a handful of cruisers and destroyers, and a collection of airplanes lacking spare parts. Yet by 1944 MacArthur was hopping along the northern coast of New Guinea in time with Nimitz's advance through the Marshalls. Propelling MacArthur was an overpowering determination to recover his lost command, the Philippines, and to achieve historical greatness by dominating the Pacific war. If he did not have a great army or fleet, he had the skills, self-confidence, and drive to make things happen, to become, in effect, an independent force fulfilling General Marshall's agenda.

He had, of course, his own agenda. Central to MacArthur's personality was a family ambition for greatness. The traditions of his family, he wrote in *Reminiscences*, "are linked with the historic lore of King Arthur and the Knights of the Round Table."[60] His grandfather, Arthur MacArthur, who arrived in America from Scotland a boy of ten with his widowed mother, became a highly respected and socially prominent federal judge in Washington. His father, Arthur MacArthur II, a Wisconsin volunteer in the Civil War at the age of seventeen, was in the van of the attack on Missionary Ridge, for which he ultimately gained a Congressional Medal of Honor. Remaining in the Army, his father became Army commander in the Philippines during the Insurrection and highest ranking officer in the Army; however, because he was engaged in a feud with William Howard Taft, governor of the Philippines, he failed to attain the position of chief of staff—to his bitter regret. Douglas's older brother, Arthur III, was pursuing a successful career in the Navy, with likelihood of high rank, when he died of appendicitis in 1923. His younger brother died of measles in childhood. The keeper of the MacArthur heritage was the mother of Douglas, Mary Pinckney Hardy MacArthur, a domineering woman from a prominent Virginia plantation and merchant family. As D. Clayton James, one of MacArthur's biographers, points out, "it was she who somehow instilled in

Douglas an almost mystical bond of unity with the family past and a burning desire to carry on and surpass the achievements of his predecessors."[61]

At West Point he was first in his class academically, with one of the highest records ever achieved, as well as First Captain of the Corps of Cadets. In World War I, as chief of staff and brigade commander in the Forty-Second Rainbow Division, he won the Silver Star Medal for gallantry seven times and the Distinguished Service Cross for "extraordinary heroism" twice.[62] Highly regarded for his troop leadership and bravery, he retained the rank of brigadier general into the peacetime army and secured the choice billet of superintendent of West Point, where he played a key role in revitalizing and modernizing the curriculum and instruction. Moving rapidly to the top, he became Army chief of staff in 1930. When he retired in 1935 to become military adviser to the Philippine government, he was only fifty-five.

Returning to the Philippines was surely a relief after five years spent fighting to save his American army in the face of Depression-era budget reductions. This was MacArthur's fourth tour (his previous tours: 1903– 1904, 1922–1925, 1928–1930) in the colony, now a commonwealth beginning transition to independence. It was becoming like a home for him, the only one he really had. The beauty of the islands appealed to him, as did the fiery and romantic temperament of its people.[63] On the transpacific crossing he met Jean Faircloth, a Tennessean proud of her southern heritage. They fell in love and were married in 1937. In 1938 Arthur MacArthur was born and, as his biographer says, the general's joy was complete.[64]

The MacArthurs relished the dramatic tropical sunsets from the terrace of their penthouse at the Manila Hotel, with its panoramic view of Manila Bay, the mountains of Bataan, and the South China Sea beyond. Here was his gateway to Asia. MacArthur's image of Asia was instilled by an inspection tour of the Far East he made as aide-de-camp to his father in 1905– 1906, at the height of European colonialism and imperial rivalry. Taking inventory of military stations at Hong Kong, Singapore, Rangoon, Calcutta, Peshawar, Bombay, Bangalore, Madras, the Dutch East Indies, Canton, Tsingtao, Tientsin, Hankow, and Shanghai, this was a Cook's Tour as well, lasting over eight months and covering almost 20,000 miles. He remembered traversing "the path to Afghanistan with the 'King of the Khyber,'

Sir Bindon Blood," and riding the "Grand Trunk Road of Kipling's *Kim.*" On the trip he heard "kings and viceroys and high commissioners lay out their hopes and fears.... We saw the strength and weakness of the colonial system, how it brought law and order, but failed to develop the masses.... We rubbed elbows with millions of the underprivileged." This pageant of "lands so rich in color, so fabled in legend, so vital to history," he wrote, was "the most important factor of preparation in my entire life."[65]

The trip inspired MacArthur with "the true historic significance" and "sense of destiny" of the region. Asia was civilization's last frontier, and America, he was convinced, was "irrevocably entwined" with it and its "island outposts." For the United States and Europe, the lure of Asia was its potential as a market for goods produced in the West, existing markets having been "feverishly competed for and exploited," as he reported in 1936.[66] American advocates of a large policy for East Asia argued that the Philippines would have a key role to play in the forthcoming international struggle for Asian markets: the United States would guide the Philippines to independence and thereafter protect them, retaining Philippine bases that would also serve as assembling points for American power in upholding the Open Door for trade and the treaty system in the region.[67] Given the strategic importance of the Philippines, MacArthur's well-established relationship with the Filipino political elite, and his love of the islands, Manila seemed an ideal place to pursue his evolving ambition.[68]

That was a vision that faded as the thirties advanced. He planned and in 1937 started to build a Philippine army of 400,000, larger than the American army at the time. Youth would be drafted, trained, and placed in reserve until an emergency arose. The program fizzled for many reasons but essentially because it came too late to build an army from the ground up, especially in an archipelago with so many different languages. Japan was on the march by this point; the War Department was trying to reduce its stake in the Far East, and the Philippine Commonwealth was looking for ways to avoid involvement.[69] With Filipino soldiers stationed throughout the islands near their homes, it was impossible to effect concentration near possible invasion sites. In July 1941 the U.S. government reversed its strategy, sending bombers and reinforcements and appointing MacArthur commander of the United States Army Forces in the Far East. The fall of the Philippines in May 1942 was the fault of the United States government, not MacArthur, but he was the officer in charge. Withdrawn by his government from the battlefield to Australia to command the southwestern Pacific front against Japan, he carried a heavy burden. What he left on Bataan was a situation that "portended the worst disaster ever suffered by an American army." In his own words: "we are very near done."[70] Whatever the practicalities and necessities of his removal, for a soldier to lose a critical battle and leave his troops to their fate was abysmally humiliating, not the stuff of Arthurian legends. His only redemption would be to win back the Philippines. Thus his promise "I came through and I shall return" became the premise of his new command, held to with steely determination. This would be the dynamic that propelled the Army toward Japan.

The MacArthur of Brisbane was a new MacArthur—a campaigner, tieless, bare of ribbons, with squashed cap and corncob pipe, a celebrity. He was also deeply embittered by the failure of his government to reinforce and save his army on Bataan. Washington, encouraging MacArthur to stand fast, had provided hope but no guarantees. It was seeking every means of sending help, he had been told. Bomber streams were headed for the Southwest Pacific by way of Africa and the Pacific. But nothing had arrived in the Philippines except by submarine. "I could have held Bataan," MacArthur told a subordinate, "if I had not been so completely deserted."[71]

What MacArthur saw as desertion his government saw as brutal necessity. It concluded within weeks of Pearl Harbor that Europe had to have first call on American military resources and that, given the power and speed of the Japanese advance, defense of Hawaii, the communication line to Australia, and Australia itself had to stand ahead of the Philippines. For MacArthur, his own command, always, wherever he was, came first. He viewed any other position as a personal challenge and threat. In the aftermath of defeat in the Philippines his attitude took on a degree of paranoia. He suspected that the "leaders in Washington"—Roosevelt and Marshall—were "against" him, indeed that they were "leaders of a clique that was maliciously trying to undermine his career." He blamed then brigadier general Dwight D. Eisenhower, who had been his chief of staff in the Philippines for four years and now was chief of war plans in the War Department, for "enhancing his own position by feeding the White House with anti-MacArthur data."[72]

Feeling "completely isolated" in his low-priority theater, suspecting enemies in Washington, MacArthur found comfort in the praise lavished on him by the American public for his gallant defense of Bataan. Babies and boulevards were named after him, awards and memberships showered on him, inspired by the anti-Roosevelt press and embraced by a "hero-hungry nation." Soon after the fall of the Philippines, he emerged in one poll among the top four considered presidential material.[73] However, public attention soon shifted to the Navy in the Central and South Pacific as the dramas of Midway and Guadalcanal unfolded in the summer of 1942. MacArthur had been infuriated at the Navy for its withdrawal of the Asiatic Fleet from the Philippines before and after Pearl Harbor. Underlying that was his memory of disputes with the Navy over air missions while he was Army chief of staff. Further, he and Admiral King detested each other.[74] Not surprisingly, therefore, he saw the Pacific Fleet as a rival and threat.

To regain the preeminence and gain the strategic priority necessary to liberate the Philippines, MacArthur believed he needed to establish a reputation at home as a winner. That required close management of communications into and out of his theater. Regarding reports of war correspondents submitted for censoring, MacArthur's public relations officer, Colonel (later Brigadier General) LeGrande A. ("Pick") Diller, bluntly stated his policy: "I wouldn't allow any stories to go out if I thought they'd hurt the Old Man." The object, according to Diller, was to ensure that the Pacific story was "attractive" (meaning successful, presumably), so MacArthur could get more troops and supplies.[75] MacArthur had press experience: in 1916, when he was the public relations officer at the War Department, he was known for his "Golden Touch With the Press." Media moguls, such as William Randolph Hearst, Roy W. Howard, Colonel Robert E. McCormick, and Henry R. Luce, were old friends. According to Carl Mydans, the *Life* photographer, the general was intensely interested in the press and kept current with clippings sent from the States daily by air express.[76] He also received from his chief signal officer copies of messages between senior officers in the War Department and his staff. In addition, his counterintelligence chief provided him with monthly roundups of troop opinion based on surveys and letters opened for censorship.[77] Believing that control depended on information, he gathered a practically universal communications system for securing it.

MacArthur thought of his command as an extension of himself. In public statements the first person singular predominated; his battle descriptions of what happened against the Japanese at Luzon sounded more like Waterloo: "I then threw the XI Corps, under General Hall, by sea to the Zambales coast.... I enveloped from the other flank with the I Cavalry Division."[78] A battle won was a MacArthur battle, as Lieutenant General Robert L. Eichelberger learned, to his chagrin. In December 1942, Eichelberger was sent to Buna on the north coast of New Guinea to reanimate the floundering Thirty-Second Division and drive it forward to capture the village; he succeeded and received favorable notices in *Life* and the *Saturday Evening Post*. MacArthur immediately saw him as a rival or replacement and sent him to Australia to train troops and learn his lesson.[79] In 1944 General Marshall encouraged a *Time* article on fighting along the New Guinea coast, but Diller weakened the article by withholding names of local commanders. In Marshall's view, successful subordinates needed recognition. MacArthur was more grudging. In 1945 he apparently refused to nominate his men for British decorations on the grounds that American decorations had already been awarded to those deserving. The War Department advised him that it had no such policy of denial and asked him to reconsider.[80] Generally, federal war agencies were unwelcome in the Southwest Pacific. The Office of Strategic Services was kept out, and the Office of War Information at General Headquarters disseminated information only to the Australian public. MacArthur had his own office of propaganda and psychological warfare.[81]

MacArthur's effort to cast his command in his own image only made the Southwest Pacific Theater seem more obscure and remote in Washington. The OPD was anxious to help MacArthur, limited though it was by European priorities. The First Cavalry Division was a Regular Army unit, mobile but not armored, and therefore arguably more suitable for Pacific than European combat. The Pacific Theater group in OPD grabbed the division from Mexican border duty and sent it to MacArthur.[82] According to Major

General John E. Hull, chief of the OPD, Southwest Pacific General Headquarters was "reluctant to go into detailed planning and discuss with us [in radio messages] back and forth the problems and the decisions they hoped to carry out." On a visit to MacArthur and knowing a two-way conversation was impossible, Hull had no difficulty finding out what General Headquarters was thinking.[83] A civilian on MacArthur's staff admitted that the general was fighting his own war and the general thought that Washington should not be "doing anything but sending what he wanted and what he thought he needed."[84]

MacArthur was Marshall's most difficult theater commander. His fulminations against the Navy and his contemptuous dismissal of rival strategies verged on insubordination and placed an unwanted burden on already strained Army-Navy relations. In a grand understatement, General Thomas T. Handy, deputy chief of staff to Marshall, suggested that his chief "felt at times that maybe he [MacArthur] didn't make our job of dealing with him too easy." Nevertheless, Marshall handled him, as Handy put it, "gingerly," with discretion and restraint. This attitude stemmed in part from the big gap between the two in career advancement: MacArthur had been a field officer who moved quickly ahead to brigadier general in World War I and on to chief of staff, while Marshall, through the war and after, lacked troop-command experience. MacArthur had substantial battle experience and was known as a fighting leader—a "piss-cutter," said a young soldier in the Rainbow Division—while Marshall did not and was not. Marshall respected MacArthur for his battle leadership, while MacArthur respected Marshall as the occupant of an office he himself had once held.[85]

Whatever Marshall's feelings about MacArthur, he had three reasons to support him. First, as all attested, MacArthur could make an army go where he wanted it to. Second, he was attack-minded; he would press ahead as fast as possible and provide the momentum Marshall desired. Finally, Marshall judged that MacArthur's path to the Philippines was the correct approach to Japan.

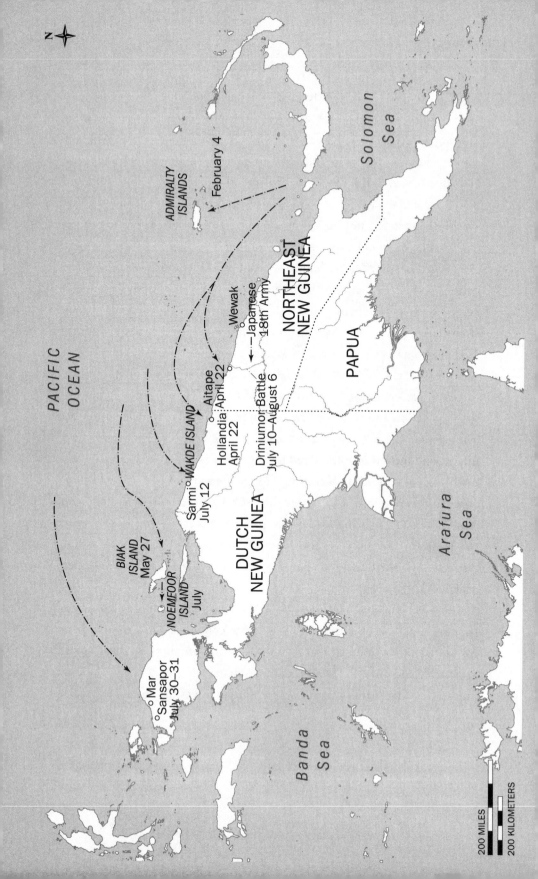

PACIFIC OCEAN

Solomon Sea

ADMIRALTY ISLANDS

February 4

NORTHEAST NEW GUINEA

Wewak

Japanese 18th Army

Aitape April 22

Hollandia April 22

Driniumor Battle July 10–August 6

PAPUA

Sarmi July 12

WAKDE ISLAND

BIAK ISLAND May 27

NOEMFOOR ISLAND July

Mar Sansapor July 30–31

DUTCH NEW GUINEA

Banda Sea

Arafura Sea

200 MILES

200 KILOMETERS

Moving Ahead on New Guinea, April–July 1944

By January 1944, Australian-American forces had recaptured the eastern portion of New Guinea (Papua) as far as the straits that separated it from the east-west island of New Britain. Now serving as rearward bases were Milne Bay, Buna, Salamaua, Lae, Finschafen, Markham Valley, Saidor, and Cape Gloucester, all of which had been the landmarks of the dismal 1942–1943 campaigns, when they had been lost to the Japanese. Ahead lay a sequence of five amphibious assaults, beginning April 22, 1944, along the northern coast of Dutch New Guinea that would bring American forces, airfield by airfield, to the western shores of that island by July 30. There they would establish the bases and staging areas for the scheduled invasion in November of Mindanao, the southernmost of the Philippine Islands. The campaign would bring about, in the span of three months, a major northwestern displacement of Southwest Pacific Area (SWPA) military power.

■ **Map 3** The Allied Advance in Northern New Guinea. Drawn by George Chakvetadze.

On the move, and when in his own self-defined sphere—beholden only to himself—MacArthur was an effective commander-in-chief. His was not a unitary command, however, meaning one that formally integrated all services. While he set the overall plan, MacArthur dealt individually with his principal land, sea, and air commanders, always reserving final decisions for himself but delegating to each commander authority to develop and manage his share and coordinate with the rest. As issues arose, he was open to individual or group discussion and change. He nonetheless demanded total loyalty and timely performance; indeed, he constantly prodded his commanders for more speed.

MacArthur gradually filled most of his senior staff and command positions with highly competent officers. Three were truly outstanding: Lieutenant General George C. Kenney, Fifth Air Force commander; Rear Admiral Daniel E. Barbey, commander of amphibious forces; and Major General Stephen J. Chamberlin, General Headquarters planner (G3). On his special staff, Hugh Casey, chief engineer, and Spencer Akin, chief signal officer, were particularly valued by MacArthur. Among his General Headquarters staff officers was a group he had brought with him from Corregidor, the so-called Bataan Gang, who served as his protective screen and whose loyalty in many cases trumped ability. However, this coterie was quite apart from the operational sphere—actual combat—in which MacArthur required loyalty but sought expertise and leadership.

MacArthur was a loner; he restricted access to his office to ensure privacy, to separate the transcendent from the routine, and to enhance his aura of power. His Cerberus and confidant was Lieutenant General Richard K. Sutherland, who had been his chief of staff since before the war. Smart, fiercely protective, a tireless manager, Sutherland was also arrogant and sharp-tongued. Later, when Sutherland came to Washington representing MacArthur in strategy conferences, General Marshall was so infuriated by his conduct that he prepared a blistering letter to MacArthur, warning him never to send Sutherland again. Then, presumably gritting his teeth, he determined to persist in his policy of patience with this most difficult theater commander and not send the letter. In the unsent letter he pointed out that the War Department no less than the Navy found Sutherland's behavior insufferable. He appeared to be "totally lacking in the faculty of dealing with others.... He antagonized almost every official in the War Department with whom he came in contact and he has made our dealings with the Navy exceptionally difficult. Unfortunately he appears utterly unaware of the effect of his methods but, to put it bluntly [striking out 'brutally'], his attitude in almost every case seems to have been that he knew it all and nobody else knew much of anything."[1] As MacArthur became more engaged with his principal operational subordinates, he depended less and less on Sutherland.

In New Guinea and after, MacArthur and his commanders all became reliant on one huge advantage: thanks to the Navy's penetration of the Japanese navy codes and an intensive Australian-American codebreaking attack within SWPA on Japanese army codes, they could read radio messages. Known by the code name ULTRA, interception and encryption were a critical element of Anglo-American cooperation.[2] Central Bureau, the SWPA cryptology organization established by MacArthur shortly after his arrival in Australia in July 1942, drew in veterans of Singapore, the desert war in Africa, and Bataan with intercept or code experience, as well as cryptanalysts from Washington. They worked in Quonset huts at the Brisbane racetrack, guarded by Australian militia and commanded by Spencer Akin, who was also in charge of MacArthur's American message traffic. Central Bureau grew to over a thousand men and women by 1943, and to 4,000 by war's end. It became a major cryptographic hub, exchanging ULTRA and technical information with Arlington Hall, the Army's principal decryption center in Washington, as well as with a Navy unit in Melbourne and a British unit in New Delhi. MacArthur had access to the entire range of military intelligence, as well as MAGIC, as the decryptions of Japanese diplomatic communications were known. Central Bureau found breaking into Japanese army codes a formidable task. Its first success, in cooperation with Arlington Hall, was deciphering the Water Transport (shipping) Code, which provided timing, routing, and composition information about Japanese convoys and data on Japanese troop movements that proved critical for operational planning.

The principal, mainline Japanese code remained invincible until an astonishing discovery occurred in the New Guinea wilderness in January 1944.[3] The rear guard of the Japanese Twentieth Division, stationed near Sio in northeastern New Guinea, packing to retreat into the mountains along jungle trails, buried a large steel trunk by a streambed. The exhausted, starved, drenched soldiers had found it impossible either to carry the load or to burn its contents. Inside were the division's cryptographic materials: codebooks, substitution tables, and key registers. Australian infantry following on began sweeping the area with a mine detector, knowing the Japanese left booby traps and mines in bivouac sites. The detector soon "brayed a shrill warning," and the trunk was unearthed. Every page was dried and then photographed, entered on punch cards, and microfilmed. They had discovered nothing less than the Imperial Army code. Among the first decrypts was a message about a major conference of high-ranking Japanese army and navy officers. Thanks to the codebooks, Arlington Hall decrypted some 36,000 Japanese army messages in March 1944.

Ultimately, the value of enemy messages depended on the interpreter and on his judgment of their significance. MacArthur's principal intelligence officer (G2) was Major General Charles A. Willoughby, who was one of the Bataan Gang. "Sir Charles" had his patrician affectations, though born in Germany of an American mother. When he came to America and became "Willoughby"—with a British-Prussian accent (his family was named Tsheppe-Weidenbach), he joined the Army as a private and worked his way up through the Command and General Staff College, where he taught, and the Army War College, specializing in military history and theory. In 1938 he begged MacArthur to let him join his staff and served with devotion.[4] All ULTRA material went first to MacArthur, who was his own intelligence officer and inclined to accept or act on those items that reinforced his intentions, but Willoughby was useful as a collector and distributor of intelligence (if unreliable in his estimates).[5] Once again, MacArthur's determination to maintain ultimate control of all communications within his theater allowed him to resist efforts by Marshall and the War Department to station its own cryptographic agents in SWPA.[6]

The first intelligence received by way of the mainline army code was immediately helpful. MacArthur learned that the nearest American objectives along the New Guinea coast—Madang, Wewak, Hansa Bay—were being reinforced, whereas Hollandia, 200 miles farther, needed reinforcement. MacArthur could skip around the intervening Japanese garrisons and make an assault landing beyond them at Hollandia, trapping the Japanese army in between. Seizing Hollandia would provide handsome returns. The consequent disorganization of Japanese forces would create momentum to transform what had been a plodding campaign into a swift advance toward the Philippines, capturing the attention of the American public, meeting the deadlines of the Joint Chiefs, and outpacing the Central Pacific offensive.

Once MacArthur had settled on an envelopment strategy for New Guinea, the key objective was protecting his seaward flank by seizing the Admiralties (which began with the First Cavalry Division foray onto Los Negros mentioned in chapter 1). MacArthur was willing to risk sending even a small force there immediately, as ULTRA indicated the Japanese garrison was small, 4,000 or less, but growing. He had the good fortune, too, that his contingent from the First Cavalry landed at a tiny harbor on Los Negros, while most of the Japanese garrison faced northward on Manus. Thus accurate intelligence, available in the nick of time, fitting the need for maneuver and speed, spiced with a bit of luck, brought success in the Admiralties and opened the way for envelopment on New Guinea. Hollandia was a bold stroke, but also one backed up by solid intelligence.[7]

The service that most extensively and profitably used ULTRA was the Fifth Air Force, which when later joined by the Thirteenth Air Force from the South Pacific was named the Far East Air Forces and commanded by General Kenney—perhaps MacArthur's most gifted commander. Kenney trained and worked as an engineer before becoming a pilot in World War I. A veteran of seventy-five combat missions, he received the Distinguished Service Cross and Silver Star. Between the wars, in addition to the Command and General Staff School and Army War College, he attended the Air Force Engineering and Tactical Schools. At the latter, where he was both student and instructor, he helped pioneer the development of attack aviation, using planes for attack on enemy forces on the ground. In 1935 Kenney took charge of Army Air Corps (renamed Army Air Forces [AAF] in June 1941) operations and training. In 1938, as war drew near and American aircraft production increased, Kenney was the Army Air Corps's troubleshooter, constantly looking for ways to facilitate completion of planes. In 1940 as a military observer in France he found that American technology lagged behind. He noted the armored seats of downed German aircraft, as well as their leak-proof fuel tanks; their pilots had better oxygen masks and flying suits.[8] After arriving in the Southwest Pacific in August 1942, Kenney immediately proved his worth. Given his forceful personality, self-confidence, and critical mind he was a first-class problem-solver and innovator. Strategically, operationally, tactically, he was offensive-minded. He also immediately recognized that getting along with MacArthur was critical to his success. For his part MacArthur recognized that Kenney was precisely what the situation called for. Sutherland, the gatekeeper, was brushed aside, and the two generals saw much of each other, formally and informally.[9]

Kenney aimed at nothing less than the destruction of Japanese airpower in the region. Only by clearing the skies could the Army move ahead. And to do that he knew that he had to strike with concentrated force at the enemy's airfields and reinforcement and supply convoys and the planes protecting them. The point was not just to hit them once but to hammer them again and again until they were left harmless. First, however, he had to revamp his own command, which, in his view, was slack, ill-trained, and wrapped in red tape. He sent home his predecessor's generals and some forty of the colonels and lieutenant colonels, bringing in those he called "operators," men who were decisive, enthusiastic, and energetic. His second in command, Major General Ennis C. Whitehead, an expert tactician, managed combat missions from an advance headquarters on New Guinea while Kenney operated from General Headquarters in Brisbane. Finding that two-thirds of his airplanes had been grounded for lack of parts or repair, Kenney moved the principal supply depot from Australia to New Guinea, increased maintenance facilities, and put them on round-the-clock shifts.[10]

With its growing mission, substantial combat losses, and the priority still being given to the European Theater, Southwest Pacific was constantly in need of more planes. Kenney flew to Washington to plead for more. He told the War Department that he would take "anything that will fly." Gradually, as Far East Air Forces scored victories, the flow increased. Initially it brought some types not in heavy demand elsewhere, such as B-25 and B-26 medium bombers, P-39 and P-40 fighters, and Kenney's favorite—the twin-engine, long-range P-38, known as the Lightning fighter. By March 1943, General Henry "Hap" Arnold, for one, judged Kenney no longer the "forgotten man." As production increased and the Luftwaffe weakened, P-47 Thunderbolts and even some P-51 Mustang fighters became available. Kenney and the Far East Air Forces started with 517 planes in 1942; by mid-1944 he had 2,629 combat aircraft.[11]

Kenney and Whitehead had concluded early on that the kind of air attack being used over Europe, by bombers flying in formation at high altitudes with fighter cover, was inadequate for their needs. They favored medium and light bombers flying close to the ground or sea with added forward-firing machine guns or cannons for strafing, and bombs that skipped across the water like flat stones into the ship's side. To attack planes parked on airfields they could both strafe and drop "parafrag" bombs, which Kenney had helped develop. These trailed a parachute that slowed the descent, allowing time for the plane to get away, and then exploded above ground, widening the area of impact. In what came to be called the Battle of the Bismarck Sea in early March 1943, the B-17s, bombing from on high, forced the convoy to disperse, making the ships vulnerable to low-level attack. To provide adequate cover for the bombers, Far East Air Forces added droppable wing fuel tanks to the P-38 fighters that accompanied them, extending their range from 350 to 650 miles.[12]

Like fast carrier admirals, Far East Air Forces generals considered tethering aircraft to defense of particular sites or formations—an air base, fleet, or convoy—wasteful and dangerous. It left initiative to the enemy. On the other hand coast watchers and radar warning systems were of limited value in gaining information about enemy intentions. Here again, radio interception and ULTRA provided critical assistance. In February 1943 reconnaissance of Rabaul indicated the gathering of a major reinforcement for Japanese garrisons in New Guinea. Navy ULTRA specified Lae as the destination and March 5 the date of arrival. In the Battle of the Bismarck Sea, Kenney attacked with all available planes and sank eight out of eight troop transports and four of eight destroyers.[13]

ULTRA also played a key role in wiping out Japanese airpower on New Guinea. In August 1943 ULTRA helped identify a major reinforcement effort, one that packed Wewak airfields with parked planes and opened the way to a major low-altitude attack, in which all but thirty-eight of 120 planes were destroyed. As the Hollandia landing neared, Kenney, following details of Japanese reinforcements from ULTRA, noted a probable "reckless and undispersed concentration" at the Hollandia airfields. On March 30, 1944, Kenney's bombers, arriving "'like clouds' over the mountains" pounded the tightly parked planes, demolishing most of them and returning to finish off the rest on March 31 and April 3. In the airpower neutralization of eastern New Guinea and Rabaul as well, Kenney and ULTRA were an extraordinarily successful team.[14]

Meanwhile, in the same time frame, Task Force 58, the name given the fast carrier forces of the Pacific Fleet, sortied from Majuro—battleships, tankers, and all—for strikes against the western Carolines, particularly the Japanese fleet anchorage in the Palau Islands. Returning to the Marshalls for resupply, they sortied again for the attacks on Hollandia and Wakde, followed by another strike on Truk. Thus in the roughly five-week period between March 22 and May 4, the Pacific Fleet was sweeping the ocean north of New Guinea and the Admiralties, guarding MacArthur's flank.[15] Commanding it was Vice Admiral Thomas C. Kinkaid, Seventh Fleet and Southwest Pacific naval commander, who arrived in November 1943 and with whom MacArthur formed a workable if muted relationship. Given MacArthur's jaundiced attitude toward the Navy and his requests for removal of both previous fleet commanders, Admiral Halsey himself accompanied Kinkaid to Brisbane to smooth the introduction. Kinkaid had impressive credentials as cruiser division and task group commander at the Eastern Solomons, Coral Sea, and Midway battles as well as North Pacific commander during the ousting of the Japanese from Attu and Kiska in the Aleutians. In that northern campaign he was known to have worked well with the Alaska Army command. With MacArthur, Kinkaid argued the Navy point of view forthrightly but nonconfrontationally.[16] Kinkaid posed no threat to MacArthur; the two would frequently sit together in the evening for a smoke and chat. MacArthur enjoyed visiting invasion sites aboard one or another of the American cruisers in the Seventh Fleet. (He was impressed with the cruiser's firepower and found Navy ice cream delectable.) This was much to Kinkaid's displeasure, concerned as he was for the supreme commander's safety (as well as by the wasteful use of time for a busy warship). The battle scene, he felt, should be left to local commanders.

Nonetheless, Kinkaid had managed what his predecessors had not, a working relationship with McArthur, principally by not reporting directly to Admiral King in Washington—who, after all, was commander of all the fleets and the source of personnel and supplies. In January 1943 when Rear Admiral Barbey arrived in theater MacArthur warned him about writing to King, on whose staff Barbey had served, adding darkly to the newcomer: "remember the echoes of what you say will come back to me." In spite of this sour beginning, Barbey came to regard MacArthur as the best commander he ever had, especially on account of his willingness to delegate authority and acknowledge expertise.[17] In the case of Barbey, dubbed "Dan, Dan, the amphibious man," this involved landings. Early recognizing the importance of landings on the enemy shore in the coming Pacific war, he wrote what most called the bible on the subject in 1940: *Landing Operations Doctrine, United States Navy*. In 1940–1941 he assisted in the training of the First Marine and Army First Divisions, and in 1942 he was the one on Admiral King's staff who took charge of amphibious readiness.[18] In the appointments of Kenney and Barbey, MacArthur brought aboard two dynamic leaders, pioneers in their specialties—tactical airpower and amphibious warfare—and innovative to the point where they could adapt these to the requirements and opportunities of Southwest Pacific warfare.

The Seventh Fleet Amphibious Forces began with luggers, lighters, Dutch interisland freighters, destroyer transports, any kind of waterborne transportation available on the New Guinea coast. In 1943 a "trickle" of the new landing ships and craft arrived from the United States, mostly manned by landlubbers: of seventy-six crew members aboard one LST only one had ever been to sea.[19] More substantial was the assignment of three engineer special brigades to the Southwest Pacific, each numbering 7,835 men. Established quite apart from the Navy, they provided Army amphibious assaults with the small landing craft and coxswains necessary to ferry troops, vehicles, and equipment from transports to shore, and the specialists to organize the beach and the bulldozed exits for moving off it. Arriving in the Southwest Pacific separately aboard cargo ships were the landing craft, cut into sections for economical stowage and reassembled on New Guinea. By the end of February 1944, MacArthur had ordered 2,334 of the fifty-six-foot LCMs (landing craft, mechanized), a heavily used small craft for one vehicle or cargo; at the rate they arrived it would take at least eleven months for all of them. Not until after the New Guinea campaign did the brigades reach assigned strength in boats, and even then they were short of spare parts.[20]

The difficulty in securing small craft was emblematic of landing craft acquisition generally. The shore-to-shore, bow-ramp LST, with large double-deck carrying capacity, was vital to an island-strewn theater such as the Southwest Pacific. The same applied to all seagoing landing craft, including the LSD (landing ship, dock), which harbored small craft within it, pumped out the water, and at the objective refloated and dispatched them. Among the small craft were LVTs (landing vehicles, tank), tank-like, tracked vehicles for crossing reefs, and DUKWs, wheeled vehicles with propellers for water. Other larger vessels were the LCT (landing craft, tank), a carry-all craft, many of which crossed the Pacific riding on an LST, and the LCI (landing craft, infantry), a troop carrier that used gangways on either side instead of bow doors and ramp. LCIs sailed from the American East Coast to Australia by way of Panama and Bora Bora. They tried to take the LCVP (landing craft, vehicle, personnel), a thirty-six-foot personnel carrier known as a Higgins Boat, on the open sea, but it was too small.[21] Amphibian engineers picked up badly needed LCMs at the Milne Bay assembly plant on the eastern tip of New Guinea and ran them, with carefully arranged refueling and rest stops, over a thousand miles to the assault at Biak.[22] Barbey used every available landing craft to the utmost, overloading them and extending their range, but for the landing on Hollandia he still had to borrow from Admiral Nimitz several LSTs, two LSDs, and five combat loaders (ships carrying their own ship-to-shore landing craft on staunch davits). The borrowed ships had to be returned promptly to serve in the invasion of Guam.[23]

The Southwest Pacific was not the only theater wanting in landing craft. By the fall of 1943, with the first amphibious craftbuilding program complete, a huge gap existed between what was available and what was needed by the European Theater for an enlarged Normandy invasion; the Mediterranean for Operation Shingle, the landing at Anzio on the coast of Italy that took place in late January 1944; and Operation Dragoon in Southern France; as well as the Pacific commands for the Marianas, Carolines, and Philippines campaigns, to say nothing of an eventual invasion of Japan. Amphibious assault now required landing craft in a wide variety of sizes and functions, slowing production. Late 1943 saw a transition from emergency programs stressing simplicity and standardization and toward varied specification for many different requirements.[24] Amphibian production would have to vie for a major portion of the national output of plate steel, cutting into programs for cargo ships, freight cars, airfield landing mats, trucks, convoy escort vessels, and tanks.

Through the fall of 1943 a succession of building programs for landing craft, instigated by Admiral King, had been approved after lengthy negotiations between the JCS, Army Service Forces, and Maritime Commission. Together these programs cost more than half again as much money as had been spent on landing craft up to that point, and they were designed for use in the Pacific, not Europe, with emphasis on oceangoing landing craft for later operations. Once the Pacific program was established, King was able to help out the Normandy invasion with some landing craft from the Pacific program's early 1944 production. MacArthur's navy would be well furnished with invasion craft for the Philippines.

But not for New Guinea.[25] There, Barbey would have to make the best of it. Only one of the New Guinea landings was contested, and that not severely; they proved to be exercises in boat handling, support fire, and beach management. Barbey sought and obtained better reconnaissance photos and interpreters, better mapping and charts, a hospital ship and repair ship fashioned from converted LSTs, a barge for drinking water, and rocket craft fashioned from converted LCTs, plus a planning ship and post office from wooden-hull coastal transports.[26] He gathered 217 ships for Hollandia and nearby operations, a designed fleet shaped to his particular needs. And the essence of his needs was getting a territorial foothold. Even the fastest-climbing fighter plane and most versatile landing craft required a chunk of land for a base, and that base would not be there unless infantry seized the land for it and held it.

The growing American ground forces in SWPA served in a command inauspiciously named Alamo Force. (Later the name was changed to the U.S. Sixth Army on the eve of the Philippines campaign. MacArthur's purpose in using that name was to separate his American troops from the command of Australian general Sir Thomas Blamey, the SWPA Land Forces commander, and keep them under his own direct control, particularly for the return to the Philippines. Blamey and his Australian troops would be left with mopping up on New Guinea and the recovery of British territory in the East Indies.)[27] The commander he chose for Alamo Force in January 1943 was Lieutenant General Walter Krueger. Born in Germany near Berlin, brought to America as a child, Krueger had joined the Army as a private in the Spanish-American War and participated thenceforth in the Philippine Insurrection and Mexican border conflict. On assignment in the Philippines he engaged in topographical map–making on the island of Luzon, which he got to know well. In World War I he was assigned as operations officer of the Twenty-Sixth Division but withdrawn because of French concerns about his German background. He attended and taught at both the Army and Navy War Colleges and served as executive officer and chief of the War Plans Division. He commanded troops at every level. In the large-scale Army maneuvers of 1941 he performed brilliantly in command of the offense and defense.

Krueger had a prickly personality; some judged him mean, others stubborn. General Marshall, for one, warned him that he seemed to have "a hard time hearing other people's views and adapting them to [his] own use" and that he struck some as unduly sensitive to criticism and resistant to policy he did not wholeheartedly agree with.[28] In the Southwest Pacific, Krueger was no more congenial but perhaps more guarded. During the New Guinea campaign, in the face of MacArthur's incessant efforts to hasten Alamo Force, resulting in nigh-impossible requirements for troop and supply movement, Krueger revamped and complied. The ground commander pointed out to Kinkaid that it was "natural" and "perfectly sound" for the supreme commander to seek the earliest possible dates for the assaults.[29]

And there were reasons beside MacArthur's obsession with the Philippines for moving fast. Shocked by the American jump to Hollandia in April 1944, the Japanese responded by reinforcing western New Guinea with troops, planes, and additional air bases while major elements of the Imperial Navy moved forward from Singapore to bases in the southern Philippines. The area around the Vogelkop of New Guinea and west through the islands of the Banda, Ceram, Molucca, and Celebes seas toward Borneo, as well as north to Mindanao, was emerging as a zone of strategic sensitivity. MacArthur, informed by ULTRA, was the more determined to seize bases before the enemy dug in.[30] While Krueger, though inherently methodical and prudent, did his best to meet the tightening deadlines, MacArthur would on occasion ease up on him. Between the two old-timers a basis of mutual respect and confidence existed. This was enhanced by Krueger's complete indifference to personal publicity; in this he was unlike Robert Eichelberger, who had enjoyed a moment in the spotlight in August 1942 at Buna and paid dearly for it.

General Krueger had strong views on the command and treatment of soldiers. Junior officers and sergeants, in his view, had to be committed to leading their men in battle. He emphasized training above all, not just in jungle and amphibious warfare schools, but in small-unit, combined arms tactics and in everyday soldiering. Surprise inspections scrutinized kitchens and latrines to ensure sanitary conditions. He established a malaria treatment center run by experts from the United States and service units to reduce mosquito breeding. Every soldier was instructed to protect himself from malaria by taking Atabrine pills, however distasteful, and keep his shirt on in spite of the infernal heat and humidity.[31] Bill Mauldin, the cartoonist who created the characters Joe and Willie, archetypal GIs ("dog-faces") in the Italian Campaign, recalled his "awesome experience" during a 1941 field exercise "when a man with three stars on each shoulder steps out of the bushes and demands to see your bare feet." Krueger was checking for blisters. If he found any, the relevant noncom lost his stripes. Mauldin added: "We in the lower echelons sort of loved the crusty old boy." Finding troops in a forward area locked into a diet of tinned corned beef hash, Krueger ordered six planeloads of fresh food from Australia for them. He believed that keeping up soldier morale so far as one could in a truly miserable environment was a matter of equity no less than military value.[32] There would be little time for field inspections in the coming months.

To manage an army that would eventually grow to over 600,000 troops, Krueger chose his staff carefully. His chief of staff, Brigadier General George H. Decker, and operations officer, Colonel Clyde D. Eddleman, eventually became, respectively, chief of staff and vice chief of the Army. Preparing an army for battle—requisitioning, gathering, provisioning, furnishing, prac-ticing, stowing—was a huge challenge, especially with the forces so scat-tered. Divisions in the New Guinea phase of the war were rarely cheek by jowl, even in battle. The Thirty-Second Division, devastated by disease and battle in the Buna campaign, spent all of 1943 in Australia rebuilding and now returned to battle from Saidor. The Forty-First Division, after the same sort of experience at Salamaua and six months in Australia, arrived at Cape Cretin in Eastern New Guinea only weeks before embarking for Hollandia. The Forty-Third Division, acquired from the South Pacific, entered battle directly from New Zealand, where it had been sent for rebuilding after heavy losses in the battle for New Georgia in the Solomons. The Twenty-Fourth Division, trained in Australia, set off for its first battle from Goodenough Island. The Sixth Division, trained in Hawaii and Papua, also setting out for its first battle, sailed from Milne Bay. The Thirty-First Division, another

untried outfit, departed from Oro Bay. Here, then, was an army of three rebuilt and three untried divisions as well as three independent regiments,
strung out in tent cities at landing sites and ports along 500 miles of the
northern Papuan coast.[33]

New Guinea, the world's second largest island, looks like a large bird on
maps, with its head at the western end and tail feathers reaching southeastward into the Coral Sea. A large mountain range runs west to east in the
center of the island, with the highest peaks reaching above 10,000 feet. In
western New Guinea, the mountain slopes give way to dense rain forests
that extend almost to the northern coastline, the area where MacArthur's
forces would be operating. The western New Guinea campaign of 1944 was
a transitional stage in the development of the Southwest Pacific's military
forces. It was the largest campaign to date, employing, as before, single regiments or divisions, but also task forces of regiments from several divisions
and several divisions under corps command. The torch of battle did not
pass from one amphibious assault to the next; more often the tight schedule and prolonged enemy resistance left battles unfinished in the rear as the
leading elements jumped forward, straining resources and communications but providing combat experience. With constant distribution and re-
distribution of reinforcements along the coast, the campaign functioned
also like a single front with depth in seaborne supply.

Hollandia was simultaneously a success and a disappointment. On invasion day, April 22, the Japanese, taken aback, offered scattered resistance,
but the beaches, mere strips of soft sand backed by mangrove swamps, offered scant access to the interior at both invasion sites, Tanamerah Bay
and Humboldt Bay. At Humboldt the beaches, already encumbered with
Japanese stores, became more and more congested with food, fuel, and
ammunition hastily unloaded from the LSTs so they could depart, as they
did before dark. On the second night after the landing, a lone enemy
bomber attacked, using a fire among Japanese stores on the beach as a
target. As ammunition ignited, fire and explosions spread up and down
the beaches, destroying the beached cargoes from eleven LSTs and sending "a solid, hideous, frightening wall of flame five hundred feet in the air."[34]
The troops had to go on half rations. Carriers of the Pacific Fleet were

providing protective cover, but not at night. The beaches should not have been overloaded, but loss of the LSTs would have seriously delayed the entire campaign. Besides, the surprise envelopment worked: the Humboldt invasion was met by Japanese service troops who—and this was rare—fled; the Tanamerah assault met Japanese resistance well past the beaches yet pushed through.

The disappointment of Hollandia was not the difficulty of acquiring it but the limited value of what had been gained. The principal objective was a cluster of airfields along a flat interior valley between the landing sites that would serve as bomber bases. Aerial photos had raised the question whether the soil there, subject to heavy rains, could sustain the weight of bombers. It proved to be sandy clay and could not. The engineers needed a month to lengthen the runways and harden them with limestone, working in soaking rain and under intense pressure. The difficulty of building and maintaining roads in from the beaches tied up many engineers and slowed the acquisition of heavy machinery at the airfields, requiring use of smaller abandoned Japanese equipment. Perhaps hastening to complete the runways, the engineers failed to remove eight inches of spongy topsoil from the airfield and installed inadequate drainage. Medium and heavy bombers could not use Hollandia airfields.[35] It therefore became a base for fighters and light bombers (the A-20).

Hollandia also became the location for most SWPA headquarters, as well as a key depot, a staging area for troops, and a Seventh Fleet naval base. The consequence of failure to secure a heavy-bomber base increased the concern at General Headquarters for securing such bases farther along and increasing pressure for speed. MacArthur was watching with alarm as the Japanese rebuilt their airpower and dispatched troop reinforcements from China to western New Guinea and nearby. In early May ULTRA revealed the devastating losses inflicted by American submarines on convoys carrying the Japanese Thirty-Second and Thirty-Fifth Divisions, but it was unclear whether this would last, making the seizure of western New Guinea while the Japanese were weak all the more important. Assurance that Japanese reinforcements were not imminent allowed MacArthur to attack at points where he remained unsure of the enemy's strength.[36] The focus of attention thus moved 140 miles westward, to Wakde-Sarmi, and beyond that to Biak.

The Wakde-Sarmi assault in mid-May 1944, the second in the campaign for New Guinea, was about an island, a bay, and a hill. Wakde is an island, roughly 1,000 by 3,000 yards, located on the shoulder of the great bird New Guinea resembles. Running down its center was an airstrip based not on spongy soil but rock-hard coral. Along the shore between Wakde and the town of Sarmi, twenty miles to the west, were several airfields, which had been objectives until suspicions about the soil arose after the failure of on-shore airfield construction at Hollandia. On the other hand Krueger liked the looks of Maffin Bay, located nearby, as a staging area for shipment of troops beyond New Guinea, so Wakde-Sarmi remained a multitask opera-tion. Overlooking the bay was a jumble of coral hills that, though no higher than 230 feet, were nonetheless steep, covered with rain forest and dense undergrowth, and honeycombed with defenses manned by veteran Japanese troops. The cartographer of the maps in use had drawn a single tree, presumably to denote forest, at the crest of the northernmost hill rising from the shore like a miniature Gibraltar. Thus "Lone Tree Hill" became an ironic signifier for a fierce, bloody jungle battle.[37]

Despite ULTRA, American intelligence was uncertain about Japanese troop strength at Wakde-Sarmi, having lost track of two of the three regi-ments in the area. Willoughby estimated 5,000–7,000 (which turned out to be roughly half the actual figure). The assault on Wakde Island by a battal-ion of the Forty-First Division met fierce resistance, which was decisively overcome within three days by tank-infantry teamwork. Attacks by Japanese forces on the mainland beachhead were poorly coordinated and unsuccess-ful. That left the hills just west of Maffin Bay, with their citadel, Lone Tree Hill, where about 850 Japanese troops occupied elaborate and extensive cave and pillbox defenses. The independent 158th Regimental Combat Team attacked, failed, withdrew, and moved on to Noemfoor, a small lime-stone and coral island sitting farther up the coast between the island of Biak and the Vogelkop Peninsula on the mainland of New Guinea. On June 22 the Regular Army Sixth Division took its turn. This was the division's first battle after training and garrison duty in Hawaii. After a day of feeling out the defenses, two battalions of the Twentieth Regiment attacked up Lone Tree Hill from the northeast and southeast. In spite of an intense preliminary bombardment by artillery and explosions of belly tanks of gasoline dropped by P-47 fighters, the battalions met intense machine gun, mortar, and rifle fire from the slopes above. Shifting its approach northward, the Third Battalion found easier going and soon reached the relatively level stretch that crowned the hill. Once on top, the battalion found itself entrapped: the Japanese had held their fire to lure the Americans up. Now, encircled and cut off from supplies, they ran out of water and nearly ran out of ammunition. Digging a foxhole was impossible: the coral turned pickaxes into fishhooks.[38] Late that afternoon two companies of Japanese, led by the hill commander, emerged from hidden positions and attacked the Third Battalion's perimeter, causing much confusion and engaging the Americans in hand-to-hand fighting that continued intermittently into the night.[39] Fortunately rain that night, captured in ponchos, refilled canteens.

Meanwhile the Second Battalion reached the plateau without great difficulty but was pinned down well short of reaching the Third Battalion, which was located more than 400 yards to the north across ground covered in dense tangled brush. A short but intense firefight occurred at dawn the next day, when Japanese soldiers, wearing parts of American uniforms and carrying American weapons, approached to within fifteen yards of the battalion perimeter before being recognized. Losses on both sides were heavy, but the Japanese retreated. The Second Battalion then went down the hill and around to the north, where it fought its way to the top, with Company G suffering very heavy casualties, and huddled down next to the embattled Third Battalion.

The following day, June 23, an effort to resupply the battalions largely failed. Company L of the First Regiment lost most of its load on the way up and was itself besieged. Even so, 300 wounded were carried down. It was on this day, according to the official history, that the task force commander, Major General Franklin C. Sibert, realized that the current estimate of Japanese troop strength and with it the tactic of frontal assault, were wrong. He now ordered an end-around, shore-to-shore assault, using amphibious tractors to move the First Regiment to the beach west of Lone Tree Hill for assault on that side, to prevent further Japanese reinforcements from arriving from that direction. Teams of infantry and engineers used flamethrowers and demolition charges to clear or seal the caves, while troops opened and secured a supply route to the battalions above. By June 25 the Japanese defense had weakened, with the remaining troops withdrawing westward, and mopping up began.

American losses in the Lone Tree Hill battle were 150 killed, 550 wounded, and another 400–500 men evacuated for injuries, heat exhaustion, psychoneurotic disorders, and other illnesses. Many of the wounded and ill returned to their units in a few days; others required hospitalization for weeks or months or returned to the United States. Losses such as these left big holes in the ranks of the infantry. By the end of June the Second Battalion, Twentieth Infantry, had only 200 men out of an authorized strength of 700; the Third Battalion had only 322 by June 24. It would take time to train replacements if replacements were even available. With replacements, about half the troops in these rifle battalions would find the next battle their first. Therefore, to claim that Lone Tree Hill was a valuable battle initiation—or "bloody-ing"—for the Sixth Division, as some have over the years, is misleading.[40] It was simply bloody.

Estimating the effectiveness of infantry units by casualty reports can be misleading. They were usually compiled and reported on a divisional basis, giving the number killed, wounded, and missing for a particular period of time. Of course the battlefield itself is the most dangerous place to be, and the farther one is from it the less likely one is to be hit. The Sixth Division consisted of 14,800 men, stretched to the rear with headquarters, service, supply, and technical units, which were of course far safer and suffered fewer losses.[41] Thus losses that seem insignificant on a divisional basis would be recognized as serious when measured against the authorized strength of the infantry battalions where they mostly originated. One historian has calculated that infantry represented one-fifth of the total American Army strength and took two-thirds of army casualties. Infantry were 67 percent of divisional strength and on average took 92 percent of the casualties.

The next assault, on Biak Island, was the fiercest and costliest of the New Guinea campaign, in part because it lasted for three months. Biak guarded Geelvink Bay, located between the head and shoulders of the New Guinea bird. One hundred eighty miles beyond Wakde, it, too, was a coral island but much bigger: fifty miles long and fifteen to twenty miles wide. The assault began May 27, ten days after the Wakde landing. Fighting was heaviest for the first month, more localized for the next two, and then declined to mopping up. Battle casualties (killed, wounded, battle injured, and missing) were 2,555 for the task force, which consisted of the Forty-First Division and attached artillery, mortar, tank, engineer, and other support units. Within that figure, casualties for the three infantry regiments amounted to 2,025 out of an authorized strength of approximately 9,700, or 21 percent.[42]

What made the losses even more severe were the nonbattle losses of 7,234, which included men suffering from psychoneurosis cases and various diseases, of which the worst was scrub typhus. A virulent strain of the disease originated on the tiny, undefended island of Owi, just south of Biak, which the Air Force wanted for an airstrip, and then spread to the main island. The warning of the indigenous people that the island was tabu was ignored. Scrub typhus, which is carried by a mite that clings to scrub on the margins of jungle, dropped onto troop clothing as it brushed by. More than a thousand soldiers were infected. Few died from the disease, but because there was no known cure before antibiotics, most suffered illness that required convalescence that kept them out of action for four to six months. In many instances, the residual effects of the disease were so severe that affected men had to be assigned to limited duty.[43]

All of these losses substantially weakened the Forty-First Division. The 163rd Regiment, for example, had already participated in the Aitape landing and Wakde assault. Its Company F after Biak was down to 42 men out of a full strength of 196, and Company G was down to 65. The official history notes that the rest of the Second Battalion was "little better off and the First and Third Battalions were also greatly understrength."[44] Aside from a few officers, the regiment had received no replacements since before Wakde. The other two regiments, which had not participated in the Wakde assault, were hurting too: the 162nd had 933 battle casualties, and the 186th had 617. Lacking replacements, soldiers without serious wounds were treated and sent back to their units the next day. Doctors removed a bullet from Private Manuel Kramer's back and returned him to his unit the same day.[45]

In the end the task force persisted, destroyed the enemy forces, and won the airdromes it desperately needed. Fortunately, the Navy's descent on the Mariana Islands drew the Japanese fleet away from what had promised to be a devastating bombardment. Nonetheless, the Biak battle was painful and costly, and for four reasons. The first involved false American expectations. The second was topography; Biak, like other places along the western coast of New Guinea, was a coral hell of a battlefield: unforgiving and impossible to dig. The third was a skilled and uncompromising defense by the Japanese, who, as throughout the New Guinea campaign and indeed through the end of the war, would simply not cede territory without nearly suicidal resistance.[46] The fourth was American command deficiencies.

False expectations were a direct result of underestimating the number of Japanese troops on Biak Island. Biak was a regimental command with its own code, sending messages short distances with low-powered transmission, too far from ULTRA receivers for adequate reception. Furthermore, Central Bureau did not have the resources to break a flock of different regimental codes. Even so, an intercepted message sent at the end of April, presumably in army mainline code, listed the Biak garrison's ration strength as 10,800.[47] Historians mostly agree that the army garrison, principally the Japanese 222nd Regiment, veterans of the China war, and attached support troops numbered 10,400. Navy units, which were used as riflemen, added 1,950 more, for a total of 12,350. In addition, about a thousand more arrived during June in increments. Willoughby, as he had for Wakde-Sarmi, underestimated the size of the Japanese force. At first, he predicted roughly half that number, 5,625, and later 5,000–7,000; the Sixth Army predicted less than 5,000. Willoughby said he expected "stubborn, but not serious, enemy resistance."[48]

MacArthur was quite prepared to accept "stubborn but not serious" as the assumption of expected Japanese resistance. His eyes were on the steps beyond New Guinea and the Marianas. He was anxious to meet his commitment to bomb the Palau Islands in support of the June 15 landings on Saipan, for which he needed the Biak coral runways, to be sure. More important, he was determined to seize the moment to move up to the Philippines before Japanese defenses hardened. Thanks to ULTRA he was able to keep tabs on the Imperial Fleet. Successful attacks on Japanese reinforcement convoys had left Biak strategically isolated. It was no longer a critical bastion in the Japanese defense perimeter but rather a garrison forfeited to slow the American offensive. As before, the strategic situation called for full speed ahead. As his subordinates, including Willoughby, well knew, MacArthur would not tolerate any delay. The consequence of a minimalist estimate of Japanese strength on Biak was an inadequate assault force. On May 27, 1944, the Forty-First Division, with one regiment already engaged in the Wakde operation, attacked with two regiments. Leaving one to guard the beachhead, it moved on the airfields with only one regiment, which was forced to retreat under heavy fire. Krueger quickly transferred the third regiment to complete the division and later sent a fourth from Hollandia. The days slid by, from May to June to July, without resolution.

The battlefield at Biak was a corridor stretching fifteen miles along the middle of the southern shore of the island, one of two large islands located above the neck of New Guinea. The eastern sector featured dense undergrowth, and there was a half mile of jungle from the beach to a sheer coral cliff, 200–250 feet high, backed up by a succession of knife-edged parallel ridges, rimming Biak's flat interior plateau. The Americans landed at the town of Bosnek on the beach, where they set up headquarters and depots. In the center of the south shore, the ridgeline bent sharply south, almost to the sea, dividing what became the fighting zone into two parts. As it doubled back to the northwest, the cliff splayed out into jungle terraces, forming a natural amphitheater above a four- by two-mile plain along the shore. Here were the airfields; the heaviest Japanese defenses were above this amphitheater. On the protruding ridgeline, which blocked the east–west corridor, were more Japanese defenses.[49]

One road ran along the shore from Bosnek westward to the airfields. What lay between the road and the forbidding cliffs behind was a mystery.

Maps were inadequate. Orientation in a jungle thick with undergrowth was guesswork. Barely south of the equator, the heat and humidity there were oppressive. Steel helmets became too hot to touch, and undergrowth blocked any breeze. Water did not collect on Biak; it seeped away through the porous coral. Troops sweated heavily, needing four canteens of water a day and getting only one. When it rained they collected more in their ponchos, but heat prostration was a serious threat. The difficulty of building supply roads and the shortage of water trailers slowed advance through the interior more than did the Japanese.[50]

The commander of Japanese forces on Biak was Colonel Kuzume Naoyuki, though in the first weeks of the campaign, May 27 to June 15, Lieutenant General Numata Takazo, chief of staff of the Japanese Second Area Army, who happened to be conducting an inspection on the island, took over the command. Time and again in the Pacific war Japanese commanders demonstrated great skill in building defenses: using terrain, siting weapons, and camouflage. Biak provided extraordinary opportunities for all three. Colonel Kuzume recognized that the Americans wanted airfields, so he designed his defenses expressly to make getting them as costly as possible. On the lower terrace of the amphitheater above the airfields was a set of three sump pits, twenty to sixty feet deep and 75–120 feet in diameter, connected to each other through underground caverns and tunnels and together capable of holding a thousand soldiers. These Kuzume developed into a stronghold called West Caves, which was at once a barracks, a supply depot, and a command center, surrounded by pillboxes, bunkers, and foxholes. On the rest of the slope, in caves and crevices, he installed his artillery, mortars, and machine guns to cover the airfields.

Meanwhile, the East Caves, located at the foot of the ridges, from which they protruded to the shoreline, provided a second stronghold. A third was located in an aboveground pocket among the ridges farther east. From these bastions he was able to send out and recover contingents to attack the Americans moving onto the airfields as well as along their shoreline supply corridor. Such a deployment made it impossible to concentrate forces for a decisive attack, but Kuzume was aiming at stringing out the battle, denying the airfields, and weakening the Americans by attrition. And this the Japanese accomplished.[51] On June 13, two and a half weeks after the landing, the assistant division commander recommended that the Third Battalion, 162nd Infantry, be withdrawn from combat because it was exhausted and unable to contribute much to the battle. The official history agrees and adds that indeed both forward regiments "were becoming fatigued" from eighteen days of continuous combat.[52] Former staff sergeant Fred Kielsigard of the 162nd Regiment Anti-Tank Company, assigned to front line duty, described the fighting:

> Our knob of coral had been denuded of any trees or bushes. So we
> were out in the open and the enemy had the advantage of cover to
> within 10–20 feet of our positions.... The attack lasted all night with
> hardly any let up. At one time I counted 3 machine guns, at least
> 2 knee mortars besides rifles and grenades lobbed at us. The usual
> [Japanese] routine was to fire the M.G.s [machine guns] and at
> times knee mortars. Then bushes would shake on one side to get our
> attention. Then a nip would try to rush us on the opposite side.
> About every hour or so we would send 2 helmets back to the
> company to be filled with grenades. The Japs were trying to get us to
> freeze on the M.G. and then rush us as we were reloading. So I fired
> the shortest bursts possible no [more] often than necessary. At one
> time a big nip rushed the M.G. and let out a piercing scream.
> Fortunately I caught him in the nick of time as he landed not far
> from the end of the barrell [sic]. Finally dawn came and the enemy
> withdrew.... There was 19 cartridges left in the M.G. belt.... As
> I tried to locate the snap that holds the barrell of the gun on the
> tripod, I found it had been shot off during the night.... I consider it a
> miracle that we came thru this ordeal with no casualties.[53]

For the "Jungleers" (the division moniker) such as Kielsigard, Biak was "bloody, awful Biak."[54]

By the end of the first week in June MacArthur and Krueger were dissatisfied with the progress of the Forty-First Division. Concern for the failure to capture the airfields was undoubtedly more pointed because of a disaster that took place on Wakde on the evening of June 5. Two Japanese bombers struck the crowded airstrip, the only one beyond Hollandia, destroying or damaging eighty-six planes.[55] Coincidentally, the Forty-First's commander, Major General Horace Fuller, was executing what seemed like a classic encirclement maneuver to seize the airfields, and it turned into a critical blunder. After an initial setback in the shoreline advance to the airfields and the arrival of a third regiment, Fuller devised a new offensive that repeated the shoreline advance but added a wide encirclement by the 186th Regiment and one battalion of the 162nd. The reinforced regiment was to cross over the ridges north of Bosnek and march west along the interior plateau until it reached a point opposite the airfield, then recross the ridges, move down the slope, and reconnoiter, and then, if no enemy was found, take the airfield. The march west began June 2, and by June 7 (the same day as the Normandy invasion, given the time difference) the encircling force had crossed the ridges and was moving onto the terraced slope above the airfield. Four American battalions were therefore above and behind the West Caves and its artillery, mortar, and machine gun emplacements, yet patrols failed to find the enemy, and the whole force moved down onto the airfield and beach. There, like fish in a barrel, they were subjected to extended bombardment from the slopes they had just passed through. Many have wondered why the division, regimental, and battalion commanders did not recognize the risks of seizing the airfields until the slope above had been secured and therefore conduct a rigorous, extensive, supervised reconnaissance. The two assault battalions began their descent at 7:30 a.m. and were on the beach and airfield by 8:50 a.m., suggesting a quick look-see rather than full reconnaissance.[56] Parched troops, anxious to finish a long march, focused on the airfields. Having already encountered enough Japanese to justify Willoughby's low estimates of 5,000–7,000, and having not yet encountered Japanese in the airfield sector, Fuller and his commanders clearly did not expect to discover many more.

On June 14, with Fuller's battalions inching their way back up the slope and under pressure from MacArthur, Krueger decided to get a new commander. He sent Robert Eichelberger, corps commander at Hollandia, to take over the task force but decided to leave Fuller in charge of the division. This was Eichelberger's second fireman's rescue; the first was at Buna in late 1942 when he relieved the commander of the Thirty-Second Division and turned the tide of battle (praise for which rankled MacArthur, as we've noted). Eichelberger found Fuller beside himself with fury at what he regarded as Krueger's hectoring and insulting messages, pushing for capture of the airfields. This had been Fuller's first chance to command the division in combat as a whole; earlier, regiments had been drawn from the division for individual deployment. He and his troops faced terrible circumstances of terrain and climate, as well as fierce and skillful Japanese defenders whose numbers were far larger than expected. Nevertheless, several representatives Krueger sent to the scene reported that Fuller did not coordinate his forces effectively; that neither he nor his staff spent enough time at the front getting information and a feel for the battle; that he did not adequately consult his subordinates; and that he had not conveyed to his commanders the imperative of speed. It was Fuller's last combat command. Krueger appointed Brigadier General Jens A. Doe, assistant division commander, to the command.[57]

The Forty-First Division finally located West Caves on June 14 and after days of intense combat was able to clear the pits and caverns. It was a sickening finale. Loudspeakers urged surrender in Japanese but without effect. Flamethrowers could not reach the interior and flashed back from the walls. Gasoline was poured into crevices above, however, and after seeping down into the caverns was then lighted and detonated ammunition. Finally, engineers winched an 850-pound block of TNT into the sump pit in front of the cavern entrance and exploded it. Later, patrols entering the bastion there were overwhelmed by the stench of rotting bodies. The operations to clear East Caves and the Ibdi Pocket bastion lasted until July 28, and mopping up continued for months.[58] But by June 30, the airfields were secured.

In assaulting Biak, SWPA forces had broken into Japanese strategic space for the first time.[59] Although the Japanese army gave up on Biak, the Japanese navy insisted on holding the island for air support in a main fleet engagement looming in the near future, an engagement that drew reinforcements from Japan, the Carolines, and the Marianas. The Japanese were building up the air forces at Sarong on the western tip of New Guinea to

200 planes, and an amphibious brigade at Mindanao was sent to Biak on destroyers, protected by three heavy cruisers, a battleship, and other destroyers. All these details—ships, units, courses, and times—were picked up by ULTRA. As Seventh Fleet cruisers and destroyers passed Biak on June 4, heading west at full speed for the encounter, artillerymen of the Forty-First Division, digging gun pits to repel an assault, waved and cheered them on: a rare intersection of the scattered elements of this campaign. However, the Japanese admiral by then had turned back, having been sighted and wrongly informed by his staff of the presence of American aircraft carriers at Biak.[60]

The Japanese navy tried twice more to reinforce Biak. On June 8 it sent destroyer transports hauling barges loaded with troops. Intercepted by the Australian-American cruiser-destroyer force alerted by ULTRA, the ships turned and fled. The final attempt was much more threatening. The two largest battleships in the world, *Musashi* and *Yamato*, along with two heavy cruisers, a light cruiser, and destroyers, formed an attack force at Batjan near the western tip of New Guinea aimed at protecting reinforcement vessels and bombarding the ships and beachhead at Biak. The date for the attack was set for June 15. The battleships' 18.1-inch guns, firing 3,200-pound shells carrying nearly thirty miles,[61] could have inflicted a devastating blow, significantly delaying the campaign. The threat of it underlay MacArthur's concern for progress on Biak. However, by June 12 it was apparent to the Japanese admirals that the American fleet was initiating a campaign against the Marianas, not the Carolines or Palaus, so the Japanese Combined Fleet gathered and departed for an encounter in the mid-Pacific. A third attempt to bring in air reinforcements was postponed when the pilots brought south for the campaign caught malaria.

The Japanese failure to reinforce Biak provides a vivid example of the value of the Joint Chiefs' dual advance strategy—MacArthur's advance along the New Guinea–Philippines axis and Nimitz's advance across the Pacific through the Marshalls, Marianas, and Carolines. Both were following deadlines set in Washington and roughly in tandem. Each was breaching Japan's security zone, one that bordered the home islands, China, and the resource lands and islands of Southeast Asia. The fast carrier forces of the

Pacific Fleet swung between the two axes, first supporting MacArthur at Hollandia, then Nimitz in his move to the Marianas. MacArthur's drive to Biak was a direct challenge, which is why it drew reaction by major elements of the Imperial Navy. Nimitz's attack on Saipan on June 15, protected by the fast carrier forces, was impossible to ignore. It was clear that a great sea battle was looming.

The Japanese were beginning to realize the scope of the threat to their security zone. Coinciding with the battles for possession of Wakde-Sarmi, Biak, and Noemfoor, Alamo Force was directing the defense of Aitape, which had been taken after an amphibious campaign, in April. Initially Alamo Force had dispatched one regiment, the 163rd of the Forty-First Division, to land at Aitape, seize the airstrip, and block any Japanese overland drive. The regiment seized the airstrip without resistance, set up a perimeter defense, left to rejoin its parent division for Wakde-Sarmi and Biak, and was replaced by a regiment of the Thirty-Second Division. Soon after the Hollandia landings on April 22, the Japanese Eighteenth Army, the force MacArthur had just outflanked at Hollandia, had set off from Wewak for a 200-mile march on half rations through the jungle. Their commander was Lieutenant General Adachi Hatazo, a veteran of the invasion of China, who was well regarded by his men for his willingness to share their hardships. Adachi concluded that if he could not recapture Aitape or Hollandia by counterattack, he could at least use his army to slow the American advance.[62]

It became increasingly clear in May, from ULTRA as well as from patrols venturing eastward along the coast, that a strong Japanese force was moving west through the coastal jungle toward Aitape. Both MacArthur and Krueger concluded that reinforcement was needed. Given that MacArthur's overriding objective was recovery of the Philippines, Aitape was a backwater inconvenience; his forces had already moved beyond it. Now he was having to redirect his forces to meet that threat instead of leaping farther ahead along the coast. From MacArthur's perspective, the looming threat to Aitape could not have come at a worse time. On June 12 the JCS sent MacArthur and Nimitz a message asking the two commanders for their thoughts on speeding up the Pacific campaign by bypassing the Philippines and striking at Formosa. MacArthur promptly denounced the suggestion and insisted on retaking Luzon for use as a base of operations against Japan. On June 24 Marshall countered that MacArthur's "personal feelings" must not interfere with "our great objective, which is the early conclusion of the war with Japan." The Japanese buildup in western New Guinea, Halmahera, and Mindanao, Marshall added, gave MacArthur "less opportunity to move against his [the enemy's] weakness and to his surprise, as has been the case in your recent series of moves."[63] The message was clear. Marshall was implying that a prolonged battle at Aitape would raise a question as to whether MacArthur could liberate the Philippines as early as he had predicted. He must keep the same fast pace even in more difficult circumstances. Needing no reminder, MacArthur approved Krueger's request for reinforcements. Ordered to Aitape were the rest of the Thirty-Second Division, together with the 112th Cavalry Regimental Combat Team and the 124th Regiment from the untried Thirty-First Division. The 112th was a small regiment (1,500 troops), consisting of two squadrons, each smaller than an infantry battalion. Later they added the Forty-Third Division, which was hastily retrieved from New Zealand.[64]

The battlefield was a jungle. The airfield, beachhead, and American defense perimeter lay seven miles east of Aitape. Ten miles farther east the Driniumor River, which alternated between being torrential and lazy, reached inland seven miles to the foothills of the Toricelli Range. The fighting was concentrated in a rectangle six miles wide, located between the sea and the foothills bisected by the Driniumor. The American maneuver unit was not the division or regiment but the infantry battalion, which to reach the fighting worked its way through jungle impassable to trucks and tanks.[65] So far as was possible, bearers hired in local villages carried food and ammunition in to the battalions and the wounded back out to the beach, where landing craft evacuated them to hospitals. The battalion scheme was more flexible and responsive, allowing quick transfer of units and formation of ad hoc task forces as the jungle battle evolved.

Shifting chains of command created difficulties in communications. A more serious problem, however, was disagreement among commanders over the distribution of battalions: whether to concentrate on defense of the beachhead-airstrip or on a covering force along the Driniumor, or to undertake a reconnaissance in force beyond that river to engage the enemy and preempt an attack. Krueger, feeling the pressure from above for speed and anxious to maintain the initiative and avoid tying down substantial forces in prolonged battle, insisted on the third course—seeking out the enemy by reconnaissance in force and defeating him quickly. Major General William H. Gill, a jungle warfare veteran and commander of the Thirty-Second Division, urged building solid defenses at the beachhead so the enemy would destroy himself attacking them. His assistant division commander, Brigadier General Clarence A. Martin, argued for meeting the attack at the Driniumor line, which would need reinforcement. On June 28, Major General Charles P. Hall and his XI Corps headquarters, newly arrived, took charge. Hall had served in Africa and was well regarded in Washington but lacked any experience in jungle warfare. He had no desire to challenge Krueger yet was inclined to retain battalions to protect the beachhead until he knew what he was up against and where. He sought reconnaissance for intelligence while Krueger would use it for battle.

Hall had been counting on having at hand one division and three regiments, that is, fifteen infantry battalions and two cavalry squadrons. The Thirty-Second Division had nine battalions, the 124th Regiment three, the 112th the equivalent of two, and the 169th Regiment of the Forty-Third Division three. The remainder of the Forty-Third would follow later. The 169th, however, arrived July 20, after the battle had started, and was inadequately armed. The Forty-Third had moved forward from New Zealand expecting to stage for future operations at Aitape, not enter directly into combat there. Therefore, its weapons had not been combat-loaded for easy retrieval and immediate use. Days were lost trying to secure replacement weapons while crews worked on uncrating and degreasing the division's weapons to make them serviceable for combat.[66] Hall repeatedly ordered reconnaissance eastward beyond the Driniumor, each patrol reporting more activity and resistance but too small to challenge the carefully screened Japanese forces moving into forward areas. On July 10 he removed one infantry battalion and a squadron of the 112th Cavalry from the Driniumor for farther search to the east, leaving the river line with only two battalions and one squadron. The Second Battalion of the 128th Regiment, Thirty-Second Division, now faced a river frontage of three and a quarter miles with not more than 700 troops. Coverage was scarcely thicker in the rest of the line. At the same time, Hall retained nine battalions at the beachhead—three of them for a later amphibious assault. ULTRA had provided plenty of evidence that the Japanese Eighteenth Army was moving forward to attack Aitape, as well as evidence of its logistical problems, progress, and even the actual date of attack. Krueger had believed it. Hall and others, for some reason, had not. Willoughby, for one, was convinced that the huge logistic difficulties of the march through jungle, as revealed by ULTRA, were bound to weaken Adachi's army to the point where it could easily be defeated even if it had the strength to attack. Hall was used to wide-open desert vistas. He could not conceive that the enemy could gather a force 20,000 strong in the impenetrable jungle without being detected.[67] ULTRA warnings specified an attack on June 29 as well as sometime in the first ten days of July. The June 29 date apparently referred to a preliminary action that was canceled in a message that was not intercepted by ULTRA. In July, as day after day passed without action, uncertainty deepened. Hall had been frozen in a state of bewilderment.[68]

The Japanese attack began near midnight on July 10. From skirmishing and tracking and finally hearing sounds across the Driniumor River, American troops knew the enemy was close. With the river lit by star shell, pretargeted concentrations of artillery as well as mortar, machine gun, and rifle fire decimated the ranks of Japanese soldiers who came splashing across the river, their bodies forming a dam. More followed, however, until American defenses collapsed. Company E, 128th Infantry, simply dissolved. Adachi had managed to punch a hole in the Driniumor line 2,000 yards wide. His troops spread north and south into the swampy country west of the river but lacked the mass, artillery support, and supply to carry on to the airstrip and beachhead. The American command responded promptly and effectively. After withdrawing his reconnaissance forces, Hall moved his forces two and a half miles from the Driniumor to a second covering line. He received a blistering criticism from Krueger for retreating at all. Chastened, Hall dug into his reserves at the airstrip and counterattacked eastward. By July 18, eight days after the first attack, the gap was closed and the Driniumor line recovered.[69]

Still left was the task of securing the jungle west and east of the Driniumor. For the western sector Hall created two multibattalion task forces, one to move south from the coast and one already in the south and heavily engaged with Japanese formations. Once the northern portion of the Driniumor was clear, he sent out four independent battalions heading east in parallel columns. About two miles east, they turned south to cut across all the east–west trails and envelop Adachi's forces in the southern sector. The farther south the battalions moved through the jungle, the more difficult things became. Their paths became scrambled, and they had to hack their way through the jungle with machetes, slipping and falling from the mud left by torrential rains, engaging the enemy when encountered.[70] Radio communication was spotty; maps were useless. At times they used triangulation by artillery spotter planes to find out where they were. Planes dropped food and ammunition into clearings. By the time the last of the battalions reached the Driniumor in the south, August 10, the fighting was over. What was left of Adachi's army was heading back to Wewak. Aitape was certifiably secure, and regiments of two rehabilitated divisions and one new one had received a rigorous lesson in jungle combat.[71]

The yoking together of battalions from several regiments made it difficult to keep track of personnel, but evidence suggests that for the battalions engaged in most or all of the fighting, losses were severe. The Aitape task force lost 440 killed, 2,550 wounded, and 10 missing, according to the official history, which acknowledges that the figures are incomplete and contradictory.[72] A 1945 Sixth Army compilation of losses in the New Guinea campaign includes injured and sick. It shows for the Driniumor (Aitape) battle 447 killed, 3,200 wounded and injured, and 16 missing, together with 3,352 evacuated (wounded, injured from all causes, sick).[73] Based on the Sixth Army figures, the total losses to the task force would be the sum of those killed, missing, and evacuated to hospitals: 3,815. Estimating that twelve battalions engaged in the battle, totaling at full strength 8,500 (7,000, for the infantry and 1,500 for the cavalry), the loss of 3,815 would amount to 45 percent, nearly half of their strength. South

Force, consisting of two squadrons and one infantry battalion, lost 936 to all causes between July 13 and 31. The Second Battalion, 127th Regiment, Thirty-Second Division, which took the full brunt of the initial attack, suffered so heavily that its task force commander moved the unit to a quieter sector so that it could rest and obtain new equipment.[74] These numbers show that Aitape was the second most costly battle after Biak in the 1944 New Guinea campaign. Nine thousand Japanese perished, 118 survived as prisoners of war, and the rest struggled back toward Wewak. After the war, Adachi, sentenced to life in prison for war crimes, committed suicide with a paring knife.[75]

The campaign in New Guinea offers a chance for understanding the degree to which the soldier in combat was a major factor in determining the nature, course, and outcome of battle in the Pacific Theater. His attitude, physical condition, and martial skills defined a unit's effectiveness. Central to the attitude of American and Australian soldiers in the South and Southwest Pacific was the conviction that battle with the Japanese army would be a fight to the death, animated by a powerful compound of fear and hate between the combatants.[76] This was a substantially different attitude toward the enemy from that of American troops in Europe.[77]

Japan, as the dominant belligerent in the months following Pearl Harbor, set the terms of conflict.[78] These reflected the newly aggressive and nationalistic Japan of the 1930s, particularly in the army, which prepared for a war to establish Japanese predominance in East Asia. Educated for their career exclusively in army schools from age twelve or thirteen, the officer leadership was "peculiarly ingrown and narrow-minded," according to military historian Fujiwara Akira. They emphasized spiritual factors, drawing on traditional Japanese ideas about the way of the warrior (Bushido) such as "loyalty, unfailing belief in victory and [the] fighting spirit of the Japanese soldier."[79] The first year of a recruit's army life was intensely painful as his seniors literally beat these values into him, but in the process he gained a place in the Japanese social order, indeed a special place as a soldier, however humble, serving his emperor, and he found in his squad's informal sanctions, hierarchy, and cohesion a substitute for the traditional Japanese family he had left behind.[80] Every morning he would bow toward the imperial palace to pay homage to the emperor, for whom he would fight to the death. In that path lay purification for himself and honor for his family. He would never surrender, which, as the imperial rescript specified, meant disgrace: for his family at home, he would cease to exist, his name expunged from the local register. "Always save the last bullet for yourself," he was told.[81] The same obliteration of identity applied to those who surrendered to Japanese soldiers, and depending on circumstances, captives were put to slave labor, starved, or simply beheaded. The Japanese soldier took an enemy with him by faking surrender or pretending to be dead while hiding a grenade. For the Japanese army, the Geneva Convention was nonexistent.

If American soldiers did not yet know details of what became known as the Bataan Death March, which were public knowledge by early 1944, or the Nanking Massacre of 1937, and other Japanese atrocities, they learned fast that they were locked in a war of kill or be killed. The First Battalion, 124th Regiment of the Thirty-First Division, new to battle, was cutting across the rear of the Japanese forces on the Driniumor in June 1944 when it came upon a Japanese hospital area. Some patients opened fire; others began committing suicide. The American troops, says the official history, "summarily dispensed with those Japanese failing to commit suicide." According to a footnote, there was no record of any prisoners being taken in the hospital area.[82] In the Forty-First Division (Hollandia, Wakde, Biak) it was understood, though not officially sanctioned, that no prisoners would be taken.[83]

Both sides engaged in the slaughter. Cooks and supply people of the Americal Division intercepted a prisoner of war going to the rear, lined up with their rifles, and killed him.[84] Ray Earl Poynter of the same division tells of a Japanese charge that left him among the wounded and dead. The Japanese bayoneted survivors but missed him. They were "sadistic," said Herschel N. McFadden, another Americal veteran. They mutilated American dead and wounded, and "we done the same to them."[85] In the Americal, after several infantrymen had been captured and killed, a verbal order came down to "take no Jap prisoners below the rank of major general."[86] Respect was due to the Japanese soldier, said a lieutenant colonel in the Fortieth Division, but since a Japanese was not a human being, he could not be accorded the benefits of captivity.[87] According to William McLaughlin of the Americal, when the stockade was full of prisoners and intelligence was not needed, "we killed the [new] prisoners." On patrol they killed those they captured because taking them in was impractical.[88] In forty-eight veterans' surveys from eight divisions that fought in the South and Southwest Pacific, the Americal, Twenty-Fourth, Twenty-Fifth, Thirty-First, Thirty-Second, Fortieth, Forty-First, and Forty-Third, each has a statement from at least one veteran to the effect that his division took few prisoners or none. Looking back, McLaughlin found something had changed for them all: "We had come to see killing as merely a reaction or in some cases as sport to relieve the monotony of patrolling." "Everyone touched by war is brutalized," he added.[89] Not everyone: on patrol Fernando Vera of the Americal came upon two dead Japanese soldiers. "One was rather young," he wrote in a memoir. "As I looked at his sightless eyes, I sadly thought to myself, we could have been friends."[90]

The veterans' surveys seldom used racist remarks or racial stereotypes. Japanese were occasionally referred to as animals and nonpersons, and adjectives such as "wild" and "fanatical" appear here and there, but generally the appraisal of the enemy was objective and professional. Of course, these surveys were conducted at least three decades after the war, when wartime passions had cooled. Nevertheless they suggest that alongside hatred of the enemy was recognition that he was a formidable soldier: in addition to "vicious," "sneaky," and "fanatical," the most common descriptives were "well-trained," "well-led," "well-armed," "tough," "adaptable," "effective," "aggressive," "tenacious," "brave," "wily," "agile," and "smart."[91]

In *War without Mercy: Race and Power in the Pacific War*, John Dower argues that racist attitudes on both sides were primarily responsible for the extraordinary viciousness of that war, and certainly dehumanizing stereotypes and epithets regarding the Japanese pervaded American speech and text. However, the Japanese soldier in combat, attacking with bayonet fixed, was a force to be reckoned with. That war with the Japanese was a battle for survival, a struggle without sanctuary, came as a shock to the American soldier. Surrender meant barbaric death; to survive meant killing. The prospect aroused two powerful human emotions, fear and anger. The adrenaline flowed; the stomach tied itself in knots. Staff Sergeant Fred Kielsigard of the Forty-First Division on Biak recalled what it was like to be close to the enemy at night. Quiet was imperative, but one squad member snored, another was panting in fright, and Kielsigard remembered that his own knees were "knocking together so loud it sounded like a wood pecker." He solved the problem "by getting these boys on each side of me so I could elbow them occasionally and getting my knees down on the coral."[92] To deal with this reality, an infantryman like Kielsigard had to detach himself from home and country; joining battle, he entered another world, a "world within war," as Gerald Linderman describes it, a world whose axis spun on survival.[93] The need for constant watchfulness was a drain on one's emotional resources.

A foot soldier in the New Guinea offensive wore a steel helmet and carried his ammunition allowance and more clips if possible, his food ration for several days, his weapon (the M1 Garand rifle, which weighed almost ten pounds), bayonet, grenades, machete for cutting through jungle, entrenching tool, and two canteens of water. Those in mortar or machine gun crews added a portion of that weapon and its ammunition. Digging a minimal foxhole two feet by three feet and four feet deep required removal of twenty-four cubic feet of soil and roots. Patrolling around the Driniumor during the Battle of Aitape made digging one a daily chore, as was hauling forward the resupply of ammunition and food. Removing those wounded who could not walk to aid stations required bearers, four to a stretcher, with more than one set, according to how slippery, long, and steep the trail was. When not otherwise engaged, the infantry unloaded supplies from ships and landing craft on account of the shortage of service battalions.

The worst was nighttime in the field. Night belonged to the enemy. The jungle was as dark as a closet. It emitted smells of rotting flesh and was punctuated by strange noises, such as the clacking of land crabs exploring empty ration cans. Heavy rains pooled in the bottom of the foxhole. To emerge from the foxhole seeking relief from diarrhea could draw friendly fire. Exhaustion battled with fear through the night as the infantryman slept with one eye open and tried to keep his weapon dry. Meals might have provided moments of ease and satisfaction, but most troops ate out of cans. In combat zones, fresh food and kitchen-prepared meals were out of the question. Standard daily fare on New Guinea, raised, prepared, and packed in Australia, was the C ration, providing 3,348 calories, fitted into six bulky twelve-ounce cans. It consisted of beef stew, pork and beans, and corned beef hash, with coffee, biscuits, sugar, and a chocolate bar. According to the official history, "In one shipment of 600,000 C rations to Biak two-thirds of the meat components consisted of corned beef hash," the meal least favored by American soldiers. Said Major General Innis P. Swift, the commander of the First Cavalry Division, "Every man is sick and tired of corned beef and corned beef hash."[94] After several days, eating the C ration, meant for short ventures beyond the range of the company kitchen, became monotonous and, for some, stomach-turning. The Sixth Army had no alternative means of sustenance. Units that endured days of no rations ate local bananas and coconuts. John Briand of the Thirty-First Division went eight weeks without coffee.[95] Later the Quartermaster Corps greatly enhanced C rations with new meat offerings, such as chicken and vegetables, meat and spaghetti, and frankfurters and beans. These did not appear, however, until 1945, just as the war in Europe was ending.[96]

Ration deficiencies stemmed from broader problems in the Southwest Pacific posed by the rapid enlargement and spread of American forces on New Guinea in 1944. The distance between Australia, the original base and source of general supply and provisions, and the combat zone was steadily lengthening, and staples were more likely to be filled through San Francisco than Sydney and Brisbane. So the supply stream was shifting from northward to westward. MacArthur's command system for supply, which was in a continual state of bureaucratic revision and tension, lagged behind the shift, moving its distribution staff from Australia to New Guinea only after the fighting ended. Meanwhile stocks of food on New Guinea were low and unbalanced.[97] With the constant shuttling of battalions, regiments, and divisions up and down the coast, it was difficult to learn how much to deliver and where. The Forty-First Division, for example, had elements at Aitape, Hollandia, Wakde, and Biak. Newly acquired bases lacked piers, cranes, forklifts, trucks, and warehousing, so unloading was slow and the number of ships awaiting discharge increasing. Offloaded cargoes were vulnerable to pilfering and weather. Food in tins deteriorated in the tropical heat, fiber cartons decomposed in the rain, and boxes split open under rough handling. Inspectors estimated losses from all causes could reach as high as 25 percent. Many other factors contributed to delay: long lines of communications, shipping, stock, rail, and storage shortages in the United States and slow processing of requisitions.[98] Most important was the low priority assigned to shipments across the Pacific at a time when the War Department was insistent on meeting the needs of the invasion of France.

Clothing was not as important to the infantryman on New Guinea as the food ration, but it was not far behind. Often weeks passed before he had a chance to wash himself and his clothes in a stream, for there was no rest area with hot showers and laundries in or near the combat zone. The only laundry on New Guinea in the first half of 1944 was at Milne Bay at the far eastern tip.[99] The infantryman's field denim was filthy and generally tattered. "People stink," recalled a member of the Thirty-Second Division.[100] Those with clothing impregnated with insect repellent found the cloth easily tore, while mold ate into the cotton stitching. Soaked boots led to rust in the lacing eyelets and decomposition of the leather.[101] New uniforms were scarce. Private Edwin E. Hanson of the Thirty-Seventh Division was one of two in his platoon to get a new pair of pants.[102] Sizes were a huge problem. Soldiers in the tropics lost weight: the average loss in the Forty-First Division was estimated by medical officers to be twenty-six pounds. The Quartermaster set of sizes with the proportion of the total for each size had too few combat denims in the thinner sizes. Only 23 percent of the Sixth Division soldiers at Wakde needed shirts in size 38 or larger, but 87 percent of those delivered were that big; only 5 percent of the division needed pants in large sizes, but 49 percent were in those sizes. Oversized clothing, said the commanding general of the division, often impaired "freedom of movement and combat efficiency."[103]

The infantryman was well aware that he shared the jungle with creatures other than the enemy. Most feared death adders, water snakes, and crocodiles, but few encountered them. Nevertheless, they thickened the net of fear cast by his environment. Far more substantial was the damage inflicted by insects. One had to keep an eye out for scorpions, centipedes, and spiders in tent and foxhole. Maggots not only feasted on corpses: one Marine awoke to find them "eating away" at tropical ulcers on his back.[104] Any penetration of the skin, even scratching a mosquito bite, opened the way for infection, leading to a festering sore they called "jungle rot." These accumulated during combat and took much time and care to heal.[105]

The Anopheles mosquito, carrier of malaria, did damage of monumental proportions in 1942–1943, infecting 85–95 percent of most units in areas such as the Solomon Islands and Papua New Guinea.[106] The rate of infection on New Guinea in February 1943 was 962 per thousand. Through extensive application of insecticide and rigorously enforced use of the suppressant drug Atabrine, the rate dropped to 45.1 per thousand in April 1944, of which 14.2 percent were recurrences, with 751 cases in SWPA hospitals. The rate for the Pacific Theater throughout 1944 in the official medical history of the war was 62.08 per thousand, with 33,475 cases.[107] This included patients with a temperature of 103 degrees or more; those with less remained with their units.[108] A bout with malaria meant a roller coaster of fever to chill and back. The strain called blackwater fever was rare but fatal. Another debilitating mosquito-borne disease (this by the Aedes species) was dengue fever, also known as breakbone fever, which caused "throbbing headaches, severe joint pains," and delirium and took months to recover from. The SWPA reported 28,292 cases in 1944 at an annual rate of 52.47 per thousand.[109]

New Guinea had its share of the typical military gastrointestinal diseases, particularly dysentery. Flies usually were the carrier of it and infected feces the source. Sanitation conditions improved by 1944, and the incidence on New Guinea was relatively low. That year, bacillary, amebic, and unclassified types altogether totaled 5,620 cases, with a rate of 10.43 per thousand per year. The rate in the Philippines in 1945 rose to 171 per thousand. The difference can be largely explained by the fact that whereas New Guinea was sparsely populated, the Philippines had a large population, with which the Americans mixed freely, and a huge sanitation problem.[110] The total reported cases of diarrhea and dysentery in the Southwest Pacific in 1944, excluding the Australian mainland and the Philippines, and thus approximating New Guinea, was 24,235, and there were undoubtedly many more instances of the "trots" unreported.[111] Dysentery and diarrhea cause loss of body weight and water and, for those already lean, further loss of tissue. Over time, this condition, combined with stomach tension, unappetizing and monotonous meals, and profound fatigue weakens the body to the point of physical and mental breakdown.[112]

One disease that emerged on New Guinea and later became a major threat in the Philippines was infectious hepatitis (now Hepatitis A). It started with 1,500 cases at Biak and Owi, sites of the scrub typhus epidemic, and spread to Hollandia, Aitape, and Finschafen, reaching a total of 5,025 cases, resulting in an estimated 85,425 man-days lost. A night-biting insect or fly seemed to be the carrier, in this case from feces to food handlers. The principal symptoms were fatigue, muscle or joint aches, nausea, vomiting, and loss of appetite, all of them, as with dysentery and diarrhea, leading to overall physical weakening.[113] The Army nonbattle hospital admission rate for the European Theater for the war as a whole was 464 per thousand; for the Southwest Pacific it was 807, the highest of all theaters.[114]

Given the instances of prolonged exposure to combat of a particularly vicious form, fatigue, inadequate sustenance, weakening from disease, and the heat, mud, and stink of the battlefield, it is not surprising that many infantrymen in New Guinea simply broke down. At Biak 423 of these went to hospitals as nonbattle casualties.[115] That year, 1944 (including the Leyte battle), there were 15,160 combat fatigue (neuropsychiatric) cases in the Southwest Pacific, enough to man a division.[116] The disorder took various forms—from incontrollable weeping and trembling to mute withdrawal and robotic movement. A traumatic episode could "trigger a loss of will."[117] The "thousand yard stare" was a warning that seemed to mirror, in the words of journalist Ernie Pyle, "the accumulated blur, and the hurting vagueness of being too long in the lines."[118] Other breakdowns originated in psychoses that preexisted army service and were not disclosed on entry. Men with these were returned to the United States for discharge.

The far larger number of neuropsychiatric patients posed a problem. Strong sentiments existed among line officers for a "clean army," and those with psychiatric problems were misfits, if not shirkers and cowards, and should be weeded out. Sending them back to the United States for therapy or discharge, however, meant further depleting rifle platoons at a moment when replacements were scarce. Facing this dilemma, divisions found the idea of providing rest and administering therapy immediately behind the front, of "salvaging on the battlefield," worth trying. The new approach put forward by Army psychiatrists was based on the premise that combat fatigue resulted not from cowardice but from a conflict between the soldier's "natural instinct for self-preservation and his desire to fight and not to run away." He "attempts to continue in the face of a biological situation that, at times, becomes overwhelming" and fails. An experimental system of front-line psychiatric treatment for combat fatigue, one that included hypnosis, was tried in the Okinawa campaign, with success. Eight hundred of nine hundred patients were returned to battle.[119] That was in 1945, however. In 1943–1944, treatment was rudimentary, given the lack of deployment of psychiatrists close to the front for more discriminating diagnosis and treatment. The Southwest Pacific began to address minor combat fatigue cases in the field in 1943, providing rest, hot food, and sedation within the division, with the aim of returning the men to their units in a few days.[120] Concurrently with the New Guinea campaign, during the Saipan invasion the hospital ship *Solace* took 150 men with combat fatigue aboard for a day or two of rest and good food and returned two-thirds of them to the battle.[121]

The infantryman's ultimate source of relief and support was his squad. It served as a forum for camaraderie, chatter, and the dry humor of soldiers that Bill Mauldin indelibly captured in his cartoons. The squad was the infantryman's world within war. This evolved through advanced training, shipment overseas, and initial combat. However, battle winnowed the circle, diminished further by transfers and promotions. New faces appeared; replacements dangerous in their ignorance required tutoring. With care, the squad reintegrated, but if the battle was prolonged or the interval between battles was too short for recuperation, the disintegration recurred, and the veteran withdrew into his own private world within war.

Opportunities to connect with the outside world were spare in the Southwest Pacific. When a radio was available, the soldiers listened to Tokyo Rose, enjoying the big band music and ignoring the propaganda (and disturbed by often accurate reports of their own troop movements). When they could find copies, they read the *Stars and Stripes*, a newspaper for soldiers by soldiers that circulated in the European Theater. As Geoffrey Perret says in his biography of MacArthur, the general was "too sensitive to slights ever to allow his troops to run a newspaper that had anything resembling freedom of expression."[122] A number of veterans remembered seeing the Bob Hope Show, then performing throughout the Pacific, but they recalled no other entertainment. Mail took months: Christmas cards arrived in July. One particular gripe was that they never saw a newspaper correspondent. Of course, the Southwest Pacific was featured less than Europe in the American press, and for the Pacific it was more dramatic and less arduous for correspondents to follow the fleet to the Marianas than, for example, to follow the Forty-First Division onto Biak. Beyond that, however, MacArthur's management of "spoon-fed" correspondents at General Headquarters left only one story and one voice emerging from the Southwest Pacific, one that drew primarily on MacArthur's daily communiqué.[123] MacArthur's supporters in the press—the anti–New Deal publishers Colonel Robert McCormick of the *Chicago Herald Tribune*, Roy Howard of the Scripps-Howard chain, and William Randolph Hearst—helped make the Southwest Pacific Theater synonymous with its commander.[124] The campaigns in North Africa, the Mediterranean, and northwest Europe made Generals Omar Bradley, George Patton, and Mark Clark household names, but it is doubtful that the average American could name any of MacArthur's subordinates. Nor was MacArthur inclined to share the limelight with the enlisted men under his command. Infantrymen in the Southwest Pacific found that their war and their division stories were not registering in the American press. The folks at home were not aware of what they were facing in the Pacific.[125] Left untold was the heavy cost being borne by GIs in the theater. Instead, MacArthur, aided by his control of news reporting in his theater and the help of powerful press magnates, cultivated the image of a general whose brilliant leapfrogging movements spared the lives of his soldiers and displayed greater finesse than his plodding rivals in the Navy and Marines.[126]

After Hollandia, Aitape, the Driniumor River, Wakde, and Biak, the remaining objectives in western New Guinea were easily taken but not without cost. Noemfoor Island, seventy-five miles west of Biak in Geelvink Bay, had a small garrison, requiring only a one-regiment assault. Krueger, however, undoubtedly stung by the Biak underestimation, sent a second. The bombardment was heavier than at Biak, and the control boats this time marked the path to the beach with searchlights and buoys to avoid the drift from the current. Inadequate communications caused extensive injuries to two battalions of the reinforcement, the 503rd Parachute Regiment, which jumped to an airstrip. They suffered an average of 9 percent casualties, mostly from landing on the very hard coral surface, causing severe fractures. Sansapor-Mar, the last objective, lay on the eyebrows of the great bird shaped by New Guinea. The landing at Mar on July 30 by the First Regiment, Sixth Division, from Wakde-Sarmi met no resistance. Set between Japanese bases at Sarong and Manokwari, Sansapor-Mar was isolated by dense jungle and spurs of the interior mountains, which came down to the sea. No longer controlling the air or sea on New Guinea, the Japanese made no counterattack. Casualties were few, but disease made up for it. In a second outbreak of scrub typhus, nine men of the First Regiment died, and 121 went to the hospital along with another 258 with fevers of undetermined origin.[127]

During August and September 1944 runways, taxiways, and hardstands, new and enlarged, poked into the jungle along the northern coast of New Guinea and all the way to the western tip. Construction battalions moved from one to the next. Planes, crews, ground crews, commanders, staff, and cooks moved from one airfield to the next, two air forces shuttling northwestward, the Fifth from Papua and the Thirteenth from the South Pacific, consolidating under Kenney and MacArthur as the Far East Air Forces. By the end of September, the Far East Air Forces and the Royal Australian Air Force had 2,719 planes. At Hollandia were two light bomber groups; at Wakde-Sarmi two heavy bomber groups and one fighter group; at Biak-Owi three heavy bomber groups, two medium bomber groups, and three fighter groups; at Noemfoor one light bomber group and three fighter groups; and at Sansapor-Mar and nearby Middleburg Island one medium bomber group and two fighter groups. Here and there were night fighter, reconnaissance, rescue, and transport squadrons as well as Australian units.[128]

Because of Biak, General MacArthur had not been able to undertake his scheduled assignment of assisting in the Marianas assault by preliminary bombardment of the Palau Islands. Nevertheless, he could take satisfaction in reaching the western tip of New Guinea at the same time that Admiral Nimitz completed his capture of the Marianas. Mopping up began on Noemfoor on July 7 and on Biak on July 23. General Gill reported the Driniumor battle had ended on August 9. Organized resistance ceased on Guam, the last capture in the Marianas, on August 12. The Sansapor-Mar airfields were operational on August 17. The Joint Chiefs' strategy of a dual drive—MacArthur and Nimitz—had proven highly successful in keeping the Japanese off guard. In the Southwest Pacific the object was acquisition of bases for projecting airpower against the Philippines, for which heavy use of infantry was found to be essential. Because of the greater attention given the Marianas then and in histories, it has overshadowed the Southwest Pacific drive. Although the naval support forces for New Guinea were far less than those for the Marianas, the number of divisions assigned was of the same order of magnitude: three for Saipan, two from Saipan for Tinian, and two additional for Guam. The equivalent of six divisions operated in New Guinea and five in the Marianas.

For the Japanese, the balance of forces tipped in the opposite direction; consistent with prewar planning, they had decided to seek a decisive confrontation with the Americans in the Central Pacific Area. That setting of priorities by the Japanese had enabled MacArthur to overcome the remorseless environment and the dogged resistance of the overmatched Japanese army to leap more than 1,000 miles closer to his ultimate objective, the Philippine Islands. The New Guinea campaign appeared to be a preview of a new kind of mobile warfare with MacArthur its premier practitioner. "The day of the frontal assault is over," MacArthur reportedly told FDR when they met in Hawaii in July. "Modern infantry weapons are too deadly," he observed, "and frontal assault is only for mediocre commanders. Good commanders do not turn in heavy losses."[129] But the Army's rapid advance to the Vogelkop peninsula had been possible, at least in part, because MacArthur sought only control of the coastline. In liberating the Philippines, however, he was determined to conquer everything. To do so, his soldiers would have to confront a larger, superbly led force committed to forcing the Americans into the protracted slugging matches MacArthur had avoided in western New Guinea.

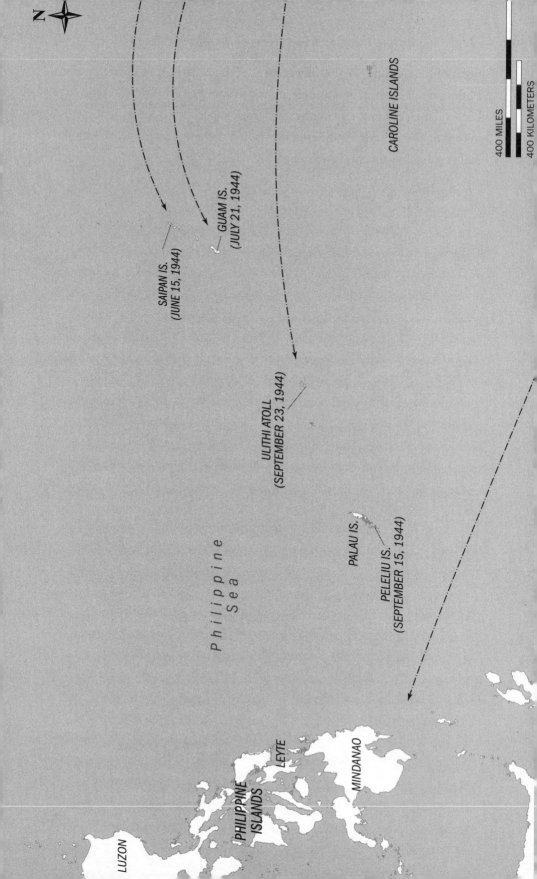

N

SAIPAN IS.
(JUNE 15, 1944)

GUAM IS.
(JULY 21, 1944)

CAROLINE ISLANDS

ULITHI ATOLL
(SEPTEMBER 23, 1944)

P h i l i p p i n e
S e a

PALAU IS.

PELELIU IS.
(SEPTEMBER 15, 1944)

PHILIPPINE
ISLANDS

LUZON

LEYTE

MINDANAO

400 MILES

400 KILOMETERS

The Marianas Campaign, June–August 1944

On June 15, 1944, as the battle for Biak entered its third week, the main body of the Japanese Combined Fleet passed through the twisting passages of the Philippine Islands and emerged into the portion of the broad Pacific known as the Philippine Sea. Joined by supply ships and the *Musashi* and *Yamato*, the pair of monster battleships that had threatened Biak, the fleet headed east toward the Marianas Islands, where the American invasion of Saipan was under way, protected by the fast carrier and battleship forces of the Pacific Fleet.

MacArthur's rapid buildup in western New Guinea and Nimitz's concentration of naval forces in the Marshalls and strikes at the Palaus and Carolines had convinced naval headquarters in Tokyo that a major American offensive was imminent. Air attacks on the Marianas and minesweeping off

■ **Map 4** The Marianas Campaign, May–September 1944. Drawn by George Chakvetadze.

Saipan removed any doubt where the Americans were headed. By now any further American advance would pose a strategic threat to Japan. Seizure of the Marianas would cut off its air and seaborne reinforcement route from the home islands to the western Pacific, in effect ceding sea control to the Americans right up to the Philippines. Furthermore, the Marianas would provide the enemy with bomber bases within range of Tokyo. The naval leadership in Tokyo decided that Japan must respond by engaging the enemy fleet covering the island assault and destroying it in a main fleet battle. Achieving a conclusive victory such as this lay at the heart of Japanese naval tradition and strategy, taken from Admiral Alfred Thayer Mahan's teaching that naval supremacy arose from the concentration of powerful warships (battleships in his day—he died in 1914; aircraft carriers with battleships by 1944) for a climactic battle of fleets.[1]

The same Mahanian logic undergirded Admiral King's assessment. The Marianas were a key communications hub for the Japanese as well as the most suitable base from which American long-range bombers such as the B-29 could attack Japan itself, and invading them would draw the Combined Fleet to its destruction. Reinforcing sentiment for taking the Marianas was the inadequacy of the original long-range bomber base at Chengtu, China. Most of Japan was beyond the B-29's range from there, and bad flying weather in the region restricted missions. Moreover, using China involved the longest and leanest of supply lines: fuel and munitions traveling by ship to India and over the Himalayas by air.[2] Despite strong resistance from MacArthur and even from members of Nimitz's staff, King and Arnold inscribed the Marianas on the campaign agenda.

The invasion plan called for seizure of three islands in the southern Marianas: Saipan, the principal and most heavily defended island, and nearby Tinian, both Japanese mandates from the League of Nations, and, 120 miles southward, Guam, an American possession captured by the Japanese after Pearl Harbor. Favored by the trade winds, Saipan and Tinian escaped the humidity of equatorial battlefields; rainfall was heavy but mostly in passing showers. Instead of unending jungle, they had open space, land under cultivation, and habitation. They had some of the New Guinea diseases—dengue, dysentery—but not as many. As benign as the climate was, the battlefield was treacherous and the combat murderous.[3] Admiral Nimitz assigned five divisions to the Marianas campaign, three Marine and two Army. The target of the Second Marine Division, survivors of Tarawa, and the Fourth Marine Division, veterans of the Marshalls, was Saipan, to be followed by Tinian; the Third Marine Division, from Bougainville in the Solomons, drew Guam. The Army Twenty-Seventh Division, units of which served at Makin in the Gilberts and in the Marshalls, waited aboard ship in reserve; the Seventy-Seventh Division, untested in battle, stood in reserve in Hawaii. Both reserve divisions would be committed, one on Saipan and the other on Guam.

Saipan is a narrow island, fourteen miles long and three to six miles wide. Hulking over the island from its center is Mount Tapotchau, 1,554 feet, topping a north–south ridge line that bisects the island. The invasion site chosen was on the western side of the island in the lee of wind and wave. The beaches selected lay along a four-mile stretch of the southwestern coast, with space for both Marine divisions to attack side by side, providing a simultaneous landing of eight battalions abreast. To cross the barrier reef and protect the assault troops, Pacific Fleet assigned 700 LVTs (landing vehicles, tank) to the two divisions. (At Tarawa the single division had 125 LVTs.)[4]

Hitting the beach was only the beginning. The V Amphibious Corps commanding the assault wanted the tracked amphibians to burst through the beach defenses and keep going all the way to the first high ground beyond by the end of the first day. The aim was to deepen the lodgment with space for maneuver and supply so as to carry the momentum of the bombardment and landing into initiation of the land offensive.[5] The command hoped to capture Saipan quickly by overwhelming the coastal defense. The American expectation of a brief campaign rested on an estimate of 15,000–17,600 Japanese army personnel on Saipan, of which 9,100–11,000 were combat troops. In fact, by June 15, the number of Japanese troops on the island was 31,629, including 6,160 Navy combatants. Revision of American intelligence had been unable to keep up with the Japanese rush to reinforce the Marianas after the recent loss of the Marshall Islands. The Japanese Forty-Third Division, transferring to Saipan from

Manchuria, lost five of seven troop transports and much equipment to American submarines, but most of the troops were saved, and the division of nearly 13,000 men reached the island in early June. On invasion day, in the absence of the regular commander on an inspection tour, the tactical command on Saipan fell to the commander of the division, Lieutenant General Saito Yoshitsugu, a skilled infantry fighter but new to island warfare.[6]

Saipan had an ideal topography for defense. The land rose gradually from the southwestern beachfront to the southern foothills and lower slopes of the central range. Emplaced along these heights, with sweeping command of the coastline, coral reef, and lagoon were well-hidden artillery—at least sixteen 150 mm howitzers and thirty 75 mm mountain guns. Smaller-bore artillery at the ends of the beachfront and on Afetna Point in the middle covered the beaches. Behind the beachfront ran barbed wire and two infantry trenches, studded with machine gun pits, mortars, and 20 mm, 37 mm, and 47 mm guns and mortars. Extensive as the defenses were, they were incomplete. Many coastal defense guns lay in storage or alongside emplacements unfinished for lack of construction materials. Furthermore, mobile artillery was immovable for lack of vehicles.[7] One can imagine what the Marines would have faced invading the following November, as originally scheduled.

The American invasion of Saipan was the largest and bloodiest amphibious assault in the Pacific to that point, more characteristic of the coming battles of Iwo Jima and Okinawa than of New Guinea and the Marshalls. Lessons learned from Tarawa and the Marshalls, the intensifying strategic importance of the objectives, and the consequent enlargement and improvement of Japanese defenses led to more powerful and elaborate American assault forces with new weapons, such as rocket-firing landing craft and amphibian tanks carrying 75 mm guns in armored turrets. Just to transport the three divisions and their equipment called for fifty-nine troopships and sixty-four LSTs.[8] The invasion began early in the morning on June 15 with a grim parade of the initial assault troops in amphibian tractors—tank and troop-carrying—from their transports to the line of departure, fifty-six vehicles in four lines for each of eight beaches. They went forward while the Japanese guns waited, climbed across the barrier reef, and entered the lagoon. Now the Japanese artillery, already on target with the reef, opened fire, as did their abundant lesser weapons, from above, ahead, and the sides.[9]

The parade dissolved. On the Second Marine Division front, imperiled troop amphtracs swung ahead of their slower, protecting armored tractors. The amphibians veered to the left under heavy enfilade fire from Afetna Point on their right and were pushed farther left, away from their assigned beaches, by the current. Battalions landed on the same beach, with following echelons adding to the pileup. Consequently the invasion formation was weakened in the center, between the two divisions, while battalions were intermingled on congested beaches to the north. These were narrow and steep beaches confined by thick vegetation on the landward side. Machine guns, mortars, and light artillery raked the beaches. In the confusion and disarray, Marines lost touch with their units and officers with their men. Amphibian crews dumped their loads and withdrew or joined the Marines digging foxholes on the beach. Here and there disabled amphibian tanks—stuck in trenches, blown open, or perforated—provided cover. Their thin armor would at best stop a bullet. Sniper fire from behind the beaches was deadly. Removing the wounded to temporary hospital ships— about 4,000 in the first three days—was difficult and at times impossible.[10] As an observer said of the Japanese artillery fire from the terraces above Mokmer airfield on Biak a week earlier, "it was like shooting fish in a barrel."

In spite of the mayhem and mounting casualties—1,575 in the Second Division on D-Day and an estimated 2,000 for the Fourth Division in the first twenty-four hours—instilled Marine discipline worked toward restoring order and cohesion and initiating movement off the beach. Individuals from the same company, scattered along the beach, found each other and, as one sergeant who was there said, "just gathered up people and tried to get something organized."[11] Officers rounding up troops made their presence felt and in so doing became targets for snipers. All four of the initial assault battalion commanders in the Second Division were wounded but quickly replaced. In the Fourth Marine Division sector, the amphtracs met the same gauntlet of fire crossing the lagoon but landed on their assigned beaches, and some did indeed burst through and reach the first day's objective, from which they had to withdraw partway. The farther south, the worse it became: heavy fire on the right flank and meager advances at great cost. The American divisions did not achieve their D-Day objectives, but they seized and held the beaches and gained a few salients beyond up to a thousand yards in depth.

Japanese counterattacks were a scourge through the following night. Three separate attacks supported by tanks came down the road from the north against the left flank of the Second Division, with flags, bugles, shouts of "Banzai!," and officers brandishing swords. Marines responded in a devastating fire of machine guns, rifles, and their single battalion of artillery. Critical support came from the 5-inch guns of three destroyers offshore, especially the star shells they shot into the sky, which illuminated the battlefield and silhouetted the attackers. Five Sherman tanks reached the beach in time for action in the third attack. Seven hundred Japanese soldiers died in that attack. In the repulse of an attack on its right flank, the Fourth Division had the support of three battalions of 105 mm howitzers and for an attack on its left, the support of the battleship *California*, a Pearl Harbor veteran, and two destroyers. In the final attack on the following night, again on the Second Division, by about 1,000 Japanese with thirty-seven tanks, the marines responded with a firestorm from artillery, tanks, and rocket launchers. Two Marines destroyed four tanks with their "bazooka," a shoulder-held rocket launcher, and a fifth by dropping a grenade through the hatch. Altogether, the Japanese lost twenty-four of their tanks. That was the end of counterattacks.[12]

The increasing availability of Sherman tanks and artillery in defense of the beachhead illustrates the thrust, sustaining power, and multiple capacities of the invading army. Sherman tanks came to the reef in ramped landing craft. In the northern sector they continued on a natural passage through the reef or a new one opened by an underwater demolition team. In the southern sector where the reef was closer to the beach and the lagoon shallower, tanks splashed into the water and followed a marked path to the beach. Later, sections of a causeway hauled across the Pacific lashed to the sides of LSTs were floated in and connected so that LSTs could unload

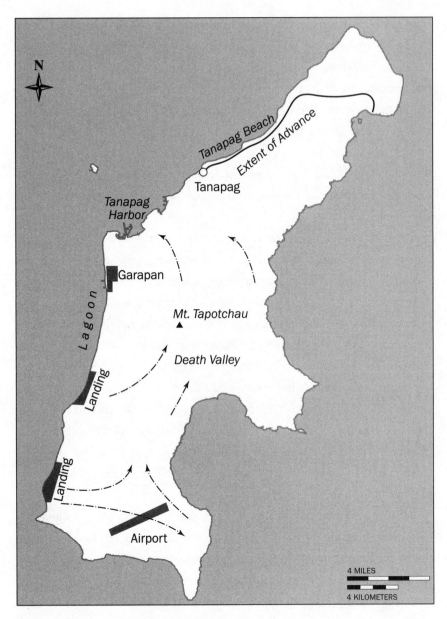

N

Tanapag Beach

Extent of Advance

Tanapag

Tanapag
Harbor

Garapan

Lagoon

Mt. Tapotchau
▲

Death Valley

Landing

Landing

Airport

4 MILES

4 KILOMETERS

■ **Map 5** Saipan. Drawn by George Chakvetadze.

from the reef directly to the beach. A constant stream of watercraft moved to the shore, carrying artillery, ammunition, and troops to manage the beaches, reserve battalions, and reserve regiments. Eight thousand troops reached the beach in the first twenty minutes and 20,000 by nightfall. Battalion, regiment, and division command posts were ashore the first day, as were seven battalions of artillery and two battalions of tanks.[13] What brought about American survival and success on the beaches of Saipan was the solidarity, skill, and offensive-mindedness of the Marines and the sense of depth and destructiveness, of irresistible mass, they presented to the enemy.

The invasion of Saipan was not in peril, but neither was it going according to expectations. During the first night, the commander of invasion forces, Vice Admiral Kelly Turner, set the Guam invasion for June 18 on the assumption that Saipan would be taken in about a week. The following morning, June 16, in conference off Saipan with General Holland Smith, troop commander, and Admiral Raymond Spruance, Fifth Fleet commander, Turner acknowledged that the battle was going badly. What the top command were looking at now was a drawn-out, bloody fight for every square mile of the island. With that dark cloud over the Saipan battle and indeed the entire Marianas campaign, Spruance informed the conference of word from American submarines that elements of the Japanese Combined Fleet were heading east into the Philippine Sea. "The Japs are coming after us," he announced.[14]

Waiting for a boat to take him from his flagship, the cruiser *Indianapolis*, to Turner's flagship, Spruance had watched "the many fat, helpless transports," wallowing in the Saipan anchorage as they unloaded supplies and reinforcements for the troops ashore. "They were all so very vulnerable," mused Spruance—"sitting ducks for an attack by the Japanese fleet."[15] The admiral was a sailor, not an airman, brought up in cruisers and battleships, yet, even so, victor in the carrier battle of Midway. Samuel Eliot Morison considered him "one of the greatest fighting and thinking admirals in American naval history."[16] Slight and taciturn, he appears deliberately unremarkable beside such vivid personalities as Admirals Halsey, King, and Nimitz. Spruance accepted the central role of airpower in the fleet. Sailor commanders, however, were supposed to have airmen as their deputies. Spruance did not even have an airman on his senior staff.[17]

The conferees agreed to the immediate landing of the Twenty-Seventh Division, standing by in floating reserve, because it was needed and its transports could then depart for safety, and they agreed to postpone the Guam invasion indefinitely and to transfer its Marine division and brigade to reserve for the Saipan forces. Furthermore, to beef up the fast carrier forces that stood between Saipan and the Japanese fleet, Spruance sent five heavy and three light cruisers and twenty-one destroyers from the Saipan gun-support group. Transports and supply ships off the beaches at Saipan would unload until the evening of the following day and then haul east out of danger. By June 18 the removal left troops on the beach viewing an empty seascape.[18]

The fast carrier forces reacted with excitement and keen anticipation to the news: at last a chance to meet and destroy the Japanese fleet. Vice Admiral Marc Mitscher gathered his fleet and prepared for battle. Attacks on airfields in the Marianas and the Volcano Islands (Iwo Jima) were hastened, and refueling begun. Mitscher repositioned his huge array of warships into five task groups, each in circular formation four miles in diameter with groups twelve miles apart. Two task groups led the way, one composed of his big guns—seven fast battleships and four heavy cruisers—the other containing a fleet carrier and two light carriers to provide protection for the big guns. Fifteen miles behind were three carrier groups, each with two fleet carriers and two light carriers. All five groups had light cruiser and destroyer screens. The armada covered an area twenty-five by thirty-five miles. With battleships forward, their hitting power would be immediately available in a surface battle. In case of air attack, battleships bristling with antiaircraft weapons would be to the fore. Meanwhile, the aircraft carriers, the offensive power of the fleet, followed behind, difficult for the enemy to reach. Mitscher intended to head west as fast as possible to find and strike the enemy.[19]

That was not the intent of the Fifth Fleet commander. Spruance was convinced that the Japanese fleet was aiming at the Saipan invasion forces and that the main engagement would occur in that context. He resisted any notion of sending his fleet westward in search of the enemy, for fear that by dividing, feinting, or flanking, all typical of Japanese naval tactics, it could get behind him and attack the Saipan beachhead. Instead, Task Force 58, the fast carrier forces, "must cover Saipan and our forces engaged in that operation" by keeping within operating distance of the island.[20] The task force, on tether west of Saipan, would sail back and forth, west during the day and east at night, on a run of about 140 miles. Furthermore, on a westerly course during the day with a prevailing easterly wind, the fleet would have to turn back to launch planes, delaying any attempt to close with the enemy. However, Spruance was not prepared to risk the troops on the island being cut off from reinforcements, ammunition, water, food, and evacuation of their wounded.[21]

Spruance had misunderstood the enemy. Vice Admiral Ozawa Jisaburo, fleet commander, had no immediate interest in the Saipan beachhead. He was not dividing his fleet but gathering it along the way, not feinting but concentrating, for what Morison called a "straight-from-shoulder punch, with all his strength behind it," at the American Pacific Fleet.[22] That was Imperial Headquarters' policy, and the Philippine Sea was where the American fleet would be challenged and destroyed "with one blow."[23] In any case, an attempt to outflank the American fleet was impossible because of his limited supply of fuel. Ozawa was not off on a "charge of the Light Brigade," however. A shrewd and perceptive strategist, he recognized that the American fleet had twice as many planes as his own. On the other hand he understood Spruance to be a conservative strategist, sticking close to the Marianas. His own planes, without protective armor, required less gasoline than the Americans', providing a longer range and allowing him to attack from a greater distance, beyond the reach of the enemy carriers. Furthermore, after attacking the American fleet, his planes could go on to Guam for fuel and ammunition, attack again, and then return to their carriers, thereby getting two strikes from one mission. In addition, Japanese planes from the Carolines in the south and Iwo Jima and neighboring airfields in the north, touted as 500 in number, could feed into the battle by way of Guam and nearby Rota. That source would greatly reduce if not eliminate his numerical inferiority in aircraft.[24]

The disparity in aircraft range meant that Mitscher would never find out where Ozawa was until Ozawa attacked. American carriers sent searches to the limits of their scout planes without success. On occasion the Japanese fleet was just over the horizon when the scouts had to turn back because of fuel. Amphibian patrol planes were hastily brought forward from the Marshalls but had an inadequate base and experienced communication failures. Long-range aerial search was one need Nimitz and his staff at Pearl Harbor had not foreseen.

A defensive deployment, despite the ire of the airmen, had significant advantages. The fleet lost no distance by turning east into the wind to launch planes, and the pilots had more time in the air to engage the enemy near or over home base. Instead of traveling to find him, the foe came to them. Furthermore, a position in defense gave full play to several strengths of the fleet. It permitted full utilization of its communications system to mobilize and manage a fighter screen against attacking forces. Radars (the SK and SM systems) picked up incoming air attacks at least forty-five miles away and in this battle much farther, indicating not only the horizontal distance but the vertical dimension as well; it could tell size, distance, and altitude. On the basis of this information the fleet fighter director could estimate how many planes he needed and at what location and altitude. Then by multiple-channel, short-range radio, he would consult with the fighter director in each task group and order up the planes, balancing the number needed against availability and requisite reserves on the fifteen attack and light carriers. From this flow of information a multiship packet of fighters would quickly rise and gather.[25]

The aircraft carrier may look like a cow, said Ernie Pyle, but it is a "ferocious thing," and its most ferocious denizen at this time was the Grumman Hellcat. The new airplane came to the Pacific as the fighter component of the new carriers. It was a burly plane like the Army's P-47 Thunderbolt, longer, taller, and wider in wingspan than its predecessor, the Wildcat, and, with protective armor and other advances, nearly a ton heavier. Though heavier, however, the Hellcat had enough thrust from its new 2,100 horsepower engine (compared to the Wildcat's 1,200 h.p.), to climb and dive faster and reach a higher ceiling than the Japanese fighter, the Zeke (the reporting name for the Zero). Six machine guns mounted in the wing delivered converging streams of .50-caliber bullets with devastating effect. The fleet carried 450 of these planes.[26]

Another advantage of the American fleet was the much more prolonged and extensive training and experience of its pilots. The Japanese navy did not have a pilot program in any way comparable to the American Navy, which ended the war with some 60,000 pilots.[27] American pilots of June 1944 had accumulated an average of 525 hours of flying, compared to 275 for Japanese pilots. The United States Navy required two years of training and 300 hours of flying even before boarding carriers. Most American pilots had completed carrier training on the West Coast followed by operational experience with the fleet in repeated strikes on the Marshalls, Carolines, and Marianas.

Carrier training in the Japanese navy involved the constant difficulty of positioning the fleet. It had to remain in the south, near its sources of fuel. In addition, as American power drew closer, stationing near access to the Pacific was critical. The Tawi Tawi anchorage, between Borneo oil fields and refineries and Mindanao, met these requirements, but carrier exercises outside the anchorage proved to be impossible because of exposure to American submarines. In spite of minimal training and carrier experience (six months training in one carrier division, three months in the second, and two months in the third), the pilots spent most of the month before the Marianas battle, as one of them said, loafing.[28] Weighing battle capabilities, a defensive deployment of the American fleet provided an opportunity to unleash enormous, concentrated, expert fighter firepower on the attacking enemy.

In justifying his deployment of the fleet, Admiral Spruance did not refer to defense advantages, either before or after the battle. However, he later introduced a historical reflection on the defense. He had studied the 1904 Russo-Japanese War at the Naval War College and had been impressed, he said, by Admiral Togo Heihachiro's victory over the Russian fleet at Tsushima. "The way Togo waited at Tsushima for the Russian fleet to come to him has always been on my mind." The Philippine Sea battle, he added, was "somewhat the same situation."[29]

June 19 dawned clear and warm with a gentle breeze and stray clouds, a "pellucid tradewind day," according to Morison. Planes left a story in contrails across the sky.[30] The American fleet, reversing course from nighttime east to daytime west and reversing again to launch planes, was hovering about 100 miles northwest of Guam and 150 miles west of Saipan. The fleet knew the Japanese attack was coming: dawn patrols had encountered a high number of enemy search planes. Whence they came remained unknown, to the intense frustration of all hands. By dawn on June 19 Admiral Ozawa had reached the location he wanted for attack—380 miles west of the American fleet. At 8:25 a.m., after pinpointing the enemy's current position, he launched his first wave, a carrier division's combination of sixty-nine fighter-bombers, fighters, and torpedo planes. A half hour later he sent a second wave of 128 planes from a second carrier division in a similar combination.

The American carriers had adequate time to respond.[31] The first wave appeared on their radar screens at a distance of 140 miles, the second at 115 miles. Just before reaching the fleet, the first wave orbited for fifteen minutes to receive final instructions for the attack, allowing more time for the American fighters to gain altitude and position and for the carriers to clear their decks of bombers and torpedo planes. Listening to the enemy's airborne instruction aboard the flagship *Lexington* was a Japanese language expert who translated and passed on to Mitscher and his fighter director the when and where of incoming attacks. Before Ozawa's first wave of sixty-nine reached the fleet, eleven Hellcats from the *Essex* pounced on them, breaking apart the close formation. As more and more Hellcats arrived from the *Hornet, Cowpens, Princeton, Cabot,* and *Monterey,* a gigantic dogfight, miles high and wide unfolded. Lieutenant Commander C. W. Brewer, leading the *Essex* fighters, blew apart the formation's lead plane on his first swoop. Diving through the bomber's flaming debris, Brewer pulled up and blew the wing off of another Japanese plane. He then sent a third fighter crashing into the sea. Next he attacked and stuck with a Zeke that used radical evasive measures until it went down in flames: four planes downed in what appears to be a minute or two.[32]

A score for the day of three or four Japanese planes shot down was not uncommon; some downed six or seven. The thick stream of slugs from the

Hellcat machine guns simply tore apart the targets. American pilots noted that the Zekes, instead of protecting their bombers, seemed to be evading the Hellcats by acrobatic maneuvers—"zooms and sideslips, skids, half rolls, barrel rolls followed by wingovers," as Morison described them.[33] The bombers, stubbornly holding course toward the American fleet, were the more vulnerable as pack after pack of Hellcats joined the fray.[34] The half-hour interval between the first and second waves allowed the American carriers to deal with each wave separately. Had the two waves joined in a mass attack of 200 planes and the preattack circling for instructions been eliminated, it would have been very difficult to mount an adequate American fighter interception in time.[35]

As it was, only a few enemy bombers and torpedo planes of the first wave got through to the battleships and heavy cruisers. A bomb struck the *South Dakota,* causing fifty-one casualties but leaving operation of the battleship unimpaired. Most of these battleships carried twenty 5-inch antiaircraft guns using proximity fuses (bursting near the target), as well as twenty mounts of four 40 mm and several dozen single 20 mm antiaircraft guns.[36] Near misses caused some slight damage, but no other ships were hit. None of the Japanese planes reached the following carrier task groups.

The second Japanese wave of 128 planes had a woeful beginning. They flew 100 miles to Ozawa's fleet vanguard, perhaps expecting to join the first wave there. Instead, they were mistaken for American planes and subjected to antiaircraft fire. Losing ten planes damaged or destroyed and then another eight to mechanical problems, the wave pushed on, following the track of the first wave, orbited for instructions, and smacked into a Hellcat barricade, this time from most of the carriers. In the following melee, an American pilot counted seventeen planes plummeting out of the sky in flames.[37] Here the second wave lost about seventy planes. However, twenty or so slid past the interception to attack the battleship force, and some of those kept on to reach the carriers. The battleships, with their protective barrage, suffered only a bruise on the *Indiana* when a plane in flames struck it at the waterline. Among the carriers, task group gunfire splashed four Japanese planes, two of which had released their loads. Both missed, but a torpedo exploded in the wake of the *Enterprise.* A bomber, just before it plunged into the sea, released its bomb close enough to spray the *Wasp* with shrapnel, killing a sailor. The *Bunker Hill* was the only carrier significantly damaged. A bomb exploded in the water alongside the ship, killing three and wounding seventy-three, damaging the port elevator, and setting several fires, which were quickly extinguished. The ship remained in action. Only twenty-seven Japanese planes of the first wave and thirty-one of the second returned to their carriers.

The third wave, forty-seven aircraft from the third and last Japanese carrier division, got off at 10:00–10:15, following a more northerly track. A shift of course in flight to a more recent sighting failed to reach twenty-seven of the planes, which found nothing and returned to their carriers. The rest found the fleet but were intercepted, losing seven planes. One got through the interceptors and loosed its bomb on the *Essex*, wide of the mark, and was shot down. The rest returned to their carriers from a fruitless mission.

The fourth wave, departing at 11:00–11:15, including eighty-two planes from two carrier divisions, aimed at a point southwest of Guam where the fleet had been sighted. That objective having been incorrectly plotted, nothing was found, and the formation broke up. Eighteen planes from the carrier *Zuikaku* set off independently and, encountering Hellcats and Avenger torpedo bombers, lost six of their number. Forty-nine of the fourth wave headed for Guam and fifteen for the small airstrip on Rota, north of Guam. The Rota contingent came upon Task Group 58.2 (the carriers *Wasp, Bunker Hill, Monterey,* and *Cabot*). Hellcats rose to intercept and shot down three but the rest slipped under and began glide bombing. With radical turns the *Wasp* narrowly avoided the bombs, and its guns downed three more planes. Again the *Bunker Hill* faced the bombers, but they also missed. Aside from the spattering of fragments and shaking up from fast maneuver, the task group came through intact.[38]

Most of the planes of Ozawa's fourth wave that headed for Guam never returned. The sprawling battle over a fleet stretching beyond the horizon was the scene of intense but punctuated combat. Guam in the southeast sector was different; it was a vital, fixed point drawing constant surveillance and frequent combat. The island was useful in servicing Ozawa's aircraft, and it was a mainstay in his strategy of narrowing the gap in air strength, by basing air groups there brought in from Japan itself, Iwo Jima, and from the Carolines to the south. However, strikes by two American carrier groups on Iwo Jima on June 16 and 17 and persistent attacks on Guam destroyed most of the garrison planes. Then, instead of the hundreds of reinforcements planned for the island, it got only fifty or so from Truk and Yap. In late morning on June 19, American scout bombers, already aloft to clear the decks for fighters, flew to Guam and cratered the runways of Orote Airfield. As the fourth wave showed up on radars, some sixty Hellcats from the *Cowpens, Essex, Hornet, Enterprise,* and *San Jacinto* joined the swarm over the island and shot down some thirty planes; the rest crashed in landing.

Dark finally ended the "Great Marianas Turkey Shoot," as the daylong battle was nicknamed and this episode over Guam demonstrated. Expert antiaircraft fire from the airfield and Japanese pilots—there were a few skilled among the ill-trained—shot down seven American planes, including that of Commander Brewer, who had opened the battle against the first wave in the morning. Only nine of the eighty-two planes in the fourth wave returned to their diminished carrier fleet. From the four waves sent out, Ozawa lost 330 planes.[39]

Meanwhile American submarines were inflicting equally major losses on the Japanese fleet. Vice Admiral C. A. Lockwood, Pacific submarine commander, set four boats in a square on the path the Japanese fleet was most likely to follow. On the morning of June 19 the fleet did indeed pass that way, and the *Albacore* found the new carrier *Taiho,* the fleet flagship, in its periscope. Among a spread of torpedoes, one ruptured the carrier's forward gasoline tanks. For some hours the *Taiho* sailed on, with fumes from the volatile and unprocessed Borneo fuel seeping through the ship. In midafternoon, wrote Morison, a huge explosion "heaved up the armored flight deck into something resembling a miniature mountain range ... blasted holes in the bottom," and sent the *Taiho* down with most of its crew. Near the same time, the submarine *Cavalla,* tracking the fleet, came upon the *Shokaku,* one of the carriers that had struck Pearl Harbor, and sank it with three torpedoes.[40] In the span of half an hour, two of Japan's largest carriers, with one-third of the fleet's aircraft capacity, disappeared. June 19, 1944, was a devastating day for the Japanese fleet.

That night Mitscher sailed west rather than east. A flank attack on Saipan—any Japanese attack—was hard to imagine. The normally conservative Spruance encouraged an attack on Ozawa the following day, yet even now with this reservation: "if we know his position with sufficient accuracy." Without location of the fleet, searches would have to continue "to ensure adequate protection of Saipan."[41] However, Spruance added, further search would be necessary only if the patrol planes, Martin Mariner flying boats, at Saipan, failed to locate Ozawa during the night. Using other means of finding the enemy—by Saipan patrols or the direction-finding system or submarines—probably fitted Mitscher's purpose, which was to close on the enemy with all possible speed. Reversing course to launch and recover search planes would prolong the chase. As it was, in the twenty-four hours after the June 19 battle ended, Mitscher managed to move his fleet about 300 miles to the west, from near Guam to the point, about 275 miles east of the Japanese fleet, he had picked for recovery of his planes after their coming attack.[42] He gained this critical mileage in spite of limiting speed to save fuel and turning east for one full recovery and one full launch.

Night searching failed, as did Mitscher's own routine dawn searches, which fell short. As the morning of June 20 passed, concern deepened that a chance to deliver an attack that day might be lost and that Ozawa would get away. Now Spruance loosened his constraint: "Desire to push our searches today as far to westward as possible."[43] Mitscher agreed to a long-range search, but as it turned out it aimed too far north and failed. Finally the American fleet came close enough for a routine search in the correct direction and found the Japanese fleet. However, this was minutes before 4:00 p.m. The sun would set before 7:00 p.m.[44] Mitscher, readying the maximum number of planes possible while still leaving room for takeoff, ordered a deckload strike by 240 planes from eleven carriers, knowing full well that his pilots had barely enough fuel at best for their four-hour round trip and that many had no experience in night landings. On a carrier ready room blackboard were the words "GET THE CARRIERS," twice underlined. Aboard the flagship *Lexington* the entire deckload got off in ten minutes.

The Americans had to settle for a twenty-minute battle in a setting sun, which allowed barely time for one bomb or torpedo run before dark. They came in three packs, one for each Japanese carrier force, deploying immediately and lining up for dive-bombing and, for torpedoes, glide bombing. The *Zuikaku*, a big carrier and a Pearl Harbor veteran, alone in its division now that submarines had sent the *Taiho* and *Shokaku* down, was the target of successive flights of bombers and torpedo planes from the *Hornet, Yorktown,* and *Bataan.* It maneuvered skillfully to avoid the torpedoes, but several bomb hits started fires, which brought it close to abandonment. However, these were overcome, and after repair it served in one more battle.

Meanwhile, flights from the *Hornet, Yorktown, Enterprise, Lexington, Belleau Wood,* and *San Jacinto* took on the next force, centered on the medium-sized, fifty-plane carriers *Ryuho, Junyo,* and *Hijo.* Bomb hits were obtained on all three, but many fewer than were later claimed. Neither of the first two carriers sank, but the third did, not by bombs but by torpedoes. Lieutenant (jg) George P. Brown, leading four torpedo planes from the *Belleau Wood,* headed for the *Zuikaku* but, seeing the *Hijo* without attackers, shifted targets. Though badly wounded by antiaircraft fire on his first run, and with his aircraft damaged, he pulled up to allow his crewmen to bail out and dove again. His torpedo probably hit, and that of Lieutenant (jg) Warren R. Omark certainly did. One of them blew a hole in the side of the ship and flooded the engine room. Later the *Hijo* sank. Brown tried to make his way back to the *Belleau Wood,* but the plane wobbled, dropped away, and was lost.

The third force of three small, thirty-plane carriers, *Chiyoda, Chitose,* and *Zuiho,* surrounded by four battleships, including the superbattleships *Musashi* and *Yamato* and eight heavy cruisers, formed a tight circle and put up a massive area antiaircraft barrage, laying what seemed like a blanket of fragmentation above the ships. Planes from the *Bunker Hill, Monterey,* and *Cabot* left the *Chiyoda* burning, but the fires were put out, and it survived. One group leader from this pack, finding six valuable fuel tankers nearby, damaged two of them so heavily that they had to be sunk.

The scene changed: deliberate and coordinated attack at first, breaking into smaller sections and individual combat, leading to what William Y'Blood describes as a "wild, incoherent melee."[45] Bombers tipped over for seventy- and eighty-degree dives, some at over 350 knots. As they slowed pulling out or as they left a flak zone, they found Zekes awaiting them. Sixty-eight Zekes rose against ninety-five Hellcats. It was "folly to dogfight Zekes" noted the commander of one of the American air groups.[46] The plane was extraordinarily maneuverable and seemed to have pilots far more skilled than the day before. To the same observer it looked like a ten-ring circus. The three Japanese forces were spread out below, eight to fifteen miles apart. Ships took radical turns and circled to avoid bombs and torpedoes. Planes plunged into and popped out of the thick cumulus clouds overhanging the battle. Fighters came darting and dodging across the sky.[47] They spiraled, flamed, and plummeted into the sea with parachutes drifting down behind. It was a circus of moving, changing color: the tracers, the multicolored puffs of flak, the smoke and fire from damaged carriers, the waterspouts from bombs that missed, the orange-red of the sun dipping into the sea. Then, suddenly, it was dark.

Mitscher's pilots, turning east toward their carriers after dispatching their bombs and torpedoes and breaking from dogfights, plunged into the first night of the new moon, blacking out even the horizon. Some of the fliers were wounded, some had damaged planes, many were exhausted by two days of combat and long-range piloting. They faced a trip of several hours, straining to keep awake and on course while managing mixture and throttle to appease both the desperate urge for speed and the absolute need to conserve fuel. A successful night landing on the carrier was the best hope; next best was a successful ditching and self-extrication from the sinking plane.

The carrier landings proved to be fearsome and brutal for everyone involved. Under ideal conditions, planes normally relied on a landing signals officer, who waved instructions to the pilot regarding his approach angle and conditions on the deck. The final instruction was either a waveoff or, if all went well, the signal to cut speed and bring the plane down on the deck, where its tailhook would grab one of several arresting wires and bring the aircraft to a jarring halt. Conditions on the night of June 20, however, were far from ideal. To aid the returning planes, the fleet switched on all lights, including searchlights pointed upward, and fired star shells. At times the glare was too much for eyes swishing in from the night. The pattern and discipline of landing broke down. Planes came in too fast, overshot the arresting wires, or failed to drop their hooks and ran into the barrier. Soon the deck was encumbered by pileups and closed to landings while deckhands unscrambled the mess and pushed damaged planes into the sea. Most planes tried to land in an orderly way, but some broke into the landing circle or ignored the waveoff and bullied their way onto the deck, forcing others in the circle who ran out of gas to ditch. At times, from fear, fatigue, and the attraction of that glowing strip of safety below, the spirit of every man for himself took hold.

The American fleet lost seventeen planes at the site of the June 20 battle. In addition, seventeen fighters, forty-two dive-bombers, and twenty-three torpedo planes were lost in the return to carriers by ditchings and damage on landing. Thus ninety-nine of the 226 planes engaged in the battle were lost. However, the fleet rescued 160 pilots and crewmen from the ocean, reducing the number of pilots and crewmen lost in the battle to forty-nine.[48] During the all-day battle on June 19, thirty-one American planes were shot down or lost in operations and search missions. Twenty-seven pilots and crewmen were lost, and thirty-one sailors were killed aboard ship.[49] Altogether in the Philippine Sea two-day battle, seventy-six American pilots and crewmen were lost, an average of five for each carrier.

The Japanese fleet lost sixty-five planes, one carrier, and two tankers in the battle of June 20. It retired to Okinawa, whence the remaining carriers and two warships went on to Japan and the rest headed for Singapore. The cost to the Japanese on June 19–20 was three carriers sunk and two, the *Chiyoda* and *Zuikaku,* damaged. The loss in planes for the two days was about 400; the fleet returned to Japan with only thirty-five operational carrier planes. This figure does not include land-based planes, lost reinforcing Guam. Y'Blood estimates that, all told, approximately 450 Japanese pilots were lost, a critical blow to the Japanese navy.[50]

Japan had lost its pilots, an outcome that had as destructive an effect on its naval aviation force as the sinking of all its carriers. Too little time remained to raise and train a new generation just as the war intensified and the momentum increased. But the combination of the loss of pilots and carriers was devastating. The *Taiho* and *Shokaku* had each carried seventy-five planes and the *Hijo* fifty-one. Turning to the surviving carriers, the *Zuikaku*, damaged, carried seventy-five, the *Ryuho* thirty-three, and the smaller three, including the damaged *Chiyoda*, each carried thirty.[51] Of the total carrier capacity of 450 planes, carrier space for 201 had been lost in the Philippine Sea, not counting the damaged carriers, cutting capacity for airplanes in the fleet by 45 percent.

The great fleet engagements occurring hundreds of miles west of Saipan guaranteed the capture of Saipan and the rest of the Marianas, but that had yet to occur. For the American troops, relief in moving off the bloody beaches by June 18—just as the Battle of the Philippine Sea was about to start—lasted no longer than a look upward at the mountain mass ahead. The sea battle had drawn on resources for the land battle. Cruisers and destroyers, which had been providing fire support, headed for the fleet, and transports withdrew to the east. Food and ammunition were in short supply, and important divisional equipment, still aboard, departed with the ships. Shipping returned on June 20, and the task of unloading resumed but was not completed until June 27. Meanwhile the invasion forces broke out of the beachhead and drove east and north.[52]

Lieutenant General Holland Smith planned to set his divisions into an east–west line across the island for a counterclockwise, circular sweep of central Saipan, pivoting on a point north of the beachhead near the west-coast town of Garapan. In the line the Second Marine Division would be on the left and the Fourth on the right, and the Army Twenty-Seventh Division would be inserted between them as the front broadened. Facing them were not only difficult terrain but veteran Japanese troops, as usual making the best defensive use of the terrain. The invasion had reduced General Saito's force by at least half, but the determination to fight to the last was undiminished.

On June 20 the Second Marine Division moved from the coastal plain into the hills below Mount Tapotchau and joined with the Fourth Marine Division, both facing north. Ahead lay "a nightmare of sheer cliffs and precipitous hills...separated in criss-cross fashion by deep gashes." Marines clambered into and out of ravines and struggled through "aerial tree-roots overgrown with a matting of vines."[53] In this terrain, attacking the enemy required dispersion to find them, so advance was slow. Lead elements of the Sixth Marine Regiment attacking Tipo Pale at an altitude of 500 feet were stopped by a machine gun position; they tried a flanking maneuver, failed, and then simply left it for the following troops. Elsewhere, they encountered a nest of six heavy machine guns and thirty riflemen that checked them the rest of the day. Troops of the Sixth and Eighth Marine Regiments found themselves under enfilade fire, gunfire from caves, grenade fusillades, and, most terrifying, close-in bayonet and knife combat. Advance up the mountain was measured in yards, but the Marines moved ahead almost every day. On June 25, the sixth day of advance, they captured the summit of Mount Tapotchau with its commanding observation of the island. Casualties for the Second Marine Division, that day alone, were thirty-one killed and 165 wounded.

The Fourth Marine Division, farther away from the pivot, covered more territory, but it was level land with hills instead of a mountain mass. Even so, casualties were heavy. Moving eastward out of the beachhead, Company C, Twenty-Third Marines, gained the top of Fina Susu Hill and started down, only to find that the defenders had moved down the reverse slope and "guns of all kinds were zeroed in on every inch" of the slope. By the third day after the landing, Company C had lost 40 percent of its men. Nearing the east coast, the Fourth Division worked its way north with its right flank on the sea. There, along Magicienne Bay, where an invasion had been expected, the division came upon extensive Japanese defenses. Ordered to cross an open field some 200 yards to a palm grove, Company G ran into "a withering fire." All who could retreated to a small ravine. Ordered to assault the palm grove, a veteran recalled, the company "raced over the bodies of their dead comrades, who lay in the field, swearing vengeance with every step." Moving north, the division passed through fields of sugarcane, which provided ideal cover for Japanese snipers. In every field, it seemed to another veteran, "the company would lose a man or two."[54] Clearing caves along the seashore, as on Biak, was dangerous work. As the two divisions advanced, their front lengthened and thinned. Increasingly important was insertion of the third division, the Twenty-Seventh, between them.

It was Smith's fundamental conviction that success required building and maintaining momentum and constant pressure against the enemy. The aim was to attack and keep attacking so that the enemy would have no chance to collect itself and improve its defenses. Speed on Saipan was essential to hasten the next invasion and thereby reduce its formidability. The JCS were pushing hard for progress. Of increasing anxiety to Smith was the progressive weakening of his Marine divisions, and his anxiety was based on experience. In World War I, he had served on the staffs of the Army's First Corps and Third Army. He had been overall troop commander in the Gilberts campaign of November 1943, in which the 165th Regiment and a battalion of the 105th Regiment from the Twenty-Seventh captured Makin atoll. They outnumbered the Japanese defenders ten to one yet took three days to do it—"a miserable, dilatory performance," according to Morison. Performance had not improved in the February 1944 seizure of Eniwetok in the Marshall campaign. The two battalions of the 106th Regiment participating were excessively cautious, "held up by groups of defenders not one-tenth their strength," wrote Morison. Observers attributed it to poor training and leadership.[55] Smith knew that he had to do better with the Twenty-Seventh and had to keep them in line. He also knew that this was not going to be easy.

The Twenty-Seventh, a National Guard division activated in the fall of 1940, had been shipped to Hawaii after Pearl Harbor to defend the outer islands, thereby missing out on the experience normally accorded to National Guard divisions before overseas deployment—shaking down, unit exercises, revamping of the officer cadre, and replacement of older men. The Twenty-Seventh did, however, experience considerable shuffling in personnel. Experienced enlisted men and NCOs (non-commissioned officers) were siphoned off to fill out other divisions and replaced by draftees and inexperienced enlisted men. By the time it went into combat, the Twenty-Seventh had only 20 percent of its original National Guardsmen and fewer of its original NCOs. The Twenty-Seventh's battalion and staff officers also suffered from inadequate training and instruction at the United States Army Command and General Staff School.[56] Over time, regiments and battalions of the Twenty-Seventh had gained considerable autonomy and established parochial attitudes that made it difficult to muster a coordinated and cohesive division advance. Confidence, a sharp fighting edge, and offensive-mindedness, qualities Major General Andrew D. Bruce was developing in his Seventy-Seventh Division, soon to be pushing forward on Guam, were lacking in officers and consequently in soldiers of the Twenty-Seventh Division.[57] Furthermore, its piecemeal exposure to combat at Makin and Eniwetok made its initial performance as a division more challenging. Just the same, the Twenty-Seventh was the only division available, Smith was told, so he would have to make the best of it. Initially Smith gave the Twenty-Seventh the task of clearing the southeastern portion of Saipan. That engagement only reaffirmed his fears. Again it was a piecemeal exposure to combat, with regiments and battalions landing and entering combat individually.

Intermingling of battalions from different regiments and shifting unit boundaries led to confusion and prolonged reorganization. The principal battleground was the Nafutan Peninsula, an eruption of cliffs and ridges featuring jagged coral, entangling vines, and open spaces without cover, defended by a mixed force of about 1,000 Japanese under the command of Captain Sasaki, a shrewd tactician. At night he set up strongpoints of rifle, machine gun, and mortar fire in the path of the American battalions. Pinned down by concentrated enemy fire, a battalion of the Twenty-Seventh would withdraw and spend hours regrouping. Squads reached the top of Mount Nafutan three times, and three times they were withdrawn because their position was too isolated. Repeatedly, battalions would advance some hundreds of yards during the day and retire to their perimeter defense of the previous night. They were not moving ahead.[58]

On June 20, preparation began for a frontal advance of three divisions. The Nafutan Peninsula force shrank as battalions moved north to the new front, finally leaving behind just one battalion, which gradually moved forward on Sasaki's weakening force. On the night of June 26 Sasaki concluded that he could better employ what was left of his troops by shifting north, toward what he thought was the hill occupied by his brigade headquarters. They passed by positions of the Twenty-Seventh but later ran into the Marines, who were now in possession of the area previously held by the brigade headquarters. Sasaki's force was effectively destroyed by the Marines. The following day the last American battalion found the peninsula clear of the enemy and secured it.

Meanwhile, on June 22 the corps advance began with attack northward by the two Marine divisions. The following morning at dawn, with the attack under way, two regiments of the Twenty-Seventh Division, the 106th and 165th, marched north to move between the Marine divisions and join the battle. Somehow the parallel columns intersected, with the 165th cutting through the 106th. The outcome was a scrambling of units and a delay while officers separated and realigned them. The 165th still arrived at the front in time for the attack, as did one assault company of the 106th, but the other assault company was nearly one hour late and thereby held up the entire division. Worse still, the Twenty-Seventh Division, once it started, barely advanced at all. One assault battalion of the 165th surrounded a hill on its right but failed to take it or advance from it. The other battalion advanced 300 yards to a tree line but no farther on account of severe cross fire. K Company of the 106th advanced into mortar and gunfire from mountain caves on its left. Tanks were sent in, but the company commander retreated to close the gap between his company and the lagging L Company. The companies dug in for the night with a gain of 100 yards.[59]

The Twenty-Seventh's faltering advance that day was enough to infuriate an already exasperated Holland Smith. It held up the entire cross-island offensive because the Marine divisions on either side could not advance farther without creating gaps on their flanks. The next day, with the approval of Admiral Spruance, he removed Major General Ralph Smith, division commander. The basic problem, as Holland Smith described it, was the "all-round poor performance of the division."[60] While the change of command was not by itself a means of propelling the division forward, "no other action," in the words of Spruance, "appeared adequate to accomplish the purpose" of getting the cross-island offensive under way.[61] On Biak, ten days earlier, a similar action occurred—the relief of General

Horace Fuller, commander of the National Guard Forty-First Division, by General Krueger under pressure from MacArthur. Fuller, too, was criticized for failure to convey to his subordinates the imperative for speed. Marshall's chief advisers, Major General Handy and Lieutenant General Joseph T. McNarney, both noted evidence of the Twenty-Seventh's "lack of aggressiveness."[62] Had Holland Smith been in the Army, there would have been no backlash in the removal of Ralph Smith. In this case, however, with a Marine general firing an Army general over the performance of an Army division, a storm of protest ensued, instigated by Lieutenant General Robert C. Richardson, Jr., commander of Army forces under Admiral Nimitz. This conflict, further shaking Army-Navy (Marine) relations and later reverberating in the American press, overshadowed the battle for control of Saipan.[63]

Meanwhile, the Twenty-Seventh infantrymen, in the middle of the advance to seize central Saipan, were stuck in a battleground of their own, which they named "Death Valley." On the west, to their left, Mount Tapotchau rose a thousand feet above the valley floor, at first gently with cultivated patches and then steeply, with a forested slope strewn with rocks and boulders, and finally featured cliffs and mesa, shaping the mountaintop like a citadel. Artillery in caves on the cliffs and machine guns among boulders below could sweep the entire valley. The valley floor, plowed land with tree borders and less than a thousand yards wide, provided troops with almost no cover. On the opposite side of the valley lay a small line of forested hills joined in a ridgeline, which provided cover and command of the valley from the east and which for good reason the troops named "Purple Heart Ridge." The Second Marine Division was fighting its way to the crest of Tapotchau, but its entire eastern slope was within the boundary of the Twenty-Seventh, as were both sides of the hill-ridgeline east of Death Valley.

Defending these eastern hills were highly maneuverable and heavily armed Japanese detachments. Infantrymen of the Twenty-Seventh, moving into the open and up the slopes, were subjected to intense cross fire from east and west. Their division artillery provided preparatory fire from the rear but could not be brought forward on the right for direct fire at the caves across the valley without endangering the Second Marine Division. The few tanks assigned lacked adequate communication, and fire direction and self-propelled gun mounts had insufficient protective armor against fire from the cliffs above.[64] A sense of helplessness was setting in among the Twenty-Seventh. A battalion would set off early in the morning to attack a particular hill or tree line. Minutes would pass, and then a sudden hail of well-timed and targeted explosives and bullets would strike. The soldiers would seek cover and remain pinned down. At the first chance the companies would retreat and reorganize, bringing in casualties, shifting leaders, realigning with other companies or battalions, and perhaps trying again, or as the sun lowered, digging in for the night or returning to their bivouac of the night before. The result was a growing passivity, and as casualties increased, fear that there was no way out of this impasse. Meager advance, in effect, meant standstill.

General Ralph Smith recognized that the existing order of attack, straight up the valley, was going nowhere. After he was relieved and before he left for Pearl Harbor, he drew up a new battle plan that provided more maneuverability and cover. His temporary successor, Brigadier General Sanderford Jarman, who had been awaiting duty as garrison commander on Saipan, implemented the plan on June 25. This would put more battalions into securing the line of hills on the right flank. Attacking and eliminating Japanese positions there would reduce the cross fire and provide cover for troops moving north on the right to circle west and strike the enemy inside the valley from the north. Meanwhile, one battalion would remain in the valley to engage and contain Japanese troops there.

The rearrangement went nowhere. Having reached the top of their assigned hill in Purple Heart Ridge, officers of the Second Battalion, 165th Regiment, were conferring when a Japanese machine gun opened fire: Lieutenant Colonel John McDonough, the battalion commander, was wounded, the commander of Company F was mortally wounded, one officer was killed, and two other officers (as well as five enlisted men) were wounded, effectively stripping the company of officers. Japanese mortar and machine gun fire halted the battalion, which withdrew down the hill and entrenched for the night. Approaching a nearby hill, the Third Battalion,

165th, met heavy fire and went no farther. The regimental commander then sent it to the far right, to connect with the Fourth Marine Division more than a mile away, removing it from the scene of action. The First Battalion of the 106th Regiment, which had withdrawn from the valley, moved to the right of the battalions and north through Purple Heart Ridge, attempting encirclement north and west. Stopped by persisting mortar and machine gun fire, it retired to a nearby crossroads for the night. The Third Battalion of the 106th followed the First but returned to the valley, reporting that road congestion by the Marines blocked their way.

In the valley, containment meant that the only avenue of attack was north, by the only battalion left—the Second of the 106th. As expected, it met heavy cross fire. In Company E, one platoon advanced 800 yards to the intermediate objective but had to withdraw 200 yards; a second platoon did not get that far before retreating to the line of departure; a third platoon "never left it." During the night, all elements of Companies E and G, with wounded in need of care, retreated to their line of departure at the south edge of the valley. That night General Jarman rebuked Colonel Russell G. Ayers, the 106th's regimental commander, for failing to make headway and threatened to relieve him if he did not succeed the next day. So far, the implementation of the Ralph Smith plan was a total failure.[65]

The next day, June 26, was the nadir of the Twenty-Seventh Division's battle for Death Valley. Movement ahead along Purple Heart Ridge was negligible. Supporting arms had proved only marginally useful. Delivery of food, water, and ammunition to the front was irregular. Casualties were now seriously reducing battalion strength. Extending the right flank had proven premature. The only way forward was complete seizure of Purple Heart Ridge and then moving back into Death Valley. The Third Battalion, 106th Regiment, advanced to the next hill along the Ridge, used its own heavy weapons to prepare the way, attacked, and within the next ten minutes lost twenty-three men. By now two of L Company's rifle platoons were down to about one-third of their strength. The battalion went no farther and dug in for the night. Following behind the Third, the Second Battalion, the 106th, battered the previous day and night, was supposed to swing out into the valley and instead dug in, too. Visiting these battalions, the division artillery commander and operations officer reported that for no apparent reason they were standing still and concluded that the 106th Regiment was in a demoralized state. That night Colonel Ayers was relieved of his command.[66]

The next day, June Twenty-Seventh, following the scheme of concentration toward the valley and hill line, the Third Battalion of the 106th Regiment and Company G of the 165th attacked two sides of Hill King, the next-to-last in the Purple Heart Ridge. Immediately running into fire, the Third Battalion withdrew for an artillery preparation and then moved forward again, this time meeting no opposition, but coming across a group of the enemy in hiding on the other side of the slope. They withdrew again, called for mortar fire, resumed their textbook advance without opposition, and completed their share in the capture of the hill. Meanwhile, Company G, 165th, mounted the same hill from the east, moved down it to the north, and came under intense fire from the last hill in the Purple Heart chain, Hill Able. With precipitous sides and a bushy top, it was more a gunnery tower than a natural formation, and with its wide range of fire down the hill line and across the valley to the west it was the key to the entire valley. Following the gunfire came a Japanese infantry charge down the slope and close combat that left thirty-five enemy dead and seven G Company casualties. With the day and the troops too far gone, the company withdrew several hills to the rear and there, digging in for the night, took a heavy mortar and machine gun barrage that killed or wounded twenty-four more men, including the battalion commander, who later died. Learning of G Company's return to its previous bivouac, General Jarman ordered that "no [future] withdrawal will be made for the night for the purpose of consolidation."[67] The Third Battalion, 106th, its task on Hill King completed, moved off Purple Heart Ridge down into Death Valley. In spite of cross fire from Hill Able and Mount Tapotchau, it gained the objective, a low ridgeline facing north on the west side of the valley. The Second Battalion, 106th, following, took up a position on the Third Battalion's right.

Finally, after five days of battle, the Twenty-Seventh Division held a forward line on the valley floor. Coincidentally, the First Battalion, 106th, was eliminating Hell's Pocket, a cove in the mountain wall that had obstructed progress along the left side of Death Valley. While one company held the mouth of the pocket, the other two climbed the cliff, circled above and behind the defenders, and cleared that portion of the pocket. At the end of the day, General Jarman congratulated the Second and Third battalions for "work well done," the first slap on the back the Twenty-Seventh Division had received on Saipan.[68]

It was short-lived. The next day, June 28, the Second Battalion, 165th, encountered unexpected resistance from the Japanese. Aimed again at Hill Able, Company G found that the enemy had reoccupied the intervening Hill King, requiring capture of the hill a second time. Gunfire from self-propelled mounts opened the way to the top, but, heading down, the company was hit with machine gun fire and a barrage of grenades. Ordered to retreat, it was thrown into disarray by mortar fire just as it was regrouping. In the ensuing confusion, Company G was withdrawn from the line, leaving Hill Able still dominating the valley. That morning the two battalions of the 106th Regiment, in line across the valley, advanced 400 yards to the north and stopped for supplies brought forward by self-propelled mounts. Hill Able opened fire, the mounts dumped their supplies and left, and twenty-nine of the soldiers sent out to retrieve the rations were struck down in a mortar barrage. The commander of Company I, Third Battalion, its fourth in three days, was killed. Then two Japanese tanks suddenly appeared from the north, firing into a grove of trees just behind the lines where the headquarters of the Second and Third Battalions, Company F, and the remnants of Companies I and K had sought cover. Twelve were killed or mortally wounded and sixty-one wounded. The commander of the Third Battalion and two company commanders were killed. Only 100 of the original 700 were left in the Third Battalion, 106th.[69]

At this dark moment the new commander of the Twenty-Seventh Division, Major General George W. Griner, formerly commander of the Ninety-Eighth Division in Hawaii, arrived on Saipan. He ordered the First Battalion of the 106th, which had just eliminated organized resistance in Hell's Pocket, to replace the decimated Third Battalion and ordered the Third Battalion of the 105th Regiment, which had been in reserve since Nafutan, to finish off Hill Able, assisted by the Second Battalion, 165th

Regiment, which so far had failed in that assignment. It took all morning the next day, June 29, and into the afternoon to bring the newly assigned Third Battalion, 105th, into the line across the valley. First it was hit with friendly artillery fire, and then one of its companies, Company K, was mistakenly led to Hill King, which had been reoccupied and was under its third assault, this time by Company E, 165th Regiment. Company K suffered both friendly and enemy barrages. Once the Third Battalion was reunified, the three-battalion advance jumped off. This time the troops made progress, gaining as much as a thousand yards, at last freed from their hellish corridor and into open country. Now they were in visual contact with the Second Marine Division, which was coming down the northern slope of Mount Tapotchau. General Holland Smith, observing from the top of the mountain, complimented General Griner on his division's performance.[70]

The following day the Second Battalion, 165th, took Hill Able against light opposition, and the Twenty-Seventh Division came in direct contact with the Fourth Marine Division. The gaps were finally closed. The ease at the end was partially due to General Saito's withdrawal of his remaining forces to their last defense line at the northern end of Saipan. On the front across central Saipan, he and his officers and troops had conducted a brilliant defense, taking full advantage of the terrain, fortifying and siting weapons skillfully, and placing and shifting blocking detachments. The Twenty-Seventh Division, boxed into a valley, never receiving the benefit of massed artillery or naval gunfire, erring, withholding, and risk-averse as it was, and devastated as it became, nevertheless persisted and weakened the enemy to the point where it left the battleground. In the central Saipan battle, the Twenty-Seventh Division had 1,465 casualties, the Second Marine Division 1,016, and the Fourth Marine Division 1,506. The Twenty-Seventh lost a regimental commander, three battalion commanders, and twenty-two company commanders to wounds or death. Major General Harry A. Schmidt, commander of the Fourth Marine Division, believed that "no one had a tougher job to do" than the men of the Twenty-Seventh Division.[71]

Meanwhile the V Amphibious Corps, the Twenty-Seventh, and the two Marine divisions, pushed northward away from Tapotchau; the three divisions moved abreast at an extraordinary pace, covering as much as 1,700 yards a day. Their spirits were lifted at the thought of completing the circular advance and ending the harrowing battle of Saipan. Saito's battalions, retrenched in the northern part of the island, were disintegrating, and his soldiers were desperately in need of food and water, so he was unable to man the last defense line. On July 4 the Twenty-Seventh Division reached the northwestern coast of Saipan at Tanapag, a town located ten miles north of the original landing beaches. The Second Marine Division, situated on its left, had taken Garapan and moved north along the coast. Now it withdrew from combat to prepare for the invasion of Tinian Island, as planned. General Holland Smith's plan at this point called for the Fourth Marine Division on the right and the Twenty-Seventh on the left to advance north and clear that end of the island, but on July 5 the Army division encountered stiff resistance in the broken terrain inland from Tanapag. With the Twenty-Seventh Division slowed down, Smith released the Marines to take the northern sector on their own while the Army finished off the Tanapag pocket. Most of the Japanese organized resistance left on the island was in or near that pocket.

North of Tanapag and next to the beach was a low, coastal plain, running north several miles to the village of Makunsha. A line of cliffs and hills rose from the plain, creating a coastal corridor about 600 yards wide. Slicing through that rise near Tanapag was a ravine fifty to sixty feet deep with caves in the walls, known to American troops as Harakiri Gulch. Japanese troops there successfully resisted attacks by the Twenty-Seventh Division's 165th Regiment. Where the gulch met the plain was the division's 105th Regiment, holding a line to the sea and stalled in the face of machine gun fire on the beach ahead as well as from hills on the right. In midafternoon on July 6, General Griner ordered the commander of the 105th to commit his reserve, the First Battalion. The commander, Colonel Leonard A. Bishop, argued that it was too late in the day for an advance and that they should dig in for the night. He was overruled, and the First and Second battalions advanced halfway to the objective, Makunsha, and formed a makeshift joint perimeter defense for the night.

A Japanese prisoner of war, captured while sleeping, revealed under interrogation that a final desperate attack by the last surviving Japanese on the island would occur that night.[72] The 105th command post sent out warnings to all units, including Holland Smith's headquarters, and requested reinforcement. No reserves were available. For troops on the line in the dark there was nothing to do but hunker down and stay alert. Gathering at Makunsha was a Japanese force composed of soldiers and sailors from all parts of northern Saipan, united by the belief that by attacking they would be making a sacrifice of the highest kind, *gyokusai,* ordered by the emperor himself. General Saito, too frail to lead it, committed suicide beforehand. His men carried every kind of weapon they could lay their hands on, even knives lashed to tree branches. How many gathered is uncertain, but estimates are between 3,000 and 4,000. Before the attack sake was distributed, and after a point the Americans could hear a growing din of voices and shouting.[73]

At approximately 4:45 a.m. the charge started down the corridor and soon hit the First and Second Battalions' perimeter. To soldiers in their foxholes, the oncoming screaming horde seemed like the tide from an exploding dam, a constant, overwhelming flow of bodies jammed together. The Japanese "just kept coming and coming and didn't stop," recalled a battalion commander.[74] Despite the frenzy, the enemy seemed to be following a plan: one group overran the forward battalions, and a second headed across the corridor for the American positions at the gulch, while the main force pressed on down the corridor through a Marine artillery battery and into Tanapag. Finally, south of Tanapag, the main force came to a stop, halted by defenders at the 105th regimental headquarters. Battle continued along the corridor all day, with Americans and Japanese intermingled, killing each other with pistols, knives, sabers, and rifles used as clubs. Army and Marine artillery were heavily engaged, with the Army battalions firing 2,666 rounds. How many of these landed exclusively on the enemy is unknown, but at least forty Americans were killed by friendly fire.[75] The troops positioned at the mouth of the gorge repelled their attackers but could not fire on the plain below without endangering their comrades and could not descend without abandoning critical positions. On the plain, war took the form of toe-to-toe slaughter. It was the largest suicide attack of the Pacific war.

The fighting petered out during the day. Tanks arrived to assist mopping up by the 106th Regiment. The next day bulldozers buried the enemy dead in trenches, indicating on makeshift signs the number of dead in each pit. The total was 4,311. Casualties in the advanced perimeter, among the First and Second Battalions of the 105th, were overwhelming: 406 killed and 512 wounded out of 1,107 men.[76] In the shock of the attack military order had collapsed; some soldiers had fled into the ocean, but most had stayed and fought as best they could. Three members of the 105th received Congressional Medals of Honor. At great cost, the Twenty-Seventh Division had eliminated a large concentration of Japanese troops, soldiers the Marines would otherwise have had to deal with. There would be other banzai attacks during the remainder of the Marianas campaign, but as terrifying as they were for the Americans, they were ultimately far more costly for the Japanese.

The American cost on Saipan was 14,111 casualties, or 20 percent of a combat force of 71,034.[77] Projected casualties of 20 percent henceforth became the standard in the planning of future operations. Of the total casualties, the Army's share was 3,674. The Twenty-Seventh Division, with four battalions virtually destroyed, went to the New Hebrides in the South Pacific for rebuilding. Saipan was declared secure on July 9, 1944, but mopping up continued into the fall.

Two weeks later, on July 24, the Second and Fourth Marine Divisions invaded Tinian, a diamond-shaped island twelve miles long, north to south, and five miles wide, lying to the southwest within artillery range of Saipan. Determined to avoid the heavy losses experienced on the beaches at Saipan, the commanders—Turner, Smith, Major General Harry A. Schmidt, Rear Admiral Harry W. Hill—chose to make a show of force at the obvious location, the beaches near Tinian Town (even sending troops down the cargo nets into boats), and then make the real landing on beaches in the northwest of the island. These beaches were comparatively tiny, with room for just two battalions at a time (compared with the eight at Saipan). To avoid potentially disastrous congestion, the commanders prohibited any unloading on the beaches; instead, supplies strapped in slings were loaded from LSTs directly onto amphibious vehicles that crossed the beaches and unloaded at inland dumps. Pontoons fitted together formed a causeway for trucks to roll from LSTs directly inland. The northern beaches provided easier access not only to supplies shipped from Saipan but also to its artillery. Thirteen battalions of guns and howitzers on the bigger island, 156 pieces altogether, supported the Marine divisions in their drive. Also supporting the drive were planes from Saipan, carrier aircraft, and naval gunfire. Napalm, a highly flammable gel that had recently been introduced into the theater, proved useful in burning off undergrowth and sugarcane fields to uncover and destroy defensive positions.[78] As the Japanese showed their determination to sacrifice their lives, the Americans brought forward more destructive equipment.

The capture of Tinian was a success, indeed, according to Admiral Spruance, "the most brilliantly conceived and executed amphibious operation in World War II."[79] The landing worked as planned. In three days the northern sector was taken. Thence the two divisions, the Second on the left, the Fourth on the right, fought their way south, reaching the southern tip of the island on August 1. The open and relatively flat terrain, ideal for airfields, was much easier for tanks than Saipan, and tank-infantry coordination and communication greatly improved. Counterattacks along the way and a last-stand attack of between 600 and 800—a small number compared to what had been assembled against the Americans on Saipan—were repulsed. The Marine defense was not penetrated, and casualties were not excessive. Soon airfield construction started for the very long-range bombers that would attack Japan's main islands. A year after Tinian was seized the *Enola Gay* would take off from one of the island's airfields on its mission to drop the first atomic bomb.

Guam, the third island taken in the Marianas campaign, initially promised to be another Saipan, given the amphibious pattern and the lineup of an Army division new to combat yoked with a Marine division and brigade under a Marine Corps commander. In fact, Guam's story was quite different from Saipan's. To begin with, it was the first American territory to be recovered from Japanese control. The islanders, Chamorros, who had been treated like serfs by the Japanese, were jubilant and grateful to the liberators. They provided intelligence and served as guides through the back country. Like Saipan, Guam is elongated, thin at the waist, but also twice as large as Saipan, measuring thirty-four miles from north to south and five to nine miles east to west. One hundred miles south of Saipan, its climate is equatorial—hot, humid, mostly jungle like New Guinea, with dense forests and thick underbrush, and subjected to incessant rain in the wet season (beginning in July).[80] On Guam's southwestern coast, the Orote Peninsula projects several miles into the ocean, at the end of which lay Orote airfield, centerpiece of air battles and bombardment a few weeks earlier. The northern shore of Orote and Cabras Island form Apra Harbor, too small for a fleet anchorage but promising as a forward base for repair, supply, and administration. The Marines were to land on the Asan beaches on the north side of Orote and on the Agat beaches on the south side. Behind the beaches stood a jumble of hills, ravines, and cliffs and behind that, still on the western side of the island, a range of mountains smaller than Mount Tapotchau. The plan called for the forces landed north and south of the peninsula to meet at the base of it, clear it, and secure the mountain chain nearby. This portion of Guam, about one-quarter of the island, was all the Americans needed, but the rest, mostly jungle, had to be cleared of organized resistance.

Invasion had originally been set for June 18, but in the face of the oncoming Japanese fleet and the heavy losses experienced in the landings on Saipan, Admiral Spruance had decided to postpone indefinitely the invasion of Guam. That way reserves could be held for Saipan and warships could concentrate on protecting its landing force. The new date was July 2. The postponement allowed time for an effective bombardment of Guam's defenses. Rear Admiral Richard L. Conolly, commander of the Southern Landing Group, was determined to show that naval gunfire, prolonged and precisely managed, would greatly reduce the terrible toll of casualties on the beaches. At his disposal were pre–Pearl Harbor battleships, heavy and light cruisers, destroyers, and, for air bombardment, escort carriers. Each day for thirteen days in July a group drawn from these vessels would strike at selected targets on Guam. Each day the damage was photographed and interpreted by specialists and repeat or new targets selected. In this longest bombardment of the Pacific war, warships fired 6,258 rounds of 14- and

16-inch ammunition, 6,292 rounds of 6- and 8-inch, and 16,214 rounds of 5-inch. The best estimate of the effect of this daily barrage, given by a Japanese staff officer who was present, was that all unprotected artillery emplacements and half of those, protected or not, in the vicinity of the landing beaches were demolished.[81]

First-day casualties on the landing beaches amounted to 697 on the northern beaches and about 350 on the southern, over a thousand altogether.[82] The landing forces were not significantly different in size from those on Saipan (six regiments on Saipan, five on Guam). On that basis, the first-day casualties on Saipan were more than three times those on Guam, supporting Conolly's claim that prolonged and methodical bombardment could save lives on the beaches. However, with the Pacific war gaining momentum, pressure being put on the infantry to speed up, and tenacious Japanese resistance, in short with a need to hasten the Pacific advance, a future extension of the bombardment time frame would be challenged.

Landing on the beaches north of Orote was the Third Marine Division, veterans of the battle for Bougainville in the northern Solomons. Landing south of Orote at the Agat beaches was the First Marine Provisional Brigade, formed from two independent Marine regiments, which would later evolve into the Sixth Marine Division. In reserve and then assigned to the southern assault was the Seventy-Seventh Division, new to combat, officered by Army regulars and filled out by Selective Service draftees. The Japanese garrison on Guam numbered about 18,500.[83] The Seventy-Seventh, a distinguished division in World War I—with Secretary of War Henry Stimson and his undersecretary, Robert P. Patterson, among its veterans—would be closely watched. Unlike the Twenty-Seventh, it was built and extensively trained for two years in the United States before overseas shipment. It underwent maneuvers in Louisiana, six months of desert training in southwestern Arizona, amphibious training in Chesapeake Bay, and, just before leaving for Guam, jungle warfare training in Hawaii. Frequent exercises at the division, regiment, and battalion levels and simply working and living together over many months created an unusual cohesiveness. A key factor was the leadership of the division commander, Major General Andrew D. Bruce. In World War I, Bruce had risen in rank from lieutenant to lieutenant colonel and won both the Distinguished Service Cross and French Legion of Honor. Placed in command in May 1943, Bruce energetically set out to prepare the Seventy-Seventh for the rigors of combat.[84] In doing so, he paid close attention to the needs of his troops while instilling an aggressive element in their attitude toward battle.

Despite the two-week bombardment of Guam the Japanese inflicted heavy losses on the Marines during and after the landings. Light artillery pieces, some in concrete blockhouses, and mortar fire put twenty-two troop-carrying amphibious tractors out of action. Broken, steep slopes and a hundred-foot cliff, cut by ravines and caves and bristling with machine guns, faced the Third Marine Division on the northern beaches. In two days of fighting on the beach, the Third Marine Regiment lost 615 men, reducing some companies to a mere thirty or forty men in total.[85] The southern beaches were less costly, but turning off the beach onto the Orote Peninsula, the First Marine Brigade faced an entrenched foe and counterattacks.

While the invasion force completed the transfer of armament, troops, and supplies from transport to beach and filled out the beachhead, the Japanese commander on Guam, Lieutenant General Takashima Takeshi, organized a set of counterattacks, primarily against the Third Marine Division in the northern beachhead, for the night of July 25. These were not rushes by frenzied masses such as the Twenty-Seventh Division had faced at Tanapag but directed movements by existing battalion and brigade formations. The attacks originated in the hill mass above the beachhead and drove downhill toward the sea. In the sector of the Third Marine Division, the Japanese launched seven counterattacks on the night of July 25–26. All seven times they were repulsed at the cost of 950 Japanese. But the Second Battalion, Ninth Marines, which bore the brunt of the attacks, suffered 50 percent casualties.[86] In the Twenty-First Regiment sector, the attack penetrated to a battalion command post, where cooks, clerks, and other headquarters personnel joined forces to stop it. Slipping through a gap between the Twenty-First and Ninth Regiments, a third Japanese attack force set up machine guns that raked American positions on both sides and pushed on as far as the division hospital, where the medical team and patients held them off until reinforcements came. A fourth but separate attack on the Orote Peninsula, a banzai charge like Tanapag but far smaller, ran into heavy artillery fire, some of it point blank, and foundered. In the July 25–27 period, the Third Marine Division had 845 casualties, mostly from this wild night on Guam. The Japanese lost 3,500 soldiers, about the same number as at Tanapag.

The Seventy-Seventh Division found coming ashore a battle in and of itself. The Second Battalion, 305th Regiment, was ordered to the line of departure on the afternoon of the invasion. They circled in their landing craft for over three hours, with many becoming seasick, waiting to be called to the beach. Reaching the fringing reef, the battalion found that the amphibious tractors that were to take them across the reef and lagoon were unavailable: some were out of action, and the rest were ferrying ammunition in and wounded out to hospital ships. Wading the coral reef, 400–700 yards wide, rough and sharp, along a winding coral ridge was the only choice. The water was waist high at low tide. Now, facing an incoming tide and waves from a storm at sea, some had to swim. Negotiating the reef laden with jungle gear and ammunition, avoiding potholes while keeping one's weapon high and dry, was a challenge, even more so in gathering darkness and at night.[87]

Eventually, the Seventy-Seventh Division took over the southern beachhead, while the Marine brigade attacked the Orote Peninsula. A critical difference from Saipan was the effective use of tanks, which, unlike those on Saipan, had trained with the infantry in Hawaii in coordination and communication.[88] A platoon of tanks from the Seventy-Seventh joined brigade tanks and tank destroyers in attacking some 250 pillboxes and entrenchments defending Orote airfield. These forces, together with massed artillery and naval gunfire, collapsed the Japanese defenses. Meanwhile all the transports were finally unloaded, hastened by working under lights at night. The Third Marine and Seventy-Seventh Divisions closed the gap between the northern and southern beachheads and extended the security zone to include the mountain line east of the beaches. By July 30, after ten days on the island, all the territory the Americans needed was held. Nevertheless, the Guam campaign was not over until organized resistance on the island was eliminated. After the failure of his counterattacks, General Takashima recognized that the enemy was on Guam to stay and that his only choice was to withdraw to the interior, there to preoccupy and weaken the Americans by fighting on to the death. He chose the northern part of the island and began setting up defense positions, leading to a last stand on Mount Santa Rosa in the northeast. To ensure that the Japanese had not gone south behind his advancing force, General Bruce initiated and gained authorization for reconnaissance teams from the Seventy-Seventh to fan out through that part of the island and report by radio. They confirmed that the Japanese had indeed not gone south. Major General Roy S. Geiger, commander of the III Amphibious Corps, therefore immediately ordered the Third Marine and Seventy-Seventh Divisions to form a line from coast to coast and head north on July 31, clearing out Japanese defenses as they went. The Marine brigade would stay and protect the beachhead. The Seventy-Seventh reached the east coast the first day and turned north, moving on the right of the Third Marine Division, and they both plunged into tropical jungle, stretching fourteen miles from the waist to the northern tip of Guam, getting denser along the way until progress quite literally meant cutting through. Digging a foxhole you scooped away only five inches of dirt before hitting unforgiving coral. The environment of heat, humidity, mud, and rain was brutal; flies multiplied on rotting flesh faster than frogs could eat them. Above them all loomed the haunting question whether the Japanese last stand on Guam would be like the one on Saipan, word of which seems to have traveled throughout the expeditionary forces.[89]

Two critical problems faced the northern advance. The first was inadequate supply routes for a two-division front. Northern Guam had a road network, but it was rarely two-lane and constantly deteriorating. Given the soft clay soil, ceaseless rain, and need for speed, road-building was impossible, so they necessarily relied on the existing road system, with engineers providing constant maintenance, regulation of traffic by military police, and twenty-four-hour usage with lights at night. All this proved sufficient but only barely. On one occasion, the Seventy-Seventh went without food and water for an entire day. The second problem, as at Driniumor on New

Guinea, was the difficulty of establishing exact location. Maps of Guam were hopeless—tracks went every which way, and the jungle encased them, above and on all sides. The result was a perpetual challenge of keeping in touch with the flank of the other division and of keeping a company and battalions moving ahead on course. Mistaken and misguided positioning and inadequate communication led to tragic firefights between Marines and soldiers and among soldiers, as well as "friendly fire" errors by artillery, mortars, and planes.

On August 2, after two days of advance with practically no opposition, the leading regiments of the Seventy-Seventh Division approached Barrigada. This village was an important road junction—the road from Agana on the west coast met a road heading due north to Finegayan—providing nearby access to a second road from the west coast and a reservoir that pumped 20,000 gallons of potable water a day. The division was advancing toward the northeast with the 307th Regiment on the left, next to the Third Marine Division, and the 305th Regiment parallel to it on the right, next to the ocean. The First Battalion of the 307th was supposed to pass just north of Barrigada while the Third Battalion swept through the village itself. The 305th Regiment would pass to the south of the village. It was at this juncture and the cleared land and woods around it that a battle developed. Along the edge of the woods east and north of the village were expertly camouflaged Japanese machine gun nests and snipers, as well as several light artillery pieces and tanks, covering roads, buildings, and open spaces.[90] At 9:30 a.m. Private John Andzelik, scout at the point of I Company, 305th Infantry, moving northeast out of the jungle and into the open, saw several Japanese soldiers crossing a trail. His company was ahead because it had already been under way when orders came down for the 305th to hold up. Andzelik reported his sighting and with others went to investigate. He was immediately killed by rifle fire, which wounded the other scout and the sergeant of the squad and brought I Company into a firefight. As the First Platoon advanced, a machine gun on the left opened fire, killing several members. I Company stopped, and other 305th Regiment companies, to the south beyond the battle, lined up with it. By moving ahead alone, I Company had become the southern end of the battle; instead of bypassing Barrigada, the 305th was stuck there. Five American light tanks attacked but were unable to find targets, and bullets ricocheting off the tanks wounded some and pinned down the rest of the accompanying infantry. Artillery fire was requested but denied for fear of hitting friendly troops. When four Sherman medium tanks finally arrived, they managed to destroy one Japanese tank and cover withdrawal of the wounded, but it became too dark to persist.

Meanwhile, in the north, C Company on the left of the 307th Regiment was feeling its way through the jungle, trying to stay in touch with the Marines on their left but losing touch with A Company on the right. Rifle fire held up A Company, and when it resumed the advance, it veered from its assigned northeast direction to almost due east, following the road from the west into Barrigada. This opened an ever-increasing gap between C Company and A Company. Furthermore, by veering into the path of Companies K and L, it pushed them to the right, squeezing them against I Company of the 305th, thereby forming a battlefront far too short for each company's firepower and exposing them all to flanking fire from the woods across the gap in the north.

With A Company and the Third Battalion exchanging fire with the enemy but unable to move forward, the First Battalion commander dispatched B Company into the gap. The Second Platoon circled north to the Finegayan-Barrigada Road and then south to seize an abandoned greenhouse with concrete walls on the first floor. As the platoon reached and crossed the road a machine gun opened fire from the woods behind the greenhouse, sending the men into the ditch and house. American artillery began firing at the greenhouse, despite frantic calls by the First Battalion executive officer to cease friendly fire. The platoon gained permission to withdraw, and those who were able left with the leader, Lieutenant Willis J. Munger, who was killed while retreating. Remaining were the wounded and those staying to cover and evacuate them, including Private First Class John E. Raley, a machine gunner, who had been hit but kept firing.

Meanwhile, another First Battalion machine gunner noted gunfire coming from a grass shack around the corner from the greenhouse and fired a burst into it. The shack caught fire and revealed a Japanese medium tank with soldiers on top of it. Thus began an extraordinary solo performance. The tank directed a burst of fire at the Americans in the greenhouse and another at A Company before heading west on the Agana road—with every weapon in American hands firing at it, to no effect except for removing the soldiers on top. Bazookas (small rocket launchers) misfired or failed to fire because the safety was on. Crashing into and out of a building, the Japanese tank nearly crushed machine gunner Raley, who was still firing. Finally it raced down the road through American lines firing wildly, past a battalion aid station and command post as well as a regimental command post, leaving wounded and wreckage in its wake. It disappeared into Marine territory, where it was eventually destroyed that afternoon.

To rescue the survivors at and near the greenhouse and to reduce the gap on the left, the regimental commander brought the Second Battalion from reserve. Company E headed out to hook up with lost Company C. Company G went to rescue those left at the greenhouse. Its First Platoon set out to cross from west to east along the northern edge of the field. The Second Platoon crossed the southern part, reached the greenhouse, and joined four light tanks that arrived by road. Heavy fire from the platoon and tanks into the woods on the east covered withdrawal of those left behind, but machine gunner Raley, the last of the wounded to leave, was killed.

The rescuers had no idea where the First Platoon was. The platoon in fact lay in the field it had been crossing, at the mercy of Japanese gunners in the woods to the north, on its left. The gunners held fire all day, waiting. When the tanks became preoccupied with the rescue, the Japanese opened fire on the platoon passing before them. Veterans of the Seventy-Seventh described the scene this way: "The enemy could see every move and had the platoon enfiladed perfectly. The only men who escaped being hit were those who found some sort of a hole in the field. But over half of the men lay there helpless. One by one they were picked off."[91] The Third Platoon was sent, but, still ignorant of where the First Platoon was located, fired to the east instead of north. Finally the battalion commander set off with three tanks, found what was left of the First Platoon, and directed the evacuation until he himself was wounded. The platoon of about forty took twenty-six casualties, most of them killed. Darkness ended the battle. The Americans dug in for the night; the Japanese used the night to withdraw to the north for another stand.

August 2 had been the Seventy-Seventh Division's first full-blown battle, and it had been a fearsome one. With the early morning tank reconnaissance, the division learned of enemy troops in the village and east of it but not their dispositions and nothing of the enemy lining the woods to the north of the open fields. The Japanese command could assume that the American forces would enter Barrigada because they needed the water supply and the road. It was worthwhile setting up carefully planned fields of fire. Skillful camouflage had hidden the weapons and troops, and smokeless powder did not betray their positions. Under tight discipline, they withheld fire until substantial numbers were in their sights. American tanks fired into the woods blind. Japanese marksmanship was excellent, increasing the number killed. On the American side, communication was inadequate. Attacks became rescues.

In a more fundamental way, the American problem was the contradiction between the campaign's need for speed and the need for greater preparation, as illustrated by what happened at Barrigada. The pressure to keep moving on was strong. General Bruce preferred to describe the march to the north of Guam as "pursuit by direct pressure" instead of merely "pursuit."[92] His troop alignment was in parallel columns from southwest to northeast. He would take Barrigada as he passed through on that axis. But the village and the enemy were on a different axis: the roads in and out were east–west and north–south. To shift axis for two regiments, while preserving adequate attack frontage for each, was a difficult maneuver, especially for a "bloody-ing" battle. Bruce chose not to change formation unless he had to. His plan the day after what had happened at Barrigada village was to undertake a bold advance. The 307th Regiment would advance up Mount Barrigada behind an artillery concentration. Meanwhile the Third Marine Division would move ahead past the mountain. He would fill the gap with his reserve.

Nevertheless, maintaining a common front remained a concern at corps and at both divisions. The Seventy-Seventh was often lagging behind the Third Marine Division and would get word to make every effort to pull up even. This lag and the gap resulting was bound to be a difficulty with a division being initiated in battle: Major General Allen H. Turnage, commander of the Third Marine Division, was impatient because his Marines were being held up; General Geiger concluded that some needling was called for, though he knew Bruce was an aggressive commander who was moving as fast as he could. Bruce understood, explained, and provided an alternative. The Geiger-Bruce relationship was one of mutual respect and cooperation, very different from the Marine-Army antagonism on Saipan.[93]

Together, the Seventy-Seventh and Third Marine Divisions pursued the Japanese forces northward for eight more days. They were to keep the enemy off balance and bring the prolonged Marianas campaign to an end. The offensive was now less a front than a set of columns tunneling through the jungle. For the Japanese, the jungle conferred an equalizing effect, limiting the firepower the enemy could bring to bear. A shrinking Japanese force could be spread across more approaches to the last stand. Tanks, surprisingly, fitted into the scheme on both sides. They opened and widened the way by battering down undergrowth and small trees and provided mobile, protected platforms for artillery and machine guns where ordinary artillery and air strikes were impossible.

The bloodiest of these encounters began with a night attack by two Japanese tanks, machine guns, and riflemen on Company A of the 305th Regiment. The tanks broke through the perimeter and, with their machine guns spraying everywhere, charged back and forth across the slit trenches, while the terrified owners flattened themselves inside them. The tanks then vanished. Company A lost forty-eight men. Later that day, Company E stumbled into an ambush by the same two tanks. They were firing down 200 yards of a single-file trail. American medium tanks came up, but the first was stopped by a shell, which brought the column to a halt. An intense firefight raged. Shells from the Japanese tanks exploded against the trees, scattering shrapnel among the Americans huddled in the woods. With the platoon leader, platoon sergeant, and battalion executive officer wounded and riflemen starting to withdraw, the lead tank also started to back out. However, the wounded leaders were partially successful in getting the men to hold in place. Meanwhile a well-aimed succession of mortar shells landed on the two tanks, ending the fusillade and the battle. Company E had lost forty-six men. It required four hours of heavy lifting to carry the Company E wounded to medical help, with eight men, changing off, to a litter.[94]

Toward the end of the northward pursuit, the Seventy-Seventh became more familiar and confident with tank fighting. The commander of the Third Battalion devised a tactical formation for tank-infantry coordination in the jungle. In an encounter August 7, three Japanese tanks and a platoon of riflemen attacked the perimeter of the Third Battalion, 306th. A bazooka carrier and two men with flamethrowers were wounded, but a light machine gun team targeted a port on the first tank and fired at close range, killing the crew. Bazooka rockets and rifle grenades eliminated the second tank, and the third fled. The same day, with American tanks held up by a Japanese antitank gun, a nearby platoon moved across and behind the gun, crept up, rushed it, and killed the crew.[95]

As the jungle wanderers emerged into more open country around Yigo and Mount Santa Rosa, American artillery, airpower, and naval bombardment prepared to destroy any massing for a last stand. By this point, however, Japanese forces were so weakened and scattered that gathering them was impossible. Lieutenant General Obata Hideyoshi, who replaced General Takashima when the latter was killed on July 27 by a Sherman tank machine gunner, was himself killed August 11. Mopping up began. An American soldier recalled throwing a grenade into a brush-covered hole. The Japanese soldier inside threw it out where it exploded harmlessly. "Me no wanna die!" "Come on out then!" shouted the American. The Japanese wanted to live, but to come out would be to surrender. He killed himself by exploding his own grenade.[96]

Guam was declared secure August 10, though some 3,000 Japanese troops had fled into the jungle, where some remained long after the war was over.[97] In the land battles of the Marianas campaign as well as the New Guinea campaign, the Americans fully appreciated how skilled and resourceful the Japanese army was on the defensive. They also understood that it was capable of unorthodox and unbridled warfare, such as sudden mass suicidal attacks and the killing spree that single tank went on at Barrigada. All that had been evident in the South Pacific, but here it played out in a wider context with larger consequences. Nearly the entire Japanese garrisons on the three islands—Saipan, Tinian, and Guam—had been killed, a number approximating 56,000 men. They killed or wounded 23,795 American soldiers, of which 19,272 were Marines.[98] Had it been worth it? Aside from giving the Americans air bases for bombing Japan, it had conferred dominance of the vast central basin of the Pacific, with direct access to the eastern face of the Philippine archipelago.

Japanese officials readily understood that the Pacific war had entered a new phase. Following the fall of Saipan, the cabinet led by General Tojo Hideki resigned. The new government, however, pledged to continue the war to the bitter end, and the army and navy began planning for the next major confrontation, which they expected to occur in the Philippines. At the same time, Imperial Headquarters reassessed its approach to island defense. The new doctrine it formulated reluctantly abandoned the idea of a waterline defense in favor of mobile defense inland organized around fortified strongpoints. The overall objective would be to draw the Americas into costly and time-consuming operations. Training still emphasized the superiority of the Japanese warrior spirit, but in keeping with the emphasis on attrition and delay, Japanese officers became less willing to squander the lives of their men in suicidal banzai attacks.[99] The Marianas campaign also provided the Americans with a grim foretaste of what could be expected when the fighting entered areas inhabited by large numbers of civilians. On Saipan, the Americans were horrified to see that Japanese soldiers expected their civilian compatriots to sacrifice themselves rather than surrender.[100] That disregard for civilian lives would be repeated in the coming campaigns and would be matched by the Americans once the strategic bombing of Japan began. By that time, the belief that all Japanese civilians should willingly give their lives for the emperor had become a fundamental principle of Japanese strategy.

Accelerating the Advance, August–October 1944

By August 1944, with the completion of the New Guinea and Marianas campaigns, the battlefront had moved from the southern reaches of the Pacific to the inner security zone of Japan itself. Its foe, having reached the western tip of New Guinea and seized the Marianas, was positioned to restrict Japan's access to the southern resource area and had moved within reach of Tokyo by long-range aircraft. The Americans would now seize or defend the approaches and staging grounds and gather their forces. So far the dual advance of Nimitz and MacArthur, with the fast carrier and land-based air forces weighing in first with one and then the other, had worked well. As American forces closed in on Japan, squeezing together, Army-Navy competition for command and resources intensified. At the same time, combat became more bloody and prolonged as the Japanese enlarged their garrisons and elaborated their fortification. Their fleet air force vanishing, the Imperial Navy turned to one-way air attack.

Meanwhile, half a world away, the invasion of Normandy had proven to be a success. Two months later, during August, came a breakout from the bridgehead in France and stunning pursuit of the Wehrmacht all the way to the German frontier, to be joined there by a largely American army that invaded southern France and pushed north. Simultaneously Soviet armies pushed into Poland and the Balkans. With the European war visibly approaching an end, it became evident how closely the Pacific and European fronts were tied together. Pacific operations ultimately depended on European reinforcement, which in turn depended on completion of European operations. And forces in the Pacific needed to be positioned for final operations when Europe was ready to reinforce. Furthermore, after the huge growth of 1940–1943, American war production would have to manage sharp swings in volume and shifts in content. And it would be a challenge for the Roosevelt administration in this period of approaching climax and sharply rising casualties to maintain unquestioning public support.

The American public followed the landing in Normandy and the campaign across France with intense interest. Now in the thirty-second month of the war, the home front had almost a million family members engaged there: by August 14, twenty-two American divisions were fighting in northwestern France. Battle casualties in the first two months of the invasion were 115,665.[1] Day after day, news of the armies' triumphal progress routinely commanded the front page of the *New York Times* and nearly the entirety of the nation's press.

For most of the summer of 1944 the fighting consisted of a succession of critical battles following the breakout from Normandy, including the German counterattack at Mortain to cut off the Allied advance from its base; the successful Allied riposte; and the entrapment and subsequent battering of German forces in the vicinity of Falaise. These engagements involved very heavy fighting by massed forces within seventy miles of the starting point, Saint-Lô in Normandy. The war correspondents' eyes were elsewhere, however, focused on the armor "spearpoints" "thundering," "dashing," "smashing," and "rampaging" down the roads of northwestern France. Armored spearheads were indeed setting out, but more typical and central at this stage was the sweat and gore of positional warfare. Correspondents saw "blitzkrieg," perhaps even a better "blitz" than in 1940. The breakout, one wrote, had the "seeds of a great victory" that would "unhinge the whole

German front." "Great things," another predicted, "are about to happen." Winston Churchill surmised "an early Allied victory" as Allied forces moved "inexorably upon Hitler's inner citadel." Others joined in. The current battle would "go far to determine the immediate fate of France and the duration of the whole war." With the American Army from the south of France joining the rest, an Allied victory "so overwhelming would occur that it is doubtful whether Hitler could survive it." Victory in Europe would arrive, it was said, before the first snowfall.[2] By mid-August, the prospect of the war in Europe ending was flourishing in the press and in American opinion.

From the beginning of the German retreat from the so-called Falaise Pocket to the attainment of the line of the Seine River on both sides of Paris (August 16–25), the Allied armies swept across northern France in a manner almost fitting the extravagant language in the press describing them. Armor-infantry spearheads spread out "with explosive force . . . with complete disdain for any German threat to their flanks . . . taking one important city after another, spanning rivers, overcoming all obstacles." Acquiring "new scope," the campaign now sought "the destruction of the German armies in the West." The Allied line swinging forward to the Seine was "threatening the Germans with a strategic defeat on a grand scale." Given good weather for Allied planes, the general retreat "should turn into a general rout." They were not merely pushing the Germans back but "chopping them up." Meanwhile all were "bathing in the delight of a freed Paris." General Sir Bernard Montgomery, British commander, saw the end of the war in sight, adding, "Let's finish off the business in record time." A *New York Times* editorial suggested that with more of the "dash and daring" of General George Patton inspiring American troops, victory in Europe "this year" would be assured.[3]

As the armor-infantry columns of the Allied armies, meeting little resistance, drew up to the Seine in the last week of August and established four bridgeheads across it, the question was "what next?" Ahead lay 100–150 miles of northeastern France. Beyond were Belgium and the German frontier, and beyond that the Rhine and Ruhr. How far the Allied armies went depended on rapidly diminishing supplies, especially gasoline. The invading armies were now 350 miles from their only deep-draught port, Cherbourg. Nevertheless, failure to sustain the drive east would allow the enemy to rally its forces and dig in. The supreme commander, General Dwight D. Eisenhower, decided to send his armies forward as far as supplies would take them toward the huge port of Antwerp, the Ruhr, and the Rhine.[4]

Correspondents witnessed an "amazing" race, "a tremendous drama of dissolution and renaissance," a "Week of Victories as the Nazis Crumble." Thanks to clear, sunny days, "swarms" of Allied planes attacked, leaving German communications in "chaos." Their divisions were "split, flanked, stripped," losing coherence and "fumbling badly." The Allied advance was "mounting" and "unrelenting." Observers variously estimated a retreat to the Rhine, a Battle of Germany, a coup de grace soon, or by October 1, or at latest by the onset of winter.[5] Undersecretary of War Robert Patterson, a critic of optimists, anticipated victory by the end of 1944. General Marshall, in a confidential press conference, had predicted early October.[6] "Victory perches on the Allied banners on every front," read an editorial in the *New York Times*. Troops were heard to say, "Won't be long now."[7]

But it *would* be long—eight months. From a hot pursuit the advance slowed abruptly in the second week of September, as one after another of the columns paused. The advance was outrunning its supplies, particularly gasoline. At a rate of consumption of 800,000 gallons a day, at a rapidly in-creasing distance, the armies' need for fuel was impossible to satisfy.[8] Gas rationing worked unevenly: some divisions got their tanks filled and dashed on; some came to a standstill others were half-filled; some infantry left their trucks and marched. Advance came in fits and starts.

The gas shortage was by no means the only impediment, however. Troops and equipment were worn out from weeks of extended pursuit. The armies slowed as they passed from the open plains of northern France into the hilly and forested region and the waterways bordering Germany. Furthermore, beyond insufficient supply and wear and tear, Allied armies were encountering a revival of serious German resistance here and there along the emerging front. In the retreat from the Falaise Pocket and the Seine, the German army had withdrawn cadre, staff, and senior officers so that a division refilled with reserves and stragglers quickly came to life. Field Marshall Gerd von Rundstedt returned to command in the West on September 4, rearming whatever forces he could gather and tying them together in a front that stretched from Holland to Switzerland. Nevertheless, in spite of their slowdown, Allied forces remained confident that they would soon over-come supply difficulties and drive through the German defenses to the Rhine.[9]

The war of pursuit in Europe shifted into a war of position, but the memory of that summer's tidal flow of armies across northern France, with victory in Europe almost in their grasp, became fixed in the mind of the American public and the leadership in Washington, with consequences at home and, as we'll show, in the Pacific. In a Gallup poll at the end of September, 67 percent were convinced that the European war would end by Christmas.[10] Thinking about postwar America was under way. Civilian managers of the economy in the Roosevelt administration were determined not to repeat the mistake made after World War I of an uncontrolled con-version to a peacetime economy, which had led to a sharp economic down-turn, unemployment, and severe labor unrest. Donald M. Nelson, chairman of the War Production Board, began devising a program to ease civilian production into the war economy gradually as peace approached. He reck-oned that once the economy had reached its peak in late 1943 and the serv-ices had received their initial equipage and armament, the war would make fewer demands on the economy, allowing factory space and materials for much-needed civilian goods, such as dairy, maintenance, baking, and har-vesting machinery, kitchen ware and appliances, metal office furniture, telephones, clocks, shoes, gloves, and steel wool[11] and employment for those workers discharged when military contracts were canceled. Of course, the military would have contingencies, would need weapon re-placements, and would want new designs, and their contracts required ab-solute priority; Nelson had in mind no radical conversion to a civilian economy. Rather, he sought to maintain full employment into the postwar period through a changing mix of military and civilian manufacturing that tipped toward the civilian side so far as military progress allowed, sopping up the unemployed.[12]

In early 1944, war production dipped and rose again, spurred by the losses and lessons of the European battle. On May 22, 1944, virtually with-out warning, the Navy terminated its contract for fighter planes with Brewster Aeronautical on Long Island. The workers tried a "stay-in" strike, but the plant closed, leaving 9,000 jobless, a sign to many of how swift and brutal the closing down of the war economy would be.[13] Nationally the early 1944 reduction involved 3,769 contract terminations and an estimate of 200,000 fewer jobs. On June 18, 1944, Nelson introduced his experimental program for production of civilian goods. It provided assignments of steel, aluminum, and magnesium for civilian production and permitted building of prototypes and necessary machine tools. Only districts with pools of unemployment could apply. He presented the program when he judged that the Normandy beachheads were secure and activated it in the cradle of the seemingly unstoppable sweep through France.[14]

At every turn in launching the program, however, Nelson found himself at war with the War Department, which enjoyed a dominant role in the War Production Board. Leading the attack were Undersecretary of War Patterson, Chief of Army Service Forces Brehon Somervell, and Major General Lucius D. Clay, assistant for materials to Somervell and member of the War Production Board. All three were hard-nosed, strong-willed bureaucratic fighters. Again and again they insisted that "reconversion," as it was called, was wholly inappropriate at this stage of the war: the entire existing war production capacity must be reserved for military programs without diversion to civilian needs.[15]

In July, the military services warned that current war production was lagging badly on 320 items, among them heavy trucks, medium tanks, artillery ammunition, and field wire. According to the Army, failure to meet quotas was due primarily to a manpower shortage, and the shortage was due to a drop in civilian morale, in particular to the loss of a disciplined and positive attitude toward the war by a cosseted American public.[16] Expectation of early victory in Europe, the Army contended, fostered a public psychology of complacency, slackening effort, and a drift of labor away from war work. Signs of this drift were slowdowns, walkouts, and strikes. Henry Kaiser, the titan of shipbuilding on the West Coast, claimed that 26,000 workers had quit during a sixty-day period. Investigation proved that claim to be false: those workers had been discharged over a six-month period on account of reduced production schedules; actually, only 900 had quit.[17] In Michigan, a major source of war production, 1944 was the year of a wartime peak and an all-time high in strikes, resulting in 8,721,000 man-days lost.[18] The home front, said Secretary of War Stimson, was "going sour."[19]

The result, according to the Army, was inadequate supply of the battle-front. The War Department campaign pictured the soldier at the front, on the Normandy or Saipan beachhead, unable to "pour it on" the enemy because of lack of ammunition. Lacking shells for big guns, the Army had to use smaller weapons requiring closer fighting and "greater loss of American lives." Ammunition shortages also changed battle plans, reducing the rate of fire and dragging out the war. Said Patterson, "If you ask some of the dough-boys who are battling it out on the front lines, whether the war isn't over, he'll [sic] tell you pretty quick...how bad the situation is for them."[20] As part of their effort to slow reconversion, War Department officials spoke to groups in cities that were eligible for Nelson's trial program. Somervell spoke in Boston on December 2 of "the war's end being delayed because thousands of men have left the shipyards, forges and foundries, and because thousands of others have sought employment away from other war industries where production is lagging...threatening to prolong the war, to multiply the number of young Americans who will lose their lives." And in New York he said, "Workers are worrying about their post-war future when all the post-war future of many of our men, for your sons, your brothers, may be under six feet of sod in Germany. This is unthinkable."[21] Admiral William D. Leahy, chairman of the JCS, warned of a "dangerous state of mind which cuts war production by causing people to throw up their jobs." It was "just as harmful as desertions on the fighting front."[22]

In this national campaign to establish a sense of urgency, the War Department, assisted by the Office of War Information, took sixty-second spots on sixty-five radio shows running on all four radio networks for speeches by generals and admirals.[23] Also brought on were road shows, movie dramatizations, and appearances by soldiers brought back from the front.[24] The reconversion battle raised concern in the mind of Robert W. Johnson, a retired official of the wartime government, about the power the armed services exerted over the nation's economy and now in forming its mindset. In January 1944, he warned Missouri senator Harry Truman, the head of the Senate Committee to Investigate the National Defense Program, known simply as the Truman Committee, that men "not qualified to judge this situation . . . are entering a zone of influence that is beyond their responsibility." He wrote Patterson that the War Department was "not qualified to direct the American economy." "Undue influence in that direction," he pointed out, "is neither appropriate nor in the course of wisdom."[25]

The War Department campaign proved immensely divisive, as well as misleading and even, to some, insulting. Leaks to the press by New Dealers on the War Production Board aroused small business, labor unions, and members of Congress. Some accused big business of dominating the war industry and seeking regulation of labor. The former Truman Committee, now the Mead Committee, chaired by Senator James M. Mead (D-NY), called in Somervell on December 4 to question his accusation that slackening on the home front had caused arms shortages on the battlefront. This time Somervell was assiduous in making it clear that the shortages arose not on account of production problems but because of problems within the war theater, mainly from difficulty in moving matériel from ships and depots to the front. "No one so far has suffered from a lack of supplies," he assured the committee. "Our problem is to keep us from suffering from a lack of supplies."[26]

Undoubtedly the prospect of peace led to some civilian slackening and a search for more stable employment than that afforded by war contracts. War work was, moreover, no bed of roses. In a constantly changing workplace in which many were learning their jobs, accidents were frequent. Hours were long, the work intense, and the commute often difficult, not to speak of temporary quarters and hasty meals.[27] Mental and physical exhaustion followed, with nervous tension, illness, and absenteeism.[28] Furthermore, manpower was not the principal cause of production shortages. A War Production Board survey found that 22 percent of critical production items were principally delayed by manpower shortage, 12 percent by shortage of factory space, 26 percent by model or design change, and 40 percent by a "sharp increase in demand or requirements."[29] Manpower shortage was characteristic of most programs, including production of artillery ammunition. The problem began with a serious underestimation and miscalculation of the amount that would be needed in the invasion and campaign in Europe and inadequate initial production in the United States.[30] Actual battle experience produced an urgent demand for much larger quantities of ammunition, requiring additional factories, machine tools, and skilled labor. However, production of the machine tools and, separately, their components, such as controls, gears, and motors, created a bottleneck. Once completed, the assembly line for the 155 mm shell, for example, featured forty different machines connected by two miles of conveyors. Packing powder charges for the larger guns required a specially trained workforce. Furthermore, the job was hazardous, with factories located in rural areas, some distance from adequate housing. Little wonder the factories were slow in starting up.[31]

The answers to these problems lay in scheduling and monitoring the manufacture and delivery of machine tools; synchronizing the inflow of new workers with the completion of plants; and using veteran arsenal crews to get the machine tools in operation. The objective was 1,500,000 shells a month. Achieving that goal was more a matter of imaginative expediency than attitude correction. By November, monthly production of heavy artillery ammunition was meeting and even slightly exceeding its quota. Only the manufacture of "heavy-heavy" artillery itself (155 mm and 240 mm) and replacements for worn-out artillery tubes and recoil mechanisms were falling seriously behind. These delays were due to the same difficulties encountered in artillery ammunition manufacture. Otherwise, quotas in critical items—combat loaders (ships with their own landing craft carrying troops and their supplies), B-29 Superfortresses, airborne radar, cotton duck (for tents), communications wire, "heavy-heavy" trucks and tires, tanks, and Navy rockets—were met and mostly exceeded. Manpower, according to the Truman Committee, was localized, unaware of conditions and opportunities elsewhere in a vast land and complex economy. Shortages were best addressed by channeling recruitment through the resources of the U.S. Employment Service and the War Manpower Commission, as well as by draft deferments, bounties, and factory ceilings on employment.[32] Meanwhile, the reconversion program shriveled in the autumn offensives and died with the German counteroffensive in the Ardennes in December 1944, only to be reborn in the spring. With the War Production Board locked in combat, the president eased Chairman Nelson out by sending him to China.

The manpower battle continued, however, in a larger framework: the drive by the administration, led by the Army, for legislation to control manpower on the platform of "work or fight." Henceforth, the Army would be more and more engaged in issues where its needs became entangled with those of the home front.

The explosive Allied advance across France, promising an early end to the war in Europe, had consequences not only for the home front but for the Pacific war as well. It reminded strategists that bringing about the defeat of Japan depended heavily on the timing of Germany's collapse, and it suddenly seemed very close. Given the determined Japanese defense in battles such as Saipan and Biak, it had become increasingly evident that only an invasion of the home islands would end the war. Conquest of that sort required additional forces, which would soon be available from Europe, extensive plans for seizure of bases within striking distance of Japan for air attack and finally, a massive concentration of troops and supplies on islands close enough to make invasion possible. No such islands or landmasses were in hand by the fall of 1944 aside from the Marianas, nor were they definitively planned. Realizing that the American public would not stand for a prolonged war, especially one dragging on past the European war, it was critical to maintain constant offensive pressure. Pacific strategists had to lay out a path or paths to Japan swiftly. They would also have to calculate how many troops being redeployed from Europe they needed, when they would arrive, and how to reequip and reorient them for battle against the Japanese. The strategists had to synchronize the two war fronts.

In early June 1944, the JCS moved to London to be nearby in case the landings in Normandy went awry. They returned to Washington in late June, assured that the landings had succeeded and heartened by the breakout from Normandy and pursuit across northern France. The limited schedule of operations in the Pacific seemed out of step with the accelerating pace of the war in Europe. Most senior officers, as we've noted, expected the war in Europe to be over before Christmas, while entry into the Philippines at Mindanao, their southernmost point, would only begin November 15. On

June 12, as we have mentioned, the JCS directed Nimitz and MacArthur to provide detailed plans for their next moves and attempted to speed them up by "advancing target dates," "by-passing presently selected objectives," and "choosing new ones including the [Japanese] home islands."[33] Later Marshall dispatched leading officers of the OPD, including Major General John E. Hull, Pacific Theater chief, to Brisbane to discuss the revamping of plans with MacArthur and his staff.

The strategic review quickly fell into a tug-of-war between King and MacArthur. King wanted to extend the westward thrust of his amphibious, battleship, and carrier forces from the Marianas across the Philippine Sea, gathering in the western Carolines and Palaus and challenging the remainder of the Japanese fleet. Then he would push farther westward into the South China Sea, without stopping at the Philippines, to seize Formosa (Taiwan) and Amoy, a major port on the coast of China. Holding Formosa, American forces could block Japan's route to the resources of Southeast Asia, especially much-needed oil and rubber; pave the way to a siege of Japan itself; and conduct long-range air attacks on the home island of Kyushu. Amoy would allow a shorter supply route for American bombers and fighters already in China. In May, the JCS Joint Strategic Survey Committee, urging a "prompt, searching and open-minded reexamination" of existing plans, suggested that with Mindanao and the Celebes now more thickly defended, it might be wise to bypass Mindanao and the Philippines and strike for Formosa.[34]

Needless to say, MacArthur "vehemently" disagreed. Reoccupation of the Philippines had of course been his central objective since he left Corregidor. The military advantages of the Philippines, he claimed, were obvious: "to cut the enemy's communications to the south and to secure a base for our further advance." Quite apart from the practical value of the islands, the United States had the "great national obligation" of liberating the Filipinos and American prisoners of war, survivors of Bataan. The Philippines were American territory, after all, where "our unsupported forces were destroyed," leaving Filipinos to suffer under Japanese army rule. Bypassing the Philippines, leaving American prisoners and loyal Filipinos to languish in captivity, would verify Japanese claims that America had abandoned them and would not risk American lives to rescue them. Such indifference would lead the Filipinos to open antagonism, ruin for years American prestige in the Far East, and raise "extremely adverse reactions" from the American public.[35]

While MacArthur was denouncing King's plan, he was designing his own. Southwest Pacific divisions would advance northward along the eastern face of the archipelago, the way they had hopped from one base to the next along the New Guinea coast, always covered by land-based planes and often by fast carrier forces. First securing airfields between New Guinea and the Philippines, MacArthur would begin his return at Sarangani Bay in southeastern Mindanao, moving on to Leyte in the central Philippines and then Bicol, the long, narrow southeastern peninsula of Luzon, followed by the island's northern tip, and, rounding the north, the beaches of Lingayen Gulf, which led southward through central Luzon to Manila. Additional landings would take place in the central and southern Philippines. The plan called for nine landings involving twenty-nine divisions. With a command of seventeen divisions, including two to be borrowed from Nimitz for Leyte, most of his divisions would be engaging in more than one operation. The campaign would last from September 1944 to April 1945. King commented that MacArthur appeared to assume that the Navy was "at his beck and call."[36]

The plan, known as Reno V, was extensive, calling for the seizure of Leyte and Luzon and minor operations in the central and southern Philippines. The latter operations could open the door to a much broader campaign than General Marshall had in mind. Clearing island after island, much of it jungle, of Japanese troops was a slow, debilitating task for infantry, requiring substantial numbers operating at a pedestrian pace. It would lead to the diffusion of forces rather than concentration for advance on Japan itself. Marshall, as we noted, advised MacArthur not to allow personal feelings to override the objective of concluding the war as quickly as possible. Bypassing the Philippines did not mean abandonment: "On the contrary," Marshall explained, "by the defeat of Japan at the earliest practicable moment the liberation of the Philippines will be effected in the most expeditious and complete manner possible."[37] In any case, Luzon remained a conditional operation. The strategy of the March 3, 1944, JCS directive, which finessed rather than resolved the Army-Navy dispute, still applied. Invasion of Formosa would come on February 15, 1945, "with the possibility of Luzon to be taken on the same date should such operations prove necessary prior to the move on Formosa."[38]

On July 27 JCS planners sent a more detailed scheme with Formosa as the prime objective to Nimitz's and MacArthur's staffs for comment. It assumed early March 1945 as the latest possible date for invasion of the island, using forces under Navy command augmented by air, ground, and service troops from the Southwest Pacific. A preliminary stage would be occupation of the Mindanao-Leyte area of the Philippines, acquiring bases that would result in the reduction of Japanese airpower on Luzon, thereby opening the way to Formosa. After Leyte, Southwest Pacific forces would continue operations within the Philippines without the cover of the fast carrier forces, extending holdings as far as possible with shore-to-shore operations by means of landing craft provided by the Nimitz command. In other words, MacArthur would have to trade a part of his army for landing craft and rely on his own airpower.[39]

MacArthur's reply in a radio message was scorching. The planners' assumptions, he asserted, not only violated the basic strategy of the country and its national obligations but also carried with them "a deeper and more sinister implication"—the imposition of a "complete blockade." Luzon depended substantially on the importation of food from the southern Philippines. To bypass it for the assault on Formosa, he would have to set up a blockade that would create widespread famine and kill millions of Filipinos. "Such a course of action," he concluded, "should *not* [emphasis by repetition in the radio message] be considered by any government even if it were proposed by the military. It is a line of action that would exceed in brutality anything that has been perpetrated by our enemies." MacArthur rejected suggestions by the Washington planners to hasten the program by canceling certain preliminary operations.[40]

In June, in the face of the shift of interest to Formosa, a defiant MacArthur had requested permission to go to Washington to defend his position. Marshall had raised no objection but did not follow through until late July, when he ordered MacArthur to Hawaii for an important conference. That proved to be a select meeting with President Roosevelt, together with Admiral Leahy, chairman of the Joint Chiefs, and Admiral Nimitz. According to MacArthur's recollection, FDR pointed to the Philippines on a huge map, and asked, "Well, Douglas, where do we go from here?" MacArthur then launched into a recitation of his previous arguments for not treating the Philippines as mere stepping stones to Japan, although one suspects he used a less minatory tone. The outcome of the debate was, as so often with a Roosevelt conclusion, ambiguous. Apparently Roosevelt was impressed and assured MacArthur that he preferred the Philippine route and that he would "push on that plan." However, according to one observer, he also did not rule out Formosa, nor would he intrude on a final decision as to which came first. MacArthur had at least the impression of presidential encouragement and responded with a more cooperative attitude toward Washington.[41]

The strategic ambiguity extended through the summer of 1944, though with growing criticism of the Formosa option. The island, 250 miles long from north to south, ceded to Japan by China in 1895, was known to have one of the most heavily organized defenses in the Japanese empire with, according to a JCS memo, "an elaborate series of mutually supporting underground type installations."[42] The Navy was learning that it faced a major assault, one that would require an estimated nine to twelve divisions. Colonel George A. Lincoln in OPD commented that "the Formosa operation begins to look almost as formidable as Kyushu."[43] Furthermore, the Navy command lacked sufficient supporting arms (tank, artillery, mortar battalions) and service troops (quartermaster, medical, engineer, port battalions) to back up its Army divisions. Indeed it estimated that it would need at least 77,000 more Army service troops. How many could the Southwest Pacific provide? The answer from MacArthur's planners was that existing forces in all categories were barely sufficient for their Philippine assignments. As it was, infantry divisions were billeted beside landing sites to provide labor in loading and unloading ships and landing craft. Too few service battalions were formed in the first place, and of these the European Theater had first choice. Furthermore, the shortage of service troops hampered the dispatch of additional supporting forces: more tank or artillery battalions would mean more troops would have to share the same number of, for example, food supply and medical care units.[44] As a result, the Navy reduced its objective from seizing the whole of Formosa to carving out an enclave in the south, which made the project seem, to some, even more dubious. Opponents of Formosa pointed out that with enemy forces still at large, the perimeter would have to be manned and would need reinforcement. Furthermore, from south Formosan bases B-29 bombers could barely reach Japan.

Meanwhile prospects for carrying the flag to the China coast faded. In May 1944 a major Japanese offensive began from south of Hankow in central China toward Canton, designed to eliminate American bomber and fighter bases assisting the Chinese and striking at Japanese industry in Manchuria. Except for strong resistance at Hengyang, Chinese forces melted away, and by August the airfields at Liuchow and Kweilin, due west of Amoy, were in peril. Troops arriving at Amoy in March 1945 could neither assist the American air bases nor receive assistance from them.

Because of all this, the weight of support shifted to Luzon over Formosa. The well-established corridor of Japanese air reinforcement from home bases to Formosa and then to Luzon posed a serious threat. With about seventy airfields and landing strips, Luzon could quickly recover from an American air attack. Enemy planes were hard to pin down; they would "fly in, top off and out of the Luzon fields."[45] The SWPA command argued that if it was impossible to seize Formosa from Leyte without neutralizing Luzon, it was also impossible to neutralize Luzon without occupying it.[46] Yet either way—attacking, in sequence, Leyte, Luzon, and Formosa, or Leyte, Formosa, and Luzon—would so preoccupy MacArthur and Nimitz's divisions in protracted, costly operations that they would be unavailable farther north, thus postponing attack on Japan proper and lengthening the war.[47] If they could only afford one operation, it therefore had to be Luzon.

As the arguments over strategy dragged on through the summer of 1944, a third potential vector of attack emerged, apart from the Philippines and Formosa. This was an advance northward toward Kyushu, the southernmost of the Japanese home islands, by way of Formosa and the Ryukyus (Okinawa) and Bonins (Iwo Jima). Encouraging the idea was Marshall, who was initially attracted to a Formosa campaign, as springboard not so much to China as to Kyushu. Marshall shared this thought with MacArthur: "After a crushing blow is delivered against the Japanese fleet, then we should go in close to Japan as quickly as possible in order to shorten the war."[48] And Marshall told MacArthur's operations officer that he "wanted to get the carriers quickly where they can effectively bomb Japan." He preferred that route over the Philippines, where, he felt, MacArthur was likely to get bogged down, though he accepted that "the shortage of troops for the Formosa campaign was a strong argument against it."[49] For Marshall the decision depended on whether the war in Europe ended by October, as he had predicted, so that reinforcements, especially service troops, could be redeployed by March 1945. Therefore, he advised a go slow approach until the outcome of the European campaign was known and he had a firmer idea of what resources could be transferred from that theater to the Pacific.[50]

Meanwhile MacArthur, with some prompting, speeded up his agenda. In their highly destructive sweeps across the Philippines in September, pilots from Admiral Halsey's fast carrier forces were amazed at the lack of Japanese response. With the central Philippines "wide open" to attack, as he put it, Halsey recommended a radical abbreviation of the Philippines attack schedule, canceling Mindanao and its supportive landings and moving directly to Leyte.[51] Given Japanese camouflage discipline, pilot reports needed to be taken with a grain of salt, as had been shown when First Cavalry troops landed in the Admiralties. Nevertheless, the Halsey message sparked impatient commanders into coming to some kind of decision.[52] Pacific Fleet leaders, including Admirals Nimitz, Halsey, Spruance, Towers, and Turner, had been turning away from King's Formosa-first postulate in favor of the idea of advancing northward, for which bases and harbors on Luzon would be more useful than any to be found on Formosa.[53] Nimitz agreed with Halsey about canceling Mindanao and hitting Leyte on October 20 and recommended that the imminent landing on Yap Island in the Western Carolines be canceled and the troops for that landing, already at sea, be switched to Leyte. Since MacArthur was aboard a cruiser keeping radio silence, his chief of staff, Sutherland, sure that the general would agree to the plan, responded affirmatively for him. He warned, however, that Leyte was not without enemy troops. The Joint Chiefs, meeting with the British at Quebec, agreed to the proposition almost instantly and sent the necessary directives.

By mid-September, any hope of the war in Europe ending in time to re-deploy troops, especially service troops, to the Formosa operation was fading fast. The agonizing failure by September 25 of an Allied airborne assault into the Netherlands to outflank the West Wall by gaining a bridgehead across the lower Rhine confirmed that the war would continue into the winter. However, there would be enough troops then present to secure Leyte and Luzon, acquiring landmass and harbors, friendly people, willing, organized labor, cooperative guerrillas, and familiar terrain for staging assaults on Japan itself. MacArthur promised that it would take no more than six weeks to take Luzon, adding that his personal conviction was that "he would not need more than thirty days."[54] Vice Admiral Robert B. Carney likened Luzon as a staging base for invading Japan to what England had been for the continent.[55]

The last stumbling block to the Philippines was the Navy's concern that MacArthur would keep the fast carrier forces on a short leash for inordi-nately long times in protecting his landings. That concern was somewhat mitigated by MacArthur's assurance that the fast carrier coverage he required for the Lingayen landing would be limited to a forty-day period before and after. Providing coverage, he now determined, didn't mean staying close to the landing but ranging far and wide, to find and attack enemy ships and aircraft that might "influence the success of our operation," while "standing ready to destroy hostile naval forces wherever found." He was allowed at least a lengthening of the leash.[56] By October 3, JCS was in agreement over issuing a directive that the Luzon landing take place on December 20. Then in late January Nimitz's forces would attack Iwo Jima in the Bonins, fol-lowed by Okinawa in the Ryukyus. No directive regarding Formosa would be issued for the time being, and none was ever issued.[57]

If any one figure dominated the question of where to go after New Guinea and the Marianas in the spring and summer of 1944, it was General Marshall. In the drawn-out interservice debate between Army and Navy, he held off taking sides until a consensus emerged, first counterbalancing

MacArthur and then King. He had continuously pressed for more studies and information and for testing propositions in the forum provided by OPD; continuously insisted on fewer landings, more bypasses, new objectives; continuously weighed the effect of outcomes elsewhere, as in Europe and China. He had consistently sought momentum and speed, the quickest end of the war possible. Marshall had limited MacArthur by directive to Leyte and Luzon and warned him against a wholesale reoccupation of the islands.[58] In September Marshall had written to Lieutenant General Stanley Embick, the Army's representative on the Joint Strategic Survey Committee, wondering if it would be better to strike directly at the Japanese homeland rather than via Formosa or Luzon. Marshall noted that southern Kyushu was currently defended by the equivalent of only one division. A "surprise attack" beginning with massed air strikes from carrier planes lasting ten days or so, followed by landings on the southernmost of Japan's main islands, would, he speculated, catch the enemy off guard and bring the Americans to one step away from their ultimate goal.[59] Embick demurred, arguing in reply that the United States should stick to its plan of seizing "intermediate objectives," including southern Formosa and Okinawa, the latter of which "should be taken at relatively small cost," and wait for Russian entry into the war to tie down Japanese troops in Manchuria.[60] Marshall asked Embick whether in counseling delay his committee had taken into account "the economic and political acceptability of deliberately extending the length of the war with Japan." Marshall also wondered if Embick's committee had considered the lives that would be lost in seizing the air bases needed for the proposed siege of Japan, to say nothing of the costs that would arise in attacking Japan's home islands after the enemy had time to reinforce them.[61]

Marshall's search for a faster route to victory in the Pacific was derailed by the slowing advance across northern France. Though victory was still in sight, the Allies would have to regroup and move toward Germany along a broad front, maximizing their material advantages and wearing down the enemy. The United States would follow a similar approach in the Pacific. There would be no more talk of "surprise attack" and dramatic stabs at the heart of the Japanese homeland. Instead, the two forces, MacArthur's and Nimitz's, would join at Leyte and then split, with MacArthur establishing bases in the Philippines and Nimitz seizing bases close to Japan for eventual invasion of the home islands. Then the two forces would join again for the invasion of Kyushu. They could not go westward, due to both the enemy's strength on Formosa and Germany's successful defense of its western frontier. American forces in the Pacific would descend on the Philippines, make a sharp right turn, and head for Japan. The action would flow north.

After victory in the Battle of the Philippine Sea and capture of the Marianas, the United States Navy became the dominant force in the huge swath of ocean between the Marianas and the Philippines. In September, only a month past the end of organized resistance in the Marianas, the Navy seized a new fleet anchorage, Ulithi, an atoll in the middle of the Philippine Sea large enough and deep enough to hold over 600 ships. Fleet service vessels—oilers, store ships, water tankers, ammunition ships, vessels for spare parts and temporary repairs—now moved forward to Ulithi from Eniwetok, thereby positioning themselves 1,400 miles closer to the enemy. When the fleet kept at sea, refueling took place at rendezvous points on the water just out of range of the enemy. Tankers also transferred mail, and escort carriers transferred replacement planes and pilots. Seagoing tugs were added to tow disabled ships to floating dry docks at Seeadler Harbor in the Admiralties or Guam. With an extended and extending supply system, the fleet had extraordinary reach.

And it started to extend that reach. Beginning in September the carrier fleet sailed westward, preparing to attack Japan's protective curtain of islands—the Philippines, Formosa, and the Ryukyus—dotted with airfields and landing strips for use by planes from the home islands and China. Meanwhile, American submarines thickened among the restricted passages and sea route junctures of the East and South China Seas.[62] As Japan's sphere of control narrowed, the American submarine commands at Fremantle, Australia, and at Pearl Harbor, now with forward bases nearer the hunting grounds on Manus and Saipan, were able to deploy more of their boats to the China seas. About fifty submarines were always at sea, of which twenty-eight were on station and the rest en route. Most of these operated in groups of three or occasionally four, patrolling assigned sectors, such as Formosa Strait, the Palawan Passage, off Hainan Island, near Camranh Bay, and other promising locations. The eight groups dispatched to Luzon Strait (between Luzon and Formosa) during the summer of 1944 altogether sank fifty-six ships, totaling 250,000 tons. Pacific submarines were credited with sinking 603 ships totaling 2,700,000 tons in 1944.[63] Japan had instituted convoys but with too few escorts and inadequate technical equipment and know-how, in effect doing the enemy a favor by collecting its targets. The American submarines now had experience, usually effective torpedoes, and, of course, the priceless advantage of using convoy data from the decoded Water Transport Code and other ULTRA intercepts.[64] In September 1944, Japanese tanker tonnage transporting oil from Southeast Asia to the home islands amounted to 700,000; by the end of the year it was 200,000. Imports of bulk commodities fell from 16,400,000 tons to 10,000,000 tons.[65] Japanese merchant tonnage declined from about 6,000,000 tons at the beginning of the war to 2,450,000 tons in December 1944.[66]

The carrier fleet's set of September strikes in the Philippines, preparing the way for invasion, was a forerunner of its multiisland air campaign. These were the strikes—September 12–14, 21, 22, and 24—that convinced Admiral Halsey that the way was open for landings on Leyte, an island in the Visayas group, roughly in the center of the Philippine islands. Carrier planes destroyed around a thousand Japanese planes in the September strikes and sank about 200,000 tons of merchant and military support shipping around Luzon. A tally of fifty-three oceangoing military support ships and merchantmen seems reasonable, given the later experience of the Manila Harbor base commander, Lieutenant General Arthur G. Trudeau. The harbor alone, he said, "was filled with over one hundred, mostly Japanese, cargo ships that had been sunk by bombers. Wherever you looked, here was another hulk half out of water."[67] Together, submarine and carrier destruction of Japanese shipping was leading to constriction of the Japanese empire.

Admiral Halsey's raids into the East China Sea began with a strike against Okinawa and other islands in the Ryukyus on October 10, the closest the carrier fleet had come to Japan so far.[68] Then, after a swipe at northern Luzon to protect his flank, he moved on to Formosa and carried out three days of attack. From seventeen carriers, he sent 1,378 planes on the first day, 974 on the second, and 246 the third. On the third strike, 100 B-29 bombers from China joined the carrier planes over Formosa. The Japanese retaliated with three raids on the carriers, totaling 761 planes, of which 321 were shot down by means of the same defense tactics and techniques used so successfully in the Battle of the Philippine Sea.[69] Taking into account losses on and above Formosa, the raids cost the Japanese army, air force, and navy somewhere between 550 and 600 planes; the cost to the American carrier fleet was eighty-nine aircraft and two cruisers, which were disabled and withdrawn.[70] Along the Ryukyu-Formosa-Philippines chain the Japanese navy had gathered in 1,485 planes from China, the home islands, and even carrier pilots in training. One Japanese strike in such numbers would have been a challenge to the American carrier fleet, but strung out as the Japanese planes were, it couldn't be. Thus each Japanese attack was inferior in numbers, and Halsey's fleet ranged across the island chain, beating down the enemy piecemeal.[71]

The American encroachment in the summer and early fall of 1944 had presented the Japanese army and navy with a cavalcade of disaster: the loss of New Guinea and the Marianas, and with that the devastation of their land-based air armada in the islands by the American carrier fleet. All signs pointed to an invasion of the Philippines. The leadership of the navy at the Japanese Combined Fleet and Imperial General Staff realized that American sea and airpower operating out of the Philippines would cut off their access to the oil of Borneo and Sumatra, leaving the fleet immobile. This would be intolerable; it would mean the end of the navy, effectively the beginning of a siege of the home islands, and ultimately the loss of the war. To prevent it, the admirals determined on a full-fleet attack to destroy the American invasion forces. The odds were heavily against them: Halsey's raids had virtually wiped out their land-based air force in the Ryukyu-Formosa-Philippines chain just as effectively as the Battle of the Philippine Sea had devastated their pool of carrier pilots. Even so, they were determined, relying on ingenuity and good fortune, with every sinew engaged, at least to delay a farther advance. If they failed, at least the honor of the navy would remain intact.[72]

What the Japanese fleet might do, of course, depended on what strength it had left. Four aircraft carriers, survivors of the Battle of the Philippine Sea, were available for action. (Three others were unfit for service.) Four new fleet carriers, bigger than the American fleet type, were completed but not yet battle-ready. Of the four available carriers, one was fleet size and three were light. Given the loss of trained pilots in the Mariana battles and of pilots taken from carrier training during the Halsey strikes of October, it was possible to provide pilots for only a total of 116 planes on the four carriers, leaving them at three-quarter capacity. The average American fleet carrier had ninety-two planes. Japanese planes were now loaded aboard carriers because the pilots were not adequately trained to fly them aboard.[73] It was, in effect, a ghost carrier fleet.

The strength of the Imperial Fleet lay in gunnery ships, that is, battleships and heavy cruisers. Of these the fleet had twenty-three: nine battleships and fourteen heavy cruisers.

This was an imposing lot, especially since among the battleships were the 18.1-inch guns of the *Musashi* and *Yamato*. As for the cruisers, in the night action off Savo Island during the Guadalcanal battles, a Japanese cruiser-destroyer force had sunk one Australian and three American heavy cruisers. Now, however, the Imperial Navy was severely deficient in light cruisers and destroyers for protection of the big-gunned ships and carriers. Available for the whole fleet were nine light cruisers, which acted as destroyer leaders, and thirty-five destroyers. These were fewer than the destroyers assigned to just two of the four task groups of the American carrier fleet.[74] The imbalance posed a baffling problem for the Japanese in devising fleet tactics and strategy for the decisive battle.

Deepening the problem was the fact that the fleet required both the Southeast Asian oil and refineries for fuel and the home ports for ammunition, repair, and training and was currently split between the two. Most battleships and cruisers were at Lingga Roads, south of Singapore and near the oil fields of Sumatra and of Brunei on Borneo. The carriers were at home ports. It was hard to imagine how these separated forces would coordinate for battle, especially with a shortage of tankers. Vice Admiral Ozawa, who led the fleet to the Marianas, recognized the hopelessness of sending his carriers in attack and advised instead using them to lure the American carrier forces away from the invasion beaches, in effect sacrificing them so that the Japanese battleships and cruisers could move in and demolish the landing forces. It seemed the only way to inflict loss on the American fleet. The plan offered a rational context for a suicidal mission.[75] Desperation in the face of a widening gap in strength between the two fleets was leading the Japanese navy toward organized suicide.

On the American side, the speedup in operations set the invasion of Leyte for October 20. Preliminary operations were necessary to seize islands along the way for air bases and prevention of enemy use. Several of these operations had been canceled in the speedup, but MacArthur and Nimitz insisted on carrying out the occupation of Morotai, located a third of the distance between the western tip of New Guinea and Mindanao, and the landings on Peleliu and Angaur, the southernmost islands of the Palau group, 600 miles east of Mindanao. The Morotai landing was virtually unopposed, but completion of runways and the air base was slowed by weeks of heavy rains, enemy air attacks, and soil and drainage problems. Morotai became a bomber and fighter base, useful against Mindanao and the Celebes, but it was too far from Leyte to protect the landings.[76]

The tiny Palaus were a different story. Their seizure would help guard the Leyte operation and provide a good airfield for staging planes and a protected anchorage in nearby Kossol Passage. From papers captured on Saipan, Admiral Nimitz knew that Peleliu, the second-southernmost island in the Palaus chain, was defended by as many as 6,300 troops, consisting of the Japanese Second Regiment of the elite Fourteenth Division, brought in from the Kwantung Army in Manchuria. It also had a mixed brigade and a navy combat force, besides 4,000 labor and air base personnel. Beyond that intelligence, Admiral Nimitz had little information and inadequate maps. Japanese camouflage and a thick mat of jungle and scrub growth hid and smoothed out the defensive features of the terrain. Nimitz did not know that Peleliu had received construction materials ahead of Saipan so that its defenses, unlike those on Saipan, were complete. Compared with the thirteen-day preliminary bombardment of Guam, assisted by continual expert assessment of damage, the nominal three-day bombardment of Peleliu, expending less ammunition than planned, suggests a lack of concern about the island's defenses.[77] The Marines would have to find out for themselves what lay under that mat of scrub jungle.

In May 1944, the First Marine Division, designated for the assault on Peleliu, came to the island of Pavuvu, a "rat-infested mudhole" in the Russell Islands near Guadalcanal, for rest and rehabilitation as well as preparation for Peleliu. Rest began with building their own encampment. This division, the first to land on Guadalcanal in August 1942, was ultimately a participant in the last battle of the war, Okinawa, in April through June 1945. It had just completed its second mission, the invasion of Cape Gloucester on New Britain, guarding MacArthur's flank for the seizure of Hollandia. The Marines had spent five sodden months through the monsoon season on the Cape. Having suffered nearly 1,500 casualties there, the division was filled with replacements in need of further training. Small and cramped by jungle, Pavuvu offered little space for rifle ranges and tactical exercises. The whole division needed training in the latest weapons and equipment, such as the flamethrower and amphibian tractor. The absence of combat was surely a luxury, but there were few others. The division was served fresh meat once a week; otherwise the Marines ate canned and dried food, saw grade-B movies, and were lucky to get three cans of 3.2 percent beer a week. Their only joyous moment was when the Bob Hope Show visited, on Hope's initiative. Eugene B. Sledge, in his famous memoir of Peleliu and Okinawa, recalls Hope asking fellow comedian and sidekick Jerry Colonna how he liked the flight to Pavuvu: "Jerry answered that it was 'tough sledding.' When asked why, he replied, 'No snow.' We thought that it was the funniest thing we had ever heard."[78]

Preparing for Peleliu was a constant challenge. The First Marine Division was something of an orphan, having moved out of the South Pacific and into the Central Pacific sphere. The III Amphibious Corps, ordered to command the Palaus operation, was still off conducting the Guam invasion. The Eighty-First Division, designated companion for the Palaus operation, as well as its planning and logistics staffs, was still in Hawaii. South Pacific depots lacked much-needed equipment for the operation. A third of the allotment of Sherman medium tanks had to be left behind for lack of transport space. Ships loaded at five different bases in the Solomons and New Hebrides. With some of them arriving at the last minute, combat loading, with immediate needs piled on top, was often impossible. Still, Major General

William H. Rupertus, division commander, assured his troops that this operation would be "a short one, a quickie. Rough but fast. We'll be through in three days. It might take only two."[79]

Peleliu was a coral-limestone island like Biak, originating in a volcanic upthrust from the ocean floor. It was much smaller than Biak and Saipan, roughly six miles long and two miles wide, with peninsulas like crab claws reaching northeastward and an air base on the flat land at their joint. Between the extended claws were a sea inlet and mangrove swamps. The claw on the southeast was low, scrub-covered wasteland, but the wider claw to the north, according to a regimental report, consisted largely of a succession of parallel ridgelines rising from a "contorted mass of decayed coral, strewn with rubble, crags, ridges, and gulches thrown together in a confusing maze."[80] This part of the island, called the Umurbrogol Pocket, like the Ibdi Pocket on Biak, was the citadel of the defenders, led by Colonel Nakagawa Kunio. The ridges were honeycombed with caves in a system that was part of a major defense installation. It had been designed by mining and engineer specialists, who had enlarged natural caves, blasted out new ones, and tunneled between caves, often on opposite sides of a ridge. Over 500 were later found. Some of the caves had steel doors; all were carefully camouflaged.[81] Almost any position in the pocket was open to multilevel, multidirectional gunfire from caves and pillboxes. Artillery and observation posts in the ridgelines covered the landing beaches and the fringing reef. The island and particularly this fastness were expertly and intensively defended.

The landings, which took place on September 15, 1944, with all three regiments abreast on five beaches along the western coast of Peleliu, were a smaller version of the Saipan assault, starting with the same succession of sea and air bombardments and with waves of amphibious craft leading the way. Heavy mortar and artillery fire from the ridgelines above struck the Marines transferring from landing craft to tractor amphibians for climbing the reef. Soon a line of vehicles could be seen burning on the reef. All told, twenty-six of the tractors were lost, slowing movement to the shore, which was raked with enfilading fire from points to the north and south.

The First Regiment, landing on the left under fire, faced a long, precipitous coral outcropping thirty feet high, shorn of cover and studded with caves and other gun positions: a foretaste of combat to come. Assaults failed, leaving the Marines pinned down. Three hundred yards north, jutting into the water from the beach on the extreme left flank, was another thirty-foot outcropping of sharp jagged coral split by deep fissures. Reinforced concrete pillboxes for heavy machine guns were on top. A casemate at the base contained a 47 mm antitank gun used to enfilade the beach to the south. It was protected by spider holes blasted into the coral for riflemen.[82] Marines fought their way to the back of the fortified rock, surmounted it, and crept down to the casemate. A smoke grenade covering the approach and a rifle grenade in the gun port ignited ammunition within and exploded the casemate. Occupants running out to escape were shot down by waiting Marines. However, concentration on the two outcroppings left a gap between them, which the Japanese promptly filled, isolating the company at the fort for thirty hours. The way was now open for Colonel Nakagawa to counterattack down the beach to the south. For some reason he failed to seize the opportunity.[83]

The Fifth Regiment, on the middle beaches, less subject to enfilade fire, had better luck. They not only reached the airport, their objective that day, but also pushed on to the eastern shore, cutting off the Japanese force in the southwest from the rest of the island. Companies in the Third Battalion, keeping to the scrub jungle south of the airfield to avoid the artillery fire, lost touch with each other in the thick vegetation and by dark were forming independent circular defenses—again, with gaps. However, the battalion commander and his runner searched for the lost companies during the night, found them one by one, and tied them together. On the right, enfilade fire from the promontory and island to the south caused heavy casualties in the Seventh Regiment. As at Saipan, the amphibians veered to the left under fire from the right and crowded the next beach north. Once the intermixed units were sorted out, one battalion of the Seventh joined the Fifth on the east shore, while another headed south to eliminate the flanking fire.[84]

The principal Japanese counterattack came in the late afternoon, an infantry-tank thrust across the airfield aimed at the juncture of the First and Fifth Regiments. Thirteen thinly armored, light tanks with infantry on top and alongside, broke onto the runways. Once in the open the tanks zoomed on ahead, leaving the infantry and any possibility of coordinated attack behind. Anticipating an attack, the Fifth Regiment commander had landed his antitank guns and heavy machine guns early, and these, along with the .30 caliber machine guns and mortars of the First Battalion, Sherman tanks on the left flank, a battery of 75 mm howitzers, and a single Navy dive-bomber thwarted the attack. Several tanks charged through the American lines, but the Marines held in place. Division casualties by the end of D-Day were high: 210 killed and 901 wounded, not including those suffering from combat fatigue and heat prostration.[85] Furthermore, the First Regiment was still pinned down on or near the beach. But the Fifth Regiment had a foothold on the air base, firm enough to set up artillery, and had reached the opposite shore. The main enemy counterattack had been withstood, and while unloading across the beaches was slow and costly, it was happening. The division had arrived and would stay.

The next task was to secure the south and east of the island, the right claw of the crab, so that all regiments could concentrate on the ridges in the north, known as the Umurbrogol. For this the division command sent forth two battalions each from the Fifth and Seventh Regiments.[86] The terrain was mainly low and uneven, covered with tangled scrub jungle into which the Japanese had built a large assortment of fortifications and guns oriented toward the ocean. The Marines came upon one of the blockhouses with walls of reinforced concrete more than five feet thick. Engineers assigned to its destruction used smoke for concealment and then explosives. Humidity was high, and the temperature reached 115 degrees in the shade. Drinking water arrived, but some of the barrels in which it came were poorly scoured, leaving a taste of oil and residue of rust. A dispatch from the Third Battalion, Seventh Regiment, reported, "Out of water. Troops having dry heaves."[87] The battalion rested until water arrived. Later, drilling located adequate subterranean sources.

Where Japanese resistance hardened, the battalion massed firepower: planes, naval gunfire, artillery, landing craft with rockets, and mortar and machine gun fire. Tanks, which by now had trained with the infantry regularly, accompanied them and provided essential protection and firepower.

In one instance, communication failed and friendly fire came down on a particular infantry assault, first from planes, then from artillery, then mortars, causing thirty-four casualties.[88] The clearing of the southern part of the island was completed on September 18 and the eastern part on September 23, allowing the battalions to turn north and address the First Division's principal objective, the ridges.

The Umurbrogol pocket, a rectangle roughly half a mile long and a quarter mile wide, was the dominant feature of the northern claw. With its vegetation scoured off by shelling, it was a stark reminder of the region's convulsive past: rock and rubble, wandering canyons, and gloomy-looking palisades. The Umubrogol area featured numerous distinctive formations and hills that the Marines named to facilitate identification in orders and after-action reports. On the day following the landing, the First Regiment on the northern beaches closed the gap in its line and headed inland toward Umurbrogol, supported by naval as well as artillery fire, tanks, mortars, and the division's only ready reserve, a battalion of the Seventh Marines. The First Marines had already lost over a thousand men in the landing. Under heavy fire from the ridges, three battalions moved into the tumbled landscape, while one battalion kept in step along the shore. The battalion on the right tackled the ridgeline it faced, one of two parallel ridges running deep into the pocket. The slope was steep; the Marines were "clawing up and over razorback crests, shinnying coral pinnacles, plunging down into sheer-sided gullies."[89] At the top they found themselves completely vulnerable, subject to incoming mortar, machine gun, and rifle fire, especially from the slightly higher parallel ridge. The coral made it worse, fragmenting and multiplying when explosives struck it, and was impossible to dig into for protection. Jagged chunks of it made for uneven footing and tore clothing and skin. Regimental casualties rose sharply. The total number of troops in the line companies of Third Battalion, for example, added up to little more than the number in one full company.

Even so, the regiment pushed ahead. By the third day of the advance, the fourth after the landing on Peleliu, there was a feeling in the First Regiment, commanded by Colonel Lewis B. Puller, that enemy collapse was imminent, so pressure must be sustained and every conceivable reinforcement sent forward, even the War Dog Platoon, the specially trained dogs that carried messages and sniffed out the enemy hiding in caves. That expectation of completion was a mirage, but the regiment did reach the center portion of Umurbrogol. Here were gaps in the sweep of ridges running from the southwest to northeast, leaving a twisting but relatively level and continuous passageway southeast across most of the pocket. This transverse valley opened into a series of walled arenas between the ridges, studded with caves housing guns, making troops entering or crossing them feel like fish in a barrel. On the third day, September 18, a series of fierce firefights occurred on the northern ends of the parallel ridges, with the Marines pinching off the Japanese hold on the higher ridge and the Japanese recapturing the nose of the lower ridge.[90]

Seeking higher ground, the Marines shifted northeast, attempting to seize a barrier angling into the valley consisting of a huddle of coral columns several hundred feet high called the Five Sisters. Intense Japanese fire from the barrier threw them back. On the extreme right the Second Battalion, First Regiment, circled outside Umurbrogol to a ridge on the southeast side of the peninsula, flanking access to the center section. Company C, attached to the Second Battalion, was ordered to seize the hill, which the Marines dubbed Walt's Ridge. Late in the afternoon, after circumventing machine gun fire, the company took the hill in a rush, only to find a higher one beyond it in the same ridge from which they received fire. They were also getting hit from a parallel ridge, called the Five Brothers, consisting of a vertical coral palisade—a narrow ridge capped by five mounds. Japanese counterattacks led to hand-to-hand fighting during the night, "with fists and rocks and throwing the enemy bodily over the cliffs."[91] Captain Everett P. Pope, ordered to withdraw, returned down Walt's Ridge with sixteen out of a company of ninety men he had taken up the day before. They were unable to bring out their dead. The following day the battalion attacked again, having gathered for the assault every man in the regiment who could be spared and every tank and gun under its control.[92] Again the attack failed when the low ground amid the rock walls "proved untenable."

After six days of battle, what remained of the First Marine Regiment was a hollow shell. Casualties amounted to 56 percent of the regiment, 71 percent in the First Battalion. In the nine rifle platoons of that battalion, a total of seventy-four men had been killed or wounded; no platoon leaders were left. The regiment claimed an estimated 3,942 Japanese killed, roughly two-thirds of the combat force. Furthermore, the regiment had reduced the size of the Umurbrogol pocket by approximately one-third and destroyed 22 pillboxes and 144 caves. Relief from combat for the regiment came on September 20, and loading commenced September 29, again for some R & R on Pavuvu.[93]

Heavy fighting continued during the following month under Marine command. With the loss of the First Regiment and the weakening of the other two, the Fifth and Seventh, reinforcement was imperative. The only immediate source was the Eighty-First Division, which had landed on Angaur, a smaller island close to Peleliu. This Wildcat Division, as it was called, untested but extensively trained, like the Seventy-Seventh (Guam), had cornered the foe on Angaur and could now dispense with one of its two regiments (the third was seizing Ulithi). Major General Roy Geiger, corps commander here as well as on Guam, so informed General Rupertus, who was "greatly alarmed" by the idea of an Army division joining them and strongly resisted, whereupon Geiger pulled rank and ordered the transfer.[94] Rupertus was undoubtedly hoping to complete the battle with his own division alone and, in the wake of the Twenty-Seventh Division affair on Saipan, likely considered all Army divisions, especially untested ones, to be laggards. The 321st Regiment landed shortly and joined the Umurbrogol encirclement.

The task given the 321st was to advance northeastward on the west side of the peninsula and seek a way to cross to the east side, thus completing the encirclement of the pocket and opening the way to its compression. The regiment found a trail across, followed it, and seized Hill 100 on the east side. It then concentrated its forces in order to assault the more dominating hill beyond the road, known as Hill B. With massed artillery and smoke covering the hill, the infantry fought their way to the top in an advance that was unstoppable.[95] The hill was taken and the peninsula divided just north of the Umurbrogol area, which was now encircled. Meanwhile, the Fifth Marine Regiment moved up the west side, passed through the

321st, and began clearing the northern tip of Peleliu and Ngesebus, an islet located 750 yards to its north. Orders to the Wildcat Division now sent it both south into the pocket and north to help the Fifth Regiment secure the hill line. Clearing the hill line in the north, and indeed everywhere on the island, often required repeated attacks, for the Japanese would reinfiltrate and reinhabit a cave unless it was sealed by demolition.

With the encirclement of the Umurbrogol, the battle for Peleliu entered a new stage. The First Regiment's losses had not been in vain: it had compressed the battlefield into a space less than a thousand yards long and half that wide. With external operations—south, east, and north—complete, the exclusive concern now was the final elimination of the pocket, which was defended by approximately 6,500 Japanese. For this General Rupertus had two Marine regiments, the Fifth and Seventh, and of course the Army's 321st Regiment, now tested and effective. The problem was that the two remaining Marine regiments were not in much better shape than the First. For example, Sledge's Company K, Fifth Regiment, lost eight killed and twenty-two wounded in successive attacks on the Five Sisters with, as he put it, "dismal results." In withdrawal, mortar-men acting as stretcher-bearers were targets of Japanese snipers. "The Japanese," recalled Sledge, "were merciless in this as in everything else in combat." In addition to heavy casualties were combat fatigue, dysentery, and heat prostration, taking Marines out of action for treatment or physically weakening them in action. As an officer present noted, the troops were "very, very tired."[96] Part of every night was taken up with guarding against Japanese infiltration. Sledge remembers with revulsion the stench of that rock-bound world. Burial of the Japanese dead was impossible, and removal of dead Marines was very slow, so bodies rotted in the heat. That odor, mixing with those of uncovered excrement and waste food, was one more burden in the "fight for survival, amid the violent death, terror, tension, fatigue, and filth that was the infantrymen's war."[97]

On the morning of October 4 the Seventh Regiment lined up for attack along the eastern side of the encirclement. Guarding the rest of the line of containment was a battalion from the Fifth, as well as Marines from the supporting services, amphibian crews, and engineers. The aim was to seize the ridgelines bordering the vital supply road on the eastern side of the peninsula, including the now infamous Walt's Ridge. Beyond lay an area of closely packed, jumbled ridges, draws, hills, and gullies, which on the south commanded the arenas and passages, the Sisters and Brothers, the Horseshoe, and the Wildcat Bowl of central Umurbrogol.

Two battalions of the Seventh took the ridges alongside the road, the third assault on Walt Ridge and the first on Boyd Ridge. The Second Battalion secured its way north along Walt Ridge by keeping behind the razorback crest on the left and using ropes, ladders, and blasting to get past a ninety-foot cliff on their side. Both ridges were taken and secured, a significant incursion into the pocket, but the east side supply road still lay open to Japanese machine gun fire from heights beyond the ridges, down the draws between them. L Company moved up the draw north of Boyd Ridge and disposed of the machine guns. Ridge 120 nearby, behind and parallel to Boyd Ridge, giving access to Baldy, a large and appropriately named hilltop in the interior, seemed undefended, so the battalion commander ordered a platoon to push on up the hill. Waiting until the platoon had reached the top, the Japanese opened fire from Baldy and below on the lower slope of Boyd Ridge, catching the Marines without cover in a deadly cross fire.[98] The Marines managed to get their wounded out, but of forty-eight men who went up the hill only five emerged unscathed. Company L was now the size of a platoon, and Company I, which assisted, counted 32 left of 235. "Companies," remembered Sledge, "looked like platoons; platoons looked like squads."[99] Division headquarters recognized that the Seventh Regiment, like the First, was practically hollow and withdrew it from battle.

That left the Fifth Regiment to carry on for the Marines, changing the character of the drive into the pocket, which took place on October 6. Maintaining constant pressure on the enemy with repeated attacks had won the Americans the eastern ridges, provided protection for the supply line, and inflicted heavy casualties on the enemy. However, that campaign had been terribly costly. Colonel Harold D. Harris, commander of the Fifth Regiment, resisted pressure from division headquarters to hasten the finish; the enemy, surrounded, posed no threat elsewhere. Harris had no desire to risk lives for the sake of speed. On the contrary, the tactical situation called for a more deliberate approach within an overall plan. He aimed to exploit the gains in the east, secure the northern jumble of hills, and turn south. "The methodical reduction of enemy positions was possible in driving southward," he explained, "due to the compartmentation of the terrain," that is, the maze of ridges and arenas. "It was this slow but steady eating away of the Jap defenses," he later wrote, "that gave the real payoff." The move across the pocket would eliminate cross fire from the north and place the Marines on the heights commanding the arenas to the south, which then could be reduced sector by sector: the Horseshoe, the Wildcat Bowl, and Death Valley.[100]

Every effort was made to maximize killing power in the sector under assault. Navy Corsairs from the Peleliu airfield used heavy bombs and napalm, but with limited success because of the constricted targets and danger to American troops. With armored bulldozers opening the way, amphibian tanks converted to flamethrowers moved in and burned off the scrub cover, revealing the caves, which tank-infantry teams or engineers then sealed with explosives. By the use of direct fire and explosives on the west side bluff, coral rubble was collected in sufficient quantity to form a ramp, opening the way to the heights above. Mortars were in heavy use: one of them fired no fewer than 3,000 rounds in this phase.

Turning south, two companies of the Fifth advanced along parallel ridges, covering each other, and then, while they were engaging the enemy in fire, a third company went through and seized the objective, Hill 140. This was a valuable piece of terrain, a commanding site above the Horseshoe, the Five Brothers, and the Wildcat Bowl.[101] The Fifth Regiment then closed up the line across the pocket on Hill 140 and tightened encirclement on the west side by several hundred yards, leaving a football-shaped pocket at the center of the original Umurbrogol that contained about 700 Japanese soldiers remaining of the initial 6,500.

Beginning October 15, the Fifth Regiment handed over the Umurbrogol to the 321st Regiment, which had been in reserve. The relief and departure of the First Marine Division occurred as soon as shipping became available. It would return to Pavuvu for another and more drastic rebuilding for the next invasion, Okinawa. The commanding general of the Eighty-First Division, Major General Paul J. Mueller, was now in charge of completing the elimination of the pocket. The 321st would be joined by the 323rd

Regiment after it completed the occupation of Ulithi atoll. The 322nd Regiment remained at Angaur, mopping up. Mueller was even less interested than Harris in a speedy completion. He wanted a caterpillar-like siege, a slow, relentless, squeeze that would expose his men to as little danger as possible.[102] Instead of a sequence of singular assaults, he wanted limited but persistent attacks by his four battalions, often concurrently, wearing down the Japanese by constant engagement.

Though this was a slow, relentless squeeze, the endgame, the remaining objective of central importance was the extension of the commanding position on Hill 140 out into the adjacent battlefield, along the narrow ridge, capped by the Five Brothers, which stood between the Horseshoe and Wildcat Bowl arenas.[103] An earlier attempt had failed because the top was bare rock, open to gunfire from several directions. This time the infantry brought sandbags hauled up the hill by an overhead cable system the engineers rigged, powered by a truck engine, and handed along from man to man on the ridge, thus extending control from mound to mound. It became common for each infantryman in the pocket to have his own sandbag, which, to advance, he would push ahead with his gun butt or a pole. The Five Brothers ridge was finally taken on October 22, and with Walt Ridge already seized, the Horseshoe was easily seized and held. A new trail could be cleared from the north by armored bulldozers, and along it came tank-infantry teams, tank destroyers, and flamethrowers. Methodically, one after another, they sealed the caves. With the eastern sector in hand, the siege-line moved west to the far side of the Five Brothers into the Wildcat Bowl. Here in the southwest, with the massive rock faces of Hill 300 and the Five Sisters, jagged, broken terrain on the northwest, and in between the treacherous gullies and ravines of Death Valley and China Wall—the location of Colonel Nakagawa's headquarters and his last resistance—progress was slower. The rainy season arrived in late October, with frequent downpours and a typhoon that stretched over four days. Nevertheless, the 323rd Regiment, relieving the 321st, succeeded in placing troops on top of Hill 300 and the Five Sisters, finally opening the way to the China Wall, a double wall alongside a narrow gulch strewn with coral rubble. This obstacle slowed the advance, from north and south, to a snail's pace.

Meanwhile tank-infantry teams and flamethrowers attacked the caves surrounding the Wildcat Bowl. With caves along the China Wall beyond the reach of flamethrowers, engineers rigged a pipeline 300 yards long to carry fuel with booster pumps from a truck on the road to the cave entrance. Lit by a white phosphorous hand grenade lobbed into the entrance, the flames killed the Japanese soldiers inside or drove them out, where they were killed. Gradually the ring closed in on the China Wall. On November 25 Nakagawa committed suicide, and resistance practically ceased. On November 27 the force working north on the China Wall met the force going south; across the way, soldiers were atop the rim of Death Valley. Soldiers from eight rifle companies, carefully searching, closed in on the spot, silently looking at one another while they slowly allowed themselves to realize that the battle was finally over.[104] Sledge recalled asking a Marine old-timer with experience in the battles of World War I what he had thought of Peleliu. This representative of the "Old Breed" answered, "I ain't never seen nothin' like it.... I've had enough after that."[105]

The casualties of the First Marine Division were 6,526, with 1,252 killed. On Peleliu the Eighty-First Division lost 1,393, with 208 killed.[106] Total casualties for both divisions on Peleliu, in other words, amounted to nearly 8,000 soldiers. On Peleliu the Eighty-First also had another 2,500 hospitalized for combat fatigue, illness, and heat prostration.[107] Peleliu has never been as prominent in public consciousness in the way Tarawa and Iwo Jima immediately became, in part because the casualties were less notable within the aggregate of American Army casualties, including those in the European war. It was a subsidiary operation, done somewhat in seclusion, with only a few correspondents along. For the First Marine Division, however, it was devastating, forcing it, regiment by regiment, to leave the battlefield because its rifle battalions were thinned almost to nonexistence. This had immediate consequences because the First Marine Division would only have until March to train replacements and rebuild squads, platoons, and companies, to say nothing of getting enough rest and good food, before they boarded ship for practice landings and Okinawa. The division would also have a new commanding general.

Peleliu was Private Sledge's first battle, and he learned to fear and hate the Japanese, particularly for disfiguring the bodies of dead Marines. At the same time he had to respect their marksmanship, their nightly infiltration of Marine lines, their discipline in withholding fire until they had substantial targets, and their skill in camouflage and siting weapons. Indeed, Colonel Nakagawa's defense of Umurbrogol was even more skilled than those of the commanders at Biak and Saipan. It would have been more consequential had he been able to mass his artillery fire on the landing and in support of his counterattack, but he nonetheless squeezed out every possible way of delaying the enemy and inflicting casualties. Tactically, the lesson Peleliu offered American planners was that storming the enemy saved time but cost lives, while maneuver saved lives but took time. However, as the end was coming into sight in the Pacific war, so too was the demand for both a faster tempo and fewer casualties.

On October 17, when the last Marine battalion was withdrawing from action on Peleliu, a new battle was beginning 600 miles to the west with the arrival of American advance detachments at Leyte Gulf. Their job was to clear the gulf of mines and install navigation lights to guide the invasion forces. Arriving on October 19 and 20 would be an armada of over 700 ships. By noon on October 17, immediately after getting word, Japanese Combined Fleet headquarters dispatched orders initiating fleet movements to attack and destroy the American landing forces.[108]

Initiation of a plan was a long way from contact in battle. The heavy guns of the Japanese navy—battleships and heavy cruisers—were mostly waiting at Lingga Roads, near Sumatra, and the carriers were still at home ports on the Inland Sea. Arranging for refueling en route, coordinating widely separated task forces, and shifting warship assignments took time, to say nothing of the 1,500-mile voyage from Lingga to Leyte. Consequently the components of the Japanese fleet did not arrive in Philippine waters until October 24, four days after the Leyte landings. The Americans, keenly aware of the vulnerability of their hundreds of ships, hastened the unloading and released most of their initial shipping after the first day. By the fifth day, when the Japanese arrived, all echelons of command had established their headquarters ashore, and the second replenishment convoy was unloading. Present in and near the gulf were several dozen LSTs and several dozen cargo ships, three command ships, and eighteen escort carriers lifting 500 planes, as well as a covering force of six pre–Pearl Harbor battleships, cruisers, and destroyers of MacArthur's Seventh Fleet under the command of Rear Admiral Jesse B. Oldendorf.[109]

Commanding the Center Force of the oncoming Japanese fleet was Vice Admiral Kurita Takeo, known as a cautious leader.[110] His command consisted of the two superbattleships *Yamato* and *Musashi*, three prewar battleships, and ten heavy cruisers, heavier than the American type—altogether a powerful force. They refueled at Brunei in north Borneo and sailed northeast along the corridor between long, narrow Palawan Island and a large expanse of water named by mariners the Dangerous Ground because of the hazards posed by its numerous reefs, shoals, and rock outcroppings. Flying his flag in a cruiser, Kurita led the way and without destroyers to protect him. The American submarines *Darter* and *Dace*, on the lookout, got ahead of the columns, sank two heavy cruisers, disabled a third, and alerted Admiral Halsey. Kurita lost his flagship and had to swim to safety. *Darter* went aground and was lost, but *Dace* managed to save its crew. In that brief spell Center Force lost 30 percent of its heavy cruisers.[111]

The next day, October 24, the Center Force entered the maze of straits and inland seas composing the Philippine archipelago. Threading his way below Luzon eastward, Kurita aimed for San Bernardino Strait and then headed south to Leyte Gulf. Meanwhile, coming from Japan, the ghost force of Vice Admiral Ozawa Jisaburo, four mostly empty carriers, two aging battleships, and three light cruisers, stationed itself northeast of Luzon to lure Halsey away from the Center Force. Paralleling Center Force but sailing south of Palawan, Vice Admiral Nishimura Shoji entered the Mindanao Sea, leading to Surigao Strait, intending an attack on Leyte Gulf from the south. His two battleships and one heavy cruiser would be followed into the Gulf by the independent command of Vice Admiral Shima Kiyohide, whose force consisted of three cruisers, two heavy and one light. Escorting the four groups were thirty-one destroyers.

Word of the approach of Japanese naval forces arrived at Admiral Halsey's command post, the battleship *New Jersey,* northeast of Luzon, at an awkward moment. As we've noted, in September and October the fast carrier forces had engaged in weeks of successive attacks on Japanese aircraft in the Ryukyus, at Formosa, and in the Philippines. Getting low on ammunition and food, they badly needed to head to Ulithi for rest, repair, and supplies. The long missions, day after day, requiring intense concentration from take-off to landing, took their toll on pilots.[112] Admiral Mitscher noted how the fatigue of ships' crews from extended combat conditions slowed down their reactions.[113] On October 22, the Leyte landings firmly established, Halsey ordered two of the four carrier task groups to Ulithi for replenishment, one to leave that day and one the next. In addition, he assigned two of the remaining attack carriers to go with them. When he learned of the approach of the Center Force early on October 23, he recalled both of the task groups. The former arrived in time to join the battle; the latter, the larger, joined at the very end. Detachments to Ulithi left Halsey with only five attack and six light carriers, from a total of seventeen.[114] Now was the time to release them, Halsey had believed, because the Japanese navy would not intervene in the Leyte landing but instead wait for the Luzon assault. However sound his logic, Halsey has been criticized by some for acting without the necessary intelligence confirming the location of the Japanese fleet.[115]

Early in the morning on October 24, American search planes found Center Force passing through the Sibuyan Sea, south of Luzon. Halsey ordered attacks from his three remaining groups situated off the eastern coasts of Luzon and Samar. The *Essex, Lexington, Princeton,* and *Langley* task group was initially unavailable because it was itself under attack by planes from the Luzon airfields. Given carrier absences, the fleet that had put over a thousand planes into an attack during the Battle of the Philippine Sea could gather this time only 251. The first two of four attacks, those in the morning, were mounted from just two vessels, the attack carrier *Intrepid* and the light carrier *Cabot*. The most effective weapon against Japanese warships was the torpedo-carrying Avenger, and of these, seventy-six were among the fighters and dive-bombers in the four attacks, though only twelve and eleven in the two morning attacks, respectively—an average of one for each heavy cruiser and battleship.[116]

Center Force was divided into two circular formations, each one four miles in diameter and located seven miles apart, with the superbattleships in the leading section. The American pilots focused on them not only because they were the biggest threats but also because of the importance of simply finding out what it took to sink these 63,000-ton behemoths. Since as flagship the *Yamato* was in the center of the circle and its sister ship, the *Musashi*, in the next ring, somewhat closer to the edge of protection, the *Musashi* received most of the attention. Pilots in attack faced a storm of bullets from the battleships, each of which had enlarged its antiaircraft batteries with 120 25 mm machine guns. However, strafing and bombing inflicted heavy casualties on the poorly protected gun crews. Estimates vary but it appears that about twenty torpedoes and seventeen bombs struck the *Musashi*. What sank the ship were torpedoes making holes in its sides and exploding in its engine room and bow. With uncontrollable flooding in the boiler and engine rooms, the breakdown of damage control systems, and loss of power, the ship fell out of the protective formation and finally sank, taking with it over a thousand of its crew.[117]

The *Musashi* was the only ship sunk in the Sibuyan Sea battle. The *Yamato* was struck by two bombs that penetrated its hull and exploded but without affecting its fighting capability. Two other battleships received minor damage. *Myoko*, slowed by a torpedo hit, retired to Brunei, reducing the heavy cruiser group once more. Kurita's force was seriously damaged but with four battleships and six heavy cruisers remained a notable threat. He withdrew west to avoid further attack. Once the battle quieted in the late afternoon, he turned back east and again headed for San Bernardino Strait.[118]

Meanwhile Japanese naval headquarters in Manila had been drawing in plane reinforcements from Japan and China along the insular flyway. It chose to ignore Kurita's plea for air support and instead used its planes against the nearest American carrier force, the *Essex, Lexington, Princeton,* and *Langley* task group. On October 24, three successive attacks were launched with fifty to sixty planes in each. The defending American planes, as in the Battle of the Philippine Sea, devastated each attack, with Commander

David McCampbell and his wingman shooting down fifteen. However, as the battle waned, a loner dove out of the clouds on the light carrier *Princeton* and landed a bomb that penetrated the flight deck, setting off explosions and fires. Despite hours of firefighting by the crew, assisting destroyers, and the light cruiser *Birmingham,* the fire persisted and finally set off weapons in a storeroom. The explosion blew a large part of the *Princeton*'s stern and flight deck over and onto the *Birmingham*'s decks, which were teeming with gun crews, rope handlers, and firefighters. Half of the ship's company were cut down—229 killed and 420 wounded. The carrier had to be sunk by torpedoes and the *Birmingham* sent home for repairs.[119]

The end of this attack on the *Princeton* group freed planes for mounting a search for the Japanese carriers, which had been encouraging such a search by dipping their bait closer to the action. Sure enough, the searchers found the battleships at 3:30 in the afternoon and the carrier section an hour later. Halsey now had everything he needed to choose his course of action. At 8:24 p.m. orders went to his task groups to gather and move north during the night, parallel with the coast of Luzon, to attack and destroy the enemy carriers in the morning. About the same time, night searchers reported that Kurita's Center Force was nearing San Bernardino Strait and navigation lights in the strait had been turned on. Halsey stayed on course to attack Ozawa, leaving the strait behind untended.[120] A few minutes after midnight the Center Force emerged one by one from the narrow strait, formed up, and headed south along the coast of Samar toward Leyte Gulf.

In Halsey's estimation, MacArthur's Seventh Fleet, with its own battleships, cruisers, destroyers, and escort carriers, should have been able to take care of Center Force by itself, especially a Center Force "badly mauled," as Morison put it, in the past day's battle. Relying on pilot after-action reports, Halsey concluded, again according to Morison, that "all of its battleships and most of its heavy cruisers" had been "tremendously reduced in fighting power and life."[121] Veteran carrier officers knew that pilots tended to exaggerate their achievements and needed questioning on specifics. The "badly mauled" Center Force had moved spryly from one side of the Philippines to the other. Senior officers were alarmed, and several sought to warn Halsey. Rear Admiral Gerald W. Bogan, a seasoned carrier group commander, urged the forming up and stationing of the battleship forces at San Bernardino Strait, covered by his own carrier group, but he was brushed off by Halsey's staff.[122]

Though Halsey had been the admiral commanding the famous Doolittle Raid on Tokyo, April 18, 1942, and then the South Pacific Theater, he was something of a newcomer to Pacific warfare. While he was known as Admiral Nimitz's fighter, a square-jawed personification of the very idea of aggressive leadership, and hailed by the American public in the gloomy months of the Solomons campaign, "Bull" Halsey had also missed the battles of Coral Sea, Midway, and the Philippine Sea; Leyte Gulf was his first experience of fleet-on-fleet combat. His flagship was a battleship rather than a carrier, and his staff lacked fast carrier fleet experience. This made little difference, given that Halsey used his staff more for carrying out orders than for discussion and debate. In contrast to the cautious, methodical Spruance, Halsey took risks and acted on instinct. Unfortunately, his impulsive style and inattention to procedures meant that his orders were often vague and out of date, leaving his carrier admirals unsure of his plans.[123] In the Battle of Sibuyan Sea, he issued a direct order to his task group commanders to attack, bypassing the task force commander, Admiral Mitscher.[124]

Despite his inexperience, Halsey was a critical player in the transformation of naval warfare occurring at this moment. He had been the one to attack the Japanese air forces on the Okinawa-Formosa-Philippines island chain, hammering at them so long and hard that even Japanese carrier trainees were transferred to the islands, leaving nearly empty carriers for Ozawa to bring to the Philippines—as sacrificial lambs to lure Halsey away from Center Force. The Japanese navy could no longer muster the fuel, ammunition, and trained pilots to conduct battle. All it could attempt to do was inflict maximum damage on the American forces. Indeed, October 25 was the first day of the next stage of the Pacific Theater, and one of the trademarks of its final year, kamikaze warfare. Halsey, at least at the strategic level, had already won his battle. Even so, Ozawa's carriers were the "fleet in being" and the essential threat, and Halsey knew that the American Navy would regard destroying them as a necessary step.[125] He therefore felt this was the moment to assemble his might and speed north to eliminate the enemy carriers, so that they could be simply removed as an element in future planning, always somewhere out there, lurking. Halsey was an aggressive commander but also was baffled by the intricacies of management and by the process of maneuvering his large and complex force. However, he had driven the front against Japan remorselessly westward and northward, carrying out in his own mind the dictum of the Joint Chiefs to keep the enemy under constant pressure.

In the formative stage for battle in the Philippines, Admiral Ozawa had urged that the noncarrier elements of his force—battleships and cruisers—be transferred to Kurita's force, where they would be able to do more than act as decoys and, by dispatching a force through the southern entry, Surigao Strait, create a pincer movement of Kurita's eastern attack into Leyte Gulf. Kurita assigned the task to Vice Admiral Nishimura, ordering him to arrive at the southern entrance to Surigao Strait at 1:00 a.m. on October 25, traverse the Strait, pass into Leyte Gulf, and strike MacArthur's shipping at precisely 4:27 a.m., two hours before sunrise. Kurita would join him at 6 a.m. Thus Nishimura would have any and all American naval forces in the Gulf to himself for ninety-three minutes. The idea was that the Americans would be fully engaged with Nishimura when Kurita charged into Leyte Gulf. Nishimura and most of his officers recognized the mission for what it was—suicidal. However, at least it would be a night action, which Nishimura preferred and at which the Japanese navy excelled, so that he just might break through and inflict heavy damage.[126] The sacrifice would not be in vain.

Vice Admiral Shima's small force of cruisers and destroyers had in the meantime been protecting troop convoys bound for Manila. Pressing hard for a role in the looming battle, Shima at the last minute secured a Combined Fleet assignment to Surigao Strait. So two entirely independent commands, each preferring not to join forces, headed toward Surigao. Shima, promising support to Nishimura, chose to follow him with an interval between.[127] Dominating Nishimura's force were the battleships *Fuso* and *Yamashiro*, pre–World War I "super dreadnoughts" pulled from duty training sailors in the Inland Sea. (The *Texas* and *New York*, serving in the Atlantic, were of the same vintage.) Extensively modernized, they retained their signature, pagoda-like foremast towers rising 144 feet above the waterline, giving them a top-heavy look.[128] On the morning of October 24, the wide-ranging searches from Halsey's carriers found Nishimura's contingent heading toward the Mindanao Sea and Surigao. Twenty-seven planes from the *Enterprise* attacked, scoring penetrating hits on the two battleships. Both suffered casualties, and the blasts shook the old hulls and started leaks. A large fire burned in the stern of *Fuso*, but the crew got the better of it. Fortunately for Nishimura, the pumps stayed ahead of the leaks, and Halsey ordered his planes to shift north to attack Kurita in the Sibuyan Sea. Despite having lost the advantage of surprise, Nishimura was determined to push on according to plan.[129]

The battle started at 10:50 p.m. on October 24, as Nishimura neared the southern entry to Surigao Strait. Patrolling these approaches and the southern part of the strait were thirty-nine American motor torpedo boats in thirteen "pods" of three. The Japanese force faced successive torpedo attacks in groups of three for over three hours. All the torpedoes missed, and several of the boats were hit. Nevertheless, they were useful in harassing Nishimura with constant attacks, requiring maneuvers to avoid torpedoes when his ships needed to maintain formation. They kept Admiral Oldendorf informed of Nishimura's location while Oldendorf's bombardment and fire support group protected the landings on Leyte. After shaking off the torpedo boats, Nishimura continued north through the strait with his two battleships, one cruiser, and four destroyers. In the center section the strait narrows to about seventeen miles and then gradually opens into Leyte Gulf. The land on either side rises sharply to nearly 2,000 feet, defeating radar sighting.

It was in this throat of the strait that the principal action of the Battle of Surigao Strait occurred, beginning at 3:00 a.m. and lasting about fifty minutes. The moon having set, the night was dark, with lightning flashes on the horizon. The sea was glassy calm, sharply defining the white of bow waves and torpedo tracks. The initial attack came from the north: three American destroyers heading for position east of Nishimura and two for the west. These were destroyers of the latest design, each mounted with two quintuple torpedo launchers. Closing to a range of about five miles, the ships on the east fired a total of twenty-seven torpedoes at the Japanese ships. After a pause for these to reach the targets, the west group fired twenty. Apparently

Nishimura had not been expecting engagement short of the Gulf, for his ships were just shifting into battle formation. The torpedoes from the east missed, except for two and possibly three critical hits on the battleship *Fuso*. It swerved out of position to the right, fighting the fires and flooding. Within the hour she sank, leaving a pool of hissing burning oil, over which could be heard the screams of the sailors trapped in its burning hulk.[130] Ten of the crew of 1,900 survived.

The torpedoes from the west were even more successful. Nishimura had ordered an all-ships 90-degree turn to starboard to evade them but then turned back to the original course too soon and ran straight into them. Three out of his four destroyers were hit, a spectacular outcome of the torpedo attack.[131] Two torpedoes struck the *Yamagumo* and probably ignited its own armed torpedoes, creating a huge explosion that broke it apart, doubling bow on stern, and sent it down. Next came *Asagumo*, struck by a torpedo in the bow that collapsed the forecastle, leaving the *Asagumo* crippled. Several hours later it was sunk by shellfire. Last was *Michishio,* which took a torpedo in the engine room and sank by flooding in ten to fifteen minutes, leaving four survivors out of a crew of about 200.[132]

The destroyer phase of the battle became more intense and confused. Next, six American destroyers in two groups charged in from the west, followed by nine more from the north and west in three groups. Their target had been reduced to only three ships from seven: the battleship *Yamashiro*, the flagship, the heavy cruiser *Mogami*, and the destroyer *Shigure*. But with thickening weather and smoke screens, surprisingly accurate and heavy fire from the enemy, orders from above to make haste, and a host of American destroyers cluttering the radar screens, together with crippled ships and landmasses, little damage was done.[133] Nonetheless, one torpedo hit the *Yamashiro* amidships, slowing it to five knots. Its engineers quickly restored power, and it forged ahead. Nishimura, apparently unaware that he had lost the *Fuso* and now informed that Shima, with his cruisers and destroyers, was near and catching up, may well have taken heart as he set course for the invasion beaches inside Leyte Gulf. He was unaware of what lay across the entrance to Leyte Gulf.

At 3:51 a.m. on October 25 the third phase of the battle began, with salvos of 8- and 6-inch guns from the four heavy and four light cruisers of the Seventh Fleet. A few minutes later the sound swelled with the opening of a barrage behind them from the big guns, 14- and 16-inch, of the six battleships of the fleet. The ships were steaming in three lines, two for cruisers and one for battleships, in single file from west to east and back across the entrance of the gulf. This was indeed capping the "T," the ideal maneuver, whereby the fleet crosses ahead of the enemy with all guns, fore and aft, and then bears down while the enemy can only employ his forward guns. However, this was a clumsy manifestation of that classic maneuver. The enemy consisted of less than a handful of Japanese ships, of which the two larger were already handicapped by hits. The six American battleships, all pre–Pearl Harbor, had a limited supply of armor-piercing shells, their principal task usually being bombardment of invasion beaches. Only three of them carried the latest fire-control radar; the rest had difficulty finding a target in the dark. The *Pennsylvania,* flagship at Pearl Harbor, found none and stayed mute, and the *Maryland* fired only one salvo. The *California* misunderstood an order to turn and lost position, almost struck the *Tennessee,* and slipped into the line of fire, forcing a general battle line cease-fire. Then word came back of Japanese long-range torpedoes under way, bringing an abrupt turn away to the north for three of the battleships. The *A. W. Grant* got caught in an overlap of the destroyer attacks and became a target for both sides; it was nearly sunk by more than twenty hits.

Altogether it was a wobbly crossing of the "T."[134] Nevertheless, the eighteen minutes of shellfire from the arc of ships had stopped Nishimura's advance. The left flank cruisers fired 3,100 rounds, the *Denver* alone 1,147. The best from the battleships was the ninety-three rounds of 16-inch shells fired from the *West Virginia.*[135] The *Yamashiro*'s tall pagoda burst into flames, the fire burning so brightly that it illuminated the ship's gun turrets. Amazingly, the ship, though burning, laid heavy, accurate fire on the right flank American cruisers. To bring its aft 14-inch guns to bear, *Yamashiro* took a wide turn to the left and came to a point where it was firing in three directions.[136] Then a torpedo struck near the starboard engine room: "She trembled considerably, and then swayed for a while. The huge iron structure squeaked as though it had been screaming," said one of the few officers saved.[137] It nonetheless started up again to twelve knots. Nishimura, resolute and calm, sent his last message: "We proceed to Leyte for *gyokusai* [total annihilation]." Now heading southwest, apparently to rendezvous with Shima, the flagship took another torpedo, capsized, and sank. Ten of its crew of approximately 1,600 survived.[138]

Nishimura had fulfilled his duty: he had fought his way to Leyte Gulf and engaged the American fleet as best he could. Now it was Kurita's turn. The *Mogami*, severely damaged, and the *Shigure*, so compromised that it had to be steered by hand, headed back toward the Mindanao Sea, the former to sink in a few hours and the latter to survive until January 1945. Shima, finally arriving in the *Nachi*, authorized a long-range torpedo attack northward by his destroyers, without results. Then he debated going northward, decided the same fate as Nishimura's would befall him, and instead went south.

The pincers did not close on Leyte Gulf. Central Force never got that far. It emerged from San Bernardino Strait shortly before Nishimura had entered Surigao Strait. Relieved at finding no enemy waiting, Admiral Kurita ordered a cruise formation and headed south along the coast of Samar. At dawn, about eighty miles north of the entrance to Leyte Gulf, his lookouts spotted aircraft carriers jutting above the horizon to the east. At almost the same time lookouts and patrol planes of these American carriers spotted the pagoda masts of Center Force rising above the horizon. Corroborating evidence for the Americans arrived in minutes, as targeting salvos from the Japanese battleships closed on their circular carrier formation.[139] For both navies, it was a surprise encounter.

Kurita had engaged the northernmost of three escort carrier groups assigned to the Seventh Fleet. The escort carrier, built on converted tanker hulls, was slower than the fleet carriers and shorter than the light fleet carrier (such as the *Princeton*). It had been invaluable in antisubmarine warfare on the Atlantic and here was providing patrolling and air support for the invasion forces. Each carrier had an assault capacity of up to thirty Wildcat fighters and bomb- or torpedo-carrying Avengers, but with only one 5-inch gun was otherwise virtually defenseless. Taffy 3 (the voice radio call sign), the northernmost group, had six of these escort carriers, collectively a substantial force from a modest source. Protecting the group were three of the same new destroyers that were attacking

Nishimura, as well as four destroyer escorts—smaller vessels, less heavily armed but more nimble. The commander of Taffy 3, Rear Admiral Clifton A. F. Sprague, recognizing that survival depended on getting his planes in the air, turned east to catch the northeast wind for launching, ordered top speed, and gained authority to engage Center Force and the promise of all available air assistance. Fortunately the Taffy 2 group was just over the horizon. The Taffy 3 group, according to Morison, "slicing planes off their flight decks faster than they had ever done before," launched forty-four Avengers in thirty minutes.[140]

Given the enemy's speed of twenty-seven knots, compared with seventeen for the escort carriers, and the overwhelming Japanese firepower advantage, it was hard to imagine that Taffy 3 could survive until substantial help arrived. Sprague therefore aimed to divert and confuse the enemy. After launching planes, hidden in a passing rain squall, he abruptly turned his carriers from east to south, toward Leyte Gulf. He ordered all ships to make smoke, which in the humid air stayed thick and low, and ordered his three destroyers to attack with torpedoes. The *Johnston* had already leaped out ahead. Their sooty black capes streaming behind, they raced at top speed, toward six Japanese heavy cruisers and, beyond them, four battleships, including the mighty *Yamato*. Pitting their 5-inch guns against 8- to 18-inch guns were the *Johnston*, joined by the *Hoel* and *Heermann*, and the destroyer escort *Roberts*, which tagged along. Only one or two of the *Johnston*'s torpedoes struck, but it was enough to retire the heavy cruiser *Kumano*, joined by the heavy cruiser *Suzuya*, which had been slowed by the near miss of a bomb. Thus two heavy cruisers were out of action; Kurita was now down from ten to four and would be down to two before the end of the chase. The destroyer torpedo spreads laid down by the Americans forced repeated evasive action by the Japanese big-gun ships, slowing them and diverting their gunfire from the carriers. The *Yamato*, making a radical turn to evade torpedoes, found itself heading away from the battle, hemmed in by a spread on either side.[141]

Admiral Kurita was slow to bring his full power to bear on the enemy. In this, his first encounter with escort carriers, his lookouts took them for fast carriers out of Halsey's fleet. Furthermore, the American destroyers, though half the size, had a silhouette quite similar to that of the current American heavy cruisers. Holding this image of fast carriers and heavy cruisers, Kurita may have failed to recognize that the enemy was much slower, thereby providing him with an opportunity to close fast and sink the carriers before an organized air attack arrived. Instead, he permitted his heavy cruisers and battleships to break formation in pursuit of potential targets and held back his destroyers.[142] As a result, two battleships moved well out on the left flank, spreading the force over fifteen miles and weakening control of the Japanese attack. Rounding the turn from east to south on the outside, they had farther to go.

At the start of the battle, Japanese gunfire was impressively accurate, straddling the American carriers and destroyers with tall geysers time after time, but the smoky scene required a shift to unreliable radar sighting.[143] Some Japanese gunners lacked persistence: the battleship *Haruna*, finally closing in on the Taffy 3 carriers, shifted target to the Taffy 2 group approaching eighteen miles away. And lack of heavy armor was not always a disadvantage for the Americans: enemy armor-piercing shells often passed through the thin sheathing of the carriers and destroyers without detonation. Nevertheless, by 9 a.m., with enemy cruisers coming abreast on the port side and battleships closing behind and to port, Taffy 3 carriers were edging into envelopment. The carrier *Gambier Bay*, vulnerable in the rear of the formation and heavily hit, dropped back from the formation and succumbed to incessant short-range fire.[144] Desperate, Sprague called on his destroyers and destroyer escorts for a second attack to draw enemy fire from the carriers, and, battered as they were, they responded. The *Johnston* charged the Japanese destroyers to starboard, prompting them to launch torpedoes from too great a distance; two were exploded by gunfire. By this time, the screen, now under incessant pounding from all sides, was breaking down. The *Roberts* had a huge hole in its side, and aft of the stack was a "yawning mass of blackened metal." Abandoned, the *Roberts* sank. The *Hoel*, badly damaged and listing severely, went down. The *Johnston*, on fire, rolled over and began sinking at 10:10, having lost power, steering, communications, the bridge, all guns except one, and the mast.[145] The *Heermann* and *Dennis* survived with flooded compartments; the *Raymond* and *Butler* escaped serious damage.

Fortunately the Taffy 3 crisis arrived just when Taffy 2 was ready to provide critical assistance. Most of Taffy 3's planes had flown off before the attack on accustomed missions. It took time to recall them and switch their loads to sea-battle weapons: torpedoes, 500-pound bombs, and rockets. Rear Admiral Felix B. Stump, Taffy 2 commander, recovered, loaded, and dispatched seventy-nine planes in an hour and a half for five strikes. Guided by controllers in the air, the Avengers and Wildcats (as noted, an earlier version of the Hellcat) began making their weight felt in the last hour of battle, delivering 49 torpedoes, 133 500-pound bombs, 276 rockets, and just plain strafing. In after-war briefings, Japanese officers stressed the skill, persistence, and impact of the air strikes. Along the heavy cruiser column, the centerpiece of the Japanese attack, Taffy 2 planes and Taffy 3 destroyers badly damaged the *Chokai* and *Chikuma*, increasing to four the number of heavy cruisers put out of action in this battle and reducing Kurita to two heavy cruisers.

At 9:11 a.m., just into the third hour of the devilish chase, to the astonishment of the Taffy 3 crews, the Japanese warships bearing down on them reversed course and headed away. Why Kurita gave up the field and his tactical advantage remains unclear. In the *Yamato* he was twelve miles away from Taffy 3, looking out on a shifting montage of low cloud, smoke, and interweaving ships. In the past two days, he had swum for his life from his sinking flagship, suffered hours of severe air attack in the Sibuyan Sea, and, probably at the highest alert the previous night, slipped through San Bernardino Strait. Just how clear his mind was in the confusion off Samar is anybody's guess. Nevertheless, historians seem to agree on a central strain in his decision: concern for the progressive destruction of Center Force. This critical time of envelopment for Taffy 3 was also, for different reasons, critical for Kurita. Center Force could not survive an engagement with their current scattered deployment in the face of repeated, widening, and skillfully directed air assaults. A further assault, this time concentrating on the battleships, began at 9:06 a.m., just as the *Chikuma* sent word that it had been struck by a torpedo and the *Yamato, Negato,* and *Kongo* were under attack from aerial torpedoes.[146] The argument for withdrawal and concentration was very strong.[147] Holding a comforting image of larger-than-life American ships sunk, Kurita gave the order to turn away and reassemble to save his remaining ships.

That brought an extraordinary interval of the Japanese looping back and forth off Samar, trying to decide what to do about the order to enter Leyte Gulf and destroy as much of the transport as possible, even if Center Force itself went down. Most communication among Japanese land, sea, and air forces in the Philippines was either delayed or nonexistent, but messages from Shima and the *Shigure,* the only surviving ship in the Nishimura force, reporting the failure of the Surigao assault may have reached the *Yamato* before dawn on October 25. More extensive reports arrived after Kurita's decision not to enter Leyte Gulf.[148] Building in Kurita's mind were three convictions. First, evidently the Americans were using the Tacloban and Dulag airfields on Leyte and thus were already established on the island and capable of defending their beachhead as well as resupplying Taffy planes. Second, to enter the Gulf would threaten his force with entrapment. He had no knowledge of what size force the Americans had in the Gulf, or how ready it was, but he expected that it was substantial and in the Gulf he would lack room for maneuver. Third, he concluded that given his assumptions of American strength and position, he would not be able to inflict on the enemy losses great enough to justify his own.

What, then, was the value of the Nishimura assault and the Ozawa diversion using carriers as bait? For Kurita, losing most or all of his ships without substantive achievement would be a waste. The thing is, he was not acting alone. Sacrifices by other elements of the fleet were designed to make it possible for him to burst into Leyte Gulf and destroy MacArthur's transports and supplies. Yet, practically at the gate of the Gulf, Kurita shied away from that responsibility. He decided to stay in the open sea, engage any elements of the fast carrier fleet he encountered, and reenter San Bernardino Strait before sunset.[149] The leadership of the Japanese navy formulated a complex plan for a final, decisive fleet engagement that could have damaged and slowed the American offensive in the western Pacific. It is suggestive of the disintegration of the navy that the plan was carried out in one way by Shima and Kurita and by Nishimura and Ozawa in another.

The aftermath of battle was horrific for the crews of the stricken Taffy ships. The destroyers were charnel houses, their decks littered with the blasted bodies of dead and wounded men. Sailors lowered their wounded into boats and rafts under continuing shellfire. The rest depended on floater nets, wooden planks, and their life jackets. More than a thousand men went into the water.[150] The rescue of survivors was miserably prolonged on account of pilot error in defining the location, preoccupation with continuing air attacks, and probably mental fatigue on the part of Admiral Kinkaid and his Seventh Fleet staff after narrowly escaping disaster in their encounter with Nishimura's and Kurita's forces. Finally Vice Admiral Barbey organized a flotilla of landing craft that swept the sea off Samar, rescuing 1,150 men who had spent two days and nights in the water holding onto life and fending off sharks. About 116 died at sea.

During the night of October 24–25, while the Battle of Surigao Strait was raging and Admiral Kurita, after threading San Bernardino Strait, was steaming south along the coast of Samar, Admiral Halsey, leaving the strait untended, headed north off Luzon with most of his fast carrier fleet to hunt down and destroy Admiral Ozawa's carriers. This time Halsey turned the attack over to the expert, Admiral Mitscher. Before he did so Halsey extracted all six fast battleships, two heavy cruisers, and six light cruisers with eighteen destroyers to form a separate battle force ahead of his five large and five light carriers. Vice Admiral John S. McCain's group with five carriers, returning from Ulithi, would join them after fueling. It was a massive force bearing down on Ozawa's four nearly empty carriers and two old battleships, three light cruisers, and nine destroyers.

At dawn on the Twenty-Fifth, Mitscher's search planes, followed by planes of the first strike, located the Ozawa group 140 miles to the northeast. With a coordinator directing planes from above, two strikes had taken place by 11:00 a.m. The light carrier *Chitose* was sunk, and its sister ship the *Chiyoda* was afire, with flooding, a sharp list, and disabled engines. More strikes were on the way. At last the Japanese carriers were within Halsey's grasp and the battleships could have their day. Suddenly at 11:15 a.m. half of his force went into reverse.[151] Halsey with all the battleships, one carrier group, four cruisers, and accompanying destroyers headed back south to engage Kurita, leaving Mitscher with two carrier groups and a cruiser-destroyer force to finish the battle with Ozawa.

What turned Halsey around was a message from his commander, Nimitz, that culminated a series of messages in a crescendo of desperation from Admiral Kinkaid relating the crisis posed by Kurita's attack and asking for, then demanding, cover and assistance. Kinkaid had made inquiries and sent search planes to ensure that San Bernardino was covered, but communication was slow and the searches were inadequate. Essentially, Kinkaid had relied on Halsey to ensure it. His pleas ran from "REQUEST" to "URGENTLY NEED" to the imperative "WHERE IS LEE [admiral commanding the battleship force] SEND LEE." In response Halsey shifted objectives for McCain's carrier group from Ozawa to Kurita, but that was all. Topping Kinkaid was the question from Nimitz: "WHERE IS REPEAT WHERE IS TASK FORCE 34 [the battleship force]."[152] The message, following standard procedure, was bracketed with additional unrelated phrases regularly used to confound enemy codebreakers. In this case the communication ended with an unfortunate phrase of cryptogram padding, "THE WORLD WONDERS," which should have been deleted from the transcribed message. Error or not, Halsey recognized that Nimitz held him responsible for the protection of the beachhead and that he must go south. In deep despair and anger, he threw his cap to the floor and began cursing. An hour after receipt of the Nimitz message, two hours in extra sailing time north and south, Halsey ordered the turnaround, following a slowdown to fuel the destroyers. Kurita beat Halsey to San Bernardino Strait by over three hours. Long-distance strikes by McCain's and Bogan's groups did no serious damage to the Center Force.

Meanwhile, Mitscher's planes went after Ozawa's force off Cape Engaño in northern Luzon during the morning and afternoon of the Twenty-Fifth. The *Zuikaku*, veteran of Pearl Harbor and the Marianas, took three simultaneous torpedo hits, settled for several hours, and sank. The *Chiyoda*, abandoned, was finally sunk by American cruiser fire. The *Zuiho* was hard to sink. It took forty planes during one onslaught and twenty-seven in a following attack after that until the *Zuiho* sank at 3:26 p.m. that afternoon. All four carriers were sunk by the end of the day. The battleships, *Ise* and *Hyuga*, elderly and damaged but tough and elusive, with the cruiser *Oyoda*, escaped to Japan.[153] Carrier and Air Force sweeps of the islands in the following days eliminated a few remnant cruisers and destroyers of the Kurita, Nishimura, Shima, and Ozawa forces.

Altogether, the Japanese navy lost three battleships, four carriers, ten cruisers, and eleven destroyers in the Battle of Leyte Gulf, amounting to a total of over 300,000 tons.[154] The battle ensured American sea and air control over the Philippines archipelago and opened the China seas to American domination. All this came in spite of American misjudgments and mismanagement, intolerably slow messaging, and feeble interfleet and interservice coordination. In the end, however, amplitude in capability on the American side and disintegration in the Japanese navy dominated the outcome. Notable on the American side was the importance of the torpedo throughout: in the submarine attacks on the Kurita force off Palawan; in the aerial onslaught against the *Musashi*; in the destroyer attacks during the Battle of Surigao Strait; in the destroyer and escort carrier attacks off Samar; and in the sinking of Ozawa's carriers.

The Japanese navy, what was left of it, sought to right the balance in weaponry on the last day of the Battle of Leyte Gulf and the following day, when it began regular use of kamikazes, this time against Taffy Groups 1 and 3. In Taffy 3, which had just lost the *Gambier Bay* to Kurita's ships, the *St. Lô* was sunk, and two more escort carriers were damaged so severely that they went to the West Coast for repair and did not return. In Taffy 1, which at the start of the battle had been far to the south, off northern Mindanao, three escort carriers were damaged seriously enough for West Coast repair, and one withdrew to Manus for repair.[155] In effect four carriers were lost, and three were out of action for a prolonged period. The Americans had demonstrated their ability to conduct sustained operations within the region Imperial Headquarters deemed vital to Japan's security but would have to endure the near constant peril of kamikaze attacks in order to remain there. The Japanese no longer had a navy that could defeat the Americans but still had one that could inflict serious damage. Meanwhile, on shore, the Americans were attempting to establish a staging area for future operations closer to Japan. The liberation of the Philippines was under way.

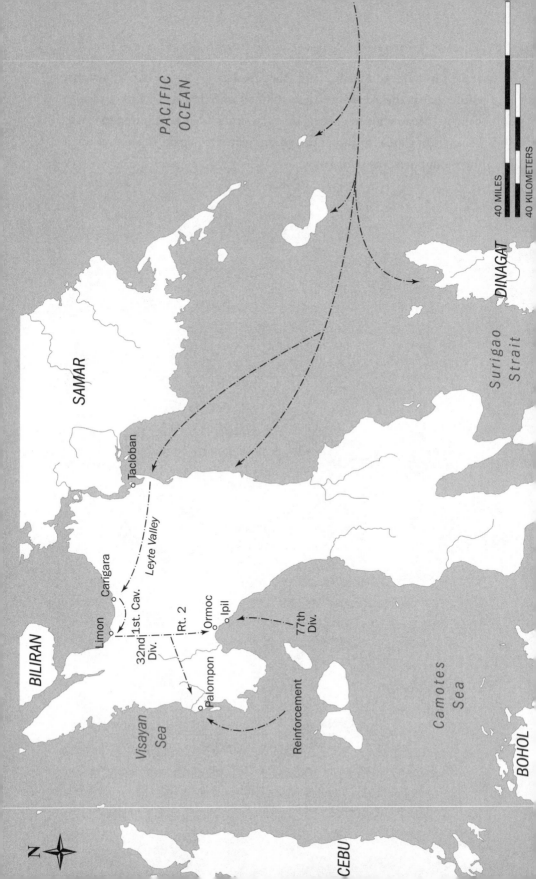

PACIFIC
OCEAN

SAMAR

DINAGAT

Surigao
Strait

Tacloban

Leyte Valley

Carigara

Limon

1st. Cav.

Rt. 2

Ormoc

Ipil

77th
Div.

32nd
Div.

Palompon

Reinforcement

BILIRAN

Visayan
Sea

Camotes
Sea

BOHOL

CEBU

N

40 MILES

40 KILOMETERS

5

Leyte to Manila,
October 1944–March 1945

n the afternoon of October 20, 1944, General MacArthur, amid a retinue of staff and correspondents, got out of a landing craft and splashed ashore to the island of Leyte to announce to the world his return to the Philippines. Ignoring warnings and orders of the beach control boat, the supreme commander's whaler had plowed ahead into a submerged sandbar, where it stuck some fifteen yards from the beach. He stepped into water up to his knees and struck out for the shore, cameras to the right and cameras to the left. As the party disappeared from sight, the crew of the control boat lost themselves in "unbuttoned hilarity." "They didn't tell me," said a sailor, "that he could walk on water."[1] After chatting awhile with soldiers and commanders and getting soaked top-down by a cloudburst, MacArthur walked to a weapons carrier with a radio and microphone to send his message. He began, "People of the Philippines, I have returned.... Rally to me." The message, transmitted to the

■ **Map 6** Leyte Operations, October–December 1944. Drawn by George Chakvetadze.

cruiser *Nashville,* was retransmitted throughout the Philippines and then re-peated in a message to the United States.

MacArthur's return had been universally established in spite of unex-pected difficulties and serious problems, which were a constant in the battle for Leyte. One was the American conviction that the decisive battle for the Philippines would be fought on Luzon, with Manila, Manila Bay, the culti-vated Central Valley, and the modern road system as the prize. The Japanese army did not share that view. Accordingly, they would not invest heavily in Leyte, which was merely a stepping stone. However, the Japanese navy had concluded that Leyte must be the place for the decisive battle and claimed success in that battle; now the Japanese army would have to do its part. The army considered the matter and concluded that it could not hold Luzon for long with American airpower planted on Leyte and began sending rein-forcements there. The Americans initially landing on Leyte faced only one Japanese division, with attachments, the total amounting to around 20,000 men. To MacArthur, who was landing four divisions on Leyte with two more in reserve, consisting of 202,500 men, taking the island would be a quick show.[2] Allied intelligence was in the dark about reinforcements be-cause the Japanese were installing new encryption systems in the army code. The Americans did not regain access to coded Japanese communications until mid-November and received only tidbits from other decryptions.[3] Enemy troop barges, transports, and destroyers slipped down to Leyte from Manila or from nearby Panay at night undetected, often shrouded by storm clouds.

A second unexpected difficulty was the weather. From September until spring the northeast trade winds bring heavy rains to Leyte, and beginning in October the island is subject to typhoons (the Pacific equivalent of hur-ricanes).[4] These powerful storms generally originate in the Marshall Islands and roll west, north of the equator. In the vicinity of the Palau Islands they tend to turn northwest to strike the northern Philippines and continue to Southeast Asia or curl north past Okinawa.[5] MacArthur's headquarters was well aware of these weather threats. They could only hope that the mon-soon would be short and light and the typhoons would pass elsewhere; postponement was unthinkable.

Leyte is an irregular island, 110 miles from northern to southern tip. Some have compared it to a human torso: short legs, thin waist, wide chest, and with a sort of wing off the right, western, shoulder. On its northeast side Leyte nudges the island of Samar, separated from it by a river-sized strait. Below the waist the island is mountainous and remote; in 1944 it was unoccupied by the Japanese, so the fight for it would take place above the waist in an area about forty by fifty miles square. The Americans landed along the northeast shore of Leyte and spread out across the low, flat land to the north and west. This was swampy rice-growing country, fed by innumerable streams carrying runoff from the mountain chain in the southwest, which rises abruptly from the plain to 3,000 or 4,000 feet. To the west, beyond the mountain barrier, lies a valley forming a strategic corridor between Ormoc Bay, south of the aforementioned wing, and Carigara Bay, north of it, a sort of hinge of the wing. The wing itself, western Leyte, is a jumble of precipitous hills, dense forests, rocky ridges, and cultivated land. Leading the American assault was the Sixth Army, under General Krueger, which now boasted two corps commands—the X Corps with two divisions from the Southwest Pacific and the XXIV Corps with two from the Central Pacific, supplemented in reserve by one division from each theater. The two corps would take different paths from the beachhead, the X Corps heading northwest alongside the mountain chain toward Carigara Bay and the northern end of the Carigara-Ormoc corridor and the XXIV Corps heading south and west, wheeling toward the Ormoc end of the corridor.

The landing, covering twenty miles of the east coast of Leyte, began at 10:00 a.m. and quickly placed the four divisions ashore.[6] As usual, the Japanese skillfully prepared defensive positions on solitary hills and foothills and at strategic villages and bridges. In one instance, they occupied aboveground crypts in a cemetery, drilling gun ports through the stone. The Americans responded with flamethrowers.[7] Though, as usual, the Japanese fought to the death, their strongpoints on Leyte were few and far between and subject to heavy American artillery fire. The Sixth Army moved steadily forward, and as steadily taking casualties, about 3,500 by November 1, and cursing the weather.[8] Rain, intermittent in the first days after the landing, grew in intensity and then seemed never to stop. Carl

F. Brandt, a medical officer in charge of a detachment for care of the sick and wounded at the battalion level, kept a diary that provides a striking picture of infantry combat on Leyte, in particular that of the First Battalion, Thirty-Fourth Infantry, Twenty-Fourth Division, the Army division on Hawaii at the time of Pearl Harbor and a participant in the Hollandia assault.[9] Rain began on October 22, Brandt notes, and continued the following day. On October 26 it was "terrific," flooding foxholes. In the next days it was raining hard and then pouring "furiously," and "like hell." On October 30 it became "a genuine typhoon." Again, it "poured steadily" all day November 8 and "turned into a typhoon" on November 9 with "terrific winds." It was again "raining like hell" on November 15, continued raining the next day, and rained "constantly" the next. In two months, Leyte was subject to three typhoons and thirty-five inches of rain. One result of the move up Leyte Valley was what Brandt calls "bad feet." Only once in ten days, sleeping under the roof of a church, was he able to take his shoes off. Soaked from water in the foxhole at night and marching and fighting in broiling heat during the day, the skin of the feet shriveled and tore (maceration). About 100 men attended sick call October 30, and nineteen were evacuated, most for feet and fever. Hospitalization for fever required a temperature of 103 degrees.

The perpetual downpour was costly in many ways. On this operation at least, the Twenty-Fourth Division had company kitchens, delivering two meals a day—provided their vehicles were not stuck in traffic. The roads on Leyte were defenseless against the rain: the roadbeds dissolved into mud, and the thin pavement was broken to pieces. Drivers kept to the center to avoid the breakable edges, turning two-lane roads into one, which needed to be shared with village refugees. Since the rations on hand required cooking, a transport tie-up meant no dinner. One company had eighty men "violently sick" with food poisoning; diarrhea became a serious problem. In joining the battle of the ridges on November 10–11, Brandt reports: "No rations all day...and it is hard to walk far without resting." The battalion, without anything substantive to eat for fifty hours, was "in a state of semi-starvation." Finally transport planes parachuted packaged food to them: "It was quite exciting as the thirty-pound cases showered down with soldiers and visiting Filipinos running in all directions." They immediately prepared a meal, though as Brandt adds, "no one could eat much."[10]

The constant downpour had a devastating impact on the construction and improvement of airfields and thereby on the establishment of American airpower on Leyte. MacArthur's headquarters had adequate warning of the danger this posed: in a written report Colonel William J. Ely, a senior engineer, described the island's wet weather and water-logged "unstable" soil that was unsuitable for airfields. The island's poor bridges and inadequate road system created additional problems. Ely did not see how it was possible for the existing engineer battalions to construct adequate bases in time under these circumstances.[11] To MacArthur and his staff, postponement or cancelation of operations on Leyte was, of course, inconceivable. This was to be an all-Pacific panoply, gathering both fleets, MacArthur's and Nimitz's, and Army corps representing both theaters, the Southwest and Central Pacific, each with scheduled battles to prepare for after Leyte. It affirmed an American strategy in the Pacific that aimed to speed up by two months American progress toward Japan. Furthermore, Leyte moved MacArthur—from the photo op on October 20 onward—onto the world stage.

The construction took seemingly forever. The best airstrip was at Tacloban City, located in the northeast corner of Leyte. During the landing it became a supply dump. Unloading LSTs on Red Beach, north of Palo, where the Twenty-Fourth Division came ashore, proved impossible. The LSTs became stuck in shallow water under enemy fire, so the ships shifted north and unloaded on the Tacloban airstrip, next to the beach. General Kenney, infuriated, threatened to send in bulldozers to clear it, which had the intended effect; the LSTs withdrew from the airstrip. Further interruption of repairing the air base for invasion purposes occurred on October 25 during the battle off Samar, when Taffy planes, unable to land on their home carriers, scooted in to rearm and refuel. Twenty-five of the sixty-five planes were damaged while landing on the incomplete runway. Finally a layer of crushed coral topped by steel matting was laid on October 27. A squadron of Kenney's P-38 Lightning fighters landed at Tacloban, all safe but one, which nose-dived on a soft spot. Through November Tacloban improved, bit by bit, with its runway redirected and extended into the bay.

By November 9, dispersal areas were added, and radar and ground observer warning stations were installed. November 19 saw completion of the reconstruction of Dulag airfield and December 16 the completion of a new airfield alongside the beach at Tenauan, between Tacloban and Dulag. The Dulag field required the efforts of no fewer than three aviation engineer battalions. The number of American planes on Leyte, mostly fighters, gradually rose to 350, but it was not until December that this Leyte force became a leading factor in the air war. For two months airfield development on Leyte suffered not only from Japanese air attacks and the miserable weather but also from the commandeering of aviation engineer battalions by the Sixth Army in order to rebuild soupy inland roads.[12]

On November 2, twelve days after landing on Leyte, troops of the Twenty-Fourth Division entered Carigara, located on the northern shore of the island. The town was important as a junction—between the road from Tacloban and Dulag on the east coast and the route west along Carigara Bay. From there the road went around the mountain barrier and to the northern entrance of the corridor to Ormoc. Adding that corridor and Ormoc itself to what he already held in the north would be, as Krueger knew, effectively winning the island. However, the day before, November 1, the Japanese First Division had disembarked at Ormoc and soon headed north in truck convoys along the corridor toward Carigara Bay. This was an elite division drawn from the Kwantung Army in Manchuria and dispatched by way of Shanghai and Manila to Leyte. Along with elements of other divisions arriving at this time, the enemy added 13,500 troops to its force of 20,000 already on the island. American air attacks, limited by lack of bases, struck at the troop convoys (camouflaged by palm leaves) moving north along the corridor but without inflicting critical damage. The Japanese First Division joined with those forces already in the north for a major counterattack aimed at pushing the Sixth Army eastward back into the sea.

The Americans from the north and the Japanese from the south were racing to seize the corridor in the mountain barrier that runs northwest to southeast on Leyte, just south of Carigara Bay.[13] Here for two miles the range thins to a ridge with precipitous slopes on the seaward side, soon named Breakneck Ridge. The beach road from Carigara turns south and zigzags over the ridge and then down into Ormoc Valley adjoining the corridor. Eastward the ridge splays into a jumble of knobs, spurs, and declivities that, together with Breakneck, form a barrier to the corridor.

On November 3 American forces passed through a deserted Carigara and advanced westward along the shore of Carigara Bay toward the corridor from Ormoc. General Krueger planned to follow the road westward as far as Pinampoan, where it abruptly heads up the mountain barrier. Leading the way was the Thirty-Fourth Regiment's First Battalion with its medical detachment (and Carl Brandt with his diary). The advance was soon stopped by a blown-out bridge but resumed when amphibious vehicles ferried them across. As the troops settled in their perimeter for the night, a friendly fire artillery shell struck among them, immediately killing two and severely wounding six.[14] The next day, a mile or so farther, they reached a second blown-out bridge, this time heavily defended. Wading across the stream, the platoon leader was killed and the platoon sergeant fatally wounded. Nevertheless, the sergeant then directed fire from the middle of the stream so accurately that two enemy machine guns were silenced and a number of riflemen hit, opening the way for a crossing. Sergeant Charles E. Mower received the Congressional Medal of Honor posthumously.[15]

The Reconnaissance Troop of the Japanese First Infantry Division had dug in on the high ground to their left, where the hills came close to the beach. The First Battalion commander planned a flanking maneuver, sending troops above and behind the Japanese and down the draw, while those below who had crossed the stream would fight their way up the draw from the other side. This led to close-quarters engagement. Brandt, with his aid station next to the platoon sergeant briefing his troops, heard him "telling his weary, footsore, unshaven, hungry men that the only way to get the Japs out would be with bayonets." The result was a fight in a small space "about 100 feet long and 30 feet wide," with about thirty on each side. The Americans killed seventeen and lost ten.[16]

Meanwhile Company K of the Thirty-Fourth Regiment circumvented roadblocks by taking to the sea in amphibian tractors, landing near Breakneck Ridge and moving quickly inland. The company had not gone far before they met resistance from leading troops of the Japanese First

Division. Despite artillery fire guided by an accompanying spotter plane, the outlook for K Company worsened as the enemy force thickened and ammunition thinned. In the late afternoon the landing craft reappeared, and with a parting barrage the company withdrew.[17]

The Japanese First Division therefore gained control of the northern barrier to the Ormoc corridor before General Krueger could gather his forces for an attack. Lieutenant General Kataoka Tadasu, division commander, hastened forward with his leading regiment and personally ordered blocking action against the American columns moving along the shore toward the mountain barrier. Immediately the Japanese began digging an elaborate defense system on the heights. The Sixth Army and X Corps had to reconceive and refashion their widely spread-out advance into a concentrated push into and down the corridor. The Thirty-Fourth Regiment was the principal force on the spot, but it was exhausted by the fight from the previous day. The Sixth Army had landed with over 12,000 men but had lost 1,000 casualties during the advance to Carigara and more every day from illness and tropical trench foot.[18]

Coming to relieve the Thirty-Fourth on November 4 and 5 was the third regiment of the Twenty-Fourth Division, the Twenty-First, which had landed at the southern tip of Leyte and encountered little resistance. The Twenty-First would reconnoiter Breakneck on November 6 and attack south on November 7. The coastal road along Carigara Bay, according to the commander of the Twenty-Fourth Division, was too fragile to carry the supplies needed for an offensive, and sure enough it collapsed into a bog with the next storm. Henceforth the troops would have to depend on seaborne supply by landing craft and parachute drops.

There was another concern: papers from a dead Japanese soldier indicated that the reinforcement through Ormoc was part of a planned offensive eastward to drive the Sixth Army back to its beaches and destroy it. This raised in General Krueger's mind the possibility that with American airpower barely functioning from Leyte, such a large and decisive operation might also include a landing in Carigara Bay, which was closer to Manila than Ormoc and which indeed the Japanese had considered for a landing. In spite of advice from Seventh Fleet officers that the Japanese probably did not have either the equipment or experience for an amphibious landing, Krueger arranged corps and division artillery so that it could be turned from mountain to seaward firing and ordered attention to beach defenses. He did this rather than attacking the heights before the Japanese could finish their defenses; at any rate, success would have been doubtful. Against a fresh Japanese division, who were trucked and not trudging into battle and were occupying higher ground, the Thirty-Fourth Regiment would probably have failed to break through the barrier on November 3 and 4. In any case, despite a typhoon, a fresh regiment, the Twenty-First, attacked the heights on November 7.[19]

Each day for three days the battalions of the Twenty-First Regiment and one of the Nineteenth pressed forward and upward, met stiff resistance, and returned to their points of departure. As usual, the Japanese defenses were well hidden and situated and the Japanese First Division soldiers "vicious fighters."[20] Heavy rain persisted, misting the terrain; maps were hopelessly inaccurate, and even Filipino guides lost their way. Trails up the steep slopes were slick with mud. Nevertheless, for Lieutenant General Franklin Sibert, X Corps commander, time was wasting. He relieved the regimental commander.[21]

Finally, on November 10, the Twenty-First Regiment, in a coordinated divisional attack plan, pushed south on the highway and western flank of the ridge and held the ground gained. That night and the next morning, corps and division artillery, as well as 4.2-inch mortars firing incendiary white phosphorous shells, bombarded the enemy and paved the way for more gains. Protected by infantry to the west, a company of tanks charged up the road to the crest and started down the other side, destroying some twenty-five automatic weapons positions along the way. Now Japanese resistance began to slack. By November 15, though the Japanese retained some spurs and ridges to the east, the regiment was over the mountain barrier and approaching the village of Limon on the valley floor of the Ormoc-Carigara corridor. The Twenty-First Regiment was exhausted, with its companies averaging 42 percent of their official strength. On November 16, after ten days of murderous battle, the Twenty-Fourth Division was relieved by the Thirty-Second Division, the X Corps reserve that had just arrived on Leyte.[22]

The conquest of Breakneck Ridge was the centerpiece but not the only objective of the Twenty-Fourth Division. No less important were two flanking advances. The division sent the Second Battalion, Nineteenth Regiment, circling southward along steep jungle trails around Kataoka's eastern flank and then westward to the Ormoc corridor, where it set up a roadblock next to the highway from the south supplying the Japanese forces at Breakneck. For eleven days the battalion held out against repeated attacks, calling in artillery fire, interrupting enemy reinforcements, and diverting supplies.[23] Carrying out the wounded was practically impossible. According to the division operations report, these were "bearded, mud-caked," emaciated soldiers; when relieved, nearly 250 men entered the hospital for "skin disorders, foot ulcers, battle fatigue, and sheer exhaustion."[24]

Above and a mile west of the roadblock was the First Battalion, Thirty-Fourth Regiment, which had come from the opposite direction in a circuitous route west along the shore in a landing craft and then south over the ridgeline, across an interior valley, and east onto a long, straight elevation facing northeast named Kilay Ridge, after a Filipino guide who had been killed. Looking northward, the valley 900 feet below and its surrounding ridges formed a bowl. The road south from Breakneck Ridge wound down into the valley at the village of Limon and thence ran straight south along the corridor to Ormoc. With the battle being waged practically at its feet, Kilay was an ideal site for directing artillery fire. Observers now could pinpoint camouflaged artillery and troops on the back slopes of the hills along the corridor. The battalion's own machine guns and mortars were firing at them too. At the village of Consuegra, west of the ridge, the battalion found Filipino litter-bearers, porters, and a unit of the guerrillas for protection of its supply route. Brandt noted in his diary that the bearers were "fantastically strong for their size," carrying the wounded "through all the mud and hills five miles back to Consuegra with hardly a jar or jolt and rarely a break." There a portable initial surgery unit prepared them for travel downriver in a tractor amphibian to the sea and back to base.[25]

The feeling of at last having gained an advantage soon began to dissipate. The fourth night on the ridge, when rumor passed that the Thirty-Second Division would relieve remaining troops of the Twenty-Fourth, someone responded, "Lord, I hope it's soon." By now the battalion had spent a month in foxholes, and it seemed to rain constantly. Cases of fever were frequent; diarrhea and macerated feet reflected normal conditions. Worst was the fact that they could feel that the Japanese were watching them, and waiting. Except for its supply route, the battalion was surrounded. Intervals between defensive positions seemed too far apart; the battalion was occupying too much ground with too few men. The line companies below, defending the ridge, withdrew one by one to the top, and the enemy followed. Overhead came the frequent "cracking" and "zipping" of bullets from the ridge opposite, and once American time-fire shells burst right over them. The roster diminished to 64 percent of full strength and then to about 50 percent. Platoons were down to twelve to fifteen men, companies to sixty to seventy.[26] As the fighting came to close quarters, smaller weapons came into use: bayonets, grenades, and the Japanese saber and knee mortar. Men's clothing and mud, "foul beyond description . . . are blown deeply into the wounds by grenades." At headquarters area, where the American dead were buried in shallow graves because of the high level of groundwater, there was "a rather putrid smell in the air."[27]

At Breakneck, neither relief nor reinforcement came. The Twenty-First Regiment was rapidly thinning out to a company average of one officer and eighty-five men.[28] On November 15, the Thirty-Second Division took operational control of the orphan flanking battalions, but orders came to hold the ridge without reinforcement, as none was available. No officer was sent to examine the situation. Now there was "no mail, in or out," and "everyone is digging deeper." Soldiers got "jittery," especially among the wounded, because of their helplessness. Most of the battalion was sinking into a "dull, stale, apathetic state." "Wanting to get off this hill is one of the greatest wants I've ever had," Brandt wrote in his diary. "At times it even supersedes wanting to go home." Finally, after the battalion commander, Lieutenant Colonel Thomas E. Clifford, Jr., had informed division that "without reinforcements we'd be off this ridge altogether," a battalion of the 128th Infantry Regiment arrived, and on December 4 and 5 the exhausted battalion returned to base.[29] The two-week missions won the two flanking battalions Presidential Unit Citations.[30]

By December 7, 1944, the third anniversary of Pearl Harbor, Breakneck Ridge and the mountain barrier had been secured. General Kataoka and his division had held off the Thirty-Fourth and Twenty-First Regiments and slowed the entire Thirty-Second Division for a month, inflicting 1,498 battle casualties. When the Thirty-Second Division entered the Ormoc corridor, the battle for Leyte had at last reached a tipping point—in favor of the Sixth Army. Leyte remained a staging area for further operations in the Philippines, with combat units arriving and then immediately being shunted into battle. By December a front had formed along the north–south mountain chain, in the following order from the north to Ormoc Bay: Thirty-Second Division, 112th Independent Cavalry Regiment, First Cavalry Division, Twenty-Fourth Division, Ninety-Sixth Division, Thirty-Eighth Division (one regiment), Eleventh Airborne Division, Seventh Division, and Seventy-Seventh Division. This amounted to seven divisions and two regiments in action, the largest single American battle force thus far assembled in the Pacific war. Furthermore, from late November to mid-December engineer battalions finally completed construction, steel matting, and extension of the three major airfields on Leyte, Tacloban, Dulag, and Tenauan. By December 14 they could service 317 fighters, assisted by the eight squadrons of bombers that now operated out of Angaur in the Palaus. More airpower was needed, but Leyte was no longer vulnerable to Japanese attack from their Philippine bases.[31]

As the engineers made headway on the airfields, in early December the Seventy-Seventh Division landed on Leyte's western shore and joined the battle for Ormoc. The Seventy-Seventh arrived by way of a very circuitous route that owed much to MacArthur's chronic tendency to underestimate the strength of the enemy. Initially, after completing the Guam campaign, the Seventy-Seventh's next assignment was to join the XXIV Corps in taking the island of Yap (in the western Carolines) as well as Ulithi. Then the Corps assignment shifted to Leyte with the Seventh and Ninety-Sixth Divisions and the Seventy-Seventh in reserve. MacArthur requested that the vessels that would have been used to transport the Seventy-Seventh be sent to load one of his Southwest Pacific divisions that was "ready, fresh, and has studied the target area." Since that transport group was too small for a Southwest Pacific division, he added, perhaps some of the ships carrying the First Marine Division to Peleliu could be used as well and then returned to the Marines after the Leyte operation.[32] What MacArthur in fact wanted was ships, not troops, and he was thinking beyond Leyte, which he expected would be a pushover. On October 29, shortly after the invasion of Leyte, MacArthur informed Nimitz that the Seventy-Seventh would not be needed. The division, which had been studying a possible landing at Ormoc, now set sail from Guam for rest and rehabilitation on New Caledonia (New Zealand). On November 10, MacArthur, under pressure from General Krueger, retreated, now asking for the Seventy-Seventh, and Nimitz agreed. The convoy, four days from New Caledonia, turned around and after a stop at Manus headed for Leyte, where it arrived on November 23. The division joined battle December 7 with an amphibious landing on the eastern shore of Ormoc Bay. Much of its equipment had been left at Guam.[33]

Major General Andrew D. Bruce was in command of a thoroughly trained and battle-hardened division in the Seventy-Seventh. He believed that the heaviest possible concentration of fire and forward momentum would be successful and imbued his troops with that confidence. The advance, however, was not monolithic but instead a combination of assault and maneuver, flanking and splitting the enemy according to terrain and the nature and size of the defense, so that the Japanese became confused and uncoordinated in their defense. The Seventy-Seventh traveled in medium-sized landing craft from Leyte Gulf south through Surigao Strait and north to a beach four miles southeast of Ormoc and seven miles north of the Seventh Division's location.

The landing met little resistance, and Bruce, knowing that speed was essential, took command ashore less than three hours after it began. Landing craft emptied quickly because supplies had been preloaded aboard tracked amphibian vehicles that had landed and joined the immediate march north. The Seventh Division, moving north from behind the Seventy-Seventh, would provide protection of the rear so that Bruce would not have to commit his infantry to defending a fixed base; he could "roll up his rear" and use all three regiments in the attack.[34] He knew that the Japanese might be waiting in strength at Ormoc, but indications were that they would be unprepared. The division was fortunate that the Japanese Twenty-Sixth Division, then engaging the Seventh Division, had been ordered east to provide infantry strength in an air-ground scheme for the destruction of American airfields and planes on Leyte. Coming by air would be demolition teams and parachuting infantry. The Japanese Twenty-Sixth together with the Japanese Sixteenth Division would attack the cluster of airstrips ten miles inland from Dulag as well as Tacloban and Dulag. The project was a failure: the airstrips had been abandoned; the demolition raiders crashed or missed the strips, only a portion of the infantry arrived, and few straggled back; communication and coordination failed. However, the parachute troops did create confusion among the American Air Force and service personnel until infantry units in the vicinity arrived and eliminated the intruders.[35]

Facing rising resistance, the Seventy-Seventh Division pushed hard to the edge of Ormoc. That critical town, with its long concrete-and-piling pier, became the division's target on December 10, the fourth day of the operation, and it was taken—entirely occupied—that day. The attack began with a storm of explosives: the guns of two divisional artillery battalions, self-propelled howitzers, white phosphorus and shrapnel mortars, self-propelled howitzers, rocket firing landing craft, and an inferno of detonating ammunition and gasoline dumps. Following were the infantry of the 307th Regiment with their own weapons, clearing the city of the Japanese, house by house. Bearing down from the right was the 306th Regiment, the two of them squeezing the enemy west, as the official history put it, "like a tube of toothpaste."[36]

Standing on a rise just north of Ormoc, across the river that formed its western boundary, was a stone house so reinforced with concrete as to be a blockhouse, held by the Japanese Imabori Detachment. This minifortress dominated a defense system standing between the Seventy-Seventh in Ormoc and the highway north up Ormoc Valley. It had to be taken. The Americans reorganized and resupplied on December 10 and then the next day swung north, attacking from both sides of the river that formed the western boundary of the town. The Americans met heavy gunfire all along the line from light artillery, mortars, machine guns set five yards apart, firing only at point-blank range, and a host of spider holes, all expertly camouflaged. Counterattacks led to an hour of intense close-in fighting.[37] When it became apparent that the cost in casualties would be too high, the battalions were withdrawn.[38] The Seventy-Seventh Division needed the tanks it had left at Guam when it departed for New Caledonia.

On December 13, after a day of reconnaissance and repositioning, the division advanced and attacked again, this time with greater extension on the left flank, which would later turn into an envelopment to the north. The day began with an artillery barrage so intense that the stunned Japanese mistakenly moved toward the Americans' front lines, where they were mowed down. The Japanese persisted, mounting five counterattacks, all of which failed, with heavy casualties on both sides.[39] One platoon of K Company, 305th Regiment, dropped from fifty-two to eleven men within minutes.[40] For seven hours chemical mortars maintained a smoke screen so that the wounded could be removed. Both sides had lost heavily, but the Japanese, after those repeated counterattacks in the face of American artillery, were badly weakened.

The blockhouse was the focus of an attack on December 14. Shellfire had removed the camouflage, and the blade of an armored bulldozer had sliced off the top of the hole leading to the inside. Riflemen used flamethrowers and grenades. One by one the blockhouse's outlying spider holes were destroyed. In its vicinity the Americans found 633 dead Japanese, a fifth of the over 3,000 Japanese who died in the Ormoc battle. The Seventy-Seventh's casualties were 421.[41] Now the division moved forward and on December 16 captured Cogon and the nearby road junction. Ormoc was sewn up in nine days, and the highway north lay open.

On December 17 the 305th Regiment set out on Highway 2 for Valencia, seven miles north at the center of the Ormoc Valley, a likely place, it was determined, for the Japanese to make a stand. The regiment met Japanese resistance here and there along the road but no organized defense, so it pushed on and formed its perimeter for the night about half way to Valencia. Meanwhile the other regiments embarked on an envelopment from the west: the 306th drove west by road two miles, turned north, and circled east to join the highway north of the 305th, while the 307th went four miles before turning north and headed directly for Valencia: three and then two parallel regimental drives converging on the town. The flanking regiments laboriously trekked through rice paddies, up to their knees and waists in mud while lugging ammunition and weapons. Filipinos helped by carrying supplies. The 307th arrived at the Valencia airstrip the same day. The 306th, also hiking though paddies, met more resistance from Japanese fleeing north from assault by the 305th and the artillery fire accompanying it. The envelopment was working well. Food and ammunition moved quickly to the distant regiments by means of an armored column that speeded north past all resistance.[42] The one-day Seventy-Seventh drive was successful not only in taking the center of communications in western Leyte but also in slicing through its system of defense.

Meanwhile, to the north the Thirty-Second Division, after taking the village Limon, had entered what might be described as the throat of the Carigara-Ormoc corridor, a highway running straight south, enclosed by jungle and parallel ridges, an ideal place for the remnants of General Kataoka's First Division to mount a defense. With hardly any room for maneuver in the corridor, the Thirty-Second could only launch one bloody assault after another, with the gain measured in yards.[43] Angered by the lack of any replacements, Major General William Gill, the commander, had told Krueger on December 6 that he needed more men and that the Thirty-Second was "too short now to do the job that I have to do. They must get me replacements." The Sixth Army on Leyte did carry replacements, just over 5,000 in all, but they were untrained and far fewer than the 19,000 Krueger had requested before the invasion.[44] By December 18 the Thirty-Second Division was about three miles south of Limon and still thirteen miles from Valencia. General Sibert decided to switch divisions and put the First Cavalry in the lead. That division, which had been fighting its way across the mountain range on the left of the Thirty-Second, now moved down onto the highway ahead of it. The Seventy-Seventh in turn moved another five miles north, to the key junction of the highway with the road to Palompon, a town on the west coast and the last Japanese port of entry. From that junction Bruce sent the 306th Regiment north along the Ormoc corridor, meeting the Twelfth Regiment, First Cavalry, near the village of

Kananga, on December 22. Finally X and XXIV Corps closed the gap, completing encirclement of the island.[45]

Next came the capture of Palompon. As the 306th Regiment went north, the 305th marched into western Ormoc Valley and the rugged hills bordering the Camotes Sea. One after another the Japanese had destroyed the bridges, and as there weren't enough prefabricated Bailey bridges, replacement was taking time. Furthermore, as the regiment moved west into the hill country, it met growing organized resistance. Bruce therefore planned an amphibious operation, seizing Palompon from the sea. One battalion and later a second took the town without a fight and pressed east along the road, threatening the enemy's rear. When the eastward- and westward-bound forces met on December 31, Japanese resistance on Leyte effectively collapsed. The Seventy-Seventh Division's campaign proved critical in bringing the land battle on Leyte to a conclusion, but the speed of it did not lower casualties, putting it third among the divisions that had suffered the most casualties, and with about two months' less combat than the Twenty-Fourth and Seventh Divisions.[46]

Disintegration of the Japanese command structure did not mean the end of fighting, which continued at the local level with heterogeneous units in the rough country north and south of Palompon. The Sixth and later the Eighth Army organized sweeps through the countryside with divisions abreast, widely deployed. Contact with the Japanese led to concentration of force and fierce engagements, which, while diminishing, nevertheless extended all the way into May 1945. The MacArthur headquarters used the term "mopping up" for this phase, but for the infantry experiencing it the term belittled a task that was life-threatening and exhausting. In his memoir, Staff Sergeant William T. McLaughlin described his experience as a member of the Reconnaissance Troop of the American Division engaged in "mopping up" on Leyte. Scouting ahead of the infantry, the troop ran into a Japanese ambush. Awaiting the arrival of the infantry company sent in reinforcement, the troops, he wrote, "sat by the trail all wrung out as the dogfaces came up armed with machine guns, bazookas and all the paraphernalia of their trade. They were as seedy as combat soldiers usually look, but they looked beautiful to us. Their green uniforms hung on their dehydrated

frames and they bent under the weight of machine guns, mortars, bando-
liers, and hand grenades." McLaughlin remembered that there was no
joking as they passed through. "We were too strung out to be humorous
and they knew they were going to bloody work." He said he finally understood there "why men fresh from combat seemed to have such staring
eyes."[47]

MacArthur may have come ashore on October 20 to assume direct com-
mand of the Leyte campaign, but mostly he stood aloof. In the preparation
stage for Leyte he had keenly enjoyed traveling aboard the light cruiser
Nashville to the Morotai and Leyte landings. However, as soon as Admiral
Kinkaid learned of the upcoming naval battle at Leyte he insisted that the
supreme commander disembark so the warship could be used in battle.
Reluctantly MacArthur went ashore to a brick-and-concrete house in
Tacloban. Now and again he met with General Krueger at Sixth Army
Headquarters, ten miles down the coast but rarely if ever visited the troops
during the weeks ahead. Despite occasional near misses from Japanese
bombing and strafing, he could be seen on his veranda, striding back and
forth, puffing on his signature corncob pipe. He seemed above the fray.[48]

MacArthur's calm demeanor did not mean that he was pleased with
progress. He had placed command responsibility on Krueger, approving
his requests but making it plain that he was dissatisfied with the slow pace
of the Sixth Army advance. Krueger did not need prodding. He had been
pressing the X Corps commander, General Sibert, for more speed. Sibert
had, as we've noted, relieved a colonel in the Twenty-Fourth Division in the
presence of the division commander, Major General Frederick Irving, and
later relieved the general himself. Irving had launched the two battalion end
runs that had earned him presidential citations. Nonetheless, there had
been differences between the commanders over whether and how the advance could be hastened. The dismissal of Irving, who was well liked and
respected in the division, was immediately seen as a mistake. MacArthur
himself told Lieutenant General Robert Eichelberger, the emerging Eighth
Army commander, that he was "sorry the action was taken."[49] When the
Thirty-Second Division replaced the Twenty-Fourth, Krueger soon found
the pace of the new Thirty-Second too slow. Even allowing for the

difficulties, he warned the division commander, Major General Gill, that "he was not pushing his regimental commanders hard enough" and his plans for Breakneck Ridge were too "defensive in tone." Gill should "pep that up a little so we'll get some results."[50]

In conversation with Eichelberger, MacArthur also vented his disgust at the funereal pace of the advance with negative remarks about several divisions. The Thirty-Second, he said, "had never been any good," and he was "very disappointed over the slow progress of the 77th and 7th."[51] MacArthur had never forgiven the performance of the hapless Thirty-Second, untried, ill-trained, and poorly supplied, at Buna, Papua New Guinea, in November 1942–January 1943. Now, however, the Thirty-Second was a substantially different division, though undermanned. Indeed, the Thirty-Second had played a crucial role in the final stage of the Breakneck Ridge battle. By late November, the Thirty-Second had endangered the Japanese western flank and forced Kataoka to shift his forces to protect his exposed position. This had created a gap along the Japanese First Division's eastern flank and allowed Gill's troops to drive through and threaten that division with complete collapse. This period, according to General Kataoka's chief of staff, "proved to be one of the most disastrous for the 1st Division."[52] To be sure, the Thirty-Second came to a dead stop deep in the Ormoc corridor, but only after almost 2,000 casualties, to say nothing of losses from disease and combat fatigue.[53] The Seventh, though no lightning division, appears to have fulfilled its missions. The division dispersed after securing the southern Leyte Valley. Three battalions dispatched to the Ormoc Gulf coast held their own under heavy attack until the Seventy-Seventh landed and initiated an advance that it would be absurd to describe as "slow."

MacArthur's misguided criticisms of the performance of his troops revealed his own poor understanding of the conditions in which they were operating. But these peevish remarks about his troops also suggest the tension and frustration he felt during late October and November in the face of multiple delays and postponements. His army was stuck, his air force sunk in mud, and his navy hounded by kamikazes. After the parade across New Guinea and the naval triumph off Leyte it was a shock to be stymied by the land battle on Leyte. The fast carriers were pressing to get away for recuperation and missions elsewhere, leaving MacArthur's navy with only the planes from the remaining six Taffy escort carriers and his air force slimmed down to one active group of fighters on one airfield, Tacloban. Luzon and redemption were so near yet still out of reach.

Like MacArthur, General Kenney had not expected heavy action on Leyte. The Japanese were "on the downhill grade" and would be saving their forces for Luzon, Formosa, or the home islands. However, Leyte did not turn out to be like New Guinea, where he had the upper hand. He had had no idea of the extent or effectiveness of the Japanese air reinforcement system for the Philippines. Even in the wake of the Leyte sea battles, planes had been moving from Kyushu to Formosa to the seventy or so airfields and airstrips on Luzon, and from the East Indies and Borneo to Cebu and Negros in the Visayas, providing significant threats from north and west to Leyte and vessels navigating among the islands. In addition to Japanese reinforcements was the new menace of kamikazes. There had been occasional suicide attacks before Leyte, most notably in the Battle of Leyte Gulf. At that time, Vice Admiral Onishi Takijiro had decided that only the most extreme measures stood a chance of stopping the United States Navy. Simply put, a plane making a crash dive was harder to stop than one on a bombing run. The Japanese navy officially adopted this frightening new weapon in October 1944. The creation of special suicide units was a mark of Japan's desperation, but it also vividly demonstrated to the Americans the lengths to which the Japanese were willing to go to defend their empire. The inauguration of these suicide missions had clear disadvantages, in that planes and pilots, usually inexperienced students, were lost after only one mission. But the willingness of pilots to aim their planes toward enemy ships regardless of antiaircraft fire increased the possibility for dramatic results.[54] The enemy was shifting tactics, too, attacking at night or at dawn or dusk. American night fighters had been too slow to catch the raiders, and the hills above Leyte Gulf blanked out their radar. Fighters at Tacloban took off at dawn and landed before dark, missing action elsewhere. In the weeks after the invasion, Kenney had been determined to do battle his way. He had brought in large numbers of planes before he had a system in place for directing them, resulting in heavy losses on the ground; he had insisted on developing all the airfields at once over engineers' advice to concentrate on Tacloban and Dulag, thus wasting time on sites with hopeless drainage problems.[55]

By late November, in this state of uncertainty and inadequacy, tempers flared, and exasperation turned to occasional infuriation. With fewer than 100 planes on his escort carriers, Admiral Kinkaid was depending on Halsey or Kenney for protection. Twice, November 27 and 29, kamikazes damaged a battleship and a destroyer in Leyte Gulf with heavy crew losses. According to Kinkaid, Kenney's planes had been assigned to protect and had failed to show up. He complained the first time. The second time he accused Kenney of not fulfilling his obligation. Kenney had explained that his planes could not get close enough because of antiaircraft fire. After Kinkaid's second accusation, Kenney angrily told Kinkaid to put it in writing so that he, Kenney, could prefer charges against Kinkaid for making false official statements. After the war Halsey sided with Kinkaid's view, recalling what he called Kenney's "failure to give Leyte effective air support," thus forcing Halsey to "stand by and attend to his knitting for him."[56]

Army-Navy relations were always tense in the Pacific. A major contribution was MacArthur and his Bataan staff's attitude of hostility toward the Navy. Naval officers scorned the Army, too, but not in the presence of Admiral Nimitz. In 1943 Captain Raymond D. Tarbuck, visiting Pacific Fleet headquarters on his way to join MacArthur's staff, mentioned in the presence of Nimitz that people seemed to be trying to prejudice him against the man to whom he would owe loyalty. He should "not have too much confidence in MacArthur," some said. The admiral leaped from his seat, pointed his finger at Tarbuck, and said, "Young man, that never came out of this office, and I want that strictly understood."[57]

What was clear, however, was that MacArthur would not be liberating Luzon until the Japanese land-based air offensive was beaten back. Following the October 25–27 American naval victories came the bitter weeks of November, when Japan kept feeding planes and one-way pilots down the flyway to the Luzon airfields. Their only obstacle was Admiral Halsey's fast carrier fleet, and that fleet, though continuing to inflict heavy losses on the enemy, was weakening from an unprecedented length of combat and sea duty without rest and refit, the piecemeal support of the Army Air Force, and the terrifying novelty of kamikaze warfare. Kamikaze pilots used dive-bombing, radical shifts of direction, or coming in at the ships just above the wave tops. They would attack singly or in a small group, pouncing on a single vessel in quick succession from widely different angles, overwhelming the defense.[58] With the constant need of its presence in battle or on guard, the carrier's stay at Ulithi was short and often interrupted, and since one or two of four task groups were continually headed to Ulithi or on their way back to the fleet, the American strikes thinned out. A prolonged mission meant repetition in launching locations and intervals between strikes, providing the enemy with clues for finding the carriers. Another path to the fleet was just following the last strike plane home. With fewer carriers in action, the size of the combat air patrol defending the carriers or the strike force itself had to be reduced.

The outcome was by no means one-sided: in a two-day strike in late November the carriers claimed that 439 Japanese planes had been destroyed. Nevertheless, the cost was high. Three fleet carriers, the *Franklin*, *Intrepid*, and *Lexington*, and two light carriers, the *Cabot* and *Belleau Wood*, had extensive damage. Three of them returned to the West Coast for repairs. This loss reduced the number of fast carriers in action from seventeen to twelve. In Halsey's judgment, the lesson was that "only strikes in great force for valuable stakes or at vital times would justify exposure of the fast carriers to suicidal attacks."[59]

Ahead lay the invasion of the principal objective, Luzon, the largest and most populous Philippine island and home to Manila. It would start with a preliminary seizure of Mindoro, a thinly inhabited island, about fifty miles at its widest point and a hundred long, lying only fifteen miles below southwestern Luzon. Mountains running north and south reaching 8,000 feet buttressed the west side against the easterly monsoons and typhoons. Blessedly drier, with promising airstrips, and barely garrisoned, Mindoro was an ideal stepping-stone to Luzon. The problem was lack of air protection for the assault and supply convoys. For MacArthur and his commanders there was now only one way to achieve command of the air over the Philippines and that was by means of the fast carrier fleet. Prior to the naval battles, he had pointed out that he was moving beyond his own land-based cover "predicated on full support by Third Fleet." That support was "essential and paramount." At the conclusion of the battles, Halsey responded cautiously that he would provide support at Leyte by October 27 but was "unable to provide any extended direct air support" on account of lack of munitions and pilot exhaustion. He asked when MacArthur's planes would take over.[60]

The general got his carriers; the admiral, however, set his limits. Nimitz recognized that they both faced a major strategic problem and opportunity. As Nimitz wrote to King, the enemy had "chosen to make a strong fight for the Philippines" on Leyte and by "committing much of his total air strength." Nimitz argued that this gave the Americans "an opportunity to inflict severe attrition on his air forces but not without some losses of our own ships and aircraft and heavy demands on the endurance of our personnel and material."[61] Attacks on the Japanese air force on Luzon would have to continue, either until MacArthur's land-based air force was fully in action or the enemy weakened. So a Luzon air battle was not only necessary but advantageous, in that the Japanese were concentrating their airpower in a position where it was open to destruction. Nimitz made clear his conditions. The carrier fleet absolutely required rest, repair, and replenishment at Ulithi. MacArthur had suggested placement of the fleet west of Luzon, standing between a conceivable enemy surface attack and his landings on Mindoro and Luzon. Nimitz responded that the fleet would stay east of Luzon, where it had sea room and proximity to seaborne replenishment and Ulithi yet could still intercept any such attack. A question therefore arose regarding protection of the Luzon landing. As soon as the old battleships completed their fire-support mission there, they would be withdrawn for fire support in the invasion of Iwo Jima. That landing depended on when MacArthur released them, and Nimitz asked him for an estimate, as durable as possible, of the date. The general replied they would "probably" be detached as planned, six days after the landing on Luzon, but suggested two fast battleships replace them with destroyer screen from the carrier fleet. Drily Nimitz replied that he did not envisage a situation that would require such a transfer.[62]

While this haggling was going on during the anxious weeks of November, the idea of postponing the landings on Luzon had taken hold. Rear Admiral Forrest Sherman, Nimitz's planner, who had flown to MacArthur's headquarters to work out Army-Navy arrangements for the use of the Philippines, painted a bleak picture in a report of November 4. General Kenney had admitted that he was unable to reach the Luzon airfields from which the Japanese attacks on Leyte came. Dulag, a second airfield on Leyte, would not be ready until November 15–20. The situation required, Sherman believed, fast carrier strikes on Luzon airfields, at least until then and indeed beyond, for "complete control of the air would be essential" in the Mindoro operation, set to begin December 5. Sherman added that the general opinion at Southwest Pacific headquarters was that a delay in the Lingayen landing on Luzon was inevitable. Indeed, all of MacArthur's commanders agreed on postponement.[63]

MacArthur stood alone in vowing to keep to the existing schedule. "The obvious intention of the enemy to make a strong fight for the Philippines can best be frustrated," he had written to Nimitz on November 16, "by immediate attack in strength to prevent his preparations for the defense of Luzon which he is pushing at top speed at the present time."[64] On November 17 Nimitz had set his terms bluntly. He was not prepared to accept—it was not "practicable"—laying on the fast carrier fleet the responsibility for cover and support of both the Mindoro and Luzon landings without adequate replenishment at Ulithi. He was prepared to furnish assistance in gaining air control during the Mindoro operation, provided the fast carrier forces secured ten days and preferably two weeks of rest and upkeep at anchor on Ulithi lagoon. The same period of replenishment would be required between the assault on Mindoro and that on Luzon.[65]

Having received no answer, Nimitz repeated the offer on November 29. First he advised MacArthur that Japanese naval forces left in southern waters were an odd lot of no great threat. He joined the rest of the Southwest Pacific headquarters in advising MacArthur to delay the Mindoro operation. The shore-based air forces needed time not just to arrive but also to establish in strength on Leyte, on the ground and in the air. At the same time, the carrier forces could recuperate and rearm at Ulithi. They had been at sea almost continuously for eighty-four days. Currently their need for carrier pilot replacements, said Nimitz, "had become critical." Then both the land-based and carrier forces could deliver powerful concurrent strikes, leading to air supremacy and protection for the assault on Mindoro.[66] Presumably the same sequence would occur in the Luzon assault. The Nimitz offer, which came with Halsey's support, provided precisely what MacArthur needed: the fast carrier fleet committed to support and cover during the critical phases of the Mindoro and Luzon landings.[67] On November 30 the general postponed the Mindoro landing from December 5 to December 15 and the Luzon landing from December 20 to January 9, 1945. These shifts had a ripple effect on later invasions, Iwo Jima and Okinawa, both postponed one month, and on shipping and staging schedules.

Still one more amphibious landing would come first: the transfer of the Seventy-Seventh Division from eastern Leyte by sea to Ormoc, feasible now because the postponement of Mindoro and Luzon freed the landing ships for that overnight trip. As we've noted, the Ormoc landing and drive north completed the encirclement and triggered the collapse of Japanese organized resistance on Leyte. As the unopposed landing and rapid unloading proceeded on December 7, a kamikaze force of about twelve bombers and four fighters appeared. Army interceptors from Tacloban downed three fighters. Nine dropped down to sea level and bored in on the destroyer *Mahan* at intervals of about 1,500 yards. Four were shot down by the ship's guns, one simply passed by, another missed and splashed, and three struck the destroyer, two in its side and one just behind the bridge. The battle was completed within four minutes. Because fires were spreading toward the forward magazine of the *Mahan* and the flooding controls were flooded, the captain ordered the crew to abandon ship. They would sink the ship with gunfire. Casualties—ten killed or missing and thirty-two wounded—were surprisingly low. The destroyer *Ward*, nearby, was the target of the last three kamikazes. Two splashed, but one struck its side and plunged into the boiler room. "A heavy explosion followed, a huge sheet of flame enveloped her amidships and broke into the troop space." The ship lost all power, was abandoned, and, like the *Mahan*, sunk by gunfire under orders. A few sailors were badly burned but otherwise there were no casualties.[68]

The record time in which the Seventy-Seventh Division unloaded the ships allowed the convoy to depart for the return trip shortly after 11 a.m. Again the kamikaze attacked the destroyer screen and destroyer transports, this time with four fighter planes. One splashed, a second and third exploded from destroyer gunfire, and a fourth coming in from dead ahead smashed into the *Liddle's* bridge, destroying communications and killing the captain. Thirty-six were killed or missing, and twenty-two were seriously wounded. Several kamikazes used a nearby small island to cover the first part of their attack. One reached the *Lamson*, weaving back and forth, hitting the second stack, and spinning into the radio shack. As Morison wrote, "flames flashed more than masthead high." The hatches jammed by the explosion sealed in the fire room crew, who burned to death. The rest gathered on the forecastle and stern for abandoning ship, but it was saved. Twenty-one of the crew were killed and fifty wounded out of about 300. During the voyage the twelve destroyers fired over 18,000 rounds of ammunition and gained assistance from Leyte of twelve P-38 fighters and a squadron of Marine Corsairs. Total casualties on the four ships were about 180.[69]

On December 8 and 9, the first resupply convoy for Ormoc went without attack or loss. The second run, on December 11, however, met an attack by ten kamikazes. Several of these were downed by the Marine patrol, but four attacked the destroyer *Reid*. One missed, and another was struck and exploded. One crashed on the bow and another on the port quarter. The bomb must have entered, for the *Reid* sank in two minutes with a huge underwater explosion, losing nearly half its crew of 255. On the return trip the *Caldwell* was simultaneously dive-bombed and crashed. One bomb broke through into No. 1 gun handling room, a second hit No. 2 gun mount, and the plane flipped, caught the bridge, and crashed on the radio room. Thirty-two were killed or missing and forty wounded. However, as terrifying as the kamikaze tactic was and as troubling the loss of three destroyers sunk and three under extensive repair (half the destroyer contingent) as well as several landing ships lost, the success of the Ormoc envelopment, breaking the back of Japanese resistance on Leyte, far outweighed the cost.[70] For the Japanese, the Mindoro assault quickly overshadowed Ormoc and indeed the whole Leyte operation.

Amphibious craft were already gathering for Mindoro for the December 14–15 invasion. The Twenty-First Regiment of the Twenty-Fourth Division, veterans of Breakneck Ridge, and the 503 Parachute Regiment, veterans of the mangled airdrop on Noemfoor in New Guinea, served as the ground force. They were conveyed in the same landing craft the Ormoc troops had used but now were more heavily protected in this venture by a screen of twelve destroyers, a cruiser flagship, and a covering force of three cruisers and seven destroyers. Protecting over the horizon in the Sulu Sea would be a powerful force consisting of three pre–Pearl Harbor battleships (mainly for their antiaircraft batteries), three cruisers, six escort carriers (Taffy 2 of the Battle of Samar), and eighteen destroyers—in short, the full array of Kinkaid's Seventh Fleet. The escort carriers would fill in whenever Kenney's fighters were unavailable on account of darkness or weather over Leyte.

Preparing for protection to the north was the fast carrier fleet. Following the Mindoro postponement and the MacArthur-Nimitz understanding about dates and restrictions, the fleet had savored an uninterrupted ten-day spell of rest and repair at anchor in Ulithi. This had helped them reorganize to improve performance in battle with the kamikazes. With carriers under repair, they strengthened the punch of the rest by consolidating the force into three instead of four task groups; and by reducing the number of their bombers and torpedo planes, they doubled the number of fighters aboard. To protect the fleet from kamikaze strikes they devised a sieve-like arrangement of radar picket destroyers and combat air patrol sixty miles ahead of the fleet, toward the Japanese. The fleet left Ulithi on December 11 to fulfill its assignment of three days of strikes on Luzon in support of the Mindoro assault. Here, too, tactics changed. The purpose was not to engage in air combat but to keep fighters over the Luzon airfields to prevent Japanese planes from taking off.[71] The plan was dubbed the Big Blue Blanket, blue being the American code color. Halsey made a claim, probably exaggerated, that in the three days and two nights, December 14, 15, and 16, they destroyed 270 planes, mostly on the ground. What counted most was that

Luzon-based attacks on Mindoro-bound American shipping were suppressed for those critical days.

Still, the Japanese were able to inflict damage. On December 13, the day before, the Attack and Heavy Covering Groups, approaching Mindoro on a southerly course through Philippine waters, not far from each other, were about to turn north around Negros Island into the Sulu Sea when they were attacked. Protecting above were thirty-five Marine Corsairs from Leyte and twelve planes from the escort carriers below. At 3 p.m. a kamikaze bomber slipped in behind the convoys and went right for the cruiser, the *Nashville,* the flagship of Rear Admiral A. D. Struble and a recent conveyor of General MacArthur. It struck just aft of the admiral's cabin, exploding two bombs, wrecking the bridge and communication centers, and igniting ready ammunition. Some of the crew were blown overboard. Killed were 133 officers and men, including the Army and Navy chiefs of staff for this operation, and 190 were wounded. The admiral, along with some fifty officers and war correspondents, transferred to a destroyer, whereupon the *Nashville* headed back to Leyte. That afternoon ten Japanese planes headed from Cebu. They were reduced by the combat patrol to three and by the battleship *West Virginia* and a destroyer to one plane, but that sole survivor swiped the bridge of the destroyer *Haraden.* Its bomb explosion knocked over the forward stack, spreading burning gasoline and broiling steam. Fires extinguished, the destroyer, too, returned to Leyte.

The landing on Mindoro on December 15 was unopposed. After months on Leyte, stable dry earth was a delight. With 1,200 soldiers from the Seventy-Seventh Division brought along to hasten the unloading, the convoy was under way for the return trip one day early. The fast carrier aircraft blanketed the Luzon airfields during the landing period, limiting kamikaze attacks to those from the Visayan Islands airfields. The first American airfield on Mindoro was ready in five days; the second opened for dry weather use on December 28, a week early, and work on a third was begun. P-38 and P-47 fighters, as well as P-61 night fighters, moved in immediately, followed by a stream of planes, building up to three fighter groups, two medium bomber groups, and two night fighter squadrons. To reach the ships, the kamikazes had to elude those fighters and the combat air patrol of the escort carriers, and few did.[72]

In spite of its gains, the Mindoro advance proved frustrating, and there were alarming signs. After the Halsey blanketing of the Luzon airfields on December 14–16, the fast carrier force retired east of Luzon to a rendezvous with its tankers and supply ships. Fueling was increasingly difficult in the face of rising wind and seas, but Halsey persisted, seeking calmer waters to complete it. Lacking any weather reporting system or local knowledge of the region's weather patterns, he had no idea that he was moving his fleet, spread over fifty by sixty miles of ocean, into the track of a powerful developing typhoon and, once in, had no idea how to get out. The larger ships survived the storm without critical damage, but 146 planes were lost aboard the carriers. Three destroyers, the *Hull, Spence,* and *Monaghan,* foundered and sank, resulting in the death of 793 officers and men. The fleet returned to Ulithi for repair, remaining until December 30. The Mindoro operation thereby lost its carrier fleet cover for at least ten days.[73]

In the latter part of December Kenney's fighters were moving from Leyte to Mindoro as the airfields on Mindoro were readied. As they still operated out of Leyte, they remained limited in the protection they could provide because of persistent bad weather and their inability to engage in dawn and dusk attacks. The escort carrier pilots were finding that their Wildcat fighters were not matching up to new kamikaze types. The Japanese were adding armor to their planes, improving attack maneuver, and maintaining extensive reconnaissance. At the same time American ships were finding their 5-inch antiaircraft guns with proximity fuses inadequate and were therefore relying more on smaller, more rapid fire and flexible 40 mm and 20 mm guns. What was most worrying about this evolution of suicidal air warfare was that destroying most or almost all of a kamikaze attack group did not constitute success: it took only one such plane to destroy a ship. In the Mindoro assault period, December 13–January 4, kamikazes sank or heavily damaged one light cruiser, two destroyers, five LSTs, and seven Liberty freighters, totaling sixteen ships. Lost were ammunition, TNT, rations, vehicles, construction materials, and aviation gasoline. A nonkamikaze night strike January 2 on Mindoro airfields took out twenty-two planes.[74]

On the map, where Luzon looks like a right-hand mitten, the gap between thumb and fingers is Lingayen Gulf. From the South China Sea, the Gulf reaches south about twenty-five miles to a twenty-mile stretch of sand beach. Rising abruptly from the eastern shore of the Gulf to 8,000 and 9,000 feet are the Cordillera Central Mountains, which keep the rain and storms from moving west. Running south from the Gulf is the Central Valley, roughly forty miles wide, of flat, cultivated, settled land, offering a network of hard-surfaced roads and even a railroad leading to Manila itself. Across that stretch of sand at the south end of the Gulf, MacArthur had a wide-open, straightaway approach to his objective. He was gathering an army for the largest assault landing in the Pacific war, the second largest in the entire war after Normandy.[75] By mid-December infantry were boarding ship at Manus in the Admiralties, Cape Gloucester on New Britain, Sansapor and Aitape on New Guinea, and New Caledonia and the Solomons in the South Pacific. Bases lining the New Guinea coast, from Milne Bay to Finschhaven, Hollandia, and Noemfoor, loaded ships with supplies, equipment, headquarters groups, and specialized troops. The divisions practiced landings, joined other groups in ever larger formations, moved on to Seeadler Harbor and Kossol Passage in the Palaus for refueling and rendezvous, and then headed for Leyte Gulf, from there to be inserted in the larger Luzon invasion scheme.

The Luzon scheme, set for January 9, called for a massive movement of ships from Leyte Gulf along the Mindoro convoy route through Surigao Strait into the Mindanao Sea, past Negros, Panay, and Mindoro to starboard. Entering the South China Sea, the ships headed north along the west coast of Luzon, past Manila Bay, to Cape Bolinao, the thumb of the mitten. It was a route beset with kamikazes throughout. The armada moved in two sections, according to function and speed. The first section of 164 vessels began with the slow minesweeping and hydrographic group; the second section searched the ocean floor of the Gulf for shoals and other obstructions. In the middle was a group of twelve escort carriers with destroyer screens. Following were the gunships of the Seventh Fleet responsible for prelanding bombardment and fire support. In line were six prewar battleships, five heavy cruisers, and one light cruiser, with destroyer screens.

About the time these leading sections arrived at Lingayen Gulf the following sections were leaving Leyte Gulf, held back from kamikaze attack as
long as possible. This included troop transports carrying all four infantry
divisions of the initial landing, the Sixth and Forty-Third on the east and
Thirty-Seventh and Fortieth on the west, and their assault landing vehicles,
tractor amphibians, aboard 148 LSTs and LSMs (landing ships, medium).
Accompanying the infantry was a second force of six escort carriers. It was,
by any measure, a formidable armada.

The eighteen escort carriers were the principal protection against kamikazes for all the warships headed for Lingayen Gulf. They maintained an
all-day airborne defense, with twelve carriers moving with the leading echelons and six with the following. It was the intent of the commanders—
MacArthur, Nimitz, Halsey, Kenney, and Kinkaid—to provide more extensive air protection. One measure, which MacArthur supported, involved
sending Halsey and the fast carriers to hit Luzon-bound Japanese air reinforcements on Formosa and Okinawa. Halsey went, but bad weather limited his strikes. Then he accepted responsibility for covering a portion of
Luzon. Limited by overcast, he nonetheless blanketed airfields in northern
Luzon, with carrier planes to demolish and ground Japanese formations.[76]
Kenney's Fifth Air Force, now growing fast on Mindoro, took on the remainder of Luzon—the airfields in the Central Valley and south.

During the first days of the voyage, the invasion force was watched and
attacked but experienced no severe damage or loss. The escort carriers had
"splashed" fifteen to twenty Japanese planes and fought off the rest. On
January 4, however, as the leading echelons approached Luzon with multiple lookouts intent on the skies, a twin-engine bomber dropped unseen in
a near vertical dive, crashed through the flight and hanger decks of the
escort carrier *Ommaney Bay*, and exploded two bombs. Overwhelming
heat and smoke from an oil fire spread and touched off stored torpedoes,
causing 158 casualties. Abandoned, the flaming wreck was ordered sunk.

On January 5, kamikazes showed how much they could achieve even
without sinking a single ship. Bad weather closed the Army's Mindoro airfields, but the escort carrier contingents intercepted and chased away two
attacks. A third, consisting of twenty planes, broke past the carrier group to

hit two heavy cruisers, the *Louisville* and the Allied ship *Australia,* causing sixty and fifty-five casualties, respectively. The captain of the escort carrier *Savo Island* avoided a fighter strike by a sharp turn and helped his gunners by ordering a twenty-four-inch searchlight to be aimed directly at the pilot in his dive, blinding him; the plane barely missed the escort carrier *Manila Bay* (her name honoring the 1898 battle, fought nearby). Two fighters came in fast and low, rose in sharp turns and loops, and dived at the carrier; one missed, and the other crashed through the deck, its bomb exploding in the radar transmitter room and hangar. Damage control saved the ship and even permitted limited operations the next day, despite seventy-eight casualties. The January 5 attacks tapered off in the late afternoon, with one destroyer escort badly damaged and another losing a mast and searchlight. A strike on the minesweepers yielded casualties aboard a landing craft at the cost of three Japanese planes.

January 6, landing day minus three, when bombardment and minesweeping began, was the highpoint of kamikaze attack. Inside Lingayen Gulf, with task-defined navigation and less room for maneuver, ships proved more vulnerable targets. The battleship *New Mexico*, using its heavy guns against targets on the eastern shore, was struck by a flaming kamikaze on the open wing of the navigation bridge, killing the captain and the personal liaison officer of Winston Churchill to MacArthur, among 110 other casualties. The destroyer *Walke* dropped three out of four attacking planes before and after the third crashed into the bridge. "Drenched with gasoline" in the strike, wrote Morison in his account, the captain "for a moment burned like a living torch."[77] He remained in control until the ship was safe and soon after died of his wounds. Another destroyer was badly damaged, as was the minesweeper *Long.* The latter was hit again and sank the following day. The Japanese suicide planes were coming in low and fast. Late in the afternoon, two came up on a destroyer; one splashed, and the second sharply rose to the left and crashed into the battleship *California* at the base of its mainmast. Indiscriminate fire from other ships struck the battleship and raised the casualty list to 196. The cruisers did not fare well. A powerful hit on the *Columbia* penetrated three decks before explosion. Quick flooding of the damaged turret magazines saved the ship, which regained steering control and finished its bombardment assignments for the day. H.M.A.S. *Australia*, victim of a strike the day before, as noted, received a second strike, raising its casualties to ninety-five, but continued fighting. The *Louisville* was stricken with a second hit that tore apart its bridge and mortally wounded Rear Admiral Theodore Chandler.

MacArthur and the other commanders were so taken aback by the extent and destructiveness of kamikaze attacks that they quickly arranged for a set of massive air attacks across Luzon on January 7. On MacArthur's invitation, Halsey had already sent his carrier groups as far south as the Clark airfields, located about forty miles northwest of Manila, the day before. On January 7, the Navy carrier planes blanketed Japanese airfields in northern and central Luzon early in the day. They were followed by sixty medium and light Army Air Force bombers, flying abreast from northwest to southeast, strafing and distributing small parachute bombs across the airfields, followed by the same number of bombers flying abreast from northeast to southwest. Two squadrons of fighters hovered over the bombers. Separately the Air Force struck the airfields around Manila.[78] Rapier-like as this bombardment was, it was intended to convince the enemy that if they planned to withdraw from Luzon, this was the time. Indeed, on January 8, the next day, the Japanese navy decided not to further reinforce its rapidly disappearing air contingent in the Philippines, judging it wiser to reserve production for battles nearer home. Ordered out by air were most of the pilots and Vice Admiral Onishi Takijiro, the organizer of the kamikazes. Presumably he would now rebuild the suicide corps. Left behind was a small group of pilots who would stay on to the end.[79]

The tide of battle slackened on January 7 and the next day. In a morning attack by conventional methods, without kamikazes, one Japanese plane released a torpedo on the minesweeper *Hovey*, and later a second dropped two bombs on the minesweeper *Palmer*. The first target sank in three minutes and the second in six minutes. Bent on sinking the seemingly unsinkable *Australia*, two kamikazes attacked. The first splashed, but the second blew a hole in its side below the bridge, flooding two compartments. Suffering its fourth hit but no casualties this time, the heavy cruiser undertook temporary repairs and returned to its assignment.

Meanwhile the heart of the invasion, the 175,000 combat troops in the rear, loaded on transports with their amphibious vehicles in LSTs, was nearing Luzon.[80] On the morning of January 8, kamikazes attacked the protective escort carrier group. One plane, though hit, persisted and struck the *Kadashan Bay* at the waterline, blowing a hole in its side and rupturing gasoline lines. The crew effectively brought the flooding and fires under control, and the *Kadashan Bay* returned to Leyte. Toward sunset six kamikazes attacked. Escort carrier planes shot down four, and antiaircraft fire dispelled two, one of which turned back and carried out the same strike at the waterline on the *Kitkun Bay*. With fire and engine room flooding and most controls lost, the *Kitkun* was towed until repaired to the point where it could steam under its own power at ten knots, enough to rejoin the escort carriers at Lingayen Gulf. In the morning attack, a plane smashed into the starboard wing of the bridge on the troop transport *Callaway*. Gasoline flames spread but were quickly doused. None of the thousand or more troops was hurt, and the ship continued on.

January 9 was the big day of troop landings and the most perilous. With all echelons present in the Lingayen Gulf, ships by the hundreds presented targets at anchor or maneuvering slowly to find their stations among swarms of landing craft. The kamikazes attacked effectively, but in dribs and drabs, reflecting dwindling numbers. They damaged two cruisers: the *Columbia,* which took a third hit with ninety-two casualties but carried on, and the *Australia,* which took a fifth hit, without casualties, and briefly carried on. Nearby a Japanese plane crashed and slewed at length along the port side of the battleship *Mississippi,* causing eighty-six casualties. At dusk a 5-inch mount nearby, firing at kamikazes above, exploded a shell on the sky control near the top of the foremast of the battleship *Colorado,* killing the entire air defense team. That night the Japanese unleashed a new weapon: eighteen-foot plywood boats manned by two or three soldiers chosen for their willingness to undertake what was virtually a suicide mission. The attackers slipped close to ships and dropped a depth charge before trying to escape.[81] Seventy of these craft were launched from Port Sual on the western shore of the gulf, attacked transports and landing ships, achieving significant damage among the latter. One of two transports was slowed by a flooded compartment but with no apparent troop loss. However, one landing craft was sunk, another hopelessly battered, and four LSTs damaged. Five of these "midget-boats"—as they were called—were sunk, and nothing more was heard of the rest.

After the landings kamikaze attacks occurred occasionally inside the gulf and along the convoy route, through January 13, after which they ceased. In the month between December 13 and January 13 (including the Mindoro operation), the Japanese lost around 600 planes, of which one-third had been on suicide missions. On the American side twenty-four ships were sunk, thirty heavily damaged, and thirty-seven lightly damaged. Navy casualties, including Australians and the American Army, wounded and dead, were just under 4,000.[82]

From its attacks in the Lingayen battles, usually accompanied by escort planes, the kamikaze corps had been developing tactics that it would use in the coming battles. For example, the pilots would aim to hit the sides of ships at the waterline (except battleships, with their protective armor) or the flight decks of carriers in order to break into the interior of the ship and explode their bombs, destroying machinery and piping, starting fires, and flooding the ship. Another frequent target was the bridge, the source of command and controls, including those on battleships. Often, to confuse gunners, the planes would come in low, weaving back and forth, and then abruptly rise and veer toward a different target.[83] The kamikaze attack was a matter of deep concern to the American Navy. So sudden and devastating, it could paralyze the gun crews in the face of what was a sort of guided missile or torpedo. Air defense must now strive to eliminate all of them, not just most of them. Radical maneuvering was the wrong tactic in ship defense, argued Vice Admiral Theodore Wilkinson, and Admiral Kinkaid agreed. Ships should maximize their gun power by staying on course and unmasking their guns. A ship at a right angle to the plane offered a slimmer target; the plane was more likely to miss by range than by deflection. No heavy ships were sunk in the Lingayen operation, but three battleships and two heavy cruisers were badly damaged and might be several months out of action, under repair at distant shipyards, while Iwo Jima was only weeks away and Okinawa due April 1. Five of the eighteen escort carriers that launched 6,152 aircraft sorties in the operation were sunk or heavily damaged.[84] What if kamikazes attacked by the hundreds?

Nonetheless, for the Americans the losses or threats were never large enough to consider withdrawal. The battleships and heavy cruisers proved to be unnecessary. The landing was virtually unopposed. From only a small segment of the beaches was there any Japanese resistance or bombardment of the landing craft. The kamikazes turned out to be the only form of defense. Troopships were targets of the highest value, and four were attacked, but two and probably the third had already been emptied of their human cargo. The 350 Army casualties were more likely aboard the fifteen amphibious craft damaged or sunk by the suicide planes, which did not blanket the skies. Most attack groups were sharply reduced in number by the escort carrier combat air patrols before they could get within striking distance. Japan would not even slow the Lingayen assault.

MacArthur came ashore on the Lingayen beaches in the middle of the landings on January 9. He had traveled in the light cruiser *Boise*, bringing along his closest aides, the so-called Bataan Gang, passing by Corregidor, the last outpost they had been forced to abandon three years earlier and enduring a kamikaze attack in the process. The beach party had formed a sand jetty for the supreme commander to use, but he ignored it and waded ashore, just as he had at Leyte. Within a few days, after the suicide attacks had ended, he set up his headquarters ashore in the provincial administrative building and school near the beach at Dagupan. He now had five-star rank, a status conferred by FDR and Congress on December 16, which he shared with Marshall, Arnold, and King, as well as Nimitz and Eisenhower. MacArthur was pleased and noted that he retained seniority over Eisenhower.[85]

Fleet Admiral Nimitz had been exceedingly cooperative in lending MacArthur a good part of his fleet for Philippines operations—fast carriers, escort carriers, battleships and heavy cruisers, amphibious craft, and infantry divisions—of course in a joint Army-Navy interest, although at some cost. Now that the Philippines had been neutralized, Central Pacific had reached the point where its direction of advance should shift sharply from west to north. Nimitz had, as he said, "introduced" MacArthur to the

Philippines. Now he was turning his attention to Iwo Jima and Okinawa and set about recovering his wandering minions. Most on his mind were the bombardment battleships he had counted on for the Iwo Jima operation, as well as the escort carriers, and many of the cruisers and destroyers. MacArthur had allowed that the battleships would "probably" be detached according to plan, six days after the Lingayen landings. That would be January 15. However, Admiral Kinkaid, dismayed at the prospect of a shrunken fleet, warned Nimitz that the Seventh Fleet would then be too weak to protect the Lingayen beachhead and its supply route from an enemy surface attack. MacArthur shared that worry. Nimitz assured Kinkaid and MacArthur that most of the remnants of the Japanese fleet were in home waters and the fast carriers would be operating between there and the Philippines. (The battleships *Ise* and *Hyuga* returned to Japan from Southeast Asia in mid-February.)[86] However, he allowed Kinkaid to keep four of the battleships for three weeks to cover forthcoming landings in western and southern Luzon. And in response to further grumbling, Nimitz allowed Kinkaid to retain twenty-two of the twenty-six destroyers he asked for and two heavy cruisers. On the matter of the return of the two heavily damaged battleships, however, Nimitz did not waver: he wanted them back immediately, adding, according to Morison, that if "a local naval defense force capable of meeting all heavy ships left in the Japanese Fleet were retained continuously on station, further major operations in the Pacific would have to be postponed indefinitely." In response MacArthur opined that his withholding of "these two veterans of the Pacific Fleet" did not seem likely to "affect the success of the massive offensive being planned" by Nimitz.[87]

Regaining ships from MacArthur was like pulling teeth. Eight escort carriers left on January 16, six more at the end of January, and the heavily damaged *New Mexico* and *California* on January 22. The four remaining battleships, on active service since the eve of the Battle for Leyte Gulf, now held for three more weeks, were finally extracted on February 14. Both the *Colorado* and *Mississippi* needed damage repair and the *Pennsylvania* non-battle repair, and they all, including the *West Virginia,* required upkeep and rehabilitation for the crew and went to Ulithi.[88] By mid-February the Clark airfield complex in central Luzon had been recaptured by the XIV Corps, so Kenney's bombers and fighters at last had an ample first-class air base from which to protect the Lingayen beachhead. By mid-February Clark Field had a still-growing number of 380 fighters and bombers.[89] The four battleships released to Ulithi came too late for Iwo Jima but not for Okinawa. Their absence from Iwo Jima would add to the difficulties of that preliminary bombardment.

Now, with the Lingayen landings a success, his army barely bruised, out of the jungle, and into relatively dry and cultivated country, his aircraft dominating the Philippine skies, and Manila at last within his grasp, MacArthur's return was almost complete. Looking beyond, the Philippines would be the mainspring for the invasion of Japan, for they alone provided sufficient landmass to mount such a large invasion. Among the islands—Luzon, Leyte, and the nearby Visayas—the troops would gather, his own and those from South and Central Pacific, pack their supplies and equipment, practice landings, and board their ships for Kyushu. On November 3 and 4 Major General Chamberlin and Rear Admiral Sherman had met at General Headquarters Hollandia and arranged troop numbers, locations, and the responsibilities of the MacArthur and Nimitz commands. The Third Amphibious Corps of three Marine divisions would use Leyte; the XXIV Corps, which had shared in the capture of Leyte, would use the Visayas from Panay to Cebu, each with its small port; and an additional corps of Central Pacific Army divisions would be located on Luzon, where most of MacArthur's divisions would prepare. In addition, Southwest Pacific would provide facilities for up to one-third of the Pacific Fleet. These the Navy would build in Leyte Gulf next to Tacloban along the southern shore of Samar, in Manila Bay, and at an undecided further location (which turned out to be Subic Bay, north of Bataan).[90] General of the Army MacArthur was well placed to command the invasion.

First was Manila. MacArthur was set for a lightning strike southward to liberate the Philippine capital, but his Sixth Army commander was not; troops of General Krueger's Forty-Third Division had been heavily engaged with Japanese forces on the left flank the day after they left the Lingayen beaches.[91] Troops moving off the center and western beaches

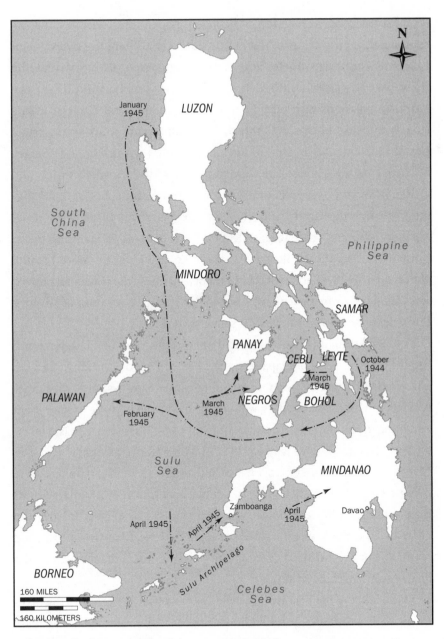

Map 7 Allied Return to the Philippines, 1944–1945. Drawn by George Chakvetadze.

found scarcely any resistance in the flat and open interior valley, but the terrain behind the eastern beaches was different. There the shoreline of Lingayen Gulf turns north, and the narrow coastal plain is broken by three parallel north–south tiers of hills. Next to the foothills of the mountain mass of northern Luzon was the Cordillera Central, rising steeply to peaks of over 8,000 feet. The countryside south of the triple tier of hills and east of the beaches was spotted with rises and solitary hills covered with grass. The topography was ideal for observation and artillery fire and, with its combination of loose stone and soil, for digging revetments, caves, and tunnels. Defenses, prepared with usual Japanese skill and with at least 13,000 Japanese troops manning them, presented a significant threat. All these enemy defenses were located within three to fifteen miles of the shoreline and inside the perimeter of what was called the Army Beachhead Line, which marked the extent of advance into enemy territory required for security of the base.[92]

For MacArthur on the other hand there was every reason to hasten south toward Manila. Now that Japanese airpower on Luzon was extinct and the Clark airfield complex, with its fifteen concrete runways, only fifty miles south of the Lingayen beaches, was empty, the time had come to seize them and bring in Kenney's air force, not only for tactical assistance to the infantry but also for long-range missions. Beyond Clark, awaiting rescue in Manila, American prisoners of war and interned civilian families were living on a starvation diet. And, of course, acquisition of Manila, with its huge, embracing bay and docks, was a prerequisite to staging the invasion of Japan. So while Krueger battled to secure his base, MacArthur had good reason to convey (without making it an outright order) that he wanted the Sixth Army marching south.

At the heart of the dispute between General Headquarters and the Sixth Army were substantially different estimates of the number of Japanese troops on Luzon.[93] When Japan was fighting the battle on Leyte, which it regarded as decisive, it sent troop reinforcements, requiring frequent signaling, which ULTRA would decode. Now that Luzon would have to fight with the troops it already had, reinforcement messages were sparse and fragmentary. Furthermore, introduction of a new edition of the Japanese codebook slowed the Allied decoding process. An additional problem was discovering and estimating the size of the several hundred unattached Japanese units—army, navy, and air force, supply and technical—mostly in the vicinity of Manila. These communicated by secure phone or an impenetrable three-digit code. To take into account noncombat units, which could be used as infantry, the Sixth Army intelligence officer, Colonel Horton V. White, multiplied the number in the combat forces by a factor of 1.5. In a November 30 report General Willoughby had estimated 137,000 troops on Luzon, and a Sixth Army report of December 5 estimated 234,500. The actual number was 267,000. MacArthur, listening to the Sixth Army chief of staff reading their estimate, repeatedly interrupted with the word "Bunk!" Estimates changed, but the actual troop figure remained at least 100,000 more than Willoughby's.[94]

General Yamashita Tomoyuki's strategy for using this army was clever and simple. The commander of the Japanese Fourteenth Area Army would not waste it in the open and flat Central Valley, which was defenseless against American tactical airpower and coordinated artillery fire. Instead he would make the Americans come to him in the broken and mountainous country bordering both sides of the valley.[95] There he had established three battle groups, each taking advantage of height, slope, defilade, and camouflage. For fifty miles along the mountains east of Lingayen Gulf and Central Valley, he had stationed the Shobu Group of 150,000 troops, a portion of which Krueger's troops had already encountered near the beaches. In the hill mass rising east of Manila was the Shimbu Group of 80,000, and in the broken, treeless hills west of the lower Central Valley, overlooking the Clark airfield runways, was the Kembu Group of 30,000. Either before or after Manila, the Sixth Army faced a set of wearying, bloody battles on its flanks.

The Forty-Third Division, landing on the easternmost of the Lingayen beaches, had engaged Shobu forces, the Japanese Fifty-Eighth Independent Mixed Brigade and Twenty-Third Division, dug in on the low hills and rises near the beaches. The Forty-Third, a New England National Guard division called to the colors before Pearl Harbor, had experienced jungle war at its worst on New Georgia in the Solomons. In three and one-half months of continuous action it had suffered over 5,000 casualties, including killed, wounded, "war neurosis" (1,171 cases), and malaria. After eight months of rehabilitation in New Zealand, the division joined the Sixth Army at Aitape in northern New Guinea, where it had a brief, limited engagement in the Driniumor battle. Several commanders of the division had been relieved along the way. Major General Leonard F. "Red" Wing, the current commander, remained through the war. Like Krueger, he entered as a private, but in the National Guard, working his way up to assistant commander of the Forty-Third in 1942. In peacetime a lawyer from Rutland, Vermont, with a wizened countenance, he was highly regarded by his men.[96]

For the Americans Luzon was a battle for roads. On the coastal road eight miles north of the beaches lies the town of Damortis, from which Route 3, a paved, two-lane road built in sections beginning in 1928, led east five miles to Rosario and just beyond reached a junction where the road to Baguio climbed into the mountains. Known today as the MacArthur Highway, Route 3 originally ran parallel to the old Manila Railroad. Holding and blocking this access to the beachhead was essential. At the junction, Route 3 turns south for twelve miles to the town of Binalonan. A line drawn from Binalonan northwest back to the beaches would represent the Forty-Third Division's battlefield, a polygon roughly the shape of the state of Nevada.

For the Americans, to capture the east–west and north–south stretches of Route 3 and the junction, the beachhead defense would have to be mobile, easily supplied, and positioned to deny the enemy on the heights above assembly in the lowlands for a counterattack. The American attack came in two parts: a drive northward toward the Damortis-Rosario section of Route 3, three regiments abreast, and an attack eastward, toward the north–south section of the road, two regiments abreast. Advancing north, east, and southeast, the regiments would be diverging, leaving gaps, so the I Corps commander, Lieutenant General Innis P. Swift, added two reserve regiments to Wing's command, the independent 158th Regimental Combat Team and the Sixty-Third Regiment of the Sixth Division. By now General Wing was maneuvering five regiments. Tying the newly attached units into division communications and setting up their artillery-infantry coordination while advancing on the enemy was a trial, to say nothing of supply mixups and shortages.

On January 12 the 158th Regimental Combat Team headed north along the coast road, found Damortis deserted, turned east on Route 3, and the following day fell into an ambush at a defile when passing through the first coastal ridge. Artillery, mortar, and machine gun fire from caves on the eastern side forced a withdrawal. The 158th returned the following day, this time advancing on both sides of the road, and gained a thousand yards. At the next ridgeline on the north, however, heavy fire from caves above struck this regiment, as well as the Sixty-Third Regiment nearby, fighting its way north along the first and second parallel ridge lines, and the 172nd Regiment on the third ridgeline. The steep upward slopes, hills above hills like a stadium, and the careful siting, enclosure, and camouflage of the enemy guns, many and large bore, brought the three regiments to a halt. There were contributing factors as well. On account of bungling and confusion, the newly attached Sixty-Third had received little or no artillery support for several days. Except for the coastal road and Route 3 itself, the hill country was roadless, and supplies were not keeping up with the advance. Fighting under a broiling sun, cut off by hills from the sea breezes, with no shade and inadequate water supply, the troops were hit with extensive heat prostration, as they had been at Biak. Stalemate was unacceptable. General Wing recognized that he had to change tactics. He began by relieving the commanding officer of the Sixty-Third Regiment, replacing him with the assistant commander. At least he had advanced three regiments onto or near the east–west section of Route 3. To secure the road and road junction, however, he would have to destroy the Japanese artillery on the steep slopes north of Route 3.

Equally important was hastening the drive eastward of the 103rd and 169th Regiments to the north–south section of Route 3 and thence north on that road to hammer Japanese forces at the junction from both directions. Japanese defenses east of the beaches were imposing but not tightly knit together. The gutted hills, from north to south, Hills 470, 355, 318, and 200, were really forts with caves, embrasures, tunnels, and galleries, even an

underground stable for horses that drew artillery. They rose above the surrounding flat land in an uneven line several miles apart, between the
beaches and Route 3. When the northern advance began, so did the eastern, and the two regiments were already engaging the forts. Rather than
attack them frontally with heavy casualties, Wing chose to slip forces
between them heading beyond for Route 3.

At 10:30 p.m. on January 15 two battalions of the 169th Regiment, leaving the third battalion to hold the enemy in place at Hill 355, moved out to
the south and then east. Carrying food and ammunition for several days,
they forded two small rivers and marched on through the night and following day, reaching Route 3 at Palecpalec, one mile north of the important
junction of Pozorrubio, at 5 p.m. Meanwhile four miles south, the 103rd
Regiment, with heavy, close support from howitzers and mortars captured
at Hill 200 and moved on to clear Pozorrubio on January 17, was opening
a supply road from the beaches to the north–south sector of Route 3. Here
and there the Japanese counterattacked in company strength but were repelled. On January 18 a battalion of the 169th moved several miles north
on Route 3, presumably to establish a blocking position to hold off any
threat from the north while the rest of the regiment attacked Mount Alava
and Hill 355 from the rear, the east. The battalion came under intense artillery fire and counterattack from troops dispatched from Mount Alava and
withdrew partway, killing nearly 400 Japanese. On January 20 the 169th
launched an attack against the remaining Japanese defenders of Mount
Alava, weakened by their losses the previous day. Making slow but costly
progress, the regiment captured Alava and nearby Hill 355 by the end of
January 24, and even then it took a week to entirely clear them. It was a
costly process. The strength of the Second Battalion, 169th, alone had been
reduced from 1,000 to 650.[97]

The elimination of the line of fortified hills in the interior of the battlefield was a long step toward securing control of Route 3 in both directions.
While the interior battle was fast moving and wide open, the battle along
the tangled slopes and ridges of Route 3 east of Damortis was confined and
prolonged. The Japanese Fifty-Eighth Independent Mixed Brigade, which
had brought three American regiments to a stop, entrenched north and

south of Route 3 with artillery, machine guns, and mortars, kept the advance of the 158th and Sixty-Third Regiments to short spurts of 500–1,000 yards. In spite of repeated calls from division to move on, the American infantry could not maintain momentum. In the period January 17–23 the two regiments took 350 casualties.[98]

Finally the "foot-to-foot" advances eastward broke out of the hill country into the flat valley near the village of Cataguintingan, opening Route 3 east to supply through the coastal road and Damortis. Ahead to the east of the 158th and Sixty-Third was the 172nd Regiment, which had crossed Route 3 at that point on January 18 and moved north of the road up the slopes to seize the heights controlling Rosario. For once a Forty-Third formation did not have to climb against enemy fire: Hills 600 and 606 were not occupied. Taking advantage of their commanding height, the regiment moved east laterally toward Hill 900, one of the two fortifications protecting the road junction below. Across the valley, above the road junction, was the second, Hill 1500, at the head of the north–south chain then under assault by the 169th and 103rd Regiments. Division planned a joint attack for January 25 by the 172nd on Hill 900 and by the Sixty-Third on Hill 1500. The Sixty-Third would advance eastward on the flat land south of Route 3, cross Route 3 where it headed south, and climb to the peak of Hill 1500. The 172nd cleverly took Hill 900 by looping north and approaching from behind, and then, according to the Army's official history, it "banged, clawed, bayoneted, and shot its way" into the enemy position and defended it successfully against several Japanese counterattacks. The Sixty-Third took the southern crest of Hill 1500 by June 28, whereupon the 172nd crossed over and took the northern peak of the same hill.[99]

South of Hill 1500, the 103rd and 169th shifted north to assault the rest of the eastern slopes of the north–south range. Krueger closed the gap by inserting the Twenty-Fifth Division, his last reserve. The two regiments struggled up the slopes but failed to reach most of the ridgeline.[100] The enemy was quick to take advantage of any blunder. The grassy, open slopes, always under observation from above, were no place to bunch up, but a battalion commander did so, gathering his officers and sergeants at his command post. Fifteen rounds of 75 mm artillery fire burst on the spot, killing him, four company commanders, and seven enlisted men and wounding thirty-five others.[101] The two regiments fought their way up as far as needed to control Route 3, and that proved to be enough. Japanese troops remained on the eastern slopes but were beginning to withdraw into the mountain mass of northern Luzon. Yamashita had inflicted as much damage as he could afford.[102]

During this part of the campaign, two-thirds of the Japanese Fifty-Eighth Independent Mixed Brigade and half of the Japanese Twenty-Third Division, close to 8,000 Japanese first-class infantry, were killed and much artillery, transport, and supply lost.[103] The battle took a large hunk out of the American Forty-Third Division's personnel: 593 killed and 1,644 wounded, not counting illness and combat fatigue. The 103rd and 169th Regiments were at close to one-half of effective strength.[104] On January 27 Krueger at last received reinforcements, the Thirty-Second and First Cavalry Divisions and the 112th Cavalry Regimental Combat Team, all from Leyte, where they had fought seemingly forever and "mopped up" through December.[105] On February 13 a third reinforcing division, the Thirty-Third, arrived with limited experience of battle at Wakde-Sarmi on New Guinea and replaced the Forty-Third along Route 3.[106] The Forty-Third withdrew for rest, which was soon to be interrupted. General Krueger had now firmly established the security of the beachhead and received sufficient forces to move south while protecting and clearing his flanks.

In fact, Krueger had been moving south since January 18, though cautiously. He expected his troops to be slowed by the shortage of trucks for supply and the repair and replacement of bridges. The XIV Corps, with no enemy on its right short of the Clark airfields, advanced from main line to outpost line, and main to outpost again, testing each for enemy concentrations. The I Corps followed on the left, spreading out to the southeast in the Central Valley while skirting the mountain mass that the Forty-Third Division had encountered in the north. Here the I Corps found resistance and engaged in battle, but in attack, not defense. Yamashita fought to slow the American advance and protect pathways—river valleys, trails, roads—into the mountains that were a sanctuary and fortress for the Shobu Group.[107]

No matter what measures Krueger took to speed the advance, MacArthur kept calling for more. On the basis of his incorrect estimate— that the Shobu Group was much smaller than the Sixth Army estimate— he insisted that Yamashita was no threat to Krueger's left flank. Indeed, contrary to Krueger's expectation, the supreme commander believed that the Japanese would offer little resistance in Manila and would simply evacuate the capital. MacArthur went further in challenging Krueger to move faster by positioning his headquarters closer to the enemy than Krueger's and, contrary to his habit of keeping to himself on Leyte, visited and even joined advancing troops. In one instance he radioed Krueger that the advance of the Thirty-Seventh Division showed "a noticeable lack of drive and aggressive initiative." The Thirty-Seventh was one of the two divisions responsible for the capture of Manila, and its pace in this instance was set by corps and division. On another occasion, two days after the opening of the Damortis-Rosario battle, MacArthur asked Krueger, "Why are you holding the I Corps back? It ought to be moving south."[108] The constant prodding was embarrassing to Krueger. Yet MacArthur did not deliver an order or relieve him of command. On the contrary, he strongly recommended him for a fourth star to become full general. Krueger, a man of stubborn and severe disposition, thoroughly versed in and bounded by the art of war, and MacArthur, a man driven by a host of imperatives, military and personal, were stuck in a tug-of-war between speed and discretion.

MacArthur was beset by an overwhelming need to capture Manila as soon as possible. His need extended beyond rational objectives, like the need for the Clark airfields, the rescue of prisoners of war and internees, and the acquisition of a critical base for advance on Japan. Above all, recovery of Manila, his home, was his key to redemption for having deserted Bataan and its soldiers. Beyond that, he now also had the opportunity of coming forth with a major victory, a military triumph registering as such in the West and the larger war. Capture of New Guinean jungle offered no such reward. Such a victory would seem the more welcome and significant at a moment when the Allied forces in Europe were laboring through the bloody setback of Hitler's winter strike in the Ardennes. No less important—indeed absolutely central to his thinking—the liberation of Manila would ensure that he would be regarded as the only conceivable general to lead Allied forces in the invasion of Japan.

To draw American public attention to the event and honor the inhabitants of Manila and the Philippine government, while anticipating little or no Japanese resistance, he planned a parade and ceremony in the city.[109] It spared no detail. The parade would consist of a column of jeeps coming in from the north headed by MacArthur's jeep, with its circle of five stars on a red background, accompanied by a motorcycle escort and two armored cars. Behind in their jeeps would be leading officers of MacArthur's headquarters and of the Sixth and Eighth Armies, corps, and divisions. The parade would move along boulevards to the government buildings south of the river and stop at the Legislative Building, a huge edifice right out of Washington, with colonnades on all sides. Massed in front of officers and guests would be the equivalent of a division (14,000) of American soldiers. They would be in combat uniform with individual weapons, "clean and neat" but not "spit and polish," their trucks nearby to avoid a long march. MacArthur's plan makes no mention of Philippine troops except the Constabulary Band. The program would include ruffles and flourishes (four each for MacArthur and President Sergio Osmena), the Philippine and American national anthems, flag raisings, and speeches by MacArthur and Osmena. Photographers and correspondents could join the jeep parade or attend just the ceremony. Colonel Diller, public relations officer at Supreme Headquarters, would arrange for "broadcast and reception coverage in the United States and Philippines." The Manila public would be notified of the parade by newspapers, radio, and sound trucks, and the city would declare an official holiday.

———

Meanwhile, passing out of the beachhead and down the Central Valley, the Sixth Army was gaining mobility and momentum. It had the rare and perhaps singular opportunity in the Pacific war of fighting in open country with road networks and room for maneuver. In the middle of the valley, on the right flank of the I Corps, were the Cabaruan Hills, a set of knolls and ridges with scrub cover, four square miles in size. It was armed and defended like the line of hill forts in the path of the Forty-Third Division. In haste to get onward, General Edwin Patrick, commanding the Sixth Division, ordered an air, artillery, infantry attack, which failed to synchronize and was followed by intense fire from the defenders, causing heavy casualties. Repeated attacks in the following days gradually made headway, but destruction of the 1,500 Japanese troops to the low hundreds, and then none, took eleven days. Impatiently, Patrick removed battalions prematurely and had to send some back. The insistence of higher command on faster progress toward Manila was settling in at division level. The Cabaruan Hills were taken on June 29, the day before the Forty-Third Division captured the Route 3 junction.[110]

The Twenty-Fifth Division, a veteran of Guadalcanal, entered the Central Valley battle positioned between the Forty-Third and Sixth Divisions, heading southeast on Route 3. After seizing Binalonan, Major General Charles L. Mullins, division commander, sent the 161st Regiment five miles east to San Manuel, a town at the foot of the mountains, alongside a valley into them, holding a detachment of 1,000 Japanese troops and a regiment of forty-five tanks, which Mullins saw as a possible threat to the left flank of the XIV Corps. The tanks were set hull down in revetments surrounded by rifle pits and supported by mortars, machine guns, and artillery. Colonel James L. Dalton, regimental commander, sent his Second Battalion around the town and up a ridge behind and above it that was lightly held. In the attack, the Second Battalion gained some ground while the First Battalion gained none. Dalton then sent part of his First Battalion to join the Second and added two battalions of 105 mm guns. All the tanks were destroyed, and most of the troops were killed, while the rest fled.[111] The battle strongly suggested that commitment of a regiment of tanks to a stationary defense meant that Yamashita was using his tank division not to attack the Sixth Army flank but to defend his Shobu Group mountain redoubt. All three divisions in I Corps, the Forty-Third, Sixth, and Twenty-Fifth, completed their assignments—the Route 3 junction, Cabaruan Hills, and San Manuel—within one day of each other

(January 29–30), and each assignment pointed to speeding up the advance on Manila.

The only one not quite ready to accept that conclusion was General Krueger. The Army commander wanted extension of the advance, indeed radical extension, but at this point primarily for reconnaissance, not assault. On the I Corps's right, the Sixth Division promptly moved south twenty miles to a line still thirty miles north of the XIV Corps and the Clark airfields. From that line reconnaissance teams scouted fifteen to twenty miles southeast and northeast to Cabanatuan and Munoz, towns on Route 5, the principal highway from Manila due north to the Shobu-held mountains. They reported Japanese forces in both towns and defensive screening but no concentration of force west of the highway and, therefore, no imminent threat to the left flank of XIV Corps. That news allowed the Corps to move on the Japanese Kembu Group forces that dominated the Clark airfields from hills to the west.[112]

The Twenty-Fifth Division was some twenty miles north of the Sixth, approaching the town of Umingan, which was twenty miles southeast of San Manuel, one more of the strongpoints along the rim of the valley. According to intelligence from various sources (apparently including some Japanese prisoners of war as well as Filipino guerrillas), a triangle of strongpoints had been established based on San José, reaching northwest to Lupao and Umingan and southwest to Muñoz. General Krueger recognized that the cluster of strongpoints looked like a system of defense, but he still believed that it had the potentiality—with the forces present adding up to an armored and an infantry division—of striking out at his army's left rear. Therefore, on January 30, before tearing for Manila, he ordered I Corps to drive into the triangle and capture the key city of San José.[113]

A hub of communications, San Jose lies in the waist of Luzon, a divide between the mountains to the north and the rugged hills north and east of Manila, forming a passageway between the Central Valley and the eastern shore. San Jose was also tied to the railroad from Lingayen to Manila. For General Yamashita it served as a transshipment and storage base for troops and supplies headed north from the Manila area to join the Shobu force. It seems somewhat hard to believe that Krueger, who had served in the Philippines, did not also have in mind the opportunity of cutting Yamashita's supply route and securing a major passageway into the northern mountains for later use. Indeed, the result of the battle for San Jose was to crystalize for the Sixth Army the conclusion that General Yamashita and his Shobu Group in northern Luzon was the immediate enemy.

It was a widespread battle, with the Twenty-Fifth Division following Route 8 from the northwest, fighting its way through or around strong-points at Umingan and Lapao, the Sixth Division striking out from the southwest on Route 5 toward Munoz, and both converging on San Jose. At the start they were fifteen miles apart. In charge was I Corps commander General Swift. To the weaponry of each division Swift added a 155 mm artillery battalion, a heavy howitzer battalion, a 4.2-inch mortar company, and a company of medium tanks. The attacks on strongpoints began February 1 across flat, dry, treeless fields. Ditches among the rice paddies ruled out use of tanks off the road. Infantrymen in frontal attack under a tropical sun without cover took heavy casualties from well dug in Japanese artillery, antitank weapons, and machine guns, in spite of preliminary artillery fire.[114]

With frontal attacks failing the following day, on February 2, and into February 3, both division commanders, Mullins and Patrick, turned to outflanking the foe. Mullins ordered a battalion of the Thirty-Fifth Regiment to move cross-country around Umingan and take a position on the San José side of Route 5. The principal objective, after all, was San Jose, not Umingan or Muñoz. The Sixth Division's First Regiment undertook a flanking maneuver with night marching along the bank of the Telavera River, which flowed parallel to Route 5 past Muñoz and north to San José. Several farther flankings occurred in both divisions. It was a promising tactic, reducing casualties and unhinging the enemy. What brought the battle to a close, however, was the fact that by February 4 all the troops and most needed supplies headed from southern Luzon to the Shobu Group had left or passed through San José on their way north. No longer needing to protect the movement north, General Yamashita that day also withdrew to the north his troops in the strongpoints guarding San José. On account of poor communications, they left at different times and in different ways, by marching north at night, by fighting escape, or by filtering north through American lines. When First Division troops entered San José it was empty.[115] By the evening of February 2 it had become absolutely clear to General Krueger that the San José defense system was not a concentration for a counterattack in the valley but a formation of individual strongpoints for the protection of the movement of troops and supplies to the north. He therefore ordered XIV Corps "to resume its drive to Manila with all speed."[116]

The other half of the Sixth Army advancing south along the Central Valley was the XIV Corps, a source of constant concern for its exposed left flank. The Corps and both its divisions were from the South Pacific, the Thirty-Seventh was from Bougainville in the Solomons, and the Fortieth was from New Britain. The corps commander, Lieutenant General Oscar W. Griswold, was according to Morison "a calm, slow-speaking officer of basic simplicity and Spartan habits" whose leadership, together with the "stern resistance" of corps infantry and artillery, won the defensive battle on Bougainville.[117] On Luzon the corps marched seventy miles in a series of bounds over sixteen days, careful not to keep too far ahead of the I Corps, here and there engaging in skirmishes. More serious than the enemy was limited supply; there were too few trucks, due to inadequate shipping space on account of an American worldwide shipping crisis brought on by movement of divisions to Europe, among other uses, as well as the need for the repair and rebuilding of bridges. On January 23, the Fortieth Division, followed by the Thirty-Seventh, reached Bamban, an outlying town of Clark Field.[118] Now to the southeast were the marshes and deltas north of Manila Bay and to the southwest the mountains of Bataan, a set of parallel ridgelines that reached from the Zambales Mountains on the northwest beyond the airfields like gnarled fingers. These heights, dominating the runways head on, formed a battlefield, fortified and occupied by the 30,000 Japanese troops of the Kembu Group.

The Kembu force was a hodgepodge of leftovers from the naval establishment in the Philippines, service troops such as construction workers from Clark, and trained army combat detachments numbering 8,500, about half of which were first-rate.[119] Nevertheless, the commanding officer, Major General Tsukada Rikichi, constructed and organized a lethal cave defense along the sides and tops of the finger-like ridges, a defense that occupied four American divisions, one after another, until April. The Kembu Group was deficient in heavy artillery but had a large supply of antiaircraft weapons that they modified for ground use. From wrecked airplanes at Clark Field, they removed and altered for ground use a large number of machine guns and cannons. South of the ridges, around the rubble of Fort Stotsenburg and the runways of Clark Field, they laid at least 1,350 mines. Tsukada set up an outpost line of strongpoints across the ridges, from north to south. Two and a half miles west of it, parallel to it, he established his heavily armed main line of resistance. West of that in the higher hills were five defined defense zones held by the naval detachments. Needless to say, all his emplacements of weapons were skillfully camouflaged. He defended from the high ground and in great depth.

All this the XIV Corps had to learn by engaging the enemy; no Southwest Pacific sources had information about how many Japanese troops were in the vicinity of Clark Field. Guesses ranged from 4,000 to 8,000, mostly service troops. General Griswold, using the Fortieth Division, decided to probe into the ridgelines in the north facing Bamban, sending the 160th Regiment, joined by the 108th on its right. What he undertook turned out by January 27 to be a much larger and more elaborate task than he had expected. At the eastern end of the ridgelines, infantry climbed a near vertical slope under fire. They reached and captured the top, moved southwest along the ridge, and then switched to the southernmost ridge that lay alongside Clark Field. It was slow going, a case of moving forward, calling for artillery, battling, and moving forward again.

Griswold now recognized that the Japanese had a "very strong natural position," as he noted in his diary, and that they were "making full use of their artillery," with automatic weapons "placed in well concealed caves covering all routes of approach." The probe had clarified the outpost line, broken through it, and disengaged its northern strongpoints so that later they could be eliminated individually. However, Griswold concluded that with the now evident Japanese strength on Clark Field, it was essential to capture the air center and Fort Stotsenburg, and for that he would have to use his other division, the Thirty-Seventh, as well as the Fortieth. He noted in the same diary entry that a Supreme Headquarters communiqué had already announced the capture of Stotsenburg and commented, referring to MacArthur: *"Why does he do this?"*[120]

On January 28, the 129th Regiment of the Thirty-Seventh Division attacked through the hangar wreckage and outpost line into Clark Field but came to a stop for that day and the next for removal of mines and defending against Japanese counterattacks, including tanks. The 129th gave up no ground, and the Japanese, their tanks destroyed, retired to their main line of resistance. That was not enough for Krueger, who warned the Thirty-Seventh and Fortieth that it was "imperative" to seize "at once" the entire air center and Fort Stotsenburg with the large hill mass to its west and three outposts lying between the two regiments. All was to be done by dark on January 30.[121] By dark on January 31 it was all done: the Thirty-Seventh had cleared the fort, airfields, and outposts and captured the massive hill called Top of the World, which was on the main line of resistance, while the 160th cut through the main line of resistance in the center; finally, the 108th eliminated the last of the outposts in the northern sector. The Americans now had the entire airfield complex and half of the main line of resistance. There was more to do, including the Japanese navy combat groups farther to the west, but XIV Corps now could withdraw the Thirty-Seventh Division, leaving the Fortieth to contain or complete the action; construction crews were already repairing the Clark runways.[122]

The Central Valley campaign generally appears in the accounts of it as a never-ending sequence of battles, when in fact they were mostly concurrent, overlapping sectors of a larger scheme to establish an army on Luzon and protect its passage to Manila. All five battles—the Route 3 junction, Cabaruan, San Manuel, San José, and Clark Field—ended successfully in the week of January 28–February 4. Indeed, it was a remarkable consequence of the MacArthur-Krueger tug-of-war between speed and security, as well as the skill of the corps commanders, Swift and Griswold, and the division commanders, Wing, Patrick, Mullins, Robert Beightler, and Brush, no less the veteran troops of the South and Southwest Pacific under their command. The number of hills named posthumously for battalion commanders suggests that officers were not leading from the rear. Nevertheless, for the infantryman, battle remained horrific, in no significant way eased by bounty or limitation.

The reminiscence of Paul M. Gerrish, a sergeant in the reconnaissance troop of the Fortieth Division, offers a darker perspective than that seen from the command point of view. The Fortieth Division, Gerrish recalled, was in action from January 9 to March 2 and in battle from late January through February. Arriving back at the Lingayen beachhead "exhausted," the soldiers spent four days cleaning, repairing, and replacing equipment, partaking of local wine, and bathing in a nearby stream before boarding LSTs for an assault on the island of Panay, to the south of Luzon. Breakfast of dehydrated eggs, bread, and coffee had been a treat after canned rations. In the Clark battle, Gerrish pointed out, the Fortieth had lost 2,500 men without replacements. With fewer than 10,000 men, less than its full strength by one-third, the Fortieth was always fighting uphill, against well-armed and entrenched foes. Furthermore, battle would begin with American attack at dawn and Japanese counterattack at night, making a twenty-four-hour fighting day. "How much of this," he asked, "is flesh and blood expected to stand?" Gerrish said they had all seen results of Japanese atrocities against Allied soldiers, including mutilation and cannibalistic acts, and now they had seen the graves of the American and Filipino soldiers who died on the Bataan Death March and thereafter. "When you hate with a passion that knows no bounds, how much more hate can you develop?" That hatred would cover any sense of guilt in setting fire (with a flamethrower presumably) to "a house containing Japanese soldiers and shoot[ing] them when they came running out." American infantry were "paying such a frightful price, in blood, for each one of those caves captured."[123] The numbers of soldiers dead, wounded, or missing are always available, but not always the numbers of those removed, battle by battle, on account of injury, illness, heat prostration, and combat fatigue. The total of these losses, for Luzon itself, from January 9 to June 30, 1945, was 93,400, probably the highest American nonbattle loss in World War II.[124]

Charged with the task of liberating Manila was the XIV Corps, with Griswold commanding, composed of the Thirty-Seventh Division and the First Cavalry Division. The Thirty-Seventh left the Clark battle on January 27, marching along Route 3 by the marshy terrain north of Manila Bay, with the 148th Regiment leading the way. The First Cavalry arrived at the Lingayen beaches on January 27, after more than two months of jungle warfare on Leyte, followed by reequipment and shipment to Luzon. The division gathered west of Cabanatuan, where MacArthur visited and gave the division commander, Major General Vernon D. Mudge, his only orders: "Go to Manila. I don't care how you do it, but get in there and get in fast. And save your men. Go around the Nips, bounce off the Nips, but go to Manila. Free the internees at Santo Tomas. Take Malacanan Palace and the Legislative Building."[125] As we've mentioned, late on February 2 General Krueger, finally satisfied that the plunge to Manila was safe, ordered XIV Corps, gathering ten to fifteen miles north of the city, to move into Manila with "all possible speed." The divisions moved on separate paths: the First Cavalry, formed into two self-supporting "flying columns," each with its own infantry aboard trucks, along with tanks, and artillery, circled southeast to southwest, finding most of its bridges intact and fordings shallow. It entered Manila from the northeast, half a day ahead of the Thirty-Seventh Division, which was marching all the way, slowed by blown bridges and small enemy points of resistance. By the evening of February 4, elements of both divisions were inside northern Manila, facing south, with the Thirty-Seventh by Manila Bay and the First Cavalry on its left.[126]

The first task of the cavalry was to save the American and British civilian internees at Santo Tomas University. Just under 4,000 of them, of all ages, had been housed there for three years and were starving to death. Packed in the lobby that night, they heard the rising "rumble of closing tanks" and then gunfire just outside, the front door crashing open, and the entrance of an American soldier pointing a rifle and wearing a rounded helmet they had never seen before. An "elderly woman...weak and feeble but with tears of happiness in her eyes...touched his arm and said, 'Soldier, are you real?' "[127] The next day, from nearby Bilibid Penitentiary, the Thirty-Seventh Division freed 1,500 Americans, 800 prisoners of war, and 700 civilians. As for the other objectives set out by MacArthur, Malacañan Palace was already in Filipino possession, but the Legislative Building, south of the Pasig, was too far to reach.

Greater Manila in 1945 was a city of over a million with many pasts, from the Intramuros, the sixteenth-century Spanish settlement fortified by walls forty feet thick at the base, to the Rizal baseball stadium; cobblestones and medieval churches stood a few hundred yards from imposing administrative buildings for the emerging Filipino government, built with reinforced concrete to guard against earthquakes. The city stretched eight miles along the eastern shore of Manila Bay and roughly five miles inland, bisected east–west by the narrow Pasig River. Manila was a capital city and a bustling interisland and international port. It had wide boulevards and public gardens, modern apartments, foreign consulates, hospitals, universities and colleges, clubs, mansions, and nipa huts. It offered an exciting broth of cultures among independence-minded people.[128]

Whatever affinity existed between the United States and the Philippines had been sorely tried in early 1942, when Washington had failed to reinforce MacArthur against the Japanese invasion, leaving Filipinos disillusioned and dubious about American reliability and faith. Many were drawn toward Japan's encouragement of independence and Asian values and rejection of Western culture. As the months went by, however, Filipinos learned that whatever role in government they were permitted would be shaped by Japan's needs. Japan's attempt to manage the rice economy by forced sale to a government corporation at set prices led to a black market, inflation, shortages, and corruption. Accompanying the Japanese mangling of the Philippine economy, imperiling food supplies, was their increasingly oppressive form of occupation. An encounter with a Japanese soldier in Manila required a bow from the waist. Failure to bow led to a slap or blow, venting vicious anger. As the American Army and Navy forces drew closer to the Philippines, Halsey's planes attacked Manila Bay, and Filipino guerrillas supplied by MacArthur became active close by, the Japanese military became increasingly concerned about subversion within the city. On November 10, 1944, they had formed a Filipino counter-guerrilla militia, called the Makapili, which General Yamashita ordered to join with the Kempeitei, the Japanese political police, in a campaign against the guerrilla bands.[129] Not far beyond lay deliberate, large-scale execution of Filipinos.[130]

MacArthur had hoped and expected that the Japanese would save Manila by withdrawing, and indeed they did, with Yamashita to the north and the Shimbu Group on the east, but they left 4,500 troops to protect removal of supplies from Manila, blow the bridges across the Pasig in retreat, and delay the American attack on the Shimbu front. The Japanese navy, with many facilities in Manila Bay, had other intentions and responsibilities: suicide boat operations, evacuation of small craft, demolition of repair facilities, destruction of supplies, and mine-laying. Furthermore, the commander, Rear Admiral Iwabuchi Sanji, and his staff firmly believed that Manila should be and could be defended. They insisted that they were under previous navy orders involving naval tasks and facilities, preempting army orders to retire to the Shimbu Group. The army conceded and placed its rearguard contingents under the navy. Thus Manila was defended, under the command of Admiral Iwabuchi, by 17,000 troops in three combat groups, one north of the Pasig River, one in the center covering the Intramuros and government buildings, and one in the south, in case the Americans landed on the southern coast and came upon Manila from that direction.[131]

The Americans did come from the south.[132] On January 31 two regiments of the Eleventh Airborne Division made an amphibious landing at Nasugbu on the southwest corner of Luzon, fifty-five miles from Manila. They moved inland quickly but were slowed by hillside defenses as they reached Tagaytay Ridge. Fighting their way through, they came to the ridge's smooth terrain tilting upward to the north, where they met the rest of the division, the 511th Parachute Regiment, which had just jumped and landed nearby. By concentrating all available transportation on the 511th in a shuttle, the commander, Major General Joseph M. Swing, moved the regiment quickly to a position just south of Manila. Attacking north, the paratroopers were held up by a Japanese strongpoint in a building with five-foot-thick walls. Technical Sergeant Robert C. Steele climbed to the roof, made a hole in it, poured in gasoline, and lit it with a white phosphorous grenade. As the Japanese ran out, they were gunned down. A few miles farther north at Las Piñas a brief firefight secured the bridge, but the next bridge, a damaged one at Parañaque, covered by Japanese fire from the north bank and artillery from Nichols Field (then held by Japanese), brought the column to a halt three miles south of Manila city limits.

On February 5, the 511th struck north, again along the shore, gaining yard by yard through pillbox defenses that had grown their own grass camouflage. Then the 511th joined the 188th in an attack on nearby Nichols Field, which met with intense artillery fire and brought the regiments to a full stop. The problem was lack of killing power. Infantry divisions have their own 105 mm and 155 mm battalions; airborne divisions carry lighter artillery. The Eleventh Airborne, an Eighth Army division, arranged artillery concentrations on Nichols Field with Sixth Army artillery, but these would not be easily coordinated with infantry in assault and adjusted. Furthermore, the Eleventh Airborne went into battle with 8,200 men, almost half the personnel of an infantry division, and by now it had taken 900 casualties.[133] General Swing persisted in the attack. On February 11, the Eleventh Airborne, now transferred from the Eighth to the Sixth Army, tried once more. The 511th pushed north along the bay, reaching within a mile of the city limits. Then the two regiments again hit Nichols Field, this time with Marine Corps Dauntless bombers that destroyed much of the enemy artillery. This time they captured the airfield. The division now stood on the southern periphery of an envelopment of Manila—a lock for which the First Cavalry would be the bolt.

North of the Pasig, the first few days, February 3–7, could be described as the discovery phase with the liberation of Santo Tomas and Bilibid, the arrival of the bulk of the Thirty-Seventh and First Cavalry Divisions, scouting, and positioning weapons. This phase also meant seizing a reservoir and water filtration plant a few miles east of the city in order to assure adequate water supply. Troops hastened to the Pasig to seize the last two bridges and were almost there when Admiral Iwabuchi's naval units blew them up. Amphibious crossings of the river would be the only way south. In the neighborhoods along the bay, the admiral's demolition parties destroyed acres of supplies, creating a gigantic fire raging northward. Soldiers of the Thirty-Seventh turned to demolition of blocks of houses to create a firebreak until the wind changed direction. Meanwhile, companies and battalions of the Thirty-Seventh and First Cavalry were moving through northern Manila eliminating pillboxes, roadblocks, and other strongpoints using artillery fire (limited to distinct targets), mortars, and tanks. The northern half of the city, lightly held because the Japanese had been expecting attack from the south, was mostly clear of the enemy by February 7.[134]

The next move was to cross the Pasig River. General Griswold chose a point just upriver from the presidential palace where the shore bends slightly, hiding the embarkation, and a landing at the Malacañan Botanical Gardens across the river, where there was no seawall to block a landing. Two battalions of the 148th Regiment crossed in amphibious tractors and boats, with Japanese mortars and machine guns downriver opening on the second wave. An observer saw "pieces of paddles and splintered chunks of boat plywood fly through the air while men paddled with shattered oars and rifles."[135] In spite of the short span, the crossing cost 145 casualties. The 129th Regiment crossed the following day. Malacañan Palace and the gardens served the Americans as a pivot in their plan of advance through Manila. Several miles to the southeast the Eighth Cavalry and a mile farther the Fifth Cavalry Regiments crossed the Pasig, in line with the 148th and 129th turning on Malacañan Palace, out to Manila Bay, circling from south to west, connecting with the Eleventh Airborne, and enveloping the enemy against the shoreline of Manila Bay.

It did not take long for the Thirty-Seventh Division to learn that they were into a far more deadly battle on the south side of the Pasig than they had experienced on the north side. Under orders to seize the electric generating plant on Provisor Island to forestall a power outage in Manila, the division assigned this task to the 129th Regiment, whose last battle had been the capture of Top of the World Hill on the Kembu front eight days earlier.

Provisor Island was 400 by 125 yards in area, set in the south shore but surrounded by small canals and the river, and dense with power plant buildings. The Americans faced the island's own garrison and were open to machine cannon, machine guns, rifles, and mortar fire from the neighbor-hood, south, southwest, and west. The regiment sent seventeen men from G Company across the eastern canal. Two in the second boat were killed, and the rest stormed the boiler room but were ejected in a counterattack and took cover behind a coal pile until night. They were withdrawn and, after a heavy barrage, were replaced by ninety men of Company E, sent in six boats. The moon emerged in midpassage, inviting another hail of bullets and the loss of three boats. This contingent was hugging the coal pile for several hours until the moon disappeared and they dashed into the boiler room and stayed, moving in and out of the machinery to flush out the enemy.[136] The following day the enemy fire, in the face of uninterrupted artillery, mortar, tank, and tank destroyer fire on the western side of the island and nearby mainland, steadily lessened and finally ceased. By the end of the third day, Provisor Island, a pile of rubble, was in American hands.[137]

South of Provisor Island, the 148th Regiment came upon thick defenses at Paco Railroad Station: pillboxes protected by spider holes outside the station and sandbagged automatic weapons inside, covered by automatic fire from school and college buildings nearby. Technical Sergeant Cleto Rodriguez and Private First Class John N. Reese, Jr., moved their machine gun and loads of ammunition close to the station and, firing from there for over two hours, killed eighty-two Japanese. Reese was killed; both received the Medal of Honor.[138]

The Paco and Provisor firefights caused a critical change in the American artillery rules of engagement. So far, to hold down civilian casualties, the guns had been limited to observed fire on specific targets. Now the batteries returned to the more devastating area bombardment, which was prohibited only against churches and hospitals "known to contain civilians," a murky distinction. The ban on air bombardment remained, which was probably a benefit, given the amount of friendly fire American troops had been receiv-ing in the Central Valley. Intelligence sources reported that the Japanese in the modern and governmental sector of Manila were making clusters of large, sturdy buildings into fortresses with interior sandbagging and exte-rior angles for cross-fire. That was a great concern to Major General Beightler, who was commanding the Thirty-Seventh Division, which now faced west toward that sector and the bay and which had taken heavy losses in the Provisor and Paco engagements. Fighting south of the Pasig had already cost the 148th about 500 casualties. The 129th Regiment was 700 under strength, the 148th was 600 with no replacements since the landings at Lingayen, except five to the 148th. The division could not sustain losses at the current rate. Now the Japanese—and Manila—would get artillery fire at full strength. Beightler had access to six 8-inch and 240 mm howitzers, twenty-four 155 mm howitzers, and forty-eight 105 mm howitzers, as well as tank, tank destroyer guns, and 4.2-inch mortars.[139]

Step by step the Americans and Japanese became engaged in a battle that engulfed thousands of civilians and destroyed the heart of Manila. At one point Admiral Iwabuchi moved his headquarters to Fort McKinley, southeast of the city, and was considering transferring his Manila Naval Defense Force to the Shimbu front, as the army command had urged and finally ordered him to do. That would have largely saved Manila and its people. However, the army officer he left in charge at Manila reported that he was unable to control the naval detachments, and Iwabuchi returned to fight in the city. Shortly thereafter the First Cavalry completed the encirclement of the city. Even so, two naval battalions, about 1,300 troops defending Fort McKinley, retreated east instead of west and joined the Shimbu Group. Iwabuchi shared the kamikaze spirit among Japanese naval officers at this stage, and he was certainly correct in arguing that prolonging a defense inside the city would inflict heavy losses on the Americans.[140]

On February 9, two days after the first American crossing of the Pasig, a Japanese program of annihilation of Filipinos began. Japanese suspicion and contempt had turned to hatred as the Americans approached and Filipino guerrillas sprang into action alongside the Americans and served as spies and couriers in Manila. "All people on the battlefield," an order read, meaning all Filipinos found in the portion of the city under attack, "will be killed."[141] The executions took place in different locations, times, and sizes, but there was a standard procedure for the men and teenage boys. An armed and officered detachment would surround a home or public building. The target group was hustled out of doors and told they needed to be moved to a safer location. The men and teenage boys were separated from the women and children and wired together. Resistance met with use of pistol, saber, or bayonet. The men who were arrested were soaked with gasoline and locked in a room stacked with inflammable materials easily catching fire. Grenades were then thrown in.

Women and children experienced different horrors. Families sought refuge in large stone or concrete public buildings, such as schools, colleges, churches, convents, the Masonic Temple, and the Red Cross. At the rounding up of 2,000 people in the Paco district, the Japanese selected groups of twenty-five girls and young women, whom they set up in hotels and apartment houses for repeated rape by Japanese marines fighting nearby. About 1,500 refugees crammed into the German Club hoping that Germany, as Japan's ally, would be a protection. They were wrong: men were killed. Babies and small boys brought forward by their mothers to show their innocence were also killed. As the battle for central Manila went on, the deliberate slaughter of civilians grew in intensity.[142] Individual Japanese soldiers intervened to rescue some of the women, but this was a time of the long knives, in this instance bayonets affixed to rifles or in hand. Use of the bayonet, it was said, saved ammunition. There were six recorded instances of babies tossed in the air to be impaled on bayonets.[143] Many women were killed offhand; many more, wounded, died slowly. All suffered from lack of water, food, and care.

By mid-February, the First Cavalry Division was pressing northward just inside the city limits on the south, while the Thirty-Seventh Division pushed west beyond the Provisor-Paco line. The ultimate objective, the Intramuros, stood in the northwest on the Pasig and near the harbor. Standing between the American lines and the Intramuros were five Japanese strongpoints. At the southern flank, the First Cavalry faced the Rizal sports stadium and baseball park next to La Salle University. After two days of fighting their way through the suburb of Passay, the First Cavalry, with 105 mm and 155 mm artillery support, took La Salle and broke into the sports complex. They were expelled the first time but returned the next day with tanks that broke through a cement wall onto the baseball field, where they used flamethrowers and explosives to clear bunkers in left field and machine guns in sandbagged emplacements under the grandstand beyond third base. Having cleared Rizal, the cavalry moved very fast and far north along the shore, taking the high commissioner's residence, the Elks Club, and the Army-Navy Club. There, on February 21, almost in the shadow of the Intramuros, with two self-propelled gun mounts and a platoon of tanks, they attacked Manila Hotel, of which the penthouse apartment had been MacArthur's prewar home. Fighting within the hotel demolished his apartment, beloved book collection, and many personal belongings.[144]

Moving westward toward the Intramuros beyond the Paco-Provisor line, the Thirty-Seventh Division came to a cluster of buildings, centering on the reinforced concrete New Police Station, that absorbed the full strength of the division for eight days. Each of the buildings—a shoe factory, the Manila Club, a church, and a college—had sandbag defenses within and open space covered by mutually supporting machine gun fire on the outside. The 129th Regiment considered it the most formidable obstacle it encountered during the entire Pacific Theater thus far. Three times division troops broke into the police station, and three times they had to withdraw. The Americans, controlling from the top down, cut holes in the floor and dropped grenades through. One by one, constant fire from an artillery battalion, self-propelled mounts, and tanks reduced the interwoven forts and finally demolished the building. The capture of the police station alone cost 105 killed and wounded.[145] The capture of City Hall and the General Post Office, solitary strongpoints farther north, went along the same lines. In the Post Office barricades in rooms and corridors were seven feet high and ten sandbags thick with barbed wire throughout. The 145th Regiment of the Thirty-Seventh Division used submachine guns, bazookas, flamethrowers, grenades, and demolitions at the police station. They finally entered by a window on the second floor and fought downward, using flamethrowers through holes in the ceiling.[146]

The last of the strongpoints was the most difficult and critical. It was a cluster of public buildings situated half a mile south of the Intramuros, blocking the old fort's encirclement. On the north side of the group was the University of the Philippines, and on the south side was the Philippine General Hospital. The reinforced concrete cluster was heavily manned by the Manila Naval Defense Force—in one building, for example, by 250 Japanese sailor infantry. Elaborate compartmental sandbagging with automatic weapons fire from the top floors and emplacements along the foundations were typical, but campus buildings with space between allowed a devastating pattern of cross fires. The hospital, showing large red crosses on the roof, did not have Japanese troops inside, though probably they manned machine guns outside. Inside the main building were 7,000 patients and refugees, packed into wards and corridors. For three days, the Thirty-Seventh Division artillery had disregarded the red crosses because the building was being defended. When the 148th Infantry learned of the refugees, it limited fire so that the 7,000 could be brought to safety.[147]

It took ten days for the 148th Regiment and the Fifth Regiment Cavalry to secure the hospital-university strongpoint. Attacking into streams of bullets from countless directions was a supreme challenge; close combat indoors for hours was totally exhausting. Sometimes the squad or platoon had to withdraw and start over again. The only way out was persistence: expanding a toehold, moving next door, and gradually reducing the arc of fire. The Fifth Regiment Cavalry, on relieving the 148th, improved the assault by following closely behind point-blank fire from medium tanks and using as primary weapons flamethrowers and rocket-firing bazookas. To deal with the enemy's use of caves in the basement, they ignited a mixture of gasoline and oil. American casualties in the reduction of this strongpoint alone were 60 killed and 445 wounded.[148] The 148th lost over a hundred as nonbattle casualties, and the Fifth Regiment Cavalry probably did also. Each of the three rifle companies of the Second Battalion, 148th, which fought the hospital engagement, was now nearly seventy-five men under strength.[149] The forces so far heavily engaged on Luzon, the Forty-Third, Fortieth, Thirty-Seventh, and First Cavalry Divisions, were winning and, without replacements, also weakening.

The paramount and conclusive objective of the American Army in Manila was the capture of the Intramuros, a relic of the Spanish conquest in the sixteenth century. Originally a fortress built to protect the Spanish inhabitants, it retained a community within, surrounded by stone-block walls forty feet thick at the base, thinning to twenty at the top, and twenty to twenty-five feet high. Even wedged between the Pasig River and the dock-yards on Manila Bay, the surrounding moat and parkland provided sweeping fields of fire. In tunnels and gun embrasures within the walls, over 1,000 last survivors of the Japanese Manila Naval Defense Force were prepared to bring the relic into one more battle.

The Thirty-Seventh Division's planning for the Intramuros battle was meticulous. The assault on the three remaining government buildings was postponed until after the capture of the Intramuros because the Intramuros provided favorable firing positions above and closer to those buildings. MacArthur vetoed aircraft bombardment. The planners agreed that the Intramuros attack would start at 8:30 a.m. after a one-hour barrage by massed artillery, allowing a full day for the infantry to carry through. The assault would follow the existing direction of attack, from east to west, except for an amphibious crossing of the Pasig by one battalion to take advantage of a gap in the northern wall through the Government Mint. American artillery would blow breaches in the wall on the northeast and east to open the way for an additional two assault battalions. Most of the heavy guns and mortars in the gathering artillery settled in the north, outside city limits: fifteen 155 mm howitzers (6.1-inch bore), four 8-inch howitzers (the bore for heavy cruisers), and two 240 mm howitzers (9.5-inch bore). Sixteen howitzers and four tank destroyer guns took position along the north bank of the Pasig to give direct fire support to the battalion of the 129th Regiment entering through the mint. Twenty-six machine guns above in office buildings would cover their crossing. The rest of the guns and howitzers massed to the east behind the two assault battalions of the 145th Regiment. This was an array of 132 artillery weapons aimed at an arena 1,000 yards long north–south and 700 yards wide east–west. Earlier pinpoint fire had eliminated Japanese artillery in the Intramuros, so the preparatory bombardment beginning on February 17 could hammer the walls and open two breaches in the eastern wall to allow the assault troops, avoiding the heavily defended gates, to enter quickly.[150]

On February 23, the seventh and last day of bombardment, the overwhelming artillery battering lasted for exactly one hour. As the guns went silent, the assault troops moved fast, across the Pasig and through the mint and clambering through the breaches. The three battalions from the 129th and 145th met within minutes inside the walls. They had been unopposed and taken no casualties. The following platoons from the east side had come in through the gates. Ten minutes after ceasing fire, the artillery resumed with a localized strike, raising a curtain of explosives, smoke, and white phosphorus across the interior of the fortress, hiding the tactical dispersion of the attacking infantry. It was not long before the enemy was roused and fighting, but the shock of one hour of explosions, followed by confusion, allowed the attacking forces to penetrate and engage without facing fields of fire. That won the battle in the first minutes.

So did the coordination and the infantry's fighting skills. That day American artillery fired nearly 8,000 rounds in support of the attack.[151] The battle became a host of firefights within the walls, ending with mopping up the next day, February 24. In the midst of the fighting the first day, the Japanese allowed 3,000 women and children refugees, with priests and nuns, to leave two churches within the walls, perhaps to save them or slow the attackers or both. Fighting was held up during the evacuation. American casualties in the Intramuros battle were 25 killed and 265 wounded. The Japanese Manila Naval Defense Force lost many more than 1,000 and possibly as many as 2,000.[152]

That left in the sights of the XIV corps 300–700 yards to the southeast and south, across the moat and parkland, the three national government buildings still held by the enemy. American commanders—and MacArthur most of all—wanted a finale to the Battle of Manila, not a siege or a prolonged and bloody struggle. Direct fire artillery provided it. The Legislative Building, an imposing structure of wings and colonnades, the culminating point of MacArthur's parade plan, received a one-hour final artillery preparation on February 26 and then an attack from the rear by the First Battalion, 148th Regiment. The battalion was stopped in its tracks by stiff resistance. It withdrew, and the artillery took over with point-blank fire for two hours by 155 mm cannon, tanks, tank destroyers, and self-propelled mounts. The destruction of this monument to representative government was so complete that it moved the author of the Army's official history to a rare instance of poetic imagery. "Only the battered central portion, roofless and gutted, still stood above its wings like a ghost arising from between toppled tombstones."[153]

On February 28, the same day the 148th was mopping up in the Legislative Building, the Fifth Regiment Cavalry was initiating a three-hour bombardment of the Agriculture and Commerce Building, with a relay of 155 mm cannon, tank, and tank destroyer gunfire, aiming only at the first floor to avoid hitting into nearby assaults, with the result that the building collapsed into its first floor. Even then the cavalry found pockets of strong resistance. It took direct fire from tanks, a flame-throwing tank, bazookas, portable flamethrowers, and finally, on March 1, demolitions and burning gas and oil. These were designed to kill anyone within.[154]

On March 2 the 148th moved on to its second objective, the Finance Building, which had experienced repeated gunfire from every bore and angle on February 28 and March 1. On March 1 the regiment held fire while a loudspeaker invited surrender. Surprisingly, twenty-two Japanese came across. The following day three more appeared under a white flag, but this time it was a ruse. As infantrymen broke cover, they were raked by rifle and machine gun fire from the interior. A fierce bombardment ensued, pulverizing the Finance Building.[155]

On February 27, while fighting continued, MacArthur formally turned over civil authority to the Philippine government. The colorful ceremony took place in Malacañan Palace, one of the few buildings still standing in the government section. In light of the circumstances, a parade no longer seemed appropriate. Finally, on March 3, 1945, the city was liberated, and the Battle of Manila was at an end. By the time the battle was over, Manila had suffered more destruction than any Allied capital except for Warsaw. More than 100,000 Filipino inhabitants of the city had been killed in the fighting. Some 16,000 Japanese Manila Naval Base troops had died. American casualties were 1,010 killed, 5,565 wounded, and presumably substantial numbers with illness, injury, and combat fatigue.[156] Robert H. Kiser, a corporal in the 148th Regiment, Thirty-Seventh Division, recalled that of the 160 men in his company who came ashore at Lingayen, "only

13 made it through the last battle for Manila." He himself was in the hospital for injured feet, for infectious mononucleosis, and twice for malaria.[157] Kiser and his weary comrades would turn next to the daunting task of securing the remainder of Luzon. General Yamashita's Shimbu and Shobu groups still controlled the Bataan Peninsula, overlooking Manila Bay, and the mountainous areas east and north of the capital. There they prepared to make the Americans' mission as costly and prolonged as possible.

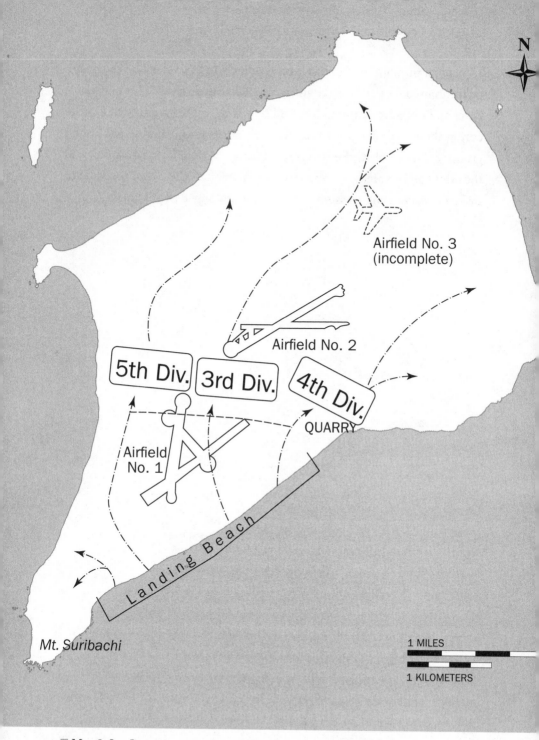

N

5th Div. 3rd Div. 4th Div.

Airfield No. 3
(incomplete)

Airfield No. 2

QUARRY

Airfield
No. 1

Landing Beach

Mt. Suribachi

1 MILES

1 KILOMETERS

■ **Map 8** Iwo Jima. Drawn by George Chakvetadze.

Iwo Jima, February–March 1945

As the stain of battle spread through the Philippines from October 1944 to March 1945, the Pacific Fleet advanced into the sheltering islands south of Japan, positioning American land, sea, and airpower for the invasion of Japan. Following were armadas of invasion craft, transports, oilers, and cargo ships aiming for Iwo Jima, a volcanic piece of rock (known in Japanese as *Iwo Tō*, or "sulfur island") of eight square miles, slightly less than half the size of Manhattan, located 660 miles south of Tokyo and approximately 1,500 miles northeast of Manila. Marines landed on the island on February 19, 1945, and nearly six weeks later Army and Marine forces invaded Okinawa on April 1, forty-four days after the Iwo landing. The campaign had suffered two postponements due to the slowness of the Leyte campaign and MacArthur's retention of ships to protect the Luzon landing. Most of the fighting ships and all of the eleven divisions, Marine and Army, in the Nimitz domain would eventually be engaged.

Early in the planning it was decided that invading Japan would require taking both islands. Capture of Iwo Jima, halfway between the Marianas and Japan, would provide rescue, refill, and repair for B-29 bombers in trouble and unable to reach home base. Admiral Spruance also wanted Iwo

Jima because it would provide a base from which land-based air support could protect the fleet as it moved into Japanese waters along the arc descending from Tokyo through the Ryukyu Islands, which included Okinawa.[1] Okinawa would offer air and supply bases to support the invasion and, in a cluster of small islands nearby, anchorage in a protective roadstead. They would be the start line for the invasion of Japan.

From above, Iwo Jima looks like an ice cream cone on its side with the contents dripping to the east. At the southern tip, almost surrounded by ocean, the burly hump of Mount Suribachi, an inactive volcano, rises to 550 feet. North from Suribachi, the island widens along a two-mile isthmus, with beaches on both sides, and then rises several hundred feet to a landmass two to three miles in length and width, with tableland fit for another airfield in the middle, surrounded by rocky land with trees and scrub, ravines and gullies, ridges and jagged hills, and edged with cliffs. By the time of the invasion, Iwo Jima had no harbor, and its small population had been removed. The isthmus was bare, with sand and soil rising smoothly from the beaches to an airfield in the middle and a second one to the north. Invasion would be more difficult on the western beaches of the peninsula because of higher winds and surf. So the Americans would land on the eastern beaches, which stretched from Suribachi to the cliffs in the north.[2]

Commanding the island was Lieutenant General Kuribayashi Tadamichi, appointed in May 1944 by Prime Minister Tojo Hideki in the face of the American Navy's move into the western Pacific. It was as clear to Tojo as to the Americans that Iwo Jima would be the jumping-off place for an invasion of Japan, and he wanted someone of experience. Of samurai lineage, Kuribayashi had been assistant military attaché in Washington in the 1920s. A veteran of the war in China, he had been most recently in command of the Imperial Guard at Tokyo. Taking up his assignment on Iwo Jima, he concluded that investing troops in defense of the beaches, as had happened at Saipan, was a critical mistake, given the Americans' concentrated firepower. Instead he would set his defense well back from the beaches, within artillery range, and wait until the beaches were crowded, as they always were, with incoming American troops and matériel, and then open bombardment. This was only the beginning. He was looking not for victory over the enemy but for ways to make his advance so costly that it would slow the advance on Japan and, perhaps, give the Japanese some bargaining power. To do this he would fortify the rest of the island—the peninsula, Suribachi, and the higher, rougher terrain in the north—so heavily that the American advance in the open would always be under fire.[3]

Iwo Jima, in other words, was a test case for the defense of Japan itself, and that meant turning the island into a fort, or rather, a fort into an island. Kuribayashi got everything he wanted in tools, materials, and labor, such as demolition and cave experts, stonemasons, Korean laborers, concrete mix, and steel reinforcing rods. Troops participated in the building, and more arrived, raising the garrison to 21,000. Kuribayashi's headquarters in the northern sector was part of a cave system reaching seventy-five feet underground. Within it was a suite for the general, a war room, staff offices, and sleeping compartments, all reached and connected by hundreds of feet of tunnels. Above it, aboveground, was a large blockhouse for radio communication with a reinforced concrete roof ten feet thick and walls five feet thick; it was so sturdy that it eventually took 8,500 pounds of explosives to destroy it. A similar blockhouse nearby, inside a hill, controlled all artillery on the island. Volcanic rock, softer and more breakable than coral, allowed enlargement of caves, multiple entries, and connecting tunnels, providing storage of supplies and ammunition as well as medical facilities. In fact, the Japanese tunneled all the way from the northern sector to Suribachi, so they could reinforce, supply, or withdraw the garrison safely and unseen. The result was eleven miles of tunnels, at an average depth of thirty feet.[4]

No American division in the Pacific theater of operations had faced a more elaborate and comprehensive defense. General Kuribayashi was also heavily supplied with big guns: 361 artillery pieces, 75 mm and larger, thirty-three naval coastal guns, 80 mm and more, and ninety-four dual-purpose (air and ground) antiaircraft guns. Except for those also engaging aircraft, these guns fired from caves or from reinforced blockhouses. Kuribayashi also had sixty-nine 37 mm and 47 mm antitank guns and over 200 of the smaller 20 mm and 25 mm dual-purpose antiaircraft guns. Of mortars, he had sixty-five 81 mm and 150 mm ones, as well as twelve of the monstrous 320 mm spigot mortars and seventy less-accurate rockets with heavy warheads and launchers. Light and heavy machine guns in concrete bunkers and pillboxes surrounded the heavier weapons, forming strong-points with mutually supporting firing lanes and all, as usual, expertly cam-ouflaged. Infantrymen selected for sniper training were among those in pillboxes and spider holes. Guarding the Airfield No. 2 area in the center of the isthmus, for example, were over 800 pillboxes.[5]

The invasion of Iwo Jima involved three Marine divisions. To weaken the defenses, Task Force 58, the fast carrier forces, now with over 700 planes and new battleships, cruisers, and carriers, would attack aircraft plants and airfields in Tokyo and its vicinity on February 16, 17, and 25. Naval minds were by now locked into a large, complex scheme for closing on Japan, and no part of it could be easily changed. That included operations on Iwo Jima.

The Marine Corps's need for extensive preparatory bombardment of Iwo Jima, however, did not fit the naval scheme. After suffering severe casu-alties the previous summer from Japanese bombardment of the beaches at Saipan, the Corps developed a more calculated approach to their prepara-tory bombardment. The weapon of choice would be the heavy guns of bat-tleships and cruisers, from 6- to 16-inch. By intensive air reconnaissance the precise location of the enemy guns would be mapped, sectored, and assigned for destruction. Expert spotters and plotters would then adjust the firing of the guns to bring them onto the target. This methodical approach had been used in the landing on Guam with success.[6]

Precise monitoring of gunfire was more thorough and successful but took time. The original plan from Nimitz's office provided for eight days of preparatory bombardment before the landing.[7] Major General Harry Schmidt, commanding the Marine V Corps, with its three Marine divi-sions, asked for ten days. Vice Admiral R. K. Turner, commander of the Joint Expeditionary Force, together with Admiral Spruance, now com-manding the Fifth Fleet, would allow only three days. Schmidt then asked for nine days; Turner would not budge. Once more Schmidt tried, asking for four days, and Turner agreed, provided the extra day could be fitted into the "general strategic situation." Spruance, however, remained opposed to any change in the larger scheme, suggesting that his forthcoming carrier air attack on Japan "could be considered at least as effective as the additional day of surface ship bombardment."⁸ Schmidt finally asked that at least the bombardment concentrate on the area of the landing; even this was not acceptable: the Navy insisted on allowing other targets such as antiaircraft guns. Two historians commissioned by the Navy after the war to write a history of amphibious warfare in the Pacific concluded from their stance on Iwo Jima that Admirals Turner and Spruance had their minds set on Okinawa and on the air strikes on Tokyo and vicinity; Iwo Jima was necessary but subsidiary and not to be a drain on the main objectives.

The objective of Spruance's attack on Tokyo and vicinity was to pin down the Japanese air force and weaken its kamikaze capability against the Okinawa as well as the Iwo invasions. His command, Task Force 58, largely post–Pearl Harbor ships, consisted of sixteen fleet carriers carrying 700 planes, eighty-one destroyers, sixteen cruisers, one large cruiser, and eight fast battleships. Two of those battleships, the *North Carolina* and *Washington*, with 16-inch guns, had been assigned to the Iwo Jima bombardment force with ground-use ammunition but were whisked away by Spruance en route to Japan because of his need for more antiaircraft guns. The two battleships were returned to Iwo on February 19, the day after the three-day preparatory gunfire, in time only to participate in the prelanding bombardment.⁹ In the end Okinawa, which was seventy times larger than Iwo Jima, would receive seven days of preparatory gunfire on the landing site. Iwo Jima received three days.

That preparatory bombardment also gained no help from Southwest Pacific. As we've mentioned, Admiral Nimitz had lent MacArthur six prewar battleships for protection against kamikaze attack during the advance from Leyte to Luzon, anticipating their return to assist in the Iwo Jima and Okinawa landings. MacArthur, wary of a return to the Philippines by what was left of the Japanese navy, which was not impossible but very unlikely, insisted on keeping them until his air force moved into Luzon. Two were released early for critical repairs and the remaining four not until February 14. Three of the latter group, needing lesser repairs, were able to join the fleet for Okinawa, and one, the *West Virginia*, hastened to Iwo Jima, arriving in time for the landing on the day after the preparatory bombardment ceased.¹⁰ Also engaged in the three-day preparatory bombardment were the battleships *Idaho* and *Tennessee,* with twelve 14-inch guns, the *New York, Texas,* and *Nevada,* with ten 14-inch guns, and the *Arkansas* with twelve 12-inch guns. The last four had gained bombardment experience in European and Mediterranean landings. Newer battleships had 16-inch guns, but shells twelve to fourteen inches thick were hugely destructive.

This was the armada that descended on the tiny island. The six battle-ships, along with five heavy cruisers (8-inch guns) and one light cruiser (6-inch guns), divided to each side of Iwo Jima. On the first of the three precious days, mist and rain frequently reduced visibility. The second day was entirely clear and the third partially reduced by rain. The second day provided a gift. During Navy preparation for the landing, twelve gunboats were heading toward the beaches to drop off underwater demolition swim-mers. Described by journalist Ernie Pyle as "half fish and half nuts," these demolition and reconnaissance teams were a recent development in the war.[11] Once the swimmers performed their mission of destroying beach ob-stacles and charting the landing sites, they were expected to swim back to the small boats from which they had been dispatched into the water. On this occasion, the Japanese coastal defense guns in that sector, perhaps as-suming this was the major assault and probably contrary to orders, opened fire, providing their precise locations to the bombardment ships. Damaged and destroyed in the three-day period were half of the Japanese heavy coastal defense and antiaircraft guns and one-fifth of the light antiaircraft guns. As to the blockhouses, artillery and antitank guns, and pillboxes, only about 25 percent were put out of action. One day more of bombardment was possible but denied. Five more days, some believe, would have pre-pared the way; as it was, according to the historians Jeter A. Isley and Peter A. Crowl in their classic 1951 study, taking Iwo Jima "was like throwing human flesh against reinforced concrete."[12]

The human flesh in the three Marine divisions came to a total of 70,647 troops.[13] Many of them were veterans by this point in the war. The Third Marine Division, Major General Graves B. Erskine commanding, consisted of veterans who had fought on Bougainville and Guam. The Fourth Marine Division, Major General Clifton B. Cates commanding, were survivors of

Saipan. The Fifth Marine Division, Major General Keller E. Rockey, was a new outfit built on former Marine raider and parachute battalions. Unlike Army divisions, Marine divisions each carried two replacement units of seventy-five officers and 1,250 men, and the corps provided a second pool of individual replacements. Joining the force were three battalions of 150 Sherman tanks, but they lacked the latest capability: flame-throwing. Those tanks had to be borrowed from other divisions.[14] By this point in the Pacific Theater napalm had established itself in both the ground and air forces and became an essential weapon against Japanese defenses.

Dawn on February 19 offered a relatively calm sea, light wind, and fleecy clouds. Blocking the horizon east of Iwo Jima was an array of transports, supply ships, landing ships, battleships, cruisers, and destroyers. Bombers and fighters from the fleet and the Marianas took their turn attacking, some so low they seemed to scrape the sand. Behind the leading waves came the thunder of battleship and cruiser guns. The eastern beach, running two miles from Mount Suribachi along the isthmus to the cliffs in the north, was the destination. Coming down the ramps of LSTs into the sea to lead the way were sixty-eight LVT(A)s (landing vehicles, tracked, armored), amphibious tractors each holding about a dozen troops. Following were LVT(A)s firing 75 mm howitzers, common LCVPs carrying reserve troops from the transports, support craft firing machine guns and rockets, and LSMs for carrying and landing tanks. Behind were LSTs with supplies. Reckoning on a stiff defense, the Marines were landing a force powerful enough to smash through just about any beach defenses.

By midday, smashing through was the only alternative. Four regiments had landed, two in the northern half of the beach and two in the southern. The land sloped upward slowly toward the center of the island but abruptly near the beach, where rows of sharply inclined terraces of volcanic ash impeded progress. The ash, light and slippery, made it almost impossible to gain a secure footing, especially for those carrying heavy weapons. Movement off the beach was slow at first, and the rapid arrival of wave after wave of landing craft and landing ships was crowding troops and supplies onto the beach. Japanese gunfire was scattered at first but steadily grew, aided by observation from Suribachi on the left and the cliffs on the right. Bombardment was particularly heavy from the west, on the far side of Airfield No. 1, an area thick with gun emplacements. Around midday the wind shifted direction from northwest to southeast, pounding the beach, while a strong current from the south set in parallel to the beach, broaching and flooding small craft and littering the congested beach. Reserve troops and supplies were landing into what must have seemed a killing basin. Orders came to move out.[15] The troops crawled or lumbered off the terraces and headed west into the gunfire. Thirty thousand troops landed the first day; nearly 600 were killed and nearly 2,000 wounded. That was a rate of roughly 8 percent, which was comparable to American losses on Omaha Beach at Normandy.[16]

According to the Marine V Corps plan for taking Iwo Jima, two divisions would land along the beach on the eastern side of the isthmus, stretching from Suribachi in the south to cliffs at the northern end where the island widens. The Fifth Division in the south would strike across the isthmus for the western shore and turn north, except for one regiment, which turned south to face Suribachi. The rest of the Fifth would drive north in line with the Fourth Division, which landed on the northern beaches and turned north. When the Third Division, in reserve, landed it would move north between the Fifth and Fourth Divisions. Then the line of three divisions would clear the wider, broken country in the north, where the enemy's principal defenses lay.

As it was impossible to tolerate the presence of enemy forces and guns at the rear of their own forces, especially from heights with observation such as Suribachi provided, the Marine command, while organizing to move north, ordered the Twenty-Eighth Regiment of the Fifth Division to drive south and take the volcano. The First Battalion of the Twenty-Eighth, landing on the southernmost portion of the eastern beach, would push as fast as possible across the isthmus, only 700 yards wide at this point, to the western beach, thereby isolating Suribachi (except for the tunnels) from the rest of the island. Then the First Battalion would link up with the Second and Third Battalions of the Twenty-Eighth Regiment to form a line facing south across the isthmus.

Usually battles take place on a larger landmass than that provided by Iwo Jima, allowing separation from action and withdrawal from the front for restitution or maneuver. On Iwo there was no such room. As one veteran put it, "this whole island is a front." Marines discovered they were never "safely out of range." At any time, as Richard Wheeler, who fought in E Company of the Second Battalion, Twenty-Eighth Regiment, wrote in his book, one of the most harrowing written about Iwo Jima, "shells were whining and crashing, machine guns and rifles were rattling, and men were shouting." Near the base of Suribachi one had the constant strain of "being watched over gun sights by hundreds of hostile eyes" from above. Rather than offering safety, taking cover in an empty crater or trench might instead invite shelling from guns zeroed on that spot. Bunkers and pillboxes already cleared were often reinhabited by stealth at night or by underground passage. Marines became isolated and helpless.[17]

Marines used backpacked flamethrowers and satchel charges of dynamite to destroy bunkers and pillboxes. Sergeant Martin J. Queeney, Wheeler remembered, "coolly took a satchel charge, made a flanking approach to the mound, and shoved the charge into its back entrance." His actions posthumously won him the Navy Cross. Corporal Conrad F. Shaker entered an enemy tunnel with his combat knife drawn and came out with it bloody. "As he climbed the mound to shout to Marines farther back, he was shot through the head and fell dead," recalled Wheeler.[18] Grenades were used heavily on both sides. Darrell S. Cole, a young sergeant in the neighboring Twenty-Third Regiment, whose squad was pinned down by machine gun fire and grenades from a group of pillboxes, "dropped back and circled around to the rear of the pillboxes with some grenades of his own, tossing them through the low entrances." Succeeding, he returned for more grenades twice, but on his third attack an enemy grenade exploded at his feet. His company completed the attack and moved ahead. Cole received the Congressional Medal of Honor posthumously.[19] Bullets from rifles and machine guns were more deadly than shellfire, but the latter, from artillery, mortars, and rockets, could explode into sizzling, jagged-edged steel fragments that gouged and sliced into men in the beach congestion and when bunching to confer.

Nighttime had its own nightmares. As soon as the sun went down, the temperature dropped and a chill set in. Most ships and planes withdrew seaward for the night, leaving a terrible feeling of isolation for those ashore. Several destroyers fired star shells into the sky from which intense yellow lights floated down, unsettling in the moving shadows they created. General Kuribayashi considered banzai suicide attacks wasteful but used night infiltration. Twice during the first night individual Japanese slipped into Company E (Easy Company in the military's alphabetical nomenclature), Twenty-Eighth Regiment, areas, once wounding a Marine with a grenade and once startling a Marine into jumping out of his foxhole screaming "Jap! Jap!" Since orders were to lie low, another Marine mistook the man shouting for a Japanese and shot him. The two Japanese got away. "The acute tension and the night's chill forced many men to clench their teeth to keep them from chattering," recalled Wheeler.[20]

The Suribachi defenses were most formidable on a shelf that protruded several hundred yards north from the volcano's sides. Lining up against these defenses on February 20, the second day of the offensive, was the Twenty-Eighth Regiment, Fifth Division, with the Second Battalion, including Company E, on the left, the Third Battalion on the right, and the First Battalion in reserve. The advance began at 8:30 a.m., with artillery, naval battery, and air attack preparing the way. The tanks assigned were delayed; beach congestion left them without fuel, ammunition, or maintenance teams. The enemy ahead, soon responding, "blanketed" a large part of the front with "roaring funnels of steel and sand," according to Wheeler. Extended enemy bombardment made survival seem hopeless. Wheeler recalled that he "could feel the fear dragging at my jowls." But, he added, "we had been ordered to attack, so we would attack." Wheeler and a companion in a shell hole each received two mortar shell wounds, Wheeler's in the jaw and leg. They immediately got first aid from a corpsman, himself wounded. The companion, "with both legs stripped of skin and missing patches of flesh," died.[21]

Leading the advance were Lieutenant Keith Wells, Sergeant Henry O. Hansen, and Private First Class Donald J. Ruhl. They were moving on the enemy in trenches on the far side of a pillbox when a grenade landed right in front of them. Ruhl "dived on the charge, absorbing its full blast," leaving "a gory cavity where his chest had been." He received the Congressional Medal of Honor. James Robeson and Louie Adrian, a Spokane Tribe Indian, took up the fight, standing up, each in turn, to fire his Browning automatic rifle into the trenches. Adrian "crumpled" with a bullet through his heart.[22] Replacement filled in for replacement. When the company ran out of grenades, two volunteers went for more, and both were killed.[23]

Next sent to the firing line were two flamethrowers with seventy-pound fuel tanks on their backs. Death by burning napalm almost defies description. The Japanese concrete bunker and pillbox, bullet- and shell-proof as they were, still required openings, at least an entry in the back and apertures for the weapon, observation, and aiming. The larger the opening, the more extensive the field of fire for the enemy and the easier a target for a lobbed grenade. For the pillbox designer, there was a fine line between protection and utility. Grenades fit through many apertures; a demolition satchel often would not. Flamethrowers, however, would spurt fire through the slits, exploding ammunition inside and incinerating occupants, while riflemen covered exit points. Rockets from shoulder-firing bazookas helped crumble the concrete. Tanks finally arrived in the afternoon of the attack on Suribachi but required guides outside, using arm signals to point out targets and steer them around land mines and wounded men. Three guides were sent, one for each tank. For the first tank heading up the slope one guide was killed, another was wounded, and the third had the tank's external phone shot from his hand. As the day wore on, the unceasing pressure of the Marine regiment and its weapons finally overcame the concrete and trench defenses at the base of Suribachi. Easy Company's sector destroyed over fifty pillboxes and bunkers. Some of the remaining Japanese in Suribachi made their way north to join the main body, leaving behind several hundred in the volcano caves, some who were wounded and others who might have formed a banzai charge had General Kuribayashi allowed it.[24]

To secure the top of Suribachi, the commander of the Twenty-Eighth Regiment selected a patrol of forty-five from Easy Company, including flamethrowers. The patrol prepared on Thursday and climbed the mountain on Friday morning, the fourth day after landing, having negotiated the steepest grades, foot by foot, on their hands and knees. Two Japanese, one of them an officer, charged out of a cave at the top and were killed; some of those left in the caves below, within the crater, attacked with grenades, but the rest were trapped inside the caves by demolition and either were burnt or, as was later learned, starved to death.

What happened next has become a storied moment in American military history. The patrol had brought an American flag to fly from the top of Suribachi, to let those below know it had been taken. They found an iron water pipe in the crater that would serve for the pole. A pistol was used to blow holes in the pipe for attachment of the flag, and rocks piled at the base supported it. However, it was determined that the flag was too small. One twice as big was found in one of the LSTs and hastened to the top, where it was fastened to a longer flagpole and raised by six Marines. The raising of the flag caught the attention of the patrol hiking up the mountain and spread to those below, as the small flag and then the large one were swung up and unfurled. A beach-master, one of the officers responsible for directing traffic through the surf and over the assault beaches, announced the event with his public address system, volume turned up as high as it would go. Shouts of joy rose from the beaches below and spread across shell holes and trenches beyond, reaching the decks of ships offshore. Thousands of Marines, gathered in an enormous coast-to-coast amphitheater, had their eyes on the scene above. Navy Secretary James V. Forrestal happened to be on the beach at Iwo Jima. It was a moment to celebrate the capture of Suribachi but, more broadly, to honor the Marines for their participation in the battle, which was described by one war correspondent as a "nightmare in hell." Recognition would help the Marine abide the losses he faced—his comrades, his physical capacity after wounds, his life. The famous picture of the raising of the larger flag, taken by Joe Rosenthal of the Associated Press, represents those who fought. Indeed, three of the six Marines who were photographed raising the flag were later killed in the battle. We find no such representation honoring the GI in MacArthur's battle publicity.[25]

The capture of Suribachi was only the beginning of the conquest of Iwo Jima. The Twenty-Eighth Regiment turned north, rejoining the rest of the

Marine Fifth Division on the main battlefront. That front could not move far until the beach was cleared and the bulk of the landing forces and their supplies landed and distributed. Storm and wind had strewn the beach with small landing craft to the point that the medium and large landing ships could scarcely find room to drop their ramps and unload. Scattered about on the sand were personal weapons and belongings and men torn apart by shellfire. Bobbing among the onshore waves and wreckage were those drowned in the landing. Soon, however, beach-masters took command of their sectors along the shoreline, clearing the way, setting priorities, and facilitating unloading. Bulldozers and cranes arrived and removed beached boats, cut passages through the terraces, laid temporary steel matting on the spongy sand, and walled in supply dumps. The rest of the Fourth and Fifth Divisions landed, as well as reserves, replacements, and parts of the Third Division. Specialty units also arrived: engineers to remove mines and set up water distilleries (there was no source of drinking water on the island); communication teams to establish a command network and control artillery and naval gunfire; graves registration teams to care correctly for the dead, including building a cemetery for each division; and construction battalions to enlarge airfields so that they could take in B-29s at the earliest possible moment. Small tractor amphibians called Weasels arrived, critical to carrying ammunition and rations to the troops at the front and wounded to the rear.

Though it was true through the Pacific campaign, it is impossible to stress enough the critical role the medical system played on Iwo Jima. Corpsmen were at the front from the start, with tourniquet and compresses to stop the bleeding, morphine for the pain, and means of protecting the wound and easing the patient, who went to the beach by litter or walking with the help of another Marine. At the beach the medical service took over with blood transfusions and identification of the individual, his wound, and his treatment. Thence, in the first days ashore, the wounded would be sent out to a hospital ship with doctors and surgical equipment, which sailed for Guam as soon as it was filled. Later, battalion aid stations just behind the front were set up, bringing doctors and medicine closer to patients, and by the end of the battle, entire hospitals were functioning on Iwo Jima. Americans from the West Coast gave blood for the Marines, which was packed in ice and flown to Iwo Jima. Whole blood was first used by medical officers on Leyte, but this was the first time whole blood, instead of plasma, was used by the Marines.[26]

Throughout the scramble of troops coming ashore in the first days of the invasion, the Marine regiments, except the Twenty-Eighth, heading for Suribachi, were fighting their way into the planned linear formation across the isthmus, headed northeast. The Twenty-Sixth and Twenty-Seventh Regiments, Fifth Division, secured Airfield No. 1 and, reaching the western coast, turned north. The Twenty-Third, Twenty-Fourth, and Twenty-Fifth Regiments, Fourth Division, fought their way westward from their landing site, met the Fifth Division at the airfield, and pivoted north as well. When the Ninth and Twenty-First Regiments, Third Division, arrived, they took their place between the two divisions, forming a line of three divisions clearing the islands as it advanced northward.

On Sunday, February 25, with almost all the combat forces landed and in line and the emplacement of headquarters and artillery substantially complete, the V Corps launched a bombardment and then attacked to the northeast. The attack began a mile northeast of Suribachi in open country, where there were no trees or scrub, no boulders or verticals, just the flat, hard runways of Airfield No. 1 and the undulating sand dunes surrounding it. The immediate objective was Airfield No. 2, located one mile to the northeast. Just behind this airfield was a ridgeline rising fifty feet and, beyond, a further rise of several hundred feet into the jumbled terrain of the northern half of Iwo Jima. Alongside, behind and above Airfield No. 2, was the most dense concentration of Japanese guns on the island, some 800 bunkers and pillboxes containing artillery, antiaircraft, antitank weapons, machine guns, and mortars, and covering from every angle and depth the flat open space of Airfield No. 2. The three American divisions formed a line across the airfields, facing north with the Third Division at the center. In the first attack the Third Division's Ninth Regiment failed to break through, and on February 24 it was the turn of the Twenty-First Regiment, who were told that the airfield had to be taken that day.

As the bombardment and air strikes lifted, the Marines spread out across Airfield No. 1, with the Second Battalion on the south side and the Third Battalion on the north. On the north side two companies set out abreast in a 400-yard front, heading for the open, sandy terrain lying between the two airfields and weighted down with their weapons as well as extra ammunition and grenades. Tanks were to join the infantry but came to a stop when two were disabled by mines and several more by antitank guns. The Pacific forces had not yet received the newly released Pershing tank, with its 90 mm gun and lower silhouette. The troops left the Sherman tanks with their 75 mm guns and higher silhouettes behind and pressed ahead. It was about 1,000 yards to the ridgeline at the far end of Airfield No. 2. The troops had been warned not to take out pillboxes, thereby slowing the charge, but to get past them. The chatter and bangs of enemy gunfire rolled down and across the runways of Airfield No. 2. Here and there Marines disappeared from view, either hit or seeking protection. Those with M1 Garand rifles had to keep sand out of the barrel and firing mechanism, which had turned out to be vulnerable. Reaching the ridge at the far side of the airfield, platoons attached bayonets and attacked up the slope, only to find themselves getting hit by friendly fire. Halting that, they tried again and were repelled by Japanese troops. They then withdrew to reorganize and allow further bombardment and came back for a third attack, this time a hand-to-hand fight involving, as Wheeler recalled it, "grenades, pistols, bayonets, knives, clubbed rifles, and even picks and shovels." The Marines of K Company, Twenty-First Regiment, killed about fifty of the enemy and, reduced from platoons to squads, took control of the ridge with I Company. They had taken only part of Airfield No. 2 but had taken that much and kept it.[27] It was a day of "mortar barrages...joined by artillery bursts, with their terrible concussion and whizzing fragments," beside steady streams of bullets. With corpsmen short of litters, wounded were carried in their ponchos. Officers were leading the troops: the captain of K Company was wounded, the captain of I Company was killed, and three of his were lieutenants wounded. For the entire corps since landing, casualties had now risen to 7,758, a staggering 25 percent of the force. Of these, 558 were cases of combat fatigue.[28]

In the battle for Airfield No. 2, as well as enemy defenses in the Fourth and Fifth Division sectors, V Corps was encountering the main line of Japanese resistance, a dense fortification east–west across the island on a rising slope of rocks, rubble, and lone, steep hills. Even with the arrival and use of almost every available artillery battalion, Fourth and Fifth Division troops barely moved ahead. The Third Division, in the center, was missing its last regiment, the Third, which was nearby but withheld. In their study of the battle, Isley and Crowl recognize that the Third Division center sector led the way in bombardment but argue that V Corps should have assigned even more bombardment to the center. They point out that the center, with its narrow, more manageable front, held a pivotal position. On February 28 General Erskine, commanding the Third Division, used all available fire-power, including artillery, mortars, naval gunfire, and air support, to drive forward while using reserves to cover.[29] On the Division's right, across the front from the ridge held by I and K Companies of the Twenty-First Regiment, a "soft spot developed." Before dark a Marine battalion pushed through and beyond what was left of Motoyama village, which stood on Motoyama Plateau. Thus on February 28, the tenth day after the landing, the Third Division had gotten past the main line of resistance and into "the guts of Iwo Jima."[30] The Marine plateau position, on terrain that had been leveled in preparation to become a third Japanese airfield, led to ridges and ravines, west, north, and east, that dropped from the plateau toward the encircling shore. The divisions now left the isthmus route north for the open plateau, allowing maneuver on enemy positions from different directions. However, the fighting became more, not less, intense among the dense system of caves, concrete gun positions, and underground fortifications toward the coast.

The Marines were weakening as a result of heavy casualties, the limited value of inexperienced and inadequately trained division replacements, and the steady drain of fighting capacity. Marines had for weeks been dealing with death all about them, becoming sleep deprived from guarding against night infiltration. In the midst of huge troop losses, Admiral Turner and General Smith rejected committing the last regiment available—the Third Regiment of the Third Division—principally on the grounds that the number of Marines already on the island should have been enough to capture it. The Third Regiment returned to the Marianas on March 5. Concern for sufficient manpower for the forthcoming campaign on Okinawa won out. Marines ashore on Iwo Jima, reporters noted, were bent forward, thin, and unshaven. Even so, throughout the drive northward, the Third Division, reduced as it was to two regiments, provided the punch and spark for advance.[31]

Pushing beyond the plateau toward the northern shore, the Third Division encountered the last line of resistance. Barring the way was the Japanese elite Twenty-Sixth Tank Regiment. Threatening the advance on the left was Hill 362C. For this assault General Erskine gained approval to attack in the dark. Before dawn on March 7, without bombardment and as silently as possible, his troops approached enemy defenses and filtered into their lines. With the defending troops pinned down, two battalions on the left attacked the hill that blocked their way, and two battalions penetrated as far as 200 yards before the enemy awoke and fought back. The battalions on the left took the first hill, but it was Hill 331, not 362C. Under division order, the left battalions continued, and by midafternoon held Hill 362C. Meanwhile the Japanese defenders attacked and besieged the troops that had penetrated their defense line. It was thirty-six hours before all the surviving Marines trapped behind the line were extricated, numbering seven of Company E and nineteen out of forty-one in Company F, Ninth Regiment. Second Lieutenant John H. Leims, commander of Company B, Ninth Regiment, after learning that a platoon had been surrounded and lacked communication, carried telephone and wire 400 yards to the platoon and there, ordered to withdraw, brought the platoon out without loss. Informed that several casualties had been left behind, he returned to them, carried one to safety, and, returning again, saved the other. For this he received the Congressional Medal of Honor.[32] It took six days for the thinning Third Division to overcome the Japanese Twenty-Sixth Tank Regiment.[33]

On March 9, eighteen days after the landing, the Third Division reached the northern seacoast, splitting the enemy's line of defense and reducing the island to a set of neighboring but independent engagements, each increasingly small but, as always on Iwo Jima, bloody. Elements of the Third Division turned left, securing the coast westward and sheltering the Fifth Division, which was fighting its way north along the west coast. The Fifth

Division had been working into the upland, capturing Hill 362A and Nishi Ridge, and now was entering a defile named the Gorge. This ravine was a confusion of angles and shapes, its walls pockmarked with hollows and caves and its ground strewn with rubble, boulders, and large slices of rock. Ideally suited for defense, the defile led to Kuribayashi's own fortress. The Fifth Division's Twenty-Eighth Regiment—those who had captured Suribachi—started up the defile, led by armored bulldozers and tanks rigged with bulldozer blades to clear the way, followed by flame-throwing tanks, which had finally arrived on the island.

In the Fourth Division sector on the eastern side of the island, the Japanese naval contingent, as had occurred in the Philippines, together with troops commanded by a traditionalist army officer, led a nighttime banzai charge to recapture Mount Suribachi, against orders issued by Kuribayashi, who had lost control as a result of the splitting of his forces. The Fourth Division, exhausted but grimly determined, killed 784 Japanese and stopped the attack, suffering 347 casualties of their own. Indeed, the Fourth Division suffered more casualties than either of the other two divisions. It had attacked what the Marines called the Meat Grinder, a cluster of separate but mutually reinforcing defenses, and Hill 382, a rock formation several hundred yards across with cave armament and underground access. The top had been carved out to accommodate artillery and anti-tank guns.[34] Nearby was the smaller hill called Turkey Knob, with a communications blockhouse made of thick concrete at the top. Next came the Amphitheater, formed by lava shaped like a bowl. At the rim on the far side were caves and tunnel entrances. Every irregular surface held gun positions creating cross lanes of fire.[35] The Fourth Division tried to capture the Amphitheater again and again, initially with five battalions abreast and with repeated bombardment by tanks, artillery, naval gunfire, and air strikes, with over a thousand gallons of napalm, and even by dismantling a 75 mm gun, carrying it close up, and reactivating it. The Fourth Division began attack on the Grinder on February 25 and ended it on March 3: Hill 382 was taken; Turkey Knob and the Amphitheater were "subdued." The remainder of the division then joined the other divisions in clearing the northern shore.[36]

The Marines suffered over 8,000 casualties in the first week of the Iwo Jima campaign.[37] It was a gigantic drain, weakening not only the troop base but also their lieutenants, captains, and majors, on whom the generals depended for frontline leadership. Consider the two-day experience of Company E, Twenty-Fourth Regiment, Fourth Division, in the assault on Hill 382 beginning on March 2. The company commander, Major Roland Carey, was wounded and replaced by Captain Pat Dolan, who was wounded and replaced by First Lieutenant Stanley Osborne, who was killed and temporarily replaced by platoon leader Second Lieutenant Dick Reich. First Lieutenant William Crecink took over and the following morning was wounded and temporarily replaced by Reich. Then a new commander arrived, Captain Charles Ireland, who was wounded that afternoon and replaced by Reich. Finally, Captain Robert M. O'Mealia, the regimental bandleader, took over and was killed. This time Company E, too small, merged with Company F.[38] Hill 382 was indeed a meat grinder. In the eight days of the battle to take it, the Fourth Division lost 2,880 troops.[39] Its combat efficiency estimate fell to 45 percent and lower. Companies in a battalion of the Fifth Division were down from about 250 to 45–85 men.[40] At the village of Nishi in the west, Marines of the Fifth hastened to the top of a knoll featuring an enemy command post inside of which was a pack of dynamite. The explosion was devastating, causing forty-three casualties.[41] By the time of the Hill 382 battle, divisional replacements had all been moved to the front, and divisions were drawing on artillery, motor transport, and other Marine service operations for troops in combat.

Early in March, a report noted that the fighting Marines seemed "very tired and listless,"[42] lacking energy and generally indifferent. Beyond listlessness was combat fatigue, experienced by a record-high 2,648 Marines.[43] Iwo Jima is generally recognized to have been among the most harrowing of fighting experiences—the constant threat of death, the endless reserves and resolve of an enemy so deeply dug in that the soldiers felt they were fighting the island itself. However, most Marines—reticent, plodding now—remained dogged, sustained by duty and loyalty.

Gradually the local fighting diminished as the Marine battalions slowly progressed. The last was the Fifth Division, which was gradually moving up the Gorge along the top and bottom of the ravine, methodically sealing off caves by fire and demolition one by one, and clearing the folds and rocks of Japanese soldiers. The battlefield was squeezed from 14,000 to 50 square yards and finally to nothing except the fortress of General Kuribayashi, which the Fifth destroyed with dynamite. The general had committed seppuku. As the firing ceased in the north it opened up on the isthmus, where 280 Japanese launched a carefully planned night attack, stealing south by tunnel and hidden paths and invading parts of the tent city. With knives, swords, grenades, and weapons that had been taken from dead Marines, they attacked awakening fighter pilots, Seabees (members of Construction Battalions), and a Fifth Division Pioneer service company made up of African Americans. The Marines seized guns and set up firing and skirmish lines that gradually overcame the attackers; particularly effective were the men in the Pioneer company. Forty-four airmen were killed and eighty-eight wounded; nine Pioneers were killed and thirty-one wounded.[44]

The Fifth Division finished its task at the Gorge on March 25 but in just two weeks of battle had taken 2,400 casualties. The troops cleaned up, packed, said their prayers and goodbyes at the Fifth Marine Division cemetery, and climbed the rope ladder from the landing craft to the troopships. Iwo Jima had taken everything out of them, and many needed assistance from the ships' crews with a lift over the rail. The Marines had taken a total of 25,851 casualties on Iwo Jima; 28,686 including Navy and Army units. The Japanese lost an estimated 20,000 of the 21,000 on the island, with the rest taken prisoner, often after weeks of holding out in small groups.[45]

The toll in lives lost on Iwo Jima produced a strong reaction at home and weighed heavily on the minds of those who directed the war. On March 15, in the midst of the battle, the Navy released an anguished letter it had received from an unidentified woman pleading "Please for God's sake stop sending our finest youth to be murdered on places like Iwo Jima." "It is too much for boys to stand," she wrote; "too much for mothers and homes to take. It is driving some mothers crazy. Why can't objectives be taken in some other way. It is most inhuman and awful—stop, stop!" Navy Secretary James Forrestal's response provided cold comfort to the author and others like her, who according to the Navy had recently sent similar entreaties to the Pentagon. Victory, Forrestal explained, depended on the "valor of the Marine and Army soldier who, with rifle and grenades, storms enemy positions, takes them and holds them." "There is no short cut or easy way," he added; "I wish there were."[46] Forrestal's willingness to publish the unidentified woman's letter and his acknowledgment that many others like it had been received suggests that he and his advisers recognized that they were reaching a critical moment in the war. As the letters made clear, a significant segment of the public was beginning to find the war's cost intolerable just as American forces were drawing closer to Japan. Harder fighting lay ahead, and that reality had to be confronted directly, Forrestal seemed to say. Toward that end, the armed forces were aiding newsreel companies in producing more realistic reports of the fighting in Europe and the Pacific. During the battle for Iwo Jima, raw footage was dispatched back to the newsreel companies in New York and was ready for distribution within two weeks of the initial landings. The newsreels produced from the film displayed the horror of war with disturbing candor. Bosley Crowther, a writer for the *New York Times*, observed that "the newsreels, thank heaven, are getting tougher. They are letting us have it right between the eyes." Of particular note, Crowther added, was *Pacific Fury*, a forthcoming film on the capture of Peleliu and nearby Anguar that looked closely into the faces of the men who fought these battles and thus personalized the strain and suffering they endured.[47]

Despite the devastating casualties—percentage-wise, the costliest of the Pacific Theater in World War II—Iwo Jima was a necessary objective. The capture eliminated Japanese airpower on the island, a threat to the Marianas as well as to B-29 raids on Japan. Furthermore, the seizure of Iwo Jima provided protection of B-29s by long-range fighters based on Iwo Jima. American aircraft were flying from the island before the fighting ended. Over 20,000 airmen bombing Japan from the Marianas landed in "crippled" planes on Iwo Jima. "Roughly one-fourth of these flyers would have been lost if the island had not been in American hands," according to Isley and Crowl.[48] The first, the B-29 *Dinah Might*, landed safely on March 4 on a contested airfield. Writing from the Marianas, war correspondent Ernie Pyle noted that B-29 airmen dreaded "'sweating out' those six or seven hours of ocean beneath them on the way back." Having an emergency airfield midway back to their base was a huge relief for the eleven-man crews, especially since the Navy managed to recover only a fifth of ditched flyers. "I suppose," Pyle wrote, "around a B-29 base you hear the word 'ditching' almost more than any other word."[49]

By early March, B-29s flying from the Marianas were shifting to nighttime bombing raids, a tactical change that further reduced the declining threat posed by Japanese fighters. Under the command of General Curtis LeMay, a demanding, cigar-chomping aviator, the bombers abandoned any pretense of precision bombing. Instead they resorted to area bombing, attacking at low altitudes armed only with incendiary bombs. LeMay's bombers inaugurated this new approach on the night of March 9–10 with an attack on Tokyo. Flying over Tokyo at only 5,000 feet, 334 bombers struck the most densely populated parts of the sprawling city, destroying sixteen square miles of buildings and homes and killing an estimated 90,000–100,000 inhabitants. As one crew member recalled, the updrafts caused by the flames were so strong that the airmen were tossed around the inside of their planes "like dice in a cup." Below, the fires ignited by the raid caused more devastation than the Great Chicago Fire of 1871, the San Francisco Earthquake of 1906, or the Tokyo Earthquake of 1923, although the latter event caused twice as many fatalities. As they ventured out after the raid, survivors confronted a ghastly spectacle of charred bodies clogging the Sumida River and area canals, where they had fled for refuge. "We were instructed to report on actual conditions," a Japanese police official later recalled; "most of us were unable to do this because of the horrifying conditions beyond imagination."[50] The massive destruction produced by a single night's raid on Japan's main city provided ample evidence of the empire's increasing vulnerability. Japanese air defenses seemed powerless to prevent other such attacks throughout the home islands. Nevertheless, the Japanese government gave no indication that it was prepared to surrender.

On March 27, eleven days after the Marines declared victory on Iwo Jima, Admiral King released his annual report surveying the Navy's accomplishments over the preceding year.[51] During that time, the Navy had moved more than 3,000 miles across the Pacific. King recounted the hard-won victories at Saipan, Tinian, and Peleliu and defended Spruance's decision not to pursue the Japanese fleet in the battle of the Philippine Sea. In describing the Navy's advance across the Pacific, King emphasized the advantages gained by the Navy's seizure in September of the unoccupied anchorage at Ulithi in the Western Caroline Islands. King further explained how Admiral Halsey's discovery of the weakness of Japanese air forces in the Philippines had led to the American attack on Leyte on October 20 and the destruction of the Japanese fleet in the Leyte Gulf. Those accumulated victories had now, with the capture of Iwo Jima, brought the Navy to the point where it had begun the assault on Japan's inner defenses.

During the same period covered in King's report, MacArthur's forces had leapfrogged along the coastline of New Guinea, overcome stiff resistance on Leyte, seized Mindoro, and landed on Luzon. Once ashore, the Americans had pushed down the Central Valley to liberate Manila. Although the battle for Manila ended on March 3, much of Luzon and the remainder of the Philippine archipelago remained in Japanese hands. As the Marines inched forward on Iwo Jima, the battle for the Philippines was already entering a new phase, the extent of which would soon test the endurance of MacArthur's men and tax the patience of his superiors in Washington.

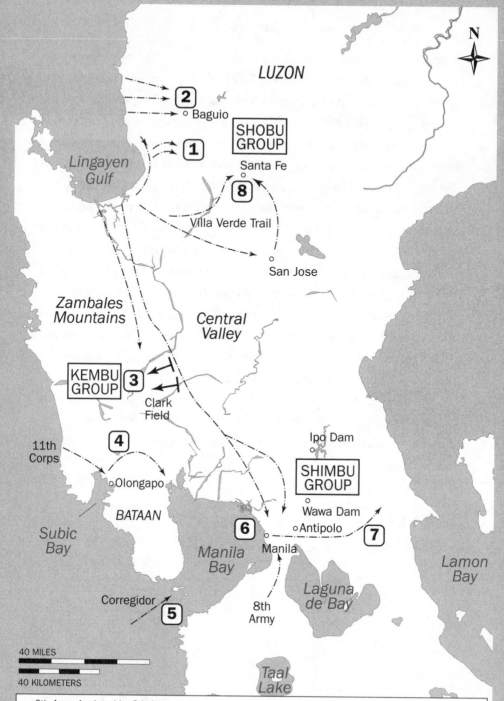

N

LUZON

2

Baguio

SHOBU GROUP

Lingayen Gulf

1

Santa Fe

8

Villa Verde Trail

San Jose

Zambales Mountains

Central Valley

KEMBU GROUP **3**

Clark Field

4

Ipo Dam

11th Corps

Olongapo

SHIMBU GROUP

Wawa Dam

Antipolo

7

BATAAN

6

Subic Bay

Manila Bay

Manila

Lamon Bay

Corregidor

5

8th Army

Laguna de Bay

Taal Lake

40 MILES

40 KILOMETERS

6th Army Assisted by 8th Army

1 43rd Division, guarding left flank of the landing, advanced east and north to the mountain wall.

2 33rd Division pierced into the mountains along three roads and took Baguio at 5,000 feet.

3 Recovery of Clark Airfield by 37th and 40th Divisions against skillful Kembu defenses.

4 11th Corps recovered Subic Bay but fought long in a Bataan barrier of rocks and twisting roads.

5 Corregidor retaken by the 503rd Paratroop Regiment, 8th Army, and landing craft of the 24th Division.

6 1st Cavalry and 37th Division strike Manila from north, 8th Army from south. Manila freed but devastated.

7 After Manila, the 1st Cavalry, 6th, 37th, and 38th Divisions moved east upon the Shimbu Group holding the nearby moutain range. After extended battle, capture of Antipolo in the south enabled encirclement, destruction of the enemy, and the holding of Manila's water sources.

8 The 25th and 32nd Divisions captured Santa Fe and broke through the northern mountain range. The battle took ninety-nine days.

Recovering Luzon,
February–June 1945

For his headquarters during the march on Manila and the monthlong battle for it from February 3 to March 3, MacArthur chose Hacienda Luisita, a sugar mill with a former country club adjoining it, situated in the middle of the Central Valley outside Tarlac. Aside from its comforts, Hacienda Luisita was close enough to the action for him to watch and even occasionally join the troops leading the way into the city. At Camp O'Donnell, located in Capas, just south of Tarlac, he visited the graves of American soldiers who died as prisoners of war. On March 2 he attended a flag-raising ceremony on Corregidor and made a trip to Bataan, where his party was sighted by one of Kenney's planes, which fortunately checked with headquarters before opening fire. These visits, together with those to the inmates of the Santo Tomas and Bilibid penitentiaries, seemed to close the wound of his departure from the Philippines in 1942.[1]

■ **Map 9** Luzon Operations, 1945. Drawn by George Chakvetadze.

The overwhelming devastation of Manila, the loss of all his personal possessions, and the advent of his sixty-fifth birthday may have given General MacArthur a sense of hopelessness about overseeing the reconstitution of the Philippines. By February 5 he was certain of the liberation of all Manila, but the rest of Luzon and a host of Philippine islands to the south remained in Japanese hands. At Hacienda Luisita in February 1945 he began to put the past behind him and turn outward, south and north. His principal task was to clear Luzon of Japanese organized resistance. The Shobu Group in the northern mountains and the Shimbu Group in similar terrain east of Manila lay in waiting. The Manila Bay region—Corregidor, Bataan, the Clark Field front—would require set battles, the harbor and docks a huge cleanup and reconstruction, and the southern coastal region extensive operations to clear it of smaller Japanese formations.

MacArthur wanted much more than just Luzon. To the south of Luzon and Mindoro a belt of islands, the Visayas—Bohol, Cebu, Negros, and Panay—ran west from Leyte through the middle of the archipelago. Several had ports with docks for interisland trade that could be used for staging troops. Once these shores and those of southern Luzon were cleared of Japanese, supplies from the United States to Luzon would arrive more quickly by going through San Bernardino Strait rather than by way of Leyte, Surigao Strait, and the Sulu Sea, which was 500 miles longer.[2] South of the Visayas lay Mindanao, whose eastern portion still held 43,000 Japanese troops. Finally, reaching like arms southwest across the Sulu Sea toward British and Dutch Borneo were the outlying islands of the Philippines: Palawan and those in the Sulu Archipelago. Considered promising as anchorages and naval bases before the war, they might now provide air bases, extending American power toward the East Indies and Southeast Asia and covering Australian troops carried by American amphibious craft to landings on Borneo. Following the Borneo extension, American amphibious forces and airpower would assist Australian and Dutch forces into Java, joined "if found necessary," MacArthur informed Marshall, by one or two American infantry divisions.[3]

MacArthur had no instructions to undertake any operations south of Luzon; his only orders were to stage forces on Luzon for the invasion of

Japan. Nevertheless, General Stephen Chamberlin, his operations officer, came to Luzon with detailed plans for a sequence of assaults throughout the islands to the south to take place over a period of seven and a half weeks. With these staggered landings, the same amphibious and covering forces of the Seventh Fleet could deliver the infantry through the nearby passages of the Philippines to one operation after another. These would be somewhat like the New Guinea campaign, only with overlapping battles and mop-ups instead of linear advance. MacArthur had pledged himself to the liberation of the Philippines, and that meant *all* the Philippines. For the southern Philippine operations he selected the Americal Division, a veteran of Guadalcanal and Bougainville; the Twenty-Fourth Division, which had been heavily engaged on Leyte; the Thirty-First Division, a new outfit that had just participated in the occupation of Morotai; the Fortieth Division, which had fought the Japanese Kembu Group forces at Clark Field; the Forty-First Division, recently heavily engaged on Biak; and finally the 503rd Parachute Regimental Combat Team.[4]

One might think that such an extensive agenda to the south, taking place on top of forthcoming operations to clear Luzon, would be too much for MacArthur's existing forces, but he was convinced it would work. He expected to complete his southern ventures by August, while General Krueger was wearing down and eliminating Japanese forces on Luzon, allowing several months to prepare for Japan. Early February 1945 saw the front in western Europe about where it had been the previous September—along the forests, hills, ravines, and concrete defenses of the German border. The Allies were recovering what they had lost in the German drive into the Ardennes but were moving very slowly against the snow, cold, and skilled German defense.[5] The redeployment of infantry and service troops from Europe to the Pacific for the invasion of Japan seemed a long way off.

MacArthur's idea of a thousand-mile plunge southward across his realm to the Dutch East Indies arose as the last stretch of the war in the Pacific seemed to be coming into view, amid helter-skelter Allied political and strategic pressures for readjustment of military boundaries, assignments, and placement of forces. MacArthur had left Australian divisions in the South Pacific and New Guinea jungles, mopping up or containing Japanese forces he had bypassed, leading Australians to protest such mean and obscure assignments and insist on grander ones, or else the demobilization of these divisions and discharge of their soldiers into war industry. British-Dutch-Australian discussions led to a mutually helpful plan: Australian and Dutch infantry, with cover from the newly formed British Pacific Fleet, would land at Batavia (Djakarta) and recover Java for the Netherlands. Java and Borneo were within the Southwest Pacific Theater, but since the Americans were heading north, toward Japan, they would presumably not object to detaching the southern portion of the Southwest Pacific zone for Commonwealth operations. MacArthur, however, would not concede an inch, but neither did he want a brawl with the Allies, so he joined the combination and set out to secure shipping. Of course, this being his own zone, he would command the colonial powers in their recovery of Borneo and Java.[6]

The campaign was necessary for several reasons, as MacArthur argued to Marshall in a letter. First, the United States was obligated to do so by the international agreement establishing the Southwest Pacific area.[7] Second, failing to assist the Dutch after freeing Australian and American territories and reestablishing governments there would be "invidious" and a "failure ... to keep faith." He had always assured them that he would assist "if means were available." Third, assisting in Dutch recovery of Java would "bring about the most favorable repercussions throughout the Far East and would raise the prestige of the United States to the highest level with results that would be felt for a great many years." Fourth, the Java initiative would resolve the Australian concern over inadequate employment of their troops. With the occupation of Batavia by August 1945, he concluded, his mission in the Southwest Pacific area would be complete and he could "prepare every resource for the major operations against Japan."[8] The southern campaign of movement and exotic landings would also be more likely to activate his public image when he needed it than would prolonged fighting on Luzon. His concern was that the Iwo Jima and Okinawa operations, which Nimitz would oversee, would get all the press attention right at the moment of the selection of the commander of the invasion of Japan. Furthermore, with American armies locked in the border forests of western Europe, MacArthur's multinational advance to the Indies would be welcome.

MacArthur's ambition to command the invasion of Japan was an unstated factor influencing his calculations about how best to employ the troops under his control. As we have mentioned, Marshall and Army planners had considered the invasion necessary to achieve America's war aim of unconditional surrender. However, plans for that final act of the war did not begin to take shape until the autumn of 1944. By November 1944, the Joint War Plans Committee had developed the initial plans for the invasion. Code-named DOWNFALL, the invasion would take place in two stages. The first stage, OLYMPIC, called for the invasion of Kyushu, the southernmost of Japan's four main islands. The objective of the landings would be to take the southern third of the island for the development of air bases that would provide ground-based air cover for the second phase, CORONET, the invasion of the Kanto Plain, the region that included Tokyo. The Joint Chiefs tentatively approved DOWNFALL in late November and subsequently confirmed that decision during the February 1945 summit conference at Yalta. Immediately after the conference, Marshall sent the Army's chief planner, Brigadier General George A. "Abe" Lincoln to confer with MacArthur and discuss the decisions made at Yalta. Planning for DOWNFALL was still in its earlier stages, however, and the JCS had not selected an overall commander for the invasion. Although MacArthur believed he was the obvious choice for that position, he and his supporters were not about to wait passively while the Joint Chiefs made their choice. On February 27, as the casualties on Iwo Jima mounted, William Randolph Hearst's *San Francisco Examiner* published an editorial praising MacArthur as "our best strategist ... he wins all objectives ... he saves the lives of his own men, not only for the future and vital operations that must be fought before Japan is defeated, but for their own safe return to their families and loved ones."[9] Closer to the locus of decision-making, *Washington Post* political columnist Drew Pearson reported on March 3 that the selection of the person to command the invasion of Japan had become the subject of considerable "wire pulling" by the Army and Navy. Pearson noted that MacArthur and his friends had been working behind the scenes to influence the decision but the Navy was emphasizing the role its forces had played in making MacArthur's operations in the Philippines successful.[10]

On March 23, as the full cost of Iwo Jima was sinking in on the home front, the *Washington Post* editorialized in favor of MacArthur's appointment to overall commander of the invasion. Titled simply "MacArthur," the editorial praised the general as a strategic and tactical genius who had caught the Japanese flatfooted in the Philippines and easily humbled the once formidable Yamashita. Most important, MacArthur had managed the conquest of the islands while sparing the lives of his men. Indeed, according to the paper, MacArthur was known to always prefer to take extra time to soften up the enemy before sending in American troops. Now only mopping up operations remained in the Philippines, and these, according to the *Post*, were not worthy of MacArthur's talents. Instead, the *Post* explained, MacArthur should be immediately named to command the invasion. That announcement would "hasten the end of the war" by striking "terror into Japanese hearts."[11] It would also inspire Americans at home and soldiers in the field. The *Post*'s depiction of events in the Philippines, which reads like one of MacArthur's press releases, left much to be desired from the standpoint of accuracy and military analysis. Contrary to the *Post*'s assertion that only mopping up operations remained in the Philippines, Yamashita was not humbled, and much hard fighting remained ahead on Luzon. Nevertheless, MacArthur had succeeded in getting his name before the public in the midst of the Iwo Jima campaign and had done so in a way that contrasted his skill with the "rapier" to the Navy's supposedly unimaginative and costly use of the bludgeon.

Throughout February and March, as his supporters lobbied for his appointment to command the invasion, MacArthur continued to seek approval to widen the scope of his operations to include the liberation of Java. Washington did not agree with MacArthur's assessment of international agreements requiring United States involvement in the Borneo and Java campaigns. Moreover, the Java portion of the operation required transoceanic shipping that Washington would have to approve, indeed provide, in the middle of the ongoing shipping crisis. In the January 1945 ship assignments, the Southwest Pacific received a reduction—from over 200 to 120—in the number of transpacific vessels it could temporarily retain for transport within its area. This must have infuriated MacArthur, who in stiff prose to Nimitz withdrew his commitment, outlined in the Filbas Agreement of November 1944, for providing Nimitz with housing, roads, and bases for the Marine and Army divisions that would be staging on Luzon for the invasion of Japan. The shipping retraction, he claimed, made it impossible to transport to Luzon the service battalions, construction equipment, and materials necessary to build the encampments. He would, however, "if desired, give domicile to these divisions by the mere allocation of adequate land areas."[12] Absent from the notification was any sense that the principal reason for occupying Luzon was its suitability for staging the invasion of Japan.

The shipping crisis of the fall and winter of 1944–1945 gripped the entire American overseas supply system right at the very moment when it was most extended and overburdened. Besides supplying existing forces in Europe, shipping was carrying the last infantry divisions in the continental United States across the Atlantic to reinforce the Allied armies as well as relief supplies for European civilians facing a brutal winter. Ports in France (except for Marseilles) were either unavailable because the Germans still held them or were of limited use because of war damage. The Allies held Antwerp, but river access still lay in enemy territory. Lend Lease supplies continued to flow to the Soviet Union's northern and Pacific ports. In the Pacific, Nimitz was shipping three Marine divisions (75,000 troops), two of which came from the Hawaiian Islands and one from the Marianas, toward the assaults on Iwo Jima and Okinawa. Entry into the Philippines at Leyte had happened two months earlier than planned and muddled schedules and priorities, exposing shipping to constant rain and frequent air attack. Port congestion was throttling movement of supplies.[13]

Idle ships awaiting unloading were not the only cause of the strain on supply. Retention was another. Commanders of the war theaters were nabbing ships for their own use, both temporarily and permanently, and the leading perpetrator was MacArthur's Southwest Pacific. Ships used as warehouses were insurance against loss or inadequacy of critical supplies such as ammunition and food, reaching beyond into less critical items. MacArthur was candid about his supply fleet, arguing that in operations among large-island bases, where enemy reactions and moves might require immediate changes of plan, a flexible supply system must be within reach to support these changes, a "sea train." This attempt to gain operational autonomy was probably inspired by the Pacific Fleet's service squadrons, and more proof that the Southwest Pacific saw itself as a world unto itself. For the War Shipping Administration and the Army Services of Supply—the bureaucracies in charge of overseas shipping operations—retention of ships abroad made it impossible to manage the thousands of ships that were now engaged in long voyages according to precise timetables. By January the government would no longer tolerate retentions. Under presidential order, penalties were imposed for retentions by reducing the number of outgoing ships.

Marshall noted that MacArthur blamed the retention penalty as his reason for the withdrawing of assistance to the Navy on Luzon. In answer, Marshall pointed out that in the Southwest Pacific from January 15 to February 19, 1945, between sixty-four and seventy-five ships were delayed for an average of forty to fifty days. He added that of the 446 ships in the Southwest Pacific Theater on February 13, 113 were loading or unloading and 102 were idle, waiting to load or unload. The rest were servicing, repairing, or en route. The number idle was "practically the same" as those working. In one of his sternest communications with MacArthur he warned, "Our global commitments cannot sustain this extraordinary tax against shipping effectiveness. Effective corrective action is a most urgent requirement if the war is not to be unduly prolonged."[14] Regarding the Borneo-Java scheme, Marshall informed MacArthur that troopships for the Australian soldiers were available but not cargo ships. Furthermore, the JCS wished to avoid use of American troops in the assault on Java.[15]

The Borneo-Java proposition—joining the Commonwealth operations— had arrived in Washington just as Marshall was heavily engaged in the issues before the Malta (British-American) and Yalta (British-American-Soviet) conferences, prolonging his communication with MacArthur on the subject. The Army chief of staff was not entirely critical, however. Although Pacific operations would have to await completion of the European war, he told MacArthur, "a policy of 'do nothing' for you and your experienced commanders and troops" would be "untenable." "The campaign from the eastern tip of New Guinea to Manila has achieved maximum results," he noted admiringly, and with "minimum resources and minimum loss of lives." The question was what farther advance beyond the southern Philippines MacArthur could undertake "without additional cargo shipping."[16]

Marshall told MacArthur that he had no objection to a Borneo operation by Australian troops, using Seventh Fleet ships to gain airfields for farther advance, essentially an extension of operations in the Philippines Palawan-Sulu area. However, Marshall suggested, in place of Java, the seizure of Hainan Island, which lay at the corner of the South China Sea, between French Indochina and China, about 350 miles west of Luzon, thus potentially providing air bases for interdiction of Japanese shipping and land communications in South China.[17] MacArthur considered Hainan and found, as he told Marshall on February 26, 1945, it "would not produce strategic benefits . . . commensurate with the means required."[18] MacArthur had suggested that Borneo oil wells and refineries would be an on-the-scene asset to Allied fleets and shipping, but Marshall found out that no shortage of oil existed "important enough to demand military operations," as MacArthur had put it, for acquisition of new fields.[19] A supporter of the Borneo idea, however, was Admiral King, who favored Brunei Bay on the west side of the island as a possible base for the oncoming British fleet. King, it seems, wanted to keep the British fleet as distant as possible from the Americans' operations in the vicinity of Japan so as to avoid placing additional demands on the Navy's intricately timed system of supply.[20] The Java mission was not formally rejected, remaining dependent on acquisition of cargo ships, but faded in importance as huge problems of logistics arose on what was now the home base, Luzon. Alongside warnings, encouragement, and suggestions, Marshall presented MacArthur with a pointed question: "If the Filbas Agreement were implemented, what specific operations to clear the southern Philippines would he have to cancel?"[21] MacArthur had sent a list of divisions involved.[22] By March 1, 1945, he recognized that he would have to reverse himself on the Filbas Agreement and do all he could to fulfill it. Thus the Java operation became "impracticable." The liberation of the Philippines, however, would not be affected.

As to the Borneo venture, MacArthur simply listed what shipping was planned, assuming that Marshall had approved by not disapproving. The Borneo landings took place in the period between May 1 and July 1, involving two, not three, Australian divisions, gathered from the New Guinea territories and staged at Morotai for landings at Tarakan (one brigade), Brunei Bay (one brigade), and Balikpapan (one division). The Seventh Fleet provided cruisers, destroyers, minesweepers, and amphibious landing craft. The operation had been expected to involve eighty-seven cargo and troopships. The landings were successful.[23]

As these operations were under way, the JCS agreed, on May 25, to make MacArthur the commander of the proposed invasion of Japan. The actual directive contained considerable qualification about the division of authority between MacArthur and Nimitz in the amphibious phase of the invasion; nevertheless, it was enough to satisfy MacArthur that he would be in charge of the biggest invasion in history. On May 30, MacArthur, now commanding the invasion of Japan, informed Marshall that any attempt to divert resources from that invasion to other operations on Borneo or Java "would prevent the execution of OLYMPIC at the time scheduled."[24] In the end, the advance on Java was not undertaken during the war. Marshall had broken MacArthur's fixation on the south and skillfully steered him north—if at some cost in ships that otherwise could have brought more of the 179,000 service troops in the South and Southwest Pacific to Luzon to build bases for invasion troops, sooner. The Borneo assaults required a total of 104 LST trips from Morotai. Some LSTs might have participated in several trips, but so might the same LSTs carrying supplies and service personnel from New Guinea to the Luzon beaches.[25] The Navy was on the verge of the Okinawa assault, scheduled for April 1, and could part with only a handful. To General Brehon Somervell, head of the Army Services of Supply, the Borneo-Java operation was "essentially a diversion in a direction opposite to our advance against our decisive objectives."[26]

Quite apart from the dearth of shipping, the task of mounting the invasion of Japan from the Philippines was gigantic. At the end of March 1945, the *Washington Post*'s assessment notwithstanding, over 100,000 Japanese troops still remained on Luzon.[27] American and Filipino troops overran the last of the Japanese Kembu Group's defenses west of Clark Field on February 21 and suffered 2,750 casualties in the following mop-up, which lasted through June. The offensive on the Shimbu Group's front in the mountains east of Manila dragged on through May, and mopping up also continued through June, as did clearing operations along the southern shore. (The principal American-Filipino offensive, against the Shobu Group in the north, was still not under way by the end of the war.)[28] Tent cities created in preparation for battle elsewhere were rising not far from skirmish and even battle itself.

With a diameter of about twenty-six miles, Manila Bay, twice the width of its passage to the ocean, had the advantage over Lingayen Gulf of substantial protection from ocean wind and wave, and thereby afforded easy anchorage. What Manila provided that was of critical importance in March, however, was a set of four piers for oceangoing vessels, one of which, long enough to tend six Liberty ships, was known as the "glamour pier" for welcoming luxury liners in better days. The piers, located in South Harbor, just south of the Pasig River, were further protected by a breakwater on the bay side and precisely what MacArthur needed most: a port at which oceangoing ships, once tied up, could unload immediately and directly onto land with flat, hard, dry surfaces, using their own masts, booms, tackle, and winches. Prolonged unloading at anchor into landing craft, which in turn unloaded on the beach, would have to continue. An additional faster system would substantially increase the rate of incoming supplies.

Tantalizing as the bay and harbor were, they had to be won. The security of Manila as the prime port in the Philippines depended on clearing the enemy from the rest of the Manila Bay area, including the south shore of the bay, Corregidor in the entrance, and Bataan, forming the western shore. The Eleventh Airborne Division, positioned south of the city, cleared the south shore, and the XI Corps, consisting of the Thirty-Eighth Division and the Thirty-Fourth Regiment of the Twenty-Fourth Division, captured the Bataan sector, though not easily.

On January 29, a few days before MacArthur's descent on Manila, XI Corps had landed on the west coast of Luzon without resistance, using the beaches north of Subic Bay, a former naval base located at the northwestern tip of Bataan. The Thirty-Eighth Division had recently gained its first experience of combat: its 149th Regiment had successfully recovered the Buri airfield on Leyte following a Japanese airborne attack in December. The Thirty-Fourth Regiment of the Twenty-Fourth Division, a veteran outfit, which had just completed the Leyte battle from landing to mop-up, losing 40 percent of its troops, had now filled its ranks with replacements new to combat. Commanding the XI Corps was Major General Charles P. Hall, a decorated veteran of World War I, known as a hard-charging corps commander.[29] He came to the Pacific from the North African campaign, joining in the Driniumor battle and running the Mindoro occupation.

Near the beaches on western Luzon the troops overran San Marcellino Airfield, which Air Force construction crews immediately began to extend and to pave for ground attack planes. Then, after overcoming brief resistance at Subic Bay, the Navy base there was recovered, and the Corps set out eastward across the Bataan Peninsula on Route 7. The purpose of the drive was to seal off Bataan, preventing Japanese troops from occupying it, and then clear the peninsula and send elements of the XI Corps to seize the fortress island of Corregidor. The Corps landing took place in the midst of the XIV Corps's drive westward from Clark Field against the Kembu Group force and MacArthur's intensive efforts to start his troops moving into Manila. Speed was the watchword. The Zambales Mountains to the north, in Kembu territory, continue down the middle of the Bataan Peninsula. Midway across the peninsula, where the mountain chain narrows and Route 7 crosses it, the road climbs into several miles of steep, jumbled, and jungled hills. This was Zig-Zag Pass, where the Nagayoshi Detachment, composed of two battalions of the Japanese Thirty-Ninth Regiment and other troops of the veteran Japanese Tenth Division, awaited the Americans.[30]

In command of the detachment was Colonel Nagayoshi Sanenobu, a skilled practitioner of the Japanese way of war with its emphasis on fortification, attrition, and last-ditch defense. Just inside Zig-Zag Pass three steep ridges approach each other, from the north, northwest, and southeast, to form a pocket around Route 7, shaped by a horseshoe curve continuing through a narrow defile in twists suggesting the number 2. Nagayoshi had fifteen companies of troops, totaling about 2,100 men, which he positioned on the heights above, at every angle that achieved maximum weapons coverage of the road and adjacent territory.[31] His main line of resistance ran along the ridgelines located about 1,500 yards northwest and 1,000 yards southeast from the road. Apart from personal weapons, each rifle company had light machine guns and small mortars. He assigned his twelve heavy machine guns to positions that seemed critical at any given moment and then moved them back to prepared positions as circumstances changed. In heavier weapons, he had only eight guns, 37 mm to 105 mm, and two 100 mm mortars, but the guns, small as they were, could be fired from inside or outside their protective caves and with deadly accuracy. Connected with the caves and bunkers by trenches and tunnels—all expertly camouflaged—were clusters of infantry spider holes. In the words of David Mann, who fought there, "each hilltop was a fortress."[32]

On February 1 the 152nd Regiment, Thirty-Eighth Division, entering its first battle, passed through the leading elements into the Zig-Zag. It was a nightmarish world. As they moved along the road into the horseshoe curve, they were subject to the "uncanny ability" of the enemy, according to Mann, "to bring down accurate artillery and mortar fire without warning on any portion of the battlefield at any time."[33] Off-road search parties looking for the sources of the gunfire and flanks got lost in the thick growth. Radios were unreliable within the enclosing hills, and maps were faulty in gauging distance, so that commanders at different levels worked from different estimates of the location of troops—the enemy's and their own. At night Japanese raiding parties, with light and heavy machine guns and mortars, descended into the American rear areas, where they caused considerable mayhem.[34] The battalions of the 152nd were gaining little during the day and being forced to retire to safer ground at night. The February 1 and 2 attacks failed. In the view of the corps commander, General Hall, the performance of the 152nd Regiment, indeed the whole Thirty-Eighth Division, was very poor, "the worst he had ever seen," as he told the division commander. This judgment, however, was based on a fundamentally mistaken estimate of the enemy. Hall believed that his troops had engaged only the outpost line, not the enemy's main line of resistance farther on. Speed was essential, he insisted. He said that the 152nd had found "nothing that an outfit ready to go forward could not overcome quickly." They must bludgeon their way through; after all, it was their four regiments against less than one. Major General Henry L. C. Jones, commander of the Thirty-Eighth Division, and Colonel William W. Jenna, commander of the Thirty-Fourth Regiment, on the other hand were certain that their troops were confronting a larger force than Hall believed was there.[35] Jones recognized the critical need for an answer to the Japanese fusillades, and that answer involved heavy American artillery bombardment, preceded by air reconnaissance for fixing enemy locations and adjustment of the guns for accuracy, and multibattalion attacks that prevented the Japanese from shifting forces. The Thirty-Eighth had four battalions of artillery and corps artillery as well. However, preparation for and use of that artillery would take at least two days.

Gradually General Hall moved toward use of bombardment and multibattalion tactics. He ordered the Thirty-Fourth Regiment onto the battlefield on February 3, leading the way and directly under his command, with General Jones and his 152nd Regiment following. The split command undermined coordination of the battalions. Companies attacking the main line of resistance on the heights were too thinly spread to outflank or overwhelm the enemy positions. Hall at last became convinced that the battle was already being waged on the main line of resistance; indeed, in a letter to General Krueger, he called the enemy position "the best fortified place I have ever seen."[36] Colonel Jenna, recognizing that using only one battalion was a mistake, took all three battalions into the Zig-Zag on February 4, while General Jones prepared the artillery battalions for opening bombardment, and Hall simplified command on the battlefield by shifting command of the Thirty-Fourth Regiment from himself to Jones. Jones began inserting artillery into his advance on February 5, but he had not had the opportunity to adjust the guns for accuracy, so he required, for safety, that they fire beyond the Santa Rita River, itself one mile beyond the fortified positions, unless they secured permission at regimental headquarters, which would entail delay. Hall found Jones still adjusting his artillery accuracy the following day, before that day's attack commenced, and warned him to "cut out such precise stuff" and get on with the attack.[37]

Six days of sundry advances in the morning, growing Japanese resistance and heavy bursts of gunfire in the afternoon, and then retreat to home ground or near it, occasionally in "disorganized fashion," and digging in for the night: this would not do. Casualties were rising sharply, and so was troop ineffectiveness. In almost three days of action the Thirty-Fourth Regiment had suffered 325 casualties and twenty-five psychoneurotic cases, which amounted to almost one-half of its total losses during seventy-eight days of fighting on Leyte. Key personnel in the regiment were lost: the regimental executive officer, a battalion commander, four company commanders, and three first sergeants. Company B, 152nd Regiment, had one officer left and none were left in Company C. The heavy junior officer and noncommissioned officer losses likely was due to their leading from ahead of the troops, many of whom were new to battle. Colonel Jenna of the Thirty-Fourth radioed General Jones with the warning that the Japanese position could not be "cracked" without a withdrawal so that the artillery and planes could "work it over with every possible means for at least 48 hours." His own troops had "suffered terrific casualties," Jenna added, "and it is becoming questionable how long they can hold up under this pounding."[38]

On February 5 circumstances began to improve with the arrival of the 149th Regiment, Thirty-Eighth Division, at Dinalupihan, about six miles east of Zig-Zag Pass and three-fourths of the way across Bataan to Manila Bay. The regiment had been ordered to advance along a trail (which did not in fact exist) parallel to the main body. Communication failed, maps went blank on the area, and the regiment got lost wandering around. Finally, orders came through for the regiment to return to its starting place, which it did. Starting east again, this time for Dinalupihan, the regiment met up with patrols of the Fortieth Division from the Kembu Group area. The regiment finally entered the battle, attacking from the east along Route 7, closing the Nagayoshi Detachment in a vice. Furthermore, by this point, with completion of the construction at San Marcellino Airfield, P-47 Thunderbolts began dropping 500-pound bombs and napalm in drums, which had been first used in the theater on Saipan. Hitting the ground, the drums exploded into what one Japanese survivor described as a "sea of fire," "unbearable" to those it touched and those who watched.[39]

The next day, February 6, Hall relieved Jones of his command, leaving in his place, temporarily, the assistant commander. General Krueger selected Brigadier General William C. Chase, commander of the First Squadron in the First Cavalry Division, as Thirty-Eighth Division commander. Chase, who had just led the "Flying Columns" of the First Cavalry into Manila, was not likely to be criticized for lack of speed. He took over the Thirty-Eighth on February 7 and prepared for a single five-battalion attack. On February 8, following three hours of artillery bombardment, pounding the fortress lines with 17,000 rounds, the battalions attacked. The enemy responded with their lashing of gun and mortar fire, holding the Americans to a 300-yard gain, but it was nonetheless a gain, and the American attacks continued for three more days, relentlessly, until the Thirty-Eighth Division from west and east broke through the pass. On February 12 the remaining leaders of the Nagayoshi Detachment in their caves and bunkers, seeing no point in dying underground, stole away with the last of the troops, a group of 120; they ultimately inhabited the wilderness of the Mount Natib area in central Bataan until the end of the war, when they surrendered.[40]

The XI Corps next began to clear organized resistance on Bataan itself. With the assistance of the Sixth Division from the Kembu Group front, Hall sent forces south along Manila Bay and across the peninsula, while the Thirty-Fourth and 151st Regiments moved by ship and landing craft from Subic Bay to Mariveles, located at the southern tip of Bataan, facing Corregidor. These troops moved northward along the roads, meeting those coming south and west. With the exception of two Japanese night attacks, which failed, little resistance was encountered. Bataan was no longer a threat to shipping in Manila Bay.

Corregidor remained. On the morning of February 16 the harbor of Mariveles became the base for an amphibious assault on the fortress island. Occupying the twenty-five LCMs selected for the invasion was the Third Battalion, Thirty-Fourth Regiment, Twenty-Fourth Division, withdrawn from the Zig-Zag battle for a few days of rehabilitation before moving south. The Twenty-Fourth was a Regular Army division on duty in Hawaii at the time of Pearl Harbor. This was the battalion's fourth combat landing, following Hollandia, Leyte, and San Antonio (as the Zig-Zag Pass is called). After seventy-eight days of combat in the jungle and mopping up in the mountains of northwest Leyte, the Twenty-Fourth Division had a month of movement to Mindoro and, for this battalion, preparation for action in the XI Corps. After Corregidor the battalion would rejoin the Twenty-Fourth and prepare for action on Mindanao in the southern Philippines, where it would be in combat from April 22 to July 25. The enlarging and unending Philippines campaign was straining MacArthur's infantry.

Corregidor is seven miles southeast of Mariveles, standing between the sea and the bay. It has the shape of a wood-chopping block, rising some 500 feet from the sea to a flat, circular top over a mile across and with precipitous sides cleaved by ravines. In the east is a mound, Malinta Hill, over 300 feet high, from which a wiggly spit extends for three miles. Overall, Corregidor gives the impression of a tadpole. Still occupied by the Japanese in February 1945, it was a formidable objective but worth taking if Manila was to be the principal staging area for the invasion of Japan, not only for its likely harassment of shipping and its site for enemy observation of ship movements but also to honor the American soldiers who died defending Bataan and Corregidor three years earlier. As to enemy strength, ULTRA remained mute, and Willoughby, as usual, underestimated Japanese numbers, this time with a figure of 850. In fact, after it was all over, at least 4,500 Japanese were killed on Corregidor.[41] It had a Japanese navy command under Admiral Iwabuchi in Manila that included some army provisional infantry and artillery units.

The foremost question in the attack was how to gain the heights, the flat top of Corregidor. An amphibious landing alone would provide access to the top on the east by way of a steep but tolerable slope up from the beaches, but if the enemy commanded the top, which of course they could, as necessary, the cost of that fight upward would be heavy. The alternative was to use, simultaneously, two kinds of assault—an amphibious attack and a parachute drop onto the top to clear the way. It would be Zig-Zag in reverse, with the Americans holding the heights, supported by Navy and Air Force bombardment. The battalion from the Twenty-Fourth would hit the beach below and the independent 503rd Parachute Regiment would land on Topside, as it was known.

The Fifth and Thirteenth Air Forces began a rising crescendo of bombardment in late January with heavy, medium, and light bombers, expending 3,125 tons of bombs. On invasion day, February 16 (three days before Iwo Jima), they used sixty-six planes, alongside offshore bombardment by three heavy cruisers, five light cruisers, and fourteen destroyers. Just before the parachutes blossomed, seventy A-20 attack planes bombed and strafed eastern Corregidor, where the amphibious landing would occur. At 8:30 a.m. C-47 transport planes approached in two columns, crossing the drop zones from southwest to northeast, carrying a thousand men of the Third Battalion, 503rd Parachute Regiment.

Since the pilot was over the drop zone for merely six seconds, he could only deliver six to eight paratroopers at a pass, each with less than one second to jump, and would have to make two or three passes to empty the plane. Piloting this parachute drop was especially difficult and meant weaving among complex and shifting dimensions. The drop zones were the Army parade ground and next to it a small golf course, both clear of cover. With the zones slightly south of the middle of Topside, a northeast course provided the most terrain below, in case the parachutes overshot the drop zone. On February 16 the wind rose and shifted from its normal direction, east, to north, increasing the drift of parachutes, especially those of the first planes, which flew 100–200 feet above the 400-foot height assigned. The error was corrected, but altogether a quarter of the first lift drifted southeast over the cliff, perhaps caught on it, or dropped to the beach or into the sea, to be rescued by PT boats.[42] This overshot was not without advantage. Navy Captain Itagaki Akira, commander on Corregidor, happened to be at an observation post on the southeastern beach with a small guard, sizing up the incoming amphibious assault, when twenty-five to thirty paratroopers, blown over the edge of the cliff, descended on him. They organized, attacked, and killed eight of the group, including Itagaki.[43]

At 10:30 a.m. the Third Battalion, Thirty-Fourth Regiment, veterans of Zig-Zag, swung around the island and came on the southern shore, where the head and tail of the tadpole join: five waves, each composed of five

LCMs. Three vehicles were lost in a beach minefield, but otherwise casualties were light; the battalion seized and held Malinta Hill, the tunnels of which had been MacArthur's headquarters in 1942. At 12:40 p.m. the second airlift brought in the Second Battalion of the 503rd for a far more successful jump. They faced the same wind but managed to land most of the troopers within or near the drop zones. Total casualties for both lifts were 280, out of 2,050. With two battalions of paratroopers now on Topside, there was no need to bring in the third by air; it arrived the following day by landing craft.

The Japanese were overwhelmed. The sudden landing of parachute troops Topside had been completely unexpected. Turning upward, the defense was left in confusion by the amphibious landing below. Within hours, every strongpoint was isolated: communication links between them were broken, and the headquarters facility had been destroyed by the bombardment.[44] The commander, as we've mentioned, was dead, and professional skill and common experience, such as those reflected in the Zig-Zag defenders, was absent. Nevertheless, resistance did not end for ten more days; it broke down into lesser, uncoordinated engagements. On Topside the paratroopers spread out from the drop zones to the north, southeast, and finally west, taking strongpoints deliberately, one at a time, using their pack howitzers for direct fire into the caves and bunkers, spraying the cave opening with Thompson submachine guns, filling the cave with gasoline vapor from a flamethrower and igniting it with white phosphorus grenades, and if necessary following up with explosives. The paratroopers were in sufficient numbers to ward off counterattacks and small banzai charges. The Third Battalion of the Thirty-Fourth Regiment from Zig-Zag did its share, engaging at sea level and Malinta Hill but also clearing the way upward toward Topside to connect with the paratroopers, so that supplies could be brought in and the wounded carried out. On February 24, with clearing on Topside practically complete, two battalions of the 503rd headed downhill to join the battalion of the Thirty-Fourth in clearing the tail of Corregidor.

They found there a carnival of self-destruction, probably inspired by the Japanese navy's suicidal strategy in the Manila area. Japanese troops in the Malinta tunnels set off the stored explosives and ammunition there on the night of February 21–22, causing the ground to shake and killing six men of the Thirty-Fourth in a landslide. On the morning of February 26 the Japanese blew up an arsenal farther along the tail, this time killing 200 of their own and wounding or killing 200 Americans: strewn over the ground was the flesh and blood of men from both sides; fragments even struck a destroyer 2,000 yards away. Three hundred of six hundred Japanese preparing for a counterattack were killed by American artillery and infantry fire. Here and there banzai charges erupted, and finally, as the final attack down the tail came to the end of it, Japanese soldiers attempted to swim to the mainland (a distance of some two miles to the shore of Bataan). Some were taken aboard PT boats, but an estimated 200 died. The Third battalion of the Thirty-Fourth, minus 200 casualties, departed before the second explosion to prepare for the invasion of Mindanao, farther south.

North of Bataan and west of Clark Field, the Fortieth Division continued its battle alone along the Kembu Group front, the Thirty-Seventh Division having been withdrawn for the battle of Manila. However, the Kembu forces were not a threat to the Sixth Army: the Fortieth had broken through in the southern portion of the main line of resistance. Now the division was summoned to battle in the Visayas, due west of Leyte, starting with Panay Island, and advised by the Sixth Army to "proceed more expeditiously with the destruction of the Kembu Group" before leaving.[45] Luckily, the 160th Regiment, situated in the center of the front, was on the verge of opening the way. Attacking and capturing a heavily defended ridge named McSevney Point, with the support of tanks, tank destroyers, and planes, the regiment beat back banzai attacks the following night and found the next day that the Japanese had abandoned the main line of resistance, their ridge-top second line of defense, and retreated to one of the last-stand defense sectors farther west. By the end of the fight, the First Battalion of the 160th had fewer than 400 effective troops, while the other battalions were about 300 under strength. That retreat had opened a wide gap in the front, giving the 185th Regiment on the north side and the 108th on the south opportunities to outflank the remainder of the front. With artillery barrages just ahead of their own troops and direct fire from tanks and tank destroyers, the attacks were successful. Six hundred eighty Japanese were killed in the flank attacks. After shredding the main line of resistance, the Fortieth moved on west, overriding one after another of the last-stand sectors, leaving a dwindling and dispirited Japanese force. By February 28, when the Forty-Third Division relieved the Fortieth, only one last-stand sector remained, which the Forty-Third eliminated and pushed several miles beyond, finding no defensive positions. Kembu Group personnel had filtered into the unmapped Zambales Mountains north of the Kembu area but were shrinking in numbers due to starvation, disease, and mop-up patrols, going from 20,000 to 12,000 and finally to 1,500 at the end of the war. Even in the later phase, February 21–June 30, mostly mop-up, the Japanese killed 550 and wounded 2,200 in the Thirty-Eighth Division. Already, by the end of February, when the Fortieth Division left for Mindanao, the Kembu Group no longer existed as an organized force.

As the Sixth Army ground down the Kembu Group, work on Manila Bay was already under way. Restoring the harbor to use was a monumental task that challenged American resources and ingenuity. The Halsey and Kenney air attacks on Luzon during the Leyte-Luzon advance and demolition by Admiral Iwabuchi's orders had strewn the bay with more than 350 sunken vessels, eighteen of them inside South Harbor itself. Weeks of minesweeping the bay resulted in the destruction of 585 mines. Warehousing on the piers was flattened or burned and some decking destroyed, leaving piles of rubble where the freight should be. Commodore W. A. Sullivan, in charge of clearing the sunken ships, had already cleared Naples, Cherbourg, and Le Havre yet found Manila "the worst."[46]

He concentrated on South Harbor. Completion of its clearance had to await arrival of heavy-lifting cranes and salvage vessels making slow progress across the Pacific, but Sullivan pushed ahead with what he had. If a sunken wreck within the breakwater did not block the docking of ships and harbor traffic, he left it where it was. If it did block traffic he moved it alongside the breakwater out of the way, or, if possible, removed it from the harbor to a nearby graveyard of ships sitting on the bottom that soon became a forest, with masts, smokestacks, and superstructures above water. Moving the vessels required a number of techniques, such as replating holes in the sides or bottom, cutting off superstructure, attaching pontoons, and removing cargo and silt. A ship would be turned upside down with straps, slings, or cable attached to special craft or cranes, buoyed with compressed air, and then towed away.[47] Meanwhile, work gangs removed rubble from the piers, and construction crews replaced damaged decking. Soon a shortage of tires for Army trucks carrying rubble away over Manila's cut-up street pavement developed. Short, two-ship piers were added between the original ones to provide total docking for twenty-four ships in South Harbor.[48] Finally, the first ship docked on March 15, and the numbers steadily increased as more wrecks were removed. Even so, Manila was consistently behind. Building more piers would take too long. What was needed after all were vessels that could unload supplies over the beaches, such as LSTs and LCTs. In late March, MacArthur submitted a request for 150 LSTs and 150 LCTs, but on the eve of the Okinawa assault on April 1, very few were available.[49] The problem persisted. In a Pacific shipping conference in early May, Lieutenant General William D. Styer, commander of the Manila Base, reiterated that it was an "urgent necessity" for the Philippines to get supplies and equipment "that can unload over the beaches," LSTs in particular.[50] Progress remained incremental; the bay was open to more shipping, but backlogs continued into the summer. By July 21 the port unloaded 13,700 tons. In port were 112 ships, however, fifty of which had been there over ten days, waiting to be discharged of 189,584 tons. Another 177,491 tons were en route.

As Commodore Sullivan worked to increase Manila Bay's capacity to receive and discharge shipping, General Krueger contended with Japanese forces east of Manila. The Sixth Army had no doubt that the Shimbu combat force, whose nearest entrenchments were less than ten miles east of Manila, posed a fundamental threat to the security of the Manila Bay region and the city itself. Sixth Army intelligence severely underestimated the size of the enemy force at 20,000 troops in the Shimbu Group zone, east and northeast of Manila; in fact the Shimbu Group had 37,500 troops in the zone and more in the vicinity. Of particular importance was Shimbu's control, within its defenses, of the dams and the waters that filled them from the Sierra Madre Mountains. The Ipo Dam provided half of Manila's requirement, and the Wawa Dam provided 15 percent.[51]

The Shimbu Group defense zone was a rectangle some thirty miles north–south and seven miles east–west. Most of the prolonged struggle occurred in the southern and central parts of the rectangle, due east of Manila. Approaching from Manila, the open land sloped down into the dry rice paddies of the Marikina River Valley, stretching north and south. Across the valley and paralleling it were the foothills of the Sierra Madre Mountains, and along these rises lay the observation posts, caves, and bunkers of the Shimbu Group's line of defense, backed up by further defensive positions in depth. Above the foothills, rising abruptly, stood a group of thousand-foot hills, tightly packed across the zone, and beyond that, rising above all on the horizon, the Sierra Madre mountain range. The southern portion of the Shimbu zone was rough, broken land with countless limestone caves and solitary hills. Commanding the Shimbu force, as well as all Japanese troops in southern Luzon, was Lieutenant General Yokoyama Shizuo. A veteran of ten years' service in Manchuria, Yokoyama commanded the Japanese Eighth Division when it was transferred to Luzon in September 1944. In December three of his infantry battalions had been sent to defend Leyte, greatly reducing his combat strength. In early 1945, as he prepared to meet the Americans on Luzon, he divided his force into three combat groups, holding the north (9,000), center (12,000), and south (9,000) of the rectangle, and a reserve of infantry (5,000) and artillery and service units (2,750) stationed behind the center and south groups. The Shimbu Group battle really consisted of two battles: first the American offensives in the center and south to protect Manila and seize Wawa Dam; and the drive in the north for Ipo Dam. Most of Yokoyama's forces were provisional, gathered in regiments and battalions for the Shimbu defense and therefore lacking in training, common experience, and coordination and depending on an inadequate supply delivery system. However, Yokoyama's force was larger than what Krueger could put in the field, and it was well-entrenched.[52]

Gathering and sustaining a force to destroy the Shimbu Group defenses was an excruciating problem for General Krueger. The First Cavalry Division, ordered to the front, was weakened and exhausted from the battle for Manila. With an assigned strength of 7,625, one-half that of an infantry division, the First Cavalry was now down to 5,100 men. Its partner in Manila, the Thirty-Seventh Division, no less weakened and exhausted, remained there on garrison duty. The independent 112th Regimental Combat Team, authorized for a complement of 2,625, had fewer than 2,000. Both the First Cavalry and the 112th were ordered to the Shimbu Group. With them would go the Sixth Division, gaining experience in Central Valley action and arriving at the front with 2,630 fewer troops than it had landed with at Lingayen Gulf. As usual, most of the casualties were in the rifle battalions. Recognizing that the First Cavalry would need relief before long, Krueger ordered the Forty-Third Division—a key performer in the Damortis-Rosario advance east of the Lingayen beaches, as well as in the breaking of the Kembu Group front—to shift across the Central Valley to the Shimbu front. The Forty-Third had had only nine days for rest and reequipment in the period from January 9, when it landed, to March 13, the day it relieved the First Cavalry. It received 1,906 replacements after the Damortis-Rosario battle and 638 wounded returning from hospital and was still 1,532 men short of a full complement.[53] The Thirty-Eighth Division, after Zig-Zag and the Zambales Mountains, would have its turn with the Shimbu Group later.

In early February, as soon as the Sixth Army arrived at Manila, MacArthur had ordered five divisions, an independent regiment, and service troops to prepare for his campaign in the central and southern Philippines. A major source of his impatience to get to Manila arose from his conclusion that the critical period of the Luzon campaign had passed once the capture of Manila was inevitable and that it was high time to reserve and prepare the forces he chose for the roundup of the rest of the Philippines. It was a shock to Krueger, who had counted on at least five divisions to overcome the Shobu Group in northern Luzon and was left with three. Two divisions, the Eleventh Airborne and, after relief from Shimbu, the First Cavalry, were to clear the southern coastline of Luzon to ensure a secure, shorter supply route to Manila from American ports. Swept away from Luzon and Leyte to the southern Philippines would be the Americal, Twenty-Fourth, Thirty-First, Fortieth, and Forty-First Divisions. MacArthur explained to Krueger that offensives against the Shobu and Shimbu groups were now of secondary importance: assaults aiming at destruction of the enemy in the mountains would be "time consuming because the terrain would probably channelize operations and limit development of full power." Instead, the enemy should be "driven into the mountains, contained and weakened." This seemed to be what was occurring after the Japanese retired to a jungle fastness, where they were more contained than engaged. The problem lay in the blood and time required to drive and weaken them to that extremity.[54]

On February 20 General Griswold, commanding the XIV Corps and the attack on the Shimbu force, ordered a general advance, west to east, across the open fields of the Marikina River Valley and into Shimbu territory. It appears to have been an exploratory strike, with hopes of seizing Wawa Dam and feeling out the placement and strength of the enemy. On the left, two and then all three regiments of the Sixth Division crossed the valley and began mounting the steep slopes of Mount Mataba and Mount Pacawagan, each over 1,000 feet, standing guard over the central Shimbu forces and the dam. For several days the division tried to take and hold the hills and failed. Only on the right could it make headway: the Twentieth Regiment drove through a river divide in the barrier of hills for an advance of two miles into the interior. For the next advance, on March 4, General Patrick, the Sixth Division commander, positioned his First Regiment south of the Twentieth, along a second river divide, opening the way for the two regiments, against light opposition, to form a wide and deep salient reaching the middle of the Shimbu rectangle.[55]

On the right, in the southern section of the rectangle, the First Cavalry moved slowly uphill through open, broken country, honeycombed with caves of all sizes housing artillery, linked to camouflaged bunkers, and bristling with mortars, machine guns, and riflemen—in short, the full panoply of Japanese attrition warfare. American practice was to eliminate each cave, assigning a squad or more with the usual weapons: rockets, flamethrowers, and explosives, besides calling in artillery and tactical bombing, more often now with delivery of napalm by air attack. The exhausted First Cavalry, heavily engaged in eliminating caves, was finally nearing the town of Antipolo, a key communications center, when two regiments of the Forty-Third Division began arriving from the Kembu front to relieve them.

The 103rd Regiment entered Antipolo and, moving on southeast, found a strong single cave position and then, according to its reconnaissance troop, no more Shimbu positions, east or south. The 103rd had rounded the Kembu southern flank. Now it headed northeast along the Morong Valley, which led into the Bosoboso Valley, and then north along the eastern side of the rectangle. The flow of battle would be a counterclockwise rotation leading to encirclement. The Twentieth and First Regiments of the Sixth Division, striking out eastward from their salient, would join the 172nd and 103rd of the Forty-Third Division driving north.[56]

Shimbu bombardment could be stunningly accurate. On March 17 the First Battalion, First Regiment, Sixth Division, after a rapid advance of several miles eastward, were digging in for the night near their objective, Mount Baytangan, when a barrage of sixty rounds or more of 150 mm mortar fire hit them, killing twelve and wounding thirty-five. Anticipating a counterattack, the battalion retreated farther than they had come that day, leaving equipment behind.[57] The nature of the Shimbu battle—bloody and sustained—helps to explain the hasty retreat. This was the twenty-sixth day of combat. On March 14, three days earlier, General Patrick had been mortally wounded, and the commander of the First Regiment, Colonel James Rees, had been killed while conferring in the open. Division casualties to March 14 were 570. In addition, 1,600 troops had left on account of sickness and combat fatigue. The Sixth Division was substantially weakening. Following the retreat, the First Regiment proceeded more cautiously, sending out patrols one day and consolidating the next, a slower tactic.[58]

Meanwhile the Forty-Third Division was moving north along the Morong River Valley, with the 172nd Regiment on the left and 103rd on the right. Rising ahead of them was a group of five hills, each heavily fortified, and the lot forming Shimbu's principal defense. The first on the right, Mount Tanauan, 1,200 feet, predominated. By evening of the first day's advance, March 18, the 103rd was "swarming" onto its nigh-vertical rock faces, spines, and ravines and then inching their way up on hands and knees "through a maze of cave and bunker defenses ... pinned down by Japanese machine gun and artillery fire."[59] The 103rd had ample protective artillery and air support and, in the last day of a three-day battle, the protection of a smoke screen. Then, by March 20 the 172nd Regiment had a foothold at the top of Mount Caymayuman, but near vertical slopes, there too, slowed full seizure. The enemy counterattacked in battalion strength, but American artillery responded with devastating effect.

On March 20, in the face of substantial but slow and costly American progress through this critical composite of hills, General Yokoyama decided to withdraw the southern sector group and those under fire from the central sector, moving them eastward, beyond the Bosoboso River, rather than lose them in cave destruction. By prolonging the battle, he would adhere to General Yamashita's principal of attrition as the best means of delaying and weakening the American invasion of Japan. With the inadequacy of communication in the Shimbu force, most of the troops did not receive the order until two days later. The American infantry noted a much easier advance on March 23, and soon the hill group was taken.[60]

The southern sector and part of the central sector were less than half of the Shimbu land, however, and neither dam had as yet been seized. Ipo Dam was more than ten miles to the northwest, but Wawa Dam was merely four miles north on the Marikina River, east of the guardian hills. General Griswold and his XIV Corps had moved on to a wider domain, managing forces engaged with smaller Japanese detachments positioned at strategic points across southern Luzon. His place was taken by General Hall of Zig-Zag Pass and his XI Corps. On March 28 Hall ordered the Sixth Division to advance northward, with the Twentieth Infantry on the left and the First Infantry on the right, toward Mounts Mataba and Pacawagan and the Marikina River and Wawa Dam. General Yokoyama was quick to adapt to this, shifting forces to meet the new line of advance with intense infantry gunfire as well as accurate artillery bombardment. For a week the infantries battled, with the Twentieth Regiment gaining only a half mile while the First Regiment, in the east, fought its way to gain 250 yards. Beginning was a slow and costly battle, just as Yamashita had hoped.[61]

Yokoyama was an expert commander, with many more troops than the Americans expected, including reinforcements. He was skilled in adjusting his defense to American advances and was persevering at and successful in wearing down the enemy in a battle of attrition. His objective in night attacks, for example, was not suicidal engagement but harrying the enemy when they slept, with his own troops hiding out in daytime. Griswold's and Hall's troops had important advantages in artillery, air bombardment, and weapons projecting fire and imposed far greater casualties on Japanese troops, almost always by death. The Shimbu force lost nearly 7,000 in thirty-four days of combat.[62]

Replenishment of American regiments was severely limited; most received no replacements during the Shimbu battle, which dragged on through May. Casualties, that is to say death and wounds inflicted by the enemy, represented by no means the only losses of personnel. Injuries, disease, especially tropical and intestinal, and cases of psychoneurosis requiring medical care and attention usually resulted in greater losses than casualties. The Sixth Division, in its period of Shimbu combat, February 22–April 30, suffered 1,335 casualties and over three times that number of noncombat evacuations, for a total loss of over 5,000 troops. Most noncombat losses were temporary, but then many sick with low fever, perhaps too many, remained in action.[63]

The American regiments thinned out, each losing fifty to sixty men a day. Rifle companies, assigned 200 troops, averaged 120 to 125 and occasionally dropped to little more than 50, about the size of a platoon. They no longer had the sense of power for en masse attack, now replaced by the fear of thinning lines and lost terrain coverage, nor did they have the physical strength to push ahead again and again, up and down steep hills. They were "bogged down," "wearing down," "worn out," exhausted, retreating into themselves but still following orders. During the winter battles in Europe along the German frontier, when possible, the Army set up rest and replenishment stations behind the lines where soldiers took their turn for twenty-four hours of bliss, consisting of, according to Private First Class Otis A. Pease, "good food, showers, new clothes, and supplies."[64] On Luzon, XI Corps did what it could but couldn't match that. The Twentieth Regiment, Sixth Division, changed places with the 145th of the Thirty-Seventh Division, joining the Manila garrison, while the 145th filled in on the Shimbu front. Finally, however, after two months on the line, the remainder of the Sixth Division was withdrawn and replaced by the Thirty-Eighth Division, which had been clearing the Zambales Mountains.

The next stage of the Shimbu battle revolved around the seizure of Wawa Dam. Previous expectation was that the dams would be taken as the advance moved north, Wawa first and later Ipo in the far north. However, the Manila water shortage worsened to the point that MacArthur told Krueger that the city, in addition to needing drinking water, was in danger of an enteric epidemic caused by the lack of water pressure to remove sewage. He wished to know when the reservoir in the vicinity of Marikina would be seized. Krueger, who by now understood the water delivery system, explained that the Wawa Dam, the only fixture near Marikina, was no longer connected to the Manila water system and hence wouldn't alleviate the city's water problems, so the Ipo Dam, currently held by the Japanese, would be the only objective. MacArthur agreed, and again the Forty-Third, the division that had already been so successful in three battles on Luzon (Damortis-Rosario, Kembu, and Shimbu), and was currently clearing enemy to the east of Shimbu, headed north to engage the rest of the Shimbu forces and seize the Ipo Dam.[65]

The Ipo battlefield was a rocky basin lying between the Sierra Madre Mountains on the east and the hills bordering the Central Valley on the west. Ipo Dam stood where the runoff from the heights flowed into the Argat River as it took a horseshoe turn, then zigzagged west to an aqueduct that diverted a portion to Manila's Novaliches Reservoir. South of the river was about nine square miles of dreary landscape, through which ran a road linked on the west to the Manila–Central Valley network and on the east to Ipo Dam. The western portion of the road ran through a jumble of ridges and palisades with caves where the Japanese had established their main line of resistance, anticipating an American attack from the west. General "Red" Wing, commanding the Forty-Third, recognizing his extreme need for a speedy conclusion to this battle, facing as he did the Manila water crisis, the imminent rainy season, and the severely limited reinforcements available, decided to avoid the route of heavy resistance and approach the Ipo Dam by positioning on the south and swinging east and then north around the enemy stronghold. While two regiments, the 103rd and 172nd, swung east, the third, the 169th, would move against the main line with limited attacks to hold it in place. A fourth regiment, attached to the Forty-Third, situated some distance north of the Argat River, would circle wide to the southeast and come upon the Ipo Dam from the rear. This regiment, a Filipino formation known as the Marking Regiment, had been assisting the Forty-Third in the clearing action east of the Shimbu zone, while receiving training and weapons.[66]

Over several days, the regiments of the Forty-Third, from west to east the 169th, 172nd, and 103rd, filtered as silently as possible into their assembly areas and points of departure south of the river and road. At 10 p.m. on May 6 they attacked, with the artillery marking initial objectives with white phosphorus. For four days the 172nd and 103rd pushed on day and night, from hill to ridge to hill, east to north, against a surprised and feeble Japanese defense. By May 11, the two regiments were within two miles of Ipo Dam on the south, as was the Filipino Marking Regiment, after a swift advance, closing in on the north. The Marking Regiment tried three times to break through the Japanese defenses and failed. Finally on May 12, the next day, with artillery support, it succeeded, at the cost of 170 casualties for the two days, and on May 13 captured a hillcrest overlooking the dam.

The battle was by no means ending: access to Ipo Dam and elimination of the Shimbu Group were essential. The 103rd and 172nd had become heavily engaged with elements of the northern Shimbu force in the vicinity of the Ipo Dam, and detachments from the main body in the hills to the west were shifting eastward. General Wing decided it was time for a full-power attack on the main body. The 169th Regiment, coming from the west along the only road to Ipo Dam, would destroy the cave defenses among the palisades and along the ridges covering the road, while the 172nd assisted from the east. This was all complicated by an early start of the wet season: at intervals, sheets of rain turned the battlefield and roads into mush and slippery rocks. The division had prepared by arranging air-drop of supplies and hiring 1,000 Filipinos to carry them, but the offensive slowed. Of singular difficulty was the evacuation of wounded, which now took twenty hours by stretcher-carry. Reaching a portable surgical unit brought as far forward as possible was still a ten-hour carry.[67]

If rainstorms were a disadvantage, artillery and airpower were certainly a boon. Initially, tactical aircraft from the many Luzon airfields, close by, eliminated enemy antiaircraft guns so that cub spotter planes could direct massed artillery fire. In their two major barrages the guns used 9,720 rounds. In air strikes, 185 planes dropped 50,000 gallons of napalm on May 16, and 240 planes dropped 62,500 gallons on May 17, all creating horrific infernos.[68] On May 17 the 169th Regiment pushed east on the road and the cliff tops above, taking out caves and then, with engineer help, smashing huge boulders that fell on the road, and joining troops of the 172nd Regiment on the far side of the narrow pass. The two regiments proceeded to clear the ridges north and south of the road of an enemy already in retreat and soon withdrawn to a rendezvous three miles east of the battlefield. Also on May 17, the Filipinos of the Marking Regiment and the Americans of the 103rd met at the Ipo Dam, for which the Japanese had prepared a demolition that had not been initiated. "Red" Wing, the Vermont lawyer and National Guard division commander, had achieved a double envelopment. The Filipino-American casualties were 590; the Japanese lost over 2,000 killed and forty captured. Once again, the Japanese refused to surrender in any significant numbers. Instead the surviving soldiers retreated east into the Sierra Madre Mountains, where, no longer a threat, they were harried by Filipino guerrillas until the end of the war.

Eleven days later the Thirty-Eighth Division secured the Wawa Dam. Engineers had bulldozed a road through to the Woodpecker (so called from the machine gun chatter) Ridge so that flamethrower tanks, medium tanks, and half-tracks mounting multiple machine guns could approach and destroy the Japanese defenses that had held up the division advance. That completed, the 149th Regiment, from the mountain south of the river, and the 151st, after taking the mountain across the river, joined to secure the Wawa Dam, intact, on May 28. Easing the seizure was a coinciding Japanese withdrawal from the Shimbu battlefront into the Sierra Madre Mountains.

While the defeat of the Shimbu force went on for over three agonizing months in the rectangle east of Manila, fighting continued beside it in that coastal swath of Luzon to the southeast, south, and southwest. Plans for the invasion of Japan called for establishing south of Manila, on Balayan and Batangas bays, landing facilities, encampment for staging troops, and hospitals for the wounded thereafter. The shorter shipping route, MacArthur insisted, required elimination of any coastal artillery and mines along the south shore. South Luzon, then, seemed no less important than clearing the Manila Bay region. The enemy here was under the largely independent command of Colonel Fujishige Masatoshi. Designated Fuji Force by the Shimbu Group commander, it consisted of 13,000 troops gathered in provisional units from all services, with only 3,000 from the infantry. Commanding the American advance was General Griswold with his XIV Corps. Doing the fighting were the Eleventh Airborne and First Cavalry Divisions and the independent 158th Regimental Combat Team. After the heavy fighting in Manila and, for the First Cavalry, against the Shimbu force as well, the divisions were badly in need of replacements and rest.[69]

The fighting would not be a frontal affair within a defined battlefield like the Shimbu operation, or a "mop-up" that sought to eliminate small units or even individuals after destruction of organized resistance. This was a clearing operation: one in which the enemy set up points of resistance in favorable locations that had to be engaged on enemy terms. In this case, a sequence of barriers—solitary hill and mountain masses and large bodies of water—shaped the path of advance. Understanding the limitations on movement imposed by the terrain, Colonel Fujishige positioned his mixed units accordingly. The Japanese had no hope of victory, but Fujishige remained committed to wearing down the Americans and exacting as high a price as possible for any ground gained. To defeat Fuji Force the Americans would have to overcome expertly placed defensive positions manned by soldiers prepared to fight to the death. And then they would have to move on to new objectives and repeat the process.

The clearing action began March 7 when the 187th Regiment of the Eleventh Airborne set out along the northern shore of Taal Lake, a hundred-square-mile expanse of volcanic origin. To the north, along the southwestern shore of Laguna de Bay, a lake four or five times larger, the 511th Parachute Regiment assembled and attacked alongside the 187th. Three days earlier the independent 158th Regimental Combat Team, which had received ten days' rest after serving in the Damortis-Rosario battle, headed around the southern side of Taal Lake and discovered the Balayan and

Batangas coastline clear of the enemy, except a base force of suicide boats, which it eliminated. Turning north on the east side of Taal Lake, the regiment found the road blocked by a Fuji Force defense that extended to the lakeshore, embracing Mount Macolod. The enemy, numbering 1,250, had some artillery and mortars, a large number of machine guns, and cannon stripped from Japanese planes at a nearby airfield. The 158th, with four battalions of artillery, attacked repeatedly for five days but failed to take the mountain by March 23, at which time it had to withdraw to form an amphibious assault on the southeastern tip of Luzon. The 158th went into that assault 900 men below its authorized strength.[70] Taking its turn, the Airborne's 187th Regiment moved south to finish the task, but not until April 1 was Mount Macolod sufficiently approached and encircled to justify a full-scale attack, which even then failed. Reduced to fewer than 1,250 men, the 187th withdrew to nearby Lipa. Reinforced with tanks, tank destroyers, 4.2-inch mortars, and 500 Filipino guerrillas, the regiment tried again on April 18, and by April 21 it had taken the mountain, a debilitating task that had required one month and two days.

With the Eleventh Airborne weakening and necessarily scattered, General Griswold had decided to reinforce the operation with elements of the First Cavalry Division.[71] As veterans of the battle for Manila and the Shimbu front, the cavalry needed reinforcement themselves, such being the state of troop strength in the Southwest Pacific. Nevertheless, cavalrymen took over and explored the sector south of Laguna de Bay as far as the mountain mass of Malepunyo, which, they learned, had been selected by Colonel Fujishige as the location of his final defense. As cavalry and airborne units cleared the rest of the southern coastline and pushed through jungle to Lamon Bay on the Pacific, what remained of Fuji Force and what could get there joined the Malepunyo defenses.

Following them were the Eleventh Airborne's 188th and 511th regiments, the Eighth Cavalry Regiment, and one squadron of the Seventh, about 1,000 guerrillas, and seven battalions of artillery. After two days of overwhelming artillery fire, the infantry-artillery force attacked while Colonel Fujishige and the remainder of the Japanese were retiring fifteen miles to Mount Banahao, an extinct volcano over 7,000 feet in height, where they remained until surrendering after the war. All resistance at Malepunyo ended by April 30, nine days after the capture of Mount Macolod.[72]

Completing the clearing of southern Luzon and the interwoven scheme of securing the Visayan Islands passages was the plan to recover the long, thin Bicol Peninsula, which projected from Lamon Bay in a succession of gulfs and headlands 170 miles to the southeast toward Samar, with which it formed San Bernardino Strait. Selected for the task was the independent 158th Regimental Combat Team, which had been outmatched at Mount Macolod. The regiment boarded landing craft at Batangas and made an easy amphibious assault at Legaspi, near the southwest tip of the peninsula, on April 1. The regiment secured the surrounding area and fought two hard and slow jungle battles in the vicinity, in which the Japanese lost some 500 and 700 troops. At the end of April, after a month of combat, Japanese resistance collapsed, and the 158th headed back, this time by road, meeting the Fifty Cavalry Regiment halfway. The 158th stayed there until mid-June, training and equipping Filipinos for mopping up Japanese stragglers from collapsed military units. The two regiments in the Bicol operation, mostly the 158th, had 570 casualties.[73] Coastlines, passages, and all but the smallest of islands were inspected and neither coastal guns nor minefields found: the Visayan Islands passages were now clear.

Indeed, all of Luzon, except the mountainous northeast (the fingers portion of the mitten), was almost free of organized resistance. The Forty-Third Division was chasing Japanese stragglers east of the Ipo Dam on June 2 when it was assigned a further mission: to relieve the Thirty-Eighth Division of the final Shimbu mission, that of taking Mount Oro and two other hills in the high country between the Wawa and Ipo dams. The 169th Regiment attacked Mount Oro, the highest, on June 6 and was repulsed and attacked again on June 8, this time with a lengthy artillery preparation, striking with infantry immediately thereafter, this time with success. The other two hills were easily taken, and the 169th returned to the straggler chase. On July 1 the division, relieved of all combat responsibility, was ordered into a rest and replenishment camp near Cabanatuan. Except for a ten-day break after the Rosario-Damortis battle, the Forty-Third Division had been in action for 175 days. Now, besides resting, they would prepare for the invasion of Japan, for which they would board ship on September 15.[74]

Sixth Army losses were heavy, but what made them unnerving was that divisions and independent regiments were shrinking, losing infantry faster than they were gaining replacements. Transports still brought replacements, but substantially fewer than SWPA had estimated it needed or requisitioned. The cause of this severe curtailment was the massive German counterattack beginning on December 16, 1944, in the rugged, forested Ardennes. This "Battle of the Bulge" quickly consumed the pool of infantry replacements in the European Theater. American battle casualties during the Ardennes battle, December 16–January 28, were the highest of the war to this point, 80,987.[75] Nonbattle losses in the European Theater for December and January together were 124,323. Along with illness and combat fatigue came trench foot, which put 46,000 men in the hospital for several months. Trench foot was an injury to blood vessels and tissue of the foot from freezing cold, wetness, and inadequate winter footwear.[76] The Ardennes, Luzon, Iwo Jima, and Okinawa proved to be the kind of devouring battles that General Marshall had in mind earlier in the war when he warned that the country had "yet to be proven in the agony of enduring heavy casualties."[77]

In spite of support in strength by artillery, armor, and tactical air, the American infantry, except for the sweep across France, gained territory slowly and with heavy casualties. Marshall recognized the problem and warned Eisenhower repeatedly that replacement training was not keeping pace with casualties and that the theater would have to partake in filling the enlarging gap out of its own service and support troops. The same hunt for infantrymen occurred in the home commands. Limited-assignment infantry trainees, those with some physical disqualification but still useful, were swapped for general assignment soldiers from the Caribbean and Alaska defense commands. Air cadets became infantry trainees alongside Army Specialized Training Program troops from college campuses. Units for which surpluses existed, such as tank destroyer and antiaircraft battalions, were decommissioned and their troops sent to infantry replacement centers. Twenty-two divisions readying to go overseas were stripped of over

75,000 badly needed infantry. Commitments of replacements to other theaters, especially the Southwest Pacific, were reduced. A positive result was that recruits high in both intelligence and physical capability from these preferred sources significantly leavened and improved the pool of replacement troops.

In response to the major threat in the Ardennes, Marshall, through the JCS, moved to send a huge reinforcement to the European front. Seven divisions would sail to France between January 11 and February 3. Two divisions on the West Coast, completing amphibious training and headed for the Pacific in May, would instead sail for France on February 19. With these nine divisions gone, the nation would have no Army divisions left on home ground. Eisenhower would also receive 23,000 additional replacements in January, for a total of 60,000. Supplies for eight new French divisions would be under way in January, and additional fast vessels would hasten troops and supplies to Europe. Eisenhower had to have an "adequate reserve" and sufficient troops to "rotate tired divisions," as Admiral Leahy wrote to President Roosevelt on January 11.[78]

After the German Ardennes breakout was halted, intense combat followed as the Americans sought to reduce the Bulge and push ahead and the Germans resisted from the forests and the West Wall. This was attrition warfare, such as the Japanese were using on Luzon. The infantry cleared, took, and held the ground while the rest of the division provided artillery, command, and services such as medical care, food, engineering, and communications. As always, the infantry took by far the most losses, from battle, disease, injury, and psychiatric disorders. Many of those remaining fought on with exhaustion and low-grade illness. In protracted combat with scarce replacements, the infantry portion weakened and diminished until the division as a whole had to be withdrawn, leaving the rest of it relatively intact but wasted without tasks.

It had been a fundamental assumption in creating the Army for World War II that it could operate with a minimum number of divisions continuously in combat by use of a rotation system for extended leave.[79] However, that would require more replacements and shipping to cover travel time. Extended leave would break up squad unity and weaken team tactics. As it was, the combat soldier grimly considered his chances of survival. General Joseph Stilwell, who became commander of Army Ground Forces Headquarters in February 1945, saw "a disappearing ground combat army." General Norman Kirk, the surgeon general of the Army, ratified the concern after a survey of troops in the Mediterranean showed high rates of psychiatric disorders in rifle battalions, induced by "prolonged exposure to battle." "The front-line soldier," he concluded, "having exhausted the reservoir of pride and devotion to his unit, and having nothing to look forward to but death or wounds, cracked under the strain." Lieutenant General Jacob L. Devers, an Army group commander, argued that a division could not be left in the line more than thirty to forty days; otherwise "everybody gets tired, then they get careless, and there are tremendous sick rates and casualty rates. . . . The result is that you feed replacements into a machine in the line, and it is like throwing good money after bad."[80]

The Southwest Pacific Theater, already anemic from troop losses, would suffer the most from replacement deductions. On January 8, 1945, the Army's monthly commitment for ground arms replacements to the Southwest Pacific dropped from 13,350 to 8,370 (7,300 for infantry only). The number actually delivered was even less, 6,583. The same month, the ground combat commitment to the European Theater rose from 43,590 to 54,874 (48,900 infantry only). From January through April, the Army delivered 195,912 infantry replacements to the European Theater.[81]

An eyewitness report of February 13 gave General Marshall and staff what appears to have been their first explicit picture, a startling one, of the Sixth Army in the early stages of the Luzon campaign. The witness, Colonel Paul L. Freeman, Jr., dispatched from the Operations Division in Washington, was struck by how many of the divisions in SWPA were "seriously depleted in strength," as Freeman wrote Marshall, with the Forty-Third at 71 percent of effective combat strength (defined as the regimental portion of the division), the independent 158th Regimental Combat Team at 66 percent, and the Thirty-Second Division, still carrying losses from the Battle of Leyte Gulf, at 88 percent. Providing a more "realistic picture" of losses, as Freeman put it, were the infantry companies, down in some cases to thirty, forty, sixty, and eighty troops. Service troop shortage, Freeman reported, was also critical: service troop replacements were "practically non-repeat non-existent," and the long supply line bringing troops forward from rear areas was causing further stringency. Freeman expected "many more months of hard fighting without respite," but "all ranks are fighting superbly and combat morale is high." However, he warned, "to continue this strain throughout many more months without opportunity for rest will tax the endurance of combat soldiers beyond the expectations of reasonable success in current and future operations."[82] General Hull, Marshall's deputy, questioned Freeman's report in a message to MacArthur, expressing surprise and concern over such a serious replacement situation. According to Hull, Southwest Pacific data did not forecast any such infantry shortages: regimental shortages on the eve of the Luzon invasion averaged 4 percent or less. Luzon forecasts were for 1.9 percent or less. To the Operations Division in Washington, the replacement requirements in Southwest Pacific had seemed tolerable up to now. Hull and the planners in Washington were surprised and shaken, however, by Freeman's report that the idea of inactivating a division and using its infantry for replacements was being considered. Concluding the message to MacArthur, Hull said that if what Freeman described were the general situation, it would be critical and could be "corrected only by drastic action" but providing more replacements was not possible at present.[83]

MacArthur's reply reflected his anger at the War Department for deepening his own replacement crisis and manifested considerable ignorance of the replacement system. Yes, he wrote to Marshall, Freeman's picture was accurate, conveying the same information as his own comprehensive reports. These, he added, had been "consistently . . . rejected and figures compiled by the War Department substituted therefor [sic] presenting an entirely erroneous picture." Of particular relevance in this "false estimate" was the War Department's insistence "in counting all sick, wounded and transients as present for duty." MacArthur overstated his case, for the opposite was true: the theater could immediately drop from its troop basis all sick and wounded (not transients) requiring hospitalization, thus opening the way for more replacements.[84] The last paragraph of MacArthur's reply differed from the rest in tone and substance. "The area is small," he said, "and the increments of personnel to keep the combat units in efficient condition is comparatively small. I recommend most earnestly that the replacements of this theater be adequate."[85]

Marshall's response was stern and direct. He wrote to MacArthur that the United States was producing "the maximum number of replacements possible at this time, and they are equably distributed to all theaters on the basis of stated requirements." Now there "must" be a "common understanding between the War Department and all theaters of the methods of replacement reporting." In Marshall's view, MacArthur's misunderstanding of the hospitalization option made "clear a serious lack of such an understanding," especially since the Southwest Pacific strength report for February carried 23,511 wounded and ill assigned to hospitalization and withdrawn from theater strength. Marshall could "find no justification" for MacArthur's claim that the War Department had substituted its own set of figures for those of the theater, presenting "an entirely erroneous picture." Requisitions, Marshall explained, had not always been filled simply for lack of available personnel. Finally, Marshall pointed out, the War Department had just received Southwest Pacific's requisition for April, which had been due in mid-February. Marshall considered it essential, not just useful, for MacArthur's personnel officer or "other authoritative representative" to come to Washington to see that "the present rather complete misunderstandings can be resolved."[86]

To MacArthur the only possible answer to the replacement crisis in his theater was "pooling," in other words establishing a reservoir of replacements in Luzon of a size that would not only cover casualties and illness but also intratheater movement, as well as providing a pipeline of troops in steady passage from home ports. The 60,000 troops he requested were denied him. It was reminiscent of the shipping fleet he had sought by holding ships within theater. The constant logistical crises and the ever-spreading opportunities of advance in 1945 led him to make his demands with absolute disregard for other fronts and zones in the war. The Southwest Pacific was his only world.

The Ardennes replacement scramble succeeded in providing enough American infantrymen in Europe in time to sustain existing divisions.

By late January they had fought their way back to the December start lines, as the Germans withdrew and shifted some of their forces to the Russian front. The Americans struck German defenses here and there and during February finally resumed the advance through the rest of the rugged border country, snow and ice, and concrete defenses of the Siegfried Line. In March and into early spring, when the Allied armies finally reached the flat lands and seized crossings of the Rhine, the end of "Hitler Germany" loomed. For the military, at each of these stages of recovery and triumph the question of infantry replacements became more historical and the issues surrounding redeployment of troops from Europe to the Pacific became more immediate.

As the manpower crisis faded, American war leaders faced a new problem on the home front. With the defeat of Germany imminent, American workers and businessmen began to prepare for the transition to a peacetime economy. A similar sentiment had arisen after the successful invasion of Normandy in June 1944 and the Allies' rapid sweep across France. The failure to take a bridge across the Rhine in September and the German offensive in the Ardennes in December temporarily dashed hopes for an early end to the war and a lifting of wartime constraints on the economy. Those hopes remained dormant through the gloomy winter of 1944–1945 but were reawakened as Allied armies began to advance again. The Joint Chiefs and the civilian department secretaries in the Pentagon firmly believed that talk about reconversion was still premature. Indeed, what they sought was a more managed and stable workforce to avoid the slump in production that had accompanied the false hopes for peace in 1944. In early January, 1945, Secretary of War Stimson and Undersecretary Robert Patterson pressed for a renewed attempt to get a National Service Bill through Congress. The president endorsed such a bill in his State of the Union address on January 6 and sent a letter to Congressman Andrew May (D-KY) of the Military Affairs Committee asking him to push for the legislation. The May Bill was a diluted National Service Bill that applied only to men aged eighteen to forty-five. It used the threat of induction into military service to herd men into war industry jobs and keep those already there in place. The bill drew immediate protests from organized labor; business leaders, including the National Association of Manufacturers; and representatives from the Farm Belt. Stimson understood that it was going to be a bruising fight for the legislation. Complicating his task was the brightening picture in Europe and the Pacific. By mid-January, the Germans were withdrawing from the Bulge, the Russians had launched offensives in Poland and East Prussia, and General Krueger's Sixth Army was ashore on Luzon. "It seems funny," Stimson wrote in his diary, "that I should be distressed by our good fortune. But the true fact is that these things are…enough to reduce our chances of…getting the legislation by fifty percent."[87]

Throughout the spring of 1945 the administration persisted in pressing for the bill, but events during that period strengthened the impression at home that the war was going well enough to make a national service bill unnecessary. On March 1, General Patton's Third Army stormed through the fortification at Trier.[88] On March 1 in the Pacific, General Krueger's Sixth Army was eliminating the last Japanese resistance in the battle for Manila. February 26 marked the end of organized resistance on Corregidor. February 20 marked the breaking of the back of Japanese resistance on the Kembu front west of Clark Field. February 21–24 marked the initial assaults on the Shimbu and Shobu fronts. And on February 28 troops of the Forty-First Division landed on Palawan Island, opening MacArthur's controversial campaign to liberate the central and southern Philippines.

Beyond Human Endurance
Taking All of the Philippines, February–June 1945

MacArthur remained absolutely determined to fulfill his promise to liberate *all* of the Philippines, in spite of Marshall's warnings against dispersing his forces. However, Marshall had been informed and did not rule out the campaign. If anything, the obstructed Luzon campaign strengthened advance southward because of the unexpected limitation of port facilities at Manila. To the south, the cities of Iloilo, Cebu City, and Zamboanga had harbors, docks, and piers, each of which could supply one division at a time. In MacArthur's conception were Palawan and the Sulu Archipelago, which stretched southwestward toward Borneo, retaken and airfields built thereon. From there, American airpower could assist the Australian campaign on Borneo and attack Japanese shipping in the South China Sea and along the China coast. The idea of recovery of Mindanao and with it completion of the liberation of the Philippines satisfied MacArthur that he would have fulfilled his pledge, though troop withdrawal from

Luzon to implement his plan dangerously burdened that island's ongoing battles throughout May and June.

In conducting these operations the Americans benefited from the support of well-armed and organized Filipino guerrilla fighters. Some of them were led by American officers, like Wendell Fertig, who took to the hills rather than surrender on Mindanao in 1942. Others were led by Filipino soldiers such as Macario Peralta, Jr., who operated on Panay, and Ruperto Kangleon on Leyte. One of the largest guerrilla armies was led by Colonel Russell Volckmann on Luzon. Volckmann, who went on to help create the Army Special Forces after the war, had brought under his command over 20,000 fighters by the time MacArthur returned to Luzon. Before 1945, indigenous resistance was never strong enough to threaten Japanese control of the islands, but the guerrillas disrupted the enemy's civil administration and provided the Americans with valuable intelligence. After the Americans returned to the islands, the guerrillas played an important role in blocking Japanese movements, dislodging the enemy from fixed positions, and pursuing them into the mountains.

The Eighth Army, which had followed the Sixth Army from New Guinea to Leyte and then Luzon, was charged with taking the islands below Luzon. This was the Eighth's first extensive assignment. Commanded by General Robert Eichelberger, the Eighth consisted of five divisions—two for Mindanao, two for the Visayas, and one for the western landings, as well as an independent parachute regiment. Amphibious groups, operating sequentially, would ferry troops every week or ten days from bases at Mindoro, Leyte, or Morotai through the interior waters of the archipelago to their landing beaches. Covering each landing force would be a Seventh Fleet task group of cruisers, destroyers, and minesweepers. Assisting at each objective would be a local Filipino guerrilla force. The Japanese had spread 102,000 troops across the islands, some infantry and the rest from a variety of sources, with meager supplies and limited artillery. Their intent was to avoid defense on the beaches and among settlements; instead they prepared skillful entrenchments on heights several miles back from the coast, which the Americans would have to assault at considerable cost in time and casualties. The enemy planned, as usual, attrition warfare.[1]

The first island attacked, Palawan, lay between the South China and Sulu Seas, extending straight as a cane over 270 miles.[2] On February 28, the 186th Regiment of the Forty-First Division, which had last fought on "Bloody Biak" island, landed beside the town of Puerto Princesa, with the Navy employing preliminary bombardment despite guerrilla reports that these shores were undefended, as indeed they were. The landing forces learned that about 150 American prisoners of war, who had been captured in 1942 and were on forced labor assignment to build an airfield, had almost all been killed two months earlier when an American convoy heading to land troops on nearby Mindoro appeared to be striking for Palawan. The prisoners had been soaked with gasoline, locked in their stockades, and burnt to death. The new arrivals buried their bones.[3] Informed by the guerrillas, the 186th marched ten miles north into the hills, where the Japanese garrison of 1,750, based on two companies of infantry, manned several strongpoints and fought to their death. Thereafter, with the remaining garrison broken into small, scattered groups, the Filipino and American forces shifted to patrolling, combing Palawan and checking the smaller islands at the northeastern and southwestern ends. Engineers finally decided not to build a new airfield but to lengthen and strengthen the existing Japanese field. The bulk of the 186th Regiment moved across the Sulu Sea to Zamboanga, leaving a guard of one battalion and an artillery detachment.

The Zamboanga Peninsula, attached to western Mindanao, forms, with the Sulu chain of islands, a strategic barrier that reaches to Borneo, dividing the Sulu and Celebes seas. The city of Zamboanga lies at the southern tip of the peninsula on Basilan Strait; at the western end of the chain, the Sulu island of Tawitawi lies near Borneo. Defending Zamboanga were 8,900 assorted troops of the Japanese Fifty-Fourth Independent Mixed Brigade, who were by no means lacking in infantry skills. The American 162nd and 163rd Regiments of the Forty-First Division, the Jungleers, commanded by Major General Jens A. Doe, landed on March 10 on beaches two to five miles west of the city after heavy and prolonged bombardment on March 8 and 9 by cruisers and destroyers as well as Air Force and Marine planes. In the face of it, the Japanese retreated from their beach defenses, a braiding of barbed wire, pillboxes, and trenches, and moved back several miles to more extended defenses in the hills. Colonel Wendell W. Fertig, commanding the local Filipino forces, had advised that unopposed landings could be made in the vicinity of Zamboanga City, one of the most scenic areas in the Philippines, which had fallen mostly to ruins from prelanding bombardment.[4]

Several miles from the coast, the ground rises through valleys and ridges to a line of hilltops at the 1,750-foot level. On these heights, five miles long, three miles in depth, and thickly overgrown, the Japanese commander, Lieutenant General Hojo Tokichi, had set a defense of caves, log pillboxes, trenches, and bunkers, with the whole entwined in barbed wire. Minefields, some with remote controls, seemed everywhere. A remote-controlled explosion, probably of bombs and torpedoes, caused eighty-three casualties in the 163rd Regiment. Valuable support for American artillery was the air spotting done by a Piper Cub aircraft that had been transported to Mindanao stuffed inside a transport plane and then reassembled. Cruisers had joined in the prelanding bombardment before leaving for a landing elsewhere; destroyers took their place. Providing especially effective close support were Marine attack planes, with three groups available.

The Forty-First Division, toughened by the Battle of Biak and fully manned and rested, kept up a steady advance, supplied near the front with ammunition and food, thanks to bulldozers carving roads out of the slopes. Facing deadly automatic weapons, mortar fire, and counterattacks every night, the 162nd and 163rd Regiments took advantage of their heavy air and artillery backup and kept moving uphill from March 12 to March 20, when the Japanese defenders began to weaken. On March 23 the division drove a wedge between two key hills, and on March 26 the 186th Regiment arrived, relieved the 163rd, and extended the front to the east, threatening the enemy rear. By April 1, the entire Japanese force was retiring northward. Blocked from moving up the eastern shore of the peninsula by the Filipino guerrilla regiment, the Japanese force turned to the interior and fell apart in the rain forest. Nearly 6,500 had been killed or died of illness or starvation; only 1,385 survived the war. Unusual was the fact that by the end of the war, 1,100 allowed themselves to be captured. Most of these were taken in isolated small bands that had become separated from the larger force. Once again, there were no large-scale surrenders. Battle casualties for the Forty-First were considerable: 220 dead and 665 wounded.[5]

Meanwhile the Forty-First Division prepared the way for a Sulu flyway to Borneo, first checking and finding no Japanese on Basilan, located across the strait. Then a battalion of the 163rd landed on Sanga Sanga and nearby Bangao, forty miles from the Borneo coast, where they met with minimal resistance. Finally they turned to Jolo Island, where they were confronted by 2,400 Japanese infantry, 1,000 army air force, and 350 naval troops entrenched on two solitary hills. With the assistance of the local Filipino guerrillas, the 163rd eliminated one hill in one week and the second in another week, completing the recapture of the Sulus by May 2. Air Force engineers established or enlarged two airfields at Zamboanga, one at Puerto Princesa on Palawan, one at Jolo, and one at Sanga Sanga. This air net was invaluable in establishing Australian forces in Borneo for the campaign aimed at Java. The airfields were also used by MacArthur's Thirteenth Air Force for search-and-destroy missions in the South China Sea. It was becoming, however, a vacant sea: American submarines had already destroyed most of the Japanese shipping. In April the submarines operating there began shifting base farther north, from Fremantle, Australia, to the Pacific Fleet base at Subic Bay on Luzon. Sanga Sanga and Puerto Princesa were useful, but the war was moving northward.[6]

On March 18, while the Forty-First Division was struggling uphill to overcome the Japanese defenses near Zamboanga, the Fortieth Division was landing twelve miles west of Iloilo City on the southern shore of Panay Island, 250 miles to the north. This was the western arm of an operation to seize the principal Visayan Islands, sandwiched together across the middle of the Philippines archipelago. Forming the eastern arm, the Americal Division landed eight days later on Cebu. The Fortieth had been in action from the initial Lingayen landing to their departure on March 18, aside from four days mostly spent replenishing supplies and repairing equipment before departure and three restful days during the LST voyage to Panay.[7]

That island was, for once, an easy assignment. Half its small garrison had been sent to reinforce Leyte, leaving 1,500 Japanese combat troops defending Iloilo. As the American division approached, the Japanese commander,

Lieutenant Colonel Totsuka Ryoichi, concluded that defending the city would only lead to annihilation of his force, so he withdrew northward from the city, breaking through a cordon of Filipino guerrillas, and took his stand in the hill country in south central Panay. Some Japanese soldiers were now surrendering, choosing to avoid an imperative death; these on Panay survived the war. Colonel Macario Peralta's Panay guerrilla force of 22,500 already controlled much of Panay. Most of the Fortieth Division moved on to Negros, the island next door to the east. Those left on Panay with Peralta made no effort to storm the Totsuka detachment. At minor cost the Eighth Army had one more staging port, Iloilo, a functioning city with an excellent harbor.[8]

On March 29 it was the turn of Negros, 125 miles long and, in the north, about 40 miles wide. The Fortieth Division, less one regiment in reserve at Leyte and one battalion left as garrison on Panay, was joined by the 503rd Parachute Regiment. The objective was to clear northern Negros; the southern portion was left to the Americal Division, which would come from Cebu, on the east. The sea between the islands was no wider than a big river, so the troops used small craft without bombardment. A detachment went ahead of the main force to prevent demolition of a key bridge to the north and succeeded. With Filipino guerrillas already in charge to the south, the 185th Regiment, followed by the 160th, moved north along the coast occupying the urban coastal area. The Division Reconnaissance Troop went farther, rounding the north and scouting south along the east coast, finding no enemy except in the north, where they had a bitter fight.

On March 30 orders came to Paul M. Gerrish's company in the Reconnaissance Troop to assault a company of Japanese entrenched in a small grove of trees near Atipuluan. Notified of an air strike to come first, the soldiers laid out three large orange panels with painted arrows pointing toward the grove, but the A-20s dropped their bombs a half mile away. Two more planes were sent, and this time all eight bombs hit the target, but seven of them were duds. Air Central cheerfully explained, "That's all right as they may explode any time as they sometimes behave that way." Gerrish later wrote that he responded, "Thanks a lot. That will be such a comfort as we go through the grove." So the infantry would have to rush into the grove, covered by support from the M8 assault guns in their armored cars. This time the advancing infantry crossed into the M8s' line of fire, shutting down the M8s and opening the way for Japanese fire. The first four riflemen collapsed all at once. Three of them were badly wounded and later died; the fourth was instantly killed with a head wound. Their comrades dashed into the grove to recover their fallen, pulling them back by the collar. The dead man, Robert R. Lowe, was laid face up on the grass. Gerrish wrote: "Tears trickled down the faces of many of those hardened veterans." Lowe, he remembered, had been one of the "best of fighting men."[9] Again the riflemen headed into the grove, this time slowly with a half-track and M8s using machine guns and canister shot, which together could mow down a swath of trees and undergrowth. They counted 114 Japanese dead the following day.[10]

In command in northern Negros was Lieutenant General Kono Takeshi. His troops, 13,500 in all, consisted of 5,500 in the Japanese 102nd Division, 7,500 of the Fourth Air Army, and 500 of the navy.[11] His plan was a fighting retreat to harm and slow the Americans and their allies while bringing his troops into a heavily protected defense zone in the middle of the northern part of the island. Negros is flat along the western coastal plain except in the center, where hills of volcanic origin, ranging from 3,000 to 4,000 feet, rise abruptly, some with interwoven ridges, others outlying sentries, described in the Fortieth Division's history as a jumble of "precipitous slopes," "jungle-filled draws," and "divergent ridges."[12] Taking full advantage of the terrain, General Kono installed an elaborate system of caves, trenches, and pillboxes, creating a formidable fortress.

Completing occupation of the urban west coast of Negros easily during the first week, the Fortieth Division lined up toward the east, with the 185th Regiment at the center, the 160th Regiment on its right, and on its left in the north the 503rd Parachute Regiment, which on February 16 had jumped and fought on Corregidor, taking 780 casualties. The 503rd was supposed to jump this time, too, but the easy assault on Negros allowed a trip from Mindoro by landing craft. With a regiment and two battalions in reserve or on garrison duty, the Negros force moved eastward toward the mountains with seven out of twelve battalions.

Initially they came upon, fought, and mostly destroyed Japanese detachments hastily removing food and military supplies to their bastion in the east. General Kono removed guns from wrecked planes on the airfields and mounted them among his defenses, gathering altogether seventy machine guns but few heavy guns.[13] Access to the slopes was itself a challenge. About halfway, the terrain roughened and defenses tightened. Needing more push, Division sent the 503rd and 185th Regiments to concentrate from two directions on Patog, at the foot of the mountains. The 503rd headed east and then south along a road on top of the narrow and steep Banana Ridge, subject to gunfire from below on both sides. The march east of the 185th was no less tortuous, eliminating enemy roadside gunfire, removing mines, widening the road, and filling in tank traps. On the night of April 13 the regiment repulsed a three-hour attack by 200 Japanese. On April 24 the 185th reached the Lantawan Plateau and joined the 503rd, taking Patog, clearing enemy emplacements on the plateau, and firing downward into adjoining jungle-covered draws. With access now to this high ground at the foot of the mountains, tanks and artillery moved forward to deliver direct fire support.

Toward the end of April the Fortieth Division and the 503rd Regiment had closed in for the critical stage of battle. The Americans had, besides six battalions and two companies of artillery and a company of tanks up close, the advantage of pounding the enemy from the air, even with B-24 bombers. In addition, the battalion of the 503rd in reserve now joined the fray. On the other hand the rainy season had arrived in the Visayas, drenching soldiers, creating mud, and postponing attacks. Most nights the enemy infiltrated, or tried to, leaving little time for sleep. For Fortieth Division troops, testing their energy supply, the Negros campaign was practically an extension of their exhausting Kembu campaign. The division and extra regiment were fighting hard and successfully, but Kono had slowed the advance and the mountains were yet to be climbed.

Dominating the scene and the path ahead was Hill 3155, named Dolan Hill in tribute to First Lieutenant John W. Dolan, the first officer killed on the hill in the attack. The hill had a broad base and reasonable incline halfway and then a near vertical wall rising to an even crest with a knob on the south end. On April 17, after two days of artillery preparation and a day of rain, the 160th Regiment, less the Second Battalion and Cannon Company, moved up the rise; on the second day, grabbing tree roots and limbs, they made it up the steep wall to within 100 yards of the top. There they were stuck for the night in a nigh-vertical perimeter, under "withering" fire, pole and dynamite charges, and grenades, unable to strike back. They were withdrawn, but the 160th tried again and again. To reduce the heavy lifting, hired Filipinos carried food and ammunition up the hill. The troops faced a network of trenches connecting caves on the reverse slope with interconnected pillboxes on the crest, all covered by nearby machine guns. Finally, withdrawal from the hill and repeated massed artillery concentrations and air attacks for four days wiped away all vegetation, uncovering and pulverizing the defensive works and 200 defenders. Still active was a spur that ran north of Dolan Hill. Despite the steep slopes, a flanking party managed to reach the opposite side, encircling the position. Precision artillery fire then landed in the middle, eliminating the last Japanese soldiers on Dolan Hill, "the core of the enemy defense on Negros," on May 3.[14] This was not the end of the battle, which went on through May, with the Fortieth Division, with scrutiny and thoroughness, eliminating every Japanese position. The Japanese force was withdrawing from its key positions more often and steadily weakening in numbers. On June 4 General Kono dispersed his forces to various parts of the island, and during the rest of the month the 503rd Regiment, with the local Filipino unit, which held two-thirds of Negros, took over the task of clearing the island by July 1. Negros was not a staging island. As they were relieved, the units of the Fortieth Division crossed back to Panay. Casualties for the Fortieth and 503rd were 370 killed and 1,025 wounded, apart from the nonrecorded ill, injured, and combat fatigued.

In June, Paul Gerrish wrote of the Fortieth Division "trying desperately to break the Jap lines." It seemed a repetition of their Kembu experience. He also noted that "more men began to suffer from 'battle fatigue' [combat fatigue] and would have to be taken out of combat and in many cases sent to hospital." It was the second time they "had been pushed far beyond the *normal* limits of human endurance." He added: "Besides being weary many of them were suffering from having been through too much heavy fire, hearing too many whistling bullets, and feeling too many concussions from exploding bombs and artillery shells. Then there was the bloodletting that has sometimes been in such proportions as to turn a man's stomach."[15] Cebu, the next island to the east, and its capital, Cebu City, the second largest city in the Philippines with the second best port facilities, was an obvious choice for staging a division. On the southeast coast of the island, Cebu City had a 5,400-foot wharf, cargo sheds, and nine berths but no cargo handling equipment.[16] The division to be staged, and thereby the one to seize it, would be the Americal, led by Major General William H. Arnold. The Americal was formed as a division from three independent regiments in the South Pacific and was a veteran of the battles of Guadalcanal and Bougainville. Moving to the Southwest Pacific in January 1945, it had participated in the exhausting clearance of northwest Leyte and Samar, which left it undermanned for the Cebu assignment. Major General Manjome Takeo commanded 12,800 troops in the Cebu City area, of which 1,800 were ground combat forces; the remainder were from auxiliary units and even included some civilians. Adhering to the current Japanese army doctrine of establishing defense away from the beaches, his pillboxes and trenches lay in the sharply rising hills behind and above Cebu City and consisted of an outpost line, a main line, and several last-ditch strongpoints. So the beaches chosen by the Americans, at Talisay, five miles southwest of the city, were empty except for an extensive and thickly sown field of mines, from just above the surf line to the tree line. Under most of the mines, blowing with them, were 111-pound aerial bombs.[17]

On March 26, just a hop and a skip from Leyte, the Cebu task force, carrying two regiments of the Americal, approached the Talisay beaches, unleashed an hour-and-a-half cruiser-destroyer bombardment, and sent in the waves of landing craft. Ten of the first fifteen tracked landing vehicles were blown apart by the mines, blocking the advance of those behind them. The troops were soon probing and taping safe corridors across the sand and setting up pontoon causeways, reopening the beach by midmorning. They encountered no further defenses during their advance eastward four miles to Cebu City, or in the city itself. However, on March 29, three days later, as the regiments moved into the heights north of the city, they met heavy machine gun and rifle fire covering the hillside.[18] Under a spur of the hill, an ammunition dump in the caves exploded by remote control, killing twenty and wounding thirty men in Company A of the 182nd Regiment. The company was already so reduced in size by mopping-up duty on Leyte that the remaining few were transferred, and the company was shut down.

The battle for the Cebu heights started on March 28 and ended on April 17, prolonged by General Manjome's complex defenses in depth, including eighty-five pillboxes on Go Chan Hill, as well as the limitation placed on the Americal Division in holding its third regiment at Leyte in reserve and the difficulty Major General Arnold had in finding out the disposition of enemy forces. When the third regiment arrived, the division was at least attacking a force about its own size. Finally, the division resorted to small-unit attacks with air and artillery support, convincing Manjome that it was time to withdraw. During the rest of April, all of May, and most of June the Americal fought through the wilderness of north and north-central Cebu, finally breaking the organized strength of the Japanese. Meanwhile, the Third Battalion of the newly arrived 164th Regiment moved east and in a week of tough fighting cleared Bohol Island of an enemy detachment of 330. Next for the Third was transfer southward across a hundred miles of sea to Macalajar Bay on Mindanao in support of the advance southward in that campaign. The rest of the regiment moved westward to clear southeastern Negros, which proved to be as unmerciful as the north end for the Fortieth Division. Under pressure to achieve thorough destruction of Japanese forces, the Americal sent out patrols to find and engage the enemy and arranged artillery fire and air bombardment. Wherever the 164th engaged, the Japanese counterattacked, making it slow, exhausting work lasting sixty days. On June 24 the division completed encampment near Cebu City for rehabilitation and preparation for the invasion of Japan.[19]

The Americal Division and attached units were severely depleted in the Battle of the Visayas. According to the division's historian, it suffered 2,427 battle casualties and 10,566 nonbattle losses. Of the noncombatant Americal losses, 8,139 were from illness, the largest being a breakout of infectious hepatitis, as well as dengue fever, venereal disease, dysentery, and recurrent malaria. The toll of Japanese dead, about 5,500, in the Visayas campaign was, as usual, high. Artillery with barrages of instantaneous and above-ground explosions as well as air attack with napalm took many lives, but for the American soldier every Japanese soldier remained a threat. Neverthe-less, the number of Japanese captured and those who survived in the wil-derness until the end of the war rose significantly. In the Zamboanga action 1,100 were captured, and 1,385 survived out of 8,900. On Panay 1,560, over half the force, were captured or survived. On Negros (north), out of 13,500, 350 were captured, and 6,150 survived the war. On Cebu out of 12,800 troops, 8,500 surrendered after the war ended. By broadcast, leaflets, and a public address system used on the battlefield, the Fortieth Division intelli-gence section, through a prisoner, urged the Japanese to surrender. This had modest success: small groups came across daily, for a total of ninety.[20]

Sergeant W. T. McLaughlin of the Twenty-First Reconnaissance Troop offers a reflection of the general state of the American GI in the Pacific Theater in April 1945. In his memoir, published years after the war, McLaughlin estimated that this was the first rest period (and preparation for battle) the Americal had in 400 days. During MacArthur's visit to Cebu on June 6, McLaughlin and another member of the Twenty-First were selected as guards for the supreme commander and presented themselves in crisp new uniforms. They concluded that MacArthur had a "pretty good reputation" in avoiding frontal assaults and "hitting them where they were not," but they were disgusted with his showing off for the cameras. After jungle life in the Solomons, Leyte, and Samar, wrote McLaughlin, the division looked for-ward to recovery near habitation, and many "eyed [Cebu City] longingly," given that Filipinos had told them that "all the business girls are there."[21]

The larger number of Japanese prisoners captured during the Visayas campaign and after showed how Japanese doctrine was adjusting to reali-ties after the Philippines campaign. The objective of the Japanese command remained to extend resistance by drawing American forces into the tangled interior of each of the Visayan Islands, a scheme that could prolong the campaign, weaken the American divisions engaged, and delay the invasion of Japan itself. Battling to suicidal death was deemed wasteful. Instead, suc-cessive lines of resistance would be prepared, sited well, and supplied. The Japanese defenders were to fight to the verge of collapse and retire to the next line. If the Americans persevered, moving into ever more remote and difficult terrain, they would pay for it in casualties. The tactics in the Visayas did inflict damage on the American divisions involved, both of which were listed for the invasion of Japan. The historian of the Americal Division describes the central Philippines at this moment as "a huge trap."[22]

These tactics—on both the American and Japanese side—persisted in the ultimate extension of MacArthur's march southward to the much larger island of Mindanao, of which Zamboanga, the western tail, had already been secured. Waiting to assist the Americans was a well-developed Filipino guerrilla force of 25,000 under the command of Colonel Wendell W. Fertig, a mining engineer and reserve officer before the war. Fertig was called to active duty shortly before the war, and when U.S. forces surrendered in 1942 he took to the hills on Mindanao to organize anti-Japanese forces. By 1945 he had assembled a potent force that controlled much of Mindanao. The body of the island, roughly 180 miles north to south and 150 in breadth, was mostly rain forest and north–south ridges, with unmapped, untrodden territory in the east–central section. The provincial capital, Davao, was located on the southeastern coast. The Eighth Army chose to land at Parang and Malabang across the waist on the southwest coast, a site with an airstrip, already under the guerrillas' control. The two divisions assigned to Mindanao landed without resistance on April 17. They were the Twenty-Fourth, which had fought on Leyte, and the Thirty-First, which had trained in the New Guinea campaign and captured Morotai against light opposition. They fought under the X Corps, Major General Sibert commanding, and General Eichelberger's Eighth Army. The Japanese had roughly 43,000 troops in eastern Mindanao, of which 15,000 were trained for combat. The Japanese 100th Division, with attachments, held the port of Davao and vicinity, and the Japanese Thirtieth Division and attachments had responsibility for the rest of eastern Mindanao. The Japanese were limited in ammunition supply and by this point were also fighting declining morale—in part because the battle for Okinawa, located on the very doorstep of Japan itself, had begun. The Americans had the advantages of naval gunfire, artillery effectiveness, and Marine air support.

The X Corps moved swiftly from its southwestern landing to the center of the island, with half of the leading force being carried in landing craft up the Mindanao River, the second largest river in the Philippines and a main transportation route on Mindanao. At Kabacan the east–west cross-island Route 1 met Route 3, the Sayre Highway, which ran north through the middle of the island. Holding that road junction, the X Corps split the two Japanese divisions. Now the Twenty-Fourth Division continued east toward Davao City, leaving the Thirty-First to clear the road north. The Twenty-Fourth reached the east coast on April 27, ten days after landing, brushing past a small contingent at the town of Digos, which had not learned that the Americans were on Mindanao until five days after they landed. The division turned north along the coast and on May 2, with light resistance, occupied a Davao devastated by earlier bombing. Facing the Twenty-Fourth on the west, throughout the delta of the Talomo and Davao Rivers and the hills rising to the northeast and southwest, were the entrenchments of nine battalions of the Japanese 100th Division, armed with artillery, machine guns, mortars, rockets, and rifles. The Twenty-Fourth faced a Japanese force roughly its size, and, as always, expertly positioned. The battlefield was fifteen miles wide and ten miles deep, contained along the two rivers by hillside gunfire from northwest and northeast, thereby forcing, in the eyes of Major General Roscoe B. Woodruff, the Twenty-Fourth Division commander, a costly frontal assault. To allow full use of the division's infantry, a battalion of the 162nd Regiment, Forty-First Division, whose mission at Zamboanga was complete, joined the Twenty-Fourth. The main American thrust began on April 30, on the left, with the Twenty-First and Thirty-Fourth Regiments attacking northwest along both sides of the Talomo River and road and running into heavy fire from the hills on the left and high ground on the right. The commander of the 100th Division, Lieutenant General Harada Jiro, followed by shifting his forces to the west, and fighting intensified. During the better part of May the two regiments, the Twenty-First and Thirty-Fourth, pushed ahead in surges, gaining depth and then clearing it, piece by piece, breaking through and tearing apart the Japanese defenses. Harada had recognized his plight and set up a second, final line of resistance. That, too, fell after further pummeling by the Thirty-Fourth with assistance from the Forty-First Division battalion and a wide western sweep by the Twenty-First. Meanwhile on the right the Nineteenth Regiment attacked toward the west, reached the Davao River, and with the Thirty-Fourth completed the encirclement.

By the night of June 10 the Japanese had vacated all their defenses and departed for their last stand or, more accurately, hideaway, in the remote jungles and mountains of the north. Harada's troops followed the same withdrawal sequence as the Japanese troops in the Visayas, suggesting they were following orders from Yamashita. The cost to the Twenty-Fourth Division and attachments was heavy: 1,965 killed and wounded in forty-two days. Its cost in the advance on Leyte had been 2,328 in seventy-two days. One gets a better sense of the disproportionate toll on Mindanao when one considers that during the war the Twenty-Fourth sustained a total of slightly more than 7,000 casualties in 260 days of combat. That meant that nearly one-third of the division's casualties were taken on Mindanao during about 15 percent of its total time in combat.[23]

During the Battle of Davao the American Thirty-First Division was securing and in effect building the Sayre Highway. Holding the ground was the Japanese Thirtieth Division, commanded by Lieutenant General Morozumi Gyosaku, a veteran of the war in China, whose regiment was implicated in the Rape of Nanking. Most recently he had been reassigned with his division from garrison duty in Korea to Mindanao.[24] He assigned each of four combat forces, totaling 13,500 troops, to a sector of the "highway" that stretched about 100 miles from Macalajar Bay at the northern end to the juncture with Route 1 at Kabacan. The highway was a dirt road in perpetual mud, severed no fewer than seventy times by guerrilla and Japanese action, which had destroyed the bridges. No advance was possible until bulldozers arrived to reestablish the surface and then engineers to restore it, bridge by bridge. Every advance meant more dependence on air supply. In a surprise encounter with a Japanese battalion just north of Kabacan, quick response by infantry and artillery of the 124th Regiment scattered the Japanese forces into the jungle. Adding a second regiment to the drive and landing the 108th Regiment, Fortieth Division, at Macalajar Bay in the north, followed there by a battalion of the 164th Regiment,

Americal Division, from Cebu, created a powerful pincer movement. At Maramag, halfway along, a Japanese battalion ordered to delay the advance did so with six days of bitter, bloody battle. In the north, inside canyon country, the 108th was stopped for four days by another delaying action. However, on May 23 the forces north and south joined twenty-three miles northwest of Malaybalay. General Morozumi now withdrew his troops from the Sayre Highway into the jungle east of the highway in the north. There he stayed without seeking engagement.

With control of the Sayre Highway, Davao, and communication on the island, the objectives of the Mindanao campaign were fulfilled—almost. The enemy now hidden in the vast jungle east of the highway and north of Davao was a threat that could not be ignored and had to be pursued and tested. Following trails from Davao and the highway, combat detachments moved into the wilderness. Trails simply disappeared or were too narrow or steep for supply and artillery, especially in the rainy season, which had just begun. Aerial supply was essential. In the south and center, enemy forces stayed ahead of the search or remained hidden. In the north, American combat groups penetrating into the hills east of the highway found the Japanese fighting tenaciously. Circulating through the islands to the south on the cruiser *Boise*, MacArthur visited Malaybalay on June 13 during an exploration of how to end the battle. Overheard by the assistant division commander of the Thirty-First, the supreme commander congratulated Eichelberger for his success but warned: "Continue patrolling and keep contact with the enemy, but do everything possible to avoid a major engagement. We don't want to lose any more men than we have to, especially at this stage of the war."[25]

It was a significant statement, reflecting his recent appointment as commander of all army forces in the Pacific and, shortly thereafter, his appointment as supreme commander of the invasion of Japan. Given the losses among his own troops, as well as the Marines at Iwo Jima, and the large, bloody, and lingering battle for Okinawa then taking place, he would have been concerned about the shortage of veteran Pacific infantrymen for his invasion of Kyushu on November 1. Divisions from Europe would arrive only in time for the second invasion in the spring of 1946. Casualties in the southern Philippines campaign had not been light: 9,060 without counting illness, combat fatigue, and injuries. Ports of the Visayas and Zamboanga were to mount three divisions, forming one of four corps at Kyushu. Thenceforward no further major engagement occurred on Mindanao, though many minor ones did, a case of mutual proximity and avoidance. The enlarging Filipino forces steadily gained ground in the jungle zone and kept track of the Japanese, of whom about 350 surrendered before war's end and 22,250 after, along with 11,900 Japanese civilians.

The conquest of the Philippines had taken about six months, with four major battles (Kembu, Manila, Shimbu, and Shobu) and five clearing campaigns (Damortis-Rosario, Central Valley, Manila Bay, southern Luzon shores, and the southern islands), which were roughly sequential but mostly coincidental or overlapping. Separated by only a few weeks, the Shobu battle was a continuation and enlargement of the initial Damortis-Rosario advance to protect the left flank of the Lingayen landing. Now the objective was a hammering of the Shobu army of 150,000 until it posed no threat. This army occupied a gigantic redoubt, that portion of Luzon east of the Lingayen beaches that projects 180 miles northward, shaped like the fingers of a mitten. Any intruder faced a wall of mountains: the Sierra Madres, partially unexplored, on the Pacific side, the Cordillera Central along the Lingayen Gulf, and the Caraballos, choking passage from the south. These were densely packed and sharply ridged mountains, many above 5,000 feet. General Yamashita, in command of the Shobu force as well as the rest of Japanese forces in the Philippines, had hastened to bring in supplies from the south and counted on food grown within the redoubt, in the Cagayan River Valley, in case of a long siege. Yamashita had gained fame as the conqueror of British Malaya and for his capture of Singapore at the start of the war. Tojo considered him a rival and dispatched him to Manchuria, but he was summoned to command the Japanese Fourteenth Area Army in the Philippines after Tojo's fall from power following the loss of Saipan.[26] Yamashita's troops were well positioned in the mountains, facing west toward Lingayen Gulf and south toward Central Valley, aiming when attacked to weaken American forces and prolong the conflict.

MacArthur's requisition of five divisions for his southern campaign, in addition to the Manila battle, and the persistent demands for reinforcements on the Kembu and Shimbu fronts had left the Shobu front thinly covered. The Thirty-Third Division, yet untested in battle, held the front along Lingayen Gulf, aiming east at Baguio, with the Thirty-Second Division, around the corner in the Central Valley, heading north. The Thirty-Second had reached Luzon on January 27, 1945, following relief on January 1 from the battle for Leyte, which wore it down with 1,949 casualties.[27] To the east of the Thirty-Second was the Twenty-Fifth Division, one of the first Army division fighting on Guadalcanal and veteran of the Solomon Islands campaign, with losses that had required extensive rebuilding.[28]

The principal route to Baguio was Highway 11, a paved two-lane extension of the Damortis-Rosario road fought for in January by the Forty-Third Division. Highway 11 followed the Bued River eastward through a cleft in the mountains and then turned north, gradually rising in the mountain corridor until reaching high ground and Baguio in the cooler atmosphere of a summer capital. As the obvious route of American attack, Highway 11 was well defended, and progress was slow and costly. Major General Percy W. Clarkson, commander of the Thirty-Third, a fresh and spirited but untested National Guard division from Illinois, looked for more ways and means to attack, as did General Swift, commander of the I Corps. They found these to the north in three roughly parallel gravel roads into the mountains from the Lingayen shore, converging on Baguio. The Highway 11 force coming up from the south would make a fourth assault. A further advantage of the western approaches was that the Shobu forces defending them appeared to be, and in fact were, withdrawing to defenses closer to Baguio and desperately needed supplies. The daily ration of rice for the Japanese combat troops had shrunk from two and a half pounds to half a pound and then even less. A valuable asset for intelligence but mostly new to battle, already operating in the northern approaches, was a Filipino guerrilla force that had recently grown to 18,000 men in five regiments, led by Colonel Russell W. Volckmann and armed by the Sixth Army.

Despite these assets and the zeal for action among the troops, Krueger moved carefully. Planning to use the Thirty-Third in the invasion of Japan, he insisted on introduction to battle, starting with limited, testing advances, and postponing the Baguio attack until he could arrange for a second division. He felt that a single division without battle experience and striking alone would be engulfed by the enemy. He sought the Thirty-Seventh Division, which was completing the Battle of Manila on March 3 and remaining there as garrison.[29] Supreme Headquarters refused, but Krueger persisted and later that month squeezed out the 129th Regiment and later the 148th Regiment. The third regiment of the Thirty-Seventh, the 145th, had been taken by the Shimbu front in exchange for the Twentieth Infantry of the Sixth Division, which then posted to Manila. The reordering of regiments placed the two from the Thirty-Seventh on Route 9, the northernmost and best of the approaches. Placed next to it, on the Galiano road, was the 130th Regiment of the Thirty-Third Division. These two approaches with three regiments formed the main striking force. The next two approaches were the Tuba Trail facing east and Route 11 striking north, each with a regiment. On the Tuba Trail the weather and terrain held up the advance, as did Japanese resistance on both routes. A critical advantage in the north was the destruction of practically all Japanese artillery by American aircraft, artillery, and tanks. As the Thirty-Seventh Division regiments advanced steadily along Route 9, the 130th of the Thirty-Third next door on the Galiano Road came to a stop at Japanese defenses in Asin. However, passage of the Thirty-Seventh opened a trail between the two routes, allowing the Thirty-Third to circle north to Route 9 and back south on the trail, behind the enemy. The envelopment opened the Galiano Road to Baguio.[30]

One more barrier on the way to Baguio lay ahead. Within five miles of Baguio, Route 9, following the Irisan River eastward, entered a gorge whose steep slopes rose into a cluster of ridges. There the road turned sharp right to cross the river on a bridge, now destroyed, and followed the river south on the opposite bank. Each quarter of the landscape, pivoting on the bridge, northwest, northeast, southeast, and southwest, had one or two ridges, each skillfully set with machine guns and mortars. Fortunately for the oncoming 148th Regiment, it had learned much about cross fire in the Battle of Manila. On April 17 at Irisan Gorge, halted by heavy gunfire from the ridges, a platoon of the Second Battalion attacked from the west, up the steep slope of the nearest ridge, while the rest of Company F infiltrated the same ridge from the northwest. By nightfall the high point and most of the ridge were taken and held against Japanese counterattack. Nearby to the northeast, two ridges, the farther one supporting the nearer with heavy gunfire, posed a challenge. It was met the following day by air attack and concentrated artillery fire on both ridges, followed by the infiltration of an American machine gun squad, which found itself on the east side of the nearby ridge with most of the Japanese defenses in their gun sights. Japanese forces' surprise by and preoccupation with this squad eased the way of the Second Battalion up the hill from the south at the same time, while the Third Battalion crossed the river and moved east along a tree-covered ridge to attack a line of small hills that paralleled Route 9 southward. The attack baffled and surprised the Japanese, who had been looking the wrong way. Many fled, and the ridge was taken. Several remaining ridges soon fell. The Irisan Gorge and Asin victories opened the way to Baguio, which American troops entered on April 27.[31]

While the Baguio offensive faced east, thereafter the line between the Central Valley and the northern mountains bent eastward for ten miles and then southeastward toward Manila. Along the eastward bent, facing north, parallel rivers in narrow valleys and canyons flowed into Central Valley, with mountain masses rising and receding to the north. Thirty-Second Division patrols up the valleys came close to Route 11 and the Baguio front but did not connect with it: the power of that front was shifting north, and the interest of the Thirty-Second Division, assigned this sector, was shifting east to prospective routes across the mountains. Hastening the shift were reports from patrols that more and more enemy were visible in the heights above, extending their defenses. That was a warning sign for the Sixth Army: it was determined to eliminate any Shobu threat of attack from the northern redoubt, and that required pinning down or destroying Shobu forces within.

As developed over the course of his engagement with MacArthur's forces, General Yamashita was equally determined to use his remaining forces in weakening American divisions presumably preparing for the invasion of Japan. A defensive battle in the heights of the Caraballo Mountains

would be an appropriate location. Route 5, a major north–south highway on Luzon, became a gravel two-lane road at San José, leading north-
northwest into the Caraballo Mountains, rising to 1,000 feet and then,
more sharply, twisting its way up the valley to Balete Pass at 3,000 feet and
the town of Santa Fe on the rim of mountains encircling northern Luzon.
Due north within the basin was the Cagayan Valley, and to its west the Shobu
forces—outlined by Bontoc in the north, sixty-five miles away, Baguio, west
thirty-five miles, and Bambang, northeast twenty miles—became the central axis of advance for the Twenty-Fifth Division. To the left, the Thirty-
Second Division would take the Villa Verde Trail from Santa Maria, on the
edge of the high country. The trail climbed north and then curved east
toward Route 5, passing through Salacsac Pass to Route 5 and Santa Fe at
the top. First Corps did not anticipate a convergence of the two divisions at
the top. They estimated that most of the enemy defenses would be along
Route 5 and ordered a rapid advance by the Thirty-Second to the top and
then down Route 5, striking the enemy from the rear and meeting the
Twenty-Fifth at Digdig, halfway back to San José. However, the convergence occurred elsewhere in a reversal of roles. On February 21 both divisions began the advance. The Twenty-Fifth Division moved smoothly north,
with one regiment on Route 5, one parallel on the left, and the third on the
right, circling wide in a flank attack. The Twenty-Fifth was a powerful force
from the South Pacific with experience, months of rest, and adequate replacements. The division worked north on this wide front, occasionally delayed by strong resistance but otherwise meeting only scattered defense.
The advance beyond Digdig pushed ahead their assigned objective: now to
enter the Caraballo Mountains and secure Balete Pass. About eight miles
north of Digdig the land tilts up toward the north, and the Digdig River
emerges from the mountain mass through a narrow ravine. Route 5 follows
the river to its source and then twists upward, rising 2,000 feet, to Balete
Pass, a distance of five miles as the crow flies. Clinging to the mountain
mass was a jumble of terrain formations: peaks, ridges, hills, and mounds.
Facing dense woods and undergrowth with hopeless maps made the movement and positioning of troops and weapons a blind man's game. Instead of
scattered resistance, the Twenty-Fifth Division now approached an enemy

main line of resistance just below the crest of ridges forming Balete Pass, as well as defenses on selected ridges below and with support troops nearby, just over the top of the mountain. Anticipating 4,000 Japanese, the Twenty-Fifth came upon 8,000–10,000.[32]

Progress was slow. The 161st Regiment, moving north against some 2,000 Japanese on the left side of the river, gained ground along Norton and Highly Ridges, including Norton's Knob, with a peak reaching 3,000 feet. Finally emplaced division artillery provided a 10,000-round bombardment while the infantry found a circuitous route to attack the Knob from three sides. The ridges and Knob were solid gains, but they took over two weeks and cost the regiment almost 200 casualties. The Thirty-Fifth Regiment, twice successful in flanking maneuvers on the right side of the division, retained that role on the mountain, following the Old Spanish Trail in a wide encirclement of Balete Pass.

Major General Konuma Haruo, a veteran of Guadalcanal and vice chief of staff for Yamashita's Fourteenth Area Army, commanding the Bambang sector, with success, sent four battalions to block the maneuver. Major General Charles L. Mullins, Jr., commanding the Twenty-Fifth, recognizing the stalemate and need to tighten his front, shifted the Thirty-Fifth Regiment east to tie in with the Twenty-Seventh Regiment. The Thirty-Fifth plunged into the forest again, heading north and then northwest to link with the Twenty-Seventh. The Japanese battalions blocking the Old Spanish Trail shifted too and gained sufficient reinforcement to counterattack the Thirty-Fifth and harass the regiment's supply line. By the end of March, the Thirty-Fifth had reached a stalemate. The Twenty-Seventh Regiment, on the east side of the river and road, had kept two battalions at the river in protection of the division's rear. Now released, one moved north along the river and the other northeast along Myoko Ridge, about halfway to Balete Ridge. The Twenty-Fifth Division had been fighting for over a month and still had not engaged the enemy's main line of resistance. For all the battalions it was always uphill, foot by foot.

Meanwhile the Thirty-Second Division, on the left, west of the Twenty-Fifth, was struggling up the mountains from Santa Maria in the Central Valley on the Villa Verde Trail. Founded on the Wisconsin and Minnesota

National Guard, the Thirty-Second went overseas in February 1942 and fought at Buna and Aitape on New Guinea. On Leyte it won the battle of Breakneck Ridge, participated in the Ormoc Corridor fighting, and chased Japanese stragglers into western Leyte. After a brief turnabout it shipped to Lingayen Gulf, where it arrived, due to the replacement crisis, 4,000 troops below its full complement.[33] In a letter home, Robert Edward Guhl, a veteran infantryman, wrote eloquently and keenly about the devastating battle: "This thing is beginning to make Leyte look like a Sunday school picnic," he stated. About the Japanese he wrote that they were "not only holding their own, but very often rear back and kick our teeth down our throats." He went on:

> I'll try and give you the picture. In the first place, we're covering a very large area which makes it hard. Then there are *plenty* of Japs, everywhere, heavily armed and well equipped and very well led. These are first line troops: they're smart, they don't make mistakes. The ground is made to order for defense. The area ahead is one mass of peaks, all perpendicular, covered with mud; it rains constantly up ahead; it's bitter cold being at 6,000 feet high. The jungle is impenetrable. Every hill is covered with a higher one and each one is defended by the Japs. They dig in caves so we can't blast 'em out and they cover the hills with machine guns and mortars. They cover our boys constantly. They can't even stick their heads above the ground. The situation is somewhat better now but a little while ago it had all the elements of a great tragedy. Make no mistake, it's gad-damned tough. That's enough of that. I feel pretty good. I'm just sick and tired of the whole thing. I guess we just need a rest.[34]

Exhausted as they were, Guhl and his comrades continued on. The Thirty-Second, like the Twenty-Fifth, began its advance on February 21 from Santa Maria, on the Central Valley floor, where division artillery was based. The 127th Regiment marched north on the Villa Verde Trail, the 126th went north on the left, parallel with the 127th, along the Ambayabang Valley, and then turned east, and the 128th remained to protect the rear and patrol.

After a slow start, the Thirty-Second made a fast climb along the grassy slopes, dislodging the enemy outpost line once and then again. However, the terrain and the foe both soon changed. The Villa Verde Trail gradually curves from north to east, moving into rain country with dense forests and jungle undergrowth. In this blanket of green, nine miles from Santa Maria as the crow flies, was the enemy's main line of resistance in the cluster of hills around Salacsac Pass. For General Konuma, the rapid appearance of the Americans before the pass and the heavy casualties they inflicted on his outpost force startled him into immediate reinforcements: four rifle companies to refill the Japanese Tenth Reconnaissance Regiment and the large supplement of the Japanese Second Tank Division (now without tanks), training as infantry; both units were heavily supplied with machine guns from a large stock of arms. Altogether his Salacsac force numbered about 6,000, and enough of the reinforcement had arrived in time to stop the American advance.

The battlefield ahead consisted of a rectangle roughly 2,000 by 3,000 yards containing a mass of hills and ridges blanketed by forest. At the western end the Villa Verde Trail passed through a saddle between hills known as Salacsac Pass No. 2 and turned sharply south and then east again to run through a trough between hills called Salacsac Pass No. 1. Emerging on the east from the passes, the trail went three and one-half miles to Santa Fe. Most of the fighting clustered around the trail, with emphasis on important flanking thrusts. The Thirty-Second Division entered the Salacsac battlefield on March 7 and exited on the east on May 28. It was, as the official history states, "a knock-down, drag-out, slug fest."[35]

On March 7 the 127th Regiment seized its first objective in the Salacsac battle, the crest of Hill 502 on the north side of the Villa Verde Trail. The plan of advance sent two battalions of the 127th Regiment eastward through the hill mass surrounding Salacsac Pass No. 2 and one battalion each of the 127th and 128th Regiments advancing separately in a wide encirclement from the south. Each of the northbound battalions reached the vicinity of the Villa Verde Trail but remained too far to close the circle and too isolated to deal with steadily reinforced defenders, so they retreated south. Meanwhile the east-bound battalions from Hill 502 advanced to

Hills 504 and 505, a distance of 600 yards, in two weeks, seizing only the southern faces, so dense was the defense and severe the artillery, mortar, and machine gun fire. The 127th Regiment by then had suffered 335 casualties and evacuated 500 with disease and combat fatigue. Almost all of the battalion and company commanders were lost, leaving privates in charge of many of the platoons.[36]

In resetting the attack, the 127th retired to Santa Maria for rest and replacements, with the 128th taking its place. The obvious need for a heavier attack meant recalling the 126th Regiment from its covering role in the three river valleys to the west. At this point General Swift at I Corps ordered the division as a whole to prepare a drive north through those valleys, joining the advance on Baguio, suggesting a fundamental misunderstanding of the battle in which the Thirty-Second was already engaged. Just at that time, General Krueger finally secured two regiments of the Thirty-Seventh Division in Manila, postponing the Baguio advance until the first of these arrived but allowing the 126th to rejoin its own division. At the Villa Verde Trail General Gill, the Thirty-Second division commander, ordered the 126th north of the 128th in a flanking position. The 128th resumed the advance on March 23; the 126th entered on April 5.

It was like starting all over again. The initial targets close by, Hills 503, 504, and 505, all required more bloodletting. The 128th took Hill 503, bypassed before, and secured more and most of Hill 504 and more of Hill 505. The Japanese responded immediately and powerfully with a nighttime artillery barrage and counterattack on Hill 504, driving off the Americans, who regained the southern face of the hill in a battalion-sized attack at dawn. The 128th held on to Hill 505 and grimly headed farther east, seeking to gain the higher ground that commanded the section of the Villa Verde Trail from where it turned south to where it turned east again. They managed to reach that stretch and set up roadblocks in the trail that limited Japanese supply, but the regiment was too weakened to capture the vital strongpoints. It had secured the Salacsac Pass No. 2 and vicinity and advanced east but then reached a point where it simply could fight no longer.

The Thirty-Second Division came to Luzon undermanned and in need of rest after prolonged fighting on Leyte. It faced a battleground ideal for defense. Cave emplacements were abundant. Bare patches here and there afforded excellent observation by the enemy of troop movements and pinpointing of artillery fire; the zigzag path of the Villa Verde Trail provided denser artillery targets. A blanketing forest blocked flank attacks, and casualties thinned the ranks in frontal attacks, but thinned ranks reduced mutual supporting fire. There could be no respite because the summer rains were coming and would flood the battlefield. Thus far the Thirty-Second Division had received no replacements, while the Japanese replenished from just over the hill. The division faced tough troops of the Japanese Second Tank Division, which had been raised in Japanese-held Manchuria and relocated to the Philippines in late 1944. This division lost its tanks in the Central Valley battles, but the survivors, under the command of Lieutenant General Iwanaka Yoshiharu, vowed to stay at their posts until death and did so. Iwanaka proved to be a determined and skilled field commander. The 128th received roughly the same number of casualties as the 127th, but these were lost in two weeks of battle instead of three.

Sixth Army observers found the 128th soldiers in a state of mental and physical exhaustion. Veterans of three to five operations became excessively cautious and talkative about home leave by rotation. The division remained in the line "long after they should have been relieved," according to the observers. But there was no division on Luzon to replace the Thirty-Second; they were all engaged. The only way was to relieve each in sequence, with relief for the 128th of ten to fourteen days by the 127th, then the same relief for the 126th with return of the 128th. Essentially, the Thirty-Second had been fighting with two regiments, each of which had only about 1,500 effective troops, against a Japanese investment, including replacements, of 8,760 troops of the Japanese Tenth Reconnaissance Regiment and Second Tank Division.[37] The Thirty-Second Division was near the breaking point.

By this point in the campaign toward Japan, the psychological cost of combat was becoming more and more clear and beginning to exert an influence on planning. Admissions for treatment of psychoneurosis (combat fatigue) at Southwest Pacific Theater hospitals in 1945 were 19,305 (admissions for all diseases in that theater in 1945 were 633,580).[38] "Combat fatigue" referred to the psychiatric breakdown of soldiers from prolonged physical and mental strain. Typical were uncontrollable weeping, shaking, and withdrawal. The soldier might be mute or screaming or berserk. According to Colonel M. Ralph Kaufman, a Harvard psychiatrist and a leader in exploring the pathology and its treatment, a crisis arises within a soldier over whether he should continue to fight. The issue, Kaufman points out, is not cowardice but conflict between the biological instinct for self-preservation and the "desire to fight and not run away." The resolution is to fight and the cost is combat fatigue.[39]

Promoting this inner strife was situational stress, that is, tension night and day, especially over the unpredictability of the enemy, but other threats and burdens as well: the threat and the almost unspeakable primitiveness of hand-to-hand combat; the sheer weight of weapons and supplies, which averaged forty pounds per soldier in the Philippines campaign and if anything was growing heavier as equipment changed; weakness from diarrhea; fear of the stalking diseases; the stink of death; the loss of buddies. Morale builders helped—hot or tasty food, movies, beer, newspapers, shows, showers, music, and rest. Combat terrain in the Philippines was likely to be uphill and thickly covered. After combat, troops followed with "mopping up" or loading and unloading ships, due to lack of port battalions. Heavy lifting between battles and the cutting short of rest periods were common. In the case of the Thirty-Second Division, it entered battle in Leyte on November 15, 1944, and had no definable rest periods thereafter until the following April 17 on the Villa Verde Trail, when the sequential withdrawals for rest occurred, altogether a span of five months or roughly 150 days. A study of combat fatigue on Saipan concluded that 140 days of combat was a threshold after which "psychiatric casualties should be expected in increasing numbers."[40] On Okinawa psychiatric treatment for combat fatigue, including hypnosis at a field hospital within hearing of the sound of guns, returned about 800 out of 900 patients to their outfits.[41]

Veterans of the Thirty-Second Division are perhaps representative of the GI experience of the Philippines campaign, starting with Luzon, which in many respects had been the most brutal part of the campaign. In letters and diaries, the overwhelming reaction was being scared all the time. The jungle and the nature of the enemy had taken away all assurances. Nothing was familiar. To say war is hell doesn't convey the degree of fear that this caused. Monte J. Howell was "scared with so many people being wounded and killed." Donald R. Dill was "frightened" fighting on when rumors of the end of the war were being thrown about in June 1945. James W. Deloach, thrice wounded in the Pacific, remembered his "extreme fatigue" and that "everyone was exhausted," while division headquarters "didn't give a damn about morale." The wounded waited from twelve to thirty-six hours for transport to the rear, which was too long for some; they died before reaching the field hospital. Roland Acheson experienced "malaria, malnutrition, trench foot, diarrhea." "People stink," he added. Edward Guhl, whose letter home is quoted above, had 670 days in combat and was sick of rations and losing weight. He was driven off a hill on Leyte and after that: "FEAR." One "had to survive all night if wounded, then survive littering out." Food was "monotonous" or lacking. "Constant combat" led to decline in morale and a "terrible physical condition." Gossip about invading Japan was too much: "I just gave up and decided I would be killed."[42]

As fighting continued under these excruciating conditions, the tide shifted, imperceptibly at first, in favor of the Americans. By April 17 the advantage in the Villa Verde Trail battle was definitely slipping across to the Thirty-Second. The 127th Regiment was returning from rest and, though not fully replenished, had received some replacements and went into action with over 2,000 effectives. Meanwhile, General Iwanaka had lost 1,125 troops and received 1,600 replacements, which were to be his last. The Salacsac Pass No. 2 area was nearly cleared, and the 127th was moving in on the Japanese strongpoints in the vicinity of the north–south stretch of the Villa Verde Trail. While that action moved along, slow and costly, the division began a major drive to the east. The 126th Regiment, which had extended its control eastward on the north side of the battleground, now drove south, with two battalions circling through the back country to the northern side of the Villa Verde Trail at Salacsac Pass No. 1, cutting through the enemy's supply lines to the west and blocking the trail itself. Artillery of the 127th west of the north–south stretch assisted the 126th. Meanwhile the 127th headed east, south of the trail, to attack Hill 508 across from the 126th Regiment. The object was to isolate Salacsac Pass No. 1. Now the battle was fought in the east toward Imugan and Santa Fe. The remaining Japanese troops in the north–south stretch were slowly taken out by the 127th, cave by cave.

The regimental sequence of ten- to fourteen-day rests gave the division a sustaining impetus, but not without heavy casualties. In the period April 17–May 4, the 126th and 127th Regiments lost 1,213 men, battle and non-battle casualties, including ten self-inflicted wounds, the latter being an ominous sign of disintegrating discipline and morale. Undoubtedly American artillery helped, but the difficulty of targeting the enemy in the mass of forest may explain why air attack is not mentioned. Two centers of action dominated the battle in late April and May: the section of the Villa Verde Trail holding Salacsac Pass No. 1 and the high ground a mile or so east of there, the holding of which would put the division close to the village of Imugan, the final objective of this division, with Santa Fe just beyond. The Second Battalion seized Hill 508 at the western edge of Salacsac Pass No. 1 and held on in the face of three successive counterattacks. Then all three battalions from west, south, and north fought their way toward the center of the pass, taking sixteen days to clear it. Iwanaka, recognizing by May 24 that he was beaten, withdrew the remnants of his forces, though not before sending a detachment to cut the supply lines of the American battalions advancing north of the Villa Verde Trail. After more delay to reopen supply, the Second Battalion, 128th, captured Hill 127, north of the Villa Verde Trail, and the Filipino Buena Vista Regiment, trained by the Thirty-Second, captured Hill 128 on the south side. These were the last stepping stones. Imugan was empty when the Filipino regiment arrived.[43]

On April 17, as the advantage on the Villa Verde Trail was shifting from the Japanese to the Americans, the same shift was occurring in the battle on Route 5 for Balete Pass. In spite of shifts of the Thirty-Fifth Regiment, the Twenty-Fifth Division was unable to gain momentum. The 161st Regiment on the left, west of the river, tackled the ridges from March 16 to April 8 and captured first Norton's Knob and then Crump Hill, overcoming strong defenses, but it had reached only halfway to the main line of resistance at Balete Ridge, and the same applied eastward for the Twenty-Seventh and Thirty-Fifth. By the end of March, division intelligence concluded that they were fighting not 4,000 Japanese but 8,000–10,000. General Mullins, deciding that he must further concentrate his forces, shortened his front by wedging the wandering Thirty-Fifth Regiment between the other two regiments. On the east, the Twenty-Seventh Regiment was entering a line of ridges and hills—Myoko Ridge, Woody Hill, Mount Myoko, Elbow Hill, Lone Tree Hill, Wolfhound Ridge—that circled north and then northwest to the Balete Pass opening. Parallel with Myoko Ridge, lying to the north, was Kapintalan Ridge. Fighting their way through this cluster from one hill or ridge to the next, one enemy strongpoint after another, were the battalions of the Thirty-Fifth and Twenty-Seventh Regiments. Essential for the battalions was the delivery of food and ammunition, either hand-carried or delivered by airdrop, and removal of the wounded. Neither would be feasible soon when the rains began to pour. Road-building bulldozers followed the troops, but progress was slow.

Colonel Philip F. Lindeman, commander of the Twenty-Seventh, was looking for a better way. A Hawaiian-born reserve officer and veteran of Guadalcanal, he would be awarded the Distinguished Service Cross, the Army's highest medal for bravery next to the Medal of Honor, for his actions on Luzon. On an aerial survey on April 17, Lindeman noticed that the terrain within the curving line of ridges and hills was flat enough for troops to cut straight across the curve to Lone Tree Hill only one and a half miles from Balete Pass, avoiding the strongpoints. Securing Kapintalan Ridge near Lone Tree Hill would provide a shorter supply route. Lindeman sent patrols followed by a platoon, then a company, then a battalion, as it became evident that the enemy had left a gap in its defense on Lone Tree Hill, only a mile from Balete Pass. Now the weight of the advance north reverted to Route 5, leaving one battalion on Kapintalan Ridge to pin down the enemy there. To engage the enemy on Mount Myoko came one more assist from the 148th Regiment, Thirty-Seventh Division, which had already played a key role in the Baguio offensive at Irisan Gorge. West of Balete Pass now stood the Third Battalion, 161st Regiment, which had fought its way up to reach Haruna Ridge on the left of Balete Pass. East of the pass the Third Battalion, Twenty-Seventh Regiment, having cleared Wolfhound Ridge, sent Company I down to Route 5, where it joined Company A of the same regiment moving into Balete Pass from Route 5. The Thirty-Fifth Regiment followed on, having reached Route 5 after eliminating scattered enemy defenses on the east side. On May 13 General Mullins announced the capture of Balete Pass as the division passed through it to reach Santa Fe and the junction with the Villa Verde Trail. From this point to the end of May the Twenty-Fifth Division and the 126th Regiment of the Thirty-Second Division scouted and cleared land two miles north and east of Santa Fe for protection.[44]

The Thirty-Second Division suffered devastating and the Twenty-Fifth Division severe casualties. Battle casualties for the Thirty-Second were 2,985 and for the Twenty-Fifth 2,775. Nonbattle evacuations (disease, injury, combat fatigue) were about 6,000 for the Thirty-Second and about two-thirds of that, 4,000, for the Twenty-Fifth. Total losses for both American divisions were 15,760, about the strength of one full division, and 13,500 of the Japanese were killed of the 20,750 committed. Japanese losses for the Philippines, except Leyte, were 380,000 and for the Americans 140,400 battle and nonbattle, of which 47,000 were battle.[45] In his oral history in which he looked back on the Villa Verde Trail battle, Major General William H. Gill, commander of Thirty-Second Division, remembered the battle as "terrible": his troops had little rest from the time of the Leyte landing, morale was dragging. Enemy machine gun and mortar positions were "perfect," so "he lost an awful lot of men," and replacements were nonexistent. There were "casualties beyond battle casualties after a long period of hard fighting and exposure to the elements, to the diseases, to all the things that go to reduce our capabilities of fighting men," such as dysentery, malaria, and cold at night.

The division came down to 50 percent effectiveness. To see the wounded and dead was "heart breaking." War was "life emphasized." He felt afterward that "the price was too high." Lower commanders were pushed to accomplish things to "pay the price that somebody didn't realize was so high." He said MacArthur and his staff violated the principle that the price can be too high.[46]

If the Twenty-Fifth and Thirty-Second Divisions thought that the fighting on Luzon would cease with the capture of Imugan and Santa Fe, they were profoundly mistaken. Each of these divisions and the Sixth, Thirty-Third, and Thirty-Seventh would participate in the encirclement and compression of the Shobu Group as it retreated into Yamashita's secluded redoubt across the mountain chain, north of Santa Fe and northeast of Baguio. General Krueger was determined to destroy any enemy capability of counterattack, even with his staff estimate of only 23,000 Japanese troops remaining.

In fact, at the end of June 1945, the Shobu Group had 65,000 men, with an organized force of 52,000. Among the American divisions, the Twenty-Fifth and Thirty-Third had to be relieved from further combat at the end of June. However, Yamashita had no thought of counterattack. As the Army's official historian R. R. Smith says, Yamashita had come to a situation where he "lacked the capability of concentrating all his forces" with counterattacks leading to "rapid, piecemeal destruction." He believed that his best and only course was "protracted delaying actions" that would weaken or hold up the invasion of Japan.[47]

The vast interior of northern Luzon, mostly encircled by mountains, stretched 160 miles from the Villa Verde Trail to Aparri on the northern coast and 120 miles from east to west coast. The Sixth Army sent a Filipino-American task force to Aparri on the north coast by way of the west coast, dropped a battalion of paratroopers from the Eleventh Airborne Division there to scout and clear the territory, and drove a regiment of the Thirty-Seventh Division down the middle of the valley to connect with them. No substantial enemy force was found. The fighting mostly occurred in the southwest quadrant of northern Luzon, among the steep hills and mountains of the Cordillerra Central in the west and the river valleys and crops to the east, the lands that stretched away below Baguio and Santa Fe. At the center was Yamashita's last redoubt, the narrow, steep-sided Asin Valley.

The last significant campaign of the battle to liberate the Philippines began June 1 with the advance from Santa Fe of the Twenty-Fifth Division, clearing the way down Route 5 to the north. Following and passing through the Twenty-Fifth was the Thirty-Seventh Division, which, after the Battle of Manila, had loaned regiments to the Shimbu front. The

Thirty-Seventh headed northeast into the Cagayan Valley, scouting and scattering bands of enemy soldiers. Following the Thirty-Seventh, the Sixth Division, which had been badly mauled on the Shimbu front, turned northwest on Route 4 toward the Cordillera Central. With the arrival of the Sixth, the Twenty-Fifth Division bowed out to prepare for Japan. Meanwhile, the Thirty-Second left the Villa Verde Trail to join the Thirty-Third at Baguio. Gradually, with the drift of enemy troops toward the south and west, the Sixth Army perceived that Yamashita's last redoubt must be somewhere in the hills and valleys north of Santa Fe and east of Baguio, between Route 11 north from Baguio and Route 4 north from Route 5. Consequently, they adopted a formation of convergence and compression to pin down what remained of the Shobu force. By June the summer rains had arrived, with daily deluges as high as ten inches, making troop movement and supply agonizingly slow.

Having stationed the Thirty-Seventh Division in the Cagayan Valley and withdrawn the Twenty-Fifth and Thirty-Third Divisions at the end of June, the Sixth Army was left with just three divisions and one large Filipino-American force of four regiments to eliminate the Shobu force as a threat. On the west, the Sixty-Sixth Filipino-American Regiment pushed south on Route 11 while the 126th and 127th Regiments of the Thirty-Second Division, just weeks away from the Villa Verde Trail, slogged north from Baguio in parallel along the Agno River and Route 11. They met the Sixty-Sixth halfway at the end of July and turned east into the Japanese defense perimeter. The Filipino-American force of 23,000, larger than a division, had been gathered, armed, and tested in battle by Colonel Volckmann. It had just completed a drive east from San Fernando on Lingayen Gulf through Bessang Pass to Cervantes and Sabangan, about twelve miles northwest and north of the Asin Valley redoubt. Two regiments of the Filipino-American force moved into the northwest sector to tie in with the Sixty-Sixth, 126th, and 127th, tightly sealing the western side of their defensive zone. On the eastern side the advance was very slow: the rain was even heavier there, marooning units from their supply. In addition, the Air Force had destroyed the bridges and buried patches of road in landslides. The south side was open, except for a regiment each

■ General George C. Marshall. Library of Congress Prints and Photographs Division, LC-USZ62-103399.

■ The Arena of Victory. From *United States and G. C. Marshall, Biennial Reports of the Chief of Staff of the United States Army to the Secretary of War: 1 July 1939–30 June 1945.* (Washington, D.C.: Center of Military History, 1996).

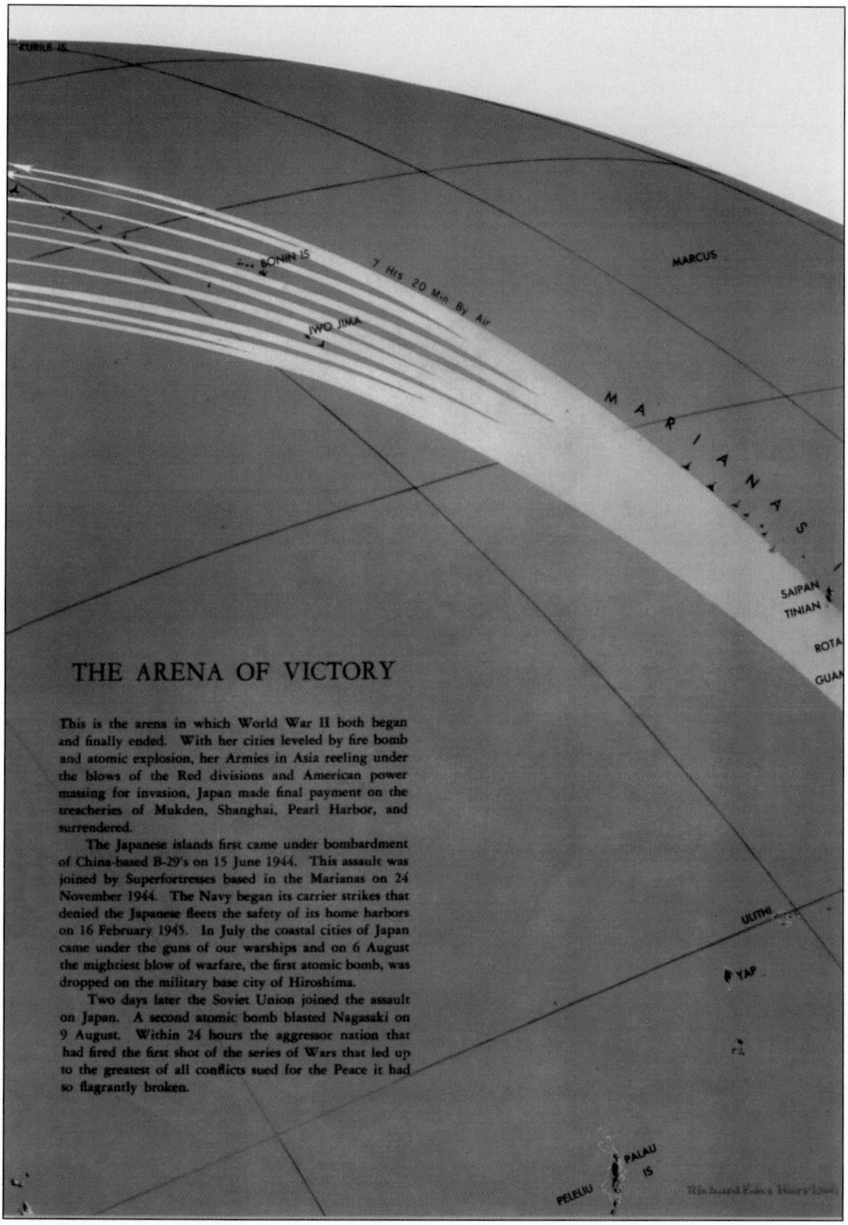

THE ARENA OF VICTORY

This is the arena in which World War II both began and finally ended. With her cities leveled by fire bomb and atomic explosion, her Armies in Asia reeling under the blows of the Red divisions and American power massing for invasion, Japan made final payment on the treacheries of Mukden, Shanghai, Pearl Harbor, and surrendered.

The Japanese islands first came under bombardment of China-based B-29's on 15 June 1944. This assault was joined by Superfortresses based in the Marianas on 24 November 1944. The Navy began its carrier strikes that denied the Japanese fleets the safety of its home harbors on 16 February 1945. In July the coastal cities of Japan came under the guns of our warships and on 6 August the mightiest blow of warfare, the first atomic bomb, was dropped on the military base city of Hiroshima.

Two days later the Soviet Union joined the assault on Japan. A second atomic bomb blasted Nagasaki on 9 August. Within 24 hours the aggressor nation that had fired the first shot of the series of Wars that led up to the greatest of all conflicts sued for the Peace it had so flagrantly broken.

KURILE IS.

...BONIN IS.

7 Hrs 20 Min By Air

IWO JIMA

MARCUS

MARIANAS

SAIPAN
TINIAN
ROTA
GUAM

ULITHI

YAP

PALAU
IS

PELELIU

General MacArthur wades ashore at Leyte. National Archives and Records Administration.

■ Admirals Chester Nimitz, Ernest J. King, and Raymond Spruance. United States Navy photo.

■ General MacArthur, FDR, Admiral William D. Leahy, and Admiral Nimitz in Honolulu. Library of Congress Prints and Photographs Division, LC-USZ62-135317.

■ Tanks blasting a cave on Peleliu. Department of Defense photo, USMC 97433.

■ An LST opens its enormous jaws on Leyte Beach. Courtesy of Wikimedia Creative Commons.

■ Drum bombs dropped on Iwo Jima. National Archives and Records Administration.

■ Clearing a cave on Iwo Jima. United States Army Signal Corps photo.

■ Paratroopers dropping on Topside, Corregidor. AP photo/United States Army Signal Corps.

■ U.S. Fast Carrier Task Force at Ulithi Atoll, February 1945. United States Navy photo.

■ Recoilless rifle, Okinawa. United States Army photo.

Name		Serial No.	Arm of Service	Unit	
MOS Title					SSN
Type of Credit		Number	Multiply By		Credits
1. SERVICE CREDIT (Number of months in Army since Sept. 16, 1940.)					
2. OVERSEAS CREDIT (Number of months served overseas.)					
3. COMBAT CREDIT (Number of decorations and bronze service stars.)					
4. PARENTHOOD CREDIT (Number of children under 18 years old.)					
				Total Credits	
Certified by -					
ADJUSTED SERVICE RATING CARD					

Sample Adjusted Service Rating Card. *Franklin Evening Star*, May 12, 1945.

Arrival in New York of the *Queen Elizabeth* bringing troops from the Eighty-Sixth Division back from Europe, June 1945. Bettmann/Contributor.

■ General Yamishita Tomoyuki surrenders, September 1945. National Archives and Records Administration.

from the Sixth and Thirty-Second Divisions stationed near the corners. The only two American divisions operating here, the Thirty-Second from the Villa Verde Trail and the Sixth from the Shimbu front, had probably been the two divisions most damaged.[48]

On June 1 Eichelberger, leader of the Eighth Army, took command of divisions on Luzon while Krueger's Sixth Army shifted to command just those slated for what was coming next: the invasion of Japan. Eichelberger, of course, had been told by MacArthur on June 4 on Mindanao to avoid a major engagement so as "not to lose any more men than we have to." In these circumstances, there would be every reason to surround and seal in the enemy and every reason to go no farther. They went no farther than the lines surrounding Asin Valley.

The basic American objective was clear: to attack and eliminate the Shobu threat in northern Luzon. The objective of Yamashita was equally clear: to concentrate his forces and attack, imposing as many casualties on the Sixth Army as possible. Yet, given the ground gained and men lost in fighting through July and even the first half of August, this last battle was different. American battle casualties for this period were 1,650, roughly 1,000 of which were taken by the Filipino force. Even though the infantry elements of the Sixth, Thirty-Second, and Thirty-Seventh Divisions had already been heavily reduced, it seems unusual that the average wounded and killed in each of those three divisions was only 217.[49] On both sides a constant pouring rain slowed movement and supply. For Yamashita, concentration of forces was incomplete: the Sixth Army task forces sent into the Cagayan Valley from several directions had broken up much of the Shobu forces on the move toward Asin Valley. By mid-August the Filipino-American encirclement had closed around the Shobu redoubt but was by no means on the doorstep. Nor were Yamashita's troops stepping out.

The campaign into the southern Philippines had been slow and bloody but essential. Without it, Luzon would not have had enough port facilities cleared and repaired to stage and mount the Sixth Army for what came next: the invasion of Japan. The ports of the Visayas, Iloilo City, and Cebu City, as well as Zamboanga, were essential for embarking one more corps of three divisions for a departure on September 15. The selected divisions for that corps were the ones that had liberated the port cities south of Luzon. However, Mindanao, apart from Zamboanga on its western tail, had no immediate military importance and only political importance in completing the liberation of the Philippines. Completing that liberation before going on to Japan was of critical importance to MacArthur in fulfilling his pledge to return. On the other hand, most of Mindanao was already in the hands of the guerrillas, and postponement would have avoided much destruction from bombardment, especially of Davao. If the Sixth Army could have retained the two divisions sent to Mindanao they would have greatly facilitated the liberation of Luzon. As it was, battle casualties in the Philippines (less Leyte) were 47,000 and nonbattle casualties 93,400. Krueger and the Sixth Army, always directing several battles at once, with great skill, managed without those divisions, but most of the divisions left behind on Luzon were now shrunken and exhausted. And with the invasion for Japan planned for November 1, this was of profound significance.

Despite the actual toll in casualties, MacArthur was able to use his control of the news from his theater to burnish his public reputation for strategic brilliance. Throughout the spring a steady stream of MacArthur communiqués touted the accomplishments of the Sixth and Eighth Armies' operations on Luzon and the islands south of it while always highlighting the disproportionate losses suffered by the enemy. MacArthur also continued his habit of declaring battles over before the shooting had stopped. On April 11, he announced that "all organized enemy resistance in northern Luzon collapsed and liberation is at hand." Ten days later, he declared that victory on Cebu had completed the liberation of the central islands. "Our losses in this campaign were extraordinarily light, due largely to the enemy's continued inability to diagnose our point of attack and understand our local tactics of combat," reported MacArthur. On April 29, more than two weeks after he declared organized enemy resistance on Luzon at an end, he announced that American forces had taken the "mountain citadel" at Baguio. American casualties were "amazingly light," according to the communiqué.[50] Reports of MacArthur's successes—the unopposed landings, the rapid movement inland, the overwhelming of fierce resistance, and the light casualties—contrasted sharply with the news from Okinawa.[51] There, after an unopposed landing on April 1, Marine and Army forces had become locked in a bloody slugging match with the enemy. The struggle for Okinawa, the first major battle on Japanese territory, gave the Americans a frightening preview of what they could expect when they invaded the home islands.

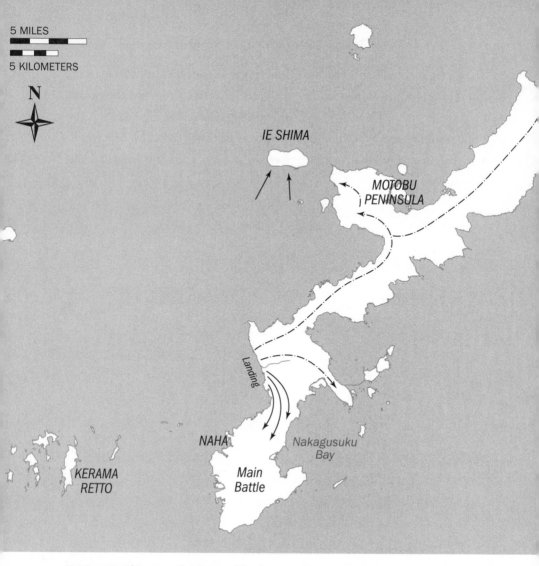

■ **Map 10** Okinawa and Adjacent Islands. Drawn by George Chakvetadze.

Okinawa, April–June 1945

Battling for Iwo Jima initiated the campaign to establish American forces within striking distance of Japan itself, and for that, despite its size, it had been perceived as critically important. But Okinawa was seen as the centerpiece of the campaign northward. It was, as noted, a far larger island than Iwo Jima, a long and raggedly thin island, sixty-five miles by two to ten miles across, stretching from northeast to southwest, with several peninsulas projecting farther. Okinawa stood at the very middle of the Ryukyu Islands, an arc stretching from Japan itself to Formosa, defining the East China Sea.

The importance of Okinawa seemed self-evident to the American military command. It was exactly what they wanted. It was 340 miles from the Japanese home island of Kyushu and about the same distance on the other side from Formosa and the China coast. Possession would open the way for tightening the blockade of Japanese shipping from the south and provide bases for air support of the invasion of Kyushu. Two bays sheltered by islands on the eastern side of Okinawa could provide anchorage. Fifteen miles west of Okinawa, a cluster of islands, the Kerama Retto, formed an excellent roadstead, with anchorage for transferring cargo and temporary ship repair. Okinawa itself, large enough for staging troops, already had five airfields and airstrips, and nearby in the north the small island of Ie Shima also boasted an airstrip.

By the middle of March most of the American Navy, from the Atlantic, the West Coast, Alaska, the South Pacific, the Marianas, and the Philippines was headed toward or moving into the northwest Pacific, in the area known as the Philippine Sea. Ulithi lagoon, four days sailing southeast from Okinawa, was harboring as many as 600 ships. Vice Admiral Mitscher's battle array now consisted of eleven fast carriers, all of which, except the *Enterprise*, were finished after 1941, and eight fast battleships, all also completed after 1941. Furthermore, three heavy cruisers and two of the new "large cruisers"—as Samuel Eliot Morison noted—"large as battleships and lean as cruisers," had joined the attack force. At last the prewar battleships, ten of them, featuring smaller guns than the newer ships, were able to gather in one place for gunfire duty in the land battle, joined by nine heavy cruisers. Supplementing these American forces would be a new British Pacific Fleet, consisting of two battleships, four aircraft carriers, cruiser squadron, destroyer screen, and fleet train, based on the harbor at Manus in the Admiralties. Servicing the whole armada were oilers, ammunition ships, mine-craft, dry food provision ships, refrigerated (reefer) ships, and many other needs. The Philippine Sea, thus far Japanese waters, was now dotted with ships—from twos and threes to fleets—crisscrossing it between Okinawa, Leyte, Ulithi, Guam, and (now) Iwo Jima. The fast carrier force was a bit faster than it had been: when it withdrew east of Okinawa to refuel, each ship could take on its ammunition supply while waiting its turn for oil.

The first landing in the expansion northwest was Kerama Retto: as mentioned above, the small islands fifteen miles west of southern Okinawa, which Admiral Kelly Turner believed, correctly, would provide an excellent protected anchorage for ship repair and servicing and a seaplane base. The Seventy-Seventh Division, under Major General Bruce, scarcely finished with "mopping up"—as the euphemism had it—on Leyte, boarded ship for Kerama Retto. Arriving on March 26, five battalions, apprised of their roles on the way north, transferred from troop transports to LCVPs (landing craft, vehicle, personnel) and from eighteen LSTs to amphtracs. These formed tendrils that penetrated the channels and seized five of the six significant islands the same day. The battalions encountered surprised and feeble Japanese defenses, fighting here and there and withdrawing to their island heights. Kerama Retto was quickly transformed into a key base: it had nets and net keepers at the entrances; a radar post to warn of Japanese air attack; a seaplane base in one of the arms of the roadstead; buoys for shipping lanes; anchorage for forty-four ships; and altogether a large base for emergency repair and replenishment of ships. Inside the roadstead one had "the feeling of security," Morison wrote. For Rear Admiral Allan Smith, Morison wrote, Kerama "gave a firmness to the Okinawa tactical situation that was felt by all." They were there to stay.[1]

Okinawa was to draw on a huge American attack force of 183,000 troops in seven divisions. Three divisions, the Army's Seventh, Seventy-Seventh, and Ninety-Sixth, came from Leyte, where they had just completed, as we've noted, a wearing campaign. Three came from training camps in the South Pacific: the First and Sixth Marine Divisions and the Army's Twenty-Seventh, which had fought with feeble leadership at Saipan. Last was the Second Marine Division, recently in Saipan. In addition, from Hawaii came Army and Corps personnel, including Lieutenant General Simon B. Buckner, Jr., commander of the expedition's new Tenth Army, and from West Coast ports came herds of supply ships.[2]

The invasion began on April 1, Easter Sunday; the landing took place on the western shore and just south of the narrow midsection of the island, near the town of Hagushi, along eight miles of smooth and straight beach. The Hagushi beaches were a good choice because the relatively flat terrain nearby and the position toward the middle of Okinawa made them an excellent place for the principal supply depot; and the immediate acquisition of two airfields lying just a mile beyond the beaches would be of great value. Preparatory gunfire by ten battleships and nine heavy cruisers worked over enemy artillery defenses for seven days, precisely what had been needed so badly at Iwo Jima. On Okinawa, however, few big Japanese guns were found in the photographs, and none were found in the landing area. The Marine III Corps advised that the extensive cover on the island might be masking the presence of heavy guns near the landing site, but it turned out that hardly any defense artillery was near the beaches; it was elsewhere.[3]

The day of the invasion was sunny, with a calm sea. The objective was shortly beforehand to concentrate the gunfire of all available weapons on the beaches and their surroundings, thereby protecting the troops during their vulnerable approach and arrival from their ships. This was done by the big guns of the nineteen older battleships and cruisers and by air attack from planes of the fast carrier and escort carrier groups. The transports and landing ships (LSTs and new, somewhat smaller LSMs) had arrived at their debarkation positions during the night from their various Pacific crossings. At sunrise they opened their bow doors, dropped their ramps, and sent forth their filled LVT-A (landing vehicle, tank-A) personnel tractors and LVT armored tractors with guns, while troops aboard transports filed onto LCVPs attached to the davits. Guide boats, many more than had been used previously, hustled them into precise positions in wave after wave of landing boats that started toward the beaches at 8:30 a.m. Counting all the boats and tractors heading for all the beaches, 1,332 craft landed. The waves moved in four masses, each consisting of one division, the Seventh and Ninety-Sixth Divisions on the south and the First and Sixth Marine Divisions on the north. The whole attack line was about 7,000 yards in depth and 10,000 in breadth. Near the shore, the boat waves stopped to cross the coral reef, easily done at high tide in the early hours but requiring transfer to boats on the other side of the reef at low tide. In one hour 16,000 troops arrived on the beaches. They met very few defenders. The American troops swept across the two airfields ahead and in a day or two pushed across the isthmus to the eastern shore with hardly any resistance.

So far the Tenth Army had done much and with apparent ease: gained a splendid anchorage in Kerama roadstead; achieved a fast and bloodless landing; acquired excellent beaches for unloading; and taken in two airfields in the immediate vicinity and, just beyond, low, sloping countryside for supply dumps. Construction crews and equipment, causeways, docks, and barges landed. The main dirt road network—roughly a lane and a half—demanded widening and hardening. Meanwhile the troops headed out immediately in every direction to find the enemy. The Sixth Marine Division, landing on the left, turned north toward the narrow middle span of Okinawa that connected with mountainous back country. The Seventh and Ninety-Sixth Army divisions spread across the isthmus to the eastern shore while turning right, forming a line across the island heading south. The Marine III Corps (First, Second, and Sixth Divisions) stood in reserve for the present. Noteworthy is the depletion of the Marine V Corps (Third, Fourth, and Fifth Divisions) on Iwo Jima by April. The III Corps would enter the main battle when needed.

Meanwhile, the Sixth Marine Division would clear Okinawa north of the landing site, a portion three-fifths the length of the island. Scattered groups of Japanese troops were spotted retiring north. The chances that these troops would organize and others from neighboring islands move in and join them called for a defensive force in the north. Sending the recently formed Sixth Marine Division would provide it with operational experience with fewer casualties. This division, built up from units that had fought on Guam, was the last Marine division created in the war. It moved out on April 7, clearing the isthmus rapidly with three files of troops, one along each shore and one in the middle, accompanied by engineers who repaired and replaced bridges quickly and landing craft that provided meals and ammunition along the way. On April 11 the division arrived at Mobutu Peninsula, a large protrusion from the western shore with a striking mountain mass named Yae-Take rising to 1,500 feet in the middle of it. Here, intelligence believed, a significant guerrilla force was gathering. The Sixth Division entered and scouted the peninsula. Meanwhile the division's Twenty-Second Regiment sent reconnaissance troops by landing craft along both sides of the rest of Okinawa to its northern tip and patrols down the middle from the east coast, without finding a trace of the enemy.

The Tenth Army was clear about what now had to be done, especially given the March 26 night attack on the tent city in Iwo Jima. Orders were to "destroy remaining enemy forces on Motobu."[4] Battalions of the Sixth Marine Division on the peninsula that had been scouting it now encircled Yae-Take, compressing the circle of defenders as they pushed toward the top. They faced a light Japanese force, well sited, with few artillery pieces but many small-bore troop weapons. Using air attack, maneuver, stratagem, and uphill charges the Marines reached the top and literally chased the enemy off the mountain. The division had many new recruits but also many skilled old-timers. They killed some 2,500 Japanese in this northern mission, though not without significant loss of their own: 1,304 killed and wounded in two weeks.[5]

The brisk acquisition of Kerama and northern Okinawa encouraged the Tenth Army to speed the agenda and seize Ie Shima while they could. On this small, flat island, located only three miles from the end of the Motobu Peninsula, the Japanese had built an airfield of three 5,500-foot landing strips. With the advent of the Americans the airfield had been so far as possible destroyed and mined, but an airfield battalion and labor battalion remained and, with local inhabitants, constructed thick fortifications within the only town, Ie. Lacking any obstacle to hinder landing and takeoff over land and sea, aside from a lonely mound with coral projection to 185 feet named Iegusugu, which the Americans called "the Pinnacle," the island was much wanted for its airfield. Tenth Army selected the Seventy-Seventh Division, just then completing its clearing of the enemy on Kerama, to undertake the task.

On April 2, their assignment at Kerama completed, the 305th Regiment, Seventy-Seventh Division, reembarked on their transports and sailed south to avoid kamikaze attack. They had gone sixteen miles when ten or more Japanese planes attacked; one plane and two bombs exploded on the bridge and in the captain's cabin. Killed were the transport division commander, the ship's captain, the commander of the 305th Regiment, his executive officer, and his personnel and operations staff officers. His intelligence and supply officers were wounded, several key enlisted men killed or wounded, and almost all the regimental records were lost. Total losses of the Seventy-Seventh aboard ship were ninety-eight men.[6] The ship returned to Kerama, where the soldiers transferred to the USS *Sarasota*. Besides the Seventy-Seventh Division's Kerama assignment, the Tenth Army withheld the division's 307th Regiment for a feint attack on the east coast of Okinawa. The commitment was reduced to a battalion, but the frequency with which the

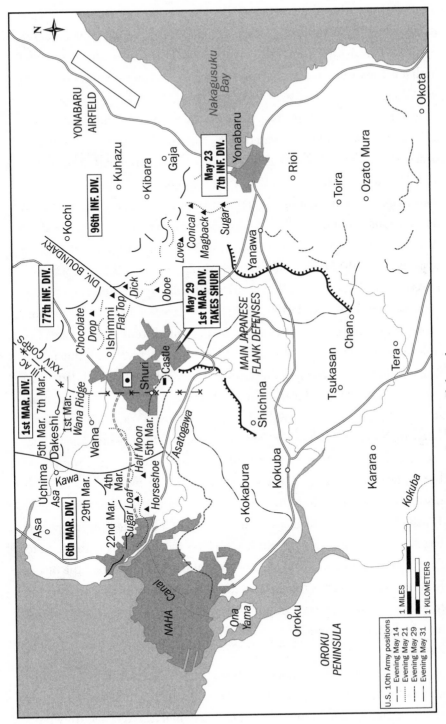

Map 11 The Battle of Okinawa, May 1945. Drawn by George Chakvetadze.

Tenth Army withheld elements of the Seventy-Seventh for other assignments added to its burden in complex amphibious warfare. The battalion withdrawn from the capture of Ie Shima would likely have been more useful in that bloody battle rather than pretending to land on the shores of southern Okinawa.[7]

Ie Shima is an east–west oval, five miles by three and a half, covered by a smooth flat plateau lying about 165 feet above the various surrounding beaches. The destroyed airstrips lay in the north–central part of the island and the Pinnacle and town in the east–central part. Beaches ran along the southwest and center south. With the town of Ie now heavily fortified and its weapons camouflaged, the Japanese commander sought to draw American forces to the beach just below the town by leaving it pristine while firing on the other beaches. The ruse did not work. Ie Shima was subjected to extensive bombardment, intermittently by Fifth Fleet ships and systematically by the battleship *Texas* and two cruisers. Further fire support came from three battalions of army artillery fired from a tiny island five miles south of Ie Shima. On April 16, landing day, two battleships, four cruisers, and seven destroyers bombarded the beaches while LCIs launched rockets and mortars and planes dropped barrels of napalm. Two battalions of the 305th Regiment (the third was garrisoning Kerama) landed separately on beaches south of the former airfield and then swung east in line, moving on Ie. The three battalions of the 306th landed on the southwest beach, headed north, and swept east abreast, clearing the western and northern coast, including the airstrip zone. On the following day, April 17, the Second and Third battalions of the 307th landed on the prized beach south of the Pinnacle and Ie (the First Battalion was withdrawn to feint a landing on Okinawa). The two battalions would protect the beach for the landing of tanks for the attack and heavy construction equipment to gain an immediate start in rebuilding the airfield. Thus by the second day the battalions provided a containment of the enemy in the southeast quarter.

Just inland the Pinnacle watched over Ie with its parallel streets running down the slope connecting the plateau to the beach. Ie was no longer a place of habitation: bombardment had flattened it. Wreckage strewn on the house plots and streets was used to hide and protect Japanese machine guns and riflemen; streets now were narrow, winding paths, mined and strung with wire entanglement and inaccessible to tanks and self-propelled artillery. Advancing uphill, the Americans were always in sight from above. Divided block by block, the infantry was unable to mass in attack. Approaching the top, "Bloody Ridge," as they called it, barred the way. From April 17 to April 20 the battalions of the 305th and 307th fought their way up toward the Pinnacle with heavy casualties. They took Bloody Ridge and another structure called Government House but, short of ammunition, could not hold them against furious enemy counterattacks. The island garrison of 5,000 included a number of local inhabitants, even women. Their weapons sometimes consisted of sharply pointed wooden staves.

Costly as it was, the American attack through Ie allowed an uninterrupted landing of the tanks and airfield machinery on the beach below. In addition, that attack allowed time for clearing the remaining enemy left behind in the north and east. On April 19 General Bruce scanned the terrain from the east in a Navy boat to judge the best assignments and routes for finishing the battle by a compression of the encirclement of Ie and the Pinnacle. The resulting plan would advance the 306th Regiment's three battalions to the west, north, and east sides of the Pinnacle and again engage the four battalions of the 305th and 307th Regiments along the southern face, pushing northeast, north, and northwest to Bloody Ridge again. It was time to squeeze the circle.

The battle began the morning of April 20 with heavy artillery concentrations on Iegusugu (the Pinnacle) and its approaches. The 306th Regiment's First Battalion, with the Third Battalion alongside, moved to the east side of the mountain and attacked, while the Second Battalion moved down the opposite side. From the bottom of the town slope to the top and from there to the peak of the Pinnacle all American battalions faced "intense small-arms fire." The assistant division commander described the Pinnacle as "a damned highly fortified position with caves three stories deep." Everywhere was "a maze of machine gun, mortar, and gun positions little affected by artillery fire we have poured on." The division report noted, however, "the

Infantry advance frequently was accomplished only by creeping, crawling, and infiltration," but the soldiers pushed forward steadily under the cover of supporting fire from artillery and self-propelled guns, and eventually created a path through the minefields surrounding the mountain.[8]

The pressure to complete operations was strong not only on Pinnacle but at Bloody Ridge as well. The Second Battalion of the 307th Regiment and First Battalion of the 305th, the same outfits that had made the first seizure of Bloody Ridge and Government House and then lost them to Japanese counterattack, now returned and this time mounted more machine guns. Forces pushing north thickened: beside these two battalions were the Third Battalion, 307th, holding ground between the Government House and the Pinnacle, and Third Battalion, 305th, closing in from the southwest.

During the night of April 20–21 small groups of Japanese tested the defenses of Company G, 307th Regiment, on the west side of Bloody Ridge near Government House. At 4:30 a.m. an hour-long mortar and gunfire attack began on the American position, with separate columns of the enemy bearing down on it, held by the Second Battalion, 307th, command post. Meanwhile that headquarters had formed a firing line on the hillcrest of everyone from colonel to driver. The platoon on the left folded, but the one on the right held on. Private First Class Martin O. May, who had covered the previous retreat with his machine gun, covered this one as well. When a mortar burst broke his machine gun and wounded him severely, he used hand grenades until he died. May was awarded the Congressional Medal of Honor. Fighting at close quarters for an hour the Americans finally regained their lost positions. The next morning they counted 364 Japanese and Okinawan bodies, among them, as noted, some women. An infantry company ordinarily carries between 100 and 200 soldiers; the three companies G, H, and E altogether had 142 men left. By April 21 the Second Battalion, 307th, had lost thirty officers, dead or wounded—almost all.[9]

Capture of the Pinnacle took all of the same day, April 21. The 306th Infantry held most of the surface, so use of artillery and naval gunfire was out of the question, but gunfire was still coming from the southwest corner of the mountain. Exterior combat continued until 2 p.m., when only the caves and tunnels remained. Fire, explosion, and tank shells soon closed these off. The six-day Ie Shima battle was over. The Americans lost 172 killed, 902 wounded, and 46 missing. In the process they killed 4,706 Japanese and took 149 prisoners. It is estimated that 1,500 of these were Okinawans. Work to expand the airfield started immediately and finished quickly; a fighter group occupied it by May 10 and three more in the next month. By mid-May Ie Shima had radar and air warning installed, as well as a 100,000-gallon freshwater basin, from filtered sea water. Perhaps the best known casualty on Ie Shima was the beloved war correspondent Ernie Pyle, outstanding in his sympathy for and depiction of the infantryman's perspective. Pyle, who had moved from the European Theater to the Pacific in January 1945, was killed by machine gun. After arriving in the Pacific, Pyle wrote about his difficulty in understanding the new enemy and struggled to comprehend the vast dimensions of the war in the Pacific. Expecting the more familiar war in Europe to end soon, he had drafted a column on that subject before he was killed. It was an attempt to sum up his experience during two and a half years in North Africa, Italy, and France, but servicemen in the Pacific would have found the sentiment disturbingly familiar. In witnessing the war he had seen "dead men in such familiar promiscuity that they become monstrous. Dead men in such monstrous infinity that you come almost to hate them. These are the things that you at home need not even try to understand. To you at home they are columns of figures."[10] Three days after the ending of the Ie Shima battle, the Seventy-Seventh Division was in the battle zone on Okinawa.[11]

The Americans were fortunate now to hold not only the two airfields, Yontan and Kadena, these right next to the landing beaches, but also Ie Shima, a third field, on an excellent site. And Kerama Retto by this point provided a handy and largely enclosed space for ships to anchor, get preliminary repair for battle damage from repair ships, transfer the wounded to hospital ships, exchange cargoes, and steal a moment of stillness from the ocean waves. Across the Hagushi beaches in the middle of the west side of Okinawa was a constant daily movement of ammunition, food, and other supplies from the mass of ships offshore, among small craft, to the nearby emptying landing ships at the beach. All this matériel was then trucked to "dumps" nearby and stacked. It was soon being drawn and carried south to soldiers and Marines in battle. Assigned to provide naval gunfire in support of the Army and Marine artillery advancing southward were ten battleships (the *Maryland, Texas, Arkansas, Colorado, Tennessee, Nevada, Idaho, West Virginia, New Mexico*, and *New York*), all with 12- to 16-inch guns. Their heavier ammunition would enlarge the damage wrought by Army artillery. For protection of the masses of troops and ships from air attack on Okinawa and the vicinity, the Navy sought to build an early warning system and defensive zone extending outward and upward. This included the Support Carrier Group, composed of eighteen escort carriers housing 495 fighter and torpedo planes, and two newly arrived Marine fighter groups of 222 planes aboard three *more* escort carriers. The Support Carrier Group maintained a day and night combat air patrol for Okinawa. The landing commander, Vice Admiral Turner, added a further dimension in the defense by encircling Okinawa with sixteen destroyer pickets posted at varied distances from headquarters in the landing zone. Each destroyer had radar and a fighter-director team aboard and patrolled in a 5,000-yard radius. Upon approach of enemy planes on the screen the destroyer sent to combat air patrol the number, direction, and distance.

Task Force 58, the fast carrier fleet that had assisted at Iwo Jima and bombarded Japan itself was present for Okinawa at its greatest capability. All eleven fast carriers were of wartime construction, *Essex* class, except one, the proud *Enterprise*. In addition, the task force had six protective light carriers for combat air patrol and five battleships. The force also took comfort in three 45,000-ton large battleships, including the *Missouri*, each of which carried, beside the big guns, 148 antiaircraft guns from 20 mm to 5-inch. Added now to the sixteen heavy cruisers and light cruisers were the *Alaska* and *Guam*, two "large cruisers" with nine 12-inch guns, described as "ships of battleship size with lean cruiser lines." Of the heavily worked destroyers the task force had about eighty. The British naval force in the Pacific was now Task Force 57, under Spruance and Nimitz and assigned the Sakishima Gunto islands in the Ryukyus, lying west of Okinawa as far as Formosa. British air attacks there would eliminate any threat to Okinawa from those islands and Formosa while Task Force 58 was engaged northward toward Japan. The Formosa sector would be covered by MacArthur's air force.

There was a reason for the size of the buildup and the vast network it created. Devastated as the Japanese navy was by now, it was organizing to strike back and weaken the American offensive however it could, and that involved mounting an effective defense on Okinawa and expanding the navy's kamikaze project. Suicidal attack, as we have noted, had proved successful in the Leyte-Lingayen battle, where kamikazes had sunk twenty-four ships and damaged sixty-seven others, including the battleships *Mississippi* and *New Mexico* and the light cruiser *Columbia*. Using their share of the fifty-five airfields on Kyushu, the home island nearest Okinawa, the Japanese navy gathered pilots, trained them, and distributed them at times alone and in joint attacks with fighter escort. Many of the pilots were college students, and most volunteered; however some were coerced into service either by peer pressure or by commanders who volunteered them for duty. The Japanese navy launched ten kamikaze surges, lasting through June, known altogether as the *kikusui*, or "floating chrysanthemums," campaign. Including nonsuicidal and army air attacks, the Japanese sent forth roughly over 5,000 planes.[12] Though the number dwindled through May and June, the kamikaze was a pressing American concern throughout the Okinawa operation. No fewer than 185 attacked on April 13, 115 more on April 27–28, and 125 on May 4.[13]

The most fearful of the weapons employed by the kamikaze was the *Ohka*, which the Americans called the *Baka*, the Japanese word for "idiot" or "fool": a bomb fitted to a piloted glider that was slung under the belly of a two-engine bomber and released over the enemy. A vertical dive and rockets provided speed up to 500 knots while the pilot drove into his target, detonating 2,645 pounds of high explosive. On March 18, two weeks before the American landing on Okinawa, Task Force 58 planes pounced on the Kyushu airfields, only to find them mostly empty: the enemy planes had left early to attack Task Force 58 carriers, the same carriers that had launched the planes now over Kyushu. In that attack three kamikazes struck the carriers: the bomb hitting the *Enterprise* was a dud; the second plane barely reached the deck of the *Intrepid* and crashed, killing and wounding forty-five; the third plunged through the flight deck of the *Yorktown* and exploded near its side, creating two large holes and killing and wounding thirty-one. On April 16, a kamikaze crashed through the flight deck of the *Intrepid*, blew a large hole in the deck, and started "intense fires," causing ninety-seven casualties. Such was the extent of the damage that this carrier too went back to a navy yard.[14]

The following day, the *Wasp*, with most of its planes away on attack, became the objective of a kamikaze directly above. He aimed his plane and dove down while he dropped its bomb, which plunged through the flight and hangar decks and crew quarters and then burst into the galley at breakfast time, killing and wounding 370 out of a crew of 2,600, including officers. The fires were out in fifteen minutes, and the *Wasp*'s planes returned and landed without incident, but she had to leave for yard repair. The *Franklin*, a new fast carrier, was hit by two bombs from an unseen attacker. They devastated the flight and hangar decks and their parked planes and set off huge fires, forcing some to abandon ship. The fire and engine rooms became too hot for the crew and brought the ship to a dead stop. By noon, with the help of two cruisers, the skeleton crew—a staggering 989 of its crew had been killed or wounded—brought the fires under control, partially stabilized the ship, and evacuated the wounded. It was towed away, gradually gaining its own power and stability, and then made the journey by way of Pearl Harbor to New York for restoration. On May 14 the only Japanese plane to survive an encounter with the shielding combat air patrol smashed the forward elevator of the *Enterprise* into a bulge; the plane's bomb burst deep in the hole. This was the third hit by a kamikaze on the "Big E." Eighty-one of the crew were killed or wounded, and the ship required a trip to a navy yard for major repairs. Neither the *Franklin* nor the *Enterprise* returned to action before the end of the war.

Kamikazes favored approaching through cloud cover, for it gave them the maximum element of surprise, on which their attacks depended. On May 11, after a quiet week, one suddenly dropped from a cloud in a dive on the fast carrier *Bunker Hill*. It hit the flight deck, Morison records, "skidded through parked planes, kindling huge fires en route, and fell over the side." Meanwhile a second kamikaze plane and its bomb damaged the flight deck and superstructure of the carrier's center island. Fires raged in the upper decks, with especially heavy smoke causing extensive suffocation. It took over five hours to put out the flames, and there were 660 casualties. The *Bunker Hill* never fought again in the war.[15] Five new *Essex*-class fast carriers required extensive structural repair in home navy yards. Three more of this class, the *Yorktown* and the *Hancock*, with holes in their flight decks, and the *Essex*, with bomb damage to its fuel tanks, needed war zone repair. Two more of this class, the *Bennington* and *Hornet*, after passing through a June typhoon, had to replace fifty feet of their forward flight deck. That left the *Randolph* the only undamaged large fast carrier in the task force.[16]

Despite all the damages caused by the kamikazes, the worst in the Pacific Theater up to this point, it could have been much worse. The carriers had been outfitted with the latest fire-safety equipment and training and provided with autonomous, mobile gasoline engines for pumping water; the fog-making nozzles emitted a fine spray that worked more effectively than a solid stream, and the hoses and couplings were all connective and interchangeable.[17] Also aboard were steel-cutting machines and breathing apparatus for crew who were dealing directly with damage. All new ships had a trained damage control party equipped with fire masks and helmets. The Navy had learned over the months of such attacks that it was critical to get at the source of flame quickly.

The Japanese navy was ready to fight to the last with what it had to prevent American forces from establishing themselves on the doorstep of Japan's home islands. In April, May, and June, the Japanese navy had sent out 3,700 sorties, by both conventional and suicide planes. Morison estimates that the Japanese army sent at least half as many, making a total for both of 5,500 sorties in three months.[18] The attacks came in surges from Kyushu; the dates depended on the acquisition of planes from the factory and completion of special training. The targets were Task Force 58, Kerama Retto anchorage, the landing beaches, and the destroyers and destroyer escorts on the "picket fence" surrounding Okinawa. The principal means of defense against them were the picket destroyers; the combat air patrol, composed of fighter planes from the airfields next to the landing area and from escort carriers of the Support Carrier Group protecting the landing;

and constant assignment of planes from the fast carriers. The stretch of sea between Kerama Retto and the landing beaches on Okinawa, as well as the air space above, formed a constantly moving three-dimensional battle sphere.

Arriving from duty in the Philippines, the destroyer escort *Abercrombie* served as one of the picket ships in this zone.[19] Now and then the *Abercrombie* served in the screen protecting transports when they moved for the night from the landing beaches to safer waters south of Okinawa. The *Abercrombie* had a crew of 216 and carried 5-inch guns, bow and stern, and 20 mm and 40 mm guns between. On April 2, the second day of the landing, the *Abercrombie* was screening transports when those on deck heard shouting from the waves. The crew found four sailors who had been in the water for nine hours, clinging to an empty oil drum. One had burned hands, and all were exhausted. They explained that they had been crew aboard the *Dickerson*, another destroyer serving as screen for transports. Ten kamikazes had attacked, and one had swept up on the stern at about 200 miles per hour and "slashed off the tops of both her stacks, ripped through the galley deck-house, toppled the mast, and came to rest in a ball of flame at the base of the bridge."[20] As the fire spread, many of the crew were forced off the ship. The crew of the rescue vessel, including the swimmers who prepared the way for landings, went searching in rubber rafts and saved about forty crewmen. Fifty-two were killed and fifteen seriously burned. These four sailors had had to wait to be rescued by the *Abercrombie*.

The attack on the *Dickerson* was becoming typical. The first surge of Japan's aerial campaign began on April 6 with an attack on American forces arriving in Okinawa. From Kyushu came 699 planes, of which 355—just over half—were kamikazes.[21] The wind was strong that day, the waves whitecapped, and the temperature sixty to sixty-five degrees. The destroyer *Newcomb*, heading toward Ie Shima, found itself a kamikaze target, with four planes heading for her. The first plane struck a smokestack, the second hit the ocean, and the third struck the remaining stack. The fourth plane was carrying a large bomb or torpedo that cut deep into the engine and fire rooms, leaving them a "rabble" and the destroyer in hundred-foot flames. The trained crew put out the fires quickly, and the *Newcomb*, its rear deck "buckled into the contour of a roller coaster," as Morison, who witnessed similar attacks, memorably put it, was towed to Kerama Retto by a tug. Forty aboard the ship were killed or missing and twenty-four wounded.[22]

It was, ironically, the positioning of solitary pickets fifty miles north of Okinawa, intended to serve as a line of defense to protect the beaches, that also made a signpost for the Japanese. From the most northerly pickets to the landing beaches, kamikazes would drop away from the main stream to target picket destroyers. These slim targets, each with six to ten guns pointing in different directions, would seem a more likely kill (and be killed) objective for the kamikaze than American cruisers and battleships off Okinawa with massed guns.

The destroyers were thin-skinned and therefore vulnerable to kamikazes, but they counted on other forms of protection in place of armor. Their gunners were well trained, and proximity fuses were available. These fuses carried a sensing device that would explode a round in proximity to its target and thus could down a plane without actually hitting it. Radio and radar operators from combat air patrol were aboard, and Marine fighter aircraft—Thunderbolts and Corsairs—were constantly in the air. Furthermore, by April 10, after the Okinawa landing was secured, the more exposed picket stations were consolidated, with two instead of one destroyer assigned as well as several landing craft with gun and lifesaving support.

The first real surge of the kamikaze program occurred three days before the landing was secured, consisting of forty to fifty planes that dropped down in midafternoon to attack the picket destroyers *Bush*, located north of Ie Jima, and *Cassin Young*, located thirty to forty miles east. The experience of these two destroyers will serve to reflect the kind of fighting involved with kamikazes. The *Bush* had downed two planes and driven off two more when a fifth dodged and darted its way to a crash between its two smokestacks, sending a bomb into the forward engine room, killing every member of the crew there and most of those in the two fire rooms. However, fires were put out, auxiliary power gained, and flooding stemmed. By this time the picket destroyer *Colhoun* had arrived to assist the *Bush* but was fully engaged in batting down the kamikazes. However, the *Colhoun* missed one, which slammed into its main deck, killing two gun crews as well as everyone in the after fire room. Even so, the engineer officer managed to shift valves so that the ship had enough steam for fifteen knots and to get the fires under control. One kamikaze was shot down nearby and yet another by the *Bush*'s antiaircraft fire and a recently arrived landing craft. A third hit exploded in the forward fire room, rupturing both boilers and blowing a four- by twenty-foot hole below the water line. Four more planes attacked, leaving a second underwater hole in the *Colhoun*'s side. The third plane skipped the *Colhoun* and smashed into the main deck of the *Bush*, starting yet another fire. The fourth kamikaze overshot, reversed in a "wing-over," and hit the port side of the *Bush*, setting flame to the wardroom. All present died instantly or shortly afterward from wounds.

At twilight a swell in the waves bent the *Bush* over to the point of sinking, and down it went. The *Colhoun* was also slowly sinking in the darkness, listing at twenty-three degrees, its deck awash. Most of the crew had been transferred to the destroyer *Cassin Young*, which arrived from the nearest picket station. The last of the skeleton crew was taken off by tug, and the *Colhoun* was sunk by request of its captain. Most of the remaining *Bush*'s crew were in or on the ocean—with waves up to twelve feet—clinging to life rafts, floater nets, and the captain's gig (taxi). They were exhausted, freezing, and suffering the agony of burns as well. Almost a third of the *Bush*'s crew were lost at sea or killed.[23]

The April kamikaze attacks made it clear that the picket line was too thin, and immediate steps were taken. The number of pickets was reduced, and some of the radio-radar teams were moved ashore, as was done, for example, on Ie Shima. Landing craft serving as gunboats and lifeboats were assigned to each picket, and some of the assigned ocean spaces were enlarged, with two destroyers working together in one picket. The 5-inch guns may not have conveyed an image of power, but their shells had proximity fuses. These changes were designed to strengthen the pickets and maintain the radio-radar-picket system that governed air defense within a radius of fifty to sixty-five miles from the landing beaches. That system was expanded when two groups of Marine fighter planes started using the Yontan and Kadena airfields and a third group of 192 was on its way.

The virtual destruction of Japan's surface fleet pushed the Japanese navy into reliance on suicidal attacks. Even Japan's last superbattleship, the *Yamato*, was called on to carry out what amounted to a suicidal mission. On April 6, the beginning of the "floating chrysanthemums" campaign, the *Yamato* left the Inland Sea, rounded Kyushu the following day, and headed south for Okinawa. The projectiles of its nine 18.1-inch guns had a range of twenty-two and a half miles. Accompanying it were a light cruiser and eight destroyers. They had already been sighted by an American submarine and kept under watch by amphibian planes from Kerama Retto and a tracking and covering group of sixteen fighters from Task Force 58, under the direction of Mitscher. The Americans sent 280 planes to attack, 98 of them Avengers carrying torpedoes, the preferred weapon against ships because they could run to their target and explode below the waterline. The battle was a disaster for what was left of the Japanese navy. The *Yamato* group had no air cover; its antiaircraft gunners, lacking practice, downed only a few American planes. Torpedo planes blew five holes in the port side of the supership. Counter-flooding drowned the crew within those compartments because they had not been warned in time. Bombs had destroyed the wireless room and medical dispensary. The ship was down to one propeller and listing to vertical decks, with its ammunition crashing and exploding, and finally sank in clouds of smoke about 200 miles north of Okinawa. The cruiser and four of the eight destroyers were also sunk.[24]

In early April, at the time of the sudden breakout by the most powerful Japanese naval vessel and the start of the first, massed kamikaze attack, Admiral Nimitz must have found encouraging the arrival and engagement of an additional four fast carriers, two battleships, five cruisers, fifteen destroyers, and fleet train (supply ships). These were the British contribution to the naval war on Japan, autonomous but attached to the American fleet as Task Force 57. Admiral Nimitz now had enough power—troops, ships, and planes—to move north but not southwest. The Ryukyus form a line extending southwest from Okinawa through the Sakishima Gunto Islands to Formosa. In reverse, the Japanese could and did build airfields on Miyako and Ishigaki islands in the Sakishima group. Miyako is only about 200 miles from Okinawa. Japanese planes in China could therefore be brought forward through Formosa for attacks from the southwest on the American invasion forces. The British Task Force 57, cruising 100 miles south of the Sakishimas, operating from Ulithi and San Pedro navy yard on Leyte Gulf, made repeated raids on the Sakishima airfields, destroying planes and cratering airstrips. The Japanese reciprocated, sending kamikaze attacks on the British carriers. On none of the British carriers did the enemy crash through the flight deck: unlike the American flight decks, which were made of wood, the British decks were made of steel, which meant that they carried about half as many planes but were also more resistant to penetration, and thus suffered only minor damage from Japanese attacks.

During replenishment following the surge in attacks, the American escort carriers and destroyers from Task Force 52 took over from the British Task Force 57, and in the process Japanese attack from the southwest was blocked.[25] The spread of ocean south of Japan was changing hands. Still, the place where this happened most slowly was in the southern part of Okinawa Island, where the weight of the Japanese army lay. On April 3, the third day of unloading at the Hagushi beaches, the American Ninety-Sixth and Seventh Divisions, having spread across the isthmus, turned south and hastened to engage. As recently as December 1944 the two divisions and their XXIV Corps commander, Major General John R. Hodge, who had fought on Guadalcanal, New Georgia, and Bougainville, had been closing the battle for Leyte, mopping up during January and part of February.[26] On Okinawa the divisions moved several miles without much resistance on April 3 and 4 and then slowed down as they began running into enemy positions. The objective of the Japanese Thirty-Second Army, under the command of Lieutenant General Ushijima Mitsuru, was to establish outposts on strategic hills along the way. Here and there Japanese infantry and artillery struck the columns advancing south, and American infantry attacked to seize strategic hilltops, but engulfment in full battle sea to sea across the isthmus arose, later, farther south from April 6 to 8 as the topography changed and large and heavily armed Japanese forces made their presence known. This slice of Okinawa, about five miles square, was crammed with hills, escarpments, ridges, fingers, gulches, crags, gorges, and pockets. The hills were often not more than 100–200 feet high but were steep and tightly packed in a jumble of positions, with one exception—the Urasoe Mura Escarpment, almost straight as a pin for a mile.

The Japanese had learned a great deal in the campaigns from Guadalcanal and Buna to Okinawa. Lieutenant General Ushijima was one of the best commanders in the region, having had both combat experience and a supervisory role at the Japanese Military Academy. He therefore knew both tactics and theory and was by all accounts an inspirational leader. He and his energetic chief of staff, Lieutenant General Cho Isamu, a seasoned staff officer with experience in China, Burma, and Malaya, reorganized the Japanese Thirty-Second Army's staff, stocking it with talented young officers. Among these was Colonel Yahara Hiromichi, chief of operations, a conservative but talented tactician.[27] Ushijima would employ the same strategy employed elsewhere, however, and as recently practiced by Yamashita: they would not meet the landing on the beaches but instead withdraw south into country featuring tightly packed hills, fortified in depth with pillboxes, trenches, caves, and underground compartments and tunnels. In this instance, falling farther back would mean creating a fortress on the tombs of the Shuri Castle, first built in the fourteenth century and a national treasure that had been the cultural and political center of the Ryukyus for hundreds of years (and, rebuilt, is today a World Heritage site). At its disposal, the Japanese Thirty-Second Army had 39,000 Japanese infantry combat troops and 38,000 special, service, and artillery troops. On top of a total of 77,000, an estimated 26,000 Okinawans were drafted, by far the largest number of local citizens to assist in the defense in the Pacific Theater.[28] The Japanese Thirty-Second Army also had the most and best available equipment: 287 large- and medium-caliber guns and howitzers; 296 smaller artillery; twenty-four of the huge spigot mortars; 1,100 knee mortars; fifty-two of the 47 mm antitank guns, which had proven so effective; and over 1,500 machine guns. The Japanese now used satchel charges as well.[29]

As the Americans' advance south slowed, they became aware that they were entering different territory, predominately tangled hill country coast-to-coast, with interlocking Japanese defenses. On April 11, the First Battalion of the American Thirty-Second Regiment, Seventh Division, pushing south along the flat eastern seaboard, seized the town of Ouki but had to withdraw north of it. Their tanks, providing critical support, had been stopped by a mined antitank ditch and Japanese artillery fire from the nearby hills. Cut off from support and open to shelling, the battalion withdrew. On the right of the Thirty-Second and also headed south were the Second and Third Battalions of the 184th Regiment, Seventh Division, which had demolished the outpost Red Hill, immediately followed on April 8 and 9 by the costly capture of two other Japanese defenses, Triangulation Hill and Tomb Hill (which featured vaults). At the latter the Japanese had dug in on the reverse (rear) slope, and a flanking maneuver by the 184th had been a complete failure.[30] Next in the American line toward the western shore stood the 382nd Regiment, Ninety-Sixth Division, all three of whose battalions were engaging or almost engaging separate enemy groups. The Second Battalion almost walked straight into the attack up Kakazu Ridge, which would have caught them in deadly cross fire, but veered away and withdrew. The other battalions advancing southwest faced constant gun, mortar, and artillery fire from Nishibaru and Tombstone Ridges. Third Battalion seized a knob in Tombstone Ridge but were forced to withdraw because of heavy gunfire. In heavy rain the Second Battalion withdrew. B and C Companies of the First Battalion became engaged in gaining the heights on Tombstone Ridge, leading to further attack, which forced the Americans to withdraw. The outpost stage had passed, and the frontal stage was unfolding: four American battle groups were linked across the island, and a fifth was attached when the 383rd Regiment, Ninety-Sixth Division, attacked Kakazu Ridge.

Kakazu was a modest ridge lying parallel to the front and to the Urasoe Mura Escarpment lying behind it. It was important because it stood in the way of the southward advance. What made Kakazu more difficult than Tombstone Ridge or Triangulation Hill was that before climbing it, one had to drop into and cross a gorge choked with brush and trees. A secondary hill, Kakazu West, was embedded in Kakazu on the north, forming a saddle. On April 8, XXIV Corps headquarters ordered the First and Third Battalions of the 383rd Regiment to take that set of hills the next day. To do so they would have to enter that night and slip through the gorge, climb the

Kakazu side, and engage what enemy was there. The companies were to attack without warning and surprise the Japanese, though without the benefit of intelligence or adequate photographs and maps of the objective. The troops crossed the gorge and climbed the hill quietly enough to reach the top before a Japanese sentry spotted them and opened fire. Almost immediately they were hit by mortar fire before they could assemble in battle order.[31] The Japanese were covering the gorge with bombardment to prevent reinforcement while closing on the enemy from the top, squeezing it back into the gorge. The Americans already on top fought with bayonets fixed, grenades, and machine guns until ammunition ran out.

Two companies, A and C, reaching the forward slope of Kakazu Ridge, were being pounded to pieces as L Company reached the top of Kakazu West. Company B was in the gorge, heading up through heavy fire, already having lost almost a fifth of its men. Lieutenant Colonel Byron King, the battalion commander, was keenly aware of the importance of holding the ridge but equally understood the peril facing the two companies on top. He radioed regiment that he had fifty men on the ridge and reinforcements were pinned down. He reported that his troops were under heavy fire and warned that if they were not reinforced they would have to withdraw. Colonel E. T. May, back at regimental headquarters, considered what little had been gained on Kakazu Ridge, small as it was, too valuable to lose and so decided that it must be held. If the battalion commander was "jumpy," the colonel said, he should be replaced by the executive officer. The word was "Hold the ridge at all costs." Company G, however, the reinforcement assigned, was 1,000 yards to the rear and arrived too late. The A Company commander, Captain Jack A. Royster, kept fighting until a smoke barrage closed in, permitting a way out for the wounded and then for the retreat off Kakazu Ridge generally. The battalion surgeon declared the survivors no longer fit for further duty.[32] April 9 was devastating for the First Battalion, 383rd Regiment: it came to half strength.

By April 10 the American southward advance had nearly halted.[33] Assessing the situation, the more aggressive Japanese officers pressed for a general counterattack north. General Ushijima, pleased by his army's defense and defenders and in order to appease his staff, agreed to a special kind of attack: six battalions would slip through American lines in the night of April 12 and spread north across the countryside just traversed by the Americans, reaching a destination a short distance away from the original invasion beaches and depots. This was not a banzai attack aimed at smashing through enemy lines. The infiltrators would be in a position to destroy the Tenth Army's supply routes. However, at the last minute, stripping six battalions from Japanese defenses in the south seemed too dangerous, and the number dispatched was reduced from six to four. On the night of April 12, after a heavy bombardment, the Japanese attack groups began infiltrating the American defense line and headed north, loaded with 110-pound packs of explosives, food, and ammunition. This time, however, the Americans held the advantage. The sky was illuminated by the American Navy's artillery, with warships laying down a coordinated bombardment. American infantry were carefully entrenched, and the Japanese were the ones exposed on the outside, in bunches and files. Some broke through, some retreated, and the rest were simply killed off.[34] The next morning, the Americans counted 317 Japanese dead.

The terrain of Okinawa provided an extraordinary benefit to the Japanese defenders. A chain of hills and escarpments, running 1,000–2,000 yards each, stood between the coasts: from the west, as we've noted, Kakazu Ridge and Kakazu West, with Urasoe Mura Escarpment behind and parallel and then Nishibaru and Tombstone Ridges in the center, Tanabaru Escarpment, and Skyline Ridge, enclosing Hill 178 and Ouki Hill near the east coast. Most if not all had caves and bunkers for artillery and tunnels capacious enough for sleeping, medical, supply, communication, and command quarters. Outside were prepared camouflaged trenches, mortar pits, pillboxes, and machine gun nests on the forward and reverse slopes of the hills. It was a far more extensive and elaborate underground and defense than had been established on Iwo Jima.

The war was revolving in a remorseless cycle of innovation and countermeasure. As Japanese defenses toughened, the Americans sought ways to pry the enemy out of his well-protected positions. What the Americans had in their favor was preparatory bombardment, which had become more extensive and accurate. They had twenty-seven battalions of artillery (numbering 324 pieces), capable of placing 19,000 rounds on the enemy lines. Battleship and cruiser guns were at their side. Massed gunfire (meaning several sources hitting in the same place) was common; timed fuses, allowing for explosion over a target, were used; coordination between naval gunnery and artillery were well established. Air attack was not as important at this stage of combat. Planes were needed on the maritime side, to protect the ships from attack. Nevertheless, 817 strike missions were flown to drop 1,000- and 2,000-pound bombs. The Japanese stayed within their forts during the initial bombardment and then manned their defenses outside for the follow-up infantry attack. The chain of hills and escarpments was the first and outer ring of principal defenses for Okinawa, with Shuri Castle several miles to the south being the ultimate center.[35]

The American drive south beginning on April 19 was manned by three divisions, the Seventh and Ninety-Sixth, already in action, and the Twenty-Seventh, just disembarked. The Seventh Division occupied the eastern portion of the front from the coastal plain uphill into the jumbled interior. Blocking the way south was Skyline Ridge, a pretzel of a hill rising from the coastal plain into a nearly vertical wall above with a narrow crest. Occupying the ridge was the Japanese Eleventh Independent Infantry Battalion, which had won a unit citation from the China war and consisted of 800–1,000 soldiers. On April 19 the Seventh Division started its advance toward Skyline after the preparatory bombardment at 6:40 a.m., heading about a thousand yards to the ridge with Company G and Company F, 184th Regiment, on the left and right and Company G of the Thirty-Second following behind. Past the halfway point, Japanese mortars and machine guns broke out from the higher slopes of Hill 178 and Ouki Hill, detachments on Skyline, and riflemen close by, hitting the advancing companies hard. All stayed flat to survive.

A second advance set out from the left, below, on the coastal plain. The Third Battalion of the Thirty-Second Regiment attacked the lower end of Skyline Ridge with the added power of a detachment of three tanks and three tank flamethrowers, which were apparently objects of fascination to infantrymen who had never seen one.[36] The tank guns and flamethrowers opened caves and emplacements in and near the start of Skyline, several of which contained carefully stacked bodies of Japanese soldiers, 200 in one vault alone, for burial or present entombment. Companies L and K moved out on the steep, forward side of the ridge, with the other, "reverse" side, held by Japanese troops with grenades, mortars, machine guns, and a "knife-edge crest" between the sides. The Company K platoon was hit first by a grenade attack and then four short rounds of their own artillery, killing or wounding all but six in the platoon. A replacement platoon was sent and a larger counterattack followed. Companies K and L left the ridge with, together, no more than twenty-five men. The tanks helped again in the morning advance on the Skyline by rescuing the remaining pocket of infantry and their wounded.

Seventh Division headquarters was concerned that the advance was being drawn toward the coastal plain, whereas pressing toward the heights—Hill 178 and Ouki Hill—would dominate Skyline from above. Before that tactic became an order, an event occurred that drew attention to the ridge. Sergeant Theodore R. MacDonnell, an observer from the Ninety-First Chemical Mortar Company, saw an infantryman in a "stalled" platoon killed without any platoon response. Furious, MacDonnell ran to the ridge, grabbed some weapons, sought out the Japanese machine gun responsible, and after many tries up and down the embankment killed the crew while managing to survive. His heroics inspired action: the emphasis shifted to closing caves and clearing Skyline Ridge and vicinity. However, the G Companies of the two regiments that had been pinned down in their advance of the morning bent forward again, reached Ouki Hill, and sought cover at the base of the hill. An hour later they suffered a heavy, concentrated 81 mm mortar attack that sent many back to their morning cover and killed many more. The next day the tank flamethrowers burned out the mortar position. Command also arranged for a mortar attack with a cover of smoke, an addition that worked. The Japanese, blinded by smoke, failed to see the Americans until they were already on the lower hill. Japanese attacks for recovery burst in all night—mortar, satchel charges, counterattacks—but the tanks resupplied, and half-tracks removed the wounded. All the attacks were repulsed and the Ouki Hill was held. The capture of Hill 178 turned out to be a fait accompli. During the night of April 23–24, in thick fog, the enemy pulled their troops off it.

One objective remained in the Seventh Division sector—Rocky Crags, a fearsome coral hill located a mile northwest of Skyline on elevated ground. It was fortified with caves and tunnels and infantry. Attacking were the 184th Infantry, with Company B of the Seventeenth attached, strengthened by tanks, flamethrowers, and a single 155 mm howitzer, which was particularly effective. Daily attacks from April 19 to April 24 pounded the hill's surface flat and eliminated almost all defense by the last day. The cost in American casualties was 243.

Next in the American battle line, filling the middle slot, was the Ninety-Sixth Division, also a veteran of Leyte, facing a daunting assignment. Before the division stood a line of three ridges, each about 500 yards long and roughly 100 feet high with 500-yard gaps between. These ridges were, from west to east, Kakazu Ridge, Nishibaru Ridge, and Tanabaru Escarpment. Nishibaru and Tanabaru were assigned to the Ninety-Sixth, Kakazu to the Twenty-Seventh Division, which was now joining battle into the added western coastal section of the line. These were large assignments: the Ninety-Sixth would have to deal with counterattacks and heavy Japanese artillery, mortar, and machine gun fire among the many avenues around the hills with cross fire positions. Furthermore, the Ninety-Sixth would first have to destroy Tombstone Ridge.

Tombstone Ridge was a burial ground alongside Kaniku village, rising seventy-five feet above its surroundings and stretching a half mile to the southwest. Now extensively tunneled, it held Japanese forces in a warren of supporting positions.[37] At 6:40 a.m. on April 19, the First Battalion of the 381st Infantry advanced down into the draw to cross over and climb Nishibaru Ridge, and the Second Battalion of the 382nd climbed onto Tombstone Ridge from the north to clear it. From among a growth of trees on the far side of the burial ground, Company L ran into Japanese emerging from their underground fort and attacking with bayonets affixed. The fight went on all afternoon until the Americans, having lost thirty-two of their company, withdrew. But the battalion remained on watch to ensure that this Japanese battle group did not repeat their attack on other American battalions moving toward the Nishibaru and Tanabaru ridges. Thus the Americans had one less battalion available for capturing the ridges. Meanwhile, Tombstone Ridge itself was thoroughly cleared by Company I.

The Ninety-Sixth Division gradually managed to put five battalions on Nishibaru Ridge and nearby Tanabaru Escarpment, not without extensive casualties. The troops moved for hours crossing the fields and stream of the draw to the foot of the ridge, under withering Japanese mortar and gunfire from above and from the right side, the eastern slope of Kakazu Ridge. Nishibaru had a large supply of the spigot mortars that lobbed large rounds, dubbed "screaming Jesus" by Marines for the sound the shell made tumbling through the air. Constant mortar fire drove a hail of jagged metal. At an early point in the advance only four officers were left for three companies. This proved a vicious struggle. The Third Battalion, 382nd Infantry, killed 198 Japanese in one day, but on April 20 both the Ninety-Sixth and Twenty-Seventh Divisions had more casualties than the enemy had, and combat fatigue was spreading among the American infantry. In the 382nd Infantry Regiment combat efficiency dropped by half.[38] Tanabaru Ridge remained to be taken. Tanks and armored flame dispensers moved in front of the ridge to blast the enemy, and infantry over from Nishibaru to the "Gate," a saddle on the near western side of the Tanabaru Escarpment, but the Ninety-Sixth, slowed by grenades and satchel charges and a setting of ten machine guns, could not reach the top. However, on the next day, April 24, the Japanese command, as they had done at Hill 178, withdrew their remaining forces from Tanabaru and Nishibaru farther south. They had decided to save their infantry for later battles.

The infantry among the ridges, especially Kakazu and Nishibaru, needed armor and got it. Landed, organized, and dispatched to the front for the general attack on April 19 was a force of thirty tanks, Company A of the 193rd Tank Battalion, with a few armored flamethrowers and assault guns besides. The tanks had objectives and maps but were not tied to the infantry for support and defense at any stage. They simply came roaring through the saddle of Nishibaru and Kakazu in columns of threes and fours looking for the village of Kakazu, finding it, and essentially destroying it. After that, the planning came to an end. Not on the part of the Japanese, however. Suicide squads were prepared with satchel charges and grenades, 47 mm antitank guns, and mines. One of these antitank guns wiped out four tanks. Only eight of the thirty tanks returned from this rash and uncoordinated attack. On the same morning, the First Battalion, 105th, of the Twenty-Seventh Division was attacking up Kakazu Ridge to join the tanks in Kakazu village. A platoon of thirty-four sent ahead entered the village easily but found it a trap. Most escaped, but the rest were killed or wounded. The Second Battalion of the same regiment struck up Kakazu on the left to eliminate the firing across Route 5 into the troops attacking Nishibaru, but that too failed. The Twenty-Seventh had had enough of what they called simply "that damned hill."[39]

Most of the battalions of the Twenty-Seventh Division were designated for Urasoe Maru Escarpment, a steep sloped ridge that dominated the center of the island south of Kakazu Ridge and gave the Japanese a commanding position from which they could block the American advance. Lieutenant Colonel D. A. Nolan, Jr., leading the Third Battalion, 381st, on Nishibaru, suggested to Captain John F. Mulhearn, commander of Company C, 105th Infantry, Twenty-Seventh Division, at Kakazu that their two battalions make a simultaneous attack with use of the five tanks that Nolan had available. Mulhearn declined, explaining that after the Kakazu attack, troops on Kakazu Ridge, among them his own, would be withdrawn toward the west and sent around the ridge and then south to Urasoe Maru Escarpment behind Kakazu. So Twenty-Seventh Division troops, like the rest, had failed to take Kakazu and were leaving it to concentrate on Urasoe Maru; troops attacking Nishibaru would have to bear heavy enemy fire from Kakazu on their right flank, across the way. The battalions of the Twenty-Seventh Division now gathered, under orders, to drive the Japanese off Urasoe Maru Escarpment.

The direction of the Okinawa coastline on the west turned sharply from south to west, adding a thousand yards or so to the zone of combat, mostly flat, marshy, coastal plain with low, finger-like hills and to the south, along the beach, the defunct Machinato Airfield. The widening of the landscape would thin the defense against counterattack by the Japanese, emerging from tunnels and caves or coming ashore from boats to destroy supplies. After the Saipan experience, and then months on the island of Espirito

Santo in the New Hebrides, now came the members of the Twenty-Seventh Division, which originated from the National Guard of New York. Originally they had been sent to Okinawa to garrison the island, not conquer it. The Urasoe Mura Escarpment stretched almost to the ocean in the west and well into the middle of the line of combat toward the east. The Twenthy-Seventh Division attack began at Machinato, a coast town by an inlet. Getting troops across this inlet meant the engineers learning to assemble two Bailey bridges and set up one 128-yard footbridge and a pontoon (floating bridge), all in the darkness of the night of April 18–19. The pontoon was a problem, but a few smoke bombs hid it adequately for the two battalions of the 106th Regiment to move across unseen, climb the tail of Urasoe Mura, and head southeast along the crest.

Soon they ran into an enemy outpost that spread the alarm. About a thousand yards farther along the ridge they met battlements and bloody battle. On top of the ridge stood West Pinnacle, essentially a fort with tunnels. Then came an intersection, cut into the crest, of roads heading to nearby towns, followed by a second lofty fort, East Pinnacle. Here was battle that took place in layers. Fortunately a map was found on a dead Japanese officer showing the minefields on the local roads, allowing their removal and delivery of supplies. On the morning of April 20 the Second and Third Battalions of the 105th Regiment fought their way up the escarpment to reach and destroy the West Pinnacle, but the Second failed to reach the top. Colonel W. S. Winn, regimental commander, then devised a different approach: the two companies, F and G, would hike around the escarpment at its base. Once past East Pinnacle, they would climb to the top, shift to the reverse slope, and head downhill on the other side. From the road below they would advance and capture the town of Nakama. As the two companies crossed over and down, they were hit with heavy mortar fire and enveloping attack from the rear. All officers and most sergeants and corporals were killed or wounded; the rest who could fled, many tumbling back down the escarpment they had just climbed. Total Twenty-Seventh Division casualties that day, April 20, were 506, the greatest loss for an Army division during any single day on Okinawa.[40] In the following three days the battalions reorganized and returned to the escarpment to eliminate the pinnacles and the enemy attacks. Finally, they succeeded. After engaging in hand-to-hand combat they killed over a hundred Japanese with gunfire, grenades, bayonets, and rifle butts. On the night of April 23, thirty Japanese, isolated and desperate, burst out with a banzai charge and were mowed down by machine gun fire.[41]

Within their combat zone the Twenty-Seventh Division engaged in three distinct battles, the Kakazu, the Pinnacles, and what has since become known as Item Pocket, which covered a portion of seacoast a mile or so northwest of the Pinnacles. The word "item" represented the letter *I* on Army maps and "pocket" the inland centerpiece from which finger ridges stretched out northeast and northwest 500–800 yards toward the beaches. The ridges ran along ravines and gulches and contained a system of tunnels and rooms with command and supply for an estimated 600 troops. The Japanese defenders were skilled infantrymen bearing—besides rifles, bayonets, and grenades—armor-piercing 47 mm antitank guns; massed, interlocking, and cross-firing machine guns; and mortars. Destruction of bridges along Route 1 severely hampered the Americans' supply. Japanese fire from the Pocket chased away engineers replacing and repairing the bridges, killing the platoon leader. The Twenty-Seventh tried a bypass, but the bulldozer driver was shot and killed. The commander of a tank battalion tried to use a tank bulldozer, the last one, but a 47 mm shell plowed through it, killing both him and his guide and blocking the bypass.[42]

The Americans who were seized were shot or suffocated to death in closed caves. Others would suddenly find themselves in hand-to-hand combat, using knife, bayonet, or rifle butt, or flattening out on the ground to survive a bombardment. One after another of the company commanders in the 165th Regiment took his turn in leading the charge of his company to the top of Ryan Ridge, which stood above Item Pocket; none succeeded in capturing it. Well-placed Japanese weapons following the American bombardment were devastating. Ammunition, medical supplies, and aid men were becoming scarce. Communication with headquarters was often broken. When it became Captain Bernard Ryan's turn to find a way to reach the top of Ryan Ridge, he added an improvement. He noted that in attack, troops in the line of the shots stand behind the explosions, leaving space for shells falling short. However, this artillery was firing perpendicularly to the direction of attack; therefore, the troops in the attack did not need protective space. The result was that more infantry could remain on the ridge before the enemy rose to defend. Earlier Company E had arrived on the ridge with eight men and could not stay. With the troops close behind the artillery fire, thirty-one made it to the ridge. No less important was that Ryan had arranged for Company I to follow him and when that failed went back and secured Company K. Its commander agreed to join, and the two companies reached the top of the ridge. Thus Ryan had accumulated more than a hundred troops at the top, enough to clear Item Pocket and rout the Japanese out the caves below.[43] By this time, the Twenty-Seventh Division commander, General Griner, had lost confidence in the commander of this 165th Regiment, Colonel Kelley, and relieved him of his command. The regiment had been slow and with the dispersal and splintering of battalions and companies was becoming increasingly disorganized.[44]

The XXIV Corps had moved south and gained ground in difficult terrain, but it had not broken the enemy line and pushed through; it had moved the line of defense several miles south with heavy losses. In the first day of the American attack, April 19, the American XXIV Corps lost 720 dead, wounded, or missing. On the second day the Twenty-Seventh Division at the Pinnacles suffered 506 casualties.[45] By the time they had left the battle in early April, the Twenty-Seventh had lost 5,224 troops as battle and nonbattle casualties.[46] In all divisions, one company commander after another was killed or wounded; combat efficiency was dropping to 50, 40, and 30 percent.[47] The Japanese army on Okinawa had the great advantage of extensive underground shelter but still had to face American artillery and infantry assaults. Japanese withdrawal would mend the ranks with replacements from infantry and specialized battalions. During the night of April 24–25 at the battlefields across the island—Hill 178, Nishibaru, Kakazu, Urasoe Mura—the enemy occupants all withdrew south. Kakazu stood silent and empty in the middle of a mile-long opening to the north.

Before engaging in further attack, the Tenth Army badly needed reinforcement. On the west the First Marine Division, waiting in the rear, took the place of the decimated Twenty-Seventh Division. At the battle for

Peleliu the First Marine Division's rifle battalions had been thinned almost to nonexistence, and the division had had to rebuild quickly.[48] The Ninety-Sixth Division, fighting hard on Okinawa after an extended Leyte campaign, badly needed rest. Stepping in for the Ninety-Sixth, the Seventy-Seventh Division, with the same recent Leyte experience, had just left battle on Ie Shima. The Seventh Division would continue until the Ninety-Sixth returned and then have a rest. The newly formed Sixth Marine Division, now ashore, would soon join the First Marine Division under the III Amphibious Corps, while the Army divisions remained under XXIV Corps. Both corps served under the Tenth Army, General Buckner commanding.

The nearly suicide attack on April 12 that had been sanctioned by General Ushijima reflected that a change in philosophy was occurring in the Japanese Thirty-Second Army. The chief of staff, Lieutenant General Cho Isamu, as well as most commanders, were disgusted with the current defensive strategy embodied by General Yamashita, consisting of withdrawal and retrenchment in a war of attrition, and were insisting on all-out attack. General Ushijima again conceded and planned a pervasive drive north. The Japanese Eighty-Ninth Regiment, next to the east coast, would drive north through Onaga. The Japanese Twenty-Fourth Division, consisting of 15,000 men and located to the west of the Japanese Eighty-Ninth, had its regiments aimed at Tanabaru Escarpment, the third ridge in the Kakazu-Nishibaru ridgeline, and the Maeda portion of the Urasoe Mura Escarpment. Breaking through these American lines, especially at Maeda, would allow the Japanese Forty-Fourth Independent Mixed Brigade to seize Oyama, a town some two miles north on the west coast, thereby cutting the Marines off from their supplies. The rest of the Japanese battalions would continue north to Futenma, near the landing beaches, where the American advance began. On both coasts assault landings would deliver suicide missions with satchel charges to destroy tanks and supplies. In the larger picture, the counterattack, which was to take place May 3–4, would occur within the fifth mass kamikaze attack of the ten planned for the "floating chrysanthemum" campaign, which brought in 125 suicide planes besides conventional two-way types.[49] Extending the land battle northward, closing in on the air battle over the Hagushi beaches, would enable the mostly underground Japanese infantrymen to regain a sense of active participation in epic battle to defend the Japanese homeland.

The amphibious part of the counterattack was a fiasco. On the west side, instead of landing near the kamikaze attack, the Japanese soldiers clambered ashore at a seawall near Naha defended by the First Marines. On the east coast, efforts to land troops on the beach behind the Seventh Division roused devastating gunfire from American Navy vessels anchored in the bay.

The Japanese land counterattack began after sundown on May 4 and was composed of formations of infantry and armor lined up facing north, from a point a short distance north of Shuri Castle to the eastern shore. If a breakthrough emerged in the east or center, the Japanese Forty-Fourth Independent Mixed Brigade on the left would turn toward the western shore and cut the supply lines of the American First Marine Division. Otherwise, the Japanese forces from center to the eastern shore would push hard to break apart the American battalions strung across the island. The Japanese Eighty-Ninth Regiment on the eastern shore faced battalions of the American Seventh Division in the hilly, open country north of Conical Hill. In the center, the Japanese Twenty-Second Regiment would reinforce the other two regiments of the Japanese Twenty-Fourth Division in drives to Maeda Escarpment, just southeast of Urasoe Mura Escarpment, and, beyond that, reaching Tanabaru Escarpment, farther north, in line east of Nishibaru Ridge.

Artillery in conjunction with offense and defense was critical to both sides. The Japanese withdrew their artillery from caves in order to widen their direction of fire, covering more front. American Cub observation planes noted and conveyed their presence. American artillery extended range to them, and the Japanese put forward antiaircraft guns. They now used air-bursting artillery shells, such as the Americans were using, and smoke shells to hide their advancing troops. The problem would be that the advancing soldier hidden in a smoke blanket or mass barrage would find it difficult to maintain his sense of direction. On the American Seventh Division front the Japanese attack persisted but uncertainly. They moved almost aimlessly in the open flatland, neither pressing forward nor retreating, and quickly became easy targets.[50]

The Battle of the Pinnacles, as it was called, involving most of Urasoe Mura Escarpment, opened the way to a corridor, roughly a mile wide, heading south along Route 5 to Shuri Castle. Where Urasoe Mura Escarpment ended the Maeda Escarpment began. Attacking from the escarpment north was the still-engaged American Ninety-Sixth Division, with the 381st Regiment on the right and the 383rd on the left, exhausted and diminished but testing and preparing for attack on the reverse slope the next day, April 26. In the battle, 1,600 American artillery shells were fired. American planes dropped napalm; tanks and flamethrowers attacked extensive underground compartments and pillboxes. Machine guns, grenades, even spears were used in close combat, but the Ninety-Sixth Division failed to close the corridor. It had been in the middle of the line for a month. Its 383rd Regiment had just fought off two attacks, killing 265 Japanese. The same day the tanks and flamethrowers killed over 200 more of the enemy. On April 29 and 30 the Seventy-Seventh Division arrived from its battle on Ie Shima to replace the Ninety-Sixth. The 381st Regiment had taken 1,021 casualties; its combat efficiency was down to about 40 percent. Company K, now reduced to twenty-four men, was combined with Company I to form one company of only seventy. In the short time the Seventy-Seventh Division fought at Maeda Escarpment, eight of its First Battalion, 307th Infantry company commanders were wounded. The Seventy-Seventh claimed over 3,000 Japanese killed.[51]

The Seventy-Seventh had sufficient strength to place a third battalion south, next to Route 5, blocking the Japanese from passage north. However, room for infiltration remained east of the road toward the town of Kochi. By this route 450 Japanese soldiers slipped north and captured Tanabaru Escarpment and town. Extending to the east of the Kakazu-Nishibaru ridgeline, Tanabaru had been vacated by the Japanese in their general withdrawal on the night of April 23–24 and left unguarded by the Americans because the battle line had gone south. Assigned to repel the intruders were companies of the Seventeenth Regiment, Seventh Division, bordering on the east. A three-day battle followed, with the Americans relying on artillery and mortar fire, as well as tank support, but engaged in close combat as well. They attacked up the Tanabaru slopes from east and then west, encircling the enemy. Under fire from below, the Americans reversed positions, securing themselves under overhanging ledges and flinging grenades until the enemy left the top. Below they destroyed defenses in the town and with portable flamethrowers step-by-step eliminated guns in caves. Especially destructive was 81 mm mortar fire. Japanese dead lay everywhere. The Japanese had threatened American supply and motor transport for the area. Though the enemy was too heavily engaged with the Seventeenth Regiment to strike the supply base, it had managed to close off access for several days.

Nonetheless, the Japanese counteroffensive was a disaster. It was costly enough for the Americans when two of their own divisions each lost over 300 troops on May 4 and 5, but the Japanese lost 5,000 of their best troops. To restore some of his losses, General Ushijima began manning his defenses with service troops in infantry training. The lineup and command of American troops was changing. Inserted now was the Sixth Marine Division, heading south along the west coast, brought south after the Yae-Take battle to join the main line next to the First Marine Division. The two Marine divisions now had their own immediate command, the III Amphibious Corps. Added to the eastern wing had been the Seventy-Seventh Division, just finished with taking Ie Shima, now alongside the Ninety-Sixth Division on the east coast, with both under the current XXIV Corps, and the Tenth Army in direct command. The Seventh Division was out of the line for a rest. Shuri Castle and its defenses, now the objective, stood on a hill in the waist of southern Okinawa with the port city of Naha on the west, the town of Yonabaru on the east coast, and about nine square miles of hill country remaining in the southern end of the island.

The terrain, continuing mostly flat along the western coast, consisted of twisting hills, ravines, gulches, mounds, cultivated fields, and open spaces. Humps and hillocks attended key hills and ridges, providing gunfire from many angles. The fortress of Shuri Castle was the headquarters of the Japanese Thirty-Second Army, and to take it the American Tenth Army ordered three advances on it: the Seventy-Seventh Division would finish its current drive capturing Maeda and follow Route 5 down the valley toward the northern side of the castle, holding its occupiers' full attention, while the Ninety-Sixth Division, on the left of the Seventy-Seventh, would circle southward along the east coast and turn inward toward the castle, while from the west the two Marine divisions would drive east. Thus the enemy would be boxed in on three sides. Such an advance, however, required staying in line with divisions on both sides.

The Seventy-Seventh objective was Ishimmi Ridge, a 125-yard rise lying east–west about 1,500 yards north of Shuri Castle. To reduce the terrible cost of a daylight attack the 307th Regiment, in charge, would seize the ridge at night. Chosen for the seizure was Company E, a heavy machine gun section, and a rifle platoon from Company C. The assault group set out at 3 a.m. and was on top of their objective, digging foxholes, before sunrise. Awakened by American gunfire, Japanese infantry began to emerge from their tunnels and engage. The American machine guns and artillery cut down many, but once the Japanese had reached their guns, mortars, and grenades they gained the upper hand, destroying the Americans' machine guns and forcing their dwindling number back toward their command post. Withdrawal became impossible. Some of the wounded—carried, walking, or pulled along the ground on ponchos—got through. A rescue force was ambushed and withdrew. Orders were to hold on. Reinforcement was sent, but only five arrived. Lacking food, water, and ammunition, the remainder of the Americans on the ridge collected rifle ammunition from the dead and wounded and engaged their bayonets. The Third Platoon fought off three bayonet attacks. American artillery, responding to requests for bombardment over the only surviving radio, did its part to help the Third Platoon hold on. After dark on the third day, Company L, Third Battalion, 306th Infantry, arrived at the front and, foxhole by foxhole, released to the rear the exhausted men of reinforced Company E, which had lost to wounds and death nearly three-quarters of its ranks.

The Seventy-Seventh captured Ishimmi Ridge, placing themselves due north of Shuri Castle, tying in with the Ninety-Sixth Division on the left and the First Marine Division on the right. The net was closing. Along the valley to the south, near the eastern border with the Ninety-Sixth Division, a jumble of twisting hills extended into the southwest. Due east of Ishimmi Ridge loomed Flat Top Hill, a giant of a hill level at its top. Alone in the valley, 700 yards north of the hill, was Chocolate Drop (fitting its name to its shape) and some 500 yards east of it was a knob called Wart. This cluster of firing positions covered passage across the valley from above and below. Attacking Chocolate Drop was very dangerous. First, it was protected by a large minefield, and the marshy approach lacked cover; second, it was a site of converging machine gun fire and thick defense on the reverse slopes, in addition to gunfire and mortar from Flat Top above. On May 11 the Third Battalion, 306th Infantry, attacked, took fifty-three casualties, and withdrew. The battalion tried again on May 13 and 14 and failed, leaving it so depleted that three companies of riflemen were regrouped into one. According to the Army's official historian, "the line of dead infantrymen at one place near Chocolate Drop looked to one observer like a skirmish line that had lain down to rest."[52] By then the battalion had lost 471 men and was replaced by the 307th Regiment. Gradually, a day at a time, the Seventy-Seventh grabbed for further hold on the little fortress without final capture, until May 20, after the Americans had extended their attack to Flat Top, a major source of Chocolate Drop's defense. The battleground expanded into the huddle of hills adjoining Flat Top, bringing the Ninety-Sixth Division and the edge of the eastern sector of the Shuri defense into the lineup.

The Flat Top–Chocolate Drop–Wart fight lasted from May 13 to May 20. The Japanese were solidly established on top with mortars, 47 mm guns, which were effective against American tanks, excellent defensive positions, and, as was nearly the case throughout the Pacific Theater by May 1945, universal acceptance of death. The defense was therefore fierce. The Seventy-Seventh and Ninety-Sixth Divisions, surely among the best in the Pacific, attacked with tanks, artillery and Navy guns, regimental self-propelled 105 mm cannon, flamethrowers, and demolition teams. There were those who attacked and failed to reach the objective, those who tried a second, third, and fourth time, and those who reached it but failed to hold it. Yet persistently, day by day, outlying positions were taken, and enemy gunfire diminished. Troops on Chocolate Drop pushed ahead some yards until, one by one, the caves were sealed and the reverse slope secured. On the hillcrest at Flat Top a fierce battle was under way. Next to Flat Top was a secondary road that passed nearby but had been mined and blocked by damaged tanks. The way had been sufficiently cleared for more American tanks on top as well as self-propelled guns. These were critical in attacking key Japanese defenses. May 20 started with a chain of men passing grenades quickly up to those along the crest, who then promptly pulled the pins and showered the enemy with explosives. Finally Flat Top was taken.

Now began in earnest the envelopment of Shuri Castle. The Seventy-Seventh Division now had the Ninety-Sixth on its left, moving southeast to drive into the castle from the northeast and east. Now joining the Seventy-Seventh on the right was the First Marine Division, whose previous fighting had been on Peleliu, pressing in from the north and northwest. The First and Sixth Marine Divisions—newly formed—had been moving south side by side, with the Sixth Marines along the west coast. The First Marine's assignment lay where rolling plain met parallel ridges and rock walls leading to Shuri Heights above. First came Dakeshi Ridge, running east–west a half mile north, and after that a complex of formidable defenses on the western edge of Shuri itself: Wana Ridge, parallel with Dakeshi and rising above Wana town, and then, almost attached to the ridge, Wana Draw, a stream basin widening to the west. Rock walls rose 200 feet above the basin, punctured with gun positions. Shuri Heights provided stellar observation of the American attack. From May 10 to May 21 this congregation of slopes was where the First fought the revamped Japanese Sixty-Third Brigade, which with the addition of survivors from other units and airfield construction troops totaled 6,700 men.

Beside rifles, lighter shorter-barreled carbines, bayonets and knives, mortars, and machine guns, these American infantrymen used loads of grenades, perhaps because with throwing skill and because the thrower would be less exposed than otherwise, they were more effective. Beyond that, they gained excellent fire support from the Navy (battleship-sized shells from the *Colorado*) and the division artillery. Cannon came to the battlefield itself in the form of single, 105 mm guns mounted on tank chassis; and tanks now joined battle with infantry assigned them for protection. Most important here were the flamethrowers, either on tanks or individuals, used to destroy the Japanese cave systems. To open the way, infantry in the Wana-Shuri battle dumped flamethrower napalm down a slope and lit it. In set battles like this, smoke screens provided useful cover. A new infantry armament was present for testing: the shoulder-fired, recoilless rocket tube called the bazooka, so-called because it vaguely resembled the musical instrument by the same name invented in the 1930s by comedian Bob Burns. Even so, with one succeeding another, the First, Fifth, and Seventh Regiments of the First Marine Division attacked the Wana slopes but failed to seize them. Casualties were always high. A company attack at Dakeshi by two platoons lost the company commander and all the squad leaders. Later, another platoon returned with thirty-two of its forty-nine killed or wounded. On May 19 the Seventh Regiment was withdrawn, having lost more than 1,000 killed, wounded, and missing since May 10.[53]

A little over a mile west of Wana Draw, bearing south, was the Sixth Marine Division. Along its way was a cluster of three Japanese fortified hills, in the middle of which was one called Sugar Loaf. The starkness of Sugar Loaf—hovering there alone, about fifty feet high, with its long side of 200 yards parallel to the road—was a grim sight, reminding the Americans of Chocolate Drop. Behind the Loaf and overlapping it by several hundred yards to the right (west) was Horseshoe Hill, about eighty feet high; and on the left (east), overlapping toward Shuri, was Half Moon (also called Crescent Hill), about 200 feet high. All three of these hills, according to the Sixth Marine Division Special Action Report, were "connected by a network of tunnels and galleries facilitating the covered movement of reserves."[54] Their proximity to one another assured gunfire from many angles and positions. Curved ridges in the hills provided protection for howitzers and mortars. Where these skilled defenses lay could only be found out by attack. On May 12, the Sixth, testing, sent Company G of the Twenty-Second, which gained the top of Sugar Loaf but suffered casualties. On the next day the division sent out the Third Battalion of the Twenty-Ninth Regiment and by the end of the day had sent the rest of it, as well as securing air attack and naval bombardment. On May 13 the Sixth Division attacked along a front extending to the east, gaining several hundred yards in the Half Moon Hill vicinity against rising resistance. The Sixth gradually came to recognize the need to concentrate on the Sugar Loaf three-hills sector and to employ the entire division. On May 14 the Second Battalion, Twenty-Second Marines, advanced to seize high ground west and north of

Sugar Loaf. Advancing farther invited heavy mortar fire and high casualties. Forty-six more Marines were sent in to hold the position. By dawn May 15 only one officer and nineteen men were left on the slope. Heavy Japanese fire from all angles, mortar attack, enemy charges, and lack of maneuvering space slowed and confined the Americans. The Second Battalion, Twenty-Second Marines, now withdrawn, had lost 400 killed and wounded in the three days of engagement.[55]

These were days with little gain and heavy loss; veterans in the Sixth found May 16 the "bitterest" day of fighting on Okinawa: "two regiments had attacked with all their available strength and had failed."[56] Yet the Division had help: naval bombardment by 16-inch guns, air attack using 1,000-pound bombs, and tank-infantry teams destroying enemy positions as well as wearing down present Japanese forces by infantry attack. On May 18, taking advantage of lessening enemy fire, Captain Howard L. Mabie, commander of Company D, Twenty-Ninth Marines, after heavy artillery and mortar preparation, advanced north of Sugar Loaf and then sent three tanks to destroy enemy defenders, withdrew them safely, and sent in a barrage of rockets, followed by another barrage of field artillery. Mabie structured his hill positions to engage the Japanese: a line of firing teams from bottom to top. On May 18 Company D, Twenty-Ninth Regiment, captured Sugar Loaf, while Company F grabbed part of Horseshoe; on May 19 they got more of it; and on May 21 Marines advanced 250 yards into the encircling hill and claimed Horseshoe. What they could not claim, because they had not captured it, was Half Moon Hill, the highest hill.[57] So the Sixth Marine Division would not go left to join the First Marine Division in the battle for Shuri Castle. Instead it would head southwest, crossing the Asatogawa (Asato River), and enter the city of Naha, Okinawa's largest. A strong force was left with the Half Moon to protect it and its connection to the First Marine Division on Shuri only a mile away.

On May 21 gusty winds arose, followed by heavy, chilling, and at times torrential rain across Okinawa that lasted every day with little interruption until the end of May. Streams and rivers overflowed; shell craters became ponds, the hastily improved road system was washed out, and paths turned into mud that went up to the knees, even hips. Motor transport, with wheels or tracks, was impossible. Each of the wounded on litters had eight carriers with four to lift and four to catch their breath. For the infantry at the front, some communication was cut and food and ammunition barely supplied. The foxhole was muddy, constantly in need of baling. The occupant and his firearms were always wet. E. B. Sledge, the mortar-man whose experience in the First Marine Division at Peleliu we mentioned earlier, arrived at Sugar Loaf just after the Sixth had left for Naha, below Shuri on the western side of the island.[58] The new arrivals set up their mortars between the Horseshoe and the Half Moon (Crescent). They dug their own foxholes and stayed in them at night, "soaked, cold, and miserable." It was "the most ghastly corner of hell," wrote Sledge in *With the Old Breed*; "choked with the putrefaction of death, decay, and destruction." Nearby "lay about twenty dead Marines, each on a stretcher and covered to his ankles with a poncho," awaiting transport to the burial ground. "The whole area was pocked with shell craters and churned up by explosions. Every crater was half full of water and many of them held a Marine corpse. The bodies lay pathetically just as they had been killed, half submerged in muck and water, rusting weapons still in hand. Swarms of big flies hovered about them."[59]

Shuri was now encircled on the north, east, and west but not the south. That would come later. The Seventy-Seventh Division held on to Ishimmi Ridge but was unable to capture several more hills in their reach. These survivors from the capture of Chocolate Drop were now mud-bound in constant rain and cut off from supply. The western side of Shuri was held by the First Marines with an outpost at Half Moon (Crescent) Hill and by the Sixth, now mostly established in Naha, southwest of Shuri, and soon to head toward engagement south of Shuri. The southeastern side of Shuri led through the hill country of Oboe and Conical Hill toward the east coast and then to the port of Yonabaru in the southern portion of Okinawa. The outstanding block was Conical Hill and its surrounding defenses of a thousand or so Japanese, with field artillery, fifty machine guns, and mortars. The principal driving force was the Ninety-Sixth Division, which had stood northeast and east in the Shuri encirclement and had fought hard and well in the Flat Top battle.

The final battle for Shuri Castle started on May 11: two battalions, attacking separately, moved downward toward the east coast into the rising ridges surrounding 476-foot Conical Hill. The First Battalion, 383rd Regiment, avoiding the Shuri defense hills and territory in the north, worked its way south through heavy fire from well-positioned guns. By May 19, in this sector, before taking on Conical, over 300 American troops had been killed or wounded. Tanks helped but quickly ran out of ammunition. Grenade duels were prolonged. Having established a position on the northwest side of Conical, the Ninety-Sixth developed a second attack, by the 383rd Regiment, which slipped south separately and emerged from the villages of Tobaru and Amaru facing the Conical's downslope toward the sea from the northeast, its finger-like ridges spreading from Conical peak like the spokes of a decrepit wheel. The objective was to capture the ridges across the slope and the peak above so that the American Seventh Infantry Division could skim south along the coast without facing Japanese gunfire from the Conical slopes on their right. Once in the southern remainder of Okinawa, the division could join with a Marine division from the opposite coast and complete the encirclement of Shuri. Colonel E. T. May, commander of the 383rd Regiment, was certain that a frontal attack uphill toward the Conical from the opposite side was necessary. Two platoons of infantry from Company F and two platoons of tanks from the 763rd Tank Battalion started uphill on the northern spur. Without officers, the two technical sergeants took charge: running into a boulder barricade but no Japanese, they agreed not to wait for orders. They and their platoons kept going until reaching high on the sides of the Conical. Their initiative was a success; the defenders had been facing the other way. However, they quickly shifted south in counterattack. An American spotting plane noted this from above, and soon a barrage of artillery and mortar fire dropped on the attacking Japanese.

The preparation for turning Conical Hill into safe passage for the Seventh Division continued with a drive east to west across the lower skirts of the hill. The Japanese held a line of small, well-defended hills dropping down the western side—Hogback, Cutaway, and Sugar—protected by nearby gun emplacements and the guns on hills identified in the military's alphabetical parlance as Mike, Love, and King. The Ninety-Sixth, with the fresh Third Battalion of the 381st Regiment, was well supported by bombing at low altitude, Navy and Army artillery, tank fire, satchel charges, light 60 mm mortars, heavy machine guns, and 1,100 grenades thrown by one company in defense. On May 21 the 381st Regiment lost fifty-six men but in the process killed eight times as many Japanese.[60] The Seventh Division, now composed of the Seventeenth, Thirty-Second, and 184th Regiments, received a rest period of twelve days, returning to the front on May 21, strengthened by 1,691 replacements and 546 returnees from hospitalization.[61] Their division was chosen to slip in single file past the Conical Hill battle and past Yonabaru into the southern portion of Okinawa. An hour before they set out it began to rain, and then to downpour. This was the prolonged Okinawa deluge, and it soaked the Seventh Division, but the division got through the corridor into the southern sector of Okinawa.

Near Naha facing east were the Marines. The Tenth Army headquarters wanted to see the forces from both the east and the west meet and complete the encirclement of Shuri and reduce, collapse, and destroy this collected Japanese army now almost within their hands. At this same time General Ushijima was planning and then effecting the removal of his army from Shuri. On May 21 he consulted his division and brigade commanders, who again expressed concern at the idea of a retreat by a Japanese army. Okinawa was more than strategic; it had tremendous symbolic importance. And there was the question as to where the army might go. The Chinen Peninsula was too rough and remote. But the territory along the southern shore made sense. Supplies had been stored and positions prepared there. Above all, the southern coast offered the opportunity of waging a longer battle and thereby imposing greater attrition and damage on the American forces and postponing use of Okinawa against Japan itself. Then, too, the gathering American success in opening passage south through the Conical defenses along the eastern shore posed for the Japanese the growing threat of being tightly encircled at Shuri and hit by devastating bombardment. The shift began on the next day, May 22, with the transfer of Japanese wounded and supplies over about seven miles to the southern coast.

The Tenth Army learned of extensive Japanese troop movement from air observation during brief breaks in the rain but also held the firm conviction that the Japanese would never retreat from Shuri Castle.[62] Once it became clear that that was exactly what was happening, though, the American troop movements turned southward. Instead of driving west to complete the encirclement of Shuri, the Seventh Division would hold at nearby Chinen Peninsula to ensure that no Japanese forces were in the hills or on the northern shore. Across the island, opposite Chinen and south of Naha, was the Oroku Peninsula, at whose tip two regiments of the Sixth made an amphibious landing from the shore to the north on June 4. Entering Oroku from the interior was the First Marine. Between the two American divisions was a Japanese naval base force led by Admiral Ota Minoru, consisting of almost all the naval personnel left on the island, scarcely effective as infantry. The battle took a week, but in the process nearly all of the 4,500 Japanese were killed. Several hundred, including Admiral Ota and his staff, committed suicide in an underground headquarters that was so well hidden that it took several days for the Marines to find it. Approximately 150 Japanese surrendered, the first large group surrender on Okinawa. This was an encouraging sign, but it had to be weighed against the grim realization that the vast majority of Japanese had chosen to fight to the death or take their own lives rather than surrender. The destruction of the Japanese naval base force was a major defeat for the Japanese, but the Americans had taken 2,608 casualties, a rate that was proportionately higher than what they had experienced at Shuri Castle when facing experienced infantrymen.[63]

And the fight wasn't over. Away to the south, bringing together its east and west shores, was what seemed like a single wall of escarpment holding the island together. On these heights and behind them the final battle for Okinawa took place. Moving south down the middle of the island was the Ninety-Sixth Infantry Division, having just finished with the Conical battle and headed for one more. Behind it was the Seventy-Seventh Division, protecting the rear. Coming southwest along the shore from the Chinen Peninsula was the Seventh Division, and down the western shore, after the Oroku battle, the First Marine and later the Sixth Marine. At last the Americans were massed and prepared.

The last battles took place in the fifteen square miles of the southwestern corner of Okinawa, enclosed by the western and southern shores, with ridges and escarpments lining all sides. Within was a tableland of intermediate height rising into two hills, Yuza-Dake and Yaeju-Dake, the latter forming the northern and eastern escarpment and then rising 290 feet high along the northern side. The Ninety-Sixth moved in for attack from the north, the Seventh from the east, and the First and Sixth Marine Divisions, when they arrived, from the west. Ushijima had collected 11,000 troops in the much-reduced Twenty-Fourth and Sixty-Second Divisions and Forty-Fourth Independent Mixed Brigade. Over 20,000 service troops and miscellaneous personnel, lacking training and equipment, were spread around the veteran Japanese infantry. Machine guns, mortars, and 47 mm cannon would cause heavy casualties in American attacks moving across the open and level approaches, climbing the escarpment, and engaging the enemy. In one squad of eight men, all were killed.

In the end, one of the most welcome sights was that of dust, at least according to one American soldier on June 10. A cloud of it was being kicked up by the tracks of a newly landed battalion of tanks—M4 medium tanks, each with a 75 mm gun and machine gun. Also landed were the same tanks converted to flamethrowers and new 200-foot detachable, flexible extensions for flamethrowing at targets inaccessible to the tank. The incessant rains had stopped, supply parachutes were no longer necessary, roads were opening, and food, water, and ammunition were reappearing. The tanks carried replacements and supplies to the front line and returned with wounded, lifted aboard through an escape hatch beneath the crew compartment. In the five-day battle for Kunishi Ridge the tanks carried ninety tons of supplies and 550 troop reinforcements to the front and returned with 1,150 wounded. Twenty-one tanks were damaged or destroyed in that battle, but their loss was far from meaningless.[64]

Circumstances were changing quickly now on Okinawa, as were American practices. Colonel Francis Pachler, commanding the Seventeenth Regiment, Seventh Division, moved the Third Battalion across the escarpment to the interior Yaeju-Dake slope for an attack using surprise and stealth. Pachler had argued that he should take a larger area on the slope with three assault companies, each with its own pathway across, and with that pathway's approach easily identified at night. "Stealth" meant no preparatory bombardment, but harassing fire earlier and protective fire was ready. Each company added a section of heavy machine guns. Plans were meticulous: every participant was required to learn all the details of the march. The hike to Yaeju-Dake was successful. Company B passed three Japanese soldiers without deviation on either side. Soon after arriving in their new position, Pachler's force ran into a Japanese column of about fifty, thirty-seven of whom Company L killed while the rest fled. By morning the battalion had destroyed the caves and established their own positions. The enemy had withdrawn for the night to avoid American artillery but had expected to return.[65]

The attack was part of a general advance, one that included the Ninety-Seventh Division, which collapsed the eastern sector along the heights and escarpment of Yaeju-Dake, Yuza-Dake, and Hill 95. In the west the First Marine Division arrived from the Oroku Peninsula and fought its way south to Kunishi Ridge, which formed the tail of the east–west hill escarpment. On its left the 382nd Regiment of the Ninety-Sixth Division cleared the slope of guns, allowing the Marines to move on June 11 directly onto Kunishi Ridge, where they held on.[66] Attacking repeatedly and without coordination with air and artillery was drawing a Japanese response that was proving costly. It was also getting nowhere. Armored support greatly eased the task of the infantry. Flamethrower tanks used no fewer than 37,000 gallons of gasoline on caves and crags on Kunishi Ridge. By comparison, the standard portable flamethrower used by infantry had a fuel tank capacity of five gallons.

Evidence finally began to show that the Japanese on Kunishi Ridge were weakening. Fresh troops of the Twenty-Second Marine Regiment began gaining ground. On June 17 the Japanese gave way, not only at the ridge but throughout Okinawa. Their forces no longer had the necessities of an army. Food was running out. Medical care meant bandaging and not much more. Their artillery sounded like a whisper. Communication lines were mostly destroyed. Reinforcements were not available. General Ushijima had done what he had planned: to delay the American Army by setting the final battle in the far south. The number of Americans killed and wounded after Shuri was abandoned added up to 8,357, approximately 17 percent of the total for the campaign. On June 18, Lieutenant General Simon B. Buckner, observing the fighting, was killed by a coral fragment from a shell explosion directly above him. As for Ushijima, he simply dismissed his army, advising his soldiers to find their way north and join guerrilla forces. Sometime during June 22 or 23, he and his chief of staff, Cho, committed ritual suicide.

Okinawa was by no means pacified on June 17; a one-week mop-up remained, through the southern portion of the island, with occasional skirmishes, much patrolling and sealing of caves, and some capture of Japanese headed north. The total number of Japanese soldiers killed in the mop-up was 8,975, as well as 2,902 military prisoners and 906 labor troops. American casualties in the roundup were 783. Total American casualties in the Okinawa battle were 49,151 of which 12,520 were killed or missing and 36,631 wounded. Nonbattle casualties (illness, psychiatric cases, accidents) were 15,613 for the Army and 10,598 for the Marines. Killed in the Japanese army were approximately 110,000, and 7,400 were taken prisoner, about half of whom were conscripted Okinawans, but the remaining number, about 3,700 Japanese, was still substantially more prisoners than taken before. American leaders were left to ponder the surprising number of Japanese who surrendered. Did it indicate a weakening of morale and discipline? Or was it more significant that over 100,000 Japanese soldiers and sailors, like the young men who piloted planes on one-way missions, chose to die rather than surrender?

The effect of the battle for Okinawa on planning the invasion of Japan was direct and deep. The Army and Marine divisions landing there would require extensive infantry reconstruction.[67] As the battle for Okinawa drew to a close, some 700 miles to the southwest on Luzon, the Forty-Third Division was withdrawn from action at Ipo Dam and the vicinity on June 26 to prepare for what lay ahead. The division had been in continual battle order for 175 days. Now the troops settled in their tent city near Cabanatuan, halfway between Manila and Lingayen Gulf. Shower baths stood waiting (using water perhaps from the Ipo Dam, which they had just recaptured).

Away from battle and the Sixth Army, troops blissfully slept off the ground on cots in tents. They ate cooked instead of boxed food and wore new or laundered uniforms. Among older men, many of them sergeants, those with sufficient "points," part of the recently enacted system for discharging veterans, departed for home; replacements arrived and began learning Pacific weaponry and tactics and fitting into their squads. So many friends lost—hospitals, home, cemeteries—and a blur of new faces.[68]

The gathering of the American forces in the Philippines, Marianas, and Hawaii for the invasion of Kyushu on November 1 and the invasion of the Tokyo area the following March would require all available Pacific troops.

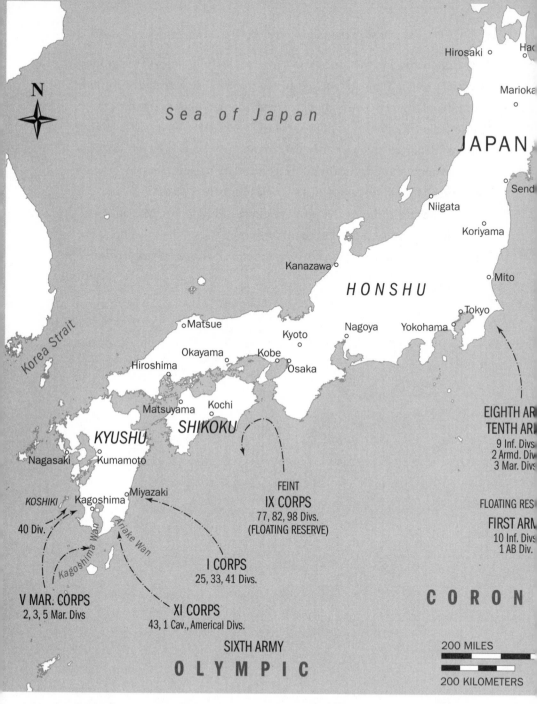

N

Sea of Japan

Hirosaki ○
Ha◌
Marioka
○

JAPAN

Send◌

Niigata ○

Koriyama ○

Kanazawa ○

H O N S H U

○ Mito

○ Matsue   Kyoto
                  ○   Nagoya   Yokohama ○ ○ Tokyo
       Okayama   Kobe   ○
Hiroshima   ○   ○ ○
                        Osaka

             Kochi
Matsuyama   ○   EIGHTH AR▮
○   TENTH AR▮
        SHIKOKU   9 Inf. Div▮
KYUSHU   2 Armd. Div▮
                         3 Mar. Div▮
Nagasaki ○ Kumamoto
         ○   FLOATING RES▮
KOSHIKI Kagoshima Miyazaki ○
           ○   FEINT   FIRST ARM▮
40 Div.   IX CORPS   10 Inf. Div▮
                                    77, 82, 98 Divs.   1 AB Div.
                                    (FLOATING RESERVE)
                    Arake Wan
Kagoshima Wan   C O R O N▮
                     I CORPS
V MAR. CORPS   25, 33, 41 Divs.
2, 3, 5 Mar. Divs   XI CORPS
                         43, 1 Cav., Americal Divs.

                    SIXTH ARMY   200 MILES
                    O L Y M P I C
                                        200 KILOMETERS

■ **Map 12** Operation DOWNFALL: The Invasion of Japan. Drawn by George Chakvetadze.

Two Down and One to Go

The Home Front,

March–June 1945

April 1945 began on a high note, bringing welcome news to the American home front from the two main theaters of war. Americans read with huge relief about unopposed landings on Okinawa, protected by the Fifth Fleet, "the world's greatest sea force." In Europe, Allied forces, having swept across the Rhine, plunged into Germany's industrial heartland. Daily reports carried news of swift encircling movements, bagging tens of thousands of Germans and reducing once formidable armies into isolated pockets of resistance. On April 1 the *Washington Post* reported that the Ninth Army had completed a seventy-five-mile "mighty drive" in one week by linking up with the First Army east of the Ruhr. The convergence of the two armies trapped more than 40,000 Germans inside the Ruhr pocket. At the same time, according to the *Post*, the Fourth Armored Division, the "breakthrough division" of Lieutenant General George S. Patton's Third Army, was "smashing along the Frankfurt–Berlin superhighway." Patton's men had captured 60,000 Germans in ten days.[1] The next day readers were told that British forces had cut across the German Twenty-Fifth Army's supply line, leaving 50,000 soldiers in danger of encirclement in the Netherlands. The same report recalculated the number caught in the Ruhr as between 40,000 and 100,000, while the total number of Germans taken in March by General Omar Bradley's Twelfth Army Group was reported as 350,000.[2] It was becoming clear that the German army was beginning to give up.

Operations in the Pacific Theater kept pace, creating at least the impression of parallel success stories. Americans landing on March 27 on Tokashiki Island, the largest of the Kerama group, located seventeen miles west of Okinawa, and several lesser islands in the same group brushed aside Japanese resistance. American forces captured approximately 300 suicide boats and tons of explosives before they could be used by the Japanese. The one-man boats were eighteen feet long, powered by a four-cylinder engine and armed with a depth charge in the rear and a torpedo in the bow. After landing on the western coast of Okinawa on April 1, American forces rapidly captured the two airfields located inland from the invasion site. "Amazing Walk-In" declared the *New York Times*; "Japanese Opposition Is Almost Entirely Lacking in Landing Expected to Be Most Bloody."[3] After those initial successes the Americans turned south toward the more densely populated third of the island and the site of the main Japanese force.

It was there that the stories in Europe and the Pacific diverged, and diverged dramatically. In the second week of combat, the American public learned from press reports that the southward advance on Okinawa had stalled in the face of "fierce" resistance and "extremely heavy mortar and artillery fire." The advance into the south was "grim." Unlike the German army, the Japanese were holding firm. The banner headlines in the *Times* and *Washington Post* told only of more gains in Europe: the Russians had entered Vienna on April 9, the British and American armies were driving for the Elbe, and on April 12 the U.S. Ninth Army was only fifty-seven miles from Berlin. A large map in the *Times* showed the commanding position of Allied forces inside Germany, graphically conveying the unmistakable message that the Reich was in its last days. By the first week of April, all eyes were on the progress of the converging Allied forces in Germany. Momentarily, at least, news from Okinawa had slipped from the headlines, receiving less space on page 1 than the fighting on the northern Italian front.[4]

With victory in Europe only days, weeks at most, away, the looming challenge of economic reconversion competed for space on the front page with news from the war front. On April 2 James F. Byrnes, the director of the Office of War Mobilization and Reconversion (OWMR), announced that he was leaving his job. In his letter of resignation, Byrnes, the "assistant president" to Roosevelt, explained that he had always planned to retire once the main part of the job switched from mobilization to reconversion. With victory "not that far distant," he wrote in his letter of resignation, it was time for a new director to take charge. Byrnes's resignation followed the release by his office of a quarterly report that predicted a gradual shift from war production to civilian output, with fewer than a million workers losing their jobs in the six months after V-E Day. According to Byrnes, munitions production would be curtailed by about 20 percent during that period and cut an additional 20 percent within a year. Overall, the report sought to assure workers that pent-up demand for consumer goods backed by as much as $140 billion in savings would provide ample employment opportunities for those displaced by the transition to a peacetime economy. Although Byrnes suggested that such unpopular measures as the nationwide curfew on bars and nightclubs and the ban on horse racing would be lifted after V-E Day, his report contained several stern reminders that the United States faced "the somber reality of the war in the Pacific against a fanatic foe who is strongly intrenched on his island bases and the mainland of Asia." In particular, he noted that restrictions on scarce materials would remain in force, as would regulations on prices, wages, and rationing of foodstuffs.[5]

Despite those reminders of sacrifices to come, many Americans, including Byrnes's former senatorial colleagues, viewed his report and subsequent resignation as further proof that the pending national service bill proposed by the Roosevelt administration was no longer needed. Roosevelt had originally endorsed the measure in his January 1944 State of the Union address, in which he spoke of an Economic Bill of Rights that was tied to workers' obligations to contribute to the nation's security.[6] As we have noted, he returned to that theme the following year in his January 1945 State of the Union speech and made it the subject of his last fireside chat before his death in April. Secretary of War Stimson and his point man on mobilization, Undersecretary of War Robert Patterson, had long wanted a stronger comprehensive service law, including a "work or fight" provision to curtail strikes, but they were willing to settle for a House bill that would allow the government to keep workers between the ages of eighteen and forty-five on the job in vital industries until replacements could be found and, if needed, direct workers into key industries.[7]

Although American public opinion supported some form of national service law, key business and labor organizations, including the American Federation of Labor and the National Association of Manufacturers, opposed any compulsory measure, although for different reasons.[8] Labor leaders feared any attempt to infringe on workers' prerogatives and were especially unwilling to trust their fate to the corporate lawyers, bankers, and businessmen who administered the departments and agencies concerned with mobilization. Businessmen, for their part, saw government direction of the workforce as evidence of the New Deal administration's insatiable appetite for power and control over the market place.

Given the reluctance of members on both sides of the aisle to antagonize such powerful constituents, administration officials were encouraged when the House passed the bill on February 1. From there it went to the Senate, where it received a chilly reception from the leaders of the Military Affairs Committee. After two weeks' delay the committee reported out a much weaker bill based on voluntarism rather than compulsion. During the subsequent debate, Senator Edwin Johnson (D-Colorado) pointedly asked, "And now with Mr. Byrnes resigning his post, presumably to take another one outside the war program, why should we 'freeze' other men to their jobs?"[9] Other defenders of the Senate version, a "powder puff bill" according to the New York Times, extolled the efforts of American workers and denounced the administration's attempt to adopt "fascist methods" of controlling workers with a "slave labor" bill when the United States had shown it could outproduce its enemies with free labor.[10] Ultimately, twelve Democrats in the Senate, under pressure from organized labor, joined with Republicans to defeat both versions of the bill.

The defeat of national service legislation illustrated the difficulty the administration faced in rallying Americans for the hard fight ahead in the Pacific. Roosevelt's warning that failure of the manpower bill would "jeopardize the war" failed to persuade senators who saw irrefutable evidence of impending victory splashed across the headlines of their constituents' newspapers. With victory in Europe so close and reconversion about to commence, as indicated by the OWMR's report and dramatized by Byrnes's resignation, an expansion of federal control over workers had no chance of success.

The mounting anxieties about the postwar economy intensified problems the administration had faced throughout the war. Those who sought to mobilize the nation never succeeded in getting Americans to agree on the level of sacrifice required for victory. Taking stock of polls that consistently showed that Americans hoped that victory would bring about a better life for themselves and their families, defined by jobs and housing, the Roosevelt administration framed its wartime goals in similarly practical terms. In his 1944 State of the Union, FDR proclaimed his support for an economic bill of rights and pledged to create sixty million jobs after the war. His program implied a contract between government and workers in which workers would be rewarded for their home front contributions to the war. But despite Roosevelt's urging, many workers were reluctant to risk seemingly secure jobs for positions in war industries.[11]

Wartime propaganda frequently packaged patriotic messages with consumer-oriented sales pitches.[12] A 1945 Buick ad assured readers that their new models would "be all that returning warriors have dreamed about," while Lucky Strike cigarettes claimed that it changed its packaging from green to white to save on allegedly scarce green ink. "Lucky Strike Green has gone to war," the company announced. "How American it is...to want something better!" exclaimed an ad for Ballantine Ale that urged female war workers to buy war bonds to save for "something better"—education, travel, or marriage. "Even in wartime," read the copy, "free America still enjoys many 'better things,' which are not available to less fortunate peoples," including, of course, Ballantine Ale, " 'something better,' in moderate beverages."[13] In short, corporate leaders embraced the opportunity to identify their endeavors with Americans' aspirations. As business rebounded during the national emergency, organizations like the National Association of Manufacturers launched a public relations campaign to drown out statist—meaning wartime—economic remedies and remind Americans that free enterprise was the key to the good life. Defenders of New Deal reforms viewed the PR onslaught with a mixture of awe and disgust. Assessing the influence of corporate propagandists, one liberal analyst in the Office of War Information sourly concluded: "Free enterprise has become the Fifth Freedom."[14]

The packaging of wartime aims in consumer-oriented advertisements both shaped and reflected widely held American attitudes. Throughout the war the public had harbored ambivalent feelings about the nature of the sacrifices they should make. Polls often showed that by large majorities Americans favored some form of "work or fight" bill even as late as 1945. But further probing raised questions about the strength of those views. For example, in 1942 polls taken by *Fortune* and by the Office of War Information showed that a large majority favored drafting workers into war work. When asked if they would be willing to leave their current jobs for one in a war industry, however, only three in ten said yes.[15]

Later experience provided further evidence for believing that American support for conscripting labor for war work was more abstract and less firm than the polls indicated. Faced with a serious tire shortage in late 1944, the War Department and War Manpower Commission sought to persuade skilled workers in New Bedford, Massachusetts, to fill 200 vacancies in that town's Firestone manufacturing plants so that Firestone could increase the supply of tire cord, a component made of rayon or nylon that was essential to the construction of tires. The targeted workers, all of whom lived in New Bedford and worked in factories making less essential cotton goods, were assured that if they switched to tire plants they would be covered by the same union and make the same wages they were earning in their current jobs. Nevertheless, the administration's efforts to recruit the workers were unsuccessful. Fearing a drop in production, labor representatives and managers in the textile plants teamed up to advise workers against changing jobs. In the end, despite the urgency of the tire shortage, few of the skilled laborers were willing to jeopardize their seniority in their current positions by taking jobs in war work that many believed would last only a few months longer.[16] The New Bedford case was only one of many that illustrated in microcosm the shortcomings of the nation's manpower policies. By 1945 the Army was coping with labor shortages in critical industries by recalling soldiers from overseas by the thousands to fill vacant positions in war industries, including the manufacture of artillery ammunition, tires, and cotton duck.

Perhaps even more frustrating for the mobilizers were the work stoppages and rising rates of absenteeism that plagued war industries. Such actions seemed a betrayal of the idea of shared sacrifice presented in wartime propaganda. GIs overseas often complained bitterly about workers who went on strike while earning unimaginably high wages in safe jobs on the home front.[17] Caricatures of workers as greedy slackers feasting on steaks and whining about gasoline rations abounded. In reality, however, "boomtown America" was a place of congestion, frayed nerves, and physical danger. Many in the war industries had worked ten-hour days for over three years with limited recreation. From 1942 to 1945, according to the Bureau of Labor Statistics, there were about two million disabling or deadly industrial accidents per year. Small wonder that workers declined to be frozen in war industry jobs when the possibility of safer, more permanent civilian jobs beckoned.[18]

War leaders were also dismayed by the growing signs of unrest within the business community. For much of the war, a kind of coalition government presided in Washington. Prominent Republicans and business leaders, like Stimson and assistant secretaries John J. McCloy and Robert Lovett, had been brought into the War and Navy Departments to manage the wartime economy and oversee military production. The migration of "dollar a year" corporate leaders into the many mobilization agencies expanded corporate influence into the second administrative tier of government, formerly controlled by New Dealers. Instead of regulating business and supervising its actions, the federal government became the principle underwriter of business expansion and windfall profits. As Stimson explained, "If you are going to go to war in a capitalist country you have to let business make money out of the process or business won't work."[19]

Even as they directed wartime production, these business leaders maintained a lively interest in preparing for the time when the economy would revert to peacetime production. As a consequence of that thinking, they shied away from total mobilization of the economy, much to the consternation of Undersecretary Patterson, and insisted that ample consideration be given to the production of consumer goods and services.[20] The close collaboration between business and government, specifically the military, as well as the impressive output of America's industries, helped to redeem the shattered Depression-era image of American business and restore the shaken confidence of those industry leaders who only years before had been held responsible for economic disaster. As the war in Europe neared conclusion, business leaders sought freer rein to begin the process of reconversion to a peacetime economy. When Stimson and Patterson refused to loosen the Army's grip on the economy, the two officials and by extension the Army came under heavy criticism from their erstwhile allies in the private sector.[21]

As the prospects for peace brightened, beginning in June 1944, so did the perception of new stakes and challenges in a different industrial environment. Workers dreaded unemployment, the bane of the Depression years. Fearing layoffs, they were leaving war plants for the security of jobs in the civilian economy, cutting plant capacity by 25 percent. The April 1945 report from the OWMR further upset the delicate sense of shared sacrifice needed for home front unity. No one wanted to be stuck in a doomed war industry as the economy shifted toward peacetime production.

On April 12 home front unity suffered a more serious blow when FDR died while on a recuperative stay at Warm Springs, Georgia. During the previous year, his congestive heart failure had mandated a limited daily regime. He managed to secure reelection and actively participated in the Allied summit conference held at Yalta in February, but at considerable physical cost. He continued cabinet meetings and press conferences and consulted with leading members of Congress, but his Oval Office hours were shorter and his rest periods longer. His exhortations on the manpower bill were among his last words to the country before he left for Warm Springs at the end of March, yet the *Times* noted that he had delayed a real fight over the issue for the previous two years. He was not the same fully engaged president he had been.

Still, Roosevelt's death seemed unimaginable, so firmly rooted in people's minds had his twelve-year presidency become. The great leader, "the greatest figure of our time" according to Republican senator Robert Taft, was gone.[22] Harry Truman followed in the same path, but the nation had lost an authoritative reminder of the values for which it was fighting, including and perhaps especially the fundamental reform of Germany and Japan, reform that could only be achieved by way of unconditional surrender. Now the political terrain was more level. Republicans had been in the wilderness for years, and the vision of an undemocratic war regime presented an inviting target. War agencies, without "the boss," spoke in many voices. On the one hand were politicians in charge of the War Manpower and War Mobilization and Reconversion presenting somewhat encouraging views of war production. On the other were the dire warnings of Patterson and Stimson. More broadly, insiders predicted that the New Dealers were on the way out and the new administration was moving to a more pragmatic centrist government.[23]

Shortly after being sworn in, Truman met with Stimson, Forrestal, and the JCS for a briefing on the military situation. The Chiefs told the new president that they expected the war with Germany to last another six months and the war with Japan a year and a half. On the evening of FDR's death, Truman summoned FDR's cabinet for a brief meeting to ask the secretaries to stay on at their posts for the time being. After the meeting ended, Secretary Stimson approached the new president and shared with him a secret of immense importance. The United States was developing a new weapon "of almost unbelievable destructive power" that would be available in about four months. That was all Stimson wished to say at the moment, but he would provide Truman with a more detailed briefing a little later.[24]

Truman's first message to Congress on April 16 and his first press conference the next day did little to bear out predictions that he would veer from

Roosevelt's policies. He proclaimed his fealty to two of his predecessor's war aims—unconditional surrender and American participation in a postwar international organization. The United States would wage war until all resistance ceased. Much hard fighting remained, he added, but Americans had sacrificed too much to settle for a "partial victory." "Our demand has been, and it remains—Unconditional Surrender!" "We will not traffic with the breakers of the peace on the terms of the peace."[25] In his first regularly scheduled press conference the next day he flatly dismissed any thought of lifting the ban on horse racing and the entertainment curfew and refused to speculate on what he might do after V-E Day.[26] Commenting on Truman's performance, *Washington Post* columnist Ernest Lindley praised his firmness in recommitting the United States to complete victory and on the bans and curfews, noting that "any sign of softness" on those issues "would have encouraged demands for letdowns from a hundred other sources." Lindley predicted that in the days to come the pressure on the president would increase but he had probably "staved off trouble with his firm stand on the first test." A bigger test lay ahead after V-E Day, when the administration would have to fend off appeals from "special interests" for deeper cuts in war production than the OWMR had predicted. At the same time, as Americans looked for relief from the war's regimentation on the home front, the armed forces would begin the complicated process of redeploying troops from the European Theater to the Pacific. Lindley explained that redeployment was necessary to defeat Japan in a timely manner but worried that the War Department had not done enough to prepare the soldiers overseas for what would be a "relatively slow and small demobilization after V-E Day."[27]

As originally conceived, the discharge of long-serving veterans, which would coincide with the redeployment of troops to the Pacific, was not meant to be slow. General Marshall was particularly concerned to avoid the months of delay in sending troops home that had occurred at the end of World War I. In July 1943 the War Department established the Special Planning Division to initiate studies in conjunction with the general staff. A period of months followed during which the criteria were devised and approval was secured from the principal commands. During this process, scientific polling methods were applied to obtain the opinions of representatives from each of the Army's constituent groups. The response showed that the GIs agreed with Marshall that discharge by units, such as divisions, as had been the case in World War I, would be grossly unfair, since each unit had both short-termers and long-termers, and the former would be released while the latter waited in frustration.

At Marshall's instigation, movie director Frank Capra, now a colonel in the Army, made a film for troops, *Two Down and One to Go*, explaining and justifying the new system.[28] The Army's V-E Day demobilization formula assigned the soldier or airman points in various multiples for service rendered as of May 12, 1945. This total was known as the Adjusted Service Rating. Each month of service earned a point; each month of overseas service was another point. Combat service was recognized by battle stars affixed to a theater ribbon (European or Pacific), each star adding five points. Each medal for merit or valor and the Purple Heart for wounds earned five points as well. Fathers received twelve points each for up to three dependent children. Initially, a point score of eighty-five or above would qualify one for discharge. To illustrate in a simplified way: a draftee entering in May 1942 might spend his first year in training in the United States (twelve points), his second in training and preparation in England (twenty-four points), and his third in France and Germany (twenty-four points), engaged in four campaigns (Northern France, Ardennes, Rhineland, and Central Europe), which earned him four battle stars (twenty points), and receive one wound (five points). He would then have eighty-five points and would qualify for discharge.

The Adjusted Service Rating system was in many ways an eminently fair means of discharging veteran troops and identifying those who should be called on to render further service in the Pacific. It was also an administrative nightmare. The program was subject to varying interpretation, misinformation, and error. War Department plans for simultaneous demobilization and redeployment sorted units into four different categories. The process called for reconstituting units such that they held men whose Adjusted Service Rating placed them in the same category. Category I units would be retained in their current command for occupation duty. Category II units were slated for redeployment to an active theater. Category II units in Europe and the Mediterranean would be redeployed to the United States. From there they would either continue on to the Pacific or remain in the States as part of a strategic reserve. Category III units in Europe or the Mediterranean would be reorganized and retrained before being moved into Categories I or II. Category IV units in Europe and the Mediterranean would be filled with high-point men, including those moving out of units with other designations and those inactivated. Units designated as Categories I–III would be composed of essential personnel, defined as men who did not have enough points for discharge or who possessed a critical Military Occupational Specialty. Men with enough points for discharge could be retained if they possessed a critical Military Occupational Specialty. Most of these were in radio, radar, cryptanalysis, and other signals jobs.[29]

The Army hoped that it could simplify this process somewhat by designating as Category I those units with the highest percentage of men with scores in the middle range. Category IV units would contain the highest percentage of men eligible for discharge. Category II units would have the highest percentage of men with low scores.[30] The goal here was to minimize the amount of reshuffling done between units. Once filled and reorganized, those Category II units in Europe and the Mediterranean designated for the Pacific would be moved back to the United States for a month furlough followed by additional training. The Army planned on moving three million men in 1945. Under the best of circumstances, moving large military units was, said a colonel in the Transportation Corps, as "complex as all get out": "You've got a hundred different variables and you've got to be able to rationalize all your variables" and rerationalize them.[31] The Army's readjustment program, specifically the shifting of soldiers from one unit to another, added to that already large list of variables and placed another layer of complexity over an already intricate process.

Speaking to the American Academy of Political Science in February 1945, Marshall called the process of redeployment "the greatest administrative and logistical problem in the history of the world." Despite the immensity of the task ahead, he remained confident, perhaps too much so, that the redeployment could be carried out in a "thoroughly businesslike manner."[32] The men could be assembled, sorted, and moved on a reasonably predictable timetable. The biggest obstacle to the smooth transfer of troops to the Pacific would be impatience on the home front. Once the fighting in Europe ended, the natural reaction of most men would be to want to return home. That sentiment would be echoed by their families, who would make their feelings known to their representatives in Congress. The press and radio broadcasters would further reflect and amplify the growing impatience at home. In this way, troop morale, a variable Marshall took very seriously, could easily be undermined by impatience on the home front.

In the meantime, despite the desire to get eligible soldiers home quickly, most of those designated for discharge, said Marshall, would have to "endure considerable delay" before they could return home.[33] There could be no diversion of resources away from the buildup in the Pacific. Speed was essential to victory over Japan at a bearable cost in lives and treasure. Nor could there be any letdown in production at home. Marshall acknowledged that citizens would naturally expect that the demand for war materials would slacken considerably after Germany's defeat. But that would not be the case. Stressing the need to limit casualties, Marshall admonished his audience: "I shall make only this comment: that we intend to expend far more ammunition and similar supplies in the Pacific than we did in the Atlantic."[34]

Delivered in the midst of accumulating victories in Europe—just after the German Ardennes offensive had been pushed back—Marshall's speech presciently described the dynamics of the war weariness unfolding at home. By mid-April, as victory came within reach, Marshall's concerns increased. Writing to General Eisenhower on April 14, Marshall warned the Allied supreme commander that the task of discharging troops not needed for occupation duty or the Pacific Theater would "demand the most unselfish and conscientious efforts on the part of everyone." Unless the process was managed properly, he added, the Army might be forced by American public opinion "to take measures which will interfere with redeployment and result in a prolongation of the Japanese war."[35] Marshall added that for psychological reasons it would be best if the first soldiers returned were combat troops from the divisions deepest in Germany, who had therefore been in combat the longest. Leaving nothing to chance, he also urged Eisenhower to "advise all of your people of my deep personal concern as to the responsibility of all commanders for a thorough and intelligent application of our readjustment and redeployment regulations."[36]

Throughout April, Marshall continued to prepare for the implementation of redeployment and partial demobilization, fearing that any snags in the process would hinder the American effort to bring the full weight of its military power to bear in the Pacific. As his first public statements indicated, Truman was also worried about a slackening in the American war effort once Germany was defeated. Toward the end of the month, however, he learned that the United States would soon have a weapon that had the potential to end the war against Japan earlier than expected. On April 25, Stimson gave Truman a more thorough briefing on the atomic bomb. Also present was Major General Leslie Groves, the commander of the Manhattan Engineering District, the code-name for the atomic bomb project. Groves had prepared a memorandum on the development and current status of the bomb. Stimson brought with him a memorandum on the political aspects of the new weapon that began "Within four months we shall have in all probability completed the most terrible weapon ever known in human history, one bomb of which could destroy a whole city."[37] The remainder of Stimson's memo explained England's role in the development of the bomb and discussed in broad terms the problems that would arise once the secret of the atomic bomb was revealed to the world. Looking beyond the war, Stimson encouraged Truman to create a committee to study the postwar implications of the new weapon, including its impact on international relations and its potential for peaceful use. Groves's memo described the history of the project and explained that the bomb would be ready by August 1 and that a second would be ready by the end of the year. The project scientists were working on a second type of bomb, an implosion device, but, Groves explained, they had run into problems. If they were able to solve those problems, an implosion device would be ready by the end of August and subsequent bombs would be ready every ten days after that. In light of the timing, Groves added that "the target is and was always expected to be Japan." The bomb would be dropped by a specially organized unit of the Twentieth Air Force, which was about to move overseas for more training.[38] Groves did not mention their destination, but Truman would eventually learn that the 509th Composite Group would be stationed on Tinian, which had been taken in the Marianas campaign the previous summer. Armed with this new knowledge, Truman could now hope that the bomb would compel Japan's surrender without an invasion. Nevertheless, he also knew that he could not count on the bomb being the winning weapon. Planning for an invasion went forward. It could hardly be otherwise. A lot could happen in four months to upset the timetable Groves had presented. Stimson and Marshall, both of whom had full knowledge of the Manhattan Project, continued to recommend that the United States prepare for the invasion.

Toward that end, Marshall nervously continued to monitor the redeployment situation as V-E Day drew near. Eisenhower assured the chief of staff that he was preparing to move quickly to return the first high-point men to the States as soon after Germany surrendered as possible. He had withdrawn two troop transport groups from action and positioned them so that the first group of returning soldiers would have "an efficient air channel all the way back."[39] On May 2 Marshall cabled Eisenhower and General Joseph McNarney, the commanding general of American forces in the Mediterranean Theater, with a request that they announce R-Day (Redeployment Day) simultaneously. Marshall followed that request with another asking Eisenhower to make R-Day as early as possible, ideally on V-E Day. Eisenhower demurred. It would take at least ten days after V-E Day, May 8, to issue instructions to all of his subordinates. Unsatisfied with that reply, Marshall won Eisenhower's agreement to the compromise date of May 12.[40]

The war in Europe had ended less than a month after Truman took office. In that brief period, the advance of Allied armies in Europe continued to dominate the news. When the American public turned its attention to the Pacific it learned of a growing stalemate and mounting casualties on Okinawa. Soldiers of the Tenth Army were meeting "bitter resistance in all areas." The pace was "damn slow and not cheap," declared one officer in an article in the *Washington Post* on April 24.[41] A little over a week later, readers were told of GIs enduring a hellish bombardment on Kakazu Ridge that left many of the shell-shocked victims little better than "walking dead."[42] On May 8, V-E Day, the *New York Times* reported that the Americans were advancing again but that the gains were being measured in hundreds of yards, a sharp contrast to the sweeping advances made by American armies in the last weeks of the German campaign. The next day, the *Washington Post* carried a grim reminder of the struggle continuing in the Pacific; "Killing Japs Only Okinawa VE Observance," read the caption.[43]

The JCS turned their attention to the final phase of the war against Japan at the very moment that the toll on Okinawa was mounting. In the unfolding debate over how best to accomplish American war aims, the Army's staff officers consistently emphasized the need for defeating Japan as quickly as possible. "Time was of the essence," asserted one staff study.[44] This emphasis on speed reflected Marshall's persistent concern that there were limits to the American people's support for the war. That concern continued to shape his strategic decisions throughout the war. The Europe First strategy, with its emphasis on an early cross-Channel invasion, was predicated on the belief that Americans would not have the patience for a protracted war on the periphery of Europe. By the same token, Marshall accepted divided command of Pacific operations between General MacArthur and Admiral Nimitz because it maintained momentum and kept the public engaged by showing steady progress toward Japan's homeland. The second part of that strategic plan, the invasion of the Japanese homeland, likewise assumed that public support could not be sustained for the time-consuming alternative of blockade and bombardment.[45]

The Combined Chiefs of Staff had formally agreed on this direct approach to defeating Japan at the OCTAGON conference in August 1944. In reality, however, key members on the American side recoiled at the anticipated costs of an invasion. Admiral William D. Leahy, the president's representative on the JCS, favored a strategy of siege, believing that it would destroy Japan's military power at less cost in American lives. To varying degrees Navy and AAF planners agreed with Leahy. Marshall and the Army's planners opposed from the beginning the strategy of blockade and bombardment, for several reasons. They noted that the United States would have to occupy strongpoints closer to Japan to make a blockade effective. In their staff papers, Army planners dismissed what they derisively called the "round the Yellow Sea idea" as time-consuming and ineffectual. Most important, they doubted that a siege would force Japan's unconditional surrender in a timely fashion.

This debate over strategy continued intermittently into the spring of 1945, when the imminent defeat of Germany compelled the Joint Chiefs to settle the issue so they could issue operational directives to MacArthur and Nimitz. The Army found reinforcement for its antiblockade position in a Joint Intelligence Committee report that warned that a siege would prolong the war and encourage Japanese leaders to believe that continued resistance would lead to war weariness in the United States. A subsequent report by the Joint Staff planners in late April endorsed invasion as the only sure way to force Japan's unconditional surrender. A strategy of blockade and bombardment, they warned, would likely lead to a protracted war and a negotiated settlement with Japan. After more wrangling, the JCS agreed that the United States should prepare for the invasion of Japan.[46]

Despite the appearance of finality, however, the JCS decision did not end the debate over strategy. Admiral King had temporarily yielded on the question of invasion but had not abandoned hope that the preinvasion softening up of Japan through blockade and bombardment would force Japan's surrender. The Navy and AAF would have several months to pursue that objective before the invasion took place. On April 30, King indicated his tentative support for the invasion by noting that, depending on the progress of the siege, the JCS could reverse their decision as late as August or September. In any case, King believed that the JCS should submit their plans to the new president for his approval. In the meantime, MacArthur's and Nimitz's staff could continue work on their plans for operation DOWNFALL.[47]

More haggling over the precise wording of the directive to MacArthur and Nimitz followed throughout May, with the main point of contention being at what point in the invasion command would be transferred from Nimitz to MacArthur. The Navy wanted Nimitz to control the amphibious part of the invasion. Once MacArthur's forces were safely ashore, he would take command. Marshall, and, even more emphatically, MacArthur wanted the Army to control the amphibious phase of the invasion. The Navy was unwilling to trust its ships to an Army commander, and the Army was opposed to having an admiral direct the initial phase of what would be the largest and most complex operation in the war. Ultimately, on May 25, the two sides settled on a compromise that left the naval and amphibious phases of the invasion under Nimitz's control except in "case of exigencies," at which time MacArthur would take command. The directive did not, however, explain what exigencies would require MacArthur to take charge. As it turned out, neither the Army nor the Navy believed the matter was actually settled. For the time being, however, the directive provided Nimitz and MacArthur the guidance they needed to begin coordinating plans for the invasion of Kyushu.[48]

Acting on early instructions from the Joint Chiefs, MacArthur's men had already begun planning and had a first draft available by May 28. As originally conceived, DOWNFALL called for units already in the Pacific to make the initial assaults in OLYMPIC and CORONET. Replacements moving from the mainland United States to the western Pacific would fill out the assault forces to be used in November, but the units redeploying from Europe were not expected until early 1946. The redeploying forces would therefore constitute the reserves and follow-up troops for CORONET. Krueger's Sixth Army would conduct the OLYMPIC operation, drawing on a total of fourteen to seventeen divisions, including three Marine divisions, with some staging as far away as Hawaii. Their goal was to seize Kagoshima Wan (Bay) and Ariake Wan and turn them into ports of entry, then move north to establish a line running diagonally from Tsuno on the east coast southwest to Sendai on the west coast, effectively taking possession of the bottom third of Kyushu. That area would be used for the development of airfields and the staging of divisions for CORONET.[49] Robert Eichelberger's Eighth Army would conduct CORONET, the assault on the main island of Honshu, along with the Tenth Army, consisting of divisions redeployed from Europe, taking the Tokyo-Yokohama area first and then moving out onto the Kanto Plain and expanding operations outward until Japan surrendered. The Eighth would use approximately fourteen divisions, two armored, for the initial assault and another ten, furnished through redeployment from Europe, for follow-up operations. According to the May 28 draft prepared by MacArthur's staff, OLYMPIC would involve a total of 776,700 personnel, including reserves and air personnel. CORONET would require a total of 1,026,000. DOWNFALL held to this basic outline in terms of objectives, but there would be significant changes through the summer as Army Forces Pacific (MacArthur's headquarters) refined its plans in coordination with the planning staffs of the Joint Chiefs in Washington and in response to changing circumstances.[50]

In the meantime, however, victory in Europe had triggered the start of demobilization and redeployment. By now, Eisenhower fully appreciated Marshall's unwavering focus on making both processes go smoothly. V-E Day was cause for thanksgiving and celebration, but, as Eisenhower explained, it was important to limit the festivities so that there was no "slackening off in intensity of our efforts against Japan," as he wrote Marshall on May 8. "To drag out receptions," he added, "would be to emphasize over too long a period what we have done rather than what we still have to do."[51] Planning and coordinating the public receptions for America's conquering heroes required sensitivity toward professional egos and alertness to public perceptions. Concerned about the latter, Eisenhower and Marshall were careful to assign representative groups of infantrymen, numbering between twenty and thirty men, to join their commanders in the stateside victory lap. In one instance, on May 30, General Mark Clark and fifty officers and enlisted men arrived in Chicago for a parade after a one-stop flight from Paris. The enlisted men, the news report explained, were there to represent "the thousands of men who had not yet come home and the thousands who never will." Clark's party was greeted by an estimated 750,000 well-wishers, was feted at the city's elegant Palmer House, and then dispersed as the men went their separate ways to visit their families.[52]

Returning larger numbers of high-point men and readying several hundred thousand more for shipment to the Pacific proved far more difficult than returning the first small groups. To begin with, American forces in Europe had to be repositioned before they could be transferred out of the theater. Troops had to be moved, lines of communication established, and new depots created. When Eisenhower requested the return of the XVIII Airborne Corps, which had been loaned to the British at the end of the war, the British commander replied that the large number of German prisoners in the area made it difficult to comply at the moment. As difficulties mounted, Eisenhower lamented to Marshall on May 15 that the requirements of redeployment were "so intricate and involved that all other considerations have had to take secondary places in our plans."[53]

The challenge of sorting out high-point men and replenishing depleted units with low-point troops was made even greater by the need to maintain morale. Trouble began almost immediately. In reality, there was always some element of subjectivity involved. After V-E Day the authorization of battle stars continued as an ongoing process as points were calculated and divisions heading for the Pacific were cleared of men with eighty-five points. At the end of May, Deputy Chief of Staff General Thomas Handy told Eisenhower: "The headaches about the campaign stars are just starting." Handy explained that his office had already received complaints from people who thought they were getting "a raw deal." "These all came in before it was known that there was a payoff on the basis of stars," he added. "I imagine such protests will increase very much in number from now."[54]

The awarding of combat stars had the potential to call into question the fairness of the adjustment system, a cardinal principle of the process, but also played havoc with the efficient readjustment of units for redeployment to the Pacific. For example, after having completed the readjustment process and stabilized its roster, the Second Division, which was slated for CORONET as part of the reserve force, was awarded two additional campaign stars, which put 2,700 men over the eighty-five-point threshold and qualified them for discharge.[55] The Fifth Division, which had already lost 6,100 men through readjustment, lost an additional 600 when they were awarded additional campaign credits. Altogether, the belated awarding of stars exempted an additional 14,000 men in the European Theater from further service.[56] Yet other complications ensued when some units, including the Second Division, were shipped before readjustment could be completed, owing to the sudden availability of more transports than had been expected. Once back in the United States, the Second Division found no experienced or specialist replacements available, while newly trained replacements were being sent exclusively to the Pacific. This called for replacement packages of low-score men from Europe. However, shipping quickly became scarce because of mounting pressure to bring home men qualified for discharge. The Second Division did not get its replacements until October 1945.

In deciding to undertake discharges and redeployment on an individual basis, the War Department had traded efficiency for fairness, which formed the basis for exempting many combat veterans from service. They had done their part and would not be asked to make further sacrifice. On May 11, a day before R-Day, Eisenhower took the underlying logic of the readjustment system a step further by exempting soldiers who had been in combat in two theaters (e.g., North Africa and Europe) from redeployment to the Pacific, even if they had not accumulated eighty-five points.[57] That decision placed additional pressure on the War Department to find replacements from other sources, including draftees, just as Congress was placing new restrictions on the deployment of eighteen-year-old draftees overseas.

The debate over the amount of training eighteen-year-old draftees should receive before combat was one of several ways Congress was beginning to reassert its authority in the waning days of the war in Europe. The United States Army, eight million strong by the spring of 1945, was the largest and most invasive arm of the wartime government. As the Army became engaged with the Germans after D-Day and correspondents and artists like Ernie Pyle and Bill Mauldin were conveying some of the misery and horror of battle to the home front, the American public adopted the foxhole point of view that they had been given on the war, a view that was sympathetic to the infantryman and critical of the "brass." Eric Sevareid reported from the Italian front how impressed he and fellow correspondents were by the "major miscalculations made in high places."[58] This increasingly populist attitude, along with steeply mounting casualties in 1944–1945—over 70 percent of whom were infantrymen—made the draft extension a volatile issue.

This was especially the case because the Army wanted young men—eighteen- and nineteen-year-olds—who could sustain the rigors of combat better and were more open to indoctrination.[59] Consequently, the debate in Congress centered on these "boys." It didn't involve changing the draft age, which was well established, but insisting on adequate training before combat.

Stimson and General Joseph Stilwell, commander of Army Ground Forces headquarters, faced the public on this issue and did not deny that some infantrymen had been killed before their nineteenth birthdays. They insisted, however, that special conditions had made these tragic sacrifices imperative. Usually, inductees were sent to divisions in the United States after fifteen to seventeen weeks of basic training for yet more weapons and tactical training and only then went overseas with that unit. By early 1945 all the divisions in the States had been sent abroad, so new soldiers went from basic training to replacement training centers, where further instruction was limited, and then overseas. Commanders in the theater of operations recommended that replacements be given a further three to six weeks of advanced instruction (in new weapons, mines, booby traps, night-fighting, scouting, and patrolling) in a combat unit in a quiet sector. That proved difficult because casualties in Europe after D-Day were far higher than anticipated, hence the new soldier went directly to a division in combat.

The American public learned of the experience of these GIs in the European Theater from an article, "Orphans of Battle," that appeared in the *Saturday Evening Post* on March 17, 1945. Correspondent Richard C. Hottelet wrote: "Bewildered, belonging to no particular outfit, the infantry replacement gets hustled into action without notice, sufficient training, or the presence of buddies." This had been going on for six months. As early as October 1944 the replacement battalions in theater were empty, and most replacements were going almost immediately to the front. There each new recruit was paired with an experienced soldier, told not to fall asleep on guard duty, to massage his feet in the cold, and to keep his rifle clean. The Pacific Theater had a lower priority for replacements than the European Theater. At a press conference on March 16, 1945, General Stilwell called to respond to Hottelet's article, ruled out division training, probably because divisions were on the move at last, and explained that replacement training centers now employed a more intensive course of preparation. Parents of young GIs were not reassured: the *New York Times* wrote of a wave of resentment against the Army. The issue was becoming more fundamental, for the people felt, according to the *Times*, "that the Army was trying to move in on the people."[60]

All this formed the background of congressional action on the extension of Selective Service with an amendment that required at least six months of training (one version called for twelve) for eighteen-year-olds. Leading the Senate fight for the amendment was Senator Robert Taft (R-Ohio). In a poll asking whether eighteen-year-olds should have a year of training before being sent overseas to fight, or be sent sooner if the Army thought they had enough training, 68 percent of respondents insisted on one year. On March 6, Marshall complained to Eisenhower that Taft had "fulminated" on the floor of the Senate because the eighteen-year-old son of a friend had been killed in Europe. Senate "attacks on the use of these young men and the inadequacy of their training," Marshall added, came at the same time that General MacArthur was "emphatically protesting against the shortage in replacements" and other commanders were opposing any further conversion of their men into infantry replacements. "The combined circumstances," Marshall concluded, "could hardly present a more illogical pressure."[61]

On April 25, the Senate "overwhelmed" the new Truman administration by a vote of fifty to twenty-five on the amendment. In doing so they ignored the expressed wishes of the president and rejected a direct appeal by Marshall, who had warned the amendment could lead to "disaster." The Senate dismissed these warnings as hyperbole. From his seat in the Senate press section, United Press reporter Allan Drury observed in his private journal that the senators had grown restive under "the continued ubiquitous presence of the military." Drury noted that after the struggle over the national service bill there was "a very strong tendency, prompted by the devious bad faith of the two service departments in that unlovely battle, to kick them in the teeth." "The handwriting is on the wall for the roll-top regulars of the Pentagon and the Navy Building," he added, "and much as they hate it their little fling at ruling America is entering its final stages with the war."[62]

Three days later, April 28, as Congress sent the draft extension bill to the president, Senator John Sparkman (D-Alabama) explained that the amendment requiring six months training rested on circumstances that had changed: the imminent defeat of Germany reduced the need for further manpower.[63] In light of the massive redeployment that was scheduled to begin after V-E Day, this was precisely the kind of thinking that Marshall was trying to prevent from taking hold in the public realm. Citing continuing casualties in Europe and troop requests from Eisenhower and MacArthur, Marshall advised Congress that the effect of the amendment would be to increase the shortage of replacements by 50,000 and slow troop discharges. Other sources pointed out that the need for young draftees would remain high as the Army began a massive redeployment under the point system.[64] Nevertheless, on May 9, one day after V-E Day, Congress extended the Selective Training and Service Act for one more year. After staving off a congressional attempt to exempt agricultural workers from the draft, Truman reluctantly approved the bill with the new requirement that no one inducted into the Army or Navy under nineteen years old would be ordered into combat service "until he has been given at least 6 months of military training of such character and to the extent necessary to prepare such inductee for combat duty."[65]

The congressional debate over renewal of the draft pointed to a broad and growing sentiment on Capitol Hill and among the American public against the continuing intrusion of the federal government into people's lives and fates. Truman prevailed on the exemption of agricultural workers by appealing to the public's sense of fairness. Did congressmen really believe that farm work was more valuable than all other forms of work? The far-reaching implications of such a blanket exemption were enough to keep most Democrats in line, including southerners, who typically voted with Republicans such as Taft. But the use of eighteen-year-olds in combat was a far more emotional issue. Congressmen were less willing to be assuaged by assurances from a War Department whose credibility they now openly questioned. In February 1945 Congressman William Hess (R-Ohio) twice accused the War Department of breaking an earlier pledge not to send eighteen-year-olds overseas until they received a year's training.

By early May, congressional suspicion of the Army was everywhere. Marshall was dismayed to learn that testimony on the demobilization and redeployment plan given in executive session to the House Military Affairs Committee had been leaked to the press. The *Washington Post* chided "irresponsible congressmen" for the leak, but the paper's editors doubted that any damage had been done and admonished the War Department that considering the current level of anxiety in the public it was best to be as open as possible about its plans. "Our soldiers, their families and the rest of the civilian population," observed the editors, "will be greatly relieved to learn that demobilization is expected to get underway speedily and proceed on a fairly broad scale after Germany's surrender."[66] Marshall, of course, would have taken issue with the *Post*'s emphasis on a "speedy and broad" demobilization. That sent the wrong message. The following day, the War Department released a detailed outline of its demobilization plans in order to prevent any misconceptions from taking hold in the public.

The press release, published on May 6, highlighted the logistical challenges involved in preparing for the final phase of fighting in the Pacific war. The Army would maintain a force of seven million men and women in uniform but hoped to discharge about two million men during the course of the year, two-thirds from the European Theater and about a third from the Pacific, but redeployment *to* the Pacific remained the top priority. Shipping would be tight, and even though 800 transport planes and three converted British ocean liners would be used, in addition to available shipping, it would take a year to get those eligible for discharge home. In what must have seemed like an understatement to all involved, the War Department conceded: "We cannot expect every phase of our plans to work to perfection." The War Department was hopeful, however, that it could count on Americans to meet the coming challenges with understanding and courage.[67]

On May 8, three days after the demobilization plans were leaked to the press, members of the House Military Affairs Committee revealed that the Army was planning for a peacetime establishment of approximately four and a half million men, four million of whom would be reserves. The committee's chairman, Andrew May (D-Kentucky), issued a written denial of the story, but several members of the committee insisted that the initial report was true. The news that Army leaders planned for a peacetime force considerably larger than its prewar predecessor and that they counted on a peacetime draft to fill the ranks and provide for the reserves was not a revelation. What was new was the specific numbers, though Marshall was on record as supporting Universal Military Training and a larger postwar army. Most congressional leaders, however, firmly opposed Universal Military Training and suspected that the Army wanted to maintain its power after the war. The leak of the Army proposal, in addition to being yet another exposure of secret testimony, fed an ongoing debate over the nature of the postwar military establishment.[68]

Skepticism bordering on cynicism toward the Army was apparent even at the moment of victory. Shortly after V-E Day, *Washington Post* columnist Marquis Childs reported that GIs in Europe viewed the Army's failure to rotate long-serving soldiers home for leave as a breach of trust. According to Childs, the Army's explanation for the breakdown—a shortage of shipping—did not hold water with the soldiers. Assessing the mood of the men overseas, Childs warned that it would be "supremely important" for the War Department to keep its promises once demobilization began. If the War Department "muffed" the discharge process, "if a few brass hats keep men in service merely to enhance the prestige of certain commanding officers," he warned, "then the problems of the Administration will be grave indeed."[69]

The gulf between enlisted men and the "brass hats" was further underscored by yet another leak, this one from secret testimony given by Marshall to the Senate Military Affairs Committee. According to political gossip columnist Drew Pearson, the chief of staff told the senators that he was worried about the large number of senior officers, notably "Blood and Guts" General George S. Patton, who were "clamoring" to fight Japan.[70]

Michigan Republican Albert Engel determined to tackle the Army head on. During an Appropriations Committee session, Engel launched what one correspondent described as "an attack on War Department's recently announced point system for demobilization." Engel, who said he was worried about the cost of dependency allowances, wanted the Army to change its system for awarding points to fathers with more than three children. Under the Army's plan, fathers received points for their first three children but no additional points if they had four or more. Engel asserted that these men were needed at home now that Germany was defeated and he threatened to attach a crippling amendment to the Army appropriations bill if the Army did not change its policy. Congressman May promised to resist any such measure and pleaded with his colleagues to have "confidence in the judgment of the Army's leaders."[71] May's plea proved futile, and the Military Affairs Committee was eventually forced to hold hearings on the subject in mid-June.

The assault on the Army's point system was only beginning. As *Time* noted in an article dated May 14, "Congressmen's mail is already heavy with letters from kin demanding to know why Joe can't come home. Congressmen themselves, breathing the air of victory, are causing the Army anxiety with their new eagerness to move in on things."[72] While Congressman Engel complained about the Army's neglecting the cost of dependency allowances, Senator Johnson of Colorado criticized the entire point system as too complicated and prone to error. In its place he recommended a simpler alternative, dubbed FIFO (First In First Out). The Army responded by pointing out that crediting only length of service did not take into account other factors essential to fairness, such as the serviceman's exposure to danger or hardship.[73] Other attacks on the Adjusted Rating System were less easily repulsed. Many of the ongoing challenges the Army faced were related to the needs of industry for laborers with special skills. Businessmen and many government administrators argued that the end of the war in Europe made it possible to release skilled workers from service according to the degree of their usefulness at home. The coal industry was particularly insistent, warning that fuel shortages would appear in the North with the onset of winter. In mid-May, Undersecretary of War Patterson fended off a request for the release of 5,000 coal miners by telling Fred Vinson, a former congressman from Kentucky who was the OWMR's new director and Byrne's successor, that it could only be accomplished "at the expense of other soldiers who had seen longer and more arduous service." Lest Vinson miss the obvious consequences for morale, Patterson added: "It would cause resentment by soldiers generally."[74]

Patterson could have added that the constant barrage of criticism directed at the Army and the War Department was already having an impact on the morale of the officers working in the newly constructed Pentagon. Writing to Eisenhower at the end of May, Deputy Chief of Staff Thomas Handy observed, "The public and the Congressional people are critical and becoming more so, of nearly everything the War Department does. I suppose it is more or less a natural reaction. From all indications it is going to be one hell of a job to keep the war in any priority." "That statement sounds strange," he admitted, "but it is literally true. From the standpoint of public relations the War Department has by far a more difficult job than it has ever had."[75]

In some respects, the Army's efforts to demonstrate that they understood the public mood further encouraged Americans to expect an accelerated transition to peacetime conditions. Statements explaining the Adjusted Rating Scores and the process of redeployment invariably contained admonitions about the huge obstacles to be overcome in the war against Japan. But they also invariably included statements, such as Eisenhower's, telling soldiers that although some men under his command would join the fight against Japan, "some—and I trust in ever-increasing numbers—will soon experience the joy of returning home."[76] "The transfer of troops, planes, and supplies to the Pacific," Marshall assured GIs, in a statement published on May 6, "will be carried out with the utmost speed to return the long-term veterans and to secure an early and final victory so that you may return to your homes." The Army added to its problems by using estimates that quickly assumed the aspect of fixed targets. For example, according to the War Department's May 6 press release explaining the process of redeployment, in the coming year the Army expected to release 1,300,000 men from service based on their Adjusted Rating Scores. But they also expected to release approximately 700,000 more because of sickness, wounds, or age. That brought the total to a neat and easily remembered figure of two million in the first year after V-E

Day.[77] Before long Army staff officers found themselves straining to provide enough seasoned troops for the Pacific while meeting their new
"obligation" to release two million men from service.

Marshall's fears about a general letdown after V-E Day were being realized. Congress, the public, and some War Program administrators were
placing domestic priorities ahead of the Pacific war. Congressional calls to
exempt agricultural laborers and discharge coal miners were intended to
provide immediate relief from some of the burdens of the war. The War
Department's refusal to budge in either instance angered some in Congress,
but business leaders and their congressional supporters were even more
critical of what they perceived as the Army's obstruction of reconversion.
"Bear in mind," explained one business publication, *"that the Army spirit is
hostile to reconversion."* The Army, according to the *Kiplinger Washington
Letter*, took that approach because it mistrusted industry leaders and accused them of desiring *"business as usual."* Industry leaders and their allies
in Congress countered that business had delivered throughout the war and
would continue to meet its obligations. Undersecretary Patterson and
Army planners were "emotional" and "impractical." Cuts in orders were already creating unemployment. Unless the civilian economy picked up the
slack there would be mass unemployment, "which will give the jitters even
to war workers, and cause instability and impair production for the Jap
war."[78] It is not going too far to say that by V-E Day the Army was becoming
the prime target for frustration and anger; it was coming to represent a war
of which Americans were tiring.

Reconversion and redeployment to the Pacific dominated the news after
V-E Day, even as the battle on Okinawa continued to rage. In the week after
Germany surrendered, the War Department and the OWMR issued a series
of reports and held several press conferences to spell out in greater detail
what Americans could expect as the United States prepared for the final
campaigns against Japan. The Army established the timetables for the overlapping processes of redeployment and demobilization, which in turn imposed limits on the pace of reconversion. The Army pressed the public to
stay the course until the final battles in the Pacific were won. Vinson accepted the Army's primacy in the process, but he also believed that there

had to be better coordination between his agency and the Army. When he learned that Secretary Stimson wanted the president to make a joint statement to Congress on redeployment, Vinson asked Truman on May 9 to instruct the War Department to consult with him before making any such statement. Vinson explained that the "entire reconversion program, as well as our ability to meet minimum domestic requirements for food and clothing and our ability to supply any of the needs of liberated areas—all of these depend in large measure on the redeployment plans as finally adopted by the Joint Chiefs of Staff."[79] Truman authorized Vinson to consult directly with the Army on the proposed message but also indicated that he was not keen on going before Congress to deliver the message in person.[80]

Vinson was fortunate in being able to count on having a close working relationship with the president, who described Vinson as "absolutely loyal and trustworthy."[81] The two men had become friends when they served in Congress, Truman in the Senate and Vinson in the House. Vinson, like Truman, was widely considered to be a political moderate, although, like Truman, he strongly supported New Deal legislation and programs. Both men had reputations as hard workers who did not seek the limelight. Neither was seen as an ideologue, a perception that owed much to their being representatives from border states. Vinson gained a reputation as an expert on tax legislation and won praise for his work on the American delegation to the Bretton Woods Conference, the July 1944 meeting in New Hampshire between America and its allies that established postwar global monetary policy. During the war he also served as director of the Office of Economic Stabilization, a position that made him the nation's chief inflation watchdog. Despite the confrontational nature of that post, he maintained his contacts with his former congressional colleagues and managed to avoid making any serious political enemies.[82] In March 1945 the Senate unanimously approved his appointment as federal loan administrator. One of his first acts in that role was to meet with members of the Senate at the invitation of Vice-President Truman.[83]

When Vinson replaced Byrnes on April 7, he was jumping onto a moving train. The American war economy required two forms of constraint, one to reconfigure business and industry so that enough resources were channeled into production of weapons and matériel to defeat the Japanese, the other, impinging on the individual, to withhold food, durables, and fuel from consumers for the same purpose while rationing and allocating enough for necessities. In the former case a major unraveling of constraint and a shift toward a market economy began in the weeks before V-E Day and gained momentum right after. Byrnes had already hinted at some of the changes in the offing, and the War and Navy Departments had begun to cancel contracts for equipment they believed they no longer needed. All could agree that with the end of the war in Europe and the defeat of the Japanese navy, the American Navy did not need all the ships, or the AAF all the airplanes, under contract. In March an order for seventy-two ships was canceled, offering a foretaste of what many feared would be a pell-mell shift to reconversion.

Germany's surrender forced Vinson to issue his first report on reconversion before he could obtain the information he needed from the Pentagon. The report, issued on May 10 and titled "The War—Phase Two," addressed the overlapping components of the one-front war; the systems of discharge and redeployment; war production and its effects on employment needs; and the availability of consumer goods in the second phase of the war. Regarding the latter, at least, Vinson gave the public little cause for joy. There would be some relaxation on controls; the dimming of lights—the "brownout"—was no longer required, and the ban on horse racing was lifted, as was the curfew that required nightclubs and bars to close early. For the most part Vinson was asking Americans to maintain what the *New York Times* described as a "Spartan regimen."[84] Of the three most in-demand items of rationed food—sugar, butter, and meat—the portions of sugar, fifteen pounds a year for household use and fifteen pounds for canning, and butter would remain the same, and meat was not expected to reach earlier levels until the late fall. The amount of leather available for shoe uppers was also reduced. A reduced workforce in the mines would lower coal supplies by 20 percent, meaning chillier homes next winter. The meager gas ration, which was determined by one's employment, was doubled, but new tire supplies were reduced by three-eighths. Cotton goods were in short supply and were expensive because planting had been reduced by half, due to labor and equipment shortages and because the Army needed cotton uniforms and tents for redeployed troops in the Pacific. Rayon stockings gave way to rayon mosquito bars to protect against malaria.[85]

Vinson predicted some easing in war production that would in turn create more consumer items such as radios, vacuum cleaners, and other appliances by the end of the summer of 1945. He emphasized, however, that achieving Japan's unconditional surrender and occupying the home islands would require "all our effort toward war, and toward production." There would be a small reduction in war production, perhaps as much as 15 percent, but most war industry workers would have to remain on the job. That meant that there would be a modest increase in unemployment, much of which would consist of workers "temporarily out of work between jobs."[86]

Labor leaders reacted sharply to what they perceived as Vinson's failure to address the looming danger of high unemployment. Ted Silvey, chair of the Congress of Industrial Organizations Reconversion Committee ridiculed Vinson's prediction of only a 10–15 percent cutback in war orders in the coming months. "It is ridiculous to use these figures," Silvey told reporters, "which the military procurement officers themselves know to be wrong, and in some Pollyanna manner expect that unemployment will somehow or other work out all right if we don't talk about it."[87] As if to underscore Silvey's point, conversion to peacetime production moved ahead even while consumer restraints remained in force. In May the AAF canceled contracts for 17,000 airplanes, with job losses in this case spread out over the coming year, totaling 450,000. Just days after Vinson issued his report, a *New York Times* headline announced: "U.S. Industry Begins Shift to Peace Basis," followed by the more sobering subheading " 'Second Phase' of War Is Expected to Pose Employment Problems, Idleness a Problem, Labor Aware of Danger." Using a procedure called "spot authorization," the government was easing into reconversion by giving seventy-two selected industries the signal and the means to return to civilian production. The object, the administration said, was to reduce the time between the cancelation of war orders and peacetime production. On May 11 the War Production Board revoked seventy-three controls, including those on metals, and promised that half of all controls would be removed in a few months.[88]

Business commentators and various members of Congress approached the OWMR report from a different perspective than labor but were no less disapproving. These observers found it difficult to believe that the armed forces would need eleven million men and women in uniform and even more food and supplies than had been required for the two-front war. Supporting that contention was a May 21 article from the business periodical *Barron's*, reporting that War Production Board director Julius Krug was hinting that deeper cuts were imminent only two weeks after Vinson released his report. The problem, according to *Barron's*, lay with the Pentagon's extravagant plans, plans that "undoubtedly envisage, as has been said of all military plans, anything up to an invasion of the moon."[89] The same journal reported that a behind-the-scenes struggle was taking place between Vinson and the Army. "There is a growing feeling among some of the wiser congressional heads," one article explained, "that General Brehon Somervell, Army Supply Chief, has set his sights too high on war production for a single enemy." These congressmen, it continued, "have some encouragement from the Vinson office." All indications were that Somervell would be on the hot seat when Congress took up the Army appropriations bill for the fiscal year beginning on July 1.[90]

It remains unclear what Vinson or members of his staff may have been saying to congressmen about the War Department's plans for the one-front war. We do know, however, that Vinson remained skeptical about the Army's manpower and procurement needs. He was present when, on May 14, Somervell met with the Advisory Board of the OWMR to explain why the Army needs remained so high after V-E Day. "The problem of staging zones in the Pacific is terrific," Somervell explained. "Manila is a shambles, the Luzon valley is destroyed." According to the minutes, Somervell "likened the transfer problem from Europe to the Pacific to moving all of Philadelphia to the Philippines, making the point that movement can only be at the rate material can be received." He estimated that overall military production would decrease by 16 percent by the end of the year. Further reductions might be possible, but the demanding conditions in the Pacific were such that he did not want to make any firm predictions. Although the members of the Advisory Board politely concluded that Somervell's was "one of the best presentations yet made to the Board," their comments the next day made it clear that he had not changed their minds about the need to step up the pace of reconversion.[91]

The day after Somervell's presentation, Vinson called Somervell's boss and asked to speak to him about the Army's requirements for the campaign against Japan. Marshall asked Vinson for a day to collect some solid information and instructed Somervell to prepare a report for the meeting. Somervell responded the same day with a defense of the Army's procurement program. He began his report by suggesting that Vinson needed to be reminded that the Army's force levels would drop only 5 percent in the coming year and that all those men, no matter where they were stationed, would need shelter, clothing, and food. Somervell explained to Marshall that Vinson questioned the relationship between procurement and strategy. In particular, Vinson wanted to know "if we intend to soften up the Japanese for three to six months, why we could not get a large amount of material in Europe into the Pacific and hence would not have to manufacture as much material here." According to Somervell, Vinson was especially concerned by domestic political reaction to the Army's plans, having said that "Congress is red-headed and in about as dangerous a mood as he has ever known" and that he wanted to have "as much information as possible to try to ward off calamity on the economic front." Here, Somervell momentarily shifted the onus to Marshall by advising him that he would need to explain to Vinson the reasons for the size of the Army and for the plan of operations.

Returning to his responsibilities as supply chief, Somervell stressed to his boss that he was already incorporating the maximum use of matériels in Europe into his estimates and that if anything "we may have counted on using a larger percentage of the equipment than we will actually be able to recover or more than we can actually move in time to meet the requirements." Somervell assured Marshall that his organization was constantly seeking to prune the estimates and reduce requirements "as fast as it was prudent to do so." He understood that the Army's requirements in some areas, such as cotton textiles, seemed onerous, but that was because production had been reduced from levels reached earlier in the war. The Army was taking a large bite, 20 percent, out of a smaller apple. Vinson could solve the problem, according to Somervell, by stimulating production to the level it had reached in 1942. The Army's requirements for textiles and other materials in short supply, such as shoe leather, had been reviewed and approved by the appropriate agencies, and in the case of shoes and boots the Army had reduced its requirements to what the quartermaster general called a "dangerously low" level. The larger problem, Somervell believed, was one of trust and confidence in the Army's judgment. He concluded that Vinson wanted to know "enough about the plans in the Pacific to convince himself that the Army which is planned for the next year is not in excess of needs and that full utilization is being made of available resources in Europe."[92]

Somervell was most disturbed by what he saw as Vinson's intrusion into the realm of military strategy. In a postscript to his memo to Marshall, Somervell said that he had come away from his conversation with Vinson with the impression that the mobilization director thought that by prolonging the period of blockade and bombardment the United States could delay the invasion and thus reduce production requirements. Somervell, like Marshall, rejected such thinking. He asserted that if the United States opted for a strategy of protracted war—for unconditional surrender—the requirements for matériel would remain the same, the loss of life would be greater, and related expenses, notably soldiers' pay, would also be greater.[93] Marshall had made these arguments before—in the meetings of the Joint Chiefs, in congressional hearings, and in off-the-record press conferences—but skepticism about American strategy remained strong in all three groups. Not surprisingly, Somervell failed to sway Vinson as well.

Following his meeting with Marshall, who had Somervell's report to rely on, Vinson remained concerned that the War Department and Army general staff did not appreciate how restive the public was getting under the constraints of the wartime economy. The mobilization director tried again to make that point when he attended a meeting of the JCS on May 22. Vinson told the group that owing to a lack of information, the public was concerned about the status of the war after V-E Day, the progress of reconversion, looming unemployment, and food shortages. Congress was very busy, he added, and was in a "strange frame of mind due to its many duties and the problems facing it." Vinson also warned of growing labor unrest, citing a trucking strike in Chicago and continuing disruption in the anthracite fields. The scarcity of food, however, was the "toughest and most irritating factor." Vinson depicted the public as "stirred up" and "susceptible to mistaken conclusions." He asked again for information on the amount of matériel needed for the war against Japan and specifically requested a review of aircraft requirements. If the military could reduce its use of strategic materials it would greatly aid the process of reconversion. According to the minutes, Vinson concluded his initial statement by saying that he was "afraid of unrest in the country. He never saw the people in their present frame of mind before."[94]

Vinson was not known as an alarmist; indeed, the opposite was true. Nevertheless, his assessment of the public mood was notably dire. Perhaps he was expressing the feelings of his congressional colleagues who were hearing complaints from their constituents. He may also have been conveying the president's determination to avoid a recession like the one that had followed World War I. Marshall tried to assure Vinson that he understood the situation but offered little hope that the Army would scale back its requirements. Instead, Marshall explained that in order to save lives in the campaign against Japan the Army would be using more troops and aircraft crews as reserves than had been the case in the European Theater. An extra regiment in each division would increase a soldier's chances of survival by 35 percent. Marshall added that he could not count on the Soviet Union's entry into the war or on the Japanese surrendering. Therefore, "production must be kept up."[95] Vinson replied that the next six months were critical and asked for realistic but gradual cutbacks in order to prevent economic problems after the war.

Admiral Leahy had the final word on the subject, declaring that he agreed with Vinson and believed that he had brought out "more clearly a view of the domestic situation."[96] The JCS minutes, which are more of a summary rather than a verbatim transcript of what was said, leave readers wondering about the import of Leahy's statement. If Leahy agreed with Vinson about the strain on the economy did he believe that the Army could reduce its requirements in manpower and supplies and still carry out its plans for the Pacific war? Or did he think that the Army should change its strategy for defeating Japan and adopt an approach that did not make such heavy exactions on the economy?

Army planners insisted that the alternative to bombardment and blockade was a recipe for protracted war, one that would not force Japan's unconditional surrender at an acceptable cost. But what if the Soviet Union entered the war? Would that reduce the size of the American force needed to subdue Japan, relieve pressure on the home front, and speed up demobilization? Marshall anticipated those questions when he addressed a subcommittee of the House Appropriations Committee in a closed session on May 25. He explained that the United States would probably need fewer troops if the Soviet Union entered the war but that whether it would remained one of the "imponderables" at present. Asked about a strategy of bombardment and blockade, Marshall identified the numerous problems with that approach, including the cost to taxpayers of a prolonged campaign. He also noted that Americans needed to consider how the Chinese would feel about the continued presence of Japanese troops in their country and warned that the occupation of strongpoints from which to launch an effective blockade could result in a costly war of attrition, with casualties approximating those expected from a direct assault.[97]

Although Marshall testified in closed session, members of the subcommittee promptly divulged much of what was said to reporters. Several congressmen told the press that the war would be longer than expected and there would be no big reduction in expenditures in the coming fiscal year. There was not much new there; the War Department and OWMR had already said as much in their public reports. More surprising, however, was the seemingly incongruous prediction by several committee members that "there may soon be another sharp reduction in the size of the Army." According to the *New York Times*, several unidentified congressmen elaborated on that point by saying that the rate of demobilization "will depend on developments of the next few months. Should the Soviet Union enter the war against Japan, they explained, this country could presumably use fewer men in the Pacific. They emphasized, however, that General Marshall did not discuss the prospect of the Soviet Union fighting Japan."[98]

This was the third time in less than a month that congressmen had revealed information presented in closed sessions. The most controversial aspect of the leaked information concerned Marshall's impromptu assessment of the

Russian factor in the Army's calculations. Congressional speculation on this subject and the reporting of it by the *New York Times* appeared to violate recently adopted censorship rules recommended by Marshall that advised against press speculation about "future war plans." In keeping with his wishes, the Office of Censorship instructed the press that speculation about the "intentions of the Soviet Union toward Japan" was a matter of particular concern and should be avoided.[99] Not surprisingly, some members of the press had protested the new strictures as yet another attempt by the War Department to impose its regimentation on the home front. Journalist I. F. Stone pointed to the folly of such efforts by noting that the Japanese were doing a lot more speculating about Russian intentions than the Americans were. Marshall and the head of the censorship office, Byron Price, knew that they could not squelch all public conjecture about the Soviet Union's entry into the war. Marshall worried, however, that such speculation, especially if it were linked to official sources, might provoke a Japanese attack on the Red Army before it had completed the transfer of forces from Europe to the Far Eastern Front. Following his testimony to the subcommittee, Marshall was surprised to see his name attached to the kind of story he wanted to suppress.

It did not help that the offending congressmen made it clear that they were drawing their own conclusions about the likelihood and probable effects of the Soviet Union's entry into the war. It was unlikely that readers would believe that the subject had not been discussed during the hearing. Perhaps even more disconcerting from Marshall's perspective was the potential effect of congressional speculation on a key component of the Army's plans. By raising the possibility of Soviet entry into the war "in the next few months," the anonymous congressmen encouraged the public to believe that the Army would not need to follow through on its redeployment plans. The timing was particularly troubling. In the next few months, Americans would be looking for relief from the Soviet Union just as hundreds of thousands of troops were crossing the United States en route to the Pacific Theater.

Marshall, his subordinates on the Army general staff, and the civilian heads of the War Department, notably Stimson and Patterson, had adopted a complex strategy for defeating Japan, one that necessitated the military's continued intrusion into the civilian economy and sustained its command of millions of the nation's young men at the moment when most Americans expected relief from such burdens. The resulting criticism of the war leaders caused them to fear that Americans' unwillingness to continue to sacrifice for the war would encourage the Japanese to hold out in the hopes that by protracting the struggle they could force the United States to accept an incomplete victory. Therefore, the Japanese had to be made to see that the United States was fully committed to invading their home islands with the overwhelming force that only an army of seven million men backed by unlimited firepower could produce. Patterson had always opposed calls for reconversion, but he found the recent actions by the officials in OWMR even less welcome now because they implicitly questioned the fundamental precepts of the Army's plan for victory. "The Vinson office," complained Patterson, "is already getting restless—due to a number of people in it who would like to be consulted on the strategy of the Pacific War."[100]

Despite the growing drumbeat of criticism directed at the Army, Truman continued to support Marshall's strategy for victory over Japan. On June 1 he submitted to Congress the address that the War Department had been working on since early May when Vinson first heard about it. Presidential counselor Judge Samuel Rosenman oversaw some revisions of the lengthy message, but the final version faithfully conveyed the War Department's concerns about the challenges the United States faced in the Pacific.[101] Nearly two-thirds of the Memorial Day message celebrated the contributions of the different branches of the armed forces and praised the courage and sacrifices of the soldiers, sailors, and airmen who had contributed to the defeat of Germany. Turning to the Pacific, the president summarized the process for demobilization and redeployment and assured Congress that everything was being done to bring eligible soldiers home from Europe as quickly as possible. The Army would need a little less than seven million men for the upcoming campaigns against Japan, which would allow for the release of 1,300,000 high-point men in the coming year. Another 700,000 would leave the Army due to wounds, sickness, or age, bringing the total to the now familiar two million discharges in the next twelve months.[102]

When Truman's message finally got to the business of winning the war against Japan, he cited the casualty figures from the ongoing battle for

Okinawa to paint a grim picture of the struggle ahead. As American forces advanced they would face the main bulk of the Japanese army for the first time. There would be no easy road to victory. Bombardment and blockade would not suffice; infantrymen backed by tanks, artillery, and flamethrowers would have to defeat an entrenched and fanatical Japanese army on the ground. The supplies required for that job would be staggeringly vast, as were the distances they would have to travel to reach the war zone. Truman cited the Navy's need for extensive repairs to damaged ships and called on shipyard workers to stay on the job. He also explained that the demands on public transportation would increase in the coming months, making domestic travel even more difficult. The material requirements of the final campaigns would allow for only small changes in war production; the home front would need to produce fewer tanks, planes, and artillery pieces, but munitions output would nearly match that of 1944. The mobilized economy would have to produce more items needed specifically for war in the Pacific, including the antimalarial drug atabrine, steel barges, wire and insect screening cloth, combat boots, cotton uniforms, amphibious trucks, raincoats, distillation units, radio relay units, special railway equipment, and motorized shop equipment. Textiles and shoe leather would remain limited on the home market, as would food, given the need to feed a seven-million-man army and the newly liberated areas in Europe.[103]

The president's message concluded with a summons to Americans to make the final exertions necessary to bring about the "unconditional surrender of Japan." The Japanese had abandoned their dreams of conquest, but they were counting on Americans becoming weary of the war's sacrifices. "They hope that our desire to see our soldiers and sailors home again and the temptation to return to the comforts and profits of peace will force us to settle for some compromise short of unconditional surrender." "They should know better," the president added. "They should realize that this Nation, now at the peak of its military strength, will not relax, will not weaken in its purpose."[104]

Truman's message served several purposes. Some observers speculated that it was a warning directed at the Japanese. But it was also aimed at the critics in the administration and Congress who thought the Army's plans placed an unnecessary burden on the home front. By submitting the message to Congress, Truman put his stamp of approval on the Army's plans and no doubt reassured Marshall that he was not wavering.

The public reaction was muted. Most of the information the message contained on redeployment, demobilization, and reconversion had appeared in print in the preceding month. The first reports were merely summaries, but later accounts raise some question, although indirectly, about the Army's ability to immediately employ all of the men and equipment it was gathering.[105] Truman's message had little impact on the government in Tokyo. It also did little to change the minds of those in Congress, business, and organized labor who demanded a more rapid reconversion to a peacetime economy. In early June, proponents of reconversion used hearings on a bill to reauthorize the Office of Price Administration to prod the administration into relaxing wartime restrictions. The most New Deal–like agency to emerge as part of the wartime mobilization of the economy, the Office of Price Administration was second only to the Army as an intrusive presence in the daily lives of citizens. Critics blamed the agency for the meat shortage and saw it as a haven for "pip-squeaks and long-haired left-wingers" who strangled free enterprise in the name of battling inflation.[106] Privately, Senator Robert Taft criticized the agency as an organization run by New Deal economists bent on appeasing labor and regulating profits. "Now," he added, "we are moving into the post-war period, and sometime before long the reconversion problems will outweigh war production in importance."[107] Publicly, Taft told the Senate that "we are beginning the reconversion period now and it is time to relax price controls."[108] On the same day, Drew Pearson reported that pressure for "swift action" on the "Reconversion Mess" was mounting within the ranks of labor. According to Pearson, R. J. Thomas, president of the Auto Workers Union of the Congress of Industrial Organizations met with Truman to express his concerns about the fates of the tens of thousands of auto and aircraft workers who were being fired daily. Truman could only promise that he would consider Thomas's recommendations on how to deal with the problem.[109] Vinson's OWMR report had predicted that the gradual shift toward a peacetime economy would absorb many of the newly unemployed workers, but as long as industry remained geared up for war and moved only selectively away from demobilization, that reshuffling process would leave the affected workers in a state of prolonged anxiety.

In the meantime, Marshall harbored his own anxieties about his ability to command the confidence of the nation's leaders in the months ahead. Despite the president's Memorial Day message, the challenges to the Army's authority continued unabated. During the first week of June Congress led off its hearings on Universal Military Training with several days' testimony by opponents of the program.[110] The press continued to speculate about "when and if" the Soviet Union would enter the war against Japan, and irate senators questioned other aspects of War Department censorship policies.[111] Perhaps most important, appropriations hearings for the Army's budget, which had begun with the leak of Marshall's testimony in closed session, had the potential to become a referendum on his strategy for the one-front war.

Marshall admitted as much when he took the unusual step of confiding his concerns to John Callan O'Laughlin, the owner and editor of the *Army and Navy Journal* and a Republican Party adviser. O'Laughlin had been an associate of Theodore Roosevelt and served briefly as assistant secretary of state before the Rough Rider left office. During the first decades of the century O'Laughlin was also a prominent journalist and, like many Republicans in the relatively quiescent 1920s, had a favorable opinion of Japan and its leaders, some of whom he met when he was secretary to the American Commission to the Tokyo Exposition of 1912.[112] As editor of the *Army and Navy Journal*, a specialized periodical dealing with service news and world affairs, O'Laughlin had access to administration figures and members of Congress. He also wrote and circulated a typewritten political newsletter to prominent Republicans, most notably former president Herbert Hoover. The newsletter of June 9 was especially informative. "The sensational development of the week," O'Laughlin wrote, "was the revelation of General Marshall's purpose to retire from the Office of Chief of Staff."[113]

According to O'Laughlin, Marshall had told him that he wanted to retire and that he would recommend Dwight Eisenhower to replace him. Marshall explained that now that Germany was defeated, "every contingency in connection with the reduction of Japan had been foreseen," and all plans and missions had been determined and deployments set in motion, he could turn the office over to a successor. O'Laughlin told Hoover that he did not know why Marshall had bared his "secret soul" in their meeting but noted that the general had said that he had received reports of "dwindling public confidence" in his conduct of the war. Marshall added that in Congress "there was a growing disposition to criticize everything he said and recommends." Marshall cited Universal Military Training as an example. O'Laughlin noted as an aside that Universal Military Training had no chance of passing and added that although Marshall had once been the most popular official on the Hill, he had "aroused resentment there by the bitter complaints he has addressed to the House Appropriations Committee at the revelation by members of confidential testimony which he had given." Marshall, according to O'Laughlin, had also drafted a sharp letter to the Senate Military Affairs Committee regarding their leaking of confidential testimony, which his aides had convinced him not to send.[114]

O'Laughlin speculated on other reasons for Marshall's readiness to retire; these included his increasingly difficult interactions with his Navy counterpart, Admiral Ernest King, and an understandable desire to put down the enormous burden that he had been shouldering since he became chief of staff in 1939. O'Laughlin also speculated that Marshall may have felt slighted by his not having been addressed by his proper title, "General of the Army," in Truman's recent Memorial Day message. The latter incident suggested to O'Laughlin that Marshall's relationship with the new president was not as close as Marshall had hoped. O'Laughlin noted on that score that Marshall had said he had been "relieved" to see that Truman endorsed the policy of unconditional surrender in his message, a reaction that indicated that Marshall had been uncertain about the president's commitment to the policy before that.

O'Laughlin's extensive account of his extraordinary meeting with Marshall was rambling and far-ranging, making it difficult to discern with any precision what precipitated Marshall's conversation. Marshall had mentioned to Eisenhower in a letter he sent immediately after V-E Day that he might retire in the next few months.[115] In O'Laughlin's account Marshall at first seemed ready to retire immediately, but later in his letter O'Laughlin speculated that Eisenhower would return to the United States for several months' leave before taking the job, a timeline that was more consistent with Marshall's earlier statement to Eisenhower. O'Laughlin did not know about Marshall's letter to Eisenhower but he surmised that Marshall had begun to think of retirement while FDR was still alive. O'Laughlin recalled that as Germany neared defeat Marshall had been greatly interested in O'Laughlin's prediction that Japan might surrender before Germany did. The sudden surrender of both enemies would have been the ideal moment for Marshall to relinquish command of the Army. Marshall told O'Laughlin that Japan had not accepted defeat at that time because the "Manchurian Gang,"—the militarists who had steered Japan into war beginning in 1931—still controlled the government. Nevertheless, Marshall said that his reports indicated that the "peace party" was growing in Japan and he expected them to prevail in a "short time," providing there was "no cessation of our attacks or the preparations we are making for a long war."[116]

At times, O'Laughlin's account makes it difficult to discern whether he was accurately summarizing the general's statements or embellishing them with his own inferences and asides. In relating Marshall's views on Japanese politics, O'Laughlin wrote that the recent bombing of several outbuildings of the imperial palace "was regretted in Washington because we want to use the Emperor both in the peace negotiations and in preventing disorders after surrender." The use of the passive voice "was regretted in Washington" obscures the author of that statement. Marshall may have said something similar, but it could just as easily have been O'Laughlin's own reading of the situation. That was almost certainly the case when in the same letter he incorrectly deduced that Lieutenant General Joseph Stilwell, who had commanded American forces in China, was meeting with MacArthur to discuss landings on the China coast. Given Marshall's stiff opposition to any operations on the China coast, that information almost certainly came from other sources.

Although we have reason to question what exactly Marshall told O'Laughlin, we can at least take him at his word that he was surprised by Marshall's announcement that he wanted to retire. Given that none of Marshall's biographers has recounted this episode, historians may share some of O'Laughlin's sense of surprise. Perhaps even more startling, however, was Marshall's explanation that he felt he could step down because "every contingency in connection with the reduction of Japan has been foreseen and that not only have all plans and missions been determined, but that down to the last detail, the movements of troops and supplies have been arranged and actually are underway." The words were O'Laughlin's, but in this case he clearly indicated that he was summarizing what Marshall told him.

Nevertheless, it is difficult to believe that Marshall thought that the situation was as settled as he let on. The Joint Chiefs had established the command structure in the Pacific for the final phase of the war and had agreed on the sequence of events—the invasion of Kyushu in the fall followed by an assault on the Kanto (Tokyo) region in the early spring—but only on the condition, as we've noted, that those operations would be subject to review and possible revision as the dates of the proposed campaigns approached. Moreover, the president had not given his final approval to those plans.[117] Nor had Congress agreed to the Army's appropriation request. There were other ways for congressmen to alter the Army's plans. The recent restrictions on the employment overseas of young draftees illustrated how Congress could interfere with the Army's redeployment plans. The full effect of those new requirements had yet to be determined by the general staff. In the meantime, Congress had scheduled hearings for mid-June to investigate the possibility of discharging servicemen with four or more children. More changes seemed possible.

There were other reasons for doubting the finality of the Army's redeployment plans. For reasons that remain unclear, the members of Eisenhower's staff anticipated a further reduction in the critical score for discharge from eighty-five to seventy-five and had begun to plan on that basis. That decision altered the availability of troops in the European Theater for redeployment and played havoc with the reshuffling of troops within units destined for the Pacific.[118]

The physical process of redeployment promised to create its own category of headaches. As noted, public officials expected the transshipment of hundreds of thousands of men across the United States to snarl rail traffic for months. Arrangements for training the redeployed units for war in the

Pacific were also unsettled. The Army expected some of the training to be completed in Europe while the GIs waited to be shipped home for furlough. They would receive the rest of their instruction when they reassembled with their units after their leaves. Publicly the War Department was confident that the transfer would go as planned, but that did not prevent others, including Colonel William Menninger, the Army's chief psychiatrist, from speculating that the Army would be faced with thousands of cases of soldiers going AWOL when their period of furlough ended.[119]

Although O'Laughlin did not voice any of these concerns about the state of the Army's plans, he nevertheless concluded that the Army, indeed the nation, still needed Marshall in command. Following their meeting, O'Laughlin scrambled to muster a public vote of confidence for the chief of staff. He began with an editorial in his journal calling on "the president to order, and the country to demand, that General of the Army Marshall abandon the idea of retirement." O'Laughlin thought the general could be dissuaded by passage "through Congress of a resolution which the president would be glad to approve, reiterating the national confidence in this great soldier which is in every citizen's heart."[120]

On June 11, Senator Thomas Hart (R-Connecticut), who had served as an admiral in the Pacific at the start of the war, referred to a "rumor around town" that Marshall planned to retire. Hart feared the rumor was well founded and asked that O'Laughlin's editorial be entered into the *Congressional Record*.[121] On the same day, according to O'Laughlin, Senator Elbert Thomas (D-Utah), the chair of the Senate Military Affairs Committee, and Warren Austin (R-Vermont), the ranking Republican on the committee, called on Marshall and asked him not to retire. Representative James Wadsworth (R-New York) and several other congressmen visited the general to make the same appeal. Finally, President Truman also told Marshall that the country needed him to stay on the job.[122]

A week after he first reported his meeting with Marshall, O'Laughlin noted with satisfaction that "as a result of all the pressure applied to General Marshall, he has agreed to remain as Chief of Staff and a statement to this effect was made by Secretary Stimson." O'Laughlin added that the senators and representatives who met with Marshall concluded that he was genuinely tired, "that he thought his job was finished; and that he needed assurances that he is essential." Unconvinced, O'Laughlin thought that "more was in back of his original decision to retire" than what Marshall told the congressmen. He was more certain, however, about the outcome of the general's brief flirtation with retirement. "Marshall's authority in the War Department will be greater, and Congress will be disposed to humor him," he predicted.[123]

It seems likely that that was what Marshall sought all along. It does not require a great leap to surmise that Marshall orchestrated events to coerce Congress and the president into giving him an unofficial vote of confidence. He would not have been the first public official to engage in such tactics. It is even possible that O'Laughlin was a willing participant in the gambit. O'Laughlin was an experienced political operator who would not have needed Marshall to spell things out to him to get him to play his part. Whatever his motives, it is clear that his recent interactions with Congress had led Marshall to wonder if the situation had deteriorated to the point where he would have to regularly defend his every decision against the criticism of increasingly assertive legislators. Certainly, the events of the previous month had seen the realization of his worst fears about how Congress would react after V-E Day. As Vinson attested, the pressure on the administration to hasten the pace of reconversion was unrelenting. The public's impatience with the pace of demobilization was also evident. Relations between Congress and the Army had reached this point at least in part because the legislators and officers operated in different spheres of discourse, the one drawing on newspaper opinion, congressional mail, and interest group lobbying and the other on highly classified sources. In the latter case, those sources told Marshall that the Japanese were watching how the Americans responded to victory in Europe and to the grueling, fearsome, and as yet unwon battle for Okinawa.

By early June Marshall could rest a little easier. He had gotten from Truman an endorsement of his strategy for war against Japan and an affirmation of his leadership as chief of staff. Congress had also fallen in line, at least for the moment. Now he could redirect his attention to the myriad problems related to the simultaneous process of demobilization and redeployment and to the daunting task of compelling Japan's unconditional surrender.

Between Peace and War, June–July 1945

As Truman had explained in his Memorial Day address on June 1, 1945, there was still a war to be won, and neither the U.S. government nor the American people could slacken in their commitment to the fight. It would take the full and unstinting use of American military power to compel Japan's unconditional surrender.

However, other problems would not wait. Reports from liberated Europe warned of mass starvation in the coming months. Disputes with the Allies, the Soviets most notably but also the French, provided a bleak backdrop to the charter meeting of the United Nations in San Francisco, which started on April 25, 1945, and lasted until June 26. The growing impatience on the home front for reconversion of the economy was another problem demanding attention. Despite the efforts of Truman, Marshall, and Patterson to explain the difficulty of waging war half a world away, for many Americans it seemed inconceivable that a conflict now reduced to one front would require nearly as much manpower and matériel as the two-front war had. For a growing number of congressmen, some of whom had spent much of the war opposing what they saw as the military's attempts to take over the economy, these demands seemed excessive, even dangerous.

In late May, Truman sought to resolve outstanding differences with the Russians by sending FDR's loyal assistant Harry Hopkins to meet with the Soviet leader, Joseph Stalin. Hopkins had served in a similar capacity in the summer of 1941 when the Soviet Union was reeling from the German onslaught. Symbolically, the choice of Hopkins as presidential emissary served to assure Stalin that there would be no abrupt change in American policy toward the Soviet Union. More concretely, Truman wanted Hopkins to convince Stalin to broaden the political composition of the Polish government and, among other goals, confirm the pledge the Soviet Union had made at the Yalta summit conference to enter the Pacific war within three months after Germany's surrender. On May 30, Hopkins reported to Truman that Stalin had agreed to a process that would lead to a broadening of the new government of national unity in Poland. Stalin also agreed to the American voting formula in the United Nations Security Council and assured Hopkins that the Soviet Union would be at war with Japan by early August and would deal only with the Chinese Nationalist government, as opposed to the Chinese Communists. This news was especially welcome in Washington. Stalin's pledge would, it was hoped, deprive the Communists of much needed support and encourage them to peacefully work out their differences with Chiang Kai-shek's Nationalist government at a time when it was still recovering from a punishing Japanese offensive the previous year that had threatened its existence. American confidence in China's contributions to the war had never been high, and after years of trying unsuccessfully to build up the military power of Nationalist China, American officials did not expect it to contribute much to victory. Nevertheless, they remained committed to Chiang's Nationalists in the hope that the government would emerge as a stronger ally after the war.

Truman was elated by the news from Moscow. According to Assistant Press Secretary Eben Ayers, the president was "so pleased and excited that he could not refrain from telling us of the good word from Hopkins and of his success in his talks with Stalin."[1] Hopkins's mission had not eliminated all potential problems with the Soviet Union, but Truman believed that enough had been accomplished to make a summit conference worthwhile. In the immediate aftermath of the Hopkins mission Truman agreed to meet with the leaders of the Soviet Union and Great Britain in mid-July in the Berlin suburb of Potsdam. Postwar problems in Europe would head the agenda, but the challenge of ending the war with Japan would have nearly equal billing.

The Joint Chiefs, with Marshall still in the lead, had never lost sight of the need to defeat Japan as quickly as possible after V-E Day. The Pentagon's strategists planned to finish the job within a year, sixteen months at most, of Germany's defeat. By June 1945, that schedule was looking less feasible, for several reasons. For one thing, as redeployment got under way it was apparent that the armed forces would be straining to meet the targets for OLYMPIC. But the other part of the equation, the assumption that the American business leaders, organized labor, consumers, and their representatives in Washington would support another year and a half of war, was equally problematic. America's military leaders continued to insist that defeating Japan remained the top priority, but other problems, chief among them the unsettled conditions in Europe and the uncertain future of the American economy, competed for attention and resources.

The battle for Okinawa dragged on. As the casualties mounted, so did the questioning of American strategy. In mid-May, following one of his *Daily War Journal* broadcasts, radio commentator Martin Agronsky received an angry letter from Mrs. C.J.H, the mother of a soldier on Okinawa, asking why the Army, War Department, and American leaders generally were not being held accountable for "all this slaughter of Am. Boys." An anguished string of questions followed. "Why haven't reinforcements reached those boys on Okinawa?" "Why must the same troops fight for 45 days?" "Why only six divisions in the first place?" "Why must every battle in the Pacific be bloody? It was bloody Tarawa, bloody Saipan, bloody Pelelu [*sic*], bloody Leyte, bloody Iwo Jima, bloody Okinawa, bloody Mindinao (ALL of three divisions there), bloody Luzon (not finished) and it will be bloody Borneo. Doesn't it ever enter anyone's mind that we are paying a needless too high a price in human blood in the Pacific[?]"[2] Had they seen her letter, the officials in the Pentagon would have tried to explain how geography and logistical constraints limited the number of divisions that could be supported in battle in these places. They would have also pointed out that mobilization of the economy and the final push to defeat Germany limited the availability of fresh reinforcements in the Pacific. It is doubtful, however, that those explanations would have offered her much solace.

The letter from Mrs. C.J.H. (she said she did not use her full name for fear her son would get in trouble) was but a prelude to more public criticism of American strategy on Okinawa. On May 28, radio commentator and news analyst H. V. Kaltenborn indirectly questioned the need for the ongoing campaign when he observed that the Americans had already secured the part of the island they needed to control.[3] A day later, war correspondent Homer Bigart reported that General Buckner's reliance on straight-ahead assaults was adding unnecessarily to the toll of killed and wounded Marines and GIs. Bigart argued that instead of making flanking landings behind the Shuri line the Americans had gone "hey diddle diddle-right down the middle," prolonging the suffering and placing a heavy strain on the Navy, which was supplying the operation and suffering kamikaze attacks. Over the next week columnist David Lawrence called the Okinawa campaign a "fiasco," demanding an investigation into its conduct and, presumably, Buckner's generalship.[4]

Privately, Navy and Army observers voiced similar concerns about Buckner's leadership. Lieutenant General Joseph Stilwell visited Okinawa on a fact-finding mission in early June in his capacity as head of Army Ground Forces. Stilwell, who was also hoping to obtain a command in the forthcoming invasion of Japan, wrote in his journal that there was "NO tactical thinking on push. No plan was ever discussed at the meetings to hasten the fight or help the divisions."[5] Admiral Raymond Spruance complained about Buckner's "go slow" approach and confessed that he wished for some of "Howland Smith's drive."[6] Less privately, MacArthur told visitors to Manila that Nimitz was also to blame for sanctioning Buckner's all-out approach to taking the entire island. There was no reason to sacrifice lives in trying to drive the Japanese off the island, MacArthur insisted. Once they secured the airfields, he argued, like Kaltenborn, the Americans should have taken up defensive positions and forced the Japanese to dislodge them. As one of

MacArthur's biographers notes, the general's criticism of Nimitz eventually reached the admiral and "contributed towards making the final weeks of the war the most tense in their relations."[7]

Publicly, Stilwell said that the press had failed to appreciate the accomplishments on Okinawa, given the hardships the Americans had to overcome.[8] Likewise, the Navy's high command, including Secretary of the Navy James Forrestal, stood by Buckner and dismissed David Lawrence's criticisms as misguided. In a statement issued on June 17, Nimitz said that Lawrence had been so badly misinformed as to give the impression that he was being used "for purposes which are not in the best interests of the United States."[9] On June 21, after frequent reports that fighting was nearly over, Buckner's successor declared that the island had been secured. Mopping-up operations continued for another ten days—during which over 11,000 Japanese were killed or captured. The controversy soon faded, but the initial story had given the American military another black eye and revealed a growing impatience and quarrelsomeness in the public and press, as well as among the Army, Marine, and Navy commanders who would have to cooperate in the coming assault on Japan.

Truman's first months in office provided daily indicators of the inseparability of the war in the Pacific from peacemaking in Europe and economic reconversion at home. Shortly after taking office, Truman received a report on Europe from White House special counsel Judge Samuel Rosenman, who had been to Europe to take stock of the situation there. Referring to Rosenman's report, Truman warned: "To a great extent the future permanent peace of Europe depends upon the restoration of the economy of these liberated countries, including a reasonable standard of living and employment. [The] United States economy, too, will be deeply affected unless these areas again resume their place in the international exchange of goods and services. A chaotic and hungry Europe is not fertile ground in which stable, democratic and friendly governments can be reared." The situation was desperate, but the demands of waging war against Japan and homefront shortages of food and coal restricted the administration's response. With these competing priorities in mind, Truman urged the heads of the government's war agencies to make every effort possible to meet the needs of America's stricken allies in northwestern Europe, "to the fullest extent that the successful prosecution of military operations and the maintenance of our essential domestic economy permit."[10]

Truman was reminded once again of the inseparability of European, Pacific, and home-front problems when he met with Herbert Hoover on May 28. Truman invited the former president to the White House to discuss the food shortage in Europe.[11] Hoover had organized the American food program during World War I and had gained international fame for his management of relief programs in Europe during and after the war. Hoover began by making recommendations on improving relief efforts in Europe and addressing food shortages at home. The latter problem, he believed, could be solved by taking food pricing out of the hands of the Office of Price Administration.[12] But during the course of his far-ranging conversation with the president, Hoover also shared his views on ending the war against Japan and restoring the economy at home.

Hoover's recommendations on ending the war were bracketed by observations critical of the Soviet Union, leaving little doubt that he saw a negotiated surrender of Japan as key to preventing Soviet domination of East Asia. According to notes he wrote after his meeting, Hoover began by cautioning Truman that the "Asiatic" nature of the Russians made them untrustworthy. Hoover then recommended that the United States, possibly in conjunction with Britain and China, issue a declaration that specified their objectives in Asia. These included Japanese withdrawal from Manchuria and restoration of Chinese control there, unconditional surrender of Japan's armed forces, disarmament of Japan for thirty to forty years, and the delivery into Allied custody for trial of specified Japanese military officials accused of breaking the rules of civilized warfare. The former president also recommended telling the Japanese that the Allies had no desire to destroy Japan's form of government and that they wanted to see Japan rejoin the family of nations. Hoover also advised Truman that the warning should include the "intimation" that Japan would be allowed to keep its colonies in Korea and Formosa. He added that the proposed declaration should also state that if the Japanese government refused to surrender it would demonstrate its complete untrustworthiness and would have to be destroyed. In response to a question from Truman about the potential success of the declaration, Hoover admitted that it had only a slight chance, but he believed that the recent formation of a new government in Tokyo headed by Admiral Suzuki Kantaro indicated that the Japanese were actively seeking a peaceful end to the war.

In his notes written after his meeting with Truman, Hoover sourly concluded that he had probably been invited to the White House for show and that little would come from the meeting "so far as I or my views were concerned." Truman's Memorial Day address on winning the war against Japan probably confirmed those fears, although in fairness to the president, he did not receive the memorandum he requested from Hoover until several days later. Nevertheless, it is clear that at this point Truman and Hoover were miles apart on the meaning of unconditional surrender and the objectives of the war. This does not mean, however, that Truman dismissed everything the former president had to say about the war with Japan.

Following the meeting, Hoover, at Truman's request, submitted a typed copy of his recommendations under the title "Memorandum on Ending the Japanese War." The memorandum presented more formally the points he had made during this meeting with Truman and in some cases provided more specific detail than his notes. Hoover prefaced his remarks by stating that he thought there was "the barest chance" of persuading the Japanese to surrender, but he believed there was little to lose and much to gain by making the effort. In addition to the terms already described—restoration of Manchuria, disarmament, and trial of Japanese militarists—Hoover recommended that all Japanese government property in China be turned over to the Chinese as reparations. Beyond those measures, he wrote, he saw no objectives that were "worth the expenditure of 500,000 to 1,000,000 American lives." He also included in his memorandum the positive inducements in the declaration that he had mentioned to Truman. These included American willingness to see Japan restored to the family of nations, a pledge not to interfere with the Japanese way of life or destroy its government, and support for Japanese control of Korea and Formosa in the form of a trusteeship. This section ended with Hoover reiterating that if Japan rejected the terms of the declaration, the United States would have to proceed with the destruction of the government in Tokyo. In his memo, Hoover stated again his belief that the recent appointment of Admiral Suzuki Kantaro as prime minister indicated that the Japanese government was looking for a way to end the war. He also asserted that the Japanese would also be more willing to surrender because they would want to preserve the "Mikado who is the spiritual head of the nation" and that they would want to end the war before the Soviet Union came in. Finally, in this section, Hoover said that there was a large liberal middle class in Japan that might exert itself if such reasonable peace terms were offered by the Allies.

Hoover concluded by assuring Truman that if Japan accepted the terms of the declaration that the United States would have achieved its every objective, "except perhaps the vengeance of an excited minority of our people."[13] The benefits, he implied, would be immediately appreciated by the majority of Americans. The United States would save the lives of 500,000–1,000,000 American boys and prevent the exhaustion of economic resources that were needed for economic recovery at home and the rehabilitation of Europe. Finally, the United States would avoid the costs and hazards inherent in trying to occupy and govern Japan.[14]

Truman's first reaction on receiving Hoover's memorandum was to share it with Fred Vinson, on whose counsel Truman was fast coming to rely. Beginning on June 2, Vinson regularly attended the president's morning conferences with his personal staff.[15] The Kentuckian, according to Truman, was "a straight shooter," "a man to trust," who knew the mind of Congress.[16] But in this case the president may also have turned to Vinson because he took seriously Hoover's warning about the disastrous economic consequences of a prolonged war with Japan. Vinson had, as we have noted, recently called attention to the lagging pace of reconversion and complained about the Army's insatiable demand for men and materials to prosecute the war against Japan. Unfortunately, we can only guess what advice Truman received from Vinson, as it was never recorded. After holding Hoover's memorandum for almost a week, Vinson returned it to Truman with the recommendation that he submit it to the secretaries of state and war and, significantly, that he also seek the advice of Cordell Hull, who had been Roosevelt's secretary of state for twelve years. Vinson's cover letter returning the memo gives no indication of his thoughts on the topic. Truman followed that advice and sent copies to Stimson, Acting Secretary of State Joseph Grew, and Hull.[17]

By the time Stimson received a copy of Hoover's memorandum from the White House he already had in hand an evaluation of a less detailed earlier version of that document that Hoover had presented to him in mid-May. Stimson had in turn asked for the views of the staff officers in the Strategy and Policy Group (S&P) of the Operations and Plans Division. S&P's response, which was sent to Stimson on June 7, cast doubt on the geopolitical basis of Hoover's memorandum. The staff officers did not believe an early peace, which they thought unlikely under any circumstances, would prevent the Soviet Union from entering the war and becoming the major power in Northeast Asia. They added that the Russians would "with some justice" view a compromise peace from which they were excluded as a breach of the agreements made at Yalta. Regarding Hoover's warnings about the economic effects of a prolonged war, the officers conceded that "this was an economic matter requiring further investigation but it appears doubtful that the U.S. economy would be 'prostrate' in 'eighteen months.'" The staff officers categorically dismissed Hoover's prediction of more than 500,000 American casualties from invasion of Japan as "entirely too high." They also thought it unwise to allow Japan to retain Formosa and Korea, given that the Allies were committed, through the 1943 Cairo Declaration, to an independent Korea and the restoration of Formosa to China. They did, however, agree that it would be advisable to issue a warning to Japan that specified the meaning of unconditional surrender, using terms that would lead to the achievement of American war aims.[18]

Stimson had S&P's comments in hand when he received Truman's request to comment on the Hoover memorandum. Stimson promptly submitted this newer version to S&P for comment, withholding Hoover's name and noting only that it was written by the same anonymous "economist" who had written the previous memorandum. On June 15, Marshall submitted S&P's comments to Stimson with the observation that he was "in substantial agreement" with its contents. For the most part, S&P repeated its earlier assessment. The staff officers agreed in principle with

Hoover's recommendation that the United States, either alone or in conjunction with its allies, should issue a warning to Japan, specifying the meaning of unconditional surrender in a manner that was consistent with previous public declarations. That ruled out Hoover's proposal to let Japan keep either Formosa or Korea, a proposal they deemed unwise in any case. The officers in S&P also stressed the importance of cooperation with the Soviet Union and emphasized that the United States would not be in a position to challenge the Russians on the mainland of Northeast Asia. Once again, the staff officers dismissed Hoover's estimate of 500,000–1,000,000 deaths as entirely too high. Unlike Hoover, S&P believed that an occupation of at least selected points in Japan would be necessary to disarm Japan. They also rejected as baseless Hoover's contention that the establishment of a military government in Japan would be "an impossible task."

Regarding the economic side, the staff officers repeated their earlier belief that there was little chance of the United States exhausting its resources in fighting Japan. They added, however, that resources used in defeating Japan and thus preventing a future war might be more worthwhile than using those same resources for the immediate relief of Europe, however dire the conditions there. The officers even more firmly rejected Hoover's analysis of the political situation in Japan. Citing input from Army intelligence, the staff officers said that there was little difference between Suzuki and the militarists controlling the government in Tokyo. They also discounted the significance of a "liberal minded" peace faction in Japan's middle classes. According to Army intelligence, the "liberals" were small in number and hardly worthy of the name. They sought the same ends as the militarists— domination of Asia—but as a consequence of greater exposure to the world outside Japan they had gained a healthier regard for American power.[19]

Stimson found S&P's explanation about the benefits to be gained from expending resources in the Pacific war, as opposed to redirecting them toward relief in Europe, puzzling. And he judged the officers' observations about Suzuki and the negligible influence of a peace party in Japan completely wrongheaded.[20] On June 16 Stimson sent S&P's comments to Truman under a cover letter that contained his own thoughts. Like Hoover, Stimson stressed the perils of invading Japan and the difficulty of occupying and governing it through military government. He also agreed with Hoover on the potential advantages of softening the peace terms by allowing Japan to maintain the emperor on the throne if the Japanese people so desired. Drawing on his prewar experience with Japan, Stimson continued to believe that there was in Japan a sizeable group of what he described as "moderate politicians" who were working secretly to bring the war to an end. This peace faction, Stimson believed, was forming around the throne, seeking to use the emperor's immense influence to challenge the militarists when the time was right. According to Stimson, a public declaration guaranteeing the safety of the emperor and preservation of the imperial institution might just give the peace faction the leverage it needed to gain control of the government and end the war.[21]

Because Secretary of State Edward Stettinius was in San Francisco for the United Nations conference, Acting Secretary of State Joseph Grew took responsibility for replying to Truman's request for comments on the Hoover memorandum. This was Grew's second opportunity to urge the president to modify unconditional surrender. In late May, Grew, who had been ambassador to Tokyo for the ten years leading up to the attack on Pearl Harbor, asked Truman to include a statement in his Memorial Day address that clarified the meaning of unconditional surrender for the Japanese. In particular, Grew wanted the president to assure the Japanese that the United States would not destroy the imperial institution. Truman appeared to agree and asked Grew to work with Judge Rosenman on a suitable statement for inclusion in the upcoming speech. But Truman also asked Grew to have the Joint Chiefs and the secretaries of the War and Navy Departments review the statement. At this point, Grew's proposal stalled.

When Grew shared a draft statement with his staff, two assistant secretaries, Dean Acheson and Archibald McLeish, both objected to any statement that tied the American government's hands in dealing with the emperor. Later the same day Grew learned that the Joint Chiefs and Secretaries Forrestal and Stimson also opposed making any statement to Japan at the present time. Grew concluded that they preferred to wait until the fighting on Okinawa had ended. But Stimson wrote in his diary that he was thinking of how the warning would fit into a timetable that included Russian entry into the war and the atomic bomb. The bomb would be ready by midsummer, and the Russians were expected to enter the war by late August. As historian Brian Villa has noted, insofar as Stimson was concerned, the schedule imposed itself, a warning followed by use of the atomic bomb, followed by Soviet entry into the war. The invasion would be a last resort.

Grew remained adamant about the need to issue a prompt warning to Japan that would clarify but also modify the meaning of unconditional surrender. Hoover's memorandum, which he received in early June, gave him a second chance to drive that point home. Truman's letter had asked for the secretary of state's views on Hoover's memorandum. Grew, however, took advantage of Stettinius's presence at the San Francisco conference to respond to Truman in his capacity as acting secretary. Like the staff officers in S&P, Grew thought that Hoover's recommendations regarding Korea and Taiwan were unrealistic in light of the Cairo Declaration. He also believed that the United States would have to occupy Japan and control it in the immediate postwar period through some form of military government. Grew stressed the importance of demilitarizing Japan but he also believed that the United States would have to enact social and political reforms (for example freedom of speech, religious freedom) that would foster democratic government in Japan. In short, Grew thought that Hoover's recommendations let Japan off too easily and would not tear out the root causes of Japanese militarism.

On the subject of the emperor, however, he and Hoover were of the same mind. The former ambassador explained that all available evidence strongly indicated that the "non-molestation of the person of the present emperor and the preservation of the institution of the throne comprise irreducible Japanese terms." Thus, according to Grew, Japanese devotion to the throne made it expedient for the United States to compromise on the fate of the emperor. If the United States guaranteed that the emperor would not be harmed and the imperial institution would not be destroyed, the United States would save "a large number of human lives," and the Japanese would be willing to undergo "drastic privations so long as these irreducible terms were met." Conversely, the Americans could expect "prolonged resistance" if Washington insisted on destroying the imperial institution and trying the emperor as a war criminal.[22]

It was not a foolproof argument. Grew, without using the word, was insisting that "fanatical" devotion to the emperor would make the Japanese fight to the bitter end if the fate of the throne remained in doubt. Were that so, Grew's critics in and out of government asked, how could the Allies be sure that the emperor would not serve as the rallying point for Japanese nationalism and militarism after the war? Grew's answer relied in part on his understanding of Japanese history. But he also believed that extraordinary measures taken during the period of occupation would make a recrudescence of Japanese militarism impossible. Grew, and other Republican statesmen who had directed American foreign policy with Japan during the more placid 1920s, such as Hoover and Stimson, emphasized Japan's impressive accomplishments in modernizing and adopting constitutional reforms following the Meiji Restoration of 1868. They believed that the desperate conditions created by the Great Depression had enabled Japanese militarists to hijack the government and steer it toward a collision with the United States. In this view, the roots of Japanese aggression were shallow and easily extracted. The United States needed to defeat Japan, punish the militarists, and restore control of the government to the moderate statesmen and business leaders who had previously guided Japan on its path to modernization.

This was a view that allowed for some variation. Grew, for example, believed that the United States would have to govern Japan in order to implement democratic reforms. Hoover believed any effort to govern Japan would be foolish and counterproductive. Admiral Leahy, the president's representative on the JCS, agreed with Hoover. In Leahy's opinion, "if Japan is to be governed by a force of occupation," U.S. forces should play only a minor role "in order to save cost and get American troops home at the earliest possible date."[23] In addition, Hoover, Grew, and many prewar antiinterventionists in the press and Congress believed that the United States had unnecessarily provoked Japan during the 1930s. American policy, most notably the embargoes imposed on Japan, had been devised by a "madman"— a term Hoover used a year later to describe FDR—who had used the war to enlarge the powers of the presidency and threaten American democracy.[24] Hoover's view represented the most extreme view on the right, but most conservatives believed that the emperor would contribute to Japan's

rehabilitation by providing a stable link to the past and a focal point of loyalty in difficult times. In this view, removing the emperor would be a disastrous mistake that would provoke resistance from the Japanese people and
necessitate a lengthy and costly military occupation by the United States.[25]

Grew had made his best pitch for modifying unconditional surrender. It
would not be his last. Over the next few weeks he continued to press the
case for making a statement on the emperor, in memoranda and in meetings with the president. To his dismay he found his efforts thwarted by
Cordell Hull, his former boss. Hull had served as FDR's secretary of state
for eleven years before he had been forced to resign because of ill health in
November 1944. He had been handed Japan's declaration of war after he
had learned of the attack on Pearl Harbor and saw little reason to trust or
compromise with Japan. Truman's Memorial Day address had served notice
to the Japanese, and that was sufficient. Hull conceded that Hoover had raised
numerous questions concerning the best methods for eliminating Japanese
militarism that would "raise broadly the question of what to do with the
Emperor, etc. etc." But Hull doubted that it would be useful for him to "discuss any of these questions to which Mr. Hoover refers in his appeasement
proposal."[26] Truman could hardly miss the significance of that last phrase.
Hull was warning the president that Hoover, and by extension Grew and
Stimson, were promoting a politically dangerous policy that could easily be
equated with appeasement. Truman respected Hoover for his technical expertise on issues like food policy and relief, but it is doubtful that he had
much regard for the former president's political acumen. On the other hand
Hull was a former congressman and a living connection to FDR, whose
policies Truman had pledged to continue. For the moment at least there
would be no modification of unconditional surrender.

That did not mean, however, that Truman had ruled out issuing another
warning to Japan that might further clarify what unconditional surrender
meant without softening the policy. But if there was to be a warning it would
have to wait until the Big Three—Churchill, Stalin, and Truman—met at
Potsdam. That was what Secretary of State Stettinius recommended. He
wired Truman from San Francisco to recommend that any warning to Japan
be made into a three- or four-power demand (Stettinius was including

China). It might be useful, he added, "to couple such a warning with some assurances to the Japanese regarding their future." Considering the joint nature of such a statement, Stettinius advised putting the subject on the agenda of the forthcoming Potsdam gathering. When Grew met with Truman on the morning of June 18, Truman said he wanted to postpone issuing a statement and asked the dejected Grew to put the subject on the agenda of the forthcoming meeting.[27]

As the battle for Okinawa neared completion in mid-June, Truman turned his attention to the invasion of Japan. Although on May 25 the Joint Chiefs had directed Nimitz and MacArthur to begin preparations for the invasion, Truman had yet to approve OLYMPIC. Before he did so, he wanted to thoroughly review the strategic options with the Joint Chiefs and civilian heads of the armed forces. The shadow of Okinawa hung over these deliberations. In advance of the meeting, Truman had Admiral Leahy request from Marshall and King an "estimate of the time required and an estimate of the losses in killed and wounded that will result from an invasion of Japan proper." Leahy added that the president intended to economize "to the maximum extent possible in the American loss of lives." In response to Truman's request, Marshall asked MacArthur for his estimate of battle casualties for the invasion of Kyushu for the first ninety days. MacArthur promptly obliged with an estimate of 105,050 battle casualties, adding approximately 12,000 more for nonbattle casualties, including injury and disease.[28]

On June 17, the day before his meeting with the JCS, Truman conferred with members of his inner circle as they sailed down the Potomac River on board the presidential yacht. He later wrote in his notes that it was a wide-ranging discussion of "plans, issues, and *decisions*" covering European affairs, particularly the food and fuel situation, as well as the "Japanese War and the relations with China, Russia, and Britain with regard to it, Supreme Commander and what to do with Mr. Prima Donna, Brass Hat, Five Star MacArthur."[29] In using of the title "Supreme Commander" Truman may have been referring to MacArthur's impending role in the invasion of Japan. It is also possible that he was thinking about MacArthur as the future head of the Allied occupation of Japan. Either way, it was clear that Truman disliked having to rely on "Mr. Prima Donna." It is equally clear that despite his tirade against that "play actor and bunco man"—as he referred to MacArthur— Truman was nonetheless not seriously considering removing him from command of the Army forces in the Pacific. Having vented his frustrations in his diary, the president turned to more dire matters; "I have to decide Pacific strategy," he wrote, "shall we invade Japan proper or shall we bomb and blockade? That is my hardest decision to date. But I'll make it when I have the facts."[30]

As Truman soon discovered, his choices were not as stark as he had presented them to be, nor was making the decision a simple matter of gathering "the facts." According to the minutes of the meeting, Marshall began by explaining that the invasion of Kyushu was "essential to the strategy of strangulation" and was the best means of "forcing capitulation by invasion of the Tokyo Plain." Marshall added that it might be possible to force Japan's surrender without defeating the entirety of the Imperial Army but it would take the continuation of the blockade and bombardment of the home islands, the Soviet Union's entry into the war, and landings on Kyushu to bring about that result.[31] On the matter of casualties, things turned murky. It readily became apparent that there was no single method for estimating casualties and the "facts" could be made to support a predetermined decision. Marshall cited the conclusion of a staff memorandum that combat experiences in the Pacific varied so widely that it was simply not possible to give a firm estimate of casualties. After some discussion of MacArthur's prior experiences on Leyte and Luzon, Marshall speculated that the availability of room for maneuver on Kyushu would help MacArthur suppress the casualty rate. In all probability, he said, casualties on Kyushu for the first thirty days might equal the 31,000 suffered by MacArthur's forces on Luzon. Marshall followed up by reading a cable from MacArthur endorsing OLYMPIC without any changes. In an unsubtle reference to the Navy's earlier support for operations in the Yellow Sea, such as landings on the Chusan Archipelago, MacArthur also urged that there be no subsidiary "wasteful operations of non-decisive character."[32] MacArthur need not have worried. Admiral King agreed that OLYMPIC was a necessary prelude to invasion of the Tokyo area. Control of Kyushu would tighten the blockade of Honshu and facilitate air operations by bringing airfields closer to the main island. Kyushu should come first, King said, after which there would be time to assess the effects on Japan of possible operations by the Russians and Chinese on the mainland.[33]

When Truman asked Admiral Leahy for his opinion the admiral reminded his colleagues that the president was particularly interested in knowing what the toll would be for OLYMPIC. Leahy wanted to apply the loss rate on Okinawa to anticipate casualties on Kyushu. That would mean that the Americans could expect to take casualties at a rate of 35 percent of the attacking force. Leahy then asked Marshall for that number. Before he could answer, King jumped in to say that he agreed with Marshall's earlier observation that Kyushu afforded greater opportunity for maneuver than Okinawa. That would help reduce casualties to a level somewhere between those suffered on Luzon and Okinawa. When King finished, Marshall told Leahy the attacking force would consist of 766,700 men. Leahy's method when applied to the attacking force would yield an estimate of nearly 270,000 killed and wounded. Marshall's and King's calculations, which were actually based on an underestimation of MacArthur's casualties throughout the island campaign and did not include losses likely to be suffered by naval forces supporting the invasion, would produce a considerably lower total—in the range of 31,000–41,000.[34] Those projections were the result of subtle methodological shifts in accounting that were not addressed in the meeting. Also omitted was any mention of an earlier cable from MacArthur's staff estimating 105,000 killed and wounded for OLYMPIC within sixty days. When Marshall received that information he promptly cabled MacArthur asking him if those were firm numbers and reminding him that the president was greatly concerned about the costs of an invasion. MacArthur took the hint and responded by saying that he did not expect casualties for OLYMPIC to come close to 105,000.[35]

The evasive and in some cases deliberately misleading manner in which the president's advisers dealt with the casualty projections is troubling to say the least. The most that can be said of this effort to attach a number to the proposed invasion is that it demonstrated that Marshall was prepared to massage the figures in order to gain approval for OLYMPIC. King's willingness to endorse Marshall's estimate is perhaps more puzzling. One possible explanation is that by agreeing with Marshall's proposition that because Kyushu's size provided greater opportunity for maneuver on the ground it would reduce casualties, King sought to absolve the Navy of any charges of mismanagement in the Okinawa campaign.[36] Ultimately, the whole matter of casualty projections was overshadowed at the meeting by the arguments presented in favor of conducting the invasion of Kyushu.

As noted, Marshall declared and King agreed that OLYMPIC was a necessary prelude to any plan to subdue Japan. Secretary Forrestal concurred, as did Lieutenant General Ira Eaker, who was representing the AAF at the meeting. Secretary Stimson likewise supported OLYMPIC, though he thought it was his duty to offer advice on the political aspects of military policy. To this end he recommended that something be done to encourage what he termed the "submerged class" in Japan that desired peace. Assistant Secretary of War John J. McCloy agreed with Stimson. Admiral Leahy went a step further and challenged the basic premise on which American strategy was being made. Leahy said that he did not agree with those who thought the United States would have fallen short of victory if it did not obtain Japan's unconditional surrender. Even without unconditional surrender, Leahy said, he "feared no menace from Japan in the foreseeable future." Leahy, who opposed an American occupation of Japan, added that an insistence on unconditional surrender would unnecessarily increase American casualties. Truman replied that it was with Leahy's thoughts in mind that he had "left the door open to Congress to take appropriate action with reference to unconditional surrender" but that he did not feel that he could do anything at the moment to change public opinion.[37]

The minutes show that the discussion before it concluded turned to "certain other matters," which historians have generally agreed is a reference to an off-the-record discussion of the atomic bomb.[38] The minutes then note that Truman approved a memo that Leahy read, recommending the reinstatement of Lend Lease supplies to the French once their troops had withdrawn from northern Italy. Truman closed the meeting by expressing his thanks to the Joint Chiefs and saying that he now felt "satisfied and reassured."[39]

Truman's June 18 White House meeting with his military advisers did not produce any irrevocable decisions on strategy. He approved the invasion of Kyushu and agreed that preparations for CORONET should continue, although he withheld formal approval of that operation. Leahy continued to oppose OLYMPIC, but Truman was not willing to abandon the basic aim of American strategy—unconditional surrender—especially when Marshall and King, as well as Forrestal and Stimson, supported it. King, however, was less committed to the Kyushu operation than his conduct at the meeting suggests. To begin with, he was on record as saying that he believed that a combination of naval blockade and strategic bombardment would compel Japan's surrender before OLYMPIC began. More important, he had in reserve a cable from Admiral Nimitz opposing any invasion of the home islands. Writing on May 25 in the midst of the seemingly endless struggle for Okinawa, Nimitz warned that an invasion of the home islands would meet resistance every bit as stiff as what the Americans were facing on Okinawa. "Unless speed is considered so important that we are willing to accept less than the best preparation and more than minimum casualties," Nimitz wrote, it would be preferable to continue the naval and air war against Japan. In stating his case for blockade and bombardment, Nimitz had framed his argument in such a way as to activate Truman's grave concern for casualties while simultaneously challenging Marshall's insistence that speed was essential to the achievement of Japan's unconditional surrender. As historian Richard Frank has noted, Nimitz's message gave King the ability to throw American strategy into turmoil. Truman had made a point of basing his approval of OLYMPIC on "the unanimous opinion" of the JCS.[40] What would happen if King withdrew his support for the invasion?

Truman's White House meeting on strategy had explored a range of options on the spectrum of force, with the atomic bomb at one end and abandonment of unconditional surrender at the other. The atomic bomb was, of course, still shrouded in near total secrecy. Everything else discussed at the meeting had already made its way into the press and had become the subject of widespread speculation and debate. As far as the public knew, the option that promised the most complete use of force against Japan was an invasion. The details of the invasion were unspecified, but public pronouncements by Truman and Marshall, as well as the beginning of redeployment, served to make the forthcoming operations the subject of constant speculation in the press. Next was the strategy of siege (blockade and bombardment) or "strangulation," as Marshall aptly put it. Blockade, bombardment, and the attendant starvation and disease would easily kill as many Japanese as invasion. But from the American perspective a siege would be less costly in lives and place fewer demands on American manpower and materials. At present the United States was employing a variant of this strategy as elements of the Third Fleet and Twentieth Air Force hunted ships venturing onto the narrow seas around Japan's home islands and pounded enemy cities with daily air raids. Preparations for an invasion and the strains they placed on transportation, manpower, and resources deprived the United States of the economic benefits offered by a siege. On the other hand the continuing naval and air war against Japan had the unintended effect of stimulating public discussion and debate over the feasibility of defeating Japan without an invasion and raised questions about the necessity of redeployment and the buildup for an invasion.

Both Stimson and McCloy had broached a third option—in the form of a diplomatic initiative that modified unconditional surrender so as to provide assurances on the preservation of the Japanese monarchy. This option was already being widely discussed by officials in the War, Navy, and State Departments. As with the various military options, the pros and cons of modifying unconditional surrender were also being openly discussed in the press and in the halls of Congress. Army planners saw advantages in using the emperor to secure the surrender of the millions of Japanese troops scattered across Asia and the Pacific. Naval officers believed that their preferred strategy of strangulation would be more likely to force Japan's capitulation if the militarists in Tokyo were assured that surrender would not mean destruction of the imperial structure. Grew, and of course Hoover, also believed that public assurances regarding the emperor would provide the members of the peace faction in Tokyo the leverage they needed to bring the war to a speedy conclusion. Stimson had obliquely referred to this course when he talked of finding some means to help the submerged peace group in Japan make its influence felt. McCloy, according to his account, was more direct. "We are crazy if we don't let them keep the Mikado," he is supposed to have said.[41] Stimson and McCloy differed from Leahy in that they did not counsel abandonment of unconditional surrender, but they were urging the president to modify it significantly. McCloy and Stimson also differed from Leahy in that they believed that a diplomatic initiative should be backed up by the threat of force, specifically the atomic bomb.

At this point—mid-June—Truman's advisers found it difficult to discern the president's views on unconditional surrender. In late May, he had given Grew the impression that he favored some modification of unconditional surrender, but he also asked the undersecretary to submit his proposal through the regular channels by clearing it with the JCS, Stimson, and Forrestal. Significantly, Truman did not reveal his thoughts to Grew on the fate of the emperor, nor did he respond to the recommendations Grew made two weeks later in his evaluation of Hoover's memorandum. When the persistent diplomat had pressed the matter again on the morning of June 18, Truman had followed Stettinius's advice and asked Grew to place the subject of a warning to Japan on the agenda of the Big Three meeting in Potsdam, which was to start on July 17. Later that day, when Stimson and McCloy broached the subject of a diplomatic solution, Truman, according to the minutes, changed the subject. Finally, when Leahy more forthrightly recommended abandoning unconditional surrender altogether, Truman said such a step would be unpopular and that it was up to Congress to take the next step. Thus, as of June 18 Truman was willing to consider making a warning to Japan after consulting with the Allies. But he did not offer any clue as to what he thought the warning should say. It is safe to assume, however, that given his previous refusal to endorse any guarantee regarding the emperor or the preservation of the imperial institution, that on this subject he was closer to Hull than Hoover.

Standing apart from the options of invasion, siege, and diplomacy, because it lay beyond American control, was the entry of the Red Army into the Pacific war. Here was another way military force might be used to hasten Japan's surrender and lighten the burden on the United States. As we have noted, despite Marshall's efforts to quash public speculation about Soviet intentions, congressmen and journalists were already wondering aloud if Soviet entry into the war would save American lives and allow for a reduction in the size of the Army. Planners on the Army general staff reasoned that at the least, and this was no small consideration, Russian troops would take on Japanese forces in Manchuria and Korea and relieve the United States of having to disperse troops onto the mainland of Asia. During the White House meeting, Marshall went so far as to hope that the shock of the Russians' entry on the "already hopeless Japanese may well be the decisive action leveraging them into capitulation at that time or shortly thereafter if we land in Japan." Admiral King conceded that the Russians' assistance would be valuable but insisted that it was not "indispensable."[42]

Truman's decisions at the June 18 meeting had been mainly negative in character; he had ignored Hoover's warnings about Soviet entry into the war and rejected his recommendation to abandon unconditional surrender and cancel OLYMPIC. Instead, Truman continued to hew to the course marked out by his predecessor. This did not mean, however, that the United States was yet firmly committed to the invasion of Japan. Truman approved OLYMPIC and implicitly rejected the strategy of siege, but for the next four and half months the United States would rely on air and sea power alone to attack Japan. American power would be augmented by the atomic bomb, if it were available, a Soviet offensive in Northeast Asia, and Chinese operations, although these received little attention at the meeting as they seemed less consequential. All of these would precede an invasion. Truman had not rejected the possibility of ending the war through diplomacy, but he made it clear that he did not plan on altering the policy of unconditional surrender while the other options remained.

Thus, in reality, not much had been settled. Despite the appearance of consensus, the president's top military and civilian advisers remained divided on the necessity of OLYMPIC. As is often the case in Washington in such situations, the dissenting parties were about to carry their debate into the public realm in the hope of changing the president's mind.

By the time Truman met with his military advisers on June 18, the simultaneous processes of demobilization and redeployment had been under way for a full month. As Eisenhower's staff assigned divisions in the European Theater to one of the four categories, soldiers moved between those divisions, depending on their Adjusted Service Rating. As planned, men with eighty-five points or more were reassigned to divisions designated for demobilization, while lower-point men in those divisions were shifted into divisions slated for redeployment to the Pacific by way of the United States, or for occupation duty in Europe. The process of reconstituting divisions in preparation for deployment to the Pacific sacrificed unit cohesion and sapped morale as inexperienced GIs left their veteran comrades behind and filtered into reorganized units composed of similarly green officers and men.

This was only the beginning of an elaborate process that moved men and equipment across two oceans and three continents, a Rube Goldberg–like system of ships, planes, and trains crisscrossing the globe, operating on tight schedules with almost no allowance for delay. Directives issued from the Pentagon, but in practice the military tradition of delegating operational decisions to theater commanders meant that there were multiple nodes of decision-making. Eisenhower's decision to exempt from redeployment those GIs who had served in two theaters as well as his staff's expectation (unfounded, as it turned out) that the Adjusted Rating Score soon would be lowered to seventy-five points were just two examples of how decisions outside Washington affected the Pentagon's plans. MacArthur's habit of hoarding cargo ships for use as floating warehouses was another.

The rush to complete the war in two theaters imposed a burden on the movement of troops and cargo to the point of testing the limits of American innovation and flexibility. By stripping divisions of all their weapons and equipment and individuals of all but their clothing and personal possessions, the Army managed to squeeze aboard troopships half again as many soldiers, who took turns in bunks. The divisions would meet their equipment on the other side. In this manner, a whole division could cross in just four transports. The downside was that much of the equipment was hastily packed and ruined in transit. Elsewhere, the momentary and unanticipated availability of troop lift in late May resulted in heavier than expected arrivals on the East Coast, leading in turn to railroad complaints and a bitter fight with Congress over discharging former railroad workers.

That did not mean, however, that high-point men were being whisked back to the United States. Army and War Department officials repeatedly explained that top priority would be given to troops redeploying to the Pacific or returning to the United States for additional training before being transferred to the Pacific. Nevertheless, GIs who were readjusted into Category IV, units designated for discharge, soon grew impatient with the delays as they saw comrades embark for home. GIs in the Service of Supply had a different set of grievances. Engineer units, construction battalions, and quartermaster troops were needed immediately in the Pacific to move supplies, rebuild harbors, and construct depots and bases in the Philippines and Okinawa. These veterans would deploy directly to the Pacific with no furlough in the United States.

Originally, most of the AAF units in the European and Mediterranean theaters were also expected to deploy directly to the Pacific and China theaters. The AAF's chief of staff, General Arnold, thought that his airmen would understand the importance of keeping well-established groups intact until the war against Japan was won. By late 1944, however, Arnold concluded that the AAF would have to implement the point system announced by the Army and that most airmen would redeploy through the continental United States. Unfortunately, commanders in the European and Mediterranean theaters did not receive the final orders explaining the process for discharging and redeploying air forces until May 25. As with the Army, AAF groups were supposed to undergo an initial reshuffling while overseas in which low-point airmen would replace those eligible for discharge. These reconstituted units would return home and be furloughed for thirty days before they returned to previously designated bases for training before shipping out to the Pacific. That was how the process was supposed to work. But, as one AAF official historian sourly noted, "the program was characterized by utter confusion pervading all echelons of command." "Theoretically it was perfect," wrote one Air Force historian; "in practice it was anything but perfect."[43]

What followed was a series of administrative snafus that would become familiar to readers of Joseph Heller's 1961 novel *Catch-22*. Delayed or conflicting orders impeded efforts to reconstitute units overseas. By mid-June the AAF had retreated completely from its original policy of redeploying air units intact from Europe and the Mediterranean to the Pacific. Instead, headquarters announced that the air groups deploying to the Pacific would be drawn from the continental United States and be composed of airmen who had not seen service overseas. In other words, having started from the premise that it was essential to employ only experienced crews in the war against Japan, the AAF had decided that it would rely on ground and air crews whose chief qualification was that they had no combat experience. According to the Air Force's history, this decision meant that "military experience had been forgotten in the desire to appease the public."[44] Shortly after announcing this decision on June 22, the AAF announced a revision that was intended to assure that each air group redeployed to the Pacific with a cadre of trained ground and air personnel. According to this new plan, approximately 10 percent of the men in the air crews and 20 percent in the ground crews would have combat experience. As an AAF internal study noted shortly after the war, "this meant that the air crews—originally not to be remanned [sic] at all—were expected to go out with proportionately fewer combat experienced elements than the ground crews."[45] In addition to the administrative mayhem created by these shifting orders, poor recordkeeping, unavailability of shipping, unexpected changes in mission or aircraft, and the reluctance of commanders to release technically skilled airmen to other units further clogged the system.

There still seemed to be time to sort out these problems. By mid-June, however, the prospects for intensifying the air war against Japan as called for in DOWNFALL were not bright. The growing complaints from airmen who felt they were being unfairly treated by the AAF's erratic processes also threatened to undermine the system. Marshall and Robert Patterson were especially sensitive to these complaints—from soldiers and airmen alike. Unmentioned in the official histories is the question how the AAF's implementation of the modified point system might affect the air forces already waging war in the Pacific. Would headquarters in Washington or the commanders in the field insist on treating their men the same as those who had seen combat in Europe? The AAF had already compromised on its commitment to combat efficiency when it changed its policy regarding the redeployment of forces to the Pacific. Would it be forced to do so again?

This was a problem that Army Ground Forces was already dealing with as it confronted the necessity of discharging high-point men from the divisions earmarked for OLYMPIC and CORONET. Once it was determined how many men were eligible for discharge, the next step was to identify replacements and provide for their transfer to the Pacific Theater so they could join their units in time to begin training for the invasion. That meant that sometime during the summer the already overtaxed shipping in the Pacific would have to accommodate a yet-to-be-determined number of replacements bound for the Philippines or Okinawa. These would be added to the more predictable need to replace soldiers lost in battle or rendered unfit for combat due to disease or injury.

In mid-June, two days before Truman's June 18 conference with the JCS, MacArthur had startled the War Department with the news that he would need a staggering 219,000 officers and enlisted men to bring the OLYMPIC forces to full strength. He based his calculations on several assumptions: that all units involved in the invasion should be at full strength; that personnel with Adjusted Rating Scores of eighty-five or higher would be removed from their units; and that a pool of replacements constituting 10 percent of the invasion force should be held in reserve to sustain the invasion after the initial landings. MacArthur explained that by July 1, the forces under his command would be short 64,000 men, 34,000 of whom would be in units scheduled for OLYMPIC. He expected to lose another 47,000 men through normal attrition over the next three months. He estimated that another 66,000 from OLYMPIC divisions would be discharged with eighty-five or more points. He also estimated that he would need another 42,000 men for his replacement pool.[46]

In declaring his personnel needs in his message to the War Department, MacArthur also specified that his most pressing need was for experienced officers and men. Readjustment would deprive him of thousands of "battle-wise seasoned veterans of long experience." The OLYMPIC divisions would also be losing "key men and specialists who due to long training are difficult to replace."[47] The prospect of inserting as many as 5,000 new men into a division slated for the November 1 Kyushu invasion was daunting enough. The current crop of untested replacements he was receiving would not do. This was especially true of the eighteen-year-olds, who were being shipped overseas before they had received six months training and thus could not be used in combat.

The War Department assured MacArthur two days later that they were doing everything to meet his needs. At present the West Coast ports had a backlog of 124,000 personnel destined for his command. But these would be augmented in the next four months, so he could expect 50,000 in June, 75,000 in July, 70,000 in August, and another 70,000 in September, for a total of 265,000 replacements.[48] The next day, recalculations in Manila and Washington revealed that MacArthur actually had 23,000 men over the amount called for in his table of organization, as opposed to a shortfall of 64,000 he had originally reported to the War Department. That meant that Washington would be able to meet all of his requirements for replacements, including the 96,000 personnel slated for readjustment, and still have 37,000 men to spare. "It must be recognized," MacArthur's headquarters was told, "that shipping capabilities will be strained to lift this number of replacements and deliver them to your theater in months as indicated."[49] Considerable exertion would be needed on both sides of the Pacific to execute these transfers. MacArthur would have to release the maximum amount of shipping he currently retained in his theater, and Washington would have to set a high priority for shipping his replacement personnel.

Even then, most of the replacement personnel would not have the desired battle experience. Soldiers who had some combat experience but were not eligible for discharge were expected to replace men with scores of eighty-five points or more in those divisions earmarked for CORONET, which was to take place in 1946. That meant that the men who would be arriving in the Pacific to fill out MacArthur's units would have minimal training beyond basic and little to no experience. Those scheduled to arrive in August and September would be joining their divisions with little time to train with their new team before mounting out for the invasion as early as mid-September.

The details of implementing simultaneous demobilization and redeployment from Europe were left to staff officers who specialized in logistics, transportation, personnel, and training. Early staff studies predicted that the shipping capabilities to accomplish both tasks existed. But these had been based on the assumption that OLYMPIC would commence on December 1, not November 1. Subsequent studies concluded that the earlier start date was possible but would create a much greater strain on the Army's capabilities and require "the closest coordination of all logistics resources during the coming months."[50] That cautious prediction, which did not reckon with the difficulties that arose in the readjustment process, proved optimistic. By June 18, when Truman met with the JCS and approved the invasion of Kyushu for November 1, the staff officers responsible for coordinating the organization, movement, and loading of redeploying units and their equipment were already running behind schedule.

All troops destined for demobilization or redeployment were funneled through the Assembly Area Command near Reims, in northern France, and thence to one of several ports in France or the Netherlands. Service troops, including engineers, redeployed directly to the Pacific through the port of Marseilles in order to meet the urgent need for construction of bases and airfields in the Philippines and other staging areas. At first these service units were expected to sail with their equipment convoy loaded for the Pacific. This procedure proved too cumbersome because of complications involved in repairing, assembling, and packing full sets of the required equipment. None of the three convoys slated to sail under this system met its scheduled departure date. As a consequence, the European Theater adopted a revised system in which a unit's equipment would be packed separately and sail ahead of the troops on slower cargo vessels while the personnel boarded faster moving transports at a later date. This new procedure made more efficient use of all of the shipping available, but it was subsequently discovered that that advantage was negated by improper packing of much of the equipment, making it unusable when it arrived in the Philippines.[51]

The divisions designated for CORONET also encountered numerous problems in trying to prepare for redeployment while discharging men with eighty-five points or more. In many cases divisions were on the move before they could identify the soldiers eligible for discharge and secure their replacements. In other cases, such as the Forty-Fifth Division, the criteria for selecting units for redeployment were utterly baffling. The Forty-Fifth, which was earmarked for CORONET, had 11,000 enlisted men and 600 officers eligible for discharge. On the other hand the Sixty-Third and Sixty-Fifth Divisions, both slated for deactivation, had far fewer personnel with scores above eighty-five.[52] The process encountered additional problems when many of the redeploying divisions failed to receive the orders directing them to the assembly area or their assigned port. In other instances, problems with the French rail net also impeded transfer of troops returning from Germany.

The Army hoped that troops waiting for redeployment would begin some of the training required for combat in the Pacific while they were waiting to disembark from Europe. This proved nearly impossible, for a variety of reasons. Equipment for training had to be secured because divisions marked for redeployment turned in all but essential personal gear for packing and shipment when they arrived at the assembly area. Fluctuations in personnel further complicated matters. There was little point in beginning training while large numbers of men in any given division were awaiting discharge and their replacements had yet to appear. The lag in training shifted the burden onto Army Ground Forces in the United States. Originally the Army expected redeploying divisions to receive the remainder of the eight-week course when they reformed at one of the designated bases after the soldiers returned from their month-long furloughs. The plan was to have redeploying units pick up where they left off in Europe. Inadequate record-keeping foiled even that modest expectation. By June, only four of the 170 arriving units submitted reports on what training had been accomplished before disembarking for home. The outgoing head of Army Ground Forces, General Joseph Stilwell, downplayed the need for extra training. While observing the action on Okinawa, Stilwell said that most GIs who had fought in Europe would be able to learn how to fight the Japanese in a week. But Stilwell's replacement, General Jacob Devers, found it necessary to reassure the public by emphasizing that the redeploying soldiers would receive a full eight-week course that would prepare them for the rigors of combat against the Japanese.[53]

The experience of the Ninety-Sixth Division, which had just completed operations on Okinawa, suggested that Devers was closer to the mark than Stilwell. Major General J. R. Bradley, the Ninety-Sixth's commander, thought that soldiers would need special training to deal with a variety of situations his division had faced on Okinawa. For example, soldiers advancing beyond

Japanese positions would need to be followed closely by reserves who would have the responsibility of mopping up the large number of bypassed Japanese soldiers who frequently remained hidden in caves and tunnels. Fortified ridges needed to be attacked longitudinally to minimize the fire from Japanese dug in on the reverse slope beyond the reach of artillery. Bradley advised that indirect fire did little to reduce fortified positions in caves. In these situations, direct fire weapons, such as recoilless rifles, a shoulder-held light artillery weapon, tanks, flamethrowers, and infantry units had to work closely together. Even then, it would take as much as three or four days before the fortifications could be properly assaulted by infantry.

Bradley also had several suggestions regarding personnel management that were of special significance for the forthcoming invasion of the Japanese homeland. "The practice of throwing a great many green replacements into battle at one time, as was necessary in this operation, resulted in a great many early casualties among these men." It would be better, Bradley recommended, to insert replacements on a daily basis so these smaller numbers of men could be more easily absorbed into their units and trained by the battle-tested veterans. Fighting the Japanese, Bradley added, forced men to stay on constant alert for the possibility of infiltration and night attacks. That stress, combined with the strain of being under near constant shellfire, meant that whenever possible, assault troops should be removed from the front lines every two weeks.[54]

The training program that Army Ground Forces began to adopt incorporated many of the lessons learned on Okinawa and elsewhere in the Pacific into a course that would include, among other subjects, modules on Japanese tactics, identification of Japanese weapons, effective employment of American weapons against caves, night fighting, and, importantly, prevention of disease.[55] The overall plan for training redeployed divisions called for soldiers to draw what was needed for training in the United States and meet up, as noted earlier, with their equipment in the Philippines. The training timetable made the "unbelievably tight" invasion schedules even tighter.[56] The first redeployed divisions arrived in late June. After a month's furlough, they would begin training in late July or early August. Two months later they would embark for the Philippines and arrive in late October or early November. At that point, they would have to unpack their equipment and make it serviceable, engage in landing and firing exercises, combat load their ships, and mount out for CORONET by January 20, 1946, the date set by MacArthur's headquarters. Subsequent divisions, arriving over the course of the summer, would have progressively less time.

Securing and then coordinating the shipping needed to simultaneously move demobilized personnel and redeploying divisions across the Atlantic provided its own set of headaches. Officers overseeing these troop movements soon found that some of the redeploying units left Europe before they had transferred out their high-point personnel. Once these units shed their high-point men in the United States, they needed replacements to bring them up to full strength. Replacements could not be obtained in the United States, however, because, as we have noted, soldiers being processed through training centers stateside were being sent directly to the Pacific to fill out MacArthur's understrength divisions. To obtain replacements for the redeploying divisions, therefore, Army Ground Forces requisitioned low-score men stationed in Europe in "packets" of 2,000. By mid-June, however, the Army found that it could not secure enough shipping to transport the low-score replacements while simultaneously meeting its quota for returning high-point personnel to the United States. Faced with the hard choice of speeding up the return of replacements or following through on its public commitment to demobilization, the Army chose the latter.[57] By mid-June, only a month into demobilization and redeployment, the accumulating inefficiencies in the system were clear to all involved.

Transportation delays, which would cut into training time, could occur at any step in the process. In contrast to the problems encountered in readying the divisions in Europe for redeployment, the return of demobilized soldiers actually moved ahead of schedule. This proved a mixed blessing. As noted, the arrival of more troops than expected in June threw the American transportation system into confusion. As soldiers crowded into trains to begin their furloughs, a public brawl ensued between the Army, the head of the civilian Office of Defense Transportation (ODT), and Congress. The head of the ODT blamed the Army for the problem. The Army's representatives, led by Undersecretary Patterson, alternated between downplaying the problem and blaming the ODT for not being properly prepared for the influx of GIs.[58]

Patterson finally yielded, but only slightly. On June 28 he announced that the Army would furlough 4,000 trainmen for thirty days to help with redeployment. But he made it clear that he did not expect the Army to grant more furloughs for the railroads or other industries. At the same time, Patterson rebuked the ODT for forcing GIs to travel in squalid conditions and insisted that the Army had fulfilled its role by giving the civilian transportation agency ample notice of the increase in demand that would follow V-E Day.[59] In reality, even the Army staff officers who were responsible for moving the returning GIs from their ships to their reception stations, from which they would board trains for their furloughs, were dismayed by the unexpected influx of soldiers from the European Theater. Colonel D. E. Farr of the Troop Control section in the Pentagon scolded his counterparts in Paris for being woefully slow in transmitting information on ship arrivals that, to compound the problem, often turned out to be inaccurate as well. "We are having considerable difficulty with you people lately," he complained. "6 Ships arrived over here within the last 24 hours and no report whatsoever has come from you people that the ships were even at sea."[60]

As originally conceived, redeployment plans relied on accurate information regarding ship capacity, sailing speed, and distance. Of course there was no way to factor in loading delays, and thus that unmeasurable variable was left out of the plans. But even seemingly concrete statistics, such as ship capacity, were subject to manipulation in ways that created further obstacles to redeployment. In early July, the beleaguered Colonel Farr learned that the redeployment of service troops from the European Theater to the Southwest Pacific was already behind schedule. The problem arose because of delays in getting vehicles to the loading areas in Marseilles. Instead of shipping out 236,000 troops with equipment by the end of July, the European Theater expected to move only 119,000, with the hope that they would catch up in September. Farr was skeptical they could do so. Simply put, the theater's arithmetic did not add up. "I'm a little mixed up on this," admitted Brigadier General Franklin, in the Troop Control section in Paris. "Somebody is," replied Farr, "because if these are facts I think we'd better call the war off in the Pacific." The problem, Farr explained, was that Franklin used eighteen freighters in June to transport equipment for 36,000 troops. But in July he expected to sail twenty-seven freighters carrying equipment for only 30,000 men. In other words, the European Theater would be using nine more freighters than in June but would be shipping equipment for 6,000 fewer troops. "The proportions don't exactly match," Farr observed. Franklin noted the discrepancy but was unable to explain it.[61] And so it went.

The delays in shipping equipment from Marseilles would have a ripple effect throughout the entire transoceanic transportation network. One solution, as we've noted, was to have service troops arrive ahead of their equipment, but no one knew whether that would be acceptable to MacArthur's headquarters. Another alternative was to use the available shipping to bring more troops back from Europe, a faster run that would make it possible for ships to return to Marseilles and then move service troops "in phase" with their equipment to the Pacific. But even here the principals could not agree on the basic facts. Franklin told Farr that there were 295,000 GIs already scheduled for indirect redeployment through the United States. Farr protested that this amounted to a 100 percent increase in the expected berthing capacity on the ships. Farr explained that his office had factored in an additional 20 percent for overberthing based on agreed estimates, but he could not imagine how the European Theater was going to load its ships with twice as many troops as originally expected.

The additional troops would, of course, add to the rail congestion on the East Coast. Nevertheless, although the clogged rail system could delay furloughs and thus interfere with the timing of redeployment to the Pacific, all concerned recognized that the real threat to the redeployment schedules would arise when more than one and half million soldiers were slated to be shipped across the country in November and December. The situation was already dire and would only get worse. "Let me tell you something for your information," Farr added in his communication with Franklin. "The backlog of troops in the United States to sail to the Pacific is reaching unmanageable proportions. The failure of the European Theater to handle these ships for direct redeployment is going to further increase that and create further difficulties."[62]

The difficulties encountered in the initial stages of redeployment did not provide much reason for optimism that they would be resolved. Of course, one could point to the Army's impressive record in the war to date as evidence that it would be able to manage any problems that stood in the way of a successful redeployment. But one could also point out that, as Marshall had noted earlier, the Army's task was unprecedented in history. The clock was ticking, and the Army was behind schedule.

In facing the challenges posed by indirect redeployment through the United States the Army confronted the unyielding physical limitations of the western trunk lines. The western rail net was not built to move such large numbers of men from the East to the West without impinging on the civilian traffic, passenger and freight, that was vital to the region's economic well-being. Manpower shortages, the lack of skilled engineers, signal men, and mechanics compounded the problem. Long-deferred maintenance on engines and track spelled trouble as the railroads geared up for the impending surge in traffic. Railroad executives and their allies in Congress saw an easy fix to the labor shortage. The Army could still discharge the thousands of skilled workers it had drafted into service, or, failing that, furlough the men until the crisis passed. Proponents of this remedy argued that by making the trains run on time, these men would be making a valuable contribution to the war effort.[63]

The Army, more specifically Undersecretary Patterson, continued to disagree with this proposal. As we've noted, almost immediately after V-E Day the War Department had been besieged with requests to make an exception to the eighty-five-point critical score and give preference to one or another group of GIs that was desperately needed at home. These included dentists, ministers, fathers, men over thirty, and coal miners. Making the case for the miners were union leaders, mine operators, and Secretary of Interior and Solid Fuels Administrator Harold Ickes. Ickes insisted that in the coming winter American cities and, equally important, much of western Europe would face a coal shortage unless the Army released men to work the mines.

Patterson viewed all requests for special exemptions, including Ickes's, as a threat to the integrity of the point system. The undersecretary of war had battled Congress and other civilian agencies over what he believed was the nation's failure to fully mobilize. After the defeat of the national service bill he went on high alert for any signs of slackening in the home front's commitment to the war. The mounting pressure for reconversion following V-E Day confirmed his worst fears. So he held the line and rebuffed the many petitions that crossed his desk asking for what he perceived as undeserved special treatment for various groups of GIs.[64]

Nothing, Patterson insisted, could be allowed to alter the Army's democratically constructed point system. Every special request was the thin end of a wedge that could crack open the whole system. Austere, stern, and tireless in conducting the duties of his office, Patterson served as an ideal villain for those in Congress, the press, and wartime agencies who pushed for reconversion. As *Look* noted in a generally favorable article, "Washington's No. 1 War Zealot" was a "paragon of personal rectitude" whose "fervor causes many less exacting public officials to pray nightly for his political demise."[65] Rather than yield to public opinion, Patterson sought to influence it through his office's public relations arm and through his many appearances before congressional committees and mobilization agencies.[66] All of these efforts were directed toward keeping the nation focused on the many sacrifices that still needed to be made to complete the daunting task of defeating Japan.

Advocates of reconversion and emergency furloughs believed that Patterson's stark ordering of priorities—the Army's needs coming first, all else relegated to secondary status—was simplistic and ultimately harmful to the country. Privately, the frustrated Ickes complained to Vinson that "Bob Patterson not only has a one track mind, the one track is just a short spur."[67] Ickes, Vinson, and Patterson's other critics worried that in winning the war the United States could still lose the peace. Widespread famine in Europe and large-scale unemployment and spiraling inflation at home would make it extremely difficult for the United States to build the kind of world millions of soldiers, sailors, and Marines were fighting for.

Vinson, who had already butted heads with General Somervell over the Army's manpower and supply needs, found Patterson's unwillingness to budge on reconversion particularly disturbing. Vinson had risen to prominence in Congress on the basis of his intellectual prowess. A "hog for work," he was also renowned for having an almost encyclopedic knowledge of the tax code. He had displayed that same ability to master complex financial matters when he served as vice-chair of the American delegation to the Bretton Woods Conference. At Bretton Woods and in his various administrative positions, Vinson was regarded as someone willing to negotiate freely and build consensus on final decisions.[68] After working with the British and Russians, Vinson found dealing with Robert Patterson a trial. Privately each man referred to the other as unreasonable and given to exaggeration. Communication between the two and between the members of their staffs took on a tone of frosty politeness that barely concealed the antagonism simmering in both offices. Beneath the clash of personalities lay a more serious difference in ideology.

As noted, Vinson was, like Truman, a solid supporter of the New Deal. He was supported by a staff of advisers, such as Robert Nathan, who shared his views on the need for government to regulate business and provide relief for the unemployed. Vinson and the New Dealers on his staff distrusted the staunch Republican Patterson, accusing him of favoring big business with war contracts and harboring an open hostility to labor.[69] Patterson, for his part, insisted that his one and only concern was making sure that American fighting men had the equipment and ammunition they needed to win the war. Military necessity trumped all other considerations. As the defeat of the national service bill and the restrictions on the use of eighteen-year-olds indicated, however, that argument was beginning to wear thin. Marshall, Patterson, and General Somervell were having to work harder to win support for the manpower, matériel, and budgetary means required to carry out the Army's strategy for subduing Japan.

Vinson, no less than the men in the Pentagon, believed that the policies he recommended were in the best interests of the country. In making his case, he was in the advantageous position of being able to speak directly to the president every morning at the White House staff meetings. Vinson could also count on Truman taking seriously what he had to say, even if he did not always side with Vinson. After all, Truman had headed the Senate's investigating committee on war expenditures and had seen more than enough evidence of chiseling by businesses and careless spending by the War Department. Indeed, he later claimed that in heading what became known as the Truman Committee he saved taxpayers $15 billion. As a senator, Truman had also cosponsored legislation to promote full employment in the postwar era. The Truman-Kilgore-Murray bill, known informally as the Reconversion Bill, made full employment a goal and recommended a national system of unemployment insurance. Privately, Truman complained that the military mobilizers "would create a fascist government if Somervell can manage it."[70] In sum, Truman's respect for Marshall and his unswerving commitment to total victory over Japan was balanced against an abiding interest in avoiding a return to Depression-era levels of unemployment and a keen awareness that the Pentagon was not always the best steward of the peoples' hard-earned money.

The task of easing the transition of the nation's economy from wartime regimentation to peacetime stability was likely to result in sharp disagreements, for this was uncharted territory for all concerned. The difference in scale between the experience after World War I and what the nation was facing in 1945 made comparisons difficult. Moreover, the process of demobilization after the Great War had not been haunted by fresh memories of depression and massive unemployment. What lay ahead was anyone's guess. This was amply demonstrated during a June 1 cabinet meeting in which Treasury Secretary Henry Morgenthau, Jr., complained about a recent statement by the War Production Board predicting 1,800,000 unemployed workers by the end of the year. Morgenthau doubted that anyone knew what the figure would be and worried that the bleak announcement would hurt the current bond drive. Navy Secretary Forrestal predicted that there would be fewer people unemployed two years hence than there were at present. Paul McNutt, head of the War Manpower Commission, was more bullish; there would be no unemployment any time in the next ten years, he said. Following the meeting, Secretary of Commerce Henry Wallace, Secretary of the Interior Ickes, and Attorney General Francis Biddle, generally regarded as the New Deal holdovers in the cabinet, privately expressed amusement at Forrestal's and McNutt's rosy predictions. The strongest reaction, however, came from the president. Clearly perturbed by the subject, Truman cut off the discussion by saying that he wanted no public statements about prospective unemployment.[71]

Vinson and the members of his staff wisely shied away from making such predictions in public, but privately they and the members of the OWMR's Advisory Board worried that the Army's continuing manpower and maté-riel needs were preventing reconversion and steering the postwar economy toward disaster. Inflationary pressure, caused by high demand for limited materials and goods, posed an immediate danger. Unemployment, a likely consequence of millions of soldiers returning home to an economy that had not begun to absorb displaced war workers, was slightly less pressing, given the expected length of the war, but an equally serious threat. Alarmed by con-tinuing inflationary pressure, the Advisory Board explained in a June report: "Reconversion plans, while assuring all-out production for the defeat of Japan, must anticipate the impact on the domestic economy which will be felt when that production is terminated." Having given the obligatory deference to the war effort, the report advised that "the prudent use of our resources calls for careful determination of military requirements with reference to the needs of the civilian economy, the minimum requirements of which are essential to continued war production." The immediate danger, as far as the Advisory Board was concerned, was inflationary pressure on civilian goods caused by continuing shortages. The answer, according to the report, was to increase pro-duction of civilian goods and services "as rapidly as possible." If military pro-duction could not be cut, although the report implied that it could, some other, unspecified means of increasing civilian production had to be found.[72]

In assessing the lagging pace of reconversion Vinson and his advisers acted on the assumption that the Army was using more men and purchas-ing more supplies than it needed to defeat Japan. Vinson had driven that point home in his meetings with Somervell and later with the JCS. That approach was already paying dividends. Robert Nathan reported to Vinson with obvious satisfaction that whereas on May 19 the Army had predicted only a 15 percent cutback in production requirements for the last quarter of 1945, by the end of May it had revised that figure upward to 31 percent. The change in estimates, he added, "certainly indicate[s] that you have hit pay dirt in your discussions with the Joint Chiefs of Staff."[73]

That was a promising start, but more opportunities for trimming existed. For example, Army Service Forces estimates for a one-front war, in contrast to the two-front campaign, showed an *increase* in purchasing in five distinct categories. Of these, the increase in bombs and chemical warfare materials was, according to one of Vinson's aides, understandable, as was the increase in the requirement for railroad cars, most of which were narrow-gauge stock for the China and India theaters. On the other hand there was probably considerable fat in the estimate for equipage and clothing, for which increases of 21 and 26 percent, respectively, were estimated. These last two items were being reviewed by the War Department and War Production Board. The Army's manpower estimates also came in for further scrutiny.[74] Of particular concern was the expectation that the Army, according to its May statement on demobilization, would have 6,968,000 men in uniform by June 1946, almost three million of whom would be in the United States. Of those kept stateside, 1,300,000 would be "operating personnel," involved in training, administrative overhead, supply, and "housekeeping." Out of the group, noted the report to Vinson, 900,000 would have had service overseas. Although the report did not make any recommendations, the presentation—"you may be interested in casting your eye over the table"; "You will be interested in this breakdown"—implied considerable skepticism about the numbers, especially the 900,000 veterans who would be kept in uniform in the United States a year after V-E Day for such duties as "housekeeping."[75]

The War Department's critics, and they were growing in number, simply could not fathom why the Army needed seven million men in uniform a year after Germany's defeat. The prospect of the Army quite literally gobbling up supplies and foodstuffs—including the figure of 400 pounds of red meat per soldier per year—for at least another year smothered all hope of reconversion. Patterson tried, without much success, to explain the Army's needs and the simultaneous processes of discharge and redeployment at a June 11 meeting of the OWMR Advisory Board. He assured the board that the Army was planning on discharging two million servicemen by June 1946 and that to reach that number it would soon be announcing a reduction in the Adjusted Rating Score needed for discharge. In the meantime, the Army and AAF were moving three million men out of Europe and between ten and fifteen million tons of supplies. To defeat Japan the Army would make use of American superiority in airpower to weaken Japan's ability to resist an invasion and thus to save lives. He dismissed as unfounded accusations that the Army was stockpiling supplies for after the war or producing surplus munitions now for fear of a mass exodus of workers from war plants. The Army was procuring material for one purpose only, he said: defeating Japan.[76] Patterson further explained that the Army would be releasing men over forty years of age soon and he hoped that the continuing discharge of high-point men would help ease the strain in key labor sectors. But he added that nothing could be done to upset the point system that was approved by the men in uniform. There would be no early discharges or special furloughs for skilled workers.

There was little in Patterson's presentation to encourage Vinson, who attended the June 11 Advisory Board meeting. Hoping that some of the soldiers discharged from service would be able to make up for the shortage in railroad workers or miners was wishful thinking. In the meantime, traffic from the West Coast carrying foodstuffs and trains on the East Coast moving redeployed soldiers home on furlough were behind schedule, overcrowded, or simply unavailable. West Coast shipyards were also experiencing a shortage of skilled labor. In late May, Vinson had received a report indicating that shipyards in California and Washington were below their personnel ceilings by more than 24,000 workers. This shortfall came at a time when work was piling up owing to the devastating effects of kamikaze attacks on the fleet supporting the Okinawa campaign. As of late May, thirty-one ships were being repaired or were heading for work at the West Coast yards, with another sixty on the way.[77] As the seriousness of the problem became apparent, Congressman James Wadsworth (R-New York) asked Patterson about the possibility of furloughing skilled workers to address the shortfall. Patterson informed Wadsworth that the Army and Navy were looking to release electricians from a special project so they could be transferred out West, but he repeated his standard explanation that there would be no furloughs. Discharges under the point system would have to take up the slack.[78]

What seemed like a quick remedy or at least a step in the right direction to some struck Patterson as a reckless overreaction to temporary problems. The furloughing or early release of soldiers with critical skills, he believed, would wreak havoc on the integrity of the point system and severely damage morale on the eve of the final campaigns of the war. In sticking to the soldier-approved Adjusted Rating Score, Patterson was following advice he had received from Winston Churchill. The prime minister had warned Patterson that after the Great War Britain's brief experiment with returning soldiers on the basis of work experience had undermined morale and provoked protest among the troops.[79] Patterson was loathe to incite that kind of response while there was a war on. On the other hand his reliance on the planned discharge of GIs to meet the shortfall in critical areas was wishful thinking at best. There was no guarantee that workers would return to their prewar jobs and a slim chance that they would do so immediately after being released from several years of military service.

Certainly there was no ready answer to the problems the United States was facing in gearing up for the last stage of the war. Coordinating the movement of ships, men, and equipment was proving exceedingly difficult. Important industries needed trained workers, while in other war industries cutbacks or cancelation of orders were producing localized spikes in unemployment. In the first week of June, Vinson was told, unemployment compensation claims had risen by 25 percent. Two-thirds of all claims were concentrated in New York, Michigan, Pennsylvania, Illinois, and California.[80] There were few options for these workers as long as the Army continued to control materials vital to civilian industry. Congressmen and local leaders at the state level sought to address their local unemployment problems by regaining control of the state employment agencies that had been nationalized as the United States Employment Service during the war. The president declined these requests, citing the continued demands of the war and the need to direct skilled workers into vital war industries.[81]

In late June, Vinson learned that these conditions were unlikely to change any time soon because of the lagging pace of redeployment and limitations in unloading and storage capacity throughout the Pacific. In June, the Army had requested 110 cargo ships to move equipment and supplies from southern France but subsequently learned that it would be able to load only fifty-seven of them. Plans called for loading 120 ships in July, but that number had been reduced to eighty-four. Across the Pacific, Manila, the main port for receiving supplies, was able to unload 9,000 tons a day. The original estimate had been 40,000. Deficiencies in roads and depots complicated storage problems. Little improvement in those conditions was expected because of the start of the rainy season. "There is considerable criticism of the Army," the report noted, "because they are now planning to clean out ETO [the European Theater of Operations] by dumping large amounts of cargo on already overstrained facilities in Pacific areas." Worse news followed. "If a conclusion may be drawn from these circumstances it is that a further delay in planned major operations would not be surprising."[82]

The Army, of course, would have rejected that conclusion. During the war, the Army had demonstrated an impressive ability to improvise solutions by reallocating personnel and resources to meet emergencies. Plans had already been developed to compensate for some of the Pacific Theater's logistical limitations by bringing divisions earmarked for OLYMPIC from the Central Pacific directly to the invasion beaches. By this time, however, Vinson was less likely to be impressed by the Army's "can-do" attitude. The possibility that operations would be delayed meant that the war would be prolonged and the Army's obstruction of reconversion would continue.

The country existed in an uneasy state, somewhere between peace and war. Mounting concerns about unemployment, inflation, and scarcity of materials for the civilian economy coexisted with alarm over conditions in Europe. Food and fuel shortages foreshadowed a winter of privation and desperation for much of liberated Europe. Soldiers were coming home for good, but many more would be passing through on the way to a front that seemed ever more distant and a war whose foregone conclusion made the prospect of greater sacrifices seem obscene. Local leaders and their representatives in Congress pressed the government to further eliminate wartime controls and questioned the Army's need for so many men and so much matériel. Officials in the civilian mobilization agencies, members of Congress, labor leaders, and state officials were reacting to what they perceived as impending problems that would lead to economic hardship after the war. In this respect they were ahead of public opinion, neither leading it nor responding to its demands.

Of course, policy-makers paid attention to public opinion. The White House monitored newspaper editorials and kept tabs on polls, measuring, among other things, the president's approval ratings. The War Department maintained its own public relations officers and regularly measured opinion in the ranks. As far as Patterson was concerned, however, the most important poll, the one used to construct the point system for discharge, had already been taken.[83] But the War Department also monitored public opinion to gauge how citizens outside the military viewed the war in general and Army policies in particular. Congressmen also watched the polls, but as historian William O'Neill notes, throughout the war legislators discounted as unreliable polling data that showed that the public was willing to endure significant hardship for the sake of the war.[84] Like Congress, the War Department seems to have treated polls the same way, citing those that confirmed department policies and ignoring those that did not.

Following Samuel Rosenman's report on the food shortages in Europe, *Time* correspondent Raymound Buell noted a poll showing that Americans supported Rosenman's recommendations calling for reductions in consumption at home in order to provide more relief to liberated Europe.[85] Buell also noted, however, that General Somervell would not agree to touch the Army's ration of 400 pounds of meat per soldier each year. (On average, civilian adults were allowed about 130 pounds per year.) "One of the greatest problems in this country," Buell wrote, "is that the military services are almost a law unto themselves." Needed was "a tough civilian authority to decide between military and civilian needs in non-military areas."[86] In light of the often contradictory findings of different polls, policy-makers in Congress and the executive branch could be forgiven for not shaping policies in conformity to the latest surveys. One did not need an opinion poll to know that most Americans wanted the war to be over. It was more difficult, however, to know what a majority of Americans were willing to do to bring an end to the fighting. On the one hand a majority insisted on unconditional surrender and complete victory over Japan. When asked about how to treat Hirohito, 33 percent wanted to execute him, 17 percent wanted to put him on trial, 11 percent wanted to imprison him for life, and only 3 percent of respondents thought the United States should keep him in place and govern Japan through him.[87]

Complicating the picture was a poll by the Cantril organization in June 1945 in which 58 percent of respondents preferred to see the Japanese brought to the brink of starvation by the Navy and American airpower before any invasion. Only 27 percent called for a prompt invasion.[88] As we have noted, however, Marshall and the Joint Staff Planners believed that a policy of siege would prolong the war and increase the likelihood of a negotiated settlement. That, in turn, would make it nearly impossible to achieve the war aims that Americans said they supported: unconditional surrender and punishment of the emperor. Other polls in June demonstrated growing public concern over casualties, the battle for Okinawa having just ended, but offered little guidance on policy preferences. In a Cantril poll, participants were offered the choice of making peace with Japan after it relinquished control of China and the Pacific islands or continuing to fight at the possible cost of "several hundred thousand American soldiers." The total wanting to fight was 56 percent, those willing to make peace 37 percent. In a *Fortune* poll that asked a similar question but omitted reference to casualties, the percentage willing to fight rose to 85 percent.[89] A concurrent survey of soldiers' views on war aims also yielded results that showed support for unconditional surrender but ambivalence about how it should be obtained. Conducted in June, the poll surveyed 2,075 soldiers who had returned to the United States from overseas duty. When asked if they supported "a peace in which both sides would have something to say about the peace terms," 1,332 answered that the United States should keep fighting until Japan was thoroughly beaten, 201 supported negotiations, and 500 were undecided. But when asked how they felt about further service in the war, 1,248 said they should be discharged now, and 381 said they should serve a while longer, but not until Japan was defeated.[90] In other words, the majority thought that the job of subduing Japan should be someone else's. That response is understandable, given that nearly all of the participants in the poll had earned at least one combat star and the vast majority had two or more.

It is easy to see why the majority believed they had done their part. Nevertheless, it seems clear that the GIs' commitment to unconditional surrender had to be qualified by the knowledge that most of the soldiers participating in the poll believed that they would not be sent to the Pacific.[91] Efforts to survey civilian attitudes about the home front, rationing, wages, and postwar economic conditions showed a general uneasiness about the future and a readiness to see wartime restrictions lifted. But the polls did not reveal the public to be as angry or weary of regimentation as congressmen and mobilization officials said they were. Shortly after V-E Day a survey showed Americans wanted relief from rationing. But, as noted, civilians also claimed they were prepared to reduce food consumption in order to alleviate shortages in Europe. Moreover, whatever they thought about rationing, 74 percent of respondents in a poll said that resorting to black market purchases was not justified. In another survey taken on June 8, 77 percent of participants said that Congress should wait until Japan was defeated before lowering income taxes.[92]

By the end of June public opinion polls generally showed a continuing commitment to winning the war against Japan, support for unconditional surrender, and recognition of the fairness of the Army's demobilization scheme. At the same time, the flood of letters calling for the immediate return of loved ones from Europe or discharge from stateside units, the expressions of dismay at the bloodletting on Iwo Jima and Okinawa, and the growing anxiousness over life after the war, demonstrated by workers leaving war-related jobs and a flurry of strikes, revealed an ambivalence that might easily crystalize into more substantive pressure on the government.

For Americans, the growing conviction of the inevitability of Japan's defeat and horror at its cost made the Pacific war seem more repugnant and less meaningful than the war against Germany. As a result, the public focus after V-E Day shifted from Europe to reconversion, rather than to Asia, as Americans began a difficult transition to a civilian economy. The shift in Washington was more rapid and radical than on Main Street. Most Americans, uncertain, confused, tired of war, and worried about casualties and jobs, held onto wartime constraints and values as far as possible. Political, labor, opinion, and corporate elites pressed harder and more insistently for the elimination of wartime regulations and the transition to a sustainable civilian economy.

In this transformed setting, the Army, the most pervasive arm of government, had become the nation's principal target of criticism and scapegoat. The Army's civilian and uniformed leaders did their best to fend off these criticisms and held their own against attempts to alter the strategy for the defeat of Japan, the demobilization process, or the budget that the Army deemed necessary for completing the war. During the first week of July, Congress, eager to leave town, voted in favor of the Army's $39 billion budget. The same week, as Truman prepared to travel to the summit conference in Potsdam, he upheld Patterson's administration of the point system in a cabinet meeting, dealing Ickes and Vinson a setback in their efforts to address what they saw as critical labor shortages at home.[93] In mid-June, the president maintained his confidence in Marshall and Stimson and reconciled himself to OLYMPIC. The Army's plans for victory held. It remained to be seen if the forces required to implement them would be ready in time.

Potsdam, July–August 1945

On July 9, as President Truman sailed east on USS *Augusta* to Europe for the Potsdam summit conference, he passed ships carrying the Fourth and Eighth Infantry Divisions back toward the United States and much needed and greatly anticipated thirty-day furloughs. The Fourth had landed on Utah Beach in the Normandy invasion, helped liberate Paris, and fought in the Hurtgen Forest, one of the bloodiest battles of the war. During its time in Europe the Fourth spent 199 days in constant contact with the enemy and suffered a staggering 30,000 casualties. It was scheduled for CORONET as part of the follow-on force. Later in its voyage, the *Augusta* passed the Second and Eighty-Seventh Infantry Divisions steaming home.[1] The Eighty-Sixth, Ninety-Seventh, 104th, and Ninety-Fifth had already arrived home. The Eighty-Sixth and the Ninety-Seventh were originally slated for service in the Pacific Theater, but after undergoing some amphibious training they were abruptly rerouted to Europe during the Battle of the Bulge. They were the last two divisions sent to Europe and the first two to return to the United States. After arriving in Europe in February, the Eighty-Sixth was in combat for forty-two days, participating in the Battles of the Rhine, Ruhr Pocket, and the Battle of Bavaria. The Eighty-Sixth arrived at the Port of New York on June 18 to the accompaniment of "hot music" played by a Women's Army Corps band in New York Harbor. Undersecretary of War Patterson took a cutter out in the harbor to meet them. The men, sweating under the weight of their souvenir-filled packs and still in winter gear, poured onto ferries that took them to New Jersey, whence they were transported to nearby Camp Kilmer. By June 20, after the best steak dinner they could remember, the Eighty-Sixth's enlisted men were setting out for their thirty-day furloughs. At the end of their leave, they would reassemble at Camp Gruber in Oklahoma. The Ninety-Seventh, veterans of the Ruhr Pocket, began arriving on June 23, along with African-American GIs from the 365th Regiment of Engineers, who had maintained the Red Ball Highway, the trucking route that rushed supplies to the front in Europe. To avoid placing more pressure on New York's overburdened rail system, the transports carrying the Ninety-Seventh and 365th sailed twenty miles up the Hudson River and deposited their passengers only four miles from Camp Shanks. Both units were slated for redeployment in the Pacific, but first they would disperse on their thirty-day furloughs.[2]

The first phase of redeployment was in full swing. All of these units, however, would need to replace soldiers who had qualified for discharge. They would then reassemble for training and move to their staging areas on the West Coast. The westward bound troopships must have reassured the president of America's power. But they may have also reminded the former artillery captain that the returning GIs would be making only a brief layover in the States before continuing on to combat in Japan.

One of Truman's main objectives at Potsdam would be to make the conquest of Japan easier by securing Soviet entry into the war against Japan's Imperial Army forces in Manchuria. Outwardly, the meeting of the Big Three looked like a conference on European issues. The Soviet Union had abrogated its neutrality treaty with Japan, but the two countries remained at peace. Moreover, although most commentators in the United States openly speculated about Soviet entry into the war, Japanese leaders continued to hope that they could persuade Stalin to help bring about a negotiated settlement of the war. Behind the scenes, the task of finishing the war against Japan consumed much of the president's attention. Even when he was engaged in meetings on European issues, the American, British, and Soviet military staffs would be conferring to coordinate their efforts in the final campaigns and delineate operational boundaries so as to avoid accidental clashes between them.

The president expected to have obtained answers to several questions of paramount importance to the defeat of Japan by the time the conference ended. In addition to determining whether and when the Soviet Union would enter the war, Truman expected to learn whether the United States would be able to deploy atomic weapons against Japan before OLYMPIC was scheduled to start. The idea of warning Japan had been rejected by the Interim Committee, a group of top officials, created by Truman and chaired by Henry Stimson, whose task it was to determine the best use of the new weapons. In addition to deciding against warning Japan, the committee recommended using the bomb against Japanese cities, an escalation of the strategic bombing already being conducted by the B-29s flying out of the Marianas. Committee members considered only briefly the possibility of a noncombat demonstration of the bombs.

The Interim Committee also reviewed and approved a target list created by the separate Target Committee, made up of military officers. The list included the ancient capital of Kyoto, Hiroshima, Nagasaki, Kokura, and Niigata. General Marshall, who sat in on committee meetings, believed that Kokura, in northern Kyushu, should top the list. He did not explain his reasoning for selecting Kokura, but it seems likely that it fit most neatly with his concern over the human cost of OLYMPIC and offered the best chance of avoiding the "opprobrium"—Marshall's word—that would come with using the new weapon against civilian targets.[3] First, by crippling a vital link between Kyushu and Honshu, the bomb would support the OLYMPIC landings should they have to be carried out. Second, Kokura's arsenal, the largest in western Japan, and its marshaling yards, which would be the ostensible targets of an attack, were located across the Murasaki River from the city's main center of population, making it possible to argue that an effort had been made to reduce civilian casualties.[4]

The committee's main task was completed once it specified how the bombs should be used. At this point, Stimson took the initiative for combining the committee's recommendations with his own firm belief that the United States should do more to clarify to Japan the meaning of unconditional surrender. Stimson had advised against issuing such a clarification while the battle of Okinawa raged, but because of the atom bomb he strongly believed that the United States should make an overture to Tokyo before launching the invasion. Before the atom bomb was dropped, there would always be the possibility that the Japanese would see a statement clarifying unconditional surrender as an offer to negotiate and a sign of weakness. Stimson was undecided whether a statement of clarification should precede or immediately follow the use of the bomb, but either way the Japanese would learn very quickly that the Americans were acting from a position of overwhelming strength.

Although he was unsure about the timing of the statement, Stimson was more certain about what it should contain. He believed that the Japanese should be told that Hirohito would be allowed to remain on the throne and that the imperial institution would be preserved. Truman's position on the emperor was less clear. In fact, it was not even clear that he favored issuing a statement of any kind to Japan. He often gave visitors to his office the impression that he agreed with them when the case might be otherwise. Moreover, the new president was acting cautiously, understandably uncertain about the best way to proceed, given the weight of the decisions on his shoulders, and had already changed his mind on several occasions.

Acting Secretary of State Joseph Grew was the first to encounter the president's wavering in this area. Truman had praised Grew's draft statement and then pointedly refrained from approving it. Grew had gotten the message. The day after Truman told him to put the item on the agenda for Potsdam, Grew told Stimson and Secretary of the Navy Forrestal that he "was of the impression that the president had indicated that he was not in accord with his point of view" regarding the desirability of issuing a statement clarifying unconditional surrender. Stimson disagreed and said that "he felt that the President did not want to proceed with such a plan at this moment and in particular did not want the Departments to abate in any way their preparations for the ultimate attack because of the existence of such a plan."[5] Stimson was taking liberties in ascribing to Truman views he had not expressed. As we have noted, when the subject of a warning to Japan had come up the day before in the president's meeting with the JCS, Stimson, and Forrestal, Truman had explicitly declined to make a public statement modifying or clarifying unconditional surrender. Instead, he said he had left the door open for Congress to take action and that as far as he was concerned, there was nothing he could do to change public opinion.[6]

Nevertheless, over the next two weeks Stimson acted on his own interpretation of the president's views and arranged for a committee, led by Assistant Secretary of War John McCloy, to draft what would become known as the Potsdam Proclamation. At the next meeting of the Committee of Three—the secretaries of the War, Navy, and State Departments—on June 26, Stimson addressed the subject of "trying to get Japan to surrender by giving her a warning *after* she had been sufficiently pounded possibly with S-1 [atomic weapons]."[7] Stimson also read a memorandum written for the president that explained why it would be sound policy to issue a statement that clarified the meaning of unconditional surrender and warned the Japanese of dire consequences if they refused. Grew and Forrestal approved the memo, and the three cabinet members appointed a subcommittee, led by McCloy, to draft the actual statement.[8] Although the subcommittee included members from the State and Navy Departments, McCloy relied primarily on several members of the Strategy and Policy Group of the Army General Staff to draft the final document. On June 30, McCloy took the draft to Stimson's home on Long Island, and after a few more minor editorial changes the document was ready for submission to the president.[9]

Stimson met with Truman late in the morning on July 2 and presented him with a sheaf of papers consisting of a cover letter from Stimson to the president, a memorandum titled "Proposed Program for Japan," also written by Stimson, and a "Draft Proclamation of the Heads of State.," which had been produced by the McCloy committee. In his letter the secretary of war reminded Truman that he had previously raised the subject of a warning to Japan and had prepared a memorandum laying out the reasons for such a warning. Noting that the warning would contain no mention of a special weapon, Stimson's letter added, "of course it would have to be revamped to conform to the efficacy of such a weapon if the warning were to be delivered, as would almost certainly be the case, in conjunction with its use."[10] Stimson's uncharacteristically imprecise language suggests that he himself had not reached a decision as to what sequence of the warning and the bomb to recommend to the president. What did "in conjunction with" mean? Before or after the bomb was dropped?

Stimson's letter explained that the memorandum and draft proclamation were prepared primarily as "a possible background" for some of the president's forthcoming meetings at Potsdam, but the memorandum itself gave the impression that its main purpose was to persuade the president of the whole idea of a warning rather than provide him with talking points for the Potsdam conference. It began by reviewing the whole decision to invade Japan and forecasting a long, difficult struggle to subdue the enemy. Stimson, for one, had visited the terrain on which the climatic battles would be fought and believed it "susceptible to a last ditch defense such as has been made on Iwo Jima and Okinawa."[11] As the memo made clear, the United States had numerous advantages in the coming campaigns, but turning those advantages into an early victory would be a serious challenge. Then Stimson made his pitch for "a warning of what is to come and a definite opportunity to capitulate." The secretary dismissed as inaccurate the American press's depiction of the Japanese as fanatical and impervious to reason. Japan's history showed that its people were industrious and responsible. He added that although the government was presently controlled by militarists, a submerged group of "liberals" was seeking to regain control of the government. The United States could help that group by issuing a warning that clarified what unconditional surrender meant and enumerating the steps that would be taken during an Allied occupation, while also outlining the steps that would be taken to restore Japan to the family of nations.[12]

Stimson's memorandum explained that all these steps were listed in the attached draft proclamation. He advised the president that the most controversial provision in the proclamation assured the Japanese that the occupying forces would leave Japan once a peacefully inclined and responsible Japanese government had been created beyond any doubt. "This may include," read the last sentence of that section "a constitutional monarchy under the present dynasty if it be shown to the complete satisfaction of the world that such a government would never again aspire to aggression."[13]

Stimson understood that he was throwing a lot at the president. Given the complexity of the subject and the tightness of the president's schedule that day, he asked for an additional appointment the following afternoon. Truman agreed. After the first meeting, Stimson confided to his office diary that Truman "was apparently very well satisfied with the way in which the subjects were presented and he was apparently acquiescent with my attitude toward the treatment of Japan and pronounced the paper which I had written as a very powerful paper."[14]

At their meeting the next day, July 3, the two men discussed the atomic bomb and how they should broach the subject with Stalin at Potsdam. According to his diary, Stimson suggested that if Stalin seemed generally cooperative, Truman should tell him that the United States was working on an atom bomb and that he knew the Soviets were as well. Truman could explain that it was nearly ready and would be used against Japan but that the United States was willing to discuss how to harness the weapon for peace when the war was over. Stimson noted that Truman seemed to agree with him.[15]

The draft proclamation consisted of Grew, Stimson, and Forrestal's efforts to produce a statement that combined a warning to Japan with a clarification of the unconditional surrender policy. The warning aspect was unmistakable. Japanese leaders would witness the "utter devastation of the Japanese homeland" should they refuse to surrender. But the proclamation also assured the Japanese that they could preserve the imperial institution under the current dynasty, pointedly offering a concession on the issue that many experts believed was preventing the peace faction in Tokyo from gaining the upper hand over the militarists. The secretaries acknowledged that the Japanese might see the proclamation as an indication of war weariness in the United States. But they believed that was a chance worth taking, as it held some promise of preventing a battle for Japan's home islands. And, of course, if Truman followed Stimson's recommendation, the proclamation would be issued "in conjunction" with the atomic bomb.

Stimson and the others were aware of the controversial nature of their recommendation. In revising the unconditional surrender formula they were guided by their own ideologically inflected analysis of Japanese history and a resolutely conservative approach to world politics. Those who opposed modifying unconditional surrender so as to permit retention of the emperor tended to be supporters of FDR's New Deal. There was more behind it than a desire for revenge against the nation that had launched the attack on Pearl Harbor. Supporters of unconditional surrender viewed the Japanese imperial institution as fundamentally undemocratic, an easily manipulated symbol of atavistic nationalism. Japanese militarists, they said, were only part of the problem. As Roosevelt had stated when he announced the policy at the January 1943 Casablanca Conference, unconditional surrender meant the "destruction of a philosophy in Germany, Italy, and Japan which is based on the conquest and subjugation of other peoples."[16] Japanese culture, it was felt, contained too many vestiges of its feudal past. Business interests and landlords retained too much power over workers and peasants. Religious and educational institutions contributed to an aggressive philosophy. To remedy the situation, labor unions would have to be protected, cartels dissolved, and tenant farmers unshackled from dependency. In short, the Japanese people needed a New Deal, and this could only be accomplished by a period of sustained occupation.

The outlines of an ideological debate over Japan's future were taking shape in public, through editorials, news reports, and congressional speeches. Similar currents ran beneath the surface of public discourse in the various State Department, military, and interdepartmental working groups.[17] Although most of the debate centered on what was needed to achieve lasting peace in the Pacific, it complicated the debate over the best means of ending the war. International and domestic politics merged. Conservatives hoped that an early end to the war and a limited occupation would eliminate wartime economic controls at home and speed the demise of New Deal–like agencies, such as the Office of Price Administration, which, from their perspective, interfered in the market, intruded into the lives of most Americans, and impeded full employment.[18]

Skeptical that the United States could sustain harmonious relations with the Soviet Union after the war, conservatives led by Hoover also challenged any policy that might work to the Soviet Union's advantage. They worried that a prolonged campaign against Japan would create ample opportunity for the Soviet Union to expand into East Asia. Some in the military supported this idea. Admiral Charles "Savvy" Cooke, the head of the Navy's Strategic Plans Division, worried about the vacuum that would be created by the absence of Japanese power. In a memorandum, Cooke advised Admiral King that the best way to end the war would be with a "strengthened CHINA and a JAPAN thrown back to her homeland, incapable of aggression, on the one hand, but, at the same time not completely eliminated as a party to the stabilization in EASTERN ASIA and the WESTERN PACIFIC."[19] Cooke's concern about the cost of an invasion, not only to American forces but to Japan as well, was shared by other officials in the administration who urged Truman to modify American demands for unconditional surrender. Forrestal, Stimson, and Grew had all privately voiced concerns about Soviet expansion in East Asia at the end of the war.[20] In recommending modification of unconditional surrender, they were also seeking to modify FDR's policy of cooperation with the Soviet Union. They feared that the ashes of Japanese cities would provide fertile ground for the growth of Japanese radicalism and, in addition, abet Soviet expansion in the region. Such thinking colored their advice to Truman, although in their formal recommendations—as we noted in our discussion of the foregoing memorandum—Grew and Stimson limited themselves to assessing the prospects for obtaining American aims through modification of unconditional surrender. Such modification and cooperation with the Soviet Union were not mutually exclusive, of course, but most officials doubted that both policies could be pursued simultaneously.[21] After Stimson handed Truman the draft proclamation, Grew worried that it would get "ditched on the way over" to Potsdam and the meeting with Stalin by officials who believed that "we cannot afford to hold out any clarification of terms to Japan which would be construed as a desire to get the Japanese war over with before Russia has an opportunity to enter."[22] Advocates of unconditional surrender did not oppose "any clarification of terms"; rather, they rejected "clarification" because they felt that the idea of it was really being used to soften the policy. As the ideologically charged debate over unconditional surrender developed in June and July 1945, the adversaries grew increasingly more suspicious of one another's motives.

Opponents of modifying unconditional surrender viewed the draft proclamation as nothing less than an attempt to scrap one of the most important objectives of the war, and without public discussion. When the McCloy draft was sent to the State Department, assistant secretaries of state Dean Acheson and Archibald MacLeish denounced the idea of allowing the emperor to remain on the throne. They argued strenuously in department meetings that it would take more than a pruning away of Japan's military extremists to transform Japan into a peaceful nation. Acheson, described by I. F. Stone as a "progressive and intelligent specimen of the corporate lawyer," thought the whole system needed to be pulled out by the roots, starting with the imperial institution. In private Acheson referred to Grew as the "prince of appeasers."[23] MacLeish denounced any attempt to change policy without a full public hearing on the issue and took his case directly to the newly appointed secretary of state, James Byrnes. Using recent public opinion polls to bolster his argument, MacLeish wrote to Byrnes that the public still strongly supported unconditional surrender. Although using the emperor to conduct the surrender might make military sense, MacLeish conceded, it might increase the danger to the peace a generation from now. There was room for disagreement on this point, he conceded, but if the administration wished to change the policy it should explain its reasons in "words that no one in the United States will misunderstand."[24]

MacLeish was as upset by the process in which policy was being changed as with the policy change itself. For MacLeish, a truly democratic foreign policy could not exist without an open discussion of the issues. Career professionals like Leahy, Stimson, and Grew on the other hand shunned electoral politics and viewed public opinion as fickle and uninformed. They believed that their professional experience had provided them with a superior basis on which to make policy decisions.

Despite their reluctance to bow to public opinion, the advocates of modifying unconditional surrender suddenly found themselves having to compete with their opponents in the public arena. They had considerable support from congressmen and conservatives in the press. The campaign to win over the public intensified when *New York Times* columnist Arthur Krock tapped his extensive sources in the Truman administration for an editorial recommending that the decision to maintain the imperial institution be made without reference to public opinion. "That is the implicit question, and it does seem one of those which must be answered by high authority on the basis of expert judgment, to which popular opinion can offer no useful contribution."[25]

MacLeish's letter to Byrnes with its pointed references to public opinion was probably enough to dissuade the new secretary of state from modifying unconditional surrender. But Byrnes also heard from one of his predecessors, Cordell Hull. Asked to comment on the draft proclamation, Hull phoned Byrnes to say that the concession on the emperor "sounded too much like appeasement"—the second time he used that word to describe the attempt to modify unconditional surrender. He underscored that verdict in a subsequent telegram. The clause pertaining to the emperor was political dynamite, Hull told Byrnes. It would be better to await the "climax of Allied bombing and Russia's entry into the war" before issuing any warning.[26]

Despite the political risks involved in supporting modification of unconditional surrender, several Republican senators publicly embraced the idea after they met with Hoover. Hugh Wilson, a former diplomat serving as an adviser to the Republican Party, welcomed Hoover's recommendations on Japan, calling them "an opportunity for the minority party to take the lead." Wilson recognized, however, that the subject had to be approached cautiously so as to avoid accusations of appeasement.[27] During the last week of June Senator Homer Capehart (R-Indiana) announced that the Japanese had contacted U.S. officials with a peace offer that he found agreeable. Without stating the precise terms, Capehart asked: "if the Japanese gave up all their conquered territories, including Manchuria, would this not be all right?" Truman, who was on the West Coast, immediately had one of his aides check with the State Department, which promptly refuted Capehart's story. Following an official denial by Grew, Capehart subsequently admitted that the Japanese in question were "influential" businessmen. The rumors briefly subsided, but the episode shows how carefully the Truman White House was monitoring congressional opinion.[28]

Several days later, on July 3, Senator Wallace White (R-Maine), the minority leader, called for a statement defining unconditional surrender. White declared that Japan should be told that it faced a choice between annihilation and surrender, "with permission to continue peaceful pursuits."[29] *Time* cor-respondent Frank McNaughton noted privately that White had said what "no inconsiderable number of Senators believe, but how to do it without giving the Japanese the impression that we are war weary is another matter, as White admitted."[30]

On July 12, as the Allied delegations began arriving for their summit conference at Potsdam, Capehart made another plea for a statement of war aims. The senator scoffed at the idea of democratizing Japan. In an indirect reference to the emperor question, Capehart said that the United States should demand Japan's demilitarization and punishment of war criminals but he saw no reason why "we must destroy Japan's form of government and then spend years in occupation and teaching a different form of gov-ernment."[31] Henry Luce's *Time* followed with a call for a statesmanlike ges-ture to try and gain Japan's surrender.[32] Luce, an ardent Presbyterian who once called the Republican Party "my other church," had tried unsuccess-fully to discuss unconditional surrender with Truman before the Potsdam conference. He had also individually lobbied more than a third of U.S. sen-ators on a recent trip to Washington. Now he was using his publishing empire to focus public attention on the issue.[33]

In the midst of the debate O'Laughlin's *Army and Navy Journal* revealed that Truman was carrying with him to Potsdam a proclamation calling on Japan to surrender and listing American terms. Someone in Washington who was privy to the drafting of Stimson's and his colleagues' proclamation wanted to make sure that it was released. The editorial, which was published on July 14, accurately described the contents and highlighted the disagree-ments over the fate of the emperor. According to the *Journal*, "Liberals and New Dealers" wanted to execute the emperor. Others blamed the warlords for Japanese aggression and believed that the emperor institution did not "involve our security and that the war would only be prolonged if we should fight to destroy Japan's religious and political systems."[34] Whoever had leaked the proclamation had done so in a way that revealed political affilia-tions. The reference to "Liberals and New Dealers" in the journal's article was not intended as a compliment. As historian Marlene Mayo has noted, for some, by 1945, "there was almost no worse epithet than New Deal."[35]

The ideological contours of the dispute prompted one Japanese commentator to observe that Truman was beginning to back away from a firm commitment to unconditional surrender. The *New York Times*, the same day it reported the *Army and Navy Journal's* scoop, noted that Kusuo Oya of the Japan Broadcasting Service viewed the recent debate over unconditional surrender as an indication of a "conservative yet considerably radical about face on the part of Truman." Oya detected a growing inclination by Americans to reassess FDR's policy of "meddling in the Far East" and predicted that Truman would "liquidate gradually the individual failures of Roosevelt which had all too strongly colored America in domestic administration and foreign policy for more than twelve years."[36]

Oya's analysis nicely captured the connections between domestic politics and foreign policy in the debate over the best means to end the war. Many of the Republican senators who criticized FDR's policy of unconditional surrender and the social engineering it would entail also opposed the way wartime emergency measures had contributed to a swollen and intrusive bureaucracy at home. As noted, the Office of Price Administration was a favorite target. But Senate Republicans also rallied in committee to challenge an extension of FDR's reciprocal trade policy. Of significance in this dispute was Senator Robert Taft's argument that the British were preparing to exploit America's open markets while the United States poured its energies into the Pacific war.[37] More generally, Republicans found themselves sympathizing with their constituents' complaints about "New Deal leftists," "globaloney," "collectivism," and lend lease giveaways while Americans rationed scarce foodstuffs at home. The remedy, as they saw it, was a return to "the American way," dissolution of "all of these government corporations," and an end to arbitrary edicts from "starry eyed" "young squirt[s]" of "little or no experience and whose main object is to please some of his superiors and of course draw a good pay check."[38]

Senators' increasing willingness to call for clarification of unconditional surrender and, in some cases, advocate a softening of terms, both reflected and influenced the public's willingness to weigh in on the subject. These often poignant pleas frequently came from Americans who had sons or husbands in the armed forces. An Omaha attorney who had lost his son on

Leyte told Truman that the public would not support a strategy that used "our boys until every last Jap is killed." The United States, he wrote, should withdraw from the Pacific Theater once it had liberated the Philippines, destroyed Japan's industries, and seized "the few necessary islands . . . to protect that area." "Respectfully," he concluded, "but with all the energy created by a broken heart—I 'cry out'—'to plan an end' to this terrible slaughter of American boys." Similar letters asked the president on behalf of mothers who had sons in the armed forces to "disregard the term 'unconditional surrender' and give the Japanese peace terms to bring about an early end to this war."[39] Some correspondents were also troubled by the moral implications of the continuing firebombing of Japan. Most acknowledged that the Japanese might not respond in a way that was acceptable to the United States but still urged their government to make more of an effort to end the war through diplomacy.[40] A steady stream rather than a flood, these letters to the White House, the State Department, members of Congress, and local newspapers showed that an active minority of citizens, having less to fear from charges of appeasement than elected officials, desired a full and open debate on the policy of unconditional surrender.

As noted, polls still showed overwhelming support for unconditional surrender and harsh treatment of the Japanese emperor. Nevertheless, by early July the public questioning of unconditional surrender became a matter of concern for the Office of War Information. A few weeks earlier, the Office's director, Elmer Davis had advised the JCS, as well as the civilian heads of various war agencies, that Japanese propaganda was emphasizing the costs of enforcing unconditional surrender with the hope that they could "involve us in a definition of what unconditional surrender meant."[41] Davis thought it wise to launch a radio campaign to counter what he saw as growing sentiment for a peace with Japan short of unconditional surrender.[42]

Those who called for clarification of unconditional surrender did so in the belief that American power was so overwhelming as to make the outcome of the war inevitable. They also believed that this fact was as unmistakably clear to the Japanese as it was to the Americans. Japanese military authorities did not see it that way. On April 8, 1945, Imperial Headquarters initiated its plans for homeland defense. Code-named KETSU-GO (Decisive

Operation), the plan called for mobilization of new military units, including "Special" (suicide) forces and guerrilla bands formed by civilians. The immediate objective of KETSU-GO was to annihilate the American beachheads several days after they were established. The larger goal was to force the United States into a negotiated settlement by making it pay a heavy price for invading the homeland. Imperial Headquarters hoped that the prospect of enormous casualties would make the Americans more amenable to negotiations. Failing that, they expected that the actual costs of the invasion would bring the Americans to the peace table. Either way, the existence of American war weariness was taken as a given in Tokyo and served as the basis for Japan's strategy for ending the war. Tokyo maintained that unconditional surrender was simply unacceptable but acted as if surrender in any form was equally objectionable. In the final months of the war, the Japanese government refused to budge from this position. At no time did the leaders in Tokyo convey to the Allies their minimum requirements for surrender.

In June the Imperial Headquarters instituted the Volunteer Military Service Law, which effectively made all citizens into combatants and commenced a propaganda program calling on all Japanese to die in the name of the emperor for the defense of the homeland.[43] The mobilization of the entire population in pursuit of a "Glorious Death" stood in contrast to what Japanese perceived as Americans' unwillingness to sacrifice and weakening commitment to the war. Tokyo propagandists, drawing on U.S. press reports, broadcast this view at home to motivate civilians. The American public, in turn, saw such efforts as a sign of desperation that even the Japanese, cut off from most outside news, could not possibly find persuasive.[44] American officials who had access to intercepted Japanese messages were not so dismissive of Japanese propaganda. Under the code name MAGIC, American cryptanalysts had been intercepting and deciphering Japanese diplomatic messages since before Pearl Harbor. As the war progressed, MAGIC had of course added to the already rich insights gained from more standard electronic surveillance that relied on the volume of traffic to discern enemy positions. By the summer of 1945, the Americans had become so proficient that they were intercepting, decrypting, and translating Japanese messages within hours of their sending.[45] The evidence gleaned from these sources revealed that despite the efforts of some isolated officials, the Japanese government remained committed to forcing the Americans into negotiations. Beginning in early spring and increasing in tempo after Germany's defeat, Japanese diplomats in several European capitals peppered their superiors in Tokyo with suggestions for ending the war. Some of them explained that American pronouncements already showed a willingness to give Japan better treatment than Germany had received. The Japanese government, headed by Baron Suzuki Kantaro, was still dominated by the military, with Army Minister General Anami Korechika and Chief of the Army General Staff Umezu Yoshijiro holding sway. Under the watchful eye of the military, the Suzuki government publicly reconfirmed its opposition to unconditional surrender and privately ordered its diplomats to cease all discussions with foreign intermediaries.[46] In mid-July, according to one MAGIC intercept, the vice chief of staff of the general staff in Tokyo admonished his subordinate in Stockholm that "Japan is firmly determined to prosecute the Greater East Asia war to the very end."[47] A little over a week later, an officer of the Imperial Navy's general staff followed suit and instructed a subordinate in Bern that Tokyo was devoting all its effort to the war. The intercepted message showed that the Navy viewed American efforts to open communication with Japanese diplomats abroad as indicative "of what difficulties the enemy is facing."[48]

By June 1945, belief in growing American war weariness had become an article of faith in Tokyo. Regardless of their own views, Japanese diplomats in Europe had to premise their recommendations on that belief. Japanese officials in Switzerland argued that Japan could take advantage of America's desire for an early end to the war, described as America's "weakness," to achieve mitigation of unconditional surrender.[49] A Japanese diplomat in Sweden took a slightly different approach by arguing that the Americans' war effort had been harmed because the "American mind" had become "relaxed with success." As long as the Japanese remained committed to the war, he added, they could count on an "ever greater war weariness developing" in the United States. The same diplomat admitted that only a minority of Americans favored moderate peace terms. He added, however, that the

British favored softening the terms and would exert themselves constantly to bring about a compromise with Japan.[50]

As the above message indicates, the prospect of divergent views among the Allies also gave the Japanese reason to hope for a more favorable outcome than the one promised by unconditional surrender. Anglo-American friction, caused by London's greater interest in European conditions, might provide one avenue of escape from unconditional surrender. Another possibility not to be ignored was that Tokyo could take advantage of Washington's desire to end the war before the Soviet Union came in. That possibility had been conveyed to the Japanese by no less an authority than the American intelligence chief in Switzerland: Allen Dulles, the future head of the CIA.[51] Growing tension between the English-speaking Allies and the Soviet Union convinced officials in Tokyo that they had something to gain by seeking Soviet assistance in ending the war. That such a move was an exercise in self-delusion was almost immediately noted by Sato Naotake, Tokyo's ambassador in Moscow. Japan could offer the Soviet Union nothing it could not take when it chose to, he pointed out. Nevertheless, he loyally persisted in trying to interest the Soviets in Tokyo's proposal to send Prince Konoye to Moscow on a high-level but unspecified mission as the emperor's representative.[52]

Finally Sato, exasperated after several failed attempts to get Soviet approval for the mission, told Foreign Minister Togo Shigenori that Japan's government would have to face the facts. If they wanted to terminate the war they would have to accept unconditional surrender or "terms closely approximating thereto." In a subsequent message Sato confessed that he remained uncertain about the government's views on ending the war. Togo replied that the "directing powers" remained convinced that Japan's armed forces could still "deliver considerable blows" against the enemy, although Japan's military leaders confessed doubt that they could withstand the repeated attacks that were likely to follow. Nevertheless, Japan would not accept anything like unconditional surrender. Lest Sato's doubts continue, Togo admonished him that "the Emperor himself has deigned to express his determination and we therefore made this request of the Russians."[53]

For American intelligence officers these and other similar cables provided compelling evidence that the Japanese militarists still controlled the government and the emperor was supportive of their efforts to force the United States to abandon its insistence on unconditional surrender. An Army Intelligence (G-2) analysis of the first several messages in the Sato-Togo exchange sent to General Marshall in a memorandum considered several interpretations of Tokyo's actions and concluded that the Japanese government "clique" was engaging in diplomatic maneuvers to stave off defeat and avoid surrendering. The proposed mission to Moscow, according to G-2, was motivated by the belief that "Russian intervention can be bought by the proper price." As for Tokyo's willingness to fight rather than accept unconditional surrender, G-2 surmised that Japanese rulers were hoping that "an attractive Japanese peace offer will appeal to war weariness in the United States."[54]

The invocations of Japan's fighting spirit and the predictions of American war weariness contained in Japanese diplomatic messages revealed the premises on which Japan's strategy rested. Decrypted Japanese army and navy communications showed how the generals and admirals in control of the government sought to implement that strategy. Beginning in June, ULTRA decryptions discovered a steady buildup of Japanese forces on Kyushu, a buildup that exceeded anything the Americans thought possible. During the June 18 meeting at the White House in which the president had approved OLYMPIC, Marshall had advised him that American air and naval forces would make Japanese reinforcement of Kyushu highly unlikely. But by July there they were anyway. The ULTRA intercepts kept locating newly formed divisions on Kyushu. Others originated in Manchuria or Honshu and had been sent south. On July 22, Marshall learned that G-2 had identified three new infantry divisions on Kyushu, raising the total to nine, at an estimated strength of 450,000 men.[55] "At the present time," Marshall told his Russian and British counterparts, "the most noticeable movements of Japanese troops have been toward Kyushu."[56] The Americans could also follow the Imperial Headquarters' efforts to convert Kyushu into a base for suicide weapons, including kamikaze planes, midget submarines, and piloted torpedoes. Staggered by the size of the escalation, American officials were also disturbed to learn that the Japanese had correctly identified the beaches where the OLYMPIC forces would be coming ashore.[57]

The ULTRA intercepts revealed the size of the Japanese reinforcement but not the quality of the troops or their equipment. Other information collected through diplomatic messages indicated that the Japanese were stretched thin in terms of food and vital supplies, especially fuel. On the other hand ULTRA revealed Imperial Headquarters' determination to inflict intolerably high casualties on the invaders through the use of suicide weapons and large-scale counteroffensives near the beaches.[58] The Japanese were pushing all their chips into the pot in a desperate gamble to prolong the war and exhaust the enemy. Imperial Headquarters identified Kyushu as the next target because the experience of the previous two years showed that the Americans would choose to direct their next assault at an objective within range of land-based aircraft, making it the most likely target. Topography dictated the landing sites on the three broad beaches in the southern and southwestern part of the island. The weather set the schedule; an attack on Kyushu sometime after September and the next assault, most likely on Honshu, early in 1946.[59]

On June 6, a report for the imperial government's Supreme War Direction Council explained the thinking behind Japanese military planning. It asserted that the United States was confronted with numerous problems. These included the death of FDR, mounting casualties, and war fatigue since V-E Day. The Americans remained committed to prosecuting the war vigorously, the report added, but there were other factors in Japan's favor, including the growing friction among the Allies over European issues and Chiang Kai-shek's concerns about his Communist rivals. An immediate break in the alliance was doubtful, but time was on Japan's side. "Should Japan resolutely continue the war and force heavy enemy attrition until the latter part of this year, it may be possible to diminish considerably the enemy's will to continue the war."[60]

On June 8, an imperial conference, with Emperor Hirohito present, unanimously approved the last-ditch strategy under the heading "Basic General Outline on Future War Direction Policy." The plan recognized that the situation for Japan was, in a colossal understatement, "pressing."[61] Army

Minister Anami insisted, however, that the battle on Okinawa was cause for optimism. Japanese forces there, though cut off from reinforcement, had inflicted heavy casualties on the Americans and demonstrated the obstacles that they would face in waging war ever farther from home. Staff officers in Imperial Army Headquarters found other reasons for hope. Reporting on the political situation in the United States, they perceptively concluded that partial demobilization might backfire by sending mixed signals to the American public. On the one hand demobilization and the initial moves toward reconversion suggested that the war would soon be over. On the other "predictions of increased casualties along with the indefinite war objectives may become factors contributing to decreased fighting morale among the people and the military." American press reports enabled the Japanese to identify many of the conditions that were troubling the Pentagon. "Rejection of the National Conscription Law, increases in labor strife, criticism of strategy, et cetera are obstacles to the success of the government's war measures," they observed. Despite these signs of restiveness in the American public, Japanese planners predicted that it would take at least one more battle on a scale larger than Okinawa to force the Americans into a negotiated settlement.[62]

The lord privy seal, Marquis Kido Koichi, Hirohito's trusted adviser, regarded that strategy as a continuation of the same failed policy that had brought Japan to the brink of ruin. He had, however, little to offer as an alternative. Working on behalf of the emperor, Kido persuaded the members of the so-called Big Six (consisting of the prime minister, foreign minister, the army and navy ministers, and the army and navy chiefs of staff) to approve the plan to seek Soviet mediation in ending the war. This was as far as the government would go in seeking an end to the war. No contact with the Americans was contemplated.[63] It thus fell to the unfortunate Ambassador Sato to endeavor to enlist the Russians in a vague plan burdened by so many conditions as to seem completely unmoored from reality. For example, Japan would be willing to withdraw its forces from colonial areas seized from the Europeans, providing that those countries gained their independence. The Japanese would consider disarmament to the minimum level required for national defense, but they clearly expected to have some say in this process.

Although the Japanese anticipated making territorial and economic concessions to the Russians, they did not contemplate relinquishing Korea. Finally, and most important, under no circumstances would the Japanese government accept unconditional surrender.[64]

The futile approach to Moscow and the reinforcement of Kyushu made it clear that the militarists remained in control in Japan and were determined to act on their publicly stated intentions to crush an invasion. Barring any unexpected developments, American planners would have to move forward with OLYMPIC. The forces for that operation were already in the Pacific, some having only recently completed mopping-up operations against the Japanese in the Philippines. With Okinawa secured by late June, engineer and construction battalions began the work of transforming the island into an air base to support the invasion of Kyushu. Redeployment from Europe was also continuing in anticipation of CORONET in March 1946—although, as noted, the president had yet to approve that operation.

The war against Japan continued apace. American-trained divisions of Nationalist Chinese soldiers began to push the Japanese out of northern Burma and southern China. Giving ground, the Japanese retreated in good order from the interior of China and consolidated their forces in anticipation of American landings on the coast. In Southeast Asia, Australian forces began the conquest of Borneo, and British forces prepared to retake Malaysia. In the Philippines, the Sixth Division continued to tighten the noose on Yamashita's Shobu force in northern Luzon. Having been in combat for over 200 days, a record for American forces, the Sixth Division stayed in the line against the Shobu Group, though it was scheduled for the assault phase of CORONET.[65] The Thirty-Second Division also remained in constant contact with the enemy through July. The fighting was reduced to small skirmishes against isolated Japanese forces who refused to surrender and often harassed the weary Americans with desperate banzai attacks. Like the Sixth, the Thirty-Second Division was slated for the assault phase of CORONET in March 1946.[66] Americans on the home front read little about the continuing action in the Philippines. After MacArthur declared the islands liberated on July 5, the fighting in the remote areas of the archipelago only occasionally made news.[67] For most Americans it appeared that the war had entered a new, less dangerous phase.

With Okinawa in hand, advocates of airpower were confidently predicting that in the next campaign American landings would be unopposed, owing to the Air Force's ability to cripple Japan's industries and destroy its communications and transportation networks. Growing evidence of dissension in Japan suggested that an invasion might be unnecessary. Was Japan on the verge of surrender, many wondered? Others cautioned against such optimism, but public discussion was rife with expressions of hope that some means of avoiding more battles like Okinawa would be found.[68] "The issue of 'soft war' vs. 'hard war' is now arising," the *Kiplinger Washington Letter* told its business readers on June 23. The author hastened to add that the reports were not true but nonetheless "there is some basis for them." The merits of "soft war," meaning blockade and bombardment, were largely economic. Kiplinger reported that economists and businessmen were concerned about the effects of invasion preparations on the economy. The government showed no sign of shifting to a "lower scale war," but Kiplinger intimated that he and most of his readers thought they should.[69]

Leading the opposition to "soft war" was the Army, whose planners had long rejected the idea that unconditional surrender could be achieved through such a means. Marshall recognized that such ideas would appeal to an American public tired of sacrifice and longing for peace. But "soft war," as Kiplinger conceded, meant a longer war. And Marshall was certain that Americans would not support a longer war under any circumstances. So redeployment continued, as did partial demobilization—Marshall's concession to public opinion. To the consternation of those who directed the program, Congress was dissatisfied with the pace of demobilization. Constituent complaints were piling up in legislators' offices. Senator Capehart was getting stacks of complaints. Senator Edwin Johnson (D-Colorado) spoke of the Army's discharging soldiers in a "leisurely" manner, taking its "own sweet time." Senator A. B. "Happy" Chandler (D-Kentucky) expected a deeper cut in the size of the Army and revision of the discharge system to improve the situation.[70]

The rising demand for faster demobilization on the Hill coincided with the lengthening Japanese order of battle being tracked in the Pentagon. The Army chose to relieve pressure at home first. Stung by the criticisms and worried about preserving the point system, War Undersecretary Patterson privately conceded the validity of some of the complaints. His own investigation showed that soldiers with scores of eighty-five or higher who had returned stateside were being held in the Army and used to perform "routine tasks of little importance," such as "cutting grass, washing windows, driving staff cars," because no replacements were immediately available. Patterson admonished commanders that it was absolutely essential that these GIs be discharged promptly or engaged in productive work, otherwise the Army would be placed in an indefensible position when critics called for changes in the point system.[71] At the same time, a War Department spokesman announced that the Army intended to lower the critical score to slightly less than eighty-five points by the end of the month so the Army could make its previously announced target of two million discharges by June 1946.

In a corresponding move, the Army sent a high-level team to Manila to make the new reduction somehow fit OLYMPIC. MacArthur was having difficulty with demobilization as it was. On the team flying to Manila were Major General Stephen Henry, War Department assistant chief of staff for personnel (G-1), and Brigadier General Claude B. Ferenbaugh, chief of the Troop Control Section of the Operations Division. On July 28, General Ferenbaugh reported that after conferring for three days, Generals MacArthur, Krueger, Eichelberger, and George Kenney, the Air Force commander, were as one in the conviction that any reduction of points below eighty-five would "increase the crisis of the impending operation to a degree that cannot be justified under any circumstances." Any number below eighty-five, they insisted in a communiqué to the War Department, would "strip divisions engaging the enemy of experienced combat leaders." The failure to assimilate replacements because of lack of time would lead to excessive casualties. The further reduction was especially critical because the divisions had "already screened out a high proportion of their skilled and experienced personnel" in getting to eighty-five. Further reduction would eliminate the rest.[72] In an additional communication on July 2, Ferenbaugh suggested that if further readjustment was insisted on, 10,000 specialists in 1,000-man blocks could be selected according to MacArthur's needs and dispatched by September 1 in shipping diverted for that purpose.[73]

Lieutenant General Handy, deputy chief of staff, responded the following day in a blunt personal message to MacArthur that it was "absolutely essential" that the commitment by the highest authorities in the government to release two million men by June 1946 be carried out. The two-million-man target, which in May had seemed like a statement of intent, had now become sacrosanct, after inclusion in speeches by Truman and War Department officials. Handy pressed the issue with MacArthur, who had stated in his message to Washington that there could be no reduction until "the operation had progressed to the point where the success of OLYMPIC could be definitely foreseen." What was that point? Handy thought those who were scheduled for discharge by June 1, 1946, would have to be removed from operations now anyway. Why should the War Department delay? Why not immediately announce a score of eighty or seventy-five but not apply it in the Pacific until later?[74] The Manila group accepted the goal of discharging two million by June 1, 1946. Their objection to reducing the score below eighty-five now arose from the fact that "only six weeks remain before OLYMPIC units mount out." That was too short a time to replace and instill the leadership and experience lost not once but twice. General Krueger was worried "that the success of OLYMPIC may be endangered if such further adjustment is ordered now." He said he would move quickly to release the required number of soldiers to meet the two million target—once the success of OLYMPIC was assured. He declined to give a date, but the War Department settled on December 1 for planning purposes. MacArthur meanwhile was "insistent" that his troops be treated no differently than those elsewhere and that accordingly he would apply the lower score if it were announced. That, however, would make impossible the execution of OLYMPIC as previously ordered by the High Command. He was "emphatic" that demobilization "should not take precedence over war operations."[75]

On August 2, the War Department issued a clarification of its demobilization policy, explaining that there were only 800,000 GIs who had earned eighty-five points or more by May 12. But in order to reach its target of two million by the following June, the Army would not lower the critical score. Instead, it would recalculate scores counting service for the period after May 12, 1945. The new calculations would favor soldiers serving in the Pacific Theater, since many of them had been in combat areas after May 12 and thus would have earned more points than those stationed in Europe. Left unsaid, however, was the date when these new calculations would be applied, although presumably that would be sometime after the invasion of Kyushu had progressed far enough to be considered secure.[76] In short, it was possible that in mid-September, some of the soldiers who had fought through May and June in the Philippines would be boarding troop transports headed for Kyushu, despite the fact that they could see that by adding in time served after May 12 they had earned the required eighty-five points. The effect on morale could not have been good.

MacArthur believed the pace of demobilization was too rapid and out of touch with basic operational needs. The civilian heads of mobilization agencies and key congressmen believed that the system was too slow, inflexible, and inattentive to pressing needs at home. Patterson's struggle to maintain the integrity of the discharge process continued while the president was away at Potsdam. Congressional criticism about the Army's sluggishness in releasing high-point men persisted, as did demands for the Army to furlough railroad workers and coal miners. The Army, it will be recalled, had furloughed 4,000 trainmen for thirty days, but this was only a drop in the bucket. On July 24, as promised, the Senate War Investigating Committee (the Mead Committee) held hearings on the railroad problem. The head of the ODT, Colonel J. Monroe Johnson, was the principle witness and foremost critic of the War Department, but other senators unleashed their own salvos against the Army as well. Johnson repeated his now familiar complaint that the War Department was not giving his agency advance warning of the arrival of troops. He also insisted that the railroads needed 75,000 additional skilled workers to maintain service and handle the increasing demand created by redeployment. Johnson alleged that instead of working with the ODT, the Army had converted a railroad battalion into an artillery unit and shipped it to the Pacific. An exasperated Johnson said that the outlook for relief was "gloomy" and that all he could do was keep "yelling my head off" to make people aware of the problem. He added, however, that the president had the authority to release the needed workers if he chose to use it. Committee chair James Mead (D-New York) took a less confrontational position, voicing his hope that the Army would release 10,000 men with railroad experience. The remaining 65,000 would be raised through an aggressive recruitment campaign sponsored by the government.[77] Less constructive was Homer Ferguson's (R-Michigan) accusation that "swivel chair" officers from the Pentagon were receiving special Pullman service for trips.

Mead's plan seemed unlikely to succeed. The same day he declared his intention to get the Army to release 10,000 railroad workers, Undersecretary Patterson told the Senate Armed Services Committee that he could not under any circumstances "break faith" with American soldiers by releasing coal miners from the Army to meet that industry's labor shortage. Unmoved, Edwin Johnson, the ranking Democrat on the committee, called the Army's manpower policies "blind, stupid and criminal."[78] Patterson's refusal to accommodate civilian needs came from his sincere conviction that the integrity of the point system had to be maintained. Of course Patterson had the president on his side, at least for now. But he and the staff officers in the Pentagon also found support for their actions in a Gallup poll that showed the public supportive of Army policies. The poll, which was initiated by the War Department, showed that the majority of Americans did not think the Army was too big for the war against Japan and did not fear its domination of civilian affairs. The majority also gave the Army favorable ratings on its training of and caring for soldiers.[79] Sustained by this information, Patterson felt secure in dismissing his critics as "certain senators" who were prone to sensationalism and exaggeration.[80]

Patterson's confidence—arrogance, his critics would say—permeated the Pentagon. Therein lay the seeds of an even more serious conflict between the War Department on the one hand and Congress and the civilian heads of mobilization agencies on the other. A weekly report on Army activities noted that on July 27, during the recent senatorial hearings, Major General John Franklin, acting chief of transportation, "testified that the Army had coordinated its plans for redeployment both with the Office of

Defense Transportation and the American Association of Railways, and that, insofar as the War Department could see, there would be no serious difficulty in obtaining adequate rail transportation for the Pacific operations."[81] This was a surprisingly positive gloss on Franklin's encounter with the irate members of the Mead Committee. When Franklin said that the head of the ODT "was unduly alarmed," Senator Mead wondered why, if there was no labor shortage, the president had recently issued a public call for 65,000 railroad workers to seek work on the western lines? More damaging was the admission by Colonel Luke Finley that in May the Army had given the ODT an estimate of troop arrivals but had not kept the agency informed on a daily basis as to what the totals would be. The Army had given that information to the American Association of Railways but not to the ODT. That, of course, was what Colonel J. Monroe Johnson, the head of the ODT, had been insisting all along. Asked why the Army kept the ODT in the dark, Finley hardly helped matters when he said he did not think they needed the updates but the agency could have had the information if it asked. At the end of the meeting Mead threatened to bring the transportation problems to the president unless the civilian agencies got more cooperation from the War Department.[82]

At the heart of this dispute lay deeper disagreements over the mobilization of American resources, disagreements dating back several years. Johnson insisted that the railroads' need for repairs, updated equipment, and workers had been systematically ignored by the military's domination of the economy. The War Department and the Army countered that their demands on civilian resources were determined by the war's objectives and the strategy chosen to achieve them. In each instance, the answer was greater sacrifice by civilians. Patterson and his colleagues believed that the alleged scarcity of sleeping cars could be eased by placing greater restrictions on civilian traffic. Similarly, the shortage of workers could have been remedied by the implementation of the national service law.[83] Whatever the merits of these arguments, Congress showed little enthusiasm for the War Department's point of view. The solution to what the legislators saw as a very real problem was greater flexibility on the part of the Army, especially in its policies governing the discharge of soldiers in critical jobs. Patterson had given ground slightly on this point when he agreed to furlough 4,000 soldiers with railroad experience, but he did not plan to go any further in appeasing Congress. A showdown was in the making.

One can understand how Patterson thought he would continue to win his battle with Congress, at least for the time being. The polls seemed to show that the soldiers and the public were on his side. Moreover, the president had told the cabinet that he did not want to tamper with the point system. It is more difficult, however, to understand the Army's general complacency on the transportation problem. On the same day that Major General Franklin was calmly saying that there was no problem, the director of the War Production Board, just back from a trip out West, declared transportation the country's number one problem and said that he did not know how it could be solved without more manpower.[84] Both men could not be right. If there was a problem, it is difficult to see how the two sides, given their mutual antagonism, could have resolved it. Perhaps the Army expected that in any emergency it would have priority on carriers and right of way. The mobilization directors and their allies in Congress may have suspected as much. But even if the Army was able to respond to an emergency, it would only be able to do so by encroaching on civilian needs. How would that affect the civilian morale that Marshall deemed so necessary to sustain the campaign against Japan?

The Army's complacency is also puzzling in light of the progress of redeployment at the end of July. Earlier in the month, Army planners identified many of the same problems impeding redeployment that Vinson's staff had reported. Unlike Vinson's staff, the Army was not predicting the postponement of OLYMPIC. But they were concerned. The main problem, according to an Army staff paper, was the conflict between the announced policy, which put redeployment ahead of readjustment, meaning the release from service of high-point men, "and actual practice in which readjustment is interfering with redeployment."[85]

Congestion in Manila harbor, the "bottleneck" in West Coast shipyards, and the lack of adequate troop transports in the Pacific continued to plague the movement of forces into the Pacific. In mid-July, officers in the Army Service Forces queried MacArthur's headquarters as to their ability to handle the influx from the European and Mediterranean theaters of the equivalent of 200 cargo ships per month in September and October, which would be superimposed on the traffic created by the mounting of the invasion force for OLYMPIC. Although there had been a "gratifying" increase in the ship discharge rates in the Philippines, the staff officers suggested that unless there were even greater increases in the turnaround of vessels by the end of July, the Army would need to reduce by thirty the number of ships set to sail for the Philippines from the West Coast. In requesting MacArthur's views on the reductions, the officers reminded him that the Army's ability to meet future requirements for the Pacific Theater would be "seriously affected" if the discharge rates were prolonged because of congestion in the Philippines. They also asked, pleaded really, for MacArthur to reconsider releasing vessels he was holding for local shipments.[86]

While they wrestled with the movement of equipment from Europe to the Pacific, the Army's planners also had to find ways to eliminate a projected backlog of troops destined for MacArthur's command. One possibility was to erect an Air Transport Command shuttle system across the Pacific like the one being used to augment the transfer of troops home from Europe in what was called the Green Project. Unfortunately, implementation would require at least 9,000 service troops to build the required housing, petroleum storage facilities, and expanded bases on the chain of islands along the projected route.[87] It was unlikely that MacArthur could spare the men for the project. Indeed, the Army had decided that MacArthur's need for service troops was so great—and the pressure to maximize available shipping capacity even greater—that they dispatched from Europe an engineer general services regiment and an engineering construction battalion, though both units lacked skilled specialists or experience in such complex tasks as port construction and heavy bridging. Slipping into a less-than-reassuring passive voice, the Army planners told MacArthur: "It is felt that units are now qualified to perform general engineering missions and that with appropriate specialized training under your command, units will be able, at an early date, to perform any specialized mission required in your area."[88]

By early August the Army arrived at a partial solution to the projected backlog of troops on the West Coast, one based on the recommendations of a high-level committee consisting of representatives from the AAF, the Transportation Corps, Army Service Forces, and the Operations Division of the General Staff. The committee's main objective was to eliminate the projected backlog of troops scheduled for transfer to the Pacific. But they had before them three other objectives that complicated achievement of the first. They needed to maintain the flow of personnel out of Europe so that they could replace low-score servicemen in the United States who were slated for transfer to the Pacific. They also had to "accelerate the return of troops from Europe to the United States as much as possible." And finally, they had to return high-score personnel from the Pacific once their replacements arrived. It quickly became apparent that the only viable options involved moving ships and planes from the Atlantic to the Pacific. That meant that achievement of the first goal, eliminating the backlog, would necessarily impinge on the accomplishment of the others.

The committee concluded that the quickest way to cut the backlog on the West Coast would be to shift the Green Project to the Pacific and convert seventy-four Victory ships currently in the Atlantic for use as troopships in the Pacific. The full use of transport planes, which were carrying 50,000 men a month across the Atlantic, and the additional Victory ships would eliminate the backlog by sometime in February 1946. On the downside, the transfer of planes and ships would reduce the number of soldiers returned from Europe by slightly more than one million. Nevertheless, the committee members believed that by returning the ships and planes to the Atlantic in April 1946, the United States could still reduce its troop presence in Europe to levels required for occupation duties by June 1946, the date, it will be recalled, by which the Army had pledged to discharge two million GIs.

By the time the committee presented its recommendation it had already had to adjust its calculations. MacArthur's headquarters informed Washington that it could accommodate only 10,000 men a month brought in by air. That necessitated scaling back the allocation of the planes and supporting forces sustaining the Green Project, although considerable construction was required to accommodate the movement of even this reduced number of troops. When Marshall received the committee's recommendation, he decided to convert and transfer to the Pacific only forty Victory ships. Decision on the remaining ships would be made by September 1. Marshall did not explain his decision, but he may have believed that Japan was on the verge of surrender and further redeployment would be unnecessary. He may also have been concerned about the political consequences of reducing the shipment home of troops in Europe. It is clear, however, that the committee's recommendation, even before Marshall rendered his decision, left the Army with a backlog of troops on the West Coast at least until the end of February and most likely through March, when CORONET was scheduled to begin. That was assuming, of course, that there would be enough trains running on schedule to move the redeploying men to their ports of embarkation on the West Coast.[89]

Elimination of the troop backlog could not be solved through use of the Army's sea and air assets alone. While the Army's high-level committee reviewed the available options for reallocating Atlantic shipping, Marshall sought Admiral King's assistance in dealing with the persistent shortage of troop lift in the Pacific. Marshall proposed that he and King send MacArthur and Nimitz a communiqué notifying them of the backlog and requesting that they undertake several specified measures to reduce it. Marshall asked that Nimitz and MacArthur review their requirements for pending operations and pare the personnel required down to "bare essentials." The Pacific commanders should also determine the unloading capacity of ports under their control so as to avoid unnecessary delays in turn-around times for shipping. Next followed the familiar problem of commanders retaining ships in their theaters for intratheater use. Starting with the assumption that each commander retained ships that could be spared for trans-Pacific use, MacArthur and Nimitz were asked to inform Washington of the maximum lift they could release each month for use in West Coast loadings. The last substantive measure asked both commanders to reexamine their plans for use of amphibious shipping, which included assault-training exercises, to permit the temporary release of attack transports before they were needed for OLYMPIC. The message ended with an exhortation that "with complete cooperation of the Pacific Commanders, combined with action taken by the War and Navy Departments, the estimated backlog can be reduced."[90] Reduced, but not eliminated. According to the Army's tables, a backlog of 188,000 troops would remain in March 1946, the start date for CORONET, assuming that the proposed measures were implemented and worked as planned.

King's reply to Marshall indicated his support for the chief of staff's proposed message, but he clearly had doubts as to its usefulness. For example, King agreed that both commanders should review their personnel requirements in light of the shortfall in shipping. But he noted: "It is my understanding that there has been a substantial increase in the necessity for Army replacements due to the point system discharges. This also has a significant impact on training requirements within the theater." In short, Nimitz would not be able to spare the amphibious assault ships for trans-Pacific use because they would be needed for training exercises for the divisions replenished by replacements. Regarding the attack transports, King reminded Marshall that in June Nimitz had said that he would not be able to spare any of those ships after August. King did not object to asking Nimitz if the situation had changed, but his tone indicated that he already knew what Nimitz's response would be. "In light of the estimated deficits shown in your memorandum," King replied, "I do not object to asking Commander in Chief, United States Pacific Fleet to reaffirm his position in this respect." As for the hoarding of shipping by the Pacific commanders, King endorsed the release of those ships for trans-Pacific troop lift, noting that two-thirds of the ships were held by MacArthur and the remainder by Nimitz.[91]

One cannot help but be struck by the icy tone in King's reply to Marshall. The implication was that the Army through its insistence on taking on OLYMPIC and partial demobilization simultaneously had created the difficulties it was now scrambling to resolve. Retention of shipping in the theaters was a problem; but, no surprise here, the lion's share of the coveted ships were held in MacArthur's theater. Rotation out of the theater of high-point men and the inflow of replacements tied up needed shipping and made the release of amphibious assault ships for troop lift impossible. Remedies might be available, but the onus fell on the Army to find them.

King may also have been influenced by ongoing difficulties over the transfer of control over troops on Okinawa from Nimitz's command to MacArthur's.

That problem had surfaced in late May, when Brehon Somervell complained that Nimitz was giving priority to preparations for operation LONGTOM (Chusan-Ningpo along the China coast) and continuation of ICEBERG (Ryukyus). Somervell pointed out that with Okinawa nearly subdued, preparations should be directed toward the invasion of Kyushu. Nimitz's priorities would "drain forces and resources from the build-up for the major operations against Japan." The Navy, it seemed, had not given up on what Army staff planners had caustically referred to as the "round the Yellow Sea idea."[92] They had hoped that the subsequent issuance by the Joint Chiefs of a firm operational directive would bring a halt to Nimitz's preparations, but he continued to withhold resources on Okinawa from MacArthur. On July 10, the day that Marshall was scheduled to leave for Potsdam, General George Lincoln approved a sharply worded memorandum for Admiral King that accused Nimitz of defying the JCS directive for OLYMPIC. Such were the contents that Lincoln thought it might be best, however, were Marshall to tell King what was in the memorandum or to read it to him without actually giving him a copy for the record.[93]

This one would have to wait. Marshall packed and left for Potsdam at midnight on the tenth. On the first leg of the trip he flew in General Arnold's plane to Mingan, Quebec, for a day of salmon fishing before boarding his own plane for the flight across the Atlantic. After another brief fishing excursion, this time in Bavaria, Marshall arrived in Berlin on July 15. The president, who had left for the conference on July 6 and taken a more leisurely voyage to Antwerp, also arrived by plane on the same day. Although Truman would be involved with daily plenary sessions, the Joint Chiefs enjoyed a lighter work schedule. They did not attend the plenary sessions but met instead with their British counterparts to finalize command responsibilities in the Pacific and reorganize theater boundaries. The Combined Chiefs of Staff (British and American) met twice with the Russian military delegation to confirm Soviet entry into the war against Japan and establish operational boundaries. While Truman was bogged down in daily meetings that resolved little and deferred decisions on European problems to postwar meetings of the foreign ministers, the Combined Chiefs moved quickly through their agenda for completing the Pacific war.

Outside the conference, the pace of world-changing events was even faster. On July 16, Stimson brought Truman news that an atomic device had been successfully detonated in the desert in New Mexico. The world had entered the atomic age. The following day, July 17, Stalin visited Truman at his residence in suburban Babelsberg, Germany, and confirmed his previous commitment to have the Soviet Union enter the war against Japan. "I've gotten what I came for," Truman wrote to his wife, Bess. "Stalin goes to war on August 15 with no strings on it," he added with some exaggeration.[94]

The atomic bomb and Soviet entry into the war, once only distant possibilities, now had to be factored into the president's calculations on ending the war. As Truman processed this new information, the Joint Chiefs reviewed the wording of the warning they expected Truman to issue to the Japanese. The warning, it will be recalled, had been drafted by an ad hoc committee led by John McCloy and dominated by representatives from the Army's S&P Group. Their version contained an explicit pledge to permit the Japanese to establish a constitutional monarchy under the present dynasty "if it be shown to the complete satisfaction of the world that such a government will never again aspire to aggression."[95] Opposition from former secretary of state Cordell Hull and from within the State Department forced a revision of the draft, changing the crucial twelfth clause to a vague assurance that once the Japanese demonstrated their commitment to live peacefully "they shall be given an opportunity to control their destiny along peaceful lines."[96] That was the draft given to Secretary of State James Byrnes at Potsdam.

In early July, however, Navy Secretary Forrestal had given a copy of the original draft to the Joint Chiefs for their comment. Admiral King had passed that version on to the Joint Strategic Survey Committee, an interservice group of senior officers empowered to think broadly about the future of American security.[97] The committee balked at the provision allowing the Japanese to preserve the monarchy "under the present dynasty." They argued that the Japanese might infer that the Allies planned to depose the current emperor and replace him with someone else. Conversely, they worried that Japanese radicals, primarily communists and socialists, might object to having the monarchy preserved in any form. To avoid misinterpretation, the committee recommended that the provision be rewritten to read: "subject to suitable guarantees against further acts of aggression, the Japanese people will be free to choose their own form of government."[98]

That revision provoked a sharp protest from the warning's original authors in S&P, who noted that the radical element in Japan was too small to be a factor in the government's decision to surrender. They were willing, however, to revise their draft to make it unmistakably clear that they did not intend to dethrone Hirohito. Most of all, they insisted that "we should not beat around the bush but should state unequivocally what we intend to do with the Emperor." In their revised draft, which was dispatched to Potsdam, the crucial clause now read, "The Japanese people will be free to choose whether they shall retain their Emperor as a constitutional monarch."[99]

That is where things stood when the Joint Chiefs took up the subject on July 17. The meeting began with Admiral Leahy explaining that "the matter had been considered on a political level and consideration had been given to the removal of the sentence in question." Leahy added, however, that he thought the Joint Chiefs could consider the Joint Strategic Survey Committee's draft from the military point of view. According to the secretary for the meeting, "the Chiefs spent considerable time discussing the application of the unconditional surrender formula to Japan." Unfortunately, the minutes provide only a terse record of this critical discussion. We know only that Marshall took the lead in warning against doing anything that would imply that the Allies planned to remove Hirohito from the throne, "since his continuation in office might influence the cessation of hostilities in areas outside of Japan proper." In addition, Marshall recommended that the Chiefs convey that idea to the president in a paper accepting the Joint Strategic Survey Committee's revised wording on the emperor. According to the minutes, the Joint Chiefs agreed with Marshall and directed the secretary to draft a memorandum with those provisions for the president.[100]

The absence of a more detailed record leaves one to wonder why Marshall accepted the views of the Joint Strategic Survey Committee over those of his staff officers in S&P. The same could be said for Admiral King and the other Navy representatives present. In light of their reluctant support for the invasion of Japan it would have made sense to support the McCloy committee's recommended modification of unconditional surrender. Perhaps Leahy's introductory remark, stating that the subject had been considered at the "political level," and consideration was given to removing the sentence referring to the emperor, was a euphemistic way of telling the Joint Chiefs that the question had been decided by Truman. The Joint Chiefs may also have concluded from their reading of the intercepted Japanese messages over the last several weeks that no proclamation, regardless of what it said about the emperor, would induce Japan to surrender. Only the day before, Ambassador Sato in Moscow had wired Tokyo to say that he was "not clear about the views of the Government and the Military with regard to termination of the war."[101] Apart from providing a revealing glimpse into the dynamics of decision-making in Tokyo, Sato's reference to the government and the military as separate entities gave the Americans little reason to hope that the Japanese were ready to surrender. Other intelligence sources reinforced that view. The alarming buildup on Kyushu revealed by ULTRA showed that Japanese war leaders were deadly serious in their determination to make the costs of an invasion unacceptable to the Americans and force a negotiated settlement.

On the following day, July 18, the Joint Chiefs approved a memorandum for the president that substituted the Joint Strategic Survey Committee's wording for that of the McCloy committee. Gone was the reference to a constitutional monarchy under the present dynasty. The crucial twelfth point in the warning now read: "Subject to suitable guarantees against further acts of aggression, the Japanese people will be free to choose their own form of government."[102] At this point, Truman had not decided when he would issue the warning. But Leahy's comments suggest that he had decided to issue one. In this respect, the concerted efforts of Grew and Stimson, the well-timed leaks at home, and the public discussion they engendered made it difficult for the president to refrain from making some statement on unconditional surrender. As noted, Leahy's statement that the emperor question had been considered "at the political level" may have been his way of indicating that Truman had already decided to omit any reference to the emperor in the warning when it was released. If the president had any lingering doubts, the Joint Chiefs memorandum would have given him the assurance he needed to strike the controversial reference to the throne from the warning.

Events away from Potsdam reinforced Truman's refusal to compromise on the status of the emperor. Although direct evidence is lacking, most historians agree on the assumption that the president continued to receive his daily briefings on the information collected through MAGIC decrypts of Japanese diplomatic messages and ULTRA analysis of Japanese troop dispositions.[103] Those two sources showed that the Japanese remained unwilling to accept anything resembling unconditional surrender. Instead, Tokyo was employing diplomacy to avoid the full consequences of defeat while simultaneously preparing for a bloody showdown on Kyushu. Under these conditions, a compromise on the fate of the emperor would have been seen as appeasement. Despite the furtive contacts made by Japanese diplomats abroad, and despite the mounting pressure on Truman to find a less costly means of compelling Japan's surrender, the positions of the two belligerents appeared to be hardening, leaving no room for diplomacy and compromise. Direct communication between them remained severed, but the Japanese nevertheless had managed to bluntly convey their intentions; if the Americans wished to avoid another costly campaign against a grimly determined foe, they would have to accept conditions laid down by Tokyo. Although Truman confided to Churchill that he worried constantly about the "effusions of blood" that would result from an invasion of Japan, he was as determined as ever not to yield on the question of the emperor.

It is not surprising, therefore, that Stalin's promise to enter the war lifted his spirits. More encouraging, however, were the updates he received on the successful test of the atomic weapon exploded in the New Mexico desert. On the morning of July 18, the same day the Joint Chiefs were preparing their recommendation for the president, Stimson gave Truman a second, more detailed report on the test. The president, Stimson wrote, was "very greatly reinforced over the message." That night, Truman summarized the day's events in his diary. He had begun the day with breakfast with his nephew, a sergeant in the field artillery, Truman's old service. Then he met with Churchill for lunch. The two leaders discussed the successful test of the atomic bomb and agreed to inform Stalin about it. The prime minister also showed Truman Stalin's reply to Hirohito's message seeking the Soviet Union's aid in negotiating an end to the war. Stalin's reply asking for clarification from Tokyo was deemed satisfactory by Truman.[104] Assessing the significance of these two developments, the atomic test and Soviet cooperation in the war, Truman allowed himself a moment of optimism: "Believe the Japs will fold up before Russia comes in. I'm sure they will when Manhattan appears over their homeland."[105]

Over the next several days Truman received news that gave him even more reason to hope that the atomic bomb would force Japan's surrender. On July 20 and 21, he received two startling messages on the state of the home front from Fred Vinson, warning him that the glacial progress of reconversion threatened to wreck the American economy and imperil the relief effort in liberated Europe. Vinson, who was slated to become secretary of the treasury at the end of the month, assured Truman that John Snyder, his replacement as head of OWMR, agreed with him about the seriousness of the situation at home. Vinson laid the blame for the impending crisis squarely on the military. Coal offered an "excellent example" of the problems created by the exorbitant demands of the military for materials and personnel. Vinson explained that he had prevailed on Harold Ickes, the coal administrator, to make some domestic supply available for Europe even though Ickes was convinced that the United States would face shortages at home in the coming winter. The United States would not be forced to make these choices, Vinson added, if the Army could be persuaded to furlough "a few thousand" coal miners. "Transportation is equally critical," Vinson added. The railroads and Colonel Johnson's office were doing "a splendid job, but the strain being placed on them is almost unbearable." Vinson reported numerous complaints of spoilage of foodstuffs on the West Coast resulting from snarled transportation and warned that "this will become worse and not better and may even threaten the Army's ability to complete redeployment in the desired length of time." Once again, the release of a few thousand skilled workers would provide substantial relief. The Army, Vinson noted, had already conceded the point by agreeing to furlough 4,000 railroad workers from service, but more were needed.

Unfortunately, Undersecretary Patterson was digging in his heels and re-fusing to furlough any more men on the grounds that to do so would under-mine the point system and constitute a breach of trust with servicemen. Vinson professed to understand Patterson's dilemma, but he dismissed the undersecretary's reasoning by pointing out that the Army had already fur-loughed several thousand men and thus could do it again. "Certainly there is nothing sacred about the figure four thousand," he added. Patterson, of course, worried that any further release of workers would unleash an ava-lanche of similar requests from other industries. Anticipating that argu-ment, Vinson proposed establishing a furlough pool with a definite number of men to be managed by the War Manpower Commission. Vinson ex-plained that this process would head off further demands for furloughs by setting the number in advance. "If something along these lines is not done," he warned the president, "I firmly believe the consequences to our econ-omy and to the world may be most serious."

After directly requesting the president's permission to act, Vinson pushed on to a subject of even more fundamental importance. The armed forces, Vinson complained, were retaining excessively large numbers of men in uniform. The Army, the real culprit, had actually raised its requirements to 270,000 over the figure announced on V-E Day. Vinson told Truman he had his staff studying the problem and promised a detailed report for submis-sion to the JCS and the president. "I urge your most serious consideration of this problem on your return," he added. "We need manpower for the war effort and for reconversion. With some help now reconversion can proceed faster, and a small impetus now will save much trouble for the economy when the shock of V-J Day comes."[106]

It is difficult to imagine a more dramatic intervention into the policy process. Vinson, who was about to be sworn in as secretary of the treasury, and his replacement at OWMR, John Snyder, an Arkansas banker and friend of the president from Army Reserve days, were among the president's most trusted and closest confidants.[107] Both of these normally cautious men had found the developments at home so troubling that they thought it neces-sary to interrupt the president's summit meeting with Stalin and Churchill. Vinson's distress over the situation was such that on the following day, again with Snyder's concurrence, he sent Truman another message. Shorter than the previous telegram, this one packed a bigger wallop. Vinson asked the president to request from the JCS an immediate "reappraisal of all military requirements and of the strategic considerations on which these requirements are based." He also wanted the OWMR involved in the study. Vinson acknowledged that recent favorable developments in the Pacific did not necessarily forecast an early end to the war, and he conceded that the United States had to be ready for the worst contingencies. "On the other hand," he added, "the demonstration of our naval and air superiority requires the continued re-examination of our needs for winning the war."[108]

Vinson elaborated on his concerns in a supporting memorandum that he sent to Truman the same day. The memo opened by referring to a statement in which Undersecretary Patterson once again scoffed at the suggestion of revising the discharge system. The Army had received special requests from over fifty industrial and trade groups, Patterson stated. "These requests have ranged from 110,000 men for the coal mines to three men to breed mice," he added. Patterson closed by calmly noting that civilian manpower requirements were being steadily eased by reductions in war production and the Army's current discharge system.[109] Vinson could not have disagreed more. "The manpower shortage has never been as acute and disturbing as it is today," he warned the president. The railroads, coal mines, metal mines, lumber industry, and textile industries were all facing critical shortages. To make matters worse, coal miners over thirty years old who had been furloughed two years ago were actually being recalled to service. Despite a request for the release of 5,000–10,000 railroad workers, the War Department had agreed to furlough only those 4,000. Something had to be done, Vinson insisted, to reduce the Army's insatiable demand for manpower. "It is by no means clear to me," he said, "that the Army needs 7,242,000 personnel plus 1,150,000 civilians to maintain 3,000,000 troops against Japan, as compared with 8,300,000 when there were 5,000,000 in active theaters last spring." A reduction in the Army's size would have an immediate salutary effect on the economy, he added. "To furlough or release men now will ease our reconversion problems, help prevent inflation, avoid criticism of the Army, and most important of all, afford badly needed relief to the railroads and coal mines which, without such assistance, will probably be in real trouble during the coming winter."[110]

In May, it will be recalled, General Somervell had complained that some of the staff members in OWMR wanted to have a say in the development of military strategy. That was not the case then, but it was now. Vinson's two messages explicitly requested action from the president, an increase in the number of furloughed servicemen and assent to a full reappraisal of strategy in the war against Japan. Vinson and Snyder had joined the ranks of those who advocated a strategy of siege or "soft war," as the Kiplinger letter had labeled it. In his first months in office, Truman had impressed observers with his decisiveness on a broad range of issues. This time, however, he opted for inaction and Rooseveltian vagueness. He responded by telling Vinson that he "very much appreciated" his memoranda. "They have been a great help to me," he added.[111]

The question is, how helpful? Vinson's and Snyder's warnings had certainly not fallen on deaf ears. After all, Truman's own experiences with the chaotic demobilization after World War I, when he, like thousands of others, endured business failure in the ensuing economic turmoil, would have made him even more sensitive to Vinson's warnings. Events would show that Vinson's alarms had registered with the president and that they would continue to influence his thinking over the next several weeks. If Truman deferred immediate action on Vinson's warnings, however, it was not because he disregarded them but because he now believed that there was a real possibility of ending the war in the next few weeks. The Japanese had not softened their position on unconditional surrender. That no longer mattered. The acquisition of the atomic bomb encouraged the president to believe that they would soon be compelled to sue for peace.

On July 21, the same day he received Vinson's second message, Truman received the first extensive report on the atomic bomb. "The test was successful beyond the most optimistic expectations of anyone," wrote Manhattan Project director General Leslie Groves. He estimated the bomb's power exceeded 20,000 tons of TNT. The explosion had dug a crater 1,200 feet wide and destroyed a forty-ton steel tower one-half mile away. In Groves's estimation the recently constructed Pentagon would not provide security from such a blast. Among the unauthorized observers in the area who caught a glimpse of the blast was a blind woman who, according to Groves, "saw the light."[112] After Stimson reviewed the report with Truman and Byrnes he confided to his diary that both men were "immensely pleased." "The President," he continued, "was tremendously pepped up by it and spoke to me again and again when I saw him."[113] The following day, July 22, Stimson told Truman that the bomb would be ready for use against Japan sooner than expected. Stimson then visited the British delegation and read Groves's report to Churchill.

One can well appreciate Truman's relief at this report. The previous two weeks had brought news that raised the stakes of OLYMPIC and called the practicality of the invasion and American war aims into question. The increased calls from the press, the Senate, and from individual citizens for a detailed warning to Japan had evolved into more forthright support for a statement assuring the status of the emperor. A growing number of Americans were willing to take that step if it prevented further bloodletting. Most of the criticism of unconditional surrender came from Republicans and their allies in the press. But Truman knew perfectly well that those criticisms would carry more weight and look more prescient if the invasion of Japan resulted in casualties on a scale comparable to Okinawa. The Japanese buildup on Kyushu made that disastrous development appear even more likely than it had in mid-June. Vinson's messages added new concerns by insisting that the current strategy for winning the war, even if successful, might well produce economic calamity at home and chaos in liberated Europe.

Although Truman did not know it at the time, more obstacles to the successful execution of DOWNFALL (the Kyushu and Honshu operations) were accumulating. Vinson alluded to current transportation problems and their likely effect on redeployment, but it appears that no one else had briefed the president on the manifold problems created by the Army's decision to carry out partial demobilization simultaneously with redeployment. As we have noted, the Army's leaders continued to deny that any problems existed, gliding serenely over the complaints from civilian agencies while at the same time Army staff officers were paddling furiously to find a way to get men and materials into place for OLYMPIC and CORONET.

The report about the bomb from General Groves enabled Truman to look past these challenges and concentrate instead on a new more welcome situation: preparation for a Japanese surrender earlier than expected. A sudden collapse of Japanese resistance promised to create new difficulties that would cast the future of much of East Asia into doubt, but the consequences for the United States would still be far more tolerable than a continuation of the war. On July 23, Truman began to explore the implications of an early surrender. Toward that end, he asked Stimson to obtain General Marshall's views on whether the Soviets were still needed in the war against Japan. Marshall was circumspect in replying. The United States did not need the Russians to defeat Japan. The massing of Red Army troops on the Manchurian border was tying down Japanese forces there, making it unlikely they would be transferred back to the home islands. In other words, even without attacking Japan, the Soviet Union was aiding the Americans. Marshall noted, however, that even if the United States forced Japan's surrender, there was nothing to stop the Russians from entering Manchuria on their own. The following day, July 24, Stimson told Truman that the United States no longer needed Soviet assistance in the war but left out Marshall's caveat about the likelihood of Soviet entry regardless of American action.[114] Stimson then informed the president that the first bomb might be ready for use as soon as August 1, and certainly no later than August 6. Truman thanked Stimson and said that was the information he needed to release the warning to Japan. He had by this point already secured Churchill's approval and had sent a message to Chiang Kai-shek requesting his approval earlier that day. As noted earlier, the JCS did not expect the Chinese to contribute much to Japan's defeat, but politically it was important to treat China as one of the great powers and seek Chiang's agreement with the warning. Internationally and in the United States, Chiang's government still received considerable sympathy for its heroic stand against Japanese aggression. There was nothing to gain by ignoring Chiang at this point, especially since Truman could be fairly certain that he would approve the warning. Once Truman received Chiang's concurrence, he would issue the declaration. Stimson tried again to change the president's mind about the importance of assuring the Japanese that the emperor would be permitted to remain on the throne. The secretary acknowledged that now that the warning had been sent to and approved by Chiang, it could not be changed to include a pledge to retain the emperor. But he implored the president to transmit the necessary assurances to the Japanese if it turned out that the emperor question was the one issue that would "make or mar" the proclamation's acceptance. Truman told Stimson that he "had that in mind and that he would take care of it."[115] This was far from the positive commitment the secretary was hoping for, but it was the best he could get.

In fact, the success of the atomic bomb test reinforced Truman's earlier decision to strike the clause referring to the emperor from the proposed warning. In this regard, he remained more confident than Stimson that the bomb would force Japan's surrender without concessions from the United States. He was also losing interest in obtaining the Soviet Union's timely entry into the war. Nevertheless, he believed that he could not use the new weapon against Japan without providing the Russians with some advance notice. After speaking with Stimson on July 24, Truman approached Stalin at the end of the evening's plenary session and casually informed him that the United States had a powerful new weapon that would soon be ready for use against Japan. Stalin appeared to take the news in stride and replied that he hoped it would help end the war quickly. Much to Truman's surprise, Stalin did not make any further inquiries. Satisfied that he had fulfilled his obligation as an ally to notify the Russians of the bomb, the president said no more on the subject. Stalin, of course, knew about the Anglo-American bomb project through the efforts of Soviet espionage agents. His outwardly calm reaction to Truman's important news was actually a studied attempt to show the Americans that he would not be intimidated by the new weapon. Privately, however, he responded by ordering his scientists to accelerate work on the Soviet atomic bomb project.[116]

In the meantime, Truman continued to seek information on the ramifications of an early Japanese surrender. On the morning of July 25, the day after he learned that the bomb would soon be ready, he met with Marshall and Admiral Lord Louis Mountbatten, the British commander of the Southeast Asian Command. Truman's diary entry for the day notes that before he met with Churchill and Stalin at 11:00 a.m., he "had a most important meeting with Lord Mountbatten & General Marshall before that." The awesome power of the atomic bomb was very much on his mind that day. "We have discovered the most terrible bomb in the history of the world," he wrote in his diary. "It may be the fire destruction prophesied in the Euphrates Valley Era, after Noah and his fabulous Ark." He then proceeded to record in detail information from Groves's report, noting, for example, the destruction of the steel tower a half mile away and the size of the bomb crater. The next several lines, dealing with the use of the bomb, appear to have been written with posterity in mind. The new weapon would be used on a strictly military target, he emphasized. "Even if the Japs are savages, ruthless, merciless, and fanatic, we as the leader of the world for the common welfare cannot drop this terrible weapon on the old capital [Kyoto] or the new [Tokyo]." Truman added that Japan would be warned to surrender, but he doubted that they would comply. His thoughts about the fearful burden imposed by possession of the new weapon led him to consider even more frightening possibilities. "It is certainly a good thing for the world that Hitler's crowd or Stalin's did not discover the atomic bomb. It seems the most terrible thing ever discovered, but it can be made the most useful." Then follows the frustratingly vague notation "at 10:15 I had General Marshall come in and discuss with me the tactical and political situation. He is a level-headed man—so is Mountbatten."[117]

What did Truman mean when he referred to "the tactical and political situation"? Some historians have speculated that during this meeting Marshall apprised Truman of the Japanese buildup on Kyushu and may have even given Truman a revised estimate of the casualties likely to result from an invasion.[118] That seems possible. After all, Marshall was receiving regular updates on conditions in the Pacific through ULTRA. But evidence from Mountbatten and Marshall indicates that the president was primarily concerned with Allied readiness for the sudden collapse of Japanese resistance. In other words, such was the impact of the bomb on Truman's thinking that he was looking *past* OLYMPIC and toward the immediate end of the war and all that this meant for American responsibilities in Asia and, significantly, the reconversion of the economy at home.

On July 24, the day he arrived at Potsdam, Mountbatten attended the meeting of the Combined Chiefs of Staff. Following that meeting Marshall invited him for drinks with General Arnold. Once the three men were together, Marshall swore Mountbatten to secrecy and told him about the atomic bomb, adding that the weapon would be ready for use by August 5. All three men agreed that the war would probably end in a few weeks. When Mountbatten asked why the Combined Chiefs had that afternoon set November 1946 as the end date of the war, Marshall explained that the planners did not know about the bomb. The November 1946 date "was a fair estimate" of how long the war would last if the Allies had to follow through on the invasion of Japan. Before the meeting ended, Marshall reminded Mountbatten of his pledge "not to tell a soul—not even the Prime Minister, with whom General Marshall knew I was dining that night."[119] Act 2 of the melodrama took place that evening. After they dined, Churchill took Mountbatten into his study and closed the doors. "I have a great secret to tell you," he said. After he shared the secret with Mountbatten, Churchill advised him to instruct his staff to begin planning for the possibility of Japanese surrender in the next few weeks.[120]

On July 25, according to Mountbatten's account of his meeting with Truman, the two men discussed the atomic bomb and the likelihood of an early Japanese surrender. "The president told me, as a great secret," he wrote, "the story of the atomic bomb." Mountbatten recommended that Truman inform MacArthur, adding that it would be best if the timing of the bombs could be arranged so that the field commanders were ready to occupy Japanese-held areas as soon as Japan surrendered. Truman demurred on this point, explaining that he did not want the war to continue a day longer than necessary. In his diary entry, Mountbatten acknowledged the soundness of the president's thinking but added that an early surrender of Japan "is clearly going to present the wretched commanders with extremely difficult problems."[121]

As Mountbatten learned from his meetings with Marshall, Churchill, and Truman, the news from General Groves was so exciting that those who knew the secret felt compelled to share it with someone else. One is struck, however, by the uncoordinated and improvised manner in which such vital information was handled. Churchill and Truman privately agreed that Truman should notify Stalin about the weapon. Everyone told Mountbatten, and the president and prime minister spoke to their own military advisers. The news about the bomb prompted an ad hoc adjustment of plans, but there was no attempt by Truman, Churchill, and the heads of the Combined Chiefs to more fully assess how the success of the atomic bomb might alter strategy, operations, or policy. The shortcomings of this approach, or lack of approach, would become evident in the weeks ahead.

Truman continued to inquire into the consequences of an early surrender when, following his appointment with Mountbatten, he met with Marshall later in the morning on July 25. The focus of the meeting shifted, however, to the impact of an early surrender on domestic policy. Our best evidence of what occurred at this meeting consists of the briefing papers that Marshall prepared for the president and a digest of those papers that Marshall sent to Stimson after both men had returned to Washington. The report, "Status of Demobilization Plans to Meet an Early Defeat of Japan," began with Marshall explaining that "this is the substance of the report I made to the President at TERMINAL (Potsdam), he being concerned over the possible adverse morale effect over jobs, etc."[122] Here was evidence that Vinson's warnings about the state of the American economy had gotten the president's attention.

Overall, Marshall's report showed that the Army would be able to shift gears and execute the transition to peace without adversely affecting the American economy. There would be no sudden shock to the system, in large part because there would be a gradual drawdown in forces matched by equally measured cutbacks in procurement. Planning for the transition, already under way, would be accelerated, and redeployment and demobilization could be adjusted to meet the new realities. The report, which covered postwar objectives in Asia and economic adjustment at home, is worth discussing in detail for what it reveals about the Army's optimistic outlook regarding the economic transition to peace.

Marshall's presentation to Truman began with the reassuring prediction that the current rate of discharge could be adjusted immediately to permit the release of larger numbers of high-point men. The current redeployment from Europe could be revised to bring home men with the highest scores first. The shipment of low-score men in Europe slated for redeployment to the Pacific would stop. Low-score men already en route to the United States would continue on to the Pacific to assist in the surrender operations or be kept as part of a strategic reserve against the resumption of hostilities. Low-score men already in the United States would either be shipped to the Pacific to assist in the occupation of Japanese-held areas or remain stateside to administer the discharge from service of their high-score comrades. These arrangements, the accelerated discharge of high-point men and reliance on troops with fewer points for occupational duties, "should solve what otherwise might be a difficult morale problem."

This new program for returning high-point men would be implemented as troops already in the Pacific occupied key areas in the Japanese empire. Fortunately, MacArthur's and Admiral Nimitz's staffs had been working on contingency plans for operations in the event of a sudden collapse of Japanese resistance. U.S. forces would be employed in the occupation of Japan and Formosa. However, the Army also anticipated opening several ports on the China coast to supply Chinese troops and facilitate their liberation of areas held by the Japanese below the Great Wall. The Army might also occupy parts of Korea, but it would need political guidance on that objective before adding it to its list of responsibilities. The report cautioned that because American forces were dispersed throughout the Pacific and were still being organized for the invasion of Kyushu, it might take up three months for them to occupy all of the strategic areas in Japan and Korea. These circumstances meant that the United States would be dependent on Japanese cooperation to occupy the home islands and disarm the millions of Japanese troops still in the field. Given the expected delays in moving troops into Japan, the Army endorsed a plan in which MacArthur would, at first, garrison key strategic points in Japan and "administer the country through the existent Japanese ministries and administrative machinery." The Army also recommended using "Japanese Imperial headquarters, or a portion thereof," to secure the surrender of Japanese troops throughout the empire. Although the briefing paper scrupulously refrained from mentioning the emperor, the reference to ministries and Imperial Headquarters tacitly reinforced the

Joint Chiefs' previous recommendation that nothing be done to prevent the U.S. forces from obtaining the cooperation of the emperor to order his subjects to surrender and not resist the occupation.

The occupation of Japan and Japanese-held areas would tax American shipping, according to Marshall's report, and the strain on transportation on the West Coast would continue, but the Army expected to be able to expedite the return of eligible high-point men from the Pacific even as it sent lower-score troops to replace them. The Army's planners also predicted that the transition from war to peace would not cause unmanageable disruptions in the economy. Production of supplies necessary for maintenance of the Army would continue but would decrease progressively as soldiers were discharged. Certain unspecified development projects would continue, as would the production of the B-29 bombers and heavy transports required to service them. South American countries were also expected to provide outlets for production of aircraft in the period of transition.

Overall, reconversion would affect only 20–25 percent of American industries. Those unaffected by reconversion would still have large military orders to fill. Moreover, there would "be a large civilian demand for goods not available during the war." Deferred maintenance on public utilities and other sectors of the economy would also take up the slack. According to the report, the Army did not see a sudden rise in unemployment stemming from the conversion of industry to peacetime production. The release of men from military service into the economy would be regulated by the amount of shipping available to bring them home. The transition would be gradual, a steady flow in increments over months, not a stampede. The picture was admittedly cloudier in cities such as Detroit and Los Angeles, where large numbers of workers had gathered for war work. There would be "difficulties" in these instances, but they could be surmounted by "careful planning" and "vigorous leadership" on the part of "government, industry, and labor."

Consideration of problems in Detroit and Los Angeles led to speculation about the broader implications of reconversion and the need to prepare the public for what lay ahead. Under the heading "Readjustment of American People," Marshall's report emphasized the importance of spelling out clearly "what is going to happen and why each particular policy or action is necessary." For example, there would undoubtedly be questions as to why low-score men already in the United States could not be released from duty. "The Army can take care of informing the soldier," the report confidently stated, but the job of informing the public at home would fall to civilian agencies like the Office of War Information. "This will require tremendous effort," concluded the report.[123]

The Army's briefing paper for the president accurately predicted the lag that would occur between the announcement of a surrender and the movement of American and Chinese troops into key areas of Japan and its continental empire. But in many other respects, the report was markedly unhelpful in preparing Truman for the sudden transition to peace. A few examples will suffice. The suggestion that problems in Detroit and Los Angeles could be handled by cooperation between labor and industry ignored the record of strikes during the war and anticipated a level of accord undreamed of by businessmen and labor leaders. The prediction that adjustments in the process of demobilization could be made that would give soldiers and the public no cause for complaint also fell wide of the mark, as events after the war would demonstrate. Moreover, the assertion that the Army could "take care of informing the soldier" would also be emphatically disproved in the immediate postwar period. Nevertheless, the defects in the Army's predictions, however significant, were not as telling as what the report revealed about the Army's assessment of the current state of demobilization, redeployment, and economic reconversion.

The Army's deadpan observation that a huge pent-up demand existed for civilian goods and services would have been taken as a small victory by the civilians concerned with reconversion. But the report's discussion of civilian needs as something that would come into play during the postwar transition tacitly demonstrated that the Army did not take seriously the OWMR's warnings about the current baleful effects of military procurement on the economy. Civilian demand could be unleashed once the war ended, but not before, and even then, the report indicated, military procurement and manpower would remain at high levels for the foreseeable future. The confidence evident in the report's discussion of redeployment and demobilization also indicated a less than candid appraisal of current conditions. The picture was of a smoothly functioning process, one requiring modest readjustments to accommodate the goal of returning high-point men to the United States for discharge from service. This ignored, however, the mounting complaints—from congressmen and GIs both—that the system was already functioning poorly and that too many high-point men were being unnecessarily held by the Army. Moreover, apart from referring to the strain on transportation on the West Coast, the report made no mention of the myriad problems plaguing demobilization and redeployment: the projected backlog in troop movements, shipping shortages, the inadequacy of port facilities in the western Pacific, the unexpected complications in assigning points, and the difficulties in sorting high- from low-point men that the Army was encountering as it moved men from Europe to the United States.

The Army's prediction of a relatively seamless transition to peace rested on the assumption that the operations already under way were proceeding smoothly and thus could be adjusted to meet the new objectives without much difficulty. But redeployment was facing mounting problems, partial demobilization had proved exceedingly complicated, and the civilians in charge of managing the wartime economy were increasingly unwilling to let the Army decide when reconversion would commence and at what pace. There was still time to apprise the president of the challenges the Army was facing in preparing for DOWNFALL. And it remained possible that the Army would solve many of the problems it faced in moving its forces into place for the invasions. Those problems would vanish, of course, if Japan surrendered. Whatever challenges the Army faced as a result of a sudden Japanese surrender would pale in comparison to those presented by the invasions. But one wonders at what point Marshall planned to give the president a detailed report on the status of redeployment and demobilization that would candidly explain the difficulties the Army was facing.

Following his meeting with Truman, Marshall instructed MacArthur to add the occupation of key points in Korea to his list of objectives in the event of a Japanese collapse. The next day, July 26, Truman released the Allied warning to Japan. Secretary of State Byrnes showed the warning, known as the Potsdam Declaration, to Soviet foreign minister Molotov as a courtesy but rejected Molotov's request for time to study the document and offer comments.[124]

Possession of the atomic bomb allowed Truman to modify policy and think more seriously about the consequences of a sudden end to the war. Preparations for the invasion proceeded, but after July 26 they were made to accommodate new objectives. A new timetable was being superimposed on the old, but the revised schedule was visible to only a few. In general terms, it encouraged American firmness toward Japan and a stiff formality in dealing with the Soviet Union. Truman had become noticeably more confident that the atomic bomb would make an invasion unnecessary. That was a source of enormous relief to him. But his attitude toward the Russians was one of resignation. Little could be done to keep them out of the war, but a sudden collapse of Japanese resistance might put the United States in a better position to resist Soviet pressure in Northeast Asia. The addition of Korea to MacArthur's occupation objectives was the clearest indication of this new attitude toward the Russians.

Although the atomic bomb remained a secret kept from most of the officers working on the Combined Chiefs of Staff, American and British leaders had been expecting to learn of the weapon's availability before the invasion of Japan began. Planning went forward for the invasion, however, because no one wanted to count on the bomb's success, nor could they be certain that the new weapon would compel Japan's surrender. As recently as June, the sudden collapse of Japanese resistance had been at best a remote possibility. That changed after Truman received the reports from General Groves. Preparations for the invasion continued in case the atomic bombs did not force Japan's surrender. With victory in sight, precautionary measures seemed warranted, especially since the preinvasion operations would put Allied forces in place to respond to Japan's surrender, if it should occur before November. The Allies still could not be certain that the war would end without an invasion, but the success of the atomic bomb test loosened some of the restraints on Allied planning and allowed Truman, Churchill, and their top commanders to begin preparations for a Japanese surrender. The end seemed in sight.

Surrender at Last, August 1945

The movement of the atomic bomb components to the Pacific—including uranium projectile, target rings, and bomb casing—and the increased tempo of Allied planning for the possibility of a sudden collapse of Japanese resistance took place behind a curtain of secrecy during and after the Potsdam conference. For those observing the proceedings at Potsdam or receiving reports secondhand through the press—meaning the entirety of the American public—it appeared that as far as the war with Japan was concerned, the Allies remained committed to subduing Japan by means of invasion. Behind the scenes, however, influential civilian and military officials continued to question the efficacy of the planned operations. Members of the OWMR Advisory Board and agency staff stepped up their criticism of the Army's procurement policies and warned about impending economic disaster. The Japanese buildup on Kyushu reinforced the Navy's initial skepticism regarding DOWNFALL and emboldened Admiral King and Navy Secretary Forrestal to challenge openly the Army's strategy for ending the war. Army staff officers remained committed to invasion, but as evidence of reinforcement on Kyushu accumulated, as it did through July, they began to search for alternatives to operation OLYMPIC. By early

August, the Army's plans were strained to the breaking point. Redeployment proceeded in fits and starts; the Atlantic leg of the journey went well, but the prospects for timely arrival in the Pacific dimmed as one contemplated the task of moving millions of men over clogged and poorly maintained rail lines, in advance of their boarding ships that had yet to be obtained and whose arrival in their ports of embarkation remained a matter of conjecture.

In the meantime, the Potsdam Declaration, the Allied warning to Japan issued on July 26, earned bipartisan support from those in Congress who had been most vocal in calling for Truman to define unconditional surrender. Republican senators Robert White, Kenneth Wherry, and Homer Capehart all declared themselves satisfied, with Wherry hedging somewhat by calling the declaration "a step in the right direction."[1] More generally, the *New York Times* reported that Washington "buzzed with speculation and rumor" that Japan might heed the Allies' warning and surrender, although no one was willing to say that on the record.[2]

Press commentary ran the gamut. Once the initial excitement of the announcement wore off, closer scrutiny of the text showed that key questions about Japan's fate remained unanswered. The declaration began with a stern warning to Japan that threatened "the utter devastation of the Japanese homeland" if the Japanese refused to surrender. "Following are our terms," it continued. "We will not deviate from them. There are no alternatives. We shall brook no delay." Japan was told that the leaders who had taken the country into war would be removed forever from positions of authority. Japanese war criminals would be brought to justice, and "points" of Japanese territory would be occupied by the Allies. Territorially, Japan would be stripped of its colonies, including Korea and Formosa, and reduced to the four main islands and such other islands as the Allies determined. The Allied warning assured the Japanese people that they would not be "enslaved as a race or destroyed as a nation." On the future of Japan's government, the Allies declared that the occupation, in addition to removing the militarists from power, would establish the basis for a democratic society, including freedom of speech, freedom of religion, and respect for basic human rights. Allied forces would withdraw from Japan as soon as those democratic objectives were achieved "and there has been established in accordance with the freely expressed will of the Japanese people a peacefully inclined and responsible government." The declaration called once more for the unconditional surrender of Japan's armed forces and ended by warning that the alternative would be "prompt and utter destruction."[3]

The ambiguous wording in some key provisions invited speculation and fed the debate over the best way to assure a lasting victory. Ernest K. Lindley, the *Washington Post* and *Newsweek* columnist, judged the declaration a "fair and final" statement of Allied war aims. Previously, Lindley had leaned toward including a pledge to keep the emperor in any warning to Japan. Nevertheless, he was unperturbed by the failure of the Potsdam warning to address the fate of the emperor. Citing the clause that promised the Japanese an opportunity to choose their own form of government, Lindley predicted that maintenance of the imperial institution would be permissible under the terms of the declaration. The ambiguity of the declaration, Lindley added, might actually work to induce Hirohito's cooperation in ending the war. The more helpful the emperor became, the more likely the Allies would be to allow him to stay on the throne, provided that the Japanese people desired it—and provided that he was not found guilty of war crimes.[4]

Hanson Baldwin, the military specialist of the *New York Times*, took the opposite view. He worried that the Allies' silence on the fate of Hirohito perpetuated the State Department's mistaken efforts to treat the militarists as separate from the emperor. Baldwin considered that approach misguided: the emperor was so closely linked to the militarists through "kinship, custom, tradition" that it was difficult to see how one could be eliminated without the other. Moreover, that "hands-off the emperor" approach, combined with recent statements by some American officials implying lenient terms for Japan, had only served to strengthen Japanese resolve to hold out for better terms. Baldwin also worried about other provisions, such as the declaration's reference to an Allied occupation of "points" in Japan, and suggested that only a full occupation of Japan could uproot Japan's military culture. Anything less, he warned, could leave Japan as capable of starting another war, as Germany had proven to be after World War I.[5]

Debate over the meaning of the Potsdam Declaration and postwar policy toward Japan was cut short by the Japanese government's announcement that it would ignore the Allied warning. The first reports that attributed the announcement to the "semiofficial" Domei News Agency left some hope that the Japanese government might actually accept the terms of Potsdam.[6] Over the next several days, however, it seemed clear that the Japanese had flatly rejected the American offer.[7] The situation in Tokyo was somewhat more complicated, reflecting disagreements between the peace advocates and those arguing for a continuation of the war, but the outcome only confirmed that the military remained in charge and the generals were unwilling to surrender on terms acceptable to the United States. Initially, Prime Minister Suzuki hoped to postpone an official statement while members of his government explored how best to respond. The government's military leaders were unsatisfied with that approach and forced Suzuki to issue a more categorical rejection of the Potsdam Declaration. "The government does not consider it a thing of any great value," he told the Japanese press; "the government will just ignore it. We will press forward resolutely to carry the war to a successful conclusion."[8] Suzuki was quoted as using the term *mokusatsu*, which could be translated variously as "withhold comment," "ignore," or even "treat with silent contempt." Obviously there is a huge difference in meaning between the first and third interpretations. However Suzuki intended his comment to be interpreted, if he even did actually comment, there was no misunderstanding as to Tokyo's basic position; the Japanese government was not prepared to surrender on the basis of the Potsdam Declaration.[9] That meant, the *New York Times* dolefully concluded, that "the war in the Pacific must and will go forward to a decision on the field of battle."[10]

Victory seemed assured, of course, but it remained to be seen if it would be achieved as the Army envisioned it—through an invasion of the home islands. Publicly, military officials sought to quell any doubts about the outcome. General James Doolittle, commander of the Eighth Air Force, declared that in a few weeks nearly 1,000 B-29 Superfortresses would begin flying from Okinawa under the protection of long-range Thunderbolt fighters. The short run from Okinawa, Doolittle explained, would allow the B-29s to carry three times the payload as the same planes flying from the Marianas. Admiral DeWitt Ramsey, chief of staff for Admiral Raymond Spruance's Fifth Fleet, likewise confidently told a radio audience that the invasion would be preceded by a massive air assault against Japan. The troops for the final onslaught were already assembling from Europe, Ramsey noted. He then added a cautionary note. Referring to an earlier comment by Admiral Nimitz, Ramsey reminded his listeners that the United States would have to overcome two enemies: the Japanese and long lines of supply.[11]

The long line of supply or, more precisely, the problem of supplying materials for the long-distance campaign against Japan, concerned civilian officials responsible for economic mobilization in ways that brought them into conflict with the officers planning for the invasion. Army planners thought almost exclusively about the logistical challenges of getting men and supplies into the Western Pacific in time to support the invasions. As Vinson's recent messages to Truman indicated, the civilians had shifted their attention to the home front and thought almost entirely about how the transfer of men and the production of supplies for the Army's plans affected economic reconversion. Heading the OWMR during this critical phase of the war was John Snyder, the banker who had been Truman's friend from Army Reserve days. This was hardly the best time for a change in leadership, but Truman wanted Vinson sworn in so that he rather than Morgenthau would be in the presidential line of succession.

Snyder, it will be recalled, had agreed with the warnings that Vinson had sent to Truman at Potsdam. Nevertheless, the members of the OWMR Advisory Board had thought it necessary to brief Snyder on the parlous state of reconversion on the day he took office. During a meeting of the board on July 23, while the president was in Potsdam, National Chamber of Commerce president Eric Johnston couched the case for reconversion in political terms calculated to gain the agreement of the new director. The American people were interested in jobs, Johnston explained. That goal, which he termed "peace at home," could only be secured through a sensible demobilization plan, "and our chore should be to help in demobilization as much as possible." He soon explained what that meant in practical terms. There had been "gross waste in the Army," he said, and "as time goes on, there will be more evidence of gross waste." He conceded that mistakes in judgment were inevitable but argued that the OWMR's job was to protect the armed forces from its own mistakes. Continuing waste would lead to more criticism, and that, he warned, would lead to criticism of Snyder and the administration. In short, when the advisory board screened procurement for evidence of waste, it was not being "supercritical"; it was sincerely trying to shield the administration. "If the Army takes too much steel," Johnston added, "the civilians cannot get it. As I view it, more material must be given to civilians in the months ahead if you are going to make democracy function and work." "The Army needs to realize that," he continued. In short, the reconversion controversy resulted from a sharp disagreement over fundamental principles. "I have sat with high people in the War Department," Johnston explained, "who said that the only thing that was important was the Army. I don't agree with that."[12]

Other board members followed up in a similar vein. The president of the American Federation of Labor, William Green, complained that the Army "won't change their attitude no matter how the whole economic situation changes. They will keep on demanding and they won't let up."[13] Speaking on the transportation situation, T. C. Cashen, head of the Switchmen's Union, worried about a shortage of brake shoes for trains and more generally a "terrific pinch on transportation" west of Chicago. The manpower shortage was acute, he added, but he hoped they could overcome it. Industrialist George H. Mead, representing the small war plants and a member of the War Labor Board, warned Snyder not to expect the Army to undertake demobilization without constant pressure from his office. The Army's leaders, Marshall included, would agree with that telegram that Vinson sent to Truman, but they would not act unless Snyder's office forced them to. "Within themselves," Mead declared, "I don't believe they can do it."[14]

In the two weeks after Snyder took over as head of the OWMR, the reconversion "muddle," as one journalist called it, became the subject of growing scrutiny in the press. Two different scenarios haunted businessmen, workers, Congress, and the civilian mobilizers. The first concerned the consequences of a protracted war lasting into 1946. Army procurement and manpower demands for a prolonged war threatened to exacerbate labor shortages and create shortfalls in essential items like coal and lumber. The continued lack of skilled railroad workers would affect the distribution of goods at home and snarl the redeployment of troops to the Pacific. The second fear was that at the current rate of reconversion, the nation would not be prepared for the economic shock that would come when Japan finally did surrender. Although commentators found that there was plenty of blame to go around, most of the criticism was aimed at the Army.

The report of the Senate War Investigating Committee (Mead Committee) released at the end of July criticized the Army's manpower policies. "The Army has a great reservoir of manpower which it is slow in releasing," complained the senators. The problem was made even more frustrating, the report added, because relatively few workers in key industries would help speed reconversion.[15] The Mead Committee also found fault with the lack of coordination between the civilian mobilization agencies. Contract termination was proceeding smoothly, the report concluded, but much better teamwork was needed on the disposal of surplus materials. "Underlying this whole problem of teamwork," wrote journalist John Crider, "is the old feud between the War Department and civilian authorities." He added that the Mead Committee's recommendation for a beefed-up OWMR was undoubtedly made with the hope that a stronger reconversion agency "clothed with enough authority might make the War Department toe the line."[16]

In the meantime the Senate Military Affairs Committee grilled Undersecretary of War Patterson in a closed session dealing with a resolution to speed the release of 10,000 miners who were eligible for discharge and furlough another 20,000 who were currently in the Zone of the Interior. The resolution received rare bipartisan support from the Democratic and Republican senators of West Virginia. When Patterson insisted that the resolution would wreck the point system and undermine morale, the usually mild-mannered Elbert Thomas (D-Utah) fired back: "You have a huge Army there Mr. Patterson. It appears to be a great deal larger than you need for a one-front war. Yet here you are refusing to take the trouble to release a relatively small number of coal miners to help relieve the most serious fuel crisis of the war period." Thomas continued at some length with a general indictment of the Army's wasteful manpower policies and arrogant disregard of the consequences of those policies for the home front. "That settled that," observed Drew Pearson. The matter would now go to the Senate for a vote.[17]

The barrage of criticism continued through the first week of August. The newly appointed secretary of agriculture, Clinton Anderson, called for faster discharges and publicly disputed the Army's need for eight million men in a one-front war. James Patton, head of the National Farmers' Union, went further in criticizing Army policies. Patton dismissed the Army's claims and sided with Senators Johnson and Taft in calling for the trimming of the total number of troops to a "sensible figure." Patton also condemned the Army for taking a "gigantic volume of materials" and refusing to release a few thousand soldiers out of the millions it held. "If it is at all possible to effect a reasonably smooth reconversion," Patton said, "it is absolutely essential that materials and manpower be released now and in increasing volume over the next few months."[18] *Washington Post* columnist Marquis Childs also rebuked the Army for failing to cooperate with the OWMR. "The civilian heads of the War Department simply will not go along on what are considered the minimum essentials of reconversion," he wrote. The Navy had been much more cooperative, Childs explained, whereas the Army thoughtlessly hoarded men and machine tools and remained oblivious to the economic consequences of its policies. Truman would have to set matters straight when he returned from Potsdam. Childs helpfully suggested that a change of leadership in the War Department would be a good place to begin. Speculating on the possible retirement of seventy-eight-year-old Secretary Stimson, Childs made cooperation with the OWMR's Snyder the number one requirement for his successor. Leaving little to chance, Childs also set out the prospective new secretary's agenda for him. Heading the list was the release of soldiers to alleviate the manpower shortages in transportation and mining, followed, "as quickly as possible," by a more general assessment of the Army's manpower necessities.[19]

The mounting public criticism had only the barest impact on thinking in the Pentagon. Surveying the situation at the end of July, the General Council of the Army staff repeated General Franklin's assertion that "so far as the War Department can see, there would be no serious difficulty in obtaining adequate rail transportation for the Pacific operations."[20] The staff officers also confidently predicted that the Senate would not act on the resolution calling for the release of coal miners before it recessed. The next day, however, Undersecretary Patterson announced that the Army was contracting with civilian airlines to fly 25,000 soldiers a month to the West Coast. Patterson also said that the Army would be expediting the release of railroad workers in the coming months. As the *New York Times* explained, these two measures were intended to "relieve the jammed transportation situation which last week brought charges before a Senate committee that the Army was not cooperating with the railroads and the Office of Defense Transportation in the redeployment of troops to the Pacific."[21] Here, at last, was some indication that the Army was acknowledging that redeployment was in trouble. Or so it seemed. In fact, Patterson, apart from announcing the airlift of some troops to the West Coast, had changed very little about the Army's operations. In explaining the "new" policy on the discharge of railroad workers, Patterson emphasized that only men with eighty-five points or more would be released, and even then it might take until December to ship some of the men home. Moreover, there would be no furloughs.

The War Department's announcement did little to quiet public concern over the slow pace of reconversion. Over the next several days, officials and commentators continued to criticize the Army for what they perceived as its obstructionist policies. On August 1, Ickes once again warned of an impending coal shortage at home and in Europe unless the Army furloughed 30,000 miners. According to the deputy director of the Solid Fuels Administration, the coal shortage would also put major factories, including steel plants, on a four-day work week by winter.[22]

And on it went. The *Washington Post*'s Ernest Lindley, like the Mead Committee, recommended revision of the Surplus Property Act. He also blamed Congress for failing to pass a bill that would have kept men deemed unfit for service from leaving war-related jobs. Lindley also called attention to the Mead Committee's concerns about the critical manpower shortages in West Coast industries and shipyards. Congressional cooperation would be needed to address some of these problems, but, Lindley noted, the president already possessed the authority to "compel the armed services to release coal miners, railroad workers, and other skilled workers who are needed more outside the armed services than in them." On his return from

Potsdam, Lindley added, Truman would have to "come to grips with home front affairs."[23]

Caught in the middle of the political maelstrom was Snyder, who, in the words of Drew Pearson, sat in meetings with "his ears literally flapping as curve balls fly at him from every direction." The conscientious but uninformed Snyder was, according to Pearson, simply not up to the task. His appointment, Pearson added, was like taking someone off the streets of New York and asking him to command a submarine. Snyder didn't "even know the terminology of various reconversion problems."[24] According to Pearson, the American people, their representatives in Congress, and the many GI's writing to him, all seemed to be directing their attention to what would happen after the war. The recent British election, in which the voters had turned out Winston Churchill and put in as prime minister Clement Atlee, head of the Labor Party, demonstrated what would happen to politicians who ignored the public's concerns on this subject.

It is doubtful that Snyder needed to be reminded of the political repercussions that would follow from a botched reconversion. During the first week of August, pressure continued to build for him to take action to curb the Army's appetite for men and materials. The OWMR staff members quickly dismissed Patterson's solution to the railroad problem as an empty gesture. There was no guarantee that men with eighty-five points would report immediately for railroad work out West once they returned home from Europe. Moreover, the 4,000 furloughs authorized in June for men still in the United States had yet to produce results. As of August 2, fewer than 1,000 men had been found with "*any* kind of railroad experience."[25]

The civilian mobilizers and the War Department appeared to be moving further apart as the war dragged on. Certainly, Patterson's response to the labor shortage suggested that he had more confidence in the Army's staff officers than the civilians who had criticized War Department practices for most of the war. In part, this was because for the civilian mobilizers the labor shortage in the railroad industry threatened economic conditions on the home front as much as redeployment. Patterson and Stimson on the other hand believed that Americans had not sacrificed enough at home and should be prepared to endure greater discomfort in the short run for the sake of total victory. In holding to those views and in treating the point system as sacrosanct, Patterson was also jeopardizing the success of redeployment to the Pacific. He could counter that there would have been no labor problems in the shipyards or in the rail industry if Congress had passed a national service bill. But that was water under the bridge now. The stark reality was that the Army needed to find ways to prevent those labor shortages from upsetting its timetables. Flying 25,000 soldiers across the country was at best a partial solution.

Patterson and the uniformed staff officers overseeing the buildup for OLYMPIC gave almost no thought to how the military's procurement and manpower policies affected reconversion. Indeed, it is probably not an exaggeration to say that Patterson thought planning for reconversion had gone too far already. The recent Gallup poll showing that most Americans did not think the Army was too big and that it was doing a good job of handling men and material gave Patterson and the Army planners all the reassurance they needed to maintain the current levels of men and equipment. The United States still faced a defiant enemy who was determined to inflict as much damage on the invaders as possible. By bringing overwhelming force to bear against Japan, the United States would minimize casualties and ensure complete victory. Thinking in the Pentagon remained focused on the immediate task of conquering Japan, crowding out operational planning about the future of mainland Asia and European recovery. The future health of the postwar U.S. economy was taken as a given and barely registered on the Army's list of concerns. When the staff officers did address economic issues, as when they responded to Hoover's memorandum of May 30, they tended to dismiss warnings of impending disaster as alarmist.

The civilian mobilizers approached victory from the opposite direction. Japan's defeat was taken as a given. The United States could achieve victory through a siege. A strategy of blockade and bombardment would still seal Japan's fate, but it would also provide greater assurance that the economy would emerge from the war strong enough to provide Americans with the fruits of victory in peacetime. Security at home mattered as much as security from foreign dangers, especially when those dangers had been all but eliminated. As peace beckoned, memories of depression and unemployment dominated the thoughts of congressmen and civilian mobilizers. Upward pressure on prices, scarcity of materials, and snarled transportation networks were taken as harbingers of an inflation-wracked stagnant economy ill-equipped to absorb the millions of men who would eventually return from overseas. Chester Bowles, the head of the Office of Price Administration, worried most about inflation. Writing to Snyder, Bowles explained that unless production was increased and military procurement and manpower reduced in the next three months, he would have to raise prices and that action would undoubtedly lead to inflation. Bowles's warning was restrained compared to the predictions of an unnamed economist who told him that if Japan did not surrender by October, or if the United States did not find a way to fight a $35 billion war instead of the current $75 billion one, "the program of economic stabilization is doomed to failure."[26] Bowles told Snyder that he could not fully accept that view but believed that it was not very far off the mark.

As the columnist John Crider had noted, Snyder did not yet have the authority to make the War Department toe the line on reconversion. But he did have the confidence of the president and the support of Vinson should he wish to confront the military. The members of the OWMR Advisory Board undoubtedly understood this when on August 6 they unanimously approved a resolution calling on Snyder to protect reconversion by cutting military spending and increasing civilian production. The Advisory Board noted that unless civilian production increased and military procurement decreased, there was "grave doubt" that the nation could make the transition to a peacetime economy with "our savings intact, mass purchasing power for products of farm and factory maintained, and jobs for returning veterans and war workers available."[27] The resolution contained the by-now standard disclaimer that nothing should be done to weaken the war effort against Japan but experience had shown that the armed forces were prone to waste and indifferent to the health of the domestic economy. "We are impelled," the resolution continued, "to recommend immediate review of the size of the armed forces and the military procurement program with a view to reductions in the interest of the National economy," whose failure would result in "the substitution of strife and chaos at home for the horrors of war abroad." Having set Snyder's agenda, the board agreed to take up at its next meeting a resolution calling on the OWMR to convene a meeting of top military and civilian heads to review the situation and bring military policies into line "with foreign and domestic needs to the end that a crisis in the civilian economy can be averted."[28]

As the Advisory Board moved to challenge the Army's procurement and manpower programs, the strategy those programs were intended to support was thrown suddenly into turmoil. As we have noted, by late July, while the president was still at Potsdam, ULTRA had shown an alarming increase in the number of Japanese soldiers on Kyushu. These reports also showed that the bulk of these forces were positioned in the areas near the three invasion beaches. There was little doubt now that Japanese Imperial Headquarters had divined American intentions and the enemy was doing everything in its power to carry out its threat to make the invaders pay dearly for daring to set foot on the sacred soil of the Japanese homeland.

When General Marshall had endorsed OLYMPIC at the June 18 White House meeting, he had done so on the assumption that the Japanese would have eight divisions on the island by November 1. By July 20, ULTRA revealed that the number of Japanese on the island had jumped from 100,000 in June to 380,000. The next day, the discovery of three more divisions raised the total of Japanese servicemen, soldiers and sailors, to 450,000.[29] At first, MacArthur's chief of intelligence, Charles Willoughby, was inclined to dismiss the reports showing the arrival of new units on Kyushu. In May he had predicted that there would be between six and eight divisions on the islands, the lower number being more likely. Like Marshall, Willoughby assumed that American air and sea power would interdict reinforcement efforts and cut the island off from the main island of Honshu as well as other parts of the empire. By mid-July, however, he was convinced that an overall increase in the number of military units in the Japanese home islands had resulted in the "tremendous influx and organization of combat units on Kyushu." Two weeks later, citing the continuing discovery of new units on the island, he filed an amended intelligence assessment warning that "this threatening trend, if not checked, may grow to a point where we attack on a ratio of one (1) to one (1) which is not a recipe for victory." Moreover,

Willoughby added, despite American dominance of the skies over Kyushu, the Japanese were able to move most of their forces to the southern half of the island.[30]

The news only got worse. By August 2, ULTRA showed that there were 545,000 Japanese servicemen on the island. Five days later, the number rose to 560,000. American cryptanalysts also kept track of the steadily rising number of aircraft moving into range of the Kyushu invasion beaches. Intercepts showed that most of these were trainers being converted into suicide planes, similar to those that had attacked the U.S. fleet off Okinawa to such devastating effect. The Japanese were also amassing a flotilla of suicide watercraft, including small surface vessels, midget submarines, and human-piloted torpedoes.

The ULTRA intercepts were less forthcoming about the quality of the troops the Americans would be facing. Willoughby noted that some of the newly discovered units were probably not fully organized or equipped. The ULTRA, as well as MAGIC, intercepts of diplomatic traffic did indicate that the Japanese were low on fuel, lacking in heavy artillery, and having difficulty moving what supplies were available, owing to American disruption of rail traffic. Nevertheless, intelligence also showed that the Japanese remained zealously committed to the defense of the homeland. Intercepts showed no sign of waning support within the military for KETSU-GO. When Admiral Toyoda Soemu was elevated to the position of supreme commander of Japanese Combined Naval Forces, American naval intelligence predicted that he and his immediate subordinate, Admiral Ozawa Jisaburo, would work closely with the "extremist" elements in the Imperial Army. Toyoda's rousing message to naval personnel on July 29 provided confirmation that the leadership of the Imperial Navy and Army were as one in their commitment to the last-ditch defense of the home islands.[31]

The alarming evidence of the Japanese buildup on Kyushu prompted the planning officers on the JCS to begin the process of considering alternatives to OLYMPIC. The first steps were tentative and exploratory but also exhibited a sense of urgency not usually found in routine contingency planning. On August 4, the Joint War Plans Committee forwarded a report to the Joint Staff Planners recommending that, in light of "The possible effect upon OLYMPIC operations of this buildup and concentration," the Joint Staff Planners instruct MacArthur and Nimitz to "review their estimates of the situation, reexamine objectives in Japan as possible alternatives to OLYMPIC, and prepare plans for operations against such alternate objectives."[32] Attached to the report was a draft memorandum for MacArthur and Nimitz explaining that conditions on Kyushu did not require an immediate change in their directive but did warrant serious consideration of OLYMPIC's prospects and an evaluation of possible alternatives.

On August 6, as the Joint War Plans Committee report made its way through the JCS bureaucracy, Marshall's deputy chief of staff notified him that the prospects for OLYMPIC would be the subject for the forthcoming meeting of the Joint Chiefs. The following day, Marshall, who had been following the progress of the buildup on Kyushu, sent MacArthur a telegram asking for his thoughts in light of the recent intelligence showing a massive increase in Japanese forces on Kyushu. Marshall noted a weakening of Japanese forces elsewhere in the home islands and raised the possibility of striking directly at the Kanto Plain or targets farther north, including Sendai, along the coast north of Tokyo, or Ominato, located at the northern tip of Honshu.[33] MacArthur promptly replied that evening. He ruled out Marshall's suggested alternatives since they would be out of range of most of the Americans' land-based aircraft, except for the B-29s flying out of the Marianas. Weather also made Ominato undesirable. Landings at Sendai, which was closer to Tokyo, might encounter reinforcements from the Kanto region. MacArthur also dismissed reports showing a concentration of Japanese air strength near the invasion sites. Throughout the war, he explained, he had always found similar reports to be greatly exaggerated. Moreover, he assured the chief of staff that once he moved his air force forward from Luzon to Okinawa in September, Japanese ground forces would be "immobilized." "There should not, repeat not, be the slightest thought of changing the OLYMPIC operation. Its fundamental purpose is to obtain air bases under cover of which we can deploy forces to the northward into the industrial heart of Japan. The plan is sound and will succeed." He concluded: "Throughout the Southwest Pacific Area campaigns, as we have neared an operation, intelligence has invariably pointed to greatly increased enemy forces. Without exception, this buildup has been found to be erroneous."[34]

More than three years of working with MacArthur had convinced Marshall that his Pacific commander was "so prone to exaggerate and so influenced by his own desires that it is difficult to trust his judgment."[35] MacArthur's impassioned defense of OLYMPIC could only confirm that harsh judgment. Marshall had asked if there was some possibility, however unlikely, that ULTRA had been a victim of Japanese deception efforts. MacArthur's unsubtle response to this query was hardly reassuring. As historian Richard Frank has noted, the Pacific commander's statement that on the eve of previous operations intelligence reports had always overestimated the size of Japanese forces was an "extraordinarily brazen lie."[36] More often than not, MacArthur's own intelligence had underestimated the size of Japanese forces, Luzon being the most recent and costly example. His confidence that American air and naval forces would prevent Japanese reinforcement of the invasion beaches once the operation was under way also seemed misplaced. Marshall had heard such categorical assertions before. Indeed, his own support for OLYMPIC at the June 18 White House meeting had been based on similar assurances that American air and naval superiority would prevent the reinforcement of Kyushu. That had not worked out well.

Marshall, of course, had firsthand experience with MacArthur's ability to conjure up numbers to suit his purposes. As recently as the June 18 White House meeting, Marshall had collaborated in one such venture when he had prodded MacArthur to lower his casualty estimates for OLYMPIC, which MacArthur had only been too happy to do. At that time, Marshall had taken advantage of MacArthur's desire to command the largest amphibious operation in history to shore up support for OLYMPIC because Marshall believed that the invasion of Kyushu was the surest way of forcing Japan's unconditional surrender in a timely fashion. The Japanese reinforcement that had turned the lightly defended island into a bastion protected by hundreds of thousands of servicemen and thousands of suicide weapons created serious doubts about the feasibility of that approach.

The Japanese buildup on Kyushu strengthened the Navy's inclination to find another route to victory and set the stage for a showdown over OLYMPIC. As we have noted, in April Admiral King had told his colleagues on the JCS that his support for OLYMPIC was conditional and he would want to review the plans sometime in August or September. In May, when the directive for OLYMPIC was being written, Admiral Nimitz had confided his doubts about the invasion to King. Those doubts only grew stronger over the next month. In late June, Nimitz and Spruance met with King in San Francisco to discuss the invasion of Japan. The tone was decidedly pessimistic. Nimitz doubted that the Army would be ready for OLYMPIC, and Spruance noted that General Bruce's Seventy-Seventh division "was in very poor shape" after fighting for a year on Guam, Leyte, and Okinawa and taking on 10,000 replacements. "Same for the divisions in Northern Luzon," he added. On the other hand, Spruance said, the Marine divisions were in good shape, and two Army divisions, the Eighty-First, on Leyte, and Ninety-Eighth, which had been on Hawaii since moving to the Pacific in April 1944, were deemed to be in good and excellent shape, respectively. Spruance questioned, however, whether newly arriving troops would have sufficient amphibious training for the invasion. Nimitz also thought there would not be enough support shipping for OLYMPIC, but Admiral Charles Cooke, the Navy's planner, said the real problem was that Luzon could not handle the supplies when they were landed. A little later, the notes of the meeting show, Spruance made the intriguing observation that plans for OLYMPIC were based on the estimate of Japanese troops on Kyushu. No elaboration followed. By itself, Spruance's observation does not seem noteworthy. In light of the developing situation on Kyushu, however, it seems far more provocative. Was Spruance making an oblique reference to the intelligence reports showing a buildup of Japanese forces on Kyushu? We cannot know for sure, but it seems likely that he was. Shortly after Spruance made his comment, Nimitz suggested that if OLYMPIC were postponed, the Navy should open a sea lane to China near Canton. Although most of the meeting was about OLYMPIC, the participants also raised serious doubts about MacArthur's plans for CORONET. In particular, Cooke stated firmly that MacArthur's plan for having an artificial harbor built for use off Tokyo was completely unworkable. There simply was not enough time, even if one could be built, which was something Cooke doubted.[37]

By late June King, Cooke, and the Pacific commanders viewed OLYMPIC as a disaster in the making. The Army was planning on invading Japan with divisions composed of battle-weary veterans and poorly trained replacements. The Army lacked the service troops and facilities on Luzon, one of the main staging areas, to land and distribute the necessary supplies to those divisions. Preparations for the invasion of Normandy from nearby England had taken two years. Now the Army was racing to launch an invasion of Japan from the Philippines, Okinawa, and Hawaii in a matter of months.

During July, the mounting evidence of Japanese reinforcement on Kyushu only confirmed the Navy's opposition to OLYMPIC. On August 9, two days after Marshall requested MacArthur's views on how the Japanese reinforcement of Kyushu affected American invasion plans, King sent a similar query to Nimitz. King appended to his message to Nimitz a copy of Marshall's cable to MacArthur and a copy of MacArthur's reply asserting that OLYMPIC should go forward. As Richard Frank has noted, King was preparing to break the fragile consensus on OLYMPIC and challenge the Army's plans for victory over Japan. Certainly, King knew that if Nimitz disapproved of OLYMPIC in May and June, the subsequent Japanese buildup on Kyushu would have only strengthened his opposition to the invasion. How Nimitz's reply would have affected the debate over OLYMPIC must, however, remain a matter of conjecture.[38]

As opposition to the Army's plan developed over the first days of August, the entire outlook for the Pacific war changed—dramatically. On August 6 (Washington time), the day on which the OWMR Advisory Board voted to have Snyder review "the size of the armed forces and the military procurement program," a B-29 dropped the first atomic bomb over Hiroshima. On August 8, the Soviet Union declared war on Japan. On August 9, at 1:00 a.m. local time, the Red Army struck at Japanese forces in Manchuria. Later that day, King asked Nimitz for his views on OLYMPIC. Before Nimitz received that message, a second atomic bomb exploded with devastating effect over Nagasaki.

Intercepts of Japanese diplomatic and military traffic once again enabled American officials to watch the drama unfolding within the highest echelon of the Japanese government. Although the Japanese had realized that Soviet belligerence was likely at some point, the sudden Soviet declaration of war and the overwhelming success of the Red Army's offensive in Manchuria left the Japanese stunned and demoralized. At the same time, the Japanese responded to the two atomic bombs with such fatalistic resignation that it left American observers uncertain about Tokyo's next step.[39]

Most of the United States was also in shock. The news of the bomb left most Americans stunned, poised between disbelief and hope. On August 7, the *Washington Post* spoke for many when it observed that "It is still impossible for most of us to believe that the grotesque dream world of the Sunday supplement editors, of the hacks who rattle out yarns for pulp magazines, of the artists who fill the so-called comic pages with fantasies of space ships, paralysis pistols and interplanetary wars . . . has at last become the world of actuality."[40] The same day, the *Washington Post* predicted that the bomb would "certainly shorten the war against Japan, if it does not end it."[41] The next day, August 8, Ernest Lindley ventured that because Japanese troops could protect themselves in underground shelters, "the bomb does not necessarily obviate an invasion of Japan."[42] The War Department took a similar view. Worried that the spectacular new weapon would prompt more insistent calls in Congress to speed up demobilization, Secretary Stimson was reported as saying that the Army had no immediate plans to cut its force of seven million men.[43] By August 9, following the destruction of Nagasaki, the *Washington Post* was less concerned about an invasion and more worried about the home front. The "successive dropping of atomic bombs until the Japanese surrender rules out the probability of an invasion and," the paper warned, "increases the possibility of a reconversion crisis."[44] The soldiers of the Eighty-Sixth Infantry Division adamantly agreed that the atomic bomb made an invasion of Japan unlikely. On August 7, the Eighty-Sixth, the first division scheduled for redeployment, left Camp Gruber, Oklahoma, for a camp outside San Francisco in preparation for being shipped overseas. By the time they arrived in California two days later, many of the soldiers were convinced that the war would be over soon. They protested to their congressmen and local newspapers the decision to send them out to the Pacific after they had served in Europe. Their complaints were unavailing. The War Department insisted that the unpredictable conditions in Japan made it imperative that MacArthur receive all the troops he needed to deal with any eventuality.[45]

Amid the uncertainty about Japan's willingness to continue the war, American officials needed to prepare for the very real possibility that the war would be over in a matter of days. OLYMPIC receded into the background as diplomats, military officers, and civilian mobilizers completely overturned the assumptions on which their planning was based. As we have noted, however, Truman had begun thinking about the possibility of an early surrender while he was at Potsdam. He had sought information from Marshall about how an early Japanese surrender would affect the Army's demobilization and procurement plans. Unaware of the atomic bomb, Vinson, Snyder, and the members of the OWMR Advisory Board had been preoccupied with the dangers to the economy posed by the continuation of Army manpower and procurement policies over a period of months. Now all that seemed like an age ago. Following the attack on Hiroshima, Snyder abruptly moved to address the problems inherent in an immediate conversion to a peacetime economy. On August 7, he met the president's ship as it docked at Norfolk, Virginia, and rode with him on the train back to Washington.[46] The next day, Truman and Snyder were joined by Chester Bowles, the head of Office of Price Administration, and War Production Board chair Julius Krug to resolve a dispute over reconversion. Fearing a sharp rise in prices, Truman sided with Snyder and Bowles and rejected Krug's advice to remove wartime controls on scarce materials. On August 9, Truman sent a carefully worded letter to Krug outlining his responsibilities as the government prepared for reconversion.[47] Truman's letter prompted additional speculation in the press about the increasingly likelihood of a Japanese surrender and the immediate onset of peace.

Meanwhile, the Japanese government moved haltingly toward surrender during a series of cabinet meetings and sessions of its Supreme War Council. Throughout this ordeal, Japanese military leaders, especially those in the Imperial Army, remained defiant. War Minister Anami Korechika insisted that Japan could not think of surrender unless the Allies agreed to four conditions: preservation of the imperial institution, no occupation of Japan's divine soil, the right of Japan to determine who might be subjected to war crimes trials, and the right of the armed forces to disarm themselves. During a meeting of the Supreme War Council that began late on August 9 and continued into the early morning of August 10, Anami declared that it would be better for the 100 million Japanese to die as one than to agree to a surrender that would allow the Allies to occupy Japan. The army chief of staff, Umezu Yoshijiro, agreed, adding that all the sacrifices of the war would have otherwise been for nothing.

Finally the emperor intervened. Japan would accept the terms of the Potsdam Declaration, providing that it did not "comprise any demands which prejudice His Majesty's prerogatives as a sovereign ruler."[48] In making his sacred decision, Hirohito had whittled the four conditions down to one, but his insistence on maintaining his prerogatives as emperor still fell short of an unconditional surrender.

On the morning of August 10, Truman met with Secretary Stimson, Admiral Leahy, Secretary Forrestal, and Secretary Byrnes to discuss the Japanese peace offer, which had not yet arrived through official channels. John Snyder was also present. It is worth noting that at this crucial juncture, Truman maintained civilian control of policy-making by calling together the civilian authorities responsible for military policy and diplomacy. Leahy, who served as the president's representative on the Joint Chiefs, would brief them and present their views to him. Records of what occurred during the meeting conflict. Byrnes complained to his assistant immediately after the meeting that when he arrived Leahy had already persuaded Truman to accept the Japanese offer. Byrnes opposed acceptance of the Japanese offer; that much is certain. But we have reason to doubt other aspects of Byrnes's account, especially his contention that Leahy had convinced the president to accept Japan's offer.[49] According to the diary of White House assistant Eben Ayers, Byrnes arrived before Leahy, making it impossible for the admiral to have swayed Truman before Byrnes arrived.[50] Truman's personal record for the day is of little help. His notes combine his meetings of August 9 and 10 under a single entry for August 10.[51] Moreover, these notes do not even mention the hastily called meeting, which according to his appointments book was held at 9:00 a.m.[52]

The various accounts do agree on some essential facts. Leahy and Stimson favored accepting Japan's offer. Byrnes was opposed. The secretary of state may have been worried about the public's response (he told his aide that acceptance would have led to the political "crucifixion" of the president), but he was later informed by the Japan experts in the State Department that there were also sound policy reasons for rejecting Japan's attempt to preserve the emperor's prerogatives, which were all-embracing.[53] Asked if maintaining the emperor's prerogatives meant "no changes in the state's governing system or no change in the position of his Imperial Majesty," a Japanese representative in Sweden replied that although he had no official instructions on that point, he thought that "the words include both interpretations."[54]

How much of this was understood by Truman and his advisers is difficult to determine. We do know that the president decided to have Byrnes draft a reply whereby the United States would ignore Tokyo's insistence on preserving the emperor's prerogatives as sovereign ruler. Instead it would place the emperor under the authority of a U.S. supreme commander, which implied a continuation of the imperial institution, at least temporarily.[55] The official American reply instructed the Japanese that "from the moment of surrender the authority of the Emperor and the Japanese government to rule the state shall be subject to the Supreme Commander of the Allied Powers who will take such steps as he deems proper to effectuate the surrender terms."[56]

Unfortunately, none of the accounts of the August 10 meeting at the White House provide a reliable account of Truman's thoughts about the Japanese offer. We do know, of course, that he ultimately rejected Leahy and Stimson's advice about accepting it. Apart from that, we do not know what, if anything, he contributed to the weighing of options. It is easy to imagine how anxious he would have been about making the right decision. He had steadfastly refused to make concessions on the emperor all summer. Yet now, if he yielded, the war would be over. No doubt Stimson remembered that at Potsdam he had advised the president that this moment might come.[57]

Military considerations appeared to tip the balance of the argument toward conceding the point to Japan. As Stimson explained, the Allies would need the cooperation of the emperor to ensure an orderly surrender of imperial forces throughout Asia.[58] The emperor could also ease the way for occupation forces entering the home islands. And still the president refused to grant the explicit assurances that the Japanese desired and that Leahy and Stimson, and before them Hoover and Grew (as well as various Republican senators), had recommended.

What was Truman thinking? Certainly he worried about the public's reaction if he appeased the Japanese at the eleventh hour. But that worry was joined by another. Simply put, Truman did not trust the Japanese. He remained wary of making any decision that could cost the United States the opportunity to achieve its postwar aims for Japan. Not long after he instructed Byrnes to draft a reply to the Japanese, Truman voiced his concerns about the impending surrender to Democratic congressman Mike Mansfield. Truman's notes say only that Mansfield, who had visited China at FDR's request in 1944, "came in to ask for a trip to China. He was once a resident there and seems to know a great deal about the country. I postponed decision on it."[59] Mansfield, however, told *Time* correspondent Frank McNaughton that he and Truman had covered considerably more ground than the president's notes indicate. Using notes he made immediately after speaking to Truman, Mansfield reported that Truman said that any Japanese surrender would have to "embrace unequivocally all Japanese forces in the field." Truman was especially worried about the potential for mayhem posed by the renegade Kwantung Army in Manchuria. Mansfield added:

> The suggestion of special guarantees to Hirohito, that his status be retained, was deeply distasteful to Truman. He favored no assurances—i.e. that to give the emperor any assurance would constitute something less than unconditional surrender, even if it is a face-saver for the Japs and a life-saving device offered us. It retains for Japan the nuclear rallying point for future nationalism. Truman was not friendly to this part of the Tokyo suggestion, but obviously

had to consult with Moscow, Chungking, and London. His idea was
to make it a complete surrender without any concessions to
Hirohito, come hell or high water.

According to McNaughton's record, Truman added that the United States
would keep the Pacific islands it needed for its security, "police the hell out
of Japan for many years, destroy its war potential, and insure the peace of
the Pacific."[60]

Truman's notes for August 10 also show that later that day he met with
Senator Warren Magnuson (D-Washington) to talk about "a road to Alaska
through British Columbia and his bill on scientific research." Magnuson told
Time's McNaughton that he and Truman had also discussed the surrender.
Magnuson found Truman "ill disposed to make special guarantees to the
emperor." According to Magnuson's account, as conveyed to McNaughton,
the president thought Hirohito was "a war criminal just as much as Hitler or
Mussolini, in many respects, and now was trying to weasel his nation out of
war, preserving meanwhile its essentially totalitarian structure." Truman realized, however, that the United States might need to retain the emperor in
place "without special concessions" to facilitate the surrender of imperial
troops. Magnuson inferred from Truman's comments that the United States
would make a counteroffer that would enable the emperor to remain "but
that the government would be made over to be essentially democratic,
using the emperor (in polite language) as a glorified figurehead."[61]

It is difficult to know how accurately Mansfield and Magnuson reported
Truman's comments and how much they were projecting their own views
onto the president. McNaughton's report does appear to be flawed in some
respects. He records Mansfield as meeting with Truman for nearly an
hour, an almost unimaginable span of the president's time, especially since
Mansfield was scheduled for only fifteen minutes in the appointments
book. On the other hand Mansfield's and Magnuson's accounts, as relayed
by McNaughton, present a consistent picture of Truman's attitudes toward
the emperor and the surrender. The most important point to emerge from
those meetings is that Truman did not accept the views of his conservative
advisers that Hirohito was a mere figurehead manipulated by Japan's

military clique. Truman judged Hirohito guilty of abetting Japan's aggression and feared that the imperial institution could serve as the focal point of Japanese nationalism in the future. Those concerns led Truman to reject Stimson and Leahy's advice that he accept Tokyo's offer on August 10. It stands to reason that he did not arrive at those views for the first time on August 10 and that they influenced his decision to reject earlier suggestions from Hoover and other conservatives to make concessions on the emperor. McNaughton's account also indicates that Truman thought in terms of a thorough occupation that would "police the hell out of Japan"—as he had put it—as it democratized Japanese society, a position that also differed from the limited occupation desired by Leahy, Stimson, Hoover, and various Republican senators. Referring to the Japanese, Truman wrote: "They wanted to make a condition precedent to the surrender. Our terms are 'unconditional.' They wanted to keep the Emperor. We told 'em we'd tell 'em how to keep him, but we'd make the terms."[62]

On the night of August 10–11, as Truman's message was transmitted to Tokyo, members of the State-War-Navy Coordinating Committee, composed of assistant secretaries from each department and the Joint Staff Planners and military staff officers from the Army, Navy, and AAF, huddled in adjoining rooms in the Pentagon to draft the documents that would spell out the steps to be taken by Japan in order to complete the surrender. The possibility of Japan's early surrender, which had been the subject of desultory contingency planning as recently as July, had become a matter of urgent necessity. It seemed that the farther one got from the Pentagon, the more willing people were to believe that the war was ending. In the Philippines, the members of MacArthur's staff considered it highly likely that Japan would surrender in a matter of weeks, if not days. On August 9, General Eichelberger, commander of the Eighth Army, described the scene to his wife. "You can imagine what is going through our heads," he wrote, "because most of us believe that Japan is going to quit soon and this is the first time we have really believed it." On August 11, after news of Japan's peace offer reached the Philippines, Eichelberger reported: "Most of the boys were awake here all night and I understand there was plenty of shooting excitement and I suppose quite a lot of free-for-all drinking."[63] On Okinawa the rejoicing took a tragic turn when six servicemen were killed and thirty wounded by celebratory bursts from antiaircraft guns that rained shrapnel down on unprotected revelers.[64]

On the home front, public speculation about the imminence of peace increased. Publicly, no one was willing to predict exactly when the war would end, but peace was on nearly everyone's mind. Wall Street responded to news of the Japanese peace offer by downgrading war-related offerings and buying up peace-related stocks.[65] The ODT, which had spent the last few weeks battling the War Department, shifted gears and announced that the prospects looked good for lifting travel bans in time for the 1945 World Series.[66] The *Washington Post* cautioned that the war was not yet over, but the paper's editors nonetheless depicted "peoples in the Allied countries waiting at the door to be ushered into a peaceful world."[67]

Shipyard workers in the Northwest vowed to stay on the job but also told reporters that they were already planning to move back to their homes in other parts of the country. War Manpower officials were urging the soon-to-be-displaced shipyard and aircraft company employees to sign up with the United States Employment Services so they could be placed in jobs that were expected to come open as the economy shifted to reconversion.[68]

A survey of major cities found most inhabitants in a state of "watchful waiting" about the possibility of Japan's surrender. In Pittsburgh a grandstand draped with bunting was erected in front of city hall. Philadelphia announced a schedule of events to commence once V-J Day was declared. Newsboys in normally staid Boston tried to drum up business by shouting "the war is over," but most workers were reported as going about their normal business. Widespread talk about layoffs and factory closings added to the mood of "tense expectation."[69]

It seems safe to say that most Americans believed that they were on the verge of peace, although they had seen too many surprises over the last four years to feel completely confident about what the Japanese would do. American military planners had even more reason to be skeptical about Tokyo's next step. Intercepts of diplomatic and military messages showed that Japanese military leaders deemed Truman's message a rejection of the emperor's proposal and argued for continuing the war. On August 12, the assistant chief of staff for Army intelligence warned that the Japanese government might drag out negotiations to weaken American resolve and predicted that any attempt by the government to surrender would be resisted by dissident elements in the Japanese military.[70] On August 13, Truman instructed Marshall to proceed with planned offensive operations against Japan, pending the Japanese government's response to American terms. That same day, Marshall had a deputy check with an officer attached to the Manhattan Project about the feasibility of using atomic weapons for tactical purposes. Speaking for Marshall, General John E. Hull wanted to know whether the bombs, as many as the nine that might be ready by November, could be used against Japanese forces and communications centers located close to the invasion beaches.[71] Fortunately for the Japanese and for the Americans who might have had to cross the beaches only twenty-four hours later, the discussion soon became moot.

On August 14, after a pause of three days, American B-29s resumed missions over Japan. Planes from the Far Eastern Air Force based on Okinawa and carrier-based aircraft from Halsey's Third Fleet also blasted targets in Japan. In one raid more than 600 planes attacked Kyushu.[72] As the aerial assault against Japan intensified, the emperor called an imperial conference consisting of cabinet members and senior advisers and instructed his subjects that he would accept the terms offered by the Allies. Later that day, U.S. officials received word through the Swiss government that the Japanese government agreed to surrender in keeping with terms of the Potsdam Declaration. The message stated further that the emperor would issue the necessary orders to all imperial forces to surrender and dispose of their arms as directed by the Supreme Commander of the Allied Forces. At a hastily called press conference that evening, a relieved and elated Truman announced: "I deem this reply a full acceptance of the Potsdam Declaration which specifies the unconditional surrender of Japan. In the reply there is no qualification."[73] After reading the Japanese message and stating that MacArthur would serve as the supreme commander to receive the surrender, Truman concluded the conference with an abrupt "That is all."

That was not quite all in Tokyo. As Army intelligence had predicted, dissidents in the Imperial Army tried to prevent the emperor from issuing the surrender decree. Officers stationed in Tokyo had been plotting a coup for several days, possibly with the support of several senior leaders in the army. On August 14, when they learned of the emperor's decision, the plotters decided to seize the imperial palace and destroy his recorded message announcing the surrender. A brief clash ensued, but by the morning of August 15 the plot had been thwarted, and the leaders, a handful of officers, realizing they had failed, committed suicide in front of the palace.[74]

Fighting continued against the Soviets in Manchuria and in the Kurile Islands until the end of August. Elsewhere, the Chinese Communist People's Liberation Army announced that it intended to disarm and accept the surrender of Japanese troops in northern China, thereby challenging the Nationalist government's authority as the sole representative of the Chinese people and setting the stage for civil war. Nationalists in Korea clashed with the Japanese occupiers, and in Hanoi the Vietnamese nationalist Ho Chi Minh proclaimed the creation of the Democratic People's Republic of Vietnam. The Pacific war had ended, but there would be no peace for Asia.

Conclusion

Despite his insistence that Japan had surrendered unconditionally, Truman had actually settled for something slightly less than that.[1] Moreover, in placing the emperor under the direction of the supreme commander of the Allied powers, MacArthur, Truman had agreed to administer the occupation indirectly through the existing Japanese government. This made it more difficult for the Americans to assure compliance with the supreme commander's edicts, though difficulties would have been much greater had Truman accepted the August 10 Japanese offer. In any case, the Japanese government wasted no time in attempting to impose its own understanding of the surrender on the Allies. On August 17, the Japanese government informed MacArthur that it would be best if "the number of points in Japanese territory to be designated by the Allies for occupation be limited to minimum number" and that "selection of the points be made in such a manner as to leave such a city as Tokyo unoccupied, and the forces to be stationed at each point be made as small as possible."[2] MacArthur ignored that request and followed through on the full-scale occupation called for in the recently completed contingency plans. Code-named BLACKLIST, the operation called for the use of twenty-two and two-thirds divisions, most of which came from the Philippines. However, as with OLYMPIC, several more—six in all—would be drawn from Okinawa, the Marianas, and Hawaii. MacArthur's planners anticipated a lag of as much as three weeks before all of the forces could reach their destination, but they assured Washington that they could obtain enough shipping to rush a sufficient number of troops forward to occupy the key strategic areas in Japan.[3]

At dawn on August 30, the Eleventh Airborne Division began arriving in force at the Atsugi air base outside Yokohama. Also at daybreak, the Navy began landing elements of the Fourth Marines at the Yokosuka naval base. According to one Marine officer, "our first wave was made up entirely of officers trying to get ashore before MacArthur." They succeeded. MacArthur arrived at Atsugi in the afternoon. Standing at the top of the mobile staircase that led to the tarmac, MacArthur, corncob pipe clenched in his teeth, paused in the doorway of the plane to survey the situation and allow photographers time to capture the historic moment. Despite the solemnity of the occasion, one of the 200 journalists present thought the atmosphere more suited to a "lawn party."[4] The official surrender took place on the deck of the USS *Missouri* on September 2, amid great pomp and ceremony, with General MacArthur presiding. On the same day, General Yamashita arrived in Baguio to surrender to representatives of the Thirty-Second Division. The formal surrender took place the next day. About 50,500 Japanese, of whom 40,000 came from the Asin valley, laid down their arms.[5] One imagines that the Americans were relieved not to have another Villa Verde Trail, and the Japanese were relieved to have preoccupied the Americans for six weeks.

The arrival of the Americans in Japan took place under far better circumstances than any had thought imaginable during the tumultuous first two weeks of August. Intelligence showing that the massive Japanese reinforcement of southern Kyushu had thrown American plans into disarray and led the Joint Chiefs seriously to question the feasibility of OLYMPIC. The dropping of the atom bombs and the Soviet entry into the war shortcircuited the looming debate over OLYMPIC and dramatically altered operational priorities. Planners shelved OLYMPIC and scrambled to prepare for an unexpectedly early and, they hoped, unopposed occupation of Japan.

The sudden collapse of the Japanese empire moved the ultimate fate of any operations into the realm of speculation. We know that the Japanese buildup on Kyushu had alarmed those with access to ULTRA in July and early August, but we cannot know with certainty whether OLYMPIC would have taken place as scheduled had the Japanese not surrendered. The mounting obstacles to invasion created by the chaotic implementation of demobilization and redeployment, the growing resistance to the Army's strategy by political leaders at home, and the demoralizing evidence of Japanese reinforcement on Kyushu compel a frank admission of uncertainty on this score.[6]

We do know that the Navy had been preparing to use the recently obtained intelligence about Kyushu to challenge the entire concept of the invasion. When Marshall learned that the Joint Chiefs were going to revisit the invasion plans at their next meeting, he was concerned enough about the outcome to request MacArthur's views on the subject. We also know that the Joint War Plans Committee produced several studies of alternative operations to take the place of OLYMPIC. These efforts had a pro forma quality about them. There was not much likelihood that the JCS would be able to change invasion sites on such short notice.[7] The real choice, however, was not Kyushu versus Honshu or Shikoku but rather—as naval officers, Admiral Leahy included, had frequently insisted—between invasion and blockade.

Naval advocates of a strategy of siege had important allies in the OWMR long before the Japanese Kyushu buildup. Beginning in May with Vinson's warning to the JCS about the mood of the American people and building throughout the summer with Vinson's and John Snyder's messages to Truman at Potsdam, the campaign to rein in the Army manpower and procurement programs was reaching a crescendo in early August with the OWMR Advisory Board's decision to confront the armed forces over the lagging pace of reconversion. Truman trusted both Vinson and Snyder and valued their council, but here, too, we can only speculate what the outcome of this showdown between the advocates of reconversion and the War

Department would have been had the war not ended abruptly. The Navy and OWMR had different reasons for opposing DOWNFALL. Their challenges to the invasion may have proceeded on different bureaucratic paths, but they were destined to intersect in the oval office.

In assessing the prospects for OLYMPIC, historians have failed to take into account the growing opposition to the Army's strategy that the advocates of reconversion were mounting. Nor have historians fully appreciated the degree to which the Army's leadership became the object of criticism and invective following V-E Day. The bitter fight over the national service bill set the tone for later complaints. The list grew longer over the summer. Critics accused the Army of seeking to regiment American society through the "work or fight" bill, for breaking its pledge not to use eighteen-year-olds in combat, for keeping men in uniform who were needed for critical civilian jobs on the home front, and for hoarding supplies, dominating the economy, and delaying reconversion. Congressional demands for reconversion abated with the summer recess but would resume when the legislators returned in October, a full month before OLYMPIC.

Behind the furor lay concern about the future at home. The Army could take comfort from the polls showing that the public still had confidence in the Army's conduct of the war. But other polls showed an aversion to taking more heavy casualties and a yearning for the pursuits of peace. In their opposition to the Army's policies, business groups, labor leaders, legislators, and the men and women charged with overseeing a smooth economic transition from war to peace gave explicit meaning and concrete form to the generalized war-weariness pervading society.

Marshall tried to remain above the fray, but he was stung by the criticisms of the Army and worried about the fracturing of unity at home. The campaign against Japan had assumed an important psychological dimension; the enemy had to be convinced of Americans' unwavering commitment to unconditional surrender. But as Japanese broadcasts revealed and ULTRA confirmed, the Japanese correctly read the public mood. Japanese strategy was counting on a slackening of American effort and a disposition to settle for something less than total victory. As Marshall had long feared, things were working against his strategy for the two-front war. He had hoped that partial demobilization would buy the Army more time to wage the final campaigns, but the Army's procedures for releasing high-point men had interfered with the redeployment of men from Europe, raised expectations at home, and drawn criticism from Congress.

The application of the Adjusted Service Rating process to forces in the Pacific further complicated matters by tying up shipping and stripping infantry units of their most experienced soldiers. The Army was losing "its first team," as Marshall admitted. As the Americans drew closer to Japan, combat became ever more demanding. Iwo Jima and Okinawa had proven this. Terrain and well-prepared fortifications, tunnels, and caves impeded reliance on artillery and offshore batteries and necessitated close engagement with the enemy, tight coordination of supporting units, and employment of new weapons, including flamethrowers and specially equipped tanks. As one historian has noted, "this was not the time for on-the-job training."[8]

Marshall also had to be worried about the condition of MacArthur's remaining troops, most of whom were scheduled for the invasion of Kyushu. MacArthur's public image as a general who avoided casualties notwithstanding, the Philippines campaigns had taken a terrible toll on the Sixth Army, with a very high percentage of units approaching combat ineffectiveness due to the loss of infantrymen to disease and exhaustion.[9] When hostilities ended on August 15, elements of the Sixth Infantry Division had been actively committed to combat for 219 straight days, a record for American units in the Pacific war. The division's infantry regiments had suffered a staggering casualty rate of 93 percent. The Sixth was still engaged with the remnants of Yamashita's Shobu force in northern Luzon when the war ended. Slated for CORONET, the Sixth would have had only several months to regroup and replace the dead and the wounded.

The divisions used in clearing the southern Philippines had ceased operations at the end of June, but they were to mount out for OLYMPIC in mid-September. First they would have to acquire replacements for dead and wounded, but also experienced soldiers who had achieved an Adjusted Rating Score of eighty-five points and would be headed home. The Forty-First Division had taken a devastatingly high percentage of casualties. The Forty-Third had been in combat for 175 days—nearly half a year—when it withdrew from mopping-up operations. Casualties from combat were not light, but disease felled far more of MacArthur's men than the Japanese. The rate of attrition due to disease exceeded levels in other areas of the Pacific and raised questions about troop discipline and morale.[10]

Most of the divisions scheduled for Kyushu would have had only a few months to rest and prepare before embarking for Japan. Compare that with the extended and meticulous preparations of American forces in England for the Normandy invasion. The Sixth Army units would lose a substantial portion of their troop leadership to discharge and would have to promote and work in new leadership. They were also receiving, and would be receiving and seeking to train through September, large numbers of replacements, mostly eighteen- and nineteen-year-olds with only fifteen weeks of basic training whose first battle experience would be one of the most frightening of all, an opposed landing. The Sixth Army would then battle on without significant numerical advantage—"not a recipe for victory," in the view of MacArthur's intelligence chief.

MacArthur was a problem in a category by himself. Marshall had tolerated his unauthorized operations in the southern Philippines mainly because they opened ports that could be used for OLYMPIC, thereby reducing reliance on Manila, which remained obstructed and limited in capacity. The costs were high, but when it came to dealing with MacArthur, the Joint Chiefs had grown accustomed to making a virtue of necessity. That is what they did when they accepted the divided command structure in the Pacific. The alternating operations of MacArthur and Nimitz unbalanced the enemy and kept before the public a picture of movement and advance across the Pacific. But as the two commanders converged on Japan, the relationship between them and their staffs became increasingly unworkable. MacArthur's criticism of the Okinawa campaign and Nimitz's reluctance to release control over resources after the campaign ended were harbingers of an approaching interservice squall that had the potential to disrupt the close coordination needed for OLYMPIC. Indeed, the Navy was ready to sail directly into that storm. On August 8, Secretary Forrestal wrote a letter to Truman asking the president to replace MacArthur with either Marshall or Eisenhower.[11] It appears that the letter was overtaken by events and not sent. Nevertheless, one does not need to speculate about what the outcome of Forrestal's challenge would have been to appreciate that the Navy had serious doubts about the existing command arrangements for OLYMPIC. Marshall, of course, had his own reservations about MacArthur. Were OLYMPIC to proceed on schedule, however, Marshall might have to defend the general that Truman disparaged as that "stuffed shirt," "play actor," "Mr. Prima Donna, Brass Hat, Five Star MacArthur."[12]

More troublesome still were the accumulating uncertainties plaguing the redeployment. Schedules for redeployment for CORONET permitted only the smallest margin of error, owing to the challenges created by distance and seasonal weather patterns. Partial demobilization further complicated an almost unbelievably complex situation by placing additional demands on transports. Army staff officers privately worried that demobilization was taking precedence over redeployment, but publicly they confidently assured Congress that redeployment was proceeding as planned. Then, immediately after the hearings, the Army announced that it was enlisting the help of commercial airlines to alleviate the backlog. Sailings from the West Coast also posed a problem. Marshall had intervened directly to approve the movement of converted Liberty ships to the West Coast, but even then, the Army's own timetables showed a backlog of troop shipments stretching into early 1946. As of mid-July, the promised eight weeks of training for redeployed troops remained an elusive goal. Units failed to catch up with new equipment sets, records were lost or unusable, and the composition of redeploying divisions changed frequently. Marshall would also have had to cope with the problems sure to arise in late September when construction equipment poorly packed in Marseilles arrived in the Philippines and was found unfit for use. How would that have affected the schedule for the construction of airfields on Kyushu after the landings? The Army's official histories offer no opinion on this question, but Marshall could not have avoided facing it.

We simply don't know what would have happened. During four long years of war, the Americans had demonstrated an impressive capacity for solving logistical problems and overcoming long odds. The gears might have all meshed perfectly and the invasions might have gone forward as planned. But that was a lot to hope for. Despite the efforts of the JCS to forge a strategy for timely and complete victory in a two-front war extending over most of the globe, the Army found itself preparing to fight the most demanding campaigns of the Pacific war with divisions replenished by green troops. Arrayed against the Army were a bitterly determined enemy, a restive public, and increasingly assertive political leaders. Under these circumstances it is not surprising that Truman and Marshall understood that the atomic bomb had been indispensable and that it alone had brought the kind of victory they sought.

NOTES

Introduction

1. Robert R. Palmer, Bell I. Wiley, and William Keast, *The Procurement and Training of Army Ground Troops* (Washington, DC: U.S. Government Printing Office, 1948), 639.
2. Charles F. Brower, *Defeating Japan: The Joint Chiefs of Staff and Strategy in the Pacific War, 1943–1945* (New York: Palgrave Macmillan, 2012), 40.
3. Peter J. Schrijvers, *The GI War against Japan: American Soldiers in Asia and the Pacific during World War II* (New York: New York University Press, 2002), 101.
4. Richard Frank, "An Overdue Pacific War Perspective," *Naval History Magazine* 24, no. 2 (April 2010), http://www.usni.org/magazines/navalhistory/2010-04/over-due-pacific-war-perspective.

Chapter 1

1. John Miller, Jr., "MacArthur and the Admiralties," chap. 11 in Kent Roberts Greenfield, ed., *Command Decisions* (Washington, DC: U.S. Government Printing Office, 1990); Samuel Eliot Morison, *Breaking the Bismarcks Barrier, 22 July 1942–May 1944* (*History of United States Naval Operations in World War II*, vol. 6) (Boston: Little, Brown, 1950), chap. 26.
2. James C. Fahey, *The Ships and Aircraft of the United States Fleet*, 2nd war ed. (New York: Ships and Aircraft, 1944), 5–6.

3. Clark G. Reynolds, *The Fast Carriers: The Forging of an Air Navy* (New York: McGraw Hill, 1968), chaps. 1–5.
4. Samuel Eliot Morison, *Aleutians, Gilberts, and Marshalls, June 1942–April 1944* (*History of United States Naval Operations in World War II*, vol. 7) (Boston: Little, Brown, 1951), 317.
5. Reynolds, *Fast Carriers*, 141.
6. Richard Overy, *Why the Allies Won* (New York: Norton, 1995), 192.
7. Hugh Rockoff, "The United States: From Plowshares to Swords," in Mark Harrison, ed., *The Economies of World War II: Six Great Powers in International Comparison* (New York: Cambridge University Press, 1998), 82.
8. Alan S. Milward, *War, Economy and Society, 1939–1945* (Berkeley: University of California Press, 1979), chaps. 3, 6–7; Overy, *Why the Allies Won*, chap. 7.
9. Overy, *Why the Allies Won*, 194. See Frederic C. Lane, *Ships for Victory: A History of Shipbuilding under the U.S. Maritime Commission in World War II* (Baltimore: Johns Hopkins University Press, 1951).
10. Mark Stoler, *Allies and Adversaries: The Joint Chiefs of Staff, The Grand Alliance, and U.S. Strategy in World War II* (Chapel Hill: University of North Carolina Press, 2000), 119; Maurice Matloff, *Strategic Planning for Coalition Warfare, 1943–1944*, United States Army in World War II, The War Department (Washington, DC: U.S. Government Printing Office, 1959), chaps. 15–17, 20.
11. Matloff, *Strategic Planning for Coalition Warfare, 1943–1944*, 317–320, 396–399, 520–521.
12. Ibid., 463.
13. On Marshall: Forrest C. Pogue, *George C. Marshall*, 4 vols. (New York: Viking, 1963–87); Larry Bland, ed., *George C. Marshall: Interviews and Reminiscences for Forrest C. Pogue* (Lexington, VA: George C. Marshall Research Foundation, 1991).
14. Bland, *George C. Marshall: Interviews*, 14, 67–68, 81.
15. Ibid., 33–34.
16. On the establishment of the Operations Division: Ray S. Cline, *Washington Command Post: The Operations Division*, United States Army in World War II: The War Department (Washington, DC: U.S. Government Printing Office, 1951; reprint, 2003), chaps. 4, 6–9, 14, 15; "odd assortment," 93.
17. On the replacement problem: Robert R. Palmer, "The Procurement of Enlisted Personnel: The Problem of Quality," xiii–86; Palmer and William R. Keast, "The Provision of Enlisted Replacements," 165–239, and Keast, "The Training of Enlisted Replacements," 365–428, in Palmer, Bell I. Wiley, and Keast, *The Procurement and Training of Ground Combat Troops* (Washington, DC: U.S. Government Printing Office, 1948); Roland G. Ruppenthal, *Logistic Support of the Armies* (Washington, DC: U.S. Government Printing Office, 1959), chap. 11.
18. Palmer et al., *Procurement and Training of Ground Combat Troops*, 206.
19. Ibid., 238.
20. Stoler, *Allies and Adversaries*, xi.
21. Charles F. Brower, *Defeating Japan: The Joint Chiefs of Staff and Strategy in the Pacific War, 1943–1945* (New York: Palgrave Macmillan, 2012).
22. Ibid., 8.

23. Ibid., 9–11; Michael Pearlman, *Warmaking and American Democracy: The Struggle over Military Strategy, 1700 to the Present* (Lawrence: University Press of Kansas, 1999), 241.

24. Brower, *Defeating Japan*, 9–10, 40.

25. Ibid., 24–28, 59; Russell F. Weigley, *The American Way of War: A History of United States Military Strategy and Policy* (Bloomington: Indiana University Press, 1973), 280.

26. Brower, *Defeating Japan*, 11, 33, 93, 103.

27. Ibid., 16–17, 27.

28. Ibid., 27.

29. Ibid., 27.

30. Waldo Heinrichs, *Threshold of War: Franklin D. Roosevelt and American Entry into World War II* (New York: Oxford University Press, 1988), 40.

31. *Time*, June 2, 1941.

32. Morison, *The Battle of the Atlantic: September 1939–May 1943* (*History of United States Naval Operations*, vol. 1) (Boston: Little, Brown, 1947), 51 n. 40, 114–116; Robert William Love, Jr., "Ernest Joseph King," in Love, ed., *The Chiefs of Naval Operations* (Annapolis: Naval Institute Press, 1980), especially 178–179.

33. Morison, *Battle of the Atlantic*, 116; Love, *Chiefs of Naval Operations*, 160–163.

34. Duncan S. Ballantine, *United States Naval Logistics in the Second World War* (Newport, RI: Naval War College Press, 1998), 275.

35. Matloff, *Strategic Planning for Coalition Warfare*, 136; John Ray Skates, *The Invasion of Japan: Alternative to the Bomb* (Columbia: University of South Carolina Press, 1994), 45.

36. Grace Person Hayes, *The History of the Joint Chiefs of Staff in World War II* (Annapolis: Naval Institute Press, 1982), 559–560.

37. E. B. Potter, *Nimitz* (Annapolis: Naval Institute Press, 1976), 268.

38. Biographical notebooks, p. 123, E. J. King folder, box 11, John H. Towers Papers, Library of Congress, Washington, DC.

39. Brower, *Defeating Japan*, 86.

40. George Baer, *One Hundred Years of Sea Power: The U.S. Navy, 1890–1990* (Stanford, CA: Stanford University Press, 1994), 214.

41. Potter, *Nimitz*, 272.

42. Robert Sherrod, *On to Westward* (New York: Duell, Stone, and Pearce, 1945), 227; Morison, *Rising Sun in the Pacific, 1931–April 1942* (*History of United States Naval Operations*, vol. 3) (Boston: Little, Brown, 1948), 256.

43. Samuel Eliot Morison, *Victory in the Pacific, 1945* (*History of United States Naval Operations*, vol. 14) (Boston: Little, Brown, 1960), 108–109.

44. Morison, *New Guinea and the Marianas, March 1944–August 1944* (*History of United States Naval Operations*, vol. 8) (Boston: Little, Brown, 1953), 172.

45. On amphibious forces: Jeter A. Isely and Philip A. Crowl, *The United States Marines and Amphibious War* (Princeton, NJ: Princeton University Press, 1951).

46. Ronald H. Spector, *Eagle against the Sun: The American War with Japan* (New York: Free Press, 1985), 484–485; Samuel Eliot Morison, *Coral Sea, Midway, and Submarine Actions, May 1942–August 1942* (*History of United States Naval*

Operations, vol. 4) (Boston: Little, Brown, 1949), 230–232; Morison, *New Guinea and the Marianas*, 15–16.

47. Spector, *Eagle against the Sun*, 482–483.

48. Ibid., 485; Morison, *New Guinea and the Marianas*, 26; Samuel Eliot Morison, *Leyte, June 1944–January 1945* (*History of United States Naval Operations*, vol. 12) (Boston: Little, Brown, 1958), 412.

49. H. P. Willmott, *The Great Crusade: A New History of the Second World War* (London: Michael Joseph, 1989), 333; Spector, *Eagle against the Sun*, 481, 485; Morison, *Coral Sea, Midway, and Submarine Activities*, 191, *Breaking the Bismarcks Barrier*, 68, *Leyte*, 398–399.

50. Spector, *Eagle against the Sun*, 483, 486, 487; Morison, *New Guinea and the Marianas*, 16, *Leyte*, 413.

51. Willmott, *Great Crusade*, 334–335.

52. Morison, *Leyte*, 414; Spector, *Eagle against the Sun*, 487.

53. On the Pacific Fleet Service Force: Morison, *Aleutians, Gilberts, and Marshalls*, chap. 6, *New Guinea and the Marianas*, chap. 18, *Victory in the Pacific*, chap. 10; Rear Admiral Worrall Read Carter, *Beans, Bullets, and Black Oil: The Story of Fleet Logistics Afloat in the Pacific during World War II* (Newport, RI: Naval War College Press, 1998); Ballantine, *Naval Logistics*, 113–156.

54. Ballantine, *Naval Logistics*, 177–180; Carter, *Beans, Bullets, and Black Oil*, 49, 90–109.

55. Ballantine, *Naval Logistics*, 153.

56. Carter, *Beans, Bullets, and Black Oil*, 46.

57. Morison, *New Guinea and the Marianas*, 345; Carter, *Beans, Bullets, and Black Oil*, 139–145.

58. On Towers: Clark G. Reynolds, *Admiral John H. Towers: The Struggle for Naval Air Supremacy* (Annapolis: Naval Institute Press, 1991).

59. Ballantine, *Naval Logistics*, 170.

60. Douglas MacArthur, *Reminiscences* (New York: McGraw-Hill, 1964), 3.

61. D. Clayton James, *The Years of MacArthur*, 2 vols. (Boston: Houghton Mifflin, 1970, 1975), I, 47.

62. Ibid., 238–239.

63. Carol Morris Petillo, *Douglas MacArthur: The Philippine Years* (Bloomington: Indiana University Press, 1981), 55.

64. James, *Years of MacArthur*, I, 555.

65. MacArthur, *Reminiscences*, 31; James, *Years of MacArthur*, I, 91–94.

66. As quoted in Michael Schaller, *Douglas MacArthur: The Far Eastern General* (New York: Oxford University Press, 1989), 32.

67. Waldo Heinrichs, "The Role of the U.S. Navy," in Dorothy Borg and Shumpei Okamoto, eds., *Pearl Harbor as History: Japanese-American Relations, 1931–1941* (New York: Columbia University Press, 1973), 202.

68. Petillo, *Douglas MacArthur*, 58.

69. James, *Years of MacArthur*, I, 501–509.

70. Ibid., II, 65 ("near done"), 95.

71. Quoted in ibid., II, 88.

72. Schaller, *Douglas MacArthur*, 74; James, *Years of MacArthur*, II, 86.

73. D. Clayton James Transcripts of Interviews, 1971, Brigadier General William L. Ritchie folder, box 4, RG 119, MacArthur Memorial Archives (hereafter MMA), Norfolk, Virginia; James, *Years of MacArthur*, II, 133–138.

74. James, *Years of MacArthur*, I, 368–371; General Thomas Handy transcript, vol. 2, 34–36, Senior Officer Oral History Program, box 1, Handy Papers, United States Army Heritage and Education Center (hereafter USAHEC), Carlisle, Pennsylvania.

75. Lewis B. Sebring, Jr., manuscript biography of MacArthur, 413, box 9, Hanson Baldwin Papers, George Marshall Research Library (MRL), Lexington, Virginia.

76. Brigadier General L. Diller folder, box 6, Oral History Transcripts, RG 32, MMA; James, *Years of MacArthur*, II, 136; Carl Mydans folder, box 7, Oral History Transcripts, RG 32, MMA.

77. George Kenney Interview, box 3, James Collection, RG 49, MMA; Geoffrey Perret, *Old Soldiers Never Die: The Life of Douglas MacArthur* (Holbrook, MA: Adams Media, 1996), 396.

78. Louis Morton Interview with MacArthur, folder 7, box 7, p. 5, Hanson Baldwin Papers, MRL.

79. Stephen R. Taaffe, *MacArthur's Jungle War: The 1944 New Guinea Campaign* (Lawrence: University Press of Kansas, 1998), 11, 83–84.

80. Marshall to MacArthur, 8 September 1944, folder 2, box 17, RG 4, MMA; Marshall to MacArthur, 29 April 1945, OPD Outgoing Secret Messages, box 56, RG 165, Record of the Army General and Special Staffs, National Archives, College Park, Maryland.

81. Marshall to Elmer Davis, 10 July 1944, folder 45, box 89, Marshall Selected Correspondence, MRL; Frederick S. Marquardt transcript, box 7, Oral History Transcripts, RG 32, MMA.

82. Thomas T. Handy transcript, vol. 2, 34, box 1, Senior Officer Oral History Program, Handy Papers, USAHEC.

83. Major General John E. Hull transcript, vol. 1, 32, vol. 2, 30, 34, box 1, Senior Officer Oral History Program, Hull Papers, USAHEC.

84. Marquardt transcript, box 7, Oral History Transcripts, RG 32, MMA.

85. Handy transcript, 38–41, 41A, vol. 2, box 1, Senior Officer Oral History Program, Handy Papers, USAHEC.

Chapter 2

1. Marshall to MacArthur, 15 April 1945, folder 2, box 75, Marshall Selected Correspondence, George Marshall Research Library (hereafter MRL), Lexington, Virginia.

2. On ULTRA and codebreaking in the Southwest Pacific: Edward J. Drea, *MacArthur's ULTRA and the War against Japan, 1942–1945* (Lawrence: University Press of Kansas, 1992).

3. Ibid., 91–93.

4. Geoffrey Perret, *Old Soldiers Never Die: The Life of Douglas MacArthur* (Holbrook, MA: Adams Media, 1996), 230–231, 367; Stephen R. Taaffe, *MacArthur's Jungle*

War: The 1944 New Guinea Campaign (Lawrence: University Press of Kansas, 1998).

5. Drea, *MacArthur's ULTRA*, 21.

6. Perret, *Old Soldiers Never Die*, 367–368.

7. Drea, *MacArthur's ULTRA*, 102–105.

8. On Kenney's background: Thomas E. Griffith, Jr., *MacArthur's Airman: General George C. Kenney and the War in the Southwest Pacific* (Lawrence: University Press of Kansas, 1998), chaps. 1–3.

9. On Kenney in the Southwest Pacific: Griffith, *MacArthur's Airman*, chaps. 4–8; Herman S. Wolk, "George C. Kenney, MacArthur's Premier Airman," and Donald M. Goldstein, "Ennis C. Whitehead, Aerial Tactician," in William M. Leary, ed., *We Shall Return! MacArthur's Commanders and the Defeat of Japan* (Lexington: University Press of Kentucky, 1988), 88–114, 178–207.

10. Griffith, *MacArthur's Airman*, 59–75.

11. Wolk, "Kenney," 94–95, 102; Wesley Frank Craven and James Lea Cate, eds., *Army Air Forces in World War II*, vol. 5, *From Matterhorn to Nagasaki, June 1944 to August 1945* (Chicago: University of Chicago Press, 1953), 337.

12. Wolk, "Kenney," 94–95, 102; Griffith, *MacArthur's Airman*, 98–99, 105–108.

13. Drea, *MacArthur's ULTRA*, 68–70; Griffith, *MacArthur's Airman*, 101–112.

14. Drea, *MacArthur's ULTRA*, 109–111.

15. Samuel Eliot Morison, *New Guinea and the Marianas, March 1944–August 1944* (*History of United States Naval Operations in World War II*, vol. 8) (Boston: Little, Brown, 1953), chap. 3.

16. On Kinkaid: Gerald E. Wheeler, "Thomas C. Kinkaid, MacArthur's Master of Naval Warfare," in Leary, *We Shall Return*, 115–128; Taaffe, *MacArthur's Jungle War*, 38, 228–229; Morison, *The Struggle for Guadalcanal, August 1942–February 1943* (*U.S. Naval Operations*, vol. 5) (London: Oxford University Press, 1949), 88 n. 13; D. Clayton James, *The Years of MacArthur*, 2 vols. (Boston: Houghton Mifflin, 1970, 1975), II, 276, 390, 562, 358.

17. Vice Admiral Daniel E. Barbey, *MacArthur's Amphibious Navy: Seventh Amphibious Force Operations, 1943–1945* (Annapolis: U.S. Naval Institute, 1969, 24; James, *Years of MacArthur*, II, 358.

18. Paolo E. Coletta, "Amphibious War Expert," in Leary, *We Shall Return*, 208–209.

19. Barbey, *MacArthur's Amphibious Navy*, ix, 43.

20. Robert W. Coakley and Richard M. Leighton, *Global Logistics and Strategy, 1943–1945*, United States Army in World War II, The War Department (Washington, DC: U.S. Government Printing Office, 1968), 490–494.

21. Barbey, *MacArthur's Amphibious Navy*, 46, 51; Coakley and Leighton, *Global Logistics and Strategy, 1943–1945*, 491.

22. Brigadier General William F. Heavey, *Down Ramp! The Story of the Army Amphibian Engineers* (Nashville: Battery Press, 1988), 122.

23. Barbey, *MacArthur's Amphibious Navy*, 19; Robert Ross Smith, *The Approach to the Philippines*, United States Army in World War II, The War in the Pacific (Washington, DC: U.S. Government Printing Office, 1953), 80; Morison, *New Guinea and the*

Marianas, app. 1, "Hollandia Task Organization," 403–406, and app. 4, "Naval Forces Engaged in the Capture of Guam," 418–420.

24. Coakley and Leighton, *Global Logistics and Strategy, 1943–1945*, 247.

25. Ibid., 252–270, 306–310, 342, 350–353, 490–499.

26. Barbey, *MacArthur's Amphibious Navy*, 62, 64, 109, 135.

27. General G. H. Decker to General Walter Krueger, 8 November 1947, folder 76, box 13, Walter Krueger Papers, U.S. Military Academy Library, West Point.

28. As quoted in Kevin C. Holzimmer, *General Walter Krueger, Unsung Hero of the Pacific War* (Lawrence: University Press of Kansas, 2007), 75–76; Leary, "Walter Krueger: MacArthur Fighting General!," in Leary, *We Shall Return*, 60–63.

29. Holzimmer, *General Walter Krueger*, 51.

30. Drea, *MacArthur's ULTRA*, 123–143.

31. Jay Luvaas, ed., *Dear Miss Em: General Eichelberger's War in the Pacific, 1942–1945* (Westport, CT: Greenwood Press, 1972), 149.

32. Holzimmer, *General Walter Krueger*, 91, 127–128; Leary, "Walter Krueger," 63, 64, 70.

33. Walter Krueger, "The Commander's Appreciation of Logistics," Army War College Lecture, 3 June 1945, box 25, Walter Krueger Papers, U.S. Military Academy Library.

34. As quoted in Taaffe, *MacArthur's Jungle War*, 91; Smith, *Approach to the Philippines*, 77–83; Morison, *New Guinea and the Marianas*, 74–85; Barbey, *MacArthur's Amphibious Navy*, 176.

35. Griffith, *MacArthur's Airman*, 166–169.

36. Drea, *MacArthur's ULTRA*, 131.

37. Smith, *Approach to the Philippines*, 244; on the Battle of Lone Tree Hill: 244–275; Taaffe, *MacArthur's Jungle War*, 130–143.

38. Fred Kielsigard to Hargis Westerfield, n.d., Westerfield Papers, 41st Division Papers, United States Army Heritage and Education Center (hereafter USAHEC), Carlisle, Pennsylvania.

39. Smith, *Approach to the Philippines*, 270.

40. Ibid., 274–275.

41. John Ellis, *The Sharp End: The Fighting Man in World War II* (New York: Scribner's, 1980), 53, 157–159.

42. On casualties: Smith, *Approach to the Philippines*, 392–393, especially n. 42; Mark Bernstein, *Hurricane at Biak: MacArthur against the Japanese, May–August 1944* (n.p.: Exlibris, 2000), 128–129; Drea, *MacArthur's ULTRA*, 137–138.

43. Smith, *Approach to the Philippines*, 392; Taaffe, *MacArthur's Jungle War*, 174.

44. Smith, *Approach to the Philippines*, 388 n. 35.

45. Ibid.; Manuel Kramer and Kenneth Baldwin, Veterans Survey Collections, 41st Division Papers, USAHEC (hereafter Veterans Surveys).

46. Drea, *MacArthur's ULTRA*, 137.

47. Bernstein, *Hurricane at Biak*, 42.

48. Smith, *Approach to the Philippines*, 300 n. 38; Bernstein, *Hurricane at Biak*, 39–42, 113; Drea, *MacArthur's ULTRA*, 131, 134–137; Holzimmer, *General Walter Krueger*, 151.

49. Maps and photos in Smith, *Approach to the Philippines*, 281–314.

50. Ibid., 319; William F. McCartney, *The Jungleers: A History of the 41st Infantry Division* (Washington, DC: Infantry Journal Press, 1948), 110.

51. Bernstein, *Hurricane at Biak*, 105–106.

52. Smith, *Approach to the Philippines*, 336–337, 344.

53. Fred Kielsigard to Hargis Westerfield, letter 1, 1971, and Westerfield, "Highlights of Our Division's History," Westerfield Papers, Veterans Surveys, 41st Division Papers, USAHEC.

54. McCartney, *Jungleers*, 16.

55. Drea, *MacArthur's ULTRA*, 137; Morison, *New Guinea and the Marianas*, 124–125, n. 9.

56. Smith, *Approach to the Philippines*, 322.

57. Ibid., 341–345; Taaffe, *MacArthur's Jungle War*; Holzimmer, *General Walter Krueger*, 166–167; Bernstein, *Hurricane at Biak*, 121–124.

58. Smith, *Approach to the Philippines*, chap. 16.

59. On Japan's naval threat to Biak: Morison, *New Guinea and the Marianas*, chap. 9; Drea, *MacArthur's ULTRA*, 135–141; Bernstein, *Hurricane at Biak*, chap. 5.

60. McCartney, *Jungleers*, 111, 119.

61. Drea, *MacArthur's ULTRA*, 141.

62. On Adachi: Edward J. Drea, "Adachi Hatazo: A Soldier of His Emperor," in *In the Service of the Emperor* (Lincoln: University of Nebraska Press, 1998), 105–108.

63. As quoted in Drea, *MacArthur's ULTRA*, 148–149; James, *Years of MacArthur*, 522–525.

64. Smith, *Approach to the Philippines*, 132–133; on the April 22–July 10 period: chaps. 5, 6; Taaffe, *MacArthur's Jungle War*, 188–200; Holzimmer, *General Walter Krueger*, 169–176.

65. Smith, *Approach to the Philippines*, 138 n. 28.

66. Ibid., 138, 168, 174.

67. Drea, *MacArthur's ULTRA*, 146–147.

68. Ibid., 147–150.

69. On the period July 10–August 9: Smith, *Approach to the Philippines*, chaps. 7, 8; Taaffe, *MacArthur's Jungle War*, 200–209; Drea, *MacArthur's ULTRA*, 150–151.

70. Paul Tillery memoir, 19–20, 31st Division Papers, USAHEC.

71. Smith, *Approach to the Philippines*, 167–205; Taaffe, *MacArthur's Jungle War*, 203–209.

72. Smith, *Approach to the Philippines*, 204–205.

73. Headquarters, 6th Army, Report on Casualties, July 2, 1945, box 7, folder 42, Walter Krueger Papers, U.S. Military Academy Library.

74. Smith, *Approach to the Philippines*, 184.

75. 6th Army Report on Casualties, July 2, 1945, Walter Krueger Papers, U.S. Military Academy Library; Drea, "Adachi Hatazo," 108–109.

76. Eric Bergerud, *Touched with Fire: The Land War in the South Pacific* (New York: Viking, 1996), 404.

77. On racism and the nature of battle see ibid., 403–425; Gerald F. Linderman, *The World within War: America's Combat Experience in World War II* (Cambridge, MA:

Harvard University Press, 1997), chap. 4, "Fighting the Japanese"; John Dower, *War without Mercy: Race and Power in the Pacific War* (New York: Pantheon, 1986).

78. Linderman, *World within War*, 143.
79. Fujiwara Akira, "The Role of the Japanese Army," in Dorothy Borg and Shumpei Okamoto, eds., *Pearl Harbor as History: Japanese-American Relations, 1931–1941* (New York: Columbia University Press, 1973), 192.
80. Drea, "Trained in the Hardest School," chap. 6 in *In the Service of the Emperor*, 77–90.
81. As quoted in John Costello, *The Pacific War* (New York: Quill, 1982), 216.
82. Smith, *Approach to the Philippines*, 199.
83. Charles N. Cripps, John L. Drugan, Richard T. Fedderson, and Fred Kielsigard, Veterans Surveys, 41st Division Papers, USAHEC; McCartney, *Jungleers*, 77.
84. William T. McLaughlin, "Recon Scout" (memoir), Americal Division Papers, box 5, USAHEC.
85. Earl Poynter and Herschel N. McFadden, Veterans Surveys, Americal Division Papers, USAHEC.
86. John H. Wood to William T. McLaughlin, 15 August 1974, Wood-McLaughlin Correspondence, box 1, Americal Division Papers, USAHEC.
87. Sidney Riches, Veterans Surveys, 40th Division Papers, USAHEC.
88. William T. McLaughlin, Veterans Surveys, Americal Division Papers, USAHEC.
89. McLaughlin, "Recon Scout" (memoir), box 5, Americal Division Papers, USAHEC.
90. Fernando Vera memoir, box 4, Americal Division Papers, USAHEC.
91. Veterans Surveys, USAHEC: Americal Division: Richard C. Lovell, George T. Kuczko, Herschel N. McFadden, David J. Rossi; 24th Division: Melvin Bulrika, Charles Card, Floyd Adams, Carl F. Brandt, Eric Diller, Ernest John Demario, Melvin Benham; 25th Division: Bryan O. Baldwin, William F. Barber, Melville C. McKenney; 31st Division: James M. Nix; 32nd Division: Edward R. Guhl, Roland Acheson, Erwin A. Pichotte, Yoshikazi Higashi, James W. DeLoach, Donald R. Dill, Newman W. Phillips, Edward S. Farmer; 41st Division: William LeGro, John M. Kelly; 43rd Division: Jay Gruenfeld; 77th Division: Gerard C. Brueders, Arthur L. Watt, Henry D. Lopez, Richard Forse, Daniel Chomin; 1st Cavalry Division: Carl Baker, Salvatore V. De Gaetano.
92. Fred Kielsigard to Bradford Westerfield, n.d., 1971, 41st Division Papers, USAHEC.
93. Linderman, *World within War*, 349–350.
94. Quotations from Alvin P. Stauffer, *The Quartermaster Corps: Operations in the War against Japan*, United States Army in World War II: The Technical Services (Washington, DC: Department of the Army, 1956), 199.
95. John P. Briand, Veterans Surveys, 31st Division, USAHEC.
96. Erna Risch, *The Quartermaster Corps: Organization, Supply, and Services*, United States Army in World War II: The Technical Services (Washington, DC: Department of the Army, 1953), I, 182–184.
97. Stauffer, *Quartermaster Corps*, 72–73, 193–200.
98. Ibid., 96–97, 144, 160–193.

99. Ibid., 234.

100. Roland Acheson, Veteran's Survey, 32nd Division Papers, USAHEC.

101. James J. Smith, Veterans Surveys, 31st Division, and Paul M. Gerrish, Veterans Surveys, 40th Division, USAHEC; Stauffer, *Quartermaster Corps*, 206.

102. Edwin E. Hanson, Veterans Survey, 37th Division Papers, USAHEC.

103. McCartney, *Jungleers*, 45; Stauffer, *Quartermaster Corps*, 206–208.

104. Bergerud, *Touched with Fire*, 101; Peter Schrijvers, *The G.I. War against Japan: American Soldiers in Asia and the Pacific in World War II* (New York: New York University Press, 2002), 121, 129; John Wood to William McLaughlin, 9 August 1974, Wood-McLaughlin Correspondence, folder 1944–1945, 1969–1976, box 1, Americal Division Papers, USAHEC.

105. Schrijvers, *G.I. War*, 118.

106. Bergerud, *Touched with Fire*, 94.

107. "Data on Malaria Incidence in U.S. Army Forces in S.W.P.A.," 1 June 1944, folder 1, War Dept., box 17, 2 April–6 August 1944, RG 4, MacArthur Memorial Archives, Norfolk, Virginia (hereafter MMA); Medical Department, United States Army, *Malaria*, Preventive Medicine in World War II, vol. 6, table 79, 579.

108. Bergerud, *Touched with Fire*, 94–97.

109. Schrijvers, *G.I. War*, 131; Colonel John Boyd Coates, Jr., ed., Medical Department, United States Army, *Infectious Diseases*, Internal Medicine in World War II, vol. 2 (Washington, DC: U.S. Government Printing Office, 1963), 60, table 3.

110. Medical Department, United States Army, *Communicable Diseases Transmitted through Respiratory and Alimentary Tracts*, Preventive Medicine in World War II, vol. 4 (Washington, DC: U.S. Government Printing Office, 1958), tables 59–61, 342–344, 400–401.

111. Ibid., 322, table 54.

112. Bergerud, *Touched with Fire*, 98–100.

113. Colonel John Boyd Coates, Jr., ed., Medical Department, United States Army, *Communicable Diseases Transmitted through Contact or by Unknown Means*, Preventive Medicine in World War II, vol. 5 (Washington, DC: U.S. Government Printing Office, 1960), 456–459.

114. Schrijvers, *G.I. War*, 133.

115. Bernstein, *Hurricane at Biak*, 128.

116. Medical Department, United States Army, *Neuropsychiatry in World War II* (Washington, DC: U.S. Government Printing Office, 1973), II, 1020, table 96.

117. Bergerud, *Touched with Fire*, 447.

118. As quoted in Linderman, *World within War*, 355.

119. Lieutenant Colonel M. Ralph Kaufman, as quoted in Lt. Colonel Robert Bernucci and Colonel Alert Glass, eds., Medical Department, United States Army, *Neuropsychiatry in World War II*, vol. 2, *Overseas Theaters* (Washington, DC: U.S. Government Printing Office, 1973), 659, 667.

120. Ibid., 525–558.

121. Sherrod, *On to Westward*, 117.

122. Perret, *Old Soldiers Never Die*, 396.

123. "Spoon-fed": Lewis B. Sebring, Jr., manuscript biography of MacArthur, 411, box 9, Hanson Baldwin Papers, MRL.
124. James, *Years of MacArthur*, 136–139, 490; Russell D. Buhite, *Douglas MacArthur: Statecraft and Stagecraft in America's East Asian Policy* (Lanham, MD: Rowman & Littlefield, 2008), 52–53, 56–57.
125. Infantrymen's opinions and experiences are drawn from the Veterans Surveys, especially the Americal, 31st, 32nd, 41st, and 43rd Divisions, USAHEC.
126. Williamson Murray and Allan R. Millet, *A War to Be Won: Fighting the Second World War* (Cambridge, MA: Harvard University Press, 2000), 207–209.
127. Smith, *Approach to the Philippines*, chaps. 17, 18.
128. Wesley Frank Craven and James Lea Cate, eds., *Army Air Forces in World War II*, vol. 5, *From Matterhorn to Nagasaki, June 1944 to August 1945* (Chicago: University of Chicago Press, 1953), 288–293.
129. MacArthur quoted in Russell F. Weigley, *The American Way of War: A History of United States Military Strategy and Policy* (Bloomington: Indiana University Press, 1973), 305.

Chapter 3

1. Sadao Asada, *From Mahan to Pearl Harbor: The Imperial Japanese Navy and the United States* (Annapolis: Naval Institute Press, 2006), chaps. 1, 2.
2. Grace Person Hayes, *The History of the Joint Chiefs of Staff in World War II* (Annapolis: Naval Institute Press, 1982), 496, 596; Wesley Frank Craven and James Lea Cate, eds., *Army Air Forces in World War II*, vol. 5, *From Matterhorn to Nagasaki, June 1944 to August 1945* (Chicago: University of Chicago Press, 1953), 118, 140.
3. Philip A. Crowl, *Campaign in the Marianas*, United States Army in World War II, The War in the Pacific (Washington, DC: U.S. Government Printing Office, 1960), 24–30.
4. Samuel Eliot Morison, *New Guinea and the Marianas, March 1944–August 1944* (*History of United States Naval Operations in World War II*, vol. 8) (Boston: Little, Brown, 1953), 195.
5. Crowl, *Campaign in the Marianas*, 85; Morison, *New Guinea and the Marianas*, 196–197.
6. Crowl, *Campaign in the Marianas*, 51–65.
7. D. Colt Denfeld, *Hold the Marianas: The Japanese Defense of the Mariana Islands* (Shippensburg, PA: White Mane, 1997), chap. 2.
8. Morison, *New Guinea and the Marianas*, 407–410.
9. On D-Day at Saipan: ibid., chap. 13; Crowl, *Campaign in the Marianas*, chap. 5; Harold J. Goldberg, *D-Day in the Pacific: The Battle of Saipan* (Bloomington: Indiana University Press, 2007), chaps. 5–6, 8–10.
10. Morison, *New Guinea and the Marianas*, 200.
11. Sergeant Jim Evans quoted in Goldberg, *D-Day in the Pacific*, 68.
12. On the counterattacks: Crowl, *Campaign in the Marianas*, 95–98; Goldberg, *D-Day in the Pacific*, 72–73, 86–87, 104–105.

13. Goldberg, *D-Day in the Pacific*, 83, 89; Crowl, *Campaign in the Marianas*, 93, 126–128.

14. Thomas B. Buell, *The Quiet Warrior: A Biography of Admiral Raymond A. Spruance* (Annapolis: Naval Institute Press, 1987), 284–285.

15. Ibid., 285.

16. Morison, *Coral Sea, Midway, and Submarine Actions*, 158.

17. Reynolds, *Fast Carriers*, 206.

18. Crowl, *Campaign in the Marianas*, 98–99; Morison, *New Guinea and the Marianas*, 241–244.

19. Morison, *New Guinea and the Marianas*, chart, 259.

20. Ibid., 250.

21. William T. Y'Blood, *Red Sun Setting: The Battle of the Philippine Sea* (Annapolis: Naval Institute Press, 1981; reprint, 2003), 81–93.

22. Morison, *New Guinea and the Marianas*, 254.

23. As quoted, ibid., 213.

24. Y'Blood, *Red Sun Setting*, 213.

25. Morison, *New Guinea and the Marianas*, 261–262; Reynolds, *Fast Carriers*, 54–55.

26. James C. Fahey, *The Ships and Aircraft of the U.S. Fleet: Second War Edition* (New York: Ships and Aircraft, 1944), 42; victory ed. (1945), 47; Reynolds, *Fast Carriers*, 57, 87.

27. H. W. Willmott, *The Battle of Leyte Gulf* (Bloomington: Indiana University Press, 2005), 44.

28. Reynolds, *Fast Carriers*, 157–160; Morison, *New Guinea and the Marianas*, 235; Y'Blood, *Red Sun Setting*, 18.

29. Buell, *Quiet Warrior*, 290–291.

30. On the battle of June 19 I am particularly indebted to Y'Blood, *Red Sun Setting*, chap. 5.

31. Morison, *New Guinea and the Marianas*, 257.

32. On the battle of June 19 I am particularly indebted to Y'Blood, *Red Sun Setting*, chap. 5.

33. Morison, *New Guinea and the Marianas*, 267.

34. Y'Blood, *Red Sun Setting*, 117.

35. Ibid., 103.

36. Morison, *New Guinea and the Marianas*, 269; Fahey, *Ships and Aircraft of the U.S. Fleet*, victory ed., 4–5.

37. Y'Blood, *Red Sun Setting*, 121.

38. Morison, *New Guinea and the Marianas*, 273.

39. Ibid., 276–277.

40. Ibid., 278–282.

41. Ibid., 284.

42. Ibid., chart after 288.

43. Quoted in Y'Blood, *Red Sun Setting*, 145.

44. On the battle of June 20: ibid., chap. 6.

45. Ibid., 153.

46. Ibid., 171.

47. Ibid., 161, 174.

48. Ibid., 193.

49. Ibid., 138.
50. Ibid., 176, 213.
51. Ibid., app. 2, 222–224.
52. On the Central Saipan campaign: Crowl, *Campaign in the Marianas*, chaps. 9–11; Goldberg, *D-Day in the Pacific*, chaps. 8–12.
53. Crowl, quoting the USMC official history of the campaign and an after-action report. Crowl, *Campaign in the Marianas*, 168, 187.
54. Goldberg, *D-Day in the Pacific*, 119–120, 123, 125.
55. Morison, *Aleutians, Gilberts, and Marshalls*, 132–134, 297–300, n.12.
56. Goldberg, *D-Day in the Pacific*, 141; Ronald H. Spector, *Eagle against the Sun: The American War with Japan* (New York: Free Press, 1985); Charles S. Kuane, "The National Guard in War: An Historical Analysis of the 27th Infantry Division (New York National Guard) in World War II," M.A. thesis (U.S. Army Command and General Staff College, Ft. Leavenworth, Kansas, 1990), 160–165.
57. Report of Military Secretary, Visit of Commander-in-Chief to Ormoc Area, 21 December 1944, box 9, Andrew D. Bruce Papers, United States Army Heritage and Education Center (hereafter USAHEC), Carlisle, Pennsylvania.
58. Crowl, *Campaign in the Marianas*, chap. 8; Goldberg, *D-Day in the Pacific*, 148.
59. Crowl, *Campaign in the Marianas*, 170–180.
60. Ibid., 200.
61. Ibid., 191.
62. Ibid., 195.
63. Holland M. Smith and Percy Finch, *Coral and Brass* (New York: Scribner's, 1949), 168–180; Crowl, *Campaign in the Marianas*, chap. 10.
64. On the Death Valley battle: Crowl, *Campaign in the Marianas*, 181–190, chap. 11.
65. Ibid., 207.
66. Ibid., 215–216.
67. Ibid., 222.
68. Ibid., 219.
69. Ibid., 222.
70. Ibid., 228.
71. Ibid., 232, quotation in ibid., 230.
72. Crowl, *Campaign in the Marianas*, 256. On the Japanese suicide attack of July 7: Goldberg, *D-Day in the Pacific*, chap. 13; Denfeld, *Hold the Marianas*, 86, 92; Smith, *Coral and Brass*, 193–198.
73. As quoted in Goldberg, *D-Day in the Pacific*, 177.
74. As quoted in ibid., 178.
75. Ibid., 182.
76. Ibid. 182, 191; Crowl, *Campaign in the Marianas*, 261.
77. Crowl, *Campaign in the Marianas*, 261.
78. Ibid., 265.
79. As quoted in ibid., 269.
80. Ibid., 307–308.
81. Ibid., 320–325.
82. Ibid., 344–345.

83. Ibid., 437.

84. "Men Who Were There" [77th Division Association], *Ours to Hold It High: The History of the 77th Division in World War II* (Washington, DC: Infantry Journal Press, 1947), 31, chaps. 3–4.

85. Crowl, *Campaign in the Marianas*, 342–343, 356–357.

86. Ibid., 364–365.

87. Ibid., 345–347; 77th Division Association, *Ours to Hold It High*, 63–65, 68–70.

88. Crowl, *Campaign in the Marianas*, 316.

89. Crowl, *Campaign in the Marianas*, chaps. 19, 20; 77th Division Association, *Ours to Hold It High*, chaps. 6–11.

90. On the Barrigada battle: 77th Division Association, *Ours to Hold It High*, chap. 9; Crowl, *Campaign in the Marianas*, 388–396.

91. 77th Division Association, *Ours to Hold It High*, 100.

92. As quoted in Crowl, *Campaign in the Marianas*, 378, n.7, 386–389.

93. Ibid., 400–403.

94. Ibid., 411–415; 77th Division Association, *Ours to Hold It High*, 108–112.

95. 77th Division Association, *Ours to Hold It High*, 118–119.

96. Ibid., 105.

97. Denfeld, *Hold the Marianas*, 203–206.

98. Crowl, *Campaign in the Marianas*, 446.

99. Edward J. Drea, *Japan's Imperial Army: Its Rise and Fall, 1853–1945* (Lawrence: University Press of Kansas, 2009), 240–242.

100. Williamson Murray and Allan R. Millet, *A War to Be Won: Fighting the Second World War* (Cambridge, MA: Harvard University Press, 2000), 360.

Chapter 4

1. Roland G. Ruppenthal, *Logistical Support of the Armies*, United States Army in World War II, The European Theater of Operations, 2 vols. (Washington, DC: U.S. Government Printing Office, 1959), II, table 7, 282–283; *New York Times*, 6 August 1944.

2. "Americans Speeding across Brittany; Big Gains Made in Day; Nazi Rout; Churchill Sees an Early Victory," 3 August 1944, 1; "Brittany Overrun: Columns 75 Miles from Brest and 38 Miles from St. Lo," 5 August 1944, 1; "American Tank Column Smashes into Brest; Other Forces Reach Loire," 6 August 1944, 1; "Four U.S. Columns Are Driving toward Paris; Allies Turn Whole German Line below Caen," 7 August 1944, 1; "The Battle in France," 10 August 1944, 16; "Germans Flee Allies' Pincers," 10 August 1944, 3; "Climax in France Declared at Hand," 13 August 1944, 7; "Falaise Gap Is Cut," 16 August 1944, 1; "Patton the Third Army's Chief; Senators Confirm His Promotion...," 16 August 1944, 1; "Norman Trap Lines 1,000 Miles of Ruin," 16 August 1944, 8; all in *New York Times*; Martin Blumenson, *Breakout and Pursuit*, United States Army in World War II, The European Theater of Operations (Washington, DC: U.S. Government Printing Office, 1984), chaps. 13–17.

3. "Dash and daring" quote in "At the Gates of Paris," 18 August 1944, 12. See also "Foe Races to River," 19 August 1944, 1; "The Great Opportunity," 21 August 1944, 14;

"Montgomery Asks for Quick Victory," 22 August 1944, 1; "Drive for Germany: 3d Army Thrusts Past Sens and the Yonne," 23 August 1944, 1; "German 7th Army Slashed to Bits," 17 August 1944, 5; all in *New York Times*; Blumenson, *Breakout and Pursuit*, chaps. 22–28; *New York Times*, 17–25 August 1944.

4. Blumenson, *Breakout and Pursuit*, chap. 31.

5. "Free Paris Marks the End of Nazi Night in Europe," 27 August 1944, E5; "The News of the Week in Review: Week of Victories," 27 August 1944, E1; "'New Order' Crumbling," 28 August 1944, 6; "Allies in the Clear," 31 August 1944, 1; "Race to Reich On," 4 September 1944, 1; all in *New York Times*.

6. H. G. Nicholas, ed., *Washington Despatches: Weekly Reports from the British Embassy* (Chicago: University of Chicago Press, 1981), 419.

7. "At the Marne Again," *New York Times*, 29 August 1944, 16.

8. Blumenson, *Breakout and Pursuit*, 691.

9. Ibid., chap. 37; Horst Boog, Gerhard Krebs, and Detleff Vogel, *The Strategic Air War in Europe, and the War in the West and East Asia, 1943–1944/5*, trans. Derry Cook-Radmore et al., vol. 7 of *Germany and the Second World War*, ed. Research Institute of Military History, Potsdam, Germany (Oxford: Clarendon Press, 2006), 599–635.

10. Nicholas, *Washington Despatches*, 426.

11. J. Carlyle Sitterson, *Development of the Reconversion Policies of the War Production Board, April 1943–January 1945*, Historical Reports on War Administration: War Production Board, Special Study No. 15 (Washington, DC: U.S. Government Printing Office; reissue, 22 March 1946), 44, 126.

12. On the Nelson reconversion plan: Sitterson, *Development of the Reconversion Policies of the War Production Board*, 21–24, 90–97, 126; Gregory Hooks, *Forging the Military-Industrial Complex: World War II's Battle of the Potomac* (Urbana: University of Illinois Press, 1991), 116, 119; Harold Stein, "The Reconversion Controversy," in Stein, *Public Administration and Policy Development: A Case Book* (New York: Harcourt Brace, 1952), 223–248.

13. Harold G. Vatter, *The United States Economy in World War II* (New York: Columbia University Press, 1985), 62–63; Stein, "Reconversion Controversy," 239–240.

14. Stein, "Reconversion Controversy," 241.

15. Vatter, *United States Economy in World War II*, 42, 62, 72; Bruce Catton, *The War Lords of Washington* (New York: Harcourt Brace, 1948), 213–217; Jean Edward Smith, *Lucius Clay: An American Life* (New York: Holt, 1990), 110–111, 143, 146, 159, 166, 169, 194.

16. Stein, "Reconversion Controversy," 226.

17. Ibid., 267.

18. Alan Clive, *State of War: Michigan in World War II* (Ann Arbor: University of Michigan Press, 1979), 75.

19. As quoted in Catton, *War Lords*, 214.

20. As quoted in Stein, "Reconversion Controversy," 252.

21. As quoted in ibid., 268–269.

22. As quoted in ibid., 243.

23. Ibid., 254.

24. Byron Fairchild and Jonathan Grossman, *The Army and Industrial Manpower*, United States Army in World War II, The War Department (Washington, DC: U.S. Government Printing Office, 1959), 259.

25. As quoted in Sitterson, *Development of the Reconversion Policies*, 43.

26. As quoted in ibid., 269.

27. Catton, *War Lords*, 270.

28. Clive, *State of War*, 66.

29. Hiland G. Batcheller, *Critical Programs: A Report to the War Production Board, November 14, 1944*, copy in box 233, Harry Hopkins Papers, Franklin D. Roosevelt Library, Hyde Park, New York; Stein, "Reconversion Controversy," 264.

30. Ruppenthal, *Logistical Support of the Armies*, I, 537–539.

31. Robert W. Coakley and Richard M. Leighton, *Global Logistics and Strategy, 1943–1945*, United States Army in World War II, The War Department (Washington, DC: U.S. Government Printing Office, 1968), 548–550; *War Production: A Report to the War Production Board, September 19, 1944*, 7–8, copy in box 233, Harry Hopkins Papers, Franklin D. Roosevelt Library; Hiland G. Batcheller, *Critical Programs*, 1, 5–8.

32. Batcheller, *Critical Programs*, 1–8; Vatter, *United States Economy in World War II*, 69; Stein, "Reconversion Controversy," 236.

33. Grace Person Hayes, *The History of the Joint Chiefs of Staff in World War II* (Annapolis: Naval Institute Press, 1982), 605.

34. As quoted in ibid., 604; on the strategic debate of May–October 1944: chap. 24; D. Clayton James, *The Years of MacArthur*, 2 vols. (Boston: Houghton Mifflin, 1970; reprint, 1975), II, chap. 13; Robert Ross Smith, "Luzon versus Formosa," in Kent Roberts Greenfield, *Command Decisions*, 461–477; Robert Ross Smith, *Triumph in the Philippines*, United States Army in World War II, The War in the Pacific (Washington, DC: U.S. Government Printing Office, 1963), chap. 1.

35. MacArthur to Chief of Staff, War Department, 18 June 1944, RG 4, box 17, folder 1, MacArthur Memorial Archives (hereafter MMA), Norfolk, Virginia.

36. MacArthur to Adjutant General, War Department, 8 July 1944, RG 4, box 17, folder 1, MMA; King quoted in Hayes, *Joint Chiefs*, 608. The divisions in his command were the Sixth, Twenty-Fourth, Twenty-Fifth, Thirty-First, Thirty-Second, Thirty-Third, Thirty-Seventh, Thirty-Eighth, Fortieth, Forty-First, Forty-Third, Ninety-Third, First Cavalry, Eleventh Airborne, and Americal.

37. Marshall to MacArthur, 24 June 1944, RG 4, box 17, folder 1, MMA.

38. Hayes, *Joint Chiefs*, 604.

39. Joint Staff Planners, Washington, to Staff Planners of Commander in Chief Pacific Ocean Area (CINCPOA) and Commander in Chief Southwest Pacific Area (CINCSWPA), signed Roberts, 27 July 1944, RG 4, box 17, folder 1, MMA.

40. MacArthur to Chief of Staff, War Department, 3 August 1944, RG 4, box 17, folder 1, MMA; Notes on Conference 1 August 1944 at GHQ, SWPA, Present General MacArthur and Colonel Ritchie, 16 August 1944, xerox 1015, OPD copies, George Marshall Research Library (hereafter MRL), Lexington, Virginia.

41. Hayes, *Joint Chiefs*, 610–611 and n. 25; James, *Years of MacArthur*, II, 530–536; Geoffrey Perret, *Old Soldiers Never Die: The Life of Douglas MacArthur* (Holbrook, MA: Adams Media, 1996), 405–407 and n. 45.

42. Memo for Chief of Policy and Strategy Group, Operations Division, War Department, initialed J.J.B., 5 September 1944, OPD copies, verifax 2232, item 2505, pt. 22, MRL.

43. General J. E. Hull, Memorandum for Generals Handy and Roberts, "Pacific Strategy, 2 September 1944, OPD copies, verifax 2233, item 2505, MRL; George A. Lincoln, Memorandum for General Roberts, 23 September 1944, RG 29C, box 1, folder 4, MMA; General George Marshall to MacArthur, 24 June 1944, RG 4, box 17, folder 1, MMA.

44. General Richard Marshall, memorandum, 4 September 1944, in R. Sutherland, Reports from War Dept., RG 4, box 17, folder 2, "War Dept. Aug. 9–Dec. 23," MMA; Coakley and Leighton, *Global Logistics and Strategy*, 412–414.

45. Notes on Conference with SWPA Planners, 7 August 1944, RG 29C, box 1, folder 4; Sigsally, (phone) Conversation between Lieutenant General Giles, Major General Hull (Brisbane), and Major General Handy (Washington), 8 August 1944, RG 4, United States Army Forces Pacific, box 17, folder 2, "War Dept., August 9–December 23, 1944," MMA.

46. Marshall to MacArthur, 24 June 1944, RG 4, box 17, folder 1, MMA; Notes on August 1, 1944, Conference, GHQ SWPA, August 16, 1944, OPD copies, xerox 1016, MRL.

47. General J. E. Hull, memorandum, 2 September 1944, OPD copies, xerox 2233, item 2505, pt. 22, MRL; Notes on Conference of General MacArthur and Colonel Richie, 10 August 1944, GHQ SWPA, RG 29C, box 1, folder 4, MRL.

48. Marshall to MacArthur, 24 June 1944, RG 4, box 17, folder 1, MMA.

49. R. J. Marshall to MacArthur, 9 September 1944, RG 4, box 17, folder 2, "War Dept.," 9 August–23 December 1944.

50. Hayes, *Joint Chiefs*, 615–616.

51. Halsey to Nimitz, 14 September 1944, RG 4, B.10, Folio Navy, 28 June 1944–8 February 1945, MMA.

52. James, *Years of MacArthur*, II, 536–542.

53. Clark G. Reynolds, *Admiral John H. Towers: The Struggle for Naval Air Supremacy* (Annapolis: Naval Institute Press, 1991), 482.

54. Notes on Conference of Colonel Ritchie and MacArthur, 10 August 1944, RG 29C, box 1, folder 4; General Somervell to General George Marshall, 17 July 1944, RG 160, AST Planning Division, Strategic Logistics Branch, Topical Files, box 6, ser. 2, folder K-1, National Archives, College Park, Maryland (henceforth NARA).

55. Smith, "Luzon versus Formosa," 468.

56. MacArthur to General George Marshall, 28 September 1944, RG 4, box 17, folder 2, 9 August–23 December 1944, MMA.

57. Smith, *Triumph in the Philippines*, 16, and chap. 1; MacArthur to Sutherland, 27 September 1944, RG 4, box 17, folder 2, "War Dept.," 9 August–23 December 1944; Marshall to MacArthur, 26 September 1944, OPD copies, xerox 1224, George C. Marshall Papers, MRL; MacArthur to Marshall, 28 September 1944, RG 4, box 17, folder 2, 9 August–23 September 1944, MMA.

58. Marshall to MacArthur, 24 June 1944, RG 4, box 17, folder 1, MMA.

59. In June, Marshall had made a similar suggestion about bypassing Luzon and Formosa in favor of Kyushu. MacArthur rejected the idea of an assault on Kyushu without direct air support and adequate shipping and bases as "suicidal." Brower, "American Strategy," 239–240. Marshall to Embick, 1 September 1944, box 67, Selected Correspondence, George C. Marshall Papers, MRL.

60. Embick to Marshall, 30 September 1944, box 67, George C. Marshall Papers, MRL.

61. Marshall to Embick, [3 October] 1944, box 67, George C. Marshall Papers, MRL. It appears that this letter was not sent. The entire exchange with Embick is printed with annotation in Larry I. Bland and Sharon Ritenour, eds., *The Papers of George Catlett Marshall*, vol. 4, *"Aggressive and Determined Leadership," June 1, 1943– December 31, 1944* (Baltimore: Johns Hopkins University Press, 1996), 566–567, 616–617.

62. H. W. Willmott, *The Battle of Leyte Gulf* (Bloomington: Indiana University Press, 2005), 45.

63. Clay Blair, Jr., *Silent Victory: The U.S. Submarine War against Japan* (Philadelphia: Lippincott, 1975), 721, 816.

64. On American submarine action: Samuel Eliot Morison, *New Guinea and the Marianas, March 1944–August 1944* (History of United States Naval Operations in World War II, vol. 8) (Boston: Little, Brown, 1953), chap. 2; Morison, *Leyte, June 1944–January 1945* (History of United States Naval Operations in World War II, vol. 12) (Boston: Little, Brown, 1958), chap. 17; Morison, *The Liberation of the Philippines, Luzon, Mindanao, the Visayas, 1944–1945* (History of United States Naval Operations in World War II, vol. 8) (Boston: Little, Brown, 1959), chap. 13.

65. Blair, *Silent Victory*, 816–817.

66. Morison, *Leyte*, 413.

67. Lt. General Arthur Gilbert Trudeau, Senior Officers Debriefing Program Interview, 11 February 1971, box 1945, Arthur Trudeau Papers, United States Army Heritage and Education Center, Carlisle, Pennsylvania; Willmott, *Battle of Leyte Gulf*, 26–29.

68. On the Formosa raids: Clark G. Reynolds, *The Fast Carriers: The Forging of an Air Navy* (New York: McGraw Hill, 1968), 260–261; Willmott, *Battle of Leyte Gulf*, 56–57, 60.

69. Willmott, *Battle of Leyte Gulf*, 56–57.

70. Morison, *Leyte*, 94 n. 10.

71. Willmott, *Battle of Leyte Gulf*, 62–63.

72. Ibid., 49–50.

73. Ibid., 40, 72–73.

74. Ibid., 40–42.

75. Ibid., 53.

76. Robert Ross Smith, *The Approach to the Philippines*, United States Army in World War II, The War in the Pacific (Washington, DC: U.S. Government Printing Office, 1953), chap. 20.

77. Major Frank D. Hough, *The Assault on Peleliu* (Washington, DC: Headquarters U.S. Marine Corps, 1950), 25.

78. E. B. Sledge, *With the Old Breed at Peleliu and Okinawa* (Novato, CA: Presidio Press, 1981), 34. On Pavuvu, Hough, *Assault on Peleliu*, 13, 25–35, and notes. Samuel Eliot Morison, *Breaking the Bismarcks Barrier, 22 July 1942–May 1944* (*History of United States Naval Operations in World War II*, vol. 6) (Boston: Little, Brown, 1950), 278–289; Morison, *New Guinea and the Marianas*, 378–379; John Miller, Jr., *Cartwheel: The Reduction of Rabaul*, United States Army in World War II: War and the Pacific (Washington, DC: U.S. Government Printing Office, 1950), 272–295; Smith, *Approach to the Philippines*, 467–475; Jeter A. Isley and Peter A. Crowl, *The U.S. Marines and Amphibious Warfare: Its Theory and Its Practice in the Pacific* (Princeton, NJ: Princeton University Press, 1951), 392–398.

79. As quoted in Isely and Crowl, *Amphibious Warfare*, 396. In other sources it was four days, maybe three: Hough, *Assault on Peleliu*, 35.

80. As quoted in Hough, *Assault on Peleliu*, 77; on Peleliu terrain and defenses, 14–16, 37, 63, 77.

81. Ibid., 194–195.

82. As quoted in ibid., 40.

83. Ibid., 37–41.

84. On the landings: ibid., chap. 3.

85. Ibid., 57.

86. Ibid., 59–74.

87. As quoted in ibid., 64 n. 13, 94.

88. Ibid., 72.

89. Ibid., 80.

90. Ibid., 74–83.

91. Ibid., 86.

92. Ibid., 87.

93. Ibid., 88 n. 60.

94. Hough, *Assault on Peleliu*, 106 n. 4.

95. Ibid., 116.

96. Sledge, *With the Old Breed*, 128; Hough, *Assault on Peleliu*, 154.

97. Sledge, *With the Old Breed*, 120, 142–144.

98. Hough, *Assault on Peleliu*, 151–154.

99. Sledge, *With the Old Breed*, 103.

100. Hough, *Assault on Peleliu*, 155, 157 n. 54, 158 n. 58, 159 n. 59.

101. Ibid., 161.

102. Ibid., 174.

103. On the Peleliu battle, 15 October–27 November: Smith, *Approach to the Philippines*, 559–575.

104. Hough, *Assault on Peleliu*, 178.

105. As quoted in Sledge, *With the Old Breed*, 156.

106. Hough, *Assault on Peleliu*, 183.

107. Smith, *Approach to the Philippines*, 573.

108. On the Battle of Leyte Gulf: Morison, *Leyte*, pt. 3; Willmott, *Battle of Leyte Gulf*; C. Vann Woodward, *The Battle for Leyte Gulf* (New York: Norton, 1965) (first

published 1947); James A. Field, Jr., *The Japanese at Leyte Gulf: The Sho Operation* (Princeton, NJ: Princeton University Press, 1947); Anthony P. Tully, *Battle of Surigao Strait* (Bloomington: Indiana University Press, 2009); Reynolds, *Fast Carriers*, chap. 8; Stanley L. Falk, *Decision at Leyte* (New York: Norton, 1966), pt. 4.

109. Morison, *Leyte*, 156.

110. Samuel Eliot Morison's more convenient name for "First Striking Force." Morison, *Leyte*, 162.

111. Ibid., 169–174.

112. Reynolds, *Fast Carriers*, 286.

113. Woodward, *Battle for Leyte Gulf*, 43.

114. Willmott, *Battle of Leyte Gulf*, 91–95, 105–107.

115. Reynolds, *Fast Carriers*, 264.

116. Willmott, *Battle of Leyte Gulf*, 113–115.

117. Ibid., 115–116.

118. Morison, *Leyte*, 187, 189.

119. Ibid., 177–183.

120. Ibid., 189; Willmott, *Battle of Leyte Gulf*, 125–126.

121. Halsey Action Report quoted in Morison, *Leyte*, 194 n. 30.

122. Morison, *Leyte*, 195–196; Reynolds, *Fast Carriers*, 269–270.

123. Reynolds, *Fast Carriers*, 256–258; Ronald H. Spector, *Eagle against the Sun: The American War with Japan* (New York: Free Press, 1985), 423.

124. Morison, *Leyte*, 175.

125. Reynolds, *Fast Carriers*, 284.

126. Tully, *Battle of Surigao Strait*, chaps. 2, 3; Willmott, *Battle of Leyte Gulf*, 43–49, 99, 140–141.

127. Willmott, *Battle of Leyte Gulf*, 89; Tully, *Battle of Surigao Strait*, 13, 21–26, 51–56; Willmott, *Battle of Leyte Gulf*, 89.

128. Tully, *Battle of Surigao Strait*, 35.

129. Ibid., chap. 5.

130. Ibid., 178. Anthony Tully's recent account of the battle and in particular of the sinking of the *Fuso*, based on extensive research in Japanese sources, has been the principal source in this account.

131. Ibid., 161.

132. Ibid., 155–163, 179–180, 250–251.

133. Ibid., 169–171.

134. Ibid., 195, 208–213.

135. Morison, *Leyte*, 223–224.

136. Tully, *Battle of Surigao Strait*, 205–207.

137. As quoted in ibid., 212.

138. As quoted in ibid., 216–218.

139. Woodward, *Battle for Leyte Gulf*, 166.

140. Morison, *Leyte*, 252; Willmott, *Battle of Leyte Gulf*, 161.

141. Morison, *Leyte*, 260–261.

142. Willmott, *Battle of Leyte Gulf*, 164.

143. Woodward, *Battle for Leyte Gulf*, 195.

144. Morison, *Leyte*, 203–204.
145. As quoted in James D. Hornfischer, *The Last Stand of the Tin Can Sailors* (New York: Random House, 2005), 298; Morison, *Leyte*, 261, 270, 273–274.
146. Field, *Japanese at Leyte Gulf*, 109.
147. See ibid., 108–109, 122–128; Morison, *Leyte*, 296–300; Woodward, *Battle for Leyte Gulf*, 194–205; Willmott, *Battle of Leyte Gulf*, 182–192, 207–208.
148. Morison, *Leyte*, 298; Tully, *Battle of Surigao Strait*, 258.
149. Woodward, *Battle for Leyte Gulf*, 197–205.
150. Hornfischer, *Last Stand*, 282, 360.
151. Woodward, *Battle for Leyte Gulf*, 147.
152. Willmott, *Battle of Leyte Gulf*, 174, 193.
153. Morison, *Leyte*, 322–336.
154. Willmott, *Battle of Leyte Gulf*, 255.
155. Ibid., 203–206; Morison, *Leyte*, 300–307.

Chapter 5

1. M. A. Adelman memoir, "Leyte Revisited," folder 26, box 3, Hanson Baldwin Papers, George Marshall Research Library (hereafter MRL), Lexington, Virginia. On MacArthur's return: D. Clayton James, *The Years of MacArthur*, 2 vols. (Boston: Houghton Mifflin, 1970, 1975), II, 553–559; Geoffrey Perret, *Old Soldiers Never Die: The Life of Douglas MacArthur* (Holbrook, MA: Adams Media, 1996), 419–424.
2. M. Hamlin Cannon, *Leyte: The Return to the Philippines*, United States Army in World War II, The War in the Pacific (Washington, DC, 1954), 22, 26.
3. Edward J. Drea, *In the Service of the Emperor: Essays on the Imperial Japanese Army* (Lincoln: University of Nebraska Press, 1998), 137–143.
4. Stanley L. Falk, *Decision at Leyte* (New York: Norton, 1966), 67.
5. Typhoon folder, box 95, Samuel Eliot Morison Papers, Navy Operational Archives, Navy Yard, Washington, DC.
6. On the land battle: Cannon, *Leyte*, chaps. 4–11; Falk, *Decision at Leyte*, chaps. 7–9, 15–18.
7. Cannon, *Leyte*, 144.
8. Ibid., 78, 123, 145, 157, 181, 183.
9. Carl F. Brandt, "Philippines Campaign of 1st Battalion, 34 Infantry" (memoir), Veterans Surveys, 24th Division, box 1, United States Army Heritage and Education Center (hereafter USAHEC), Carlisle, Pennsylvania.
10. Ibid., 3–15.
11. Falk, *Decision at Leyte*, 68.
12. Thomas E. Griffith, Jr., *MacArthur's Airman: General George C. Kenney and the War in the Southwest Pacific* (Lawrence: University Press of Kansas, 1998), 191–192, 205; Wesley Frank Craven and James Lea Cate, eds., *Army Air Forces in World War II*, vol. 5, *From Matterhorn to Nagasaki, June 1944 to August 1945* (Chicago: University of Chicago Press, 1953), 373–389; Major General Hugh J. Casey, *Engineer Memoirs* (Washington, DC: U.S. Army Corps of Engineers, 1993), 230–235; Cannon, *Leyte*, 185–190.

13. Cannon, *Leyte*, 208–209.
14. Brandt, "Philippines Campaign," 7–8.
15. Cannon, *Leyte*, 207.
16. Brandt, "Philippines Campaign," 8–9.
17. Falk, *Decision at Leyte*, 243.
18. Cannon, *Leyte*, 181, 183.
19. Falk, *Decision at Leyte*, 245–247.
20. James W. Deloach, Veterans Surveys, 32nd Division, unprocessed box, World War II, USAHEC.
21. Cannon, *Leyte*, 218.
22. Falk, *Decision at Leyte*, 250; Cannon, *Leyte*, 218–220.
23. Falk, *Decision at Leyte*, 250–251.
24. As quoted in Cannon, *Leyte*, 225, 227.
25. Brandt, "Philippines Campaign," 14.
26. Ibid., 11–19.
27. Ibid., 16, 18.
28. Falk, *Decision at Leyte*, 250.
29. Brandt, "Philippines Campaign," 18.
30. Cannon, *Leyte*, 225, 235.
31. Craven and Cate, *Army Air Forces in World War II*, vol. 5, *From Matterhorn to Nagasaki, June 1944 to August 1945*, 372–375, 384–387.
32. MacArthur to Nimitz, 17 September 1944, folder 6 [Navy, 28 June 1944–8 February 1945], box 10, RG 4, MacArthur Memorial Archives (hereafter MMA), Norfolk, Virginia; Cannon, *Leyte*, 276–277.
33. "Men Who Were There" [77th Division Association], *Ours to Hold It High: The History of the 77th Division in World War II* (Washington, DC: Infantry Journal Press, 1947), 127, 141; Cannon, *Leyte*, 275–283; Kevin C. Holzimmer, *General Walter Krueger, Unsung Hero of the Pacific War* (Lawrence: University Press of Kansas, 2007), 200–202; Falk, *Decision at Leyte*, chap. 20.
34. Cannon, *Leyte*, 286.
35. Ibid., chap. 17; Falk, *Decision at Leyte*, chap. 19.
36. Cannon, *Leyte*, 292; 77th Division Association, *Ours to Hold It High*, 157–159.
37. 77th Division Association, *Ours to Hold It High*, 161; Cannon, *Leyte*, 315–321.
38. Falk, *Decision at Leyte*, 297–303.
39. Cannon, *Leyte*, 318–319.
40. 77th Division Association, *Ours to Hold It High*, 166.
41. Cannon, *Leyte*, 321.
42. Ibid., 329–336.
43. Ibid., 339–342.
44. Holzimmer, *General Walter Krueger*, 199.
45. Cannon, *Leyte*, 342–346.
46. Ibid., table 4, 368.
47. William T. McLaughlin, "Recon Scout" (memoir), Veterans Surveys, Americal Division, box 5, USAHEC.
48. James, *Years of MacArthur*, II, 584–587; Perret, *Old Soldiers Never Die*, 427.
49. James, *Years of MacArthur*, II, 576–577; Cannon, *Leyte*, 213.

50. Holzimmer, *General Walter Krueger*, 199; Cannon, *Leyte*, 356.

51. As quoted in James, *Years of MacArthur*, II, 593.

52. Falk, *Decision at Leyte*, 261.

53. Cannon, *Leyte*, table 4, 368.

54. Ronald H. Spector, *Eagle against the Sun: The American War with Japan* (New York: Free Press, 1985), 440–441; Griffith, *MacArthur's Airman*, 194.

55. Griffith, *MacArthur's Airman*, 190, 202.

56. Ibid., 198, 204–205.

57. E. B. Potter, *Nimitz* (Annapolis: U.S. Naval Institute Press, 1976), 221.

58. Samuel Eliot Morison, *Leyte, June 1944–January 1945* (*History of United States Naval Operations in World War II*, vol. 12) (Boston: Little, Brown, 1958), 354–360.

59. Ibid., 360, chap. 15.

60. MacArthur to Halsey, 21 October 1944, folder 6, Navy: 28 January–6 February 1945, box 10, RG 4, MMA; Halsey to MacArthur, 26 October 1944, box 104, Map Room Files, Franklin D. Roosevelt Library (hereafter FDRL), Hyde Park, New York.

61. Nimitz to King, copy to MacArthur, 13 November 1944, box 104, Map Room Files, FDRL.

62. Nimitz to MacArthur, 17 November 1944, box 104, Map Room Files, FDRL; MacArthur to Nimitz, 16 November 1944, folder 6, Navy: 28 June 1944–6 February 1945, box 10, RG 4, MMA; Nimitz to MacArthur, 17 November 1944, and Nimitz to Halsey, 21 November 1944, box 104, Map Room Files, FDRL.

63. Kinkaid [Sherman] to Nimitz, 4 November 1944, box 104, Map Room Files, FDRL.

64. MacArthur to Nimitz, 16 November 1944, folder 6, Navy: 28 June 1944–6 February 1945, box 10, RG4, MMA.

65. Nimitz to MacArthur, 17 November 1944, box 104, Map Room Files, FDRL.

66. Nimitz to MacArthur, 29 November 1944, Navy: 28 June–8 February 1945, folder 6, box 10, RG4, MMA.

67. Griffith, *MacArthur's Airman*, 210.

68. Morison, *Leyte*, 375–382.

69. Ibid., 382–385.

70. Ibid., 389.

71. Morison, *The Liberation of the Philippines, Luzon, Mindanao, the Visayas, 1944–1945* (*History of United States Naval Operations in World War II*, vol. 8) (Boston: Little, Brown, 1959), 55, 57.

72. On the Mindoro assault: Morison, *Liberation of the Philippines*, chap. 2; Robert Ross Smith, *Triumph in the Philippines*, United States Army in World War II, The War in the Pacific (Washington, DC: U.S. Government Printing Office, 1963), 43–53; Griffith, *MacArthur's Airman*, 207–212.

73. On the typhoon of December 18, 1944: Morison, *Liberation of the Philippines*, 59–87; Bob Drury and Tom Clavin, *Halsey's Typhoon: The True Story of a Fighting Admiral, an Epic Storm, and an Untold Rescue* (New York: Atlantic Monthly Press, 2007).

74. Smith, *Triumph in the Philippines*, 51, 60–67; Morison, *Liberation of the Philippines*, 22–36, 43–51.

75. On the Lingayen Gulf landings and the kamikaze attacks: Morison, *Liberation of the Philippines*, 96–156; Smith, *Triumph in the Philippines*, 54–69.

76. Craven and Cate, *The Army Air Forces in World War II*, vol. 5, *From Matterhorn to Nagasaki, June 1944 to August 1945*, 409.

77. Morison, *Liberation of the Philippines*, 106.

78. Craven and Cate, *Army Air Force in World War II*, vol. 5, *From Matterhorn to Nagasaki, June 1944 to August 1945*, 410–411; Morison, *Liberation of the Philippines*, 106–107.

79. Smith, *Triumph in the Philippines*, 58; Morison, *Liberation of the Philippines*, 152.

80. Spector, *Eagle against the Sun*, 520.

81. Morison, *Liberation of the Philippines*, 139.

82. Ibid., 152; Smith, *Triumph in the Philippines*, 65–66.

83. Morison, *Liberation of the Philippines*, 96–156.

84. Smith, *Triumph in the Philippines*, 65–67.

85. James, *Years of MacArthur*, II, 590–591.

86. Clark G. Reynolds, *The Fast Carriers: The Forging of an Air Navy* (New York: McGraw Hill, 1968), 297.

87. Morison, *Liberation of the Philippines*, 175–178.

88. Nimitz to MacArthur, 6 February 1945, box 97, file 300, Map Room Files, FDRL; Morison, *Liberation of the Philippines*, 155–156, 174–179; Morison, *Victory in the Pacific, 1945* (*History of United States Naval Operations in World War II*, vol. 14) (Boston: Little, Brown, 1960), 26–27.

89. Craven and Cate, *Army Air Forces in World War II*, vol. 5, *From Matterhorn to Nagasaki, June 1944 to August 1945*, 419.

90. FILBAS [Philippines Bases] Agreement, Report of Conferees as to Logistical Support in the Philippine Islands for Pacific Ocean Area Forces, 4 November 1944, folder 6, box 1, RG 29A, Richard Marshall Papers, MMA.

91. Smith, *Triumph in the Philippines*, 84.

92. Ibid., 80–87, map 1.

93. On intelligence estimates: Edward J. Drea, *MacArthur's ULTRA and the War against Japan, 1942–1945* (Lawrence: University Press of Kansas, 1992), chap. 7.

94. Ibid., 181–186.

95. Smith, *Triumph in the Philippines*, 94–100.

96. On the Forty-Third Division attack: Smith, *Triumph in the Philippines*, chap. 6, 147–155; Joseph E. Zimmer, *The History of the 43rd Infantry Division, 1941–1945* (Nashville: Battery Press, 1982), 7, 34, 36, 38.

97. Smith, *Triumph in the Philippines*, 148–149.

98. Ibid., 152–153.

99. Ibid., 153–155.

100. Ibid., 140, 154–155.

101. Ibid., 150.

102. Ibid., 165.

103. Ibid., 151.

104. Ibid., 151; Zimmer, *History of the 43rd Infantry Division*, 61.

105. Smith, *Triumph in the Philippines*, 181.

106. Zimmer, *History of the 43rd Infantry Division*, 61.

107. Smith, *Triumph in the Philippines*, 139–146, 155–171.

108. Ibid., 212; Holzimmer, *General Walter Krueger*, 216.

109. The plan is in Richard Connaughton, John Pimlott, and Duncan Anderson, *The Battle of Manila* (Novato, CA: Presidio Press, 2002), 209–214.

110. Smith, *Triumph in the Philippines*, 161–164.

111. Ibid., 155–160.

112. Ibid., 164–166.

113. Ibid., 187–188.

114. Ibid., 187–196.

115. Ibid., 196–202.

116. Ibid., 198.

117. Samuel Eliot Morison, *Breaking the Bismarcks Barrier, 22 July 1942–May 1944* (*History of United States Naval Operations in World War II*, vol. 6) (Boston: Little, Brown, 1950), 364, 431.

118. Smith, *Triumph in the Philippines*, 121–122, 130.

119. On the capture of the Clark airfields to January 27: ibid., 167–179.

120. Lt. Gen. Oscar Griswold, Diary, 26 January 1945, box 1, Griswold Papers, USAHEC.

121. Smith, *Triumph in the Philippines*, 184.

122. On the capture of the Clark airfields, January 27–31: ibid., 179–186.

123. Paul M. Gerrish, "My Army Days" (memoir), 84–85, 91–93, Veterans Surveys, 40th Infantry Division Papers, USAHEC.

124. Smith, *Triumph in the Philippines*, 652.

125. As quoted in Perret, *Old Soldiers Never Die*, 446.

126. Smith, *Triumph in the Philippines*, 237–256.

127. As quoted in Connaughton et al., *Battle of Manila*, 93.

128. Ibid., chap. 1.

129. Ibid., 69–70.

130. On the deteriorating Japanese-Filipino relationship: ibid., chap. 2.

131. On the Japanese navy force in defense of Manila: Smith, *Triumph in the Philippines*, 240–248.

132. On the Eleventh Airborne assault: ibid., 221–231, 265–269.

133. Ibid., 268.

134. On the clearing of the city north of the Pasig and the crossing of the river: ibid., 251–265.

135. As quoted in Connaughton et al., *Battle of Manila*, 109.

136. Smith, *Triumph in the Philippines*, 263.

137. Ibid., 260–263.

138. Ibid., 260 and n. 24; Connaughton et al., *Battle of Manila*, 112.

139. Smith, *Triumph in the Philippines*, 261–264, table 3, 296.

140. Ibid., 271–275; Connaughton et al., *Battle of Manila*, 141–144, 183–186; on the Manila massacre, ibid., chaps. 4–6.

141. As quoted in Connaughton et al., *Battle of Manila*, 107–108.

142. Smith, *Triumph in the Philippines*, 275.

143. Connaughton et al., *Battle of Manila*, 129, 135.

144. Smith, *Triumph in the Philippines*, 275–280.

145. Ibid., 280–283.
146. Ibid., 283–285.
147. Ibid., 285–287.
148. Ibid., 288–289.
149. Ibid., 289–290.
150. On the Intramuros battle: ibid., 291–301, table 3.
151. Ibid., table 4, 297.
152. Ibid., 300–301.
153. Ibid., 304.
154. Ibid., 304–306.
155. Ibid, 306.
156. Ibid., 307.
157. Robert H. Kiser, memoir, Veterans Surveys, 37th Division Papers, USAHEC.

Chapter 6
1. Thomas B. Buell, *The Quiet Warrior: A Biography of Admiral Raymond Spruance* (Annapolis: Naval Institute Press, 1987), 307, 322–323.
2. On the Iwo Jima battle: Richard Wheeler, *Iwo* (New York: Lippincott and Crowell, 1980); Richard F. Newcomb, *Iwo Jima* (New York: Holt, 1965); Jeter A. Isley and Peter A. Crowl, *The U.S. Marines and Amphibious Warfare: Its Theory and Its Practice in the Pacific* (Princeton, NJ: Princeton University Press, 1951); Eric Hammel, *Iwo Jima* (Minneapolis: Zenith, 2009).
3. On Kuribayashi and his defense system: Newcomb, *Iwo Jima*, chap. 1, 41–44, 274; Wheeler, *Iwo*, 12, 25–26.
4. Hammel, *Iwo Jima*, 36; Newcomb, *Iwo Jima*, 43–44, 274.
5. Hammel, *Iwo Jima*, 33–36; Newcomb, *Iwo Jima*, 179, 274.
6. On the Guam preparatory gunfire: Isley and Crowl, *U.S. Marines and Amphibious Warfare*, 380–383.
7. On the preparatory bombardment issue: ibid., 439–451.
8. Ibid., 443.
9. Ibid., 443.
10. Samuel Eliot Morison, *The Liberation of the Philippines, Luzon, Mindanao, the Visayas, 1944–1945* (*History of United States Naval Operations in World War II*, vol. 8) (Boston: Little, Brown, 1959), 174–179.
11. Dick Camp, *Iwo Jima Recon: The U.S. Navy at War, February 17, 1945* (Minneapolis: Zenith, 2007), 49.
12. Isley and Crowl, *U.S. Marines and Amphibious Warfare*, 474–475.
13. Newcomb, *Iwo Jima*, 27.
14. Isley and Crowl, *U.S. Marines and Amphibious Warfare*, 458–459, 516.
15. Newcomb, *Iwo Jima*, 103.
16. Ibid., 132.
17. Wheeler, *Iwo*, 79–84.
18. Ibid., 84–85.
19. Ibid., 81; Hammel, *Iwo Jima*, 83.
20. Wheeler, *Iwo*, 107–108.

21. Ibid., 126–127.
22. Ibid., 128–129; Hammel, *Iwo Jima*, 110.
23. Wheeler, *Iwo*, 129–130.
24. Ibid., 134–135, 141.
25. On the Suribachi flag event: ibid., chap. 11; Newcomb, *Iwo Jima*, chap. 4.
26. Newcomb, *Iwo Jima*, 200; Stanley K. Fink, U.S.M.C., "Blood Use in Pacific War," *Hygeia* 23 (May 1945), 397–398.
27. On the Twenty-First Regiment advance across Airfield No. 2: Wheeler, *Iwo*, 156–160; Newcomb, *Iwo Jima*, 179–180.
28. On casualties: Wheeler, *Iwo*, 158, 160; Newcomb, *Iwo Jima*, 183.
29. Isley and Crowl, *U.S. Marines and Amphibious Warfare*, 489–493.
30. Ibid., 494.
31. Ibid., 528.
32. Hammel, *Iwo Jima*, 213.
33. Newcomb, *Iwo Jima*, 266; Wheeler, *Iwo*, 188–191.
34. Newcomb, *Iwo Jima*, 198.
35. Ibid., 188.
36. Ibid., 204–205, 215–218.
37. Ibid., 192.
38. Ibid., 215–216.
39. Ibid., 218.
40. Wheeler, *Iwo*, 206.
41. Newcomb, *Iwo Jima*, 252.
42. Wheeler, *Iwo*, 181.
43. Newcomb, *Iwo Jima*, 296.
44. Ibid., 282–284.
45. Ibid., 296.
46. "Woman's Pleas to End Iwo Battles Revealed," *New York Times*, 17 March 1945, 7. The letter was also published in the 26 March edition of *Time*; Geoffrey Perret, *Days of Sadness Years of Triumph* (New York: Coward, McCann, and Geoghegan, 1972), 410.
47. Bosley Crowther, "Matters of Actual Fact, Iwo Jima between the Eyes Pacific Fury," *New York Times*, 18 March 1945, X1.
48. Isley and Crowl, *U.S. Marines and Amphibious Warfare*, 529. For differing views on the value of Iwo Jima to the United States, see Ronald H. Spector, *Eagle against the Sun: The American War with Japan* (New York: Free Press, 1985), 502–503; William L. O'Neill, *A Democracy at War: America's Fight at Home and Abroad in World War II* (New York: Free Press, 1993), 405–407; Robert S. Burrell, "Breaking the Cycle of Iwo Jima Mythology: A Strategic Study of Operation Detachment," *Journal of Military History* 68, no. 4 (October 2004), 1143–1186; Brian Hanley and Robert S. Burrell, "The Myth of Iwo Jima: A Rebuttal [and Response]," *Journal of Military History* 69, no. 3 (July 2005), 801–809.
49. David Nichols, ed., *Ernie's War: The Best of Ernie Pyle's World War II Dispatches* (New York: Random House, 1986), 375.

50. Richard B. Frank, *Downfall: The End of the Imperial Japanese Empire* (New York: Penguin, 1999), 3–19; Spector, *Eagle against the Sun*, 504–505; Francis Pike, *Hirohito's War: The Pacific War, 1941–1945* (London: Bloomsbury, 2015), 1024–1028.

51. "3,000-Mile Stride on the Tokyo Road: Sees No Quick and Easy Victory over Japan," *New York Times*, 28 March 1945, 14.

Chapter 7

1. As quoted in D. Clayton James, *The Years of MacArthur*, 2 vols. (Boston: Houghton Mifflin, 1970, 1975), II, 647.

2. Robert Ross Smith, *Triumph in the Philippines*, United States Army in World War II, The War in the Pacific (Washington, DC: U.S. Government Printing Office, 1963), 362–363.

3. MacArthur to Marshall, 26 February 1945, folder 3, box 17, RG 4, MacArthur Memorial Archives (MMA), Norfolk, Virginia.

4. Smith, *Triumph in the Philippines*, 583–586.

5. Charles B. MacDonald, *The European Theater of Operations: The Last Offensive* (New York: Barnes and Noble, 1995), chaps. 1–6.

6. For MacArthur's determination to maintain the existing boundaries and command of the Southwest Pacific area: MacArthur to Marshall, 27 August 1944, folder 2, War Dept., 9 August–23 December 1944, box 17, RG 4, MMA. On the diplomatic and strategic context of the Java project: Christopher Thorne, *Allies of a Kind: The United States, Britain, and the War against Japan, 1941–1945* (New York: Oxford University Press, 1978), 256, 415–416, 480–487, 614, 645–652; Thorne, *The Issue of War: States, Societies, and the Far Eastern Conflict of 1941–1945* (New York: Oxford University Press, 1985), 152, 168–169, 188–189, 194–195, 198–199, 212, 223–224, 258; James, *Years of MacArthur*, II, 702–717, 751–763; Grace Person Hayes, *The History of the Joint Chiefs of Staff in World War II* (Annapolis: Naval Institute Press, 1982), 695–701; Samuel Eliot Morison, *The Liberation of the Philippines, Luzon, Mindanao, the Visayas, 1944–1945* (*History of United States Naval Operations in World War II*, vol. 8), chap. 12.

7. J. E. Hull, Memo for General Lincoln, 5 March 1945, 2892, reel 119, George Marshall Research Library (MRL), Lexington, Virginia.

8. MacArthur to Marshall, 10 and 26 February 1945, folder 3, box 17, RG 4, MMA.

9. Francis Pike, *Hirohito's War: The Pacific War, 1941–1945* (London: Bloomsbury, 2015), 989.

10. Drew Pearson, "Merry Go-Round," *Washington Post*, 3 March 1945, 5.

11. "MacArthur," *Washington Post*, 20 March 8.

12. MacArthur to Nimitz, 26 February 1945, folder 7, Navy, 8 February–30 July 1945, box 10, RG 4, MMA.

13. On the fall–winter shipping crisis: Robert W. Coakley and Richard M. Leighton, *Global Logistics and Strategy, 1943–1945*, United States Army in World War II, The War Department (Washington, DC: U.S. Government Printing Office, 1968), chaps. 19, 22–24; H. B. Whipple, extracts from journal, 1945, Wartime folder, R.G. 29A, Richard Marshall Papers, MMA; Whipple memo, February 1945, folder 1, box 1,

RG 29A, MMA; C. H. Unger memo, 30 March 1945, 1945 Wartime folder, box 2, RG 29A, MMA.

14. Marshall to MacArthur, 27 February 1945, folder 3, War Department, December 1944–April 1945, box 17, RG 4, MMA.

15. Ibid.; Marshall to MacArthur, 7 February 1945, and MacArthur to Marshall, 26 February 1945, both in folder 3, box 17, RG 4, MMA.

16. Marshall to MacArthur, 7 February 1945.

17. Ibid.; Marshall to MacArthur, 1 March 1945, folder 3, box 17, RG 4, MMA.

18. MacArthur to Marshall, 26 February 1945, folder 3, box 17, RG 4, MMA.

19. MacArthur to Marshall, 28 February 1945, 2882, reel 119, George C. Marshall Papers, MRL; MacArthur to Marshall, 26 February 1945, folder 3, box 17, MMA.

20. Marshall to MacArthur, 26 March 1945, box 55, Outgoing, RG 165, National Archives (NARA), College Park, Maryland.

21. Marshall to MacArthur, 28 February 1945, 2882, reel 119, George C. Marshall Papers, MRL.

22. MacArthur to Marshall, 26 February 1945, folder 3, box 17, RG 4, MMA.

23. Morison, *Liberation of the Philippines*, chap. 12.

24. MacArthur to Marshall, 30 May 1945, folder 4, box 17, RG 4, MMA.

25. MacArthur to Marshall, 5 April 1945, Incoming, box 35, RG 165, NARA.

26. Somervell, Memorandum for General Hull, 6 February 1945, 2892, reel 119, MRL.

27. Edward J. Drea, *MacArthur's ULTRA and the War against Japan, 1942–1945* (Lawrence: University Press of Kansas, 1992), 200.

28. Smith, *Triumph in the Philippines*, 203–208, 418–445, 577.

29. B. David Mann, "Japanese Defense of Bataan, Luzon, Philippine Islands, 16 December 1944–4 September 1945," *Journal of Military History* 67 (October 2003), 1149–1176, n. 36, 1167.

30. On the battle at Zig-Zag Pass: ibid., and Smith, *Triumph in the Philippines*, chap. 17.

31. Smith (*Triumph in the Philippines*, 315) puts the number of Nagayoshi's force at 2,750, but Mann's number, 2,100 ("Japanese Defense of Bataan," 1159), is based on more recent Japanese sources.

32. Mann, "Japanese Defense of Bataan," 1163.

33. Ibid., 1167.

34. Ibid., 1168.

35. Smith, *Triumph in the Philippines*, 319–320.

36. Mann, "Japanese Defense of Bataan," 1166.

37. Smith, *Triumph in the Philippines*, 322, 328.

38. Ibid., 323, 325.

39. Mann, "Japanese Defense of Bataan," 1169–1170.

40. Ibid., 1172–1174; Smith, *Triumph in the Philippines*, 327–330.

41. Drea, *MacArthur's ULTRA*, 199–200.

42. Smith, *Triumph in the Philippines*, 33.

43. Ibid., 345.

44. Ibid. On the Corregidor battle: ibid., chap. 18.

45. Ibid., 203.
46. As quoted in Morison, *Liberation of the Philippines*, 206–207.
47. W. A. Sullivan, Estimate of Situation, Harbor Clearance Activities, Philippine Islands, folder 6, box 2, RG 4, MMA.
48. Photographs, 1 May 1945, 212139, and 13 July 1945, 262756, Signal Corps Photograph Archives, NARA.
49. MacArthur to War and Navy Departments, Incoming, 28 March 1945, box 34, RG 165, NARA.
50. Summary of Ships in Port, 21 July 1945, XI-D-Diary and Day File to Krueger File, General Subject File, Planning Division: Theater Branch, Divisions of Plans and Operations, Army Service Forces, box 63, RG 160, NARA; Lt. Gen. William D. Styer, Joint Conference on Supply and Shipping Problems, 1–6 May 1945, box 11, Strategic Logistics Branch, Planning Division, Army Service Forces, RG 160, NARA.
51. On the capture of the dams: Smith, *Triumph in the Philippines*, 367–368, 391, 404–405; James, *Years of MacArthur*, II, 677–678. On the Shimbu campaign: Smith, *Triumph in the Philippines*, chaps. 20–22.
52. Smith, *Triumph in the Philippines*, 368–371.
53. Ibid., 376–377; Joseph E. Zimmer, *The History of the 43rd Infantry Division, 1941–1945* (Nashville: Battery Press, 1982), 62.
54. Smith, *Triumph in the Philippines*, 362; on the Southern Philippines strategy: ibid., chap. 20.
55. Ibid., 375, 378.
56. Ibid., 367–384.
57. Ibid., 387.
58. Ibid., 384.
59. Ibid., 386; Zimmer, *History of the 43rd Division*, 69–70.
60. Smith, *Triumph in the Philippines*, 379–381.
61. Ibid., 392–398.
62. Ibid., 389.
63. On casualties: ibid., 384, 387, 389, 394, 396, 398.
64. Otis A. Pease, *Blueberry Pie: The Meaning of WWII for the Americans Who Fought in It* (Lincoln, NE: i Universe, 2007), 61.
65. On the Ipo Dam: Smith, *Triumph in the Philippines*, 404–405; James, *Years of MacArthur*, II, 674–678.
66. Smith, *Triumph in the Philippines*, 403–408; Zimmer, *History of the 43rd Division*, chap. 17.
67. Zimmer, *History of the 43rd Division*, 78–82.
68. Smith, *Triumph in the Philippines*, 412–413.
69. On the clearing of southern Luzon: ibid., 415–445.
70. Ibid., 443.
71. Ibid. 433.
72. Ibid., 432–433.
73. Ibid., 439–445.
74. Zimmer, *History of the 43rd Division*, 81–82.
75. MacDonald, *European Theater of Operations*, 53.

76. Roland G. Ruppenthal, *Logistic Support of the Armies* (Washington, DC: U.S. Government Printing Office, 1959), II, 220–232, 316–317.

77. Brower, "American Strategy," 16.

78. Fleet Admiral William D. Leahy to President Roosevelt, 11 January 1945, 319.1 sec. 1, Ca 1–50, Operations Division Decimal File, 1945, RG 165, entry 419, box 116, NARA.

79. Leonard L. Lerwill, *Personnel Replacement System in the U.S. Army*, Department of the Army Pamphlet No. 20-211, Office of the Chief of Military History, Washington, DC, 1953, 85, 123.

80. Robert R. Palmer and William R. Keast, "The Provision of Enlisted Replacements," 165–239, in Palmer, Bell I. Wiley, and Keast, *The Procurement and Training of Ground Combat Troops* (Washington, DC: U.S. Government Printing Office, 1948), 227–228.

81. Ibid., 218–223.

82. Freemen to Marshall for Hull, CA 50542, 13 February 1945, folder 3, box 17, RG 4, MA; also box 32, 11–13 February 1945, RG 165, NARA.

83. Hull to MacArthur, for Sutherland, 22 February 1945, folder 3, box 17, RG 4, MMA.

84. Hull to General Marshall, 5 March 1945, reel 118, 2861, OPD Executive File, MRL.

85. MacArthur to Marshall, 3 March 1945, box 33, RG 165, NARA.

86. Marshall to MacArthur, 6 March 1945, folder 1, box 75, Marshall Selected Correspondence, MRL.

87. Keith E. Eiler, *Mobilizing America: Robert P. Patterson and the War Effort, 1940–1945* (Ithaca, NY: Cornell University Press, 1997), 417–423, Stimson quoted on 419; John Morton Blum, *V Was for Victory: Politics and American Culture in World War II* (New York: Harcourt Brace Jovanovich, 1977), 253; "The Nation: Dispute on Manpower Labor's View," *New York Times*, 21 January 1945, 64.

88. On the ending of the war on the European front: Trevor N. Dupuy, David L. Bongard, and Richard C. Anderson, Jr., *Hitler's Last Gamble, The Battle of the Bulge, December 1944–January 1945* (New York: Harper, 1994), 358; MacDonald, *European Theater of Operations*, 134.

Chapter 8

1. Robert Ross Smith, *Triumph in the Philippines*, United States Army in World War II, The War in the Pacific (Washington, DC: U.S. Government Printing Office, 1963), 583–589.

2. On the Palawan capture: Smith, *Triumph in the Philippines*, 589–591; Samuel Eliot Morison, *The Liberation of the Philippines, Luzon, Mindanao, the Visayas, 1944–1945* (*History of United States Naval Operations in World War II*, vol. 8), 213–222; William F. McCartney, *The Jungleers: A History of the 41st Infantry Division* (Washington, DC: Infantry Journal Press, 1948), chap. 13.

3. Morison, *Liberation of the Philippines*, 220.

4. On the Zamboanga battle: McCartney, *Jungleers*, 145–147; Smith, *Triumph in the Philippines*, 591–597; Morison, *Liberation of the Philippines*, 213–222.

5. Smith, *Triumph in the Philippines*, 597–600.

6. H. W. Willmott, *The Battle of Leyte Gulf* (Bloomington: Indiana University Press, 2005), 234–235; Morison, *Liberation of the Philippines*, 280–286.

7. Paul M. Gerrish, "My Army Days" (memoir), 91–93, Veterans Surveys, 40th Infantry Division, United States Army Heritage and Education Center (USAHEC), Carlisle, Pennsylvania.

8. Smith, *Triumph in the Philippines*, 601–602.

9. Gerrish, "My Army Days," 102.

10. Ibid., 102–103.

11. Smith, *Triumph in the Philippines*, 605; on the battle for Negros: ibid., 604–608.

12. 40th Infantry Division, *The Years of World War II* (Nashville: Battery Press, 1946), 130.

13. Smith, *Triumph in the Philippines*, 605 n. 9.

14. 40th Infantry Division, *Years of World War II*, 135.

15. Gerrish, "My Army Days," 106.

16. "Geographic/Topographic Intelligence for Cebu," folder of Lt. F. H. Gilbert, Co. B, 182nd Infantry, Americal Division, box 4, Infantry, World War II, U.S.A., USAHEC. Sources for the Cebu battle: Smith, *Triumph in the Philippines*, 608–617; Captain Francis D. Cronin, *Under the Southern Cross: The Saga of the Americal Division* (Washington, DC: Combat Forces Press, 1951), 268–308; Morison, *Liberation of the Philippines*, 233–237, 240.

17. Smith, *Triumph in the Philippines*, 608–613; the landing on Cebu: ibid., 610–613.

18. Ibid., 613–614.

19. Cebu battles: ibid., 613–617; Cronin, *Under the Southern Cross*, 267–328.

20. Troop loss and Japanese survivors: Cronin, *Under the Southern Cross*, 340; Smith, *Triumph in the Philippines*, 597, 602, 605, 607–609, 615, 617; 40th Infantry Division, *Years of World War II*, 137.

21. Staff Sergeant W. T. McLaughlin, 21st Reconnaissance Troop, Americal Division, "Recon Scout" (memoir), box 5, Americal Division, Infantry Collection, USAHEC.

22. Cronin, *Under the Southern Cross*, 266.

23. Invasion of Mindanao, battle of Davao, and capture of the Sayre Highway: Smith, *Triumph in the Philippines*, 620–642; Morison, *Liberation of the Philippines*, 240–241.

24. Richard Fuller, *Shōkan: Hirohito's Samurai* (London: Arms and Armour Press, 1991), 157; Pacific War Online Encyclopedia, http://pwencycl.kgbudge.com/M/o/Morozumi_Gyosaku.htm.

25. Suspension of battle on Mindanao, casualties, and surrender: D. Clayton James, *The Years of MacArthur*, 2 vols. (Boston: Houghton Mifflin, 1970, 1975), II, 758, 803; Smith, *Triumph in the Philippines*, 636–648.

26. Fuller, *Shōkan*, 236–238; Pacific Online Encyclopedia, http://pwencycl.kgbudge.com/Y/a/Yamashita_Tomoyuki.htm.

27. Fuller, *Shōkan*, 181; M. Hamlin Cannon, *Leyte: The Return to the Philippines*, United States Army in World War II, The War in the Pacific (Washington, DC, 1954), 358, table 4, 368.

28. Melvin C. Walthall, *Lightning Forward: A History of the 25th Division (Tropic Lightning), 1941–1978* ([Bradenton, FL]: 25th Infantry Division Association, 1978), 51.

29. Smith, *Triumph in the Philippines*, 306.

30. Ibid., 468–481.

31. Ibid., 481–485.

32. Ibid., 525; on the Twenty-Fifth Division advance: ibid., chap. 27.

33. Ibid. 504.

34. Edward R. Guhl to his mother and George, 30 March 1945, 32nd Division, World War II Survey, USAHEC.

35. Smith, *Triumph in the Philippines*, 498; on the Villa Verde Trail battle: ibid., chap. 26, maps 11, 12.

36. Ibid., 499.

37. Ibid., 503, 505. The 126th Regiment, when it joined the battle, had 2,100 effectives.

38. Lt. Colonel Robert Bernucci and Colonel Alert Glass, eds., Medical Department, U.S. Army, *Neuropsychiatry in World War II*, vol. 2, *Overseas Theaters* (Washington, DC: U.S. Government Printing Office, 1973), tables 89 and 96, 1008, 1020.

39. Ibid., 661, 666–667.

40. Ibid., 663, 1002–1003, 1011–1027.

41. Ibid., 659.

42. Monte J. Howell, James W. Deloach, Roland Acheson, Donald R. Dill, Edward Guhl Surveys, in Veterans Surveys, 32nd Division, USAHEC.

43. Smith, *Triumph in the Philippines*, 505–511.

44. Ibid., 525–37.

45. Ibid.; losses: battle, 538–539; nonbattle, 503, 532.

46. William H. Gill Papers, tape 9, box 1, USAHEC.

47. Smith, *Triumph in the Philippines*, 578–579; on the northern encirclement: chap. 29.

48. Ibid., chap. 29.

49. Ibid., table of casualties, 577.

50. "Jolo in Sulu Isles Won by MacArthur," *New York Times*, 11 April 1945, 1; "Big Cebu Victory Won in Philippines," *New York Times*, 21 April 1945; 8; "Philippines' Summer Capital Falls to Americans after Long Battle," *New York Time*, 29 April 1945, 1; "Another Mindanao Airfield Won; Japan's Philippine Loss 369,818," *New York Times*, 21 May 1945, 3.

51. Williamson Murray and Allan R. Millet, *A War to Be Won: Fighting the Second World War* (Cambridge, MA: Harvard University Press, 2000), 502–503.

Chapter 9

1. Samuel Eliot Morison, *Victory in the Pacific, 1945* (*History of United States Naval Operations*, vol. 14) (Boston: Little, Brown, 1960), 129.

2. Roy E. Appleman, James M. Burns, Russell A. Gugeler, and John Stevens, *Okinawa: The Last Battle*, United States Army in World War II, The War in the Pacific (Washington, DC, 1948) (hereafter Appelman), 36.

3. Jeter A. Isley and Peter A. Crowl, *The U.S. Marines and Amphibious Warfare: Its Theory and Its Practice in the Pacific* (Princeton, NJ: Princeton University Press, 1951); *U.S. Marines*, 553.

4. Appleman, *Okinawa*, 144.

5. Ibid., 148; chap. 6.

6. 77th Division Association, *Ours to Hold It High*, 253–254; Morison, *Victory*, 176–177.

7. Appleman, *Okinawa*, 154.

8. Ibid., 175–176.

9. Ibid., 179–180.

10. David Nichols, ed., *Ernie's War: The Best of Ernie Pyle's World War II Dispatches* (New York: Random House, 1986), xi; James Tobin, *Ernie Pyle's War: America's Eyewitness to World War II* (New York: Free Press, 1997), 1–5.

11. Appleman, *Okinawa*, 180–183.

12. Ibid., 233, 235; George Feifer, *Tennozan: The Battle of Okinawa and the Atomic Bomb* (New York: Ticknor and Fields, 1992), 195–229.

13. Commander Edward P. Stafford, USN (Ret.), *Little Ship, Big War: The Saga of DE343* (New York: Morrow, 1984), 230, 234, 239.

14. Morison, *Victory*, 248.

15. Ibid., 262.

16. Ibid., 305.

17. Ibid., 98–99.

18. Ibid., 133, 135.

19. On the picket ship–kamikaze battle: Stafford, *Little Ship, Big War*, 212–265.

20. Ibid., 225.

21. Morison, *Victory*, 181.

22. Ibid., 224.

23. Ibid., 181–191.

24. Ibid., 199–209.

25. Ibid., 102–107, 211–214, 249–250, 264–266.

26. M. Hamlin Cannon, *Leyte: The Return to the Philippines*, United States Army in World War II, The War in the Pacific (Washington, DC, 1954), 26, 365.

27. Appleman, *Okinawa*, 84–85.

28. Ibid., 89, 91.

29. Ibid., 91–92.

30. Ibid., 112.

31. Ibid., 116.

32. Ibid., 113–118.

33. Ibid., 130.

34. Ibid., 130–137.

35. Ibid., 194; Isley and Crowl, *U.S. Marines and Amphibious Warfare*, 557–568.

36. Appleman, *Okinawa*, 196–197.

37. Ibid., 198.

38. Ibid., 230–235.

39. Ibid., 242.

40. Ibid., 238.

41. Ibid., 235–241.

42. Ibid., 211.

43. Ibid., 210, 217, 218.

44. Ibid., 219.

45. Ibid., 238.

46. Ibid., 490.

47. Ibid., 200, 207, 213, 231, 234, 279.

48. Ibid., chap. 4, p. 37.

49. Morison, *Victory*, 233.

50. Appleman, *Okinawa*, 291.

51. Appleman, 276, 279–282.

52. Ibid., 341–342.

53. Ibid., 326, 330.

54. Sixth Marine Division Special Action Report, Phase III, Pt. III, 5, Ike Skelton Combined Arms Research Library Digital Library, http://cgsc.contentdm.oclc .org/cdm/ref/collection/p4013coll8/id/3365, Charles S. Nichols and Henry I. Shaw, Jr., *Okinawa: Victory in the Pacific, Historical Branch, Headquarters, U.S. Marine Corps* ([Washington, DC]: Historical Branch, G-3 Division, Headquarters, U.S. Marine Corps, 1955), 176.

55. Nichols and Henry I. Shaw, Jr., *Okinawa*, 320.

56. Ibid.

57. Ibid., 373.

58. E. B. Sledge, *With the Old Breed at Peleliu and Okinawa* (Novato, CA: Presidio Press, 1981), 251–252.

59. Ibid., 252–253.

60. Appleman, *Okinawa*, 357–359.

61. Ibid, 377.

62. Ibid., 388–392.

63. Ibid., 433–434; Feifer, *Tennozan*, 441–443.

64. Appleman, *Okinawa*, 452, 454.

65. Ibid., 443–447.

66. Ibid., 454.

67. Ibid., 461–474.

68. Robert Ross Smith, *Triumph in the Philippines*, United States Army in World War II, The War in the Pacific (Washington, DC: U.S. Government Printing Office, 1963), 597, 617–619; Joseph E. Zimmer, *The History of the 43rd Infantry Division, 1944–1945* (Nashville: Battery Press, 1945), 82.

Chapter 10

1. "Yanks Invade Okinawa, Cost Very Light; Ruhr Cut Off with 40,000 Nazis in Trap." This was the banner headline in the *Washington Post*, 2 April 1945, 1. The same page also printed a map showing the American landings on Okinawa.

2. The information was under the heading "North Reich Cut Up," which was subsumed under another banner headline linking Okinawa and Germany: "British

Sweep Menaces Foe in Holland; Patton's Tanks 155 Miles from Berlin; American Thrust Cuts Okinawa in Two," *New York Times*, 3 April 1945, 1.

3. "Amazing Walk-In," *New York Times*, 2 April 1945, 1. The banner headline in the *Times* linked the successes in the Pacific and Germany in the same manner as the *Post* reporting "Americans Invade Okinawa in the Ryukyus; Seize Two Airfields; First Resistance Light; 9th and 1st Armies Join, Circling Ruhr."

4. "Fierce Battle Blazes in South on Okinawa"; "Okinawa Fighting Grim in South," *New York Times*, 10 and 12 April 1945, both on p. 1. "Jap Bayonet Charge Drives Yanks off Key Okinawa Hills"; "Real Barrage Helps Force Yanks Back: Artillery Battles on European Scale Seen as Nips Mass Their Most to Date," both in *Washington Post*, April 10 April 1945, 1.

5. Ben W. Gilbert, "Byrnes Sets Slow Let-up for VE-Day," *Washington Post*, 1 April 1945, M1. "Byrnes Report," *Washington Post*, 2 April 1945, 6; "Byrnes Will Quit Mobilization Post," *New York Times*, 3 April 1945, 1.

6. James T. Sparrow, *Warfare State: World War II Americans and the Age of Big Government* (New York: Oxford University Press, 2011), 197–200.

7. "Radio Address Summarizing the State of the Union Message, 6 January 1945," and "The President Reemphasizes the Need for National Service Legislation," 17 January 1945, in *The Public Papers and Addresses of Franklin D. Roosevelt, 1944–45, Victory and the Threshold of Peace*: compiled with special material and explanatory notes by Samuel I. Rosenman (New York: Harper, 1950), 507–517, 517–519; Keith E. Eiler, *Mobilizing America: Robert P. Patterson and the War Effort, 1940–1945* (Ithaca, NY: Cornell University Press, 1997), 417–426.

8. Hadley Cantril, ed., *Public Opinion, 1935–1946*, prepared by Mildred Strunk (Princeton, NJ: Princeton University Press, 1951), 1126; George H. Gallup, *The Gallup Poll: Public Opinion, 1935–1971* (New York: Random House, 1972), I, 487.

9. "Manpower Defeat Is Seen as Certain," *New York Times*, 3 April 1945, 1.

10. "The War Service Fiasco," *New York Times*, 5 April 1945, 21; C. P. Trussell, "Manpower Legislation Remains Up in the Air," *New York Times*, 8 April 1945, 61; Eiler, *Mobilizing America*, 423, Nancy Beck Young, *Why We Fight: Congress and the Politics of World War II* (Lawrence: University Press of Kansas, 2013), 129–131.

11. Sparrow, *Warfare State*, 196–198.

12. Susan Brewer, *Why America Fights: Patriotism and War Propaganda from the Philippines to Iraq* (New York: Oxford University Press, 2009), 117; Mark H. Leff, "The Politics of Sacrifice on the American Home Front in World War II," *Journal of American History* 77, no. 4 (March 1991), 1296–1318, especially 1313; John Morton Blum, *V Was for Victory: Politics and American Culture in World War II* (New York: Harcourt Brace Jovanovich, 1977), 100–101.

13. John Chappell, *Before the Bomb: How American Approached the End of the Pacific War* (Lexington: University Press of Kentucky, 1996), 65; Geoffrey Perret, *Days of Sadness Years of Triumph* (New York: Coward, McCann, and Geohegan, 1972), 390–391; Sue Hart, "Madison Avenue Goes to War: Patriotism in Advertising during World War II," in M. Paul Holsinger and Mary Anne Schofield, eds., *Visions of War: World War II in Popular Literature and Culture* (Bowling Green, OH: Bowling Green State University Popular Press, 1992), 120.

14. Brewer, *Why America Fights*, 117. On the corporate campaign see also Robert Griffith, "Forging America's Postwar Order: Domestic Politics and Political Economy in the Age of Truman," in Michael J. Lacey, ed., *The Truman Presidency* (New York: Cambridge University Press, 1991), 63; Elizabeth A. Fones-Wolf, *Selling Free Enterprise: The Business Assault on Labor and Liberalism, 1945-60* (Urbana: University of Illinois Press, 1995); Perret, *Days of Sadness*, 390-391.

15. Sparrow, *Warfare State*, 193.

16. "New Bedford Order Unchanged," *New York Times*, 22 March 1945, 38; "Most Pleas Fail to WMC in New Bedford," *New York Times*, 25 March 1945, 32; Eiler, *Mobilizing America*, 415-417.

17. Gerald F. Linderman, *The World within War: America's Combat Experience in World War II* (Cambridge, MA: Harvard University Press, 1997), 335-343.

18. Andrew Edmund Kersten, *Labor's Home Front: The American Federation of Labor during World War II* (New York: New York University Press, 2006), 166-171; "The Human Machinery of War: Disability of the Front Lines and Factory Floor, 1941-1945," ehistory, http://ehistory.osu.edu/exhibitions/machinery/index. accessed 19 October 2014. Working and living conditions for war workers are described in Mary Heaton Vorse, "And the Workers Say," *Public Opinion Quarterly* 7, no. 3 (autumn 1943), 443-456. For the rise of juvenile delinquency see Perret, *Days of Sadness*, 346-350. The rigors of life for workers who migrated into the boomtowns and crowded cities are succinctly described in Williamson Murray and Allan R. Millet, *A War to Be Won: Fighting the Second World War* (Cambridge, MA: Harvard University Press, 2000), 545-546.

19. Blum, *V Was for Victory*, 122.

20. Alan Gropman argues that given the industrial base in the United States, American production for the war was something less than the miracle it is often called. Gropman, *Mobilizing Industry in World War II* (Washington, DC: Diane Publishing, 1996), 127-135; Russell F. Weigley, "The American Military and the Principle of Civilian Control of the Military from McClellan to Powell," *Journal of Military History* 57, no. 5 (October 1993), 50.

21. Paul A. C. Koistinen has written the most thorough analysis of mobilization. While he is highly critical of the overall corporate-military relationship in the war, he is particularly scathing in his assessment of the Army's opposition to reconversion. Koistinen, *Arsenal of World War II: The Political Economy of World War II, 1940-1945* (Lawrence: University Press of Kansas, 2004), 498-516. See also William H. Miller, "'P' Was for Plenty," 875-892, and Edward G. Miller, "Generating American Combat Power in World War II," 893-908, both in Thomas W. Zeiler with Daniel DuBois, eds., *A Companion to World War II* (Malden, MA: Wiley-Blackwell, 2013).

22. Lewis L. Gould, *Grand Old Party: A History of the Republicans* (New York: Random House, 2003), 300.

23. "Turn to Right Seen," *New York Times*, 14 April 1945, 1; Marquis Childs, "Washington Calling: Utilizing Advisers," and Arthur Krock, "Influence of Congress is Looming Large Again," *New York Times*, 15 April 1945, E3; Roy Roberts, "Truman to Shelve Person Rule," *New York Times*, 15 April 1945, 6; Barnet Nover, "Closing of the Ranks:

President Truman at the Helm," *Washington Post*, 17 April 1945, 6; Luther Huston, "Truman's Record Shows Practical, Prudent Man," *New York Times*, 15 April 1945, E5. Roy Roberts was managing editor of the *Kansas City Star*.

24. Martin Sherwin, *A World Destroyed: The Atomic Bomb and the Grand Alliance* (New York: Vintage Books, 1977), 150; Robert James Maddox, *Weapons for Victory: The Hiroshima Decision Fifty Years Later* (Columbia: University of Missouri Press, 1995), 24.

25. Address before Joint Session of Congress, 16 April 1945, Public Papers of the Presidents, Harry S. Truman, 1945–1953 (hereafter HST PP), Harry S. Truman Library and Museum, Independence, Missouri, http://www.trumanlibrary.org/publicpapers/index.php?pid=2&st=&st1=.

26. "The President's News Conference," 17 April 1945, HST PP, http://www.truman-library.org/publicpapers/index.php?pid=4&st=&st1=.

27. Ernest Lindley, "Home Front Demands: Truman Stands Firm," *Washington Post*, 20 April 1945, 8.

28. "The Operation of the Army Personnel Readjustment Plan," Hearings before the Committee on Military Affairs, House of Representatives, 79th Congress, 1st session, 19 June 1945, 8–9.

29. Mildred V. Hester, *Occupation Forces in Europe Series, 1945–1946: Redeployment*, Office of the Chief Historian, European Command, Frankfurt-Am-Main, Germany, manuscript history accessed 24 July 2014, Combined Arms Research Library Digital Library, http://cgsc.contentdm.oclc.org/cdm/singleitem/collection/p4013coll8/id/2952/rec/12, 8–11.

30. Ibid., 22.

31. John Hersey, "Reporter at Large: Long Haul with Variables," *New Yorker*, 8 September 1945, 44.

32. The quotations come from Marshall's notes for the speech. "Draft of Speech to the Academy of Political Science," 4 April 1945, in Larry I. Bland and Sharon Ritenour, eds., *The Papers of George Catlett Marshall*, vol. 5, *"The Finest Soldier," January 1, 1945–January 7, 1947* (Baltimore: Johns Hopkins University Press, 2003) (hereafter *GCM*),121.

33. Ibid.

34. Ibid., 122.

35. Marshall to Eisenhower, 14 April 1945, *GCM*, 143.

36. Ibid. Marshall sent the same message to General Joseph McNarney, the commanding general of United States Army forces in the Mediterranean Theater. See Eisenhower to Marshall, 18 April 1945, and Eisenhower to Jacob Devers, 19 April 1945, for Eisenhower's response and subsequent messages to subordinates; *The Papers of Dwight David Eisenhower: The War Years* (Baltimore: Johns Hopkins University Press) (hereafter *DDE*), IV, 2621–2622, 2626–2627, n. 1.

37. Memorandum discussed with the president, 25 April 1945, in William Burr, ed., *The Atomic Bomb and the End of World War II: A Collection of Primary Sources*, National Security Archive Electronic Briefing Book no. 162, http://nsarchive.gwu.edu/NSAEBB/NSAEBB162/.

38. Memorandum for the Secretary of War from General L. R. Groves, "Atomic Fission Bombs," 23 April 1945, in Burr, *Atomic Bomb and the End of World War II.*

39. Eisenhower to Marshall, 27 April 1945, in *DDE,* IV, 2651–2653.

40. The exchanges between Marshall and Eisenhower are summarized in the footnotes for Eisenhower to Marshall, 4 May 1945, in *DDE,* IV, 2678–2679.

41. "Hand to Hand Battle Rages for Kakazu" and "Army Restores Kakazu Ridge Walking Dead," *Washington Post,* 24 April 1945, 1, and 6 May 1945, M2, respectively.

42. "Army Restores Kakazu Ridge Walking Dead," *Washington Post,* 6 May 1945, M2.

43. "Killing of Japs Only Okinawa VE Observance: Warships, Planes Batter Enemy as Yanks Push Ahead," *Washington Post,* 9 May 1945, 1; "Island-Wide Drive," *New York Times,* 8 May 1945, 1, and "All Okinawa Guns Fire V-E Day Salvo," 9 May 1945, 1.

44. Charles Brower, *Defeating Japan: The Joint Chiefs of Staff and Strategy in the Pacific War, 1943–1945* (New York: Palgrave Macmillan, 2012), 103.

45. Ibid., 134.

46. Ibid., 132–135.

47. Grace Person Hayes, *The History of the Joint Chiefs of Staff in World War II* (Annapolis: Naval Institute Press, 1982), 704–706; Richard B. Frank, *Downfall: The End of the Imperial Japanese Empire* (New York: Penguin, 2001), 34–37.

48. Grace Person Hayes believes that the directive was a victory for the Navy, but Michael Pearlman believes that although it fell short of giving MacArthur the authority that Eisenhower had over the Normandy invasion, it nevertheless gave him a "leg up" over Nimitz. Hayes, *Joint Chiefs,* 706–707; Michael Pearlman, *Warmaking and American Democracy: The Struggle over Military Strategy from 1700 to the Present* (Lawrence: University Press of Kansas, 1999), 270.

49. "DOWNFALL Strategic Plan," General Headquarters, U.S. Army Forces in the Pacific, 28 May 1945, copy in U.S. Military History Institute, Carlisle Barracks, Carlisle, Pennsylvania. Detailed discussion of DOWNFALL, including revisions, can be found in D. Clayton James, *The Years of MacArthur,* 2 vols. (Boston: Houghton Mifflin, 1970, 1975), II, 765–773; John Ray Skates, *The Invasion of Japan: Alternative to the Bomb* (Columbia: University of South Carolina Press, 1994); Frank, *Downfall,* 117–130; D. M. Giangreco, *Hell to Pay: Operation Downfall and the Invasion of Japan, 1947–1947* (Annapolis: Naval Institute Press, 2009).

50. In one change, MacArthur requested three infantry divisions in place of the two armored divisions envisioned in the original plan. In another major change, the Tenth Army was dropped from CORONET, and the First Army, which was initially to be used in reserve, assumed the tasks previously assigned to the Tenth.

51. Eisenhower to Marshall, 8 May 1945, in *DDE,* VI, 21–22.

52. Despite these efforts to include enlisted men, the generals received most of the attention as prominent commanders, including Omar Bradley, Courtney Hodges, George Patton, visited their hometowns when they returned in May and June. "General Hodges Takes Atlanta by Storm," *New York Times,* 25 May 1945, 5; "Clark and Fifty Men Feted in Chicago," *New York Times,* 31 May 1945, 7; "Salute to the

Generals, *New York Times*, 10 June 1945, E2; "Topic of the Times," *New York Times*, 12 June 1945, 18.

53. Eisenhower to Bernard Law Montgomery, 15 May 1945, and Eisenhower to Marshall, 18 May 1945, in *DDE*, VI, 49–50, 65–67, respectively.

54. Thomas T. Handy to Eisenhower, 27 May 1945, Eisenhower Correspondence, Pre-Presidential Papers, Dwight D. Eisenhower Library, Abilene, Kansas.

55. Frank, *Downfall*, 124–125.

56. Army Ground Force Study no. 2, box 33, Army Ground Forces File, RG337, Records of Headquarters Army Ground Forces, National Archives (NARA), College Park, Maryland.

57. Hester, *Occupation Forces in Europe Series, 1945–1946*, 49.

58. *Reporting World War II*, 2 pts. (New York: Library of America, 1995), pt. 2, 567.

59. Henry Lewis Stimson, diary entry, 21 February 1945, Diaries of Henry Lewis Stimson, Henry Lewis Stimson Papers, Yale University Library, New Haven, Connecticut (Microfilm); George C. Marshall to Elbert Thomas, 17 April 1945, in *GCM*, 145–147.

60. "Stilwell Answers Critics of Training," *New York Times*, 16 March 1945, 5; C. P. Trussell, "House Likely to Vote Draft Curb on Combat Use," *New York Times*, 26 April 1945, 1.

61. Marshall to Eisenhower, 6 March 1945, in *GCM*, 76–79.

62. Allen Drury, *A Senate Journal, 1943–1945* (New York: McGraw Hill, 1963), 420.

63. Mary Spargo, "Senate Votes Ban on Raw Boys into Draft Act," *Washington Post*, 25 April 1945, 1; C. P. Trussell, "House Likely to Vote Draft Curb on Combat Use," *New York Times*, 26 April 1945, 1; Trussell, "Draft Extension Sent to President, *New York Times*, 28 April 1945, 1.

64. C. P. Trussell, "Army Slash Will Be Slow, General Marshall Cautions," *New York Times*, 5 May 1945, 1.

65. Mary Spargo, "Truman Wins First Skirmish with Congress," *Washington Post*, 4 May 1945, 1; "Truman Approves New Draft Bill, Hits It," *New York Times*, 10 May 1945, 17; Bertram D. Hulen, "Truman Vetoes Farm Deferment," *New York Times*, 4 May 1945, 1; Truman's veto message is in "Amending section 5 (k) of the Selective Training and Service Act of 1940, as amended. Message from the President of the United States transmitting without approval the Joint Resolution (H.J. Res. 106) to amend section 5 (K) of the Selective Training and Service Act of 1940, as amended... May 3, 1945," Serial Set Vol. No. 10969, Session Vol. No. 16 H.Doc. 166, http://docs.newsbank.com.ezp1.villanova.edu/openurl?ctx_ver=z39 .88-2004&rft_id=info:sid/iw.newsbank.com:SERIAL &rft_val_format=info:ofi/ fmt:kev:mtx:ctx&rft_dat=1215CBE5ECF8E4C8&svc_dat=Digital: ssetdoc&req_dat=0E8515E56BD9D19F.

66. "Demobilization, *Washington Post*, 6 May 1945, B4.

67. "Plans of War Department for Redeployment," *Washington Post*, 6 May 1945, 26.

68. "Standing Army of 4,500,000 Being Planned," *Washington Post*, 9 May 1945, 14; "Peacetime Goal Set for 4,500,000 for Army," *New York Times*, 9 May 1945, 20.

69. Marquis Childs, "Demobilization," *Washington Post*, 11 May 1945, 6.

70. Pearson, "Washington Merry-Go-Round," *Washington Post*, 15 May 1945, 5.

71. Mary Spargo, "Army Considers Giving Points to GI Dads for All Children," *Washington Post*, 16 May 1945, 11.

72. Army and Navy," *Time*, 14 May 1945, 34.

73. Ibid., 36.

74. Eiler, *Mobilizing America*, 434.

75. Thomas T. Handy to Eisenhower, 27 May 1945, Eisenhower Correspondence, Pre-Presidential Papers, Dwight D. Eisenhower Library.

76. V-E Day Speech, recorded 4 May 1945, in *DDE*, IV, 2673–2676.

77. "Plans of War Department for Redeployment," *Washington Post*, 11 May 1945, 26; "Army and Navy," *Time*, 14 May 1945, 34.

78. Emphasis in the original. *Kiplinger Washington Letter*, 31 March 1945, 3.
    The War Department surveyed how its policies were represented in the *Kiplinger Washington Letter* and found that reporting had become more critical of the Army in the last six months. The author of the study recommended meeting with the newsletter's reporter to get across the Army's point of view. Major Walter Power to Patterson, 8 March 1945, Public Relations, box 165, Robert P. Patterson Papers, Library of Congress (hereafter RPP, LC), Washington, DC.

79. Memo for the President, 4 May 1945, Presidents Official File, 121B–122, box 687, Truman Papers, Harry S. Truman Library and Museum, Independence, Missouri (hereafter HST).

80. Truman to Vinson, 9 May 1945, Presidents Official File, 121B–122, box 687, Truman Papers, HST.

81. Vinson met with Truman at least six times in between May 7 and May 31; Subject File, box 8, Eben Ayers Papers, HST. The quotation is in Truman diary entry, 17 June 1945, in Robert H. Ferrell, ed., *Off the Record: The Private Papers of Harry S. Truman* (Columbia: University of Missouri Press, 1980), 46.

82. Drew Pearson, "Washington Merry-Go-Round," 14 May 1945, *Washington Post*, 13; "Fred Vinson" (profile), Frank McNaughton Papers, HST.

83. Truman to Vinson, 7 March 1945, Personal and Congratulatory Letters, box 60, Fred M. Vinson Papers (hereafter Vinson Papers), University of Kentucky, Lexington.

84. For press reports of Vinson's report see Walter Waggoner, "What We Face Told," *New York Times*, 10 May 1945, 1, and the text of the nineteen-page report on p. 16 of the same issue. The *Washington Post* led with a more upbeat headline but conveyed the same message of "severe" demands on the home front as the *Times*: Fred Brandeis, "Racing Ban, Curfew End, More Civilian Goods Ahead," 10 May 1945, 1.

85. "Vinson's Report on the Prospects Facing Americans in the Second Phase," *New York Times*, 10 May 1945, 16.

86. Ibid.

87. "CIO Hits at Vinson on Post War Report," *New York Times*, 13 May 1945, 18.

88. Walter Waggoner, "U.S. Industry Begins Shift to Peace Basis," *New York Times*, 13 May 1945, E7; Fred Brandeis, "Labor Asks U.S. to Make Jobs for Aircraft Help," *Washington Post*, 19 May 1945, 6.

89. "How's Business?," *Barron's National Business and Financial Weekly*, 21 May 1945, 1.

90. Julius Hirsch, "The Enigmas of Our Demobilization Plans," *Barron's*, 28 May 1945, 3; Edson Blair and Henley Davenport, "Both Sides of the Curtain: Inside Reports on Latest Developments in National Affairs," *Barron's*, 28 May 1945, 4, 6.

91. Meeting of the Advisory Board, OWMR, 14–15 May 1945, copy in box 153, RPP, LC.

92. An abridged version of Marshall's memo and Somervell's response memorandum for General Marshall is published in Somervell, 15 May 1945, *GCM*, 190–191, and notes 1–3.

93. Ibid.

94. Joint Chiefs of Staff, Minutes of the JCS and Heads of Civilian War Agencies, 22 May 1945, Meetings of the JCS, box 216, Record Group 218, Records of the Combined and Joint Staffs, NARA.

95. Ibid. A summary of the meeting is also in *GCM*, 190–191, n. 2.

96. Joint Chiefs of Staff, Minutes of the JCS and Heads of Civilian War Agencies, 22, 1945 May Meetings of the JCS, box 216, RG 218, NARA.

97. "Testimony before the House War Department Subcommittee," 25 May 1945, *GCM*, 200–204. Marshall's impromptu remarks are contained in n. 1, 204.

98. "House Group Told of Blows at Japan," *New York Times*, 27 May 1945, 4.

99. Quotations in Michael S. Sweeney, *Secrets of Victory: The Office of Censorship and the Press and Radio in World War II* (Chapel Hill: University of North Carolina Press, 2001), 207–209; "Way of the Censor," *Washington Post*, 29 May 1945, 6; Drew Pearson, "Merry-Go-Round," *Washington Post*, 7 June 1945.

100. Eiler, *Mobilizing America*, 433.

101. Truman joked about the length of the message at his press conference that day, telling reporters: "I am releasing a message to the Congress this morning, which will have—[laughter]—a summary on the war. It will be released at noon. Read that summary very carefully. You can't read the message, it's too thick! [Laughter]." The message was approximately 5,700 words, about twenty-two pages typed and double spaced. Partial drafts of the message are in War Messages to Congress, June 1945, Subject File, box 7, Samuel Rosenman Papers, HST. President's News Conference, 1 June 1945, HST PP, http://www.trumanlibrary.org/publicpapers/index.php.

102. "Special Message to the Congress on Winning the War with Japan," 1 June 1945, War Messages to Congress, June 1945, Subject File, box 7, Samuel Rosenman Papers, HST. President's News Conference, 1 June 1945, HST PP, http://www.trumanlibrary.org/publicpapers/index.php.

103. Ibid.

104. Ibid.

105. C. P. Trussell, "Report by Truman," *New York Times*, 2 June 1945, 1; Robert C. Albright, "President Calls for Maintained Production Till Final Victory," *Washington Post*, 2 June 1945, 1; "Writing on the Wall," *Washington Post*, 3 June 1945, B4.

106. *Kiplinger Agricultural Letter*, 5 May 1945.

107. Taft to Herbert Hoover, 23 May 1945, in Clarence Wunderlin, ed., *The Papers of Robert Taft*, vol. 3, *1945–1948* (Kent, OH: Kent State University Press, 2003), 47–48.

108. Republican Senator E. H. Moore of Oklahoma called the Office of Price Administration a "bureaucratic tyranny." "Senators Debate Price Control Law," *New York*

Times, 7 June 1945, 14. See also "Radio Statement at Columbus Town Meeting," 7 June 1945, in Wunderlin, ed., *Papers of Robert Taft, 3, 1945–1948*, 55–56.
109. Drew Pearson, "Merry-Go-Round," *Washington Post*, 7 June 1945, 5.
110. "Youth Draft Foes Call for Delay," *New York Times*, 7 June 1945, 11.
111. Mark Sullivan, "Russian Tangle," *Washington Post*, 4 June 1945, 6; Pearson, "Merry-Go-Round," *Washington Post*, 28 May 1945, 5.
112. "Colonel O'Laughlin, Publisher, Dies," *New York Times*, 15 March 1949, 1; Peter Mauch, *Sailor Diplomat: Nomura Kichisaburo and the Japanese-American War* (Cambridge, MA: Harvard University Press, 2011), 52.
113. O'Laughlin to Herbert Hoover, 9 June 1945, O'Laughlin Correspondence, Herbert Hoover Presidential Library and Museum (hereafter HHL), West Branch, Iowa.
114. Ibid.
115. Marshall to Eisenhower, 16 May 1945, *GCM*, 192–193.
116. O'Laughlin to Herbert Hoover, 9 June 1945, O'Laughlin Correspondence, HHL.
117. Hayes, *Joint Chiefs*, 706.
118. Hester, *Occupation Forces in Europe Series, 1945–1946, 1945–1946*, 50. The likelihood that the critical score would be lowered was discussed in *Kiplinger Washington Letter*, 12 May 1945.
119. Pearson, "Washington Merry-Go-Round," *Washington Post*, 30 April 1945, 5.
120. 91 *Congressional Record* 5842 (1945) Senate—Monday, 11 June 1945, 5842.
121. Ibid.
122. O'Laughlin to Herbert Hoover, 16 June 1945, O'Laughlin Correspondence, HHL.
123. Ibid.; "Denies Marshall Leaving," *New York Times*, 15 June 1945, 5; Stimson Scotches Talk of Marshall Retirement," *Washington Post*, 15 June 1945, 1.

Chapter 11
1. Truman made similar comments to Secretary of the Treasury Henry Morgenthau, entry, 1 June 1945, Presidential Diaries, Henry Morgenthau Papers, Franklin D. Roosevelt Library, Hyde Park, New York (hereafter FDRL); entries for 6, 7 June 1945, Diary of Eben Ayers, Eben A. Ayers Papers, Harry S. Truman Library and Museum (hereafter HST), Independence, Missouri.
2. Mrs. C.J.H. to Martin Agronsky, 17 May 1945, box 3, Correspondence, Martin Agronsky Papers, Manuscripts Division, Library of Congress (hereafter LC), Washington, DC.
3. John Chappell, *Before the Bomb: How American Approached the End of the Pacific War* (Lexington: University of Kentucky Press, 1996), 76.
4. Ibid., 76–78; Nicholas Evan Sarantakes, ed., *Seven Stars: The Okinawa Battle Diaries of Simon Bolivar Buckner, Jr. and Joseph Stilwell* (College Station: Texas A & M Press, 2004), 80–81; Williamson Murray and Allan R. Millet, *A War to Be Won: Fighting the Second World War* (Cambridge, MA: Harvard University Press, 2000), 514–515.
5. Buckner entry, 7 June 1945, in Sarantakes, *Seven Stars*, 75.
6. Ronald H. Spector, *Eagle against the Sun: The American War with Japan* (New York: Free Press, 1985), 539.

7. D. Clayton James, *The Years of MacArthur*, 2 vols. (Boston: Houghton Mifflin, 1970, 1975), II, 732–733.

8. Buckner entry, 7 June 1945, in Sarantakes, *Seven Stars*, 75.

9. "Nimitz Defends Okinawa Campaign," *New York Times*, 17 June 1945, 3; "Forrestal Denies Okinawa Bungling," *New York Times*, 6 June 1945, 3.

10. Letter to the Heads of War Agencies on the Economic Situation in the Liberated Countries of Northwestern Europe, 22 May 1945, Public Papers of Harry S. Truman, http://trumanlibrary.org/publicpapers/index.php?pid=42&st=&st1=.

11. In later years, Truman liked to portray his invitation to Hoover as a courtesy from one president to his predecessor, an unplanned act of friendliness and respect. The documentary record shows otherwise. Hoover went to considerable lengths to wrangle an invitation to the White House on his terms. For his part, Truman hoped his bipartisan gesture would warm a few Republican hearts in Congress. Truman told his staff that he had written Hoover on the spur of the moment. Entry for 24 May 1945, Diary of Eben Ayers, Eben Ayers Papers, HST. Years later he told an interviewer that he had called Hoover when Hoover was in Washington. Robert H. Ferrell recounts that story but also indicates his doubts about its veracity. Ferrell, *Harry S. Truman: A Life* (Columbia: University of Missouri Press, 1994), 194–195, 421 n. 32. For Hoover's desire for a meeting and the preliminary arrangements see Gary Dean Best, *Herbert Hoover: The Post-presidential Years, 1933–1964* (Stanford, CA: Hoover Institution Press, 1983), 266–270.

12. Joan Hoff Wilson, "Herbert Hoover's Plan for Ending the Second World War," *International History Review* 1, no. 1 (January 1979), 84–102.

13. Critics of unconditional surrender often described the doctrine's supporters as seeking vengeance or as animated by "blind prejudice." See Joseph Grew to Secretary of State, 3 January 194[5], in U.S. Department of State, *Foreign Relations of the United States*, vol. 6, *1945* (Washington, DC: U.S. Government Printing Office, 1969) (hereafter *FRUS*), 515–516.

14. Hoff Wilson, "Hoover's Plan for Ending the Second World War," 84–102; Fred M. Vinson to Harry S. Truman, 7 June 1945, enclosing [Herbert Hoover], "Memorandum on Ending the Japanese War," WWII, White House Confidential File, box 43, Harry S. Truman Papers, HST.

15. Ayers, Presidential Staff folder, Eben Ayers Papers, HST.

16. Truman might have also wanted to show the memorandum to James F. Byrnes, a former senate colleague, the previous head of OWMR, and already a close adviser, but Byrnes was home in South Carolina during this period. Byrnes was also the secretary of state in waiting. Diary entry, 17 June 1945, Robert H. Ferrell, ed., *Off the Record: The Private Papers of Harry S. Truman* (Columbia: University of Missouri Press, 1980), 46; David Robertson, *Sly and Able: A Political Biography of James F. Byrnes* (New York: Norton, 1994), 400–403.

17. Vinson to Truman, 7 June 1945, enclosing [Herbert Hoover], "Memorandum on Ending the Japanese War"; Truman to Cordell Hull; Truman to Edward Stettinius, Secretary of State; Truman to Henry Stimson, all 9 June 1945; State Department, WWII, White House Confidential File, box 43, Harry S. Truman Papers, HST. As historian D. M. Giangrecco has argued, Truman's handling of the Hoover memo,

which contained dire casualty projections of 500,000–1,000,000 lives lost, shows that he did not conjure those numbers out of thin air when, after the war, he sought to justify his use of the atomic bombs. D. M. Giangrecco, "A Score of Okinawas: President Truman and Casualty Estimates for the Invasion of Japan,'" *Pacific Historical Review* 72, no. 1 (February 2003), 93–132.

18. General Handy to Stimson, Memorandum, 4 June 1945, copy in item 2840, reel 117, General Staff Papers, George C. Marshall Papers, George Marshall Research Library (hereafter MRL), Lexington, Virginia.

19. Marshall to Stimson, 15 June 1945, transmitting "Memorandum of Comments on 'Ending the Japanese War,'" 14 June 1945, facsimile in William Burr, ed., *The Atomic Bomb and the End of World War II: A Collection of Primary Sources*, National Security Archive Electronic Briefing Book no. 162, http://nsarchive.gwu.edu/NSAEBB/NSAEBB162/18.pdf.

20. Ibid. Stimson drew a vertical line in the margin and penciled a question mark next to the comments about Europe. He drew another vertical line alongside the comments about Suzuki and the liberals and wrote "no" with a "#" above it in the margin.

21. Richard B. Frank, *Downfall: The End of the Imperial Japanese Empire* (New York: Penguin, 2001), 133, and 390–391, note for 133.

22. Joseph Grew to President Truman, 13 June 1945, State Department, WWII, White House Confidential File, box 43, Harry S. Truman Papers, HST.

23. Entry for 18 July 1945, Diary of William D. Leahy, Leahy Papers, LC; and Memorandum, "Size of U.S. Occupation Forces for Japan," 6 July 1945, JCS 13982, ABC 014 Japan (13 Apr 1944), sec. 16-A, RG 165, National Archives (henceforth NARA), College Park, Maryland. On Leahy's conservatism see Martin Weil, *A Pretty Good Club: The Founding Fathers of the U.S. Foreign Service* (New York: Norton, 1978), 122–123, 253–254.

24. Hoover called Roosevelt a madman during a conversation with General MacArthur in May 1946. Haruo Iguchi, "The First Revisionists: Bonner Fellers, Herbert Hoover, and Japan's Decision to Surrender," in Marc Gallicchio, ed., *The Unpredictability of the Past: Memories of the Asia-Pacific War in U.S.-East Asian Relations* (Durham, NC: Duke University Press, 2007), 65.

25. Michael Schaller, *Douglas MacArthur: The Far Eastern General* (New York: Oxford University Press, 1989), 123–124; Marlene Mayo, "American Wartime Planning for Occupied Japan: The Role of Experts," in Robert Wolfe, ed., *Americans as Proconsuls: United States Military Government in Germany and Japan* (Carbondale: Southern Illinois University Press, 1984), 3–52; Frank Ninkovich, "History and Memory in Postwar U.S.-Japanese Relations," in Gallicchio, *Unpredictability of the Past*, 85–120.

26. Hull to Truman, 12 June 1945, folder: State Department. World War II–1945, White House Confidential File, HST.

27. Memorandum of Joseph Grew, 18 June 1945, 740.00119 PW/7-945, RG 59, General Records of the Department of State, NARA.

28. John Ray Skates, *The Invasion of Japan: Alternative to the Bomb* (Columbia: University of South Carolina Press, 1994), 79–82; Frank, *Downfall*, 138–148.

29. Emphasis in original. Entry for 17 June 1945, in Ferrell, *Off the Record,* 46–47.

30. Ibid., 47.

31. Minutes of the Meeting Held at the White House, 18 June 1945, http://nsarchive .gwu.edu/NSAEBB/NSAEBB162/20.pdf.

32. Ibid.

33. Ibid.

34. Frank, *Downfall,* 138–148.

35. Ibid., 138–139; Skates, *Invasion of Japan,* 79–82. Marshall thanked MacArthur for his prompt revision of the casualty estimates, noting that it arrived thirty minutes before the White House meeting. Marshall to MacArthur, 19 June 1945, MacArthur Correspondence, May–July 1945, box 75, Pentagon Office, 1938–1951, George C. Marshall Papers, MRL.

36. King had made a similar argument about the problem of comparing the Navy's island campaigns with campaigns in Europe or the Southwest Pacific. Frank, *Downfall,* 391, note for page 135.

37. All quotes from the meeting are in Minutes of the Meeting Held at the White House, 18 June 1945, http://nsarchive.gwu.edu/NSAEBB/NSAEBB162/20.pdf.

38. Ibid. According to McCloy's recollections, as the meeting was ending Truman asked for his opinion, saying "no one gets out of here without committing himself." McCloy recommended that the United States tell the Japanese that they could keep the emperor provided they surrendered immediately. "I think we ought to have our heads examined," he recalled saying, "if we don't let them keep the emperor." He added that the United States should link that offer to a warning that it would soon have the atomic bomb, which it would use against Japan. There is, however, reason to doubt McCloy's melodramatic account. The minutes show that McCloy had not been silent during the meeting; he had already expressed his views when he supported Stimson's views on seeking a diplomatic alternative to an invasion. McCloy quoted in Marc S. Gallicchio, *The Cold War Begins in Asia: American East Asian Policy and the Fall of the Japanese Empire* (New York: Columbia University Press, 1988), 14.

39. Minutes of the Meeting Held at the White House, 18 June 1945. http://nsarchive .gwu.edu/NSAEBB/NSAEBB162/20.pdf.

40. Frank, *Downfall,* 147.

41. John J. McCloy, interview with Marc S. Gallicchio, 2 August 1984.

42. Minutes of the Meeting Held at the White House, 18 June 1945, in Burr, *Atomic Bomb and the End of World War II,* http://nsarchive.gwu.edu/NSAEBB/ NSAEBB162/20.pdf.

43. Chauncey Saunders, *Redeployment and Demobilization,* USAF Historical Study No. 77, USAF Historical Division, 1953, Air University, Maxwell Air Force Base, http://www.ibiblio.org/hyperwar/AAF/AAFHS/AAFHS-77.pdf, 22, 27–28, accessed 30 April 2015. For further discussion of AAF redeployment see W. F. Craven and J. L. Cate, eds., *The Army Air Forces in World War II,* vol. 7, *Services around the World,* chap. 7, http://www.ibiblio.org/hyperwar/AAF/VII/AAF-VII-17.html, accessed 30 April 2015; D. M. Giangreco, *Hell to Pay: Operation*

Downfall and the Invasion of Japan, 1947-1947 (Annapolis: Naval Institute Press, 2009), 36; Skates, *Invasion of Japan*, 70-72.

44. Saunders, *Redeployment and Demobilization*, 24. During the war, Heller was in the AAF and was a veteran of sixty combat missions as a bombardier on a B-25 in northern Italy.

45. The study was completed in June 1946. Quoted in ibid., 25.

46. MacArthur did not include in his total of 219,000 an additional 30,000 men he expected to lose through readjustment in units not slated for OLYMPIC. Presumably he thought that shortfall could be addressed later. MacArthur to War Department, 16 June 1945, box 56, OPD Incoming Top Secret Messages, RG 165, NARA.

47. Ibid. See also *Reports of General MacArthur: The Campaigns of MacArthur in the Pacific* (Washington, DC: U.S. Government Printing Office, 1966), I, 393-394.

48. The staff officers in Washington reminded MacArthur that officers with eighty-five or more points were exempted from discharge until suitable replacements could be obtained. War Department, Chief of Staff to Commander in Chief Army Forces Pacific, 18 June 1945, box 56, OPD Outgoing Top Secret Messages, RG 165, NARA.

49. Conference between General J. D. Barker (Washington) and Major General Chamberlain (Manila), 19 June 1945, box 56, OPD Outgoing Top Secret Messages, RG 165, NARA.

50. The November 1 D-Day for OLYMPIC meant that less time would be available to use amphibious assault shipping to transport redeploying troops from the West Coast because it would be needed in the invasion sooner than previously expected. Memorandum by the Chief of Staff, Cargo and Personnel required for "OLYMPIC," [11 April 1945], and JCS, Revised Estimate on Personnel Shipping Including Air Transport, 18 May 1945, box 213, RG 218, CCS 381 (2-8-43), sec. 9, NARA.

51. Mildred V. Hester, *Occupation Forces in Europe Series, 1945-1946: Redeployment*, Office of the Chief Historian, European Command, Frankfurt-Am-Main, Germany, manuscript history, accessed 24 July 2014, Combined Arms Research Library Digital Library, http://cgsc.contentdm.oclc.org/cdm/singleitem/collection/p4013coll8/id/2952/rec/12, 59, 73.

52. Robert R. Palmer, Bell I. Wiley, and William R. Keast, *The Procurement and Training of Ground Combat Troops* (Washington, DC: U.S. Government Printing Office, 1948), 639.

53. "Europe's Veterans to Train for Asia," 20 July 1945, *New York Times*, 8; "7,000,000 Troops for Single Blow at Japan Planned, Says Devers," *New York Times*, 27 July 1945, 1.

54. Action Report, 96th Infantry Division, Ryukyu Campaign, 1 April 1945 [28 July 1945], copy in authors' possession.

55. "Ground Training for the Pacific," *Army and Navy Journal*, 21 July 1945, 1415, and "Outlines Pacific Training," *Army and Navy Journal*, 28 July 1945, 1442,

56. The quotation is from the Army's official history, Robert W. Coakley and Richard M. Leighton, *Global Logistics and Strategy, 1943-1945*, United States Army in

World War II, The War Department (Washington, DC: U.S. Government Printing Office, 1968), 564.

57. The first "packets" of 2,000 men did not reach the United States until October. Ibid., 639.

58. ODT and WMC Ask Army Release of 35,000 Skilled Rail Workers, *New York Times*, 23 June 1945, 15.

59. "Train Reservations Cut to Five Days; 4,000 Soldiers to Take Rail Jobs," *New York Times*, 30 June 1945, 19; Veterans Protest Using Day Coaches," *New York Times*, 7 July 1945, 11; Patterson to Col. Johnson, 5 July 1945, and Patterson to Col. Johnson, 9 July 1945, both in Letters vol. 5, box 26, Robert P. Patterson Papers, LC (hereafter RPP, LC).

60. Conference between Colonel D. E. Farr and Colonel G. Bartlett, 13 June 1945, box 56, OPD Outgoing Top Secret Messages, RG 165, NARA.

61. Conference between Colonel Farr and Brig. Gen. Franklin, 2 July 1945, box 56, OPD Outgoing Top Secret Messages, RG 165, NARA.

62. Ibid.

63. Cabbell Phillips, "Rail Travel Crisis Mounts over U.S," *New York Times*, 15 July 1945, 44; Hanson Baldwin, "Kure Strike Goads Foe," *New York Times*, 25 July 1945, 4.

64. Harold Ickes to Robert Patterson, 2 July 1945; Patterson to Ickes, 13 July 1945, box 165, RPP, LC; Keith E. Eiler, *Mobilizing America: Robert P. Patterson and the War Effort, 1940–1945* (Ithaca, NY: Cornell University Press, 1997), 434–435.

65. Eiler, *Mobilizing America*, 433 n.

66. For example "Speech before the Advisory Board of Office of War Mobilization and Reconversion," 12 June 1945, OWMR, box 153; Patterson to Chief of Staff, "War Department Conference," 23 April 1945, box 167; and materials in Public Relations folder, in box 165, all in RPP, LC.

67. Harold Ickes, diary entry for 21 July 1945, folder 21, July–26 August 1945, Papers of Harold Ickes, LC.

68. Frank McNaughton to Jack Beal, 28 June 1945, biographical sketch of Fred Vinson, Reports, June 1945, box 9, Frank McNaughton Papers, HST; H. G. Nicholas, ed., *Washington Despatches: Weekly Reports from the British Embassy* (Chicago: University of Chicago Press, 1981), 538.

69. Paul A. C. Koistinen, *Arsenal of World War II: The Political Economy of World War II, 1940–1945* (Lawrence: University Press of Kansas, 2004), 489.

70. Alonzo Hamby, *Man of the People: A Life of Harry S. Truman* (New York: Oxford University Press, 1995), 259, 273.

71. John Morton Blum, ed., *The Price of Vision: The Diary of Henry A. Wallace, 1942–1946* (Boston: Houghton Mifflin, 1973), 457–458.

72. W. R. Davlin, Executive Secretary, Advisory Board, to Joseph Livingston, OWMR, submitting Quarterly Report, 16 June 1945, Director's Office file, box 170, OWMR, RG 250, Records of the Office of War Mobilization and Reconversion, NARA.

73. Robert Nathan to Vinson, 1 June 1945, box 118, OWMR, RG 250, NARA.

74. A week later, one of Vinson's staff members reported that the Navy was releasing 500,000 raincoats it had purchased but would not need. Noting that the Navy

had 3,500,000 personnel, this action showed that the Navy's estimating process was highly ineffective. The report also complained that the Army and Navy were duplicating purchases of textiles and storing them for later use when the materials could be better used by civilians. J. Anthony Panuch to Vinson, 16 June 1945, and William Lawrence to Donald Russell, 22 June 1945, both in Vinson folder, box 118, OWMR, RG 250, NARA.

75. William Haber to Vinson, 11 June 1945, Vinson file, box 118, OWMR, RG 250, NARA.

76. Advisory Board Meeting, 11–12 June 1945, Stenographer's transcriptions, box 391, OWMR, RG 250, NARA; Robert Patterson, Outline of Speech before Advisory Board, 11 June 1945, OWMR, OWMR file, box 153, RPP, LC.

77. Fred Searles, Jr., to Vinson, 23 May 1945, Vinson folder, box 117, OWMR Central Files, RG250, NARA.

78. Patterson to Wadsworth, 4 June 1945, Letters, vol. 5, RPP, LC.

79. Patterson to Herbert Bayard Swope, 1 August 1945, Letters, vol. 5, RPP, LC.

80. Nathan to Vinson, 20 June 1945, Vinson folder, box 118, RG 250, OWMR, NARA.

81. Summaries of these requests are in Official File 88–90, box 538, Harry S. Truman Papers, HST.

82. William F. Schneider, Notes on Redeployment, 27 June 1945, Vinson folder, box 118, OWMR, RG 250, NARA.

83. Another poll taken in early August 1945 showed that GIs would have opposed the release of soldiers on the basis of special categories such as job skills if it meant they would have to serve longer. S. A. Stouffer et al., *The American Soldier.*, vol. 2, *Combat and Its Aftermath* (New York: Wiley, 1965), 541.

84. William L. O'Neill, *A Democracy at War: America's Fight at Home and Abroad in World War II* (New York: Free Press, 1993), 14–15, 132–133, 142.

85. The Gallup Organization asked the following question: "Would you be willing to continue to put up with present shortages of butter, sugar, meat, and other rationed food products in order to give food to people who need it in Europe?" Eighty-five percent of the 1,500 respondents answered yes. A second question asked if consumers would be willing to "eat about one-fifth less than you are now eating in order to send more food to Europe?" This time 70 percent of the respondents answered yes. The poll was conducted from May 18 to 23, 1945 (accessed through Roper Opinion online).

86. Buell wrote that American civilians ate 100 pounds of meat a year, but according to historian Meg Jacobs, consumption increased during the war from 127 pounds per capita to 150. Raymond Buell to Messrs. Billings, Gottfried, et al., "The Food Situation and Western Europe," 23 June 1945, Buell folder, Time Inc., box 523, Henry Luce Papers, LC; Meg Jacobs, "How About Some Meat?," *Journal of American History* 84, no. 3 (December 1997), 932.

87. Only 56 percent of respondents correctly named the emperor, 5 percent identified Tojo as the monarch, and other answers included Hara Kiri, Yokohama, and Fujiyama. Gallup, *Public Opinion, 1935–1971* survey 348, 511–512.

88. Hadley Cantril, ed., *Public Opinion, 1935–1946* (Princeton, NJ: Princeton University Press, 1951), Poll no. 88, 27 June 1945, 1185.

89. *Fortune* poll cited in Bell, "War Weariness," 3; Poll no. 87, 27 June 1945, in Cantril, *Public Opinion, 1935–1946*, 1185.

90. "The American Soldier in World War II: Reactions to the Enemy and Further Duty," survey directed by Dr. Samuel A. Stouffer for the Research Branch, Information and Education Division, War Department, June 1945. In a related question, the same soldiers were asked how they felt about their service in the war; 1,317 said they had done their part and should be discharged.

91. Ibid.

92. Polls for 26 May, 8 June, and 27 June, in Gallup, *Public Opinion, 1935–1971*, 506, 508, 511.

93. "OPA Bill Is Passed in Time, Flown to Truman to Sign," *New York Times*, 1 July 1945, 1; Notes on Cabinet Meeting, 6 July 1945, Letters, vol. 5, box 26, RPP, LC; Henry A. Wallace, entry for 6 July 1945, in Blum, *Price of Vision*, 465–466.

Chapter 12

1. D. M. Giangreco, *Hell to Pay: Operation Downfall and the Invasion of Japan, 1945–1947* (Annapolis: Naval Institute Press, 2009), 1–3.

2. "86th Division Here on Way to Pacific," *New York Times*, 18 June 1945 1; "1,463 of 97th Steam up Hudson," *New York Times*, 24 June 1945, 5.

3. Memorandum of conversation with General Marshall and the Secretary of War, 29 May 1945, John Jay McCloy Papers, Amherst College Library, Amherst, Massachusetts.

4. Memo to Files, 14 June 1945 [Marshall's views], and Kokura Arsenal, 2 July 1945, both in Documents from General Groves Locked box, in *Correspondence Top Secret of the Manhattan Engineering District, 1942–1946*, National Archives Microfilm Publication M1109, reel 3, RG 77, Records of the Office of Chiefs of Engineers, National Archives (hereafter NARA), College Park, Maryland.

5. State-War-Navy Meeting, 19 June 1945, in Walter Millis, ed., *The Forrestal Diaries* (New York: Viking Press, 1951), 69.

6. Minutes of the Meeting Held at the White House, 18 June 1945, in William Burr, ed., *The Atomic Bomb and the End of World War II: A Collection of Primary Sources*, National Security Archive Electronic Briefing Book no. 162, http://nsarchive.gwu.edu/NSAEBB/NSAEBB162/20.pdf.

7. Emphasis added. Entry for 26–30 June 1945, Diaries of Henry Lewis Stimson, Henry Lewis Stimson Papers, Yale University Library, New Haven, Connecticut (Microfilm).

8. Entry for 26 June 1945, in Millis, *Forrestal Diaries*, 71–72.

9. Entry for 26–30 June 1945, Diaries of Henry Lewis Stimson, Henry Lewis Stimson Papers, Yale University Library, New Haven, Connecticut (Microfilm).

10. Stimson to the President, 2 July 1945, ABC 387 Japan (15 Feb 45), Sec 1-B, RG 165, NARA.

11. Memorandum for the President, Proposed Program for Japan, 2 July 1945, ABC 387 Japan (15 Feb 45), Sec 1-B, RG 165, NARA.

12. Ibid.

13. Proclamation by the Heads of State, Draft of 1 July 1945, ABC 387 Japan (15 Feb 45), Sec 1-B, RG 165, NARA.

14. Entry for 2 July 1945, ABC 387 Japan (15 Feb 45), Sec 1-B, RG 165, NARA .

15. Entry for 3 July 1945, ABC 387 Japan (15 Feb 45), Sec 1-B, RG 165, NARA.

16. Brian Loring Villa, "The U.S. Army, Unconditional Surrender, and the Potsdam Proclamation," *Journal of American History* 63 (June 1976), 70. On the background and meaning of unconditional surrender see Robert James Maddox, *Weapons for Victory: The Hiroshima Decision Fifty Years Later* (Columbia: University of Missouri Press, 1995), 6–19.

17. Marlene Mayo, "American Wartime Planning for Occupied Japan: The Role of Experts," in Robert Wolfe, ed., *Americans as Proconsuls: United States Military Government in Germany and Japan* (Carbondale: Southern Illinois University Press, 1984), 3–52; Villa, "Unconditional Surrender," *passim*.

18. Robert Taft, "Radio Statement at Columbus Town Meeting," 7 June 1945, in Clarence E. Wunderlin, Jr. ed., *The Papers of Robert A. Taft*, vol. 3, 1945–1948 (Kent, OH: Kent State University Press, 2003), 55–57.

19. Admiral Charles Cooke to Admiral King, 4 April 1945, Charles M. Cooke Papers, Hoover Institute on War Revolution and Peace, Stanford, CA.

20. Waldo Heinrichs, *American Ambassador: Joseph C. Grew and the Development of American Diplomatic Tradition* (reprint, New York: Oxford University Press, 1986), 374–375; Marc S. Gallicchio, *The Cold War Begins in Asia: American East Asian Policy and the Fall of the Japanese Empire* (New York: Columbia University Press, 1988), 6–10.

21. Stimson continued to council cooperation with Stalin at least until the war was over. Mark Stoler, *Allies and Adversaries: The Joint Chiefs of Staff, The Grand Alliance, and U.S. Strategy in World War II* (Chapel Hill: University of North Carolina Press, 2000), 246–247.

22. Grew mentioned Russian specialist and interpreter Charles Bohlen in this connection. Entry for 6 July 1945, in Millis, *Forrestal Diaries*, 73.

23. David McLellan and David Acheson, *Among Friends: Personal Letters of Dean Acheson* (New York: Dodd, Mead, 1980), 55; Martin Weil, *A Pretty Good Club: The Founding Fathers of the U.S. Foreign Service* (New York: Norton, 1978), 213; Mayo, "Wartime Planning for Occupied Japan," 42–44.

24. McLeish to Byrnes, 6 July 1945, U.S. Department of State, *Foreign Relations of the United States* (hereafter *FRUS*), vol. 1, *Berlin* (Washington, DC: U.S. Government Printing Office, 1960), 903–910, 895–897.

25. Arthur Krock, "Our Policy toward the Emperor of Japan," *New York Times*, 5 July 1945, 12.

26. Heinrichs, *American Ambassador*, 377. Hull's message was conveyed in Grew to Byrnes, 16 July 1945, Papers of Joseph Grew, Harvard University Library, Cambridge, Massachusetts. Earlier, as we have noted, Hull had referred to Hoover's memo on ending the war as an "appeasement proposal." Hull to Truman, 12 June 1945, State Department, World War II, White House Confidential File, Harry S. Truman Library and Museum (hereafter HST), Independence, Missouri.

27. Several days after his White House visit, Hoover had met with nine Republican senators at the home of William R. Castle, formerly Hoover's undersecretary of state and, briefly, ambassador to Japan. According to Castle, Hoover's advocacy

of a negotiated settlement with Japan was well received by the senators. Shortly afterward, Castle discussed the matter with Hugh Wilson. William R. Castle to Herbert Hoover, 2 June 1945, Herbert Hoover Papers, Post-Presidential Individual Files, Herbert Hoover Presidential Library and Museum, West Branch, Iowa.

28. Truman's response to the story is in Frank McNaughton to Jack Beal, 7 July 1945, Frank McNaughton Papers, HST. McNaughton was a correspondent for *Time*. "Grew Flatly Denies Japan Seeks Peace," *New York Times*, 30 June 1945, 3.

29. "White Urges Truman to Give Terms to Tokyo," *New York Times*, 3 July 1945, 3.

30. Frank McNaughton to Jack Beal, "Jap Peace Offers," 7 July 1945, box 9, Frank McNaughton Papers, HST.

31. "Big Three Asked to Tell Foe Price of Peace," *New York Times*, 13 July 1945, 3.

32. "Power v. Statesmanship," *Time*, 16 July 1945, 15.

33. Luce worried about Soviet encroachment in Asia if the war continued. He recommended making a concession on the emperor. He expected a demilitarized Japan to regain entry into the family of nations and access to Southeast Asian markets. Robert Edwin Herzstein, *Henry R. Luce, Time, and the American Crusade in Asia* (New York: Cambridge University Press, 2005), 48–50.

34. The editorial gained wider circulation when it was reported in "Japan Warned to Give Up Soon," *New York Times*, 22 July 1945, 1.

35. Mayo, "Wartime Planning for Japan," 50.

36. "Japanese Expect Concessions," *New York Times*, 22 July 1945, 4.

37. Frank McNaughton to Don Bermingham, "Reciprocal Trade—Bretton Woods," June 8, 1945, box 9, Frank McNaughton Papers, HST.

38. This summary is drawn from the following letters to and from Senator Alexander Wiley (R-Wisconsin). Wiley, who attended Hoover's meeting at Castle's home, favored a statement clarifying unconditional surrender. F. M. Rosekrans to Wiley, 16 June 1945, and Wiley to Rosekrans, 22 June 1945; George Washington Robnett to Wiley, 22 June 1945; Verne Kaub to Louis Muharsky, cc Wiley, 9 June 1945; Wiley to Emil Tehl, 6 June 1945; K. M. Haugen to Wiley, 29 June 1945, and Wiley to Haugen, 2 July 1945; Mark Catlin to Wiley, 12 July 1945, and Wiley to Catlin, 16 July 1945; all in boxes 3 and 20, Personal Correspondence, Papers of Alexander Wiley, Wisconsin Historical Society, Madison.

39. Quotation marks are in the original letter. Russell A. Robinson to President Harry Truman, 22 May 1945, box 800, Official File 190-Misc. 1945, HST; Unconditional Surrender File, Letters Referred to the Department of State, 14 June–2 August 1945, General File, HST.

40. For a representative sample and thoughtful discussion of these citizen comments see John Chappell, *Before the Bomb: How Americans Approached the End of the Pacific War* (Lexington: University Press of Kentucky, 1996), 116–131.

41. JCS and Heads of Civilian War Agencies, 26 June 1945, CCS 334 (2-2-45), Joint Chiefs of Staff Papers, RG 218, Combined Chiefs of Staff, NARA.

42. Quoted in Chappell, *Before the Bomb*, 124.

43. Williamson Murray and Allan R. Millet, *A War to Be Won: Fighting the Second World War* (Cambridge, MA: Harvard University Press, 2000), 520–521.

44. Barnet Nover, "Tightening the Vise," *Washington Post*, 3 July 1945, 6.

45. Edward J. Drea, *MacArthur's ULTRA and the War against Japan, 1942–1945* (Lawrence: University Press of Kansas, 1992), xiii–xiv; Richard B. Frank, *Downfall: The End of the Imperial Japanese Empire* (New York: Penguin, 1999), 103–105.

46. "Fatal Phrase," *Washington Post*, 11 June 1945, 6; Gallicchio, *Cold War Begins*, 49–52; Frank, *Downfall*, 113–116.

47. Summary of message 11 July 1945, MAGIC Diplomatic Summaries, Intercepted Japanese Messages (reel 14), RG 457, Records of the National Security Agency/ Central Security Service, NARA.

48. Summary of message, 22 July 1945, in Japanese Navy Orders Berne Official to Withdraw from Peace Negotiations, 28 July 1945, MAGIC Diplomatic Summaries, Intercepted Japanese Messages (reel 14), RG 457, Records of the National Security Agency/Central Security Service, NARA.

49. Japanese in Switzerland Argue for Peace, 27 July 1945, box 18, RG 457, MAGIC Diplomatic Summaries, Intercepted Japanese Messages (reel 14), RG 457, Records of the National Security Agency/Central Security Service, NARA.

50. Continued Japanese Interest in Peace, 26 July 1945, MAGIC Diplomatic Summaries, Intercepted Japanese Messages (reel 14), RG 457, Records of the National Security Agency/Central Security Service, NARA.

51. The American, Allen Dulles, was working for the Office of Strategic Services. His statements about the Soviet Union were not authorized by his superiors in Washington. Gallicchio, *Cold War Begins*, 50.

52. Japanese Peace Move, 12 July 1945, and Follow-Up Message on Japanese Peace Move, 13 July 1945, both in MAGIC Diplomatic Summary, in Burr, *Atomic Bomb and the End of World War II*, http://nsarchive.gwu.edu/NSAEBB/NSAEBB 162/29.pdf.

53. Frank, *Downfall*, 225–227; Ronald Lewin, *The American MAGIC: Codes, Cyphers and the Defeat of Japan* (New York: Farrar, Straus and Giroux, 1982), 280–282.

54. The memorandum contains a message intended for Marshall. Memorandum for the Deputy Chief of Staff, Japanese Peace Offer, 13 July 1945, Burr, *Atomic Bomb and the End of World War II*, http://nsarchive.gwu.edu/NSAEBB/NSAEBB 162/30.pdf.

55. Owing to the time differences, Marshall probably received the message on July 23. The next day he informed British and Russian military leaders that an estimated 500,000 troops were on Kyushu. General H. A. Craig to Marshall, July 22, 1945, item 2190, reel 117, General Staff Papers, George C. Marshall Papers, George Marshall Research Library (hereafter MRL), Lexington, Virginia; Maddox, *Weapons for Victory: The Hiroshima Decision Fifty Years Later*, 118.

56. Tripartite Military Meeting, 24 July 1945, in FRUS, vol. 2, *The Conference of Berlin (Potsdam) (1945)* (1960), 346.

57. The buildup is expertly explained in Drea, *MacArthur's ULTRA*, 206–221. See also Frank, *Downfall*, 198–211, especially for discrepancies between MacArthur's and the Navy's analyses and estimates.

58. Drea, *MacArthur's ULTRA*, 213.

59. At first, the Japanese feared a direct assault on Honshu because they overestimated the speed with which the United States would be able to redeploy divisions from Europe. Once they recognized their error, Japanese planners predicted that the first

assault would come against Kyushu; John Ray Skates, *The Invasion of Japan: Alternative to the Bomb* (Columbia: University of South Carolina Press, 1994), 103; Drea, *MacArthur's ULTRA*, 203; Takushiro Hattori, *The Complete History of the Greater East Asia War* ([Tokyo?]: [Headquarters, United States Army Forces Far East], [1953–54], 176.

60. Hattori, *Greater East Asia War*, 289.

61. Ibid., 297.

62. Report of Imperial Headquarters Army Department, [1 July 1945], in *Defense of the Homeland and End of the War*, vol. 12, Donald Detwiler and Charles Burdick, eds., *War in Asia and the Pacific: A Fifteen Volume Collection* (New York: Garland, 1980); this is the Japanese official history written under the supervision of the American Military Intelligence Section following the end of the war.

63. This group excluded other staff officers from attending meetings. The subordinate officers in the Army staff were known to be especially adamant about fighting a climactic battle in the home islands. Tsuyoshi Hasegawa, *Racing the Enemy: Stalin, Truman, and the Surrender of Japan* (Cambridge, MA: Harvard University Press, 2005), 72.

64. Hasegawa, *Racing the Enemy*, 72–73; No. 1208–16 July 1945, SRS-1730; and "Tokyo Says No Unconditional Surrender," 17 July 1945, SRS-1732, MAGIC Diplomatic Summaries, Intercepted Japanese Messages (reel 14), RG 457, Records of the National Security Agency/Central Security Service, NARA.

65. 6th Infantry Division, After Action Report, Final Phase of the Luzon Campaign, 1 July–21 August 1945, 41, Ike Skelton Combined Arms Research Library Digital Library, http://cgsc.contentdm.oclc.org/cdm/ref/collection/p4013coll8/id/3365.

66. Harold Whittle Blakely, *The 32d Infantry Division in World War II. Blakeley* ([Madison, WI: Thirty Second Infantry Division History Commission, 1957), 257–276, https://babel.hathitrust.org/cgi/pt?id=mdp.39015015377172;view=1 up;seq=13

67. "Yanks Capture 3 Jap Holdouts in North Luzon," *Washington Post*, 15 July 1945, M4; "4879 More Jap Dead," *Washington Post*, 16 July 1945, 2. The latter was a small notice of about one column inch.

68. Sheldon Menefee, "Pacific Affairs: Japan's Staying Power," *Washington Post*, 10 June 1945, 28; Barnet Nover, "Tightening the Vise," *Washington Post*, 3 July 1945, 6; "Kenney Sees Little Fight on Japan Beaches," *Washington Post*, 26 July 1945, 5; "U.S. at War," *Time*, 16 July 1945; "Japanese Jitters," *New York Times*, 13 July 1945, 8; "Patterson Sees Japan 'Formidable to Finish,'" *New York Times*, 14 July 1945, 2; "At Japan's Homeland/Threefold Halsey's Strikes/Gathering Forces Isolating the Foe/Tension in Tokyo/Discussions in Washington/Question of the Cabinet," *New York Times*, 22 July 1945, 59.

69. *Kiplinger Washington Letter*, 23 June 1945.

70. "Army Will Reduce Discharge Points Soon, but Men with Surplus Say They Are Held," *New York Times*, 23 July 1945, 11.

71. Patterson to Deputy Chief of Staff, 24 July 1945; GI to Walter Winchell, 12 July 1945, Demobilization, box 129, Robert P. Patterson Papers, Library of Congress (hereafter RPP, LC), Washington, DC.

72. Commander in Chief Army Forces Pacific to War Department, 28 July 1945, box 39, OPD Top Secret Incoming Messages, RG 165, NARA.

73. Commander in Chief Army Forces Pacific to War Department, 2 July 1945, box 39, OPD Top Secret Incoming Messages, RG 165, NARA.

74. Handy to MacArthur, 29 July 1945, box 57, OPD Top Secret Outgoing Messages, RG 165, NARA.

75. Commander in Chief Army Forces Pacific to War Department, 31 July 1945, box 39, OPD Top Secret Incoming Messages, RG 165, NARA.

76. "War Department Demobilization Plans," 2 August 1945, Demobilization after Defeat of Germany, box 129, RPP, LC; "Stimson Refuses Speedier Release," *New York Times*, 4 August 1945, 1.

77. Mary Spargo, "Senate Unit Acts to Provide Badly Needed Rail Workers," *Washington Post*, 25 July 1945, 1.

78. "Stimson Refuses Speedier Release," *New York Times*, 4 August 1945, 1.

79. The results of the poll were first reported in General Council Meeting, 23 July 1945, item 2397, reel 84, MRL. Patterson conveyed the results to Stimson while Stimson was at Potsdam; Patterson to Stimson, 27 July 1945, Letters vol. 5, box 26, RPP, LC.

80. Patterson to Secretary of War, 3 August 1945, and Patterson to General Robert E. Wood, 13 August 1945, both in Letters vol. 5, box 26, RPP, LC.

81. General Council Meeting, Office of the Deputy Chief of Staff, 30 July 1945, item 2397, reel 84, MRL.

82. Quotations in C. P. Trussell, "Mead Threatens to Take Dispute over Rail Jam to President, *New York Times*, 28 July 1945, 1; Mary Spargo, "Senate Unit Threatens to Send Rail Problem to White House, *Washington Post*, 28 July 1945, 1.

83. Charles Wardlow, *The Transportation Corps: Movements, Training, and Supply*, United States Army in World War II, The Technical Services (Washington, DC: U.S. Government Printing Office, 1990), 193.

84. Spargo, "Senate Unit Threatens," *Washington Post*, 28 July 1945, 1.

85. Memorandum on Redeployment, [c. July 5, 1945], ABC 320.2 (3-13-43), sec. 10, OPD box 162, RG 165, NARA.

86. The message was sent out over Somervell's name; Somervell to MacArthur, 18 July 1945, OP DTS incoming and Outgoing Messages, box 57, RG 165, NARA.

87. Craig to Hull, 24 July 1945, OP DTS incoming and Outgoing Messages, box 57, RG 165, NARA.

88. Hull to MacArthur, 21 July 1945, OP DTS incoming and Outgoing Messages, box 57, RG 165, NARA.

89. Memorandum for the Deputy Chief of Staff, Army Air Force Plan for Increasing Pacific Troop Lift, 4 August 1945, Directive from the Chief of Staff, 7 August 1945, and Directive from the Chief of Staff, August 8, 1945, all in ABC 320.2 (3-13-43), sec. 10, OPD box 162, RG 165, NARA.

90. Memorandum for Admiral King, with proposed message to MacArthur and Nimitz enclosed, 6 July 1945, OPD 320.2 TS Sec IV (10 Jul 45), in item 2812, reel 117, MRL.

91. Memorandum for General Marshall, July 10, 1945, OPD 320.2 TS Sec IV (10 Jul 45), in item 2812, reel 117, MRL.

92. Brower, *Defeating Japan*, 131.
93. Memorandum for the Chief of Staff by Brehon Somervell, re: Logistic Support of Pacific Forces, n.d., item 3327, reel 127, and George A. Lincoln to John E. Hull, July 10, 1945, item 2776, reel 117, both in MRL.
94. Robert H. Ferrell, ed., *Dear Bess: The Letters from Harry to Bess Truman, 1910–1959* (New York: Norton, 1983), 519.
95. Gallicchio, *Cold War Begins*, 17.
96. Ibid., 48.
97. Matthias Correa to James Forrestal, 4 July 1945, and Admiral King to JCS, 6 July 1945, both in file 331-21, box 65, Forrestal-Secretary of the Navy, RG80 (General Correspondence of the Secretary of the Navy), Old Army and Navy Branch, NARA.
98. Military Aspects of Unconditional Surrender Formula, JCS 1275/6, 19 July 1945, w/enclosure ABC 387 Japan (15 Feb 45), sec. 1-B, RG 165, MMRB, NA.
99. Memorandum for General Handy from General Craig, 14 July 1945, sec. 1-B, RG 165, MMRB, NA.
100. Minutes of Meeting of the JCS, 17 July 1945, in *FRUS*, vol. 2, *Conference of Berlin (Potsdam), 1945* (1960), 39–40.
101. Gallicchio, *Cold War Begins*, 56.
102. Memorandum for the President, 18 July 1945, in *FRUS*, vol. 2, *Conference of Berlin (Potsdam), 1945* (1960), 1268–1269.
103. Richard Frank explains how the process of informing Truman might have worked. Frank, *Downfall*, 241. See also Barton J. Bernstein, "The Alarming Japanese Buildup on Southern Kyushu, Growing U.S. Fears, and Counterfactual Analysis: Would the Planned November 1945 Invasion of Southern Kyushu Have Occurred?," *Pacific Historical Review* 68, no. 4 (November 1999), 576 n. 24.
104. Maddox, *Weapons for Victory*, 92–93; Robert J. Donovan, *Conflict and Crisis: The Presidency of Harry S. Truman, 1945–1948* (New York: Norton, 1977), 92.
105. Entry, 18 July 1945, in Robert H. Ferrell, ed., *Off the Record: The Private Papers of Harry S. Truman* (Columbia: University of Missouri Press, 1980), 53–54.
106. All quotes in this section from Vinson to Truman, 19 July 1945, Naval Aide to President, 1945–1953, Berlin Conference, Communications from the Map Room, 15–25 July, box 6, Harry S. Truman Papers, HST.
107. Truman thought so highly of Vinson that he was originally supposed to travel with the president to Potsdam. At the last minute, however, Truman changed his mind and asked Vinson to stay behind so he could be sworn in as secretary of the treasury while the president was out of the country. Truman was worried that if any calamity should befall him and Secretary of State Byrnes, who was next in the line of succession, there being no vice president, then outgoing secretary of the treasury, Henry Morgenthau, would become president. Truman disliked and mistrusted Morgenthau and felt it absolutely necessary to have Vinson in the line of succession for president. Entries for 14 and 21 July 1945, folder 1 July–26 August 1945, Diary of Harold Ickes, Harold Ickes Papers, LC; "The President on His Way," *Time*, 16 July 1945. On Snyder see Alonzo Hamby, *Man of the People: A Life of Harry S. Truman* (New York: Oxford University Press, 1995), 90–91.

108. Vinson to Truman, 20 July 1945, Naval Aide to President, 1945–1953, Berlin Conference, Communications from the Map Room, 15–25 July, box 6, Harry S. Truman Papers, HST.

109. "Patterson Defends Discharge System," *New York Times*, 20 July 1945, 10.

110. Memorandum for the President, [20 July 1945], Correspondence with the President, 1945, Political File, 1945–1946, box 139, Fred M. Vinson Papers, HST.

111. Truman's reply is quoted in a cross-reference file that records action on presidential correspondence. Vinson, Hon. Fred M., Official File 122 (1945), HST.

112. Martin Sherwin, *A World Destroyed: The Atomic Bomb and the Grand Alliance* (New York: Vintage Books, 1977), 223.

113. Entry for 21 July 1945, Diaries of Henry Lewis Stimson, Henry Lewis Stimson Papers, Yale University Library, New Haven, Connecticut (Microfilm).

114. Entry for 23 July 1945, Diaries of Henry Lewis Stimson, Henry Lewis Stimson Papers, Yale University Library.

115. Entry for 24 July 1945, Diaries of Henry Lewis Stimson, Henry Lewis Stimson Papers, Yale University Library.

116. Reports from witnesses vary as to what specifically Truman said to Stalin. Hasegawa, *Racing the Enemy*, 154; Maddox, *Weapons for Victory*, 99; Donovan, *Conflict and Crisis*, 93.

117. All quotations in this passage are from the entry for 25 July 1945, in Ferrell, *Off the Record*, 55–56. The president's log for the Potsdam trip states that Truman met with Mountbatten at 9:20 a.m. and that Marshall called on the president at 10:00 a.m. Entry for 25 July 1945, Log of the President's Trip to the Berlin Conference, 6 July–7 August 1945, Harry S. Truman Library and Museum, http://www.truman-library.org/calendar/travel_log/documents/index.php?documentdate=1945-07-25&groupid=1281&documentid=17&studycollectionID=TL&pagenumber=62&nav=ok.

118. Frank, *Downfall*, 243; Maddox, *Weapons for Victory*, 118.

119. Philip Ziegler, ed., *Personal Diary of Admiral the Lord Louis Mountbatten: Supreme Allied Commander, South-East Asia, 1943–1946* (London: Collins, 1988), 230.

120. Mountbatten records that Churchill said that the bomb would be dropped on August 5 and Japan would surrender on August 15. Historians Barton Bernstein and Richard Frank agree that the accuracy of Churchill's prediction that Japan would surrender on August 15 was so uncanny as to lead one to wonder if Mountbatten's editor supplied that date when he was preparing the diaries for publication. No one else who knew about the bomb dared try to fix a specific date to Japan's surrender. Instead, they spoke more generally in terms of the next few weeks. Frank, *Downfall*, 414, 244 n.; Ziegler, *Mountbatten Diary*, 231.

121. Ziegler, *Mountbatten Diary*, 232.

122. "Status of Demobilization Plans to Meet an Early Defeat of Japan," Memorandum for the Secretary of War, 1 August 1945, item 2338, reel 79, MRL.

123. All quotations in this section are from Memorandum for the President, [25 July 1945], item 2595, reel 109, MRL.

124. Gallicchio, *Cold War Begins*, 45; Donovan, *Conflict and Crisis*, 95.

Chapter 13

1. "Washington Surprised: Ultimatum News to State Department—Senators Are Pleased," *New York Times*, 27 July 1945, 4.
2. "Japanese Cabinet Weighs Ultimatum," *New York Times*, 28 July 1945, 1.
3. The text of the Potsdam Declaration appeared in American newspapers on July 27. "Swift, Utter Destruction Alternative, Foe Is Told," *Washington Post*, 27 July 1945, 1; "Text of Offer to Japan," *New York Times*, 27 July 1945, 4.
4. Lindley, "People Laud Ultimatum for Japan," *Washington Post*, 29 July 1945, B5. See also Lindley, "The Decision We Face on Japan," *Newsweek*, 30 July 1945, 25. Lindley did not think the emperor would pose a threat if Japan were disarmed and watched from nearby bases. Lindley, "Vote on Emperor," *Washington Post*, 16 July 1945, 7.
5. Baldwin, "Terms for Japanese," *New York Times*, 27 July 1945, 4.
6. "Japanese Cabinet Weighs Ultimatum," *New York Times*, 28 July 1945, 1.
7. The *New York Times* treated Domei's statement as authoritative, but the *Washington Post* waited for official word from Suzuki before concluding that the proclamation had been rejected. "The Ultimatum," *New York Times*, 28 July 1945, 10; "Jap Premier Scorns Peace Demand, *Washington Post*, 30 July 1945, 1; Barnet Nover, "Road of Surrender," *Washington Post*, 31 July 1945, 6.
8. Robert J. Butow, *Japan's Decision to Surrender* (Stanford, CA: Stanford University Press, 1954), 148.
9. Tsuyoshi Hasegawa cites a Japanese journalist who was present at Suzuki's press conference as being certain that the prime minister never said "mokusatsu." According to the reporter, Suzuki said only "no comment" but the press embellished his remark. Tsuyoshi Hasegawa, *Racing the Enemy: Stalin, Truman, and the Surrender of Japan* (Cambridge, MA: Harvard University Press, 2005), 168.
10. "The Ultimatum," *New York Times*, 28 July 1945, 10.
11. "Crushing Invasion of Japan Planned," *New York Times*, 30 July 1945, 3.
12. Minutes of Advisory Board Meetings, 23–24 July 1945, box 392, OWMR, RG 250, National Archives (hereafter NARA), College Park, Maryland.
13. Ibid.
14. Ibid.
15. "Drastic War-Agency Control Change Asked by Senate Unit," *Washington Post*, 30 July 1945, 12. The committee went so far as to recommend giving Snyder actual supervisory authority over the entire demobilization process, as opposed to a mediating role, but that would have required a significant enlargement of his office, and it was unlikely that Truman would have made drastic changes so late into the war.
16. John H. Crider, "Reconversion Conflict Seethes in Washington," *New York Times*, 5 August 1945, 68.
17. Drew Pearson, "Releasing GI Miners Hot Subject," *Washington Post*, 29 July 1945, B5. The resolution was titled "Manpower for the Bituminous-Coal Industry," 19 July 1945, 79th Congress, 1st Session, Report 501.
18. "Farmers' Union Calls for Cut in Army's Size: Sec. Anderson Sees No Need for Force of 8 Million," *Washington Post*, 6 August 1945, 1.

19. Marquis Childs, "Washington Calling: Reconversion Mix-Up," *Washington Post* 31 July 1945, 6.
20. General Council Meeting, 30 July 1945, item 2397, reel 84, George Marshall Research Library (MRL), Lexington, Virginia.
21. "Army to Fly Men to Coast to Aid Rail Redeployment," *New York Times*, 1 August 1945, 1.
22. "Ickes Urges Army to Free 30,000 Miners," *Washington Post*, 1 August 1945, 1.
23. Ernest Lindley, "Urgent Business: Reconversion Muddle," *Washington Post*, 3 August 1945, 8.
24. Drew Pearson, "Merry-Go-Round," *Washington Post*, 3 August 1945, 16.
25. J. Anthony Panuch, Memo for Mr. Nathan, 2 August 1945, box 118, OWMR, RG 250, NARA.
26. Chester Bowles to John Snyder, 6 August 1945, Advisory Board Minutes
27. Minutes of Advisory Board Meetings, 6 August 1945, box 392, OWMR, RG 250, NARA.
28. Ibid.
29. The buildup and the U.S. response is described in Edward J. Drea, *MacArthur's ULTRA and the War against Japan, 1942–1945* (Lawrence: University Press of Kansas, 1992), 215–217; Richard B. Frank, *Downfall: The End of the Imperial Japanese Empire* (New York: Penguin, 2001), 206–213; Douglas J. MacEachin, *The Final Months of the War with Japan: Signals Intelligence, U.S. Invasion Planning, and the A-Bomb Decision* (Central Intelligence Agency, 2007), https://www.cia.gov/library/center-for-the-study-of-intelligence/csi-publications/books-and-mono graphs/the-final-months-of-the-war-with-japan-signals-intelligence-u-s-invasion-planning-and-the-a-bomb-decision/csi9810001.html#rtoc6.
30. General Headquarters, U.S. Armed Forces Pacific, Military Intelligence Summary, General Staff, "Amendment No. 1 to G-2 Estimate of the Enemy Situation with Respect to Kyushu (dated 25 April 1945)," 29 July 1945, Stephen Chamberlain Papers, United States Army Heritage and Education Center (hereafter USAHEC), Carlisle, Pennsylvania. A copy of the April 25 G-2 estimate is also in this file.
31. Frank, *Downfall*, 204.
32. Ibid., 272–273.
33. MacEachin, *Final Months of the War with Japan*; Drea, *MacArthur's ULTRA*, 222.
34. Drea, *MacArthur's ULTRA*, 222–223.
35. Frank, *Downfall*, 276.
36. Ibid., 275; also Drea, *MacArthur's ULTRA*, 223.
37. Notes, Conferences, 1944–1945, box 20, Ernest J. King Papers, Library of Congress (hereafter LC), Washington, DC; E. B. Potter, *Nimitz* (Annapolis: U.S. Naval Institute Press, 1976), 384. On the artificial harbor see also D. M. Giangreco, *Hell to Pay: Operation Downfall and the Invasion of Japan, 1945–1947* (Annapolis: Naval Institute Press, 2009), 176–182.
38. Frank, *Downfall*, 276.
39. "Magic"—Far East Summary, War Department, Office of Assistant Chief of Staff, G-2, no. 507, 9 August 1945, Document 61; "Magic"—Far East Summary, War Department, Office of Assistant Chief of Staff, G-2, no. 508, 10 August 1945,

Document 63, in William Burr, ed., *The Atomic Bomb and the End of World War II: A Collection of Primary Sources*, National Security Archive Electronic Briefing Book no. 162, http://nsarchive.gwu.edu/NSAEBB/NSAEBB162/63.pdf; Drea, *MacArthur's ULTRA*, 223–225.

40. "The Haunted Wood," *Washington Post*, 7 August 1945, 6.
41. "Single Atomic Bomb Rocks Army Base," *Washington Post*, 7 August 1945, 1.
42. Lindley, "The Atomic Bomb: Will Japan Surrender Now?," *Washington Post*, 8 August 1945, 7.
43. "New Weapon Not to Bring Army Cut Now," *Washington Post*, 8 August 1945, 1.
44. "Second Thoughts," *Washington Post*, 9 August 1945, 6.
45. Richard Arthur Briggs, *Blackhawks over the Danube: The History of the 86th Infantry Division in World War II* (Louisville, KY: Western Recorder Printing, 1955), 104–105.
46. Log of the President's Trip to the Berlin Conference, 6 July–7 August 1945, Harry S. Truman Library and Museum (hereafter HST), Independence, Missouri, http://www.trumanlibrary.org/calendar/travel_log/documents/index.php?page number=103&documentid=17&documentdate=1945-08-07&studycollectionid =TL&nav=OK.
47. Letter to the Chairman, War Production Board, on Measures to Speed Reconversion, HST, http://trumanlibrary.org/publicpapers/viewpapers.php?pid=102; "Post-VJ-Day," *Washington Post*, 12 August 1945, B4; entry for 10 August 1945, Robert H. Ferrell, ed., *Off the Record: The Private Papers of Harry S. Truman* (Columbia: University of Missouri Press, 1980), 60.
48. "Hoshina Memorandum" on the Emperor's "Sacred Decision [go-seidan]," 9–10 August 1945, Document 62, in Burr, *Atomic Bomb and the End of World War II*, http://nsarchive.gwu.edu/NSAEBB/NSAEBB162/62.pdf; Herbert Bix, "Japan's Delayed Surrender, A Reinterpretation," *Diplomatic History* 19, no. 2 (spring 1995), 218–223.
49. Byrnes's memoir also inaccurately omits crucial details about how the final response to Japan was written. See John K. Emerson, *The Japanese Thread: A Life in the U.S. Foreign Service* (New York: Holt, Rinehart and Winston, 1978), 237–238.
50. Byrnes's account is in Walter Brown's Book, entry for 10 August 1945, folder 102, Conferences 2-1, Potsdam, Special Collections, James Francis Byrnes Papers, Clemson University Libraries Special Collections, Clemson, South Carolina; Ayers Diary, entry for 10 August 1945, Eben Ayers Papers, HST.
51. This error may have gone unnoticed by historians because the editorial note that precedes Truman's entry states that he arrived at the White House on August 9. Truman's ship docked at Hampton Roads at 5:25 p.m. on August 7; editorial note and entry for 10 August 1945, in Ferrell, *Off the Record*, 59–62; "Truman Back from Europe, Holds Cabinet Conference," *New York Times*, 8 August 1945, 1; "The President's Homecoming," *New York Times*, 8 August 1945, 22. The 9:00 a.m. meeting on August 10 is also reported in "Japan Offers to Surrender: U.S. May Let Emperor Remain," *New York Times*, 11 August 1945, 1.
52. Entries for Thursday, 9 August 1945, and Friday, 10 August 1945, Appointments, box 20, Rose Conway Files, Harry S. Truman Papers, HST. See also the entry for

10 August 1945 in James V. Forrestal's diary, in Walter Millis, ed., *The Forrestal Diaries* (New York: Viking Press, 1951), 82–84.

53. Walter Brown's Book, entry for 10 August 1945, folder 102, Conferences 2-1, Potsdam, James Francis Byrnes Papers, Clemson University Libraries Special Collections; and Emerson, *Japanese Thread*, 237–238.

54. "Japan's Surrender Maneuvers," SRH-090, Record Group 457 (Special Research Histories), Modern Military Records Branch, NARA.

55. The tenor of the American reply was most likely suggested by Forrestal. Coincidentally, the head of Army intelligence made a similar recommendation to Marshall. There is no evidence to indicate that anyone at the White House meeting on the morning of August 10 was aware of the Army's recommendation when the president issued his instructions to Byrnes. The G-2 report advised Marshall that the United States should "accept the Japanese offer in language that does not bind the United States to maintain the Emperor in power but which will permit the utilization of his position to secure the occupation of the Japanese homeland and disarming of Japanese military forces." Millis, *Forrestal Diaries*, 83; Maj. General Clayton Bissell to Marshall, 10 August 1945, OPD 387.4 TS, sec. II, case 20, RG 165, NARA.

56. Byrnes to Swiss Chargé, 11 August 1945, in U.S. Department of State, *Foreign Relations of the United States*, vol. 6, *1945* (1969), 631–632.

57. At that time, Secretary of War Stimson had worried that the Potsdam Declaration's silence on the future of the emperor might cause the Japanese to balk at accepting its terms. Stimson had suggested that "if they were hanging fire on that one point" it would be advisable to assure Tokyo through diplomatic channels that they could keep the emperor. Truman had responded vaguely that "he had that in mind, and that he would take care of it." Entry for 24 July 1945, Diaries of Henry Lewis Stimson, Henry Lewis Stimson Papers, Yale University Library, New Haven, Connecticut (Microfilm).

58. Stimson recorded that he thought Leahy had taken the "good plain horse-sense position that the question of the Emperor was a minor matter compared with delaying a victory in the war which was now in our hands." Entry for 10 August 1945, Diaries of Henry Lewis Stimson, Henry Lewis Stimson Papers, Yale University Library.

59. Entry for 10 August 1945, in Ferrell, *Off the Record*, 61.

60. McNaughton to Eleanor Welch, "Surrender," 10 August 1945, box 9, Frank McNaughton Papers, HST. For Mike Mansfield's version of the meeting, see Don Oberdorfer, *Senator Mansfield: The Extraordinary Life of a Great American Statesman and Diplomat* (New York: Random House, 2003), 84–86.

61. McNaughton to Welch, "Surrender," 10 August 1945, box 9, Frank McNaughton Papers, HST.

62. Entry for 10 August 1945, in Ferrell, *Off the Record*, 61.

63. Jay Luvaas, ed., *Dear Miss Em: General Eichelberger's War in the Pacific, 1942–1945* (Westport, CT: Greenwood Press, 1972), 298–299.

64. "Celebration on Okinawa Leaves 6 Dead, 30 Hurt," *New York Times*, 12 August 1945, 17.

65. "War Stocks Drop, Peace Shares Rise," *Washington Post*, 11 August 1945, 1; and Hudson Phillips, "Wall Street Left Groggy by War News," *Washington Post*, 12 August 1945, M8.
66. "Prospects for World Series Brighter, Says ODT Official," *Washington Post*, 12 August 1945, M6.
67. "Allied Reply," *Washington Post*, 12 August 1945, B4.
68. Lawrence E. Davies, "Thousands to Quit Far West in Peace," *New York Times*, 12 August 1945, 4.
69. "Cities Prepare for Celebrations," *New York Times*, 12 August 1945, 7.
70. Memorandum from Major General Clayton Bissell, Assistant Chief of Staff, G-2, for the Chief of Staff, "Estimate of Japanese Situation for Next 30 Days," 12 August 1945, Top Secret, Document 70, in Burr, *Atomic Bomb and the End of World War II*, http://nsarchive.gwu.edu/NSAEBB/NSAEBB162/70.pdf.
71. Entry for 13 August 1945, Diary of William D. Leahy, Leahy Papers, LC; Marc Gallicchio, "After Nagasaki: General Marshall's Plan for Tactical Nuclear Weapons in Japan," *Prologue* 23 (winter 1991), 396–404.
72. "Third Fleet Fliers Smash Suicide Blow, 138 Planes," *Washington Post*, 14 August 1945, 1.
73. Harry S. Truman: "The President's News Conference," 14 August 1945, in Gerhard Peters and John T. Woolley, eds., *The American Presidency Project*, http://www.presidency.ucsb.edu/ws/?pid=12383.
74. Hasegawa, *Racing the Enemy*, 225–228; Frank, *Downfall*, 316–321.

Conclusion

1. As one War Department analysis subsequently explained, the Potsdam Declaration amounted to a contractual arrangement that included an American pledge to preserve Japan's sovereignty over the home islands and, among other guarantees, to permit Japanese troops to return to their homes in return for their surrender. No such offer had been made to Germany; Robert P. Newman, *Truman and the Hiroshima Cult* (East Lansing: Michigan State University Press, 1995), 70.
2. War Department to MacArthur, 17 August 1945, TS, Incoming-Outgoing Messages, OPD, box 57, RG 165, National Archives (hereafter NARA), College Park, Maryland.
3. Marc S. Gallicchio, *The Cold War Begins in Asia: American East Asian Policy and the Fall of the Japanese Empire* (New York: Columbia University Press, 1988), 60–62.
4. Marc Gallicchio, *The Scramble for Asia: U.S. Military Power in the Aftermath of the Pacific War* (Lanham, MD: Rowman and Littlefield, 2008), 55, 75–76.
5. Robert Ross Smith, *Triumph in the Philippines*, United States Army in World War II, The War in the Pacific (Washington, DC: U.S. Government Printing Office, 1963), 579.
6. Historians have devoted considerable attention to counterfactual analyses of the events surrounding the end of war, including speculation whether OLYMPIC and CORONET would have taken place and, if so, their costs. See, for example, Barton Bernstein, "Understanding the Atomic Bomb and the Japanese Surrender," *Diplomatic History* 19, no. 2 (spring 1995), 227–274; Bernstein, "The Alarming

Japanese Buildup on Southern Kyushu, Growing U.S. Fears and Counterfactual Analysis: Would the Planned November 1945 Invasion of Southern Kyushu Have Occurred?" *Pacific Historical Review* 68 (1999), 561–609; John Ray Skates, *The Invasion of Japan: Alternative to the Bomb* (Columbia: University of South Carolina Press, 1994), 254–257; Edward S. Miller, *War Plan Orange: The U.S. Strategy to Defeat Japan, 1897–1945* (Annapolis: Naval Institute Press, 1991), 366–369; D. M. Giangreco, *Hell to Pay: Operation Downfall and the Invasion of Japan, 1945-1947* (Annapolis: Naval Institute Press, 2009), 169–186, and 246–274, app. B for G-2 Report prepared in December 1945.

7. Giangreco, *Hell to Pay*, 105–106.
8. Michael Pearlman, *Warmaking and American Democracy: The Struggle over Military Strategy from 1700 to the Present* (Lawrence: University Press of Kansas, 1999), 274.
9. Williamson Murray and Allan R. Millet, *A War to Be Won: Fighting the Second World War* (Cambridge, MA: Harvard University Press, 2000), 502–503.
10. Ibid. MacArthur's biographer was also critical of his handling of the Philippines campaign. D. Clayton James, *The Years of MacArthur*, 2 vols. (Boston: Houghton Mifflin, 1975), II, 690. Geoffrey Perret, *Old Soldiers Never Die: The Life of Douglas MacArthur* (Holbrook, MA: Adams Media Corp., 1996), defends the general.
11. James Forrestal to Harry S. Truman, 8 August 1945, box 1, Forrestal Diaries, James Forrestal Papers, Seeley Mudd Library, Princeton University, Princeton, New Jersey.
12. Entry for 17 June 1945, in Robert H. Ferrell, ed., *Off the Record: The Private Papers of Harry S. Truman* (Columbia: University of Missouri Press, 1980), 47.

SELECTED BIBLIOGRAPHY

Official Historical Series, United States Army in World War II, Published by U.S. Government Printing Office, Washington, DC

The War in the Pacific

Roy E. Appleman, James M. Burns, Russell A. Gugeler, and John Stevens, *Okinawa, the Last Battle,* 1948.

M. Hamlin Cannon, *Leyte: The Return to the Philippines,* 1954.

Philip A. Crowl, *Campaign in the Marianas,* 1960.

Robert Ross Smith, *The Approach to the Philippines,* 1953.

Robert Ross Smith, *Triumph in the Philippines,* 1963.

The European Theater of Operations

Martin Blumenson, *Breakout and Pursuit,* 1984.

Ray S. Cline, *The Operations Division,* 2003.

Robert W. Coakley and Richard M. Leighton, *Global Logistics and Supply, 1943–1945,* 1968.

Byron Fairchild and Jonathan Grossman, *The Army and Industrial Manpower,* 1959.

Kent Roberts Greenfield, ed., *Command Decisions,* 1990.

Maurice Matloff, *Stategic Planning for Coalition Warfare, 1943–1944,* 1959.

Roland Ruppenthal, *Logistical Support of the Armies,* 2 vols., 1959. The War Department, Washington Command Post

The Medical Department
Communicable Diseases Transmitted Through Respiratory and Alimentary Tracts, Vol. 4, 1958.
Diseases Transmitted Through Contact or by Unknown Means (Preventive Medicine in World War II), Vol. 5, 1960.
Infectious Diseases (Internal Medicine in World War II), Vol. 2, 1958.
Malaria (Preventive Medicine in World War II), Vol. 6.
Neuropsychiatry in World War II, Vol. 2, 1973.

Technical Services
Major General Hugh Casey, *Engineer Memoirs* (U.S. Army Corps of Engineers), 1993.
Erna Risch, *The Quartermaster Corps: Organization, Supply, and Services*, 1953.
Alvin P. Stauffer, *The Quartermaster Corps: Operations in the War Against Japan*, 1956.

Army Ground Forces
Robert R. Palmer, Bell I. Wiley, and William R. Keast, *The Procurement and Training of Ground Combat Troops*, 1948.

Army Air Force
Wesley F. Craven and James L. Cate, *Army Air Forces in World War II*, (Chicago: University of Chicago Press, 1948–1958), Vols. II, V.

History of United States Naval Operations in World War II
Samuel Eliot Morison, Published by Little, Brown, Boston. Volumes Relating to the Pacific War.
Aleutians, Gilberts, and Marshalls, June 1942–April 1944, Vol. 7.
Breaking the Bismarcks Barrier, 22 July 1942–1May 1944, Vol. 6.
Leyte, June 1944–January 1945, Vol. 12.
The Liberation of the Philippines: Luzon, Mindanao, the Visayas, 1944–1945, Vol. 13.
New Guinea and the Marianas, March 1944–August 1944, Vol. 8.
Victory in the Pacific, 1945, Vol. 14.

Selected Books and Articles
Asada, Sadao, *From Mahan to Pearl Harbor: The Imperial Japanese Navy and the United States* (Annapolis: Naval Institute Press, 2006).
Ballantine, Duncan S., *United States Naval Logistics in the Second World War* (Newport, RI: Naval War College Press, 1998).
Barbey, Vice Admiral Daniel E., *MacArthur's Amphibious Navy: Seventh Amphibious Operations, 1943–1945* (Annapolis: Naval Institute Press, 1969).
Bergerud, Eric, *Touched with Fire: The Land War in the South Pacific* (New York: Viking, 1996).
Blair, Clay, *Silent Victory: The U.S. Submarine War Against Japan* (Philadelphia: Lippincott, 1975).
Bland, Larry, ed., *George C. Marshall: Interviews and Reminiscences for Forrest C. Pogue* (Lexington, VA: George C. Marshall Research Foundation, 1991).

Boog, Horst, Gerhard Crebs, and Detleff Vogel, trans. by Derry Cook-Radmore et al., *Germany and the Second World War*, Research Institute of Military History, Potsdam, Germany, Vol. 7, *The Strategic Air War in Europe, and the War in the West and East Asia, 1943–1944/5* (Oxford: Clarendon Press, 2006).

Borg, Dorothy, and Shumpei Okamoto, eds., *Pearl Harbor as History* (New York: Columbia University Press, 1973).

Brower, Charles, *Defeating Japan: The Joint Chiefs of Staff and Strategy in the Pacific War, 1943–1945* (New York: Palgrave Macmillan, 2012).

Buell, Thomas B., *The Quiet Warrior: A Biography of Admiral Raymond A. Spruance* (Annapolis: Naval Institute Press, 1981).

Carter, Rear Admiral Worrall Read, *Beans, Bullets, and Black Oil: The Story of Fleet Logistics Afloat in the Pacific During World War II* (Newport, RI: Naval War College Press, 1953).

Catton, Bruce, *The War Lords of Washington* (New York: Harcourt Brace, 1948).

Clive, Alan, *State of War, Michigan in World War II* (Ann Arbor: University of Michigan Press, 1979).

Connaughton, Richard, John Pimlott, and Duncan Anderson, *The Battle of Manila* (Novato, CA: Presidio Press, 2002).

Costello, John, *The Pacific War* (New York: Quill, 1982).

Denfeld, D. Colt, *Hold the Marianas: The Japanese Defense of the Mariana Islands* (Shippensburg, PA: White Mane Publishing Co., 1997).

Dower, John, *War Without Mercy: Race and Power in the Pacific War* (New York: Pantheon, 1986).

Drea, Edward, *MacArthur's ULTRA and the War Against Japan, 1942–1945* (Lawrence: University Press of Kansas, 1992).

Dupuy, Trevor N., David L. Bongard, and Richard C. Anderson, Jr., *Hitler's Last Gamble: The Battle of the Bulge, December 1944–January 1945* (New York: Harper, 1994).

Ellis, John, *The Sharp End: The Fighting Man in World War II* (New York: Scribner, 1980).

Falk, Stanley L., *Decision at Leyte* (New York: Norton, 1966).

Field, James A., Jr., *The Japanese in Leyte Gulf: The Sho Operation* (Princeton, NJ: Princeton University Press, 1947).

Frank, Richard B., *Downfall: The End of the Imperial Japanese Empire* (New York: Penguin Books, 2001).

Goldberg, Harold J., *D-Day in the Pacific: The Battle of Saipan* (Bloomington: Indiana University Press, 2007).

Griffeth, Thomas E., Jr., *MacArthur's Airman: General George C. Kenney and the War in the Southwest Pacific* (Lawrence: University Press of Kansas, 1998).

Hayes, Grace Person, *The History of the Joint Chiefs of Staff in World War II* (Annapolis: Naval Institute Press, 1982).

Hooks, Gregory, *Forging the Military-Industrial Complex: World War II's Battle of the Potomac* (Urbana: University of Illinois Press, 1991).

Hough, Major Frank D., *The Assault on Peleliu* (Washington, DC: Headquarters U.S. Marine Corps, 1950).

Isely, Jeter A., and Philip A. Crowl, *The United States Marines and Amphibious War* (Princeton, NJ: Princeton University Press, 1951).

James, D. Clayton, *The Years of MacArthur* (2 vols., Boston: Houghton Mifflin, 1970, 1975).

Lane, Frederic C., *Ships for Victory: A History of Shipbuilding Under the Maritime Commission in World War II* (Baltimore: Johns Hopkins University Press, 1951).

Leary, William M., ed., *We Shall Return! MacArthur's Commanders and the Defeat of Japan* (Lexington: University of Kentucky Press, 1988).

Linderman, Gerald E., *The World Within War: America's Combat Experience in World War II* (Cambridge, MA: Harvard University Press, 1997), chapter 4, "Fighting the Japanese."

Love, Robert William, ed., *The Chiefs of Naval Operations* (Annapolis: U.S. Naval Institute, 1980).

MacArthur, Douglas, *Reminiscences* (New York: McGraw Hill, 1964).

Milward, Alan S. *War Economy and Society* (Berkeley: University of California Press, 1979).

Overy, Richard, *Why the Allies Won* (New York: Norton, 1995).

Pease, Otis, *Blueberry Pie: The Meaning of World War II for the Americans Who Fought in It* (Lincoln, NE: iUniverse, 2007).

Pogue, Forrest C., *George C. Marshall* (4 vols., New York: Viking, 1963–1987).

Potter, E., *Nimitz* (Annapolis: U.S. Naval Institute Press, 1976).

Reynolds, Clark G., *Admiral John H. Towers: The Struggle for Naval Air Supremacy* (Annapolis: Naval Institute Press, 1991).

Rockoff, Hugh, "The United States: From Plowshares to Swords," in *The Economies of World War II: Six Great Powers in International Comparison*, Mark Harrison, ed., (New York: Cambridge University Press, 1998).

Schaller, Michael, *Douglas MacArthur: The Far Eastern General* (New York: Oxford University Press, 1989).

Schrijvers, Peter, *The G.I. War against Japan: American Soldiers in Asia and the Pacific during World War II* (New York: New York University Press, 2002).

Sitterson, J. Carlyle, *Development of the Reconversion Policies of the War Production Board (Historical Reports on War Administration: War Production Board, Special Study No. 15)* (Washington, DC: U.S. Government Printing Office, Reissue March 22, 1946).

Sledge, E. B., *With the Old Breed at Peleliu and Okinawa* (Novato, CA: Presidio Press, 1981).

Smith, Holland M., and Percy Finch, *Coral and Brass* (New York: Scribners, 1949).

Spector, Ronald H., *Eagle Against the Sun: The American War With Japan* (New York: Free Press, 1985).

Stein, Harold, *Public Administration and Policy Development: A Case Book* (New York: Harcourt Brace, 1952).

Stoler, Mark, *Allies and Adversaries: The Joint Chiefs of Staff, the Grand Alliance, and U.S. Strategy in World War II* (Chapel Hill: University of North Carolina Press, 2000).

Taaffe, Stephen R., *MacArthur's Jungle War: The New Guinea Campaign* (Lawrence: University Press of Kansas, 1998).

Thorne, Christopher, *The Issue of War: States, Societies, and the Far Eastern Conflict of 1941–1945* (New York: Oxford University Press, 1985).

Tully, Anthony P., *Battle of Surigaro Strait* (Bloomington: Indiana University Press, 2014).

Vatter, Harold V., *The United States Economy in World War II* (New York: Columbia University Press, 1985).

Willmott, H. P., *The Battle of Leyte Gulf* (Bloomington: Indiana University Press, 2005).

Willmott, H. P., *The Great Crusade: A New History of the Second World War* (London: Michael Joseph, 1989).

Woodward, C. Vann, *The Battle of Leyte Gulf* (New York: Norton, 1965, first published, 1947).

Y'Blood, William T., *Red Sun Setting: The Battle of the Philippine Sea* (Annapolis: Naval Institute Press, 1981).

INDEX

Maps are indicated by "m" following the page number.